A SEMANTIC AND STRUCTURAL ANALYSIS OF ROMANS

Summer Institute of Linguistics

SEMANTIC AND STRUCTURAL ANALYSIS SERIES

JOHN BANKER, GENERAL EDITOR

A SEMANTIC AND STRUCTURAL ANALYSIS OF ROMANS

Ellis W. Deibler, Jr.

Summer Institute of Linguistics

The Greek text used in this SSA is from the fourth revised edition
of the United Bible Societies' *Greek New Testament*.

© 1998 by the Summer Institute of Linguistics, Inc.
ISBN: 1-55671-072-0
Library of Congress Catalog Card Number: 98-61142
Printed in the United States of America

**Summer Institute of Linguistics
7500 W. Camp Wisdom Road
Dallas, TX 75236, U.S.A.**

CONTENTS

Preface 7

Abbreviations 8

GENERAL INTRODUCTION
Theoretical Basis 9
Assumptions about Language 9
Conventions Used in This Volume 10
Use of a Semantic and Structural Analysis 11

INTRODUCTION TO THE ANALYSIS OF ROMANS
The Communication Situation 15
The Status of the Roman Church 16
Occasion and Purpose of the Letter 17
Date of Composition 22
The Constituent Organization of Romans 23
Overview: Thematic Outline of Romans 24

THE SEMANTIC UNITS OF ROMANS
Epistle 35
Epistle Constituent 1:1–7 36
Epistle Constituent 1:8–15:33 41
        Part Cluster Constituent 1:8–15 42
        Part Cluster Constituent 1:16–15:13 46
        Part Cluster Constituent 15:14–33 344
Epistle Constituent 16:1–27 360

Figures
Paragraph-Pattern Types in Various Discourse Genres 10
Chart of Communication Relations 13
The Constituent Organization of Romans 23

Bibliography 379

PREFACE

My first efforts on materials which were early forerunners of what are now called *Semantic and Structural Analyses* began after interaction with John Beekman, SIL's first International Translation Coordinator, at a translation workshop in Mexico in 1966. After returning to the field I produced a number of materials called "Basic Structures of New Testament Books." Further stimulation came in 1973 when a number of us assembled in Dallas to work on a preliminary analysis of Colossians, which later evolved into *A Semantic Structure Analysis of Colossians* by John Callow (1983). Several years later it appeared that if we wanted to be serious about producing more of these analyses we would have to put together a team to work on them. I joined this team and began work on Romans in 1989.

Actually I had done a lot of preliminary work on Romans during a workshop in Guatemala in 1982. For that workshop I drew on material previously worked out by John Werner. The material developed in the Guatemala workshop was further revised in a workshop in Papua New Guinea in 1984. I am indebted to the participants in those workshops for insights received.

I am also very grateful for the contributions and theoretical insights given me by my colleagues Dennis Newton, John Tuggy, and George Hart as we have worked on various books and been able to interact with each other. I am grateful for the continual encouragement given by the current International Translation Coordinator, Katy Barnwell. Especially am I grateful to John Banker, the series editor, who has gone over all the material twice, first on his own and then with me.

Almost all the keyboarding was done by two ladies to whom I am greatly indebted for their patience: Doris Reynhout keyboarded most of the notes; my wife, Katherine, keyboarded the displays. Copy editor Betty Eastman went through the material many times and also keyboarded the revisions in the final stage; in a very real sense the quality of this work is due to her patient and persistent attention to accuracy and consistency. Dick Blight and John Banker and others in the Translation Department at Dallas have done great work in preparing the camera-ready copy and seeing the book off to the printer as well as arranging for it to be available on a CD. My thanks to all these people.

I would also like to express my appreciation to those whose faithful financial contributions have kept us going during these years.

Finally, but not the least, I would like to express my thanks to the Lord for sustaining all of us and for his gifts of wisdom and understanding and insight into the meaning of this portion of his inspired Word.

ABBREVIATIONS IN THE DISPLAYS

[CHI]	chiasm	[LIT]	litotes
[DOU]	doublet	[MET]	metaphor
[EUP]	euphemism	[MTY]	metonymy
(exc)	exclusive	¶ PTRN	paragraph pattern
(f)	feminine	[PRS]	personification
[HEN]	hendiadys	[RHQ]	rhetorical question
[HYP]	hyperbole	(sg)	singular
[IDM]	idiom	[SIM]	simile
[IRO]	irony	[SYN]	synecdoche

ABBREVIATIONS IN THE TEXT

ABS	American Bible Society	NEB	New English Bible
BAGD	Bauer, Arndt, Gingrich, Danker	NCV	New Century Version
BDF	Blass, Debrunner, and Funk	NIV	New International Version
CEV	Contemporary English Version	NJB	New Jerusalem Bible
GNT*	Greek New Testament (Aland et al.)	NLT	New Living Translation
ISBE	International Standard Bible Encyclopedia	NRSV	New Revised Standard Version
		NT	New Testament
JB	Jerusalem Bible	OT	Old Testament
JBP	J. B. Phillips's *New Testament in Modern English*	REB	Revised English Bible
		RSV	Revised Standard Version
KJV	King James Version	TCNT	Twentieth Century New Testament
LB	Living Bible	TEV	Today's English Version (Good News for Modern Man)
LXX	Septuagint		
NASB	New American Standard Bible	UBS	United Bible Societies

*The third edition of GNT was used in the early stages of writing this SSA. In the late stages the fourth edition was consulted, and references to it are noted specifically.

GENERAL INTRODUCTION

Theoretical basis

This special translation and commentary on Paul's Epistle to the Romans is one of a series designed to assist translators, especially those translating into non-European languages. But because the analysis pays careful attention to meaning at all levels of discourse, it should be useful to all serious students of the Scriptures. It is firmly based on discourse analysis, and the epistle is therefore viewed as an integrated whole. Although the grammar and the lexicon of the original are carefully considered, this is particularly a semantic analysis, concerned about giving a semantically oriented translation of the text and presenting both the grammatical and semantic evidence for all the decisions made in the translation.

This work is based on the theory of discourse analysis first set forth in Beekman, Callow, and Kopesec's *Semantic Structure of Written Communication* (1981). More recently Kathleen Callow's *Man and Message* (forthcoming) presents a broader basis for this theory. The reader who is interested in a more detailed presentation of the theory is referred to the introductions to previous volumes of the Semantic Structure Analysis Series, especially those on Colossians and 2 Thessalonians. (The charts on pp. 10 and 13 present a condensed view of it.)

This study is called *A Semantic and Structural Analysis* (SSA) because it is greatly concerned with how meaning is organized, from the lowest to the highest level. It presents that overall organization believed to be in the mind of the author and which he wanted to convey to his audience. It also makes a thorough semantic analysis of even the smallest units, phrases, and clauses.

Assumptions about language

Several assumptions about the nature of language as a vehicle of communication underlie this work:

(1) An author uses written language signals in an attempt to communicate cognitive content, emotive feelings, and desires for an appropriate response from his audience.

(2) An author shares a vast amount of information with his intended audience, such as world view, culture, and specific circumstances involved in the communication situation. Much can therefore be left unexpressed because the author is confident the audience will infer it aright.

(3) Although a biblical author's purpose and meaning are largely available to us today only through the written text, his purpose and the meaning he intends to communicate are prior to and have priority over the written surface forms he uses.

(4) Meaning is conveyed through a hierarchically arranged set of units which are related in semantically appropriate ways to other units.

(5) Within a given unit some constituents of meaning are nuclear (central) and others satellitic (supportive) of them. The units that are nuclear have natural prominence.

(6) An author can use various grammatical and lexical devices to signal that certain meaning units have marked prominence.

(7) The basic unit of communication is the "proposition," a semantic unit that expresses an event (or experience or state) to which other concepts are related appropriately by a system of case relations (e.g., agent, location). Propositions are related to each other by semantically appropriate communication relations (see the chart on p. 13). These relations are universal, basic to human experience. They are expressed by surface forms, but there is not necessarily a one-to-one correlation between communication relations and surface forms: certain relations are expressed by a variety of surface forms depending on the author's purpose or style, and certain surface forms may in various contexts signal different communication relations.

(8) The basic unit that expresses author intent is the paragraph, defined as a semantic unit consisting of a set of propositions appropriately related to each other and together intended to convey the author's intent to influence the ideas, actions, or emotions of his audience. Paragraphs combine into higher-level units in semantically appropriate patterns that correlate with the discourse genre the author utilizes.

		SOLUTIONALITY	CAUSALITY	VOLITIONALITY
IDEAS	EXPOSITORY –sequence	+problem (exp)+SOLUTION ±evidence^n ±(complication+SOLUTION) [(objection+REFUTATION)/ query+RESPONSE)]	+cause^n+EFFECT; +major+minor+INFER- ENCE; +evidence^n+INFERENCE; +PRINCIPLE+application^n	+justification^n+CLAIM
IDEAS	NARRATIVE +sequence	+problem+RESOLUTION ±resolving incident^n ±(complication+RESOLUTION)	+occasion+OUTCOME	+step^n+GOAL
EMOTIONS	EXPRESSIVE –sequence	+problem (emo)+SOLUTION ±seeking/belief ±(complication+SOLUTION)	+situation^n+REACTION ±belief	+belief^n+CONTROL
EMOTIONS	DESCRIPTIVE +sequence	+problem (dsc)+SOLUTION ±experience^n ±(complication+SOLUTION)	+situation^n+REACTION	+description^n+DECLAR- ATION
BEHAVIOR	HORTATORY –sequence	+problem (hrt)+APPEAL ±basis^n ±(complication+SOLUTION)	+basis^n+APPEAL; +APPEAL+application^n; +basis^n+COMMISSIVE	+motivation+ENABLE- MENT^n; +motivation^n+APPEAL
BEHAVIOR	PROCEDURAL +sequence	+problem (prc)+SOLUTION ±step^n ±(complication+SOLUTION)	+APPEAL+outcome	+STEP^n+accomplishment

Paragraph-Pattern Types in Various Discourse Genres (With a few exceptions one formula serves for each paragraph-pattern type; alternate formulas are separated by a semi-colon.)

Conventions used in this volume

The reader needs to understand certain conventions used in this volume:

(1) Implicit material in the propositions of the displays has been supplied and shown as italicized. (However, in the case of an obvious ellipsis of a word that was explicit in a preceding parallel clause or phrase the supplied words are not normally written in italics.) In general, italicized words are material which has by careful analysis been determined to fall under assumption 2 (see p. 9). Every effort has been made to identify the implicit information accurately, but in some cases it is difficult to decide what is truly implicit and what is a component of meaning actually in the Greek.

(2) In making the translation, the forms of the Greek have been rendered in English using those forms which correspond most closely with their semantic functions. For example, verbal nouns or abstract nouns are rendered as complete clauses using verbs because verbs are the most straightforward way of expressing event propositions. This process is referred to as propositionalization (i.e., rendering the content by appropriate propositions). The peculiar use of the word *semantically*, in commenting on such renderings, should be noted. It is used with some frequency to mean "from the point of view of the semantic theory upon which the SSAs are based."

(3) In the notes on individual verses, the parts of propositions that are quoted from the displays are in bold type. Only that part discussed in the note is given. The full Greek text is not included in the interest of saving space. (Readers may refer to interlinear texts.)

(4) In the relational structure shown in the displays, the word NUCLEUS signifies a prominent or central proposition. In some cases, two NUCLEI are considered to be of equal prominence with no subordinate propositions relating to them. In other cases, the NUCLEUS is the central proposition with a restatement or clarification relation (not a logical relation) subordinate to it.

A difference between this SSA and previously published ones is that a word identified or described by a succeeding proposition appears in single quotation marks on the horizontal line leading to the proposition in which it occurs, and on the next horizontal line the label "identification" or "description" appears.

(5) A distinction is made in the displays between communication relations on lower levels and those on higher levels. The communication relations between the highest level units *within* a paragraph are referred to as the "paragraph pattern" (abbreviated in the displays as ¶ PTRN). Relations between paragraphs or higher-level units are referred to as macrostructure relations. Paragraph patterns and macrostructures are shown in the left-hand column of the displays under these headings. (Paragraph-pattern constituents are usually propositional clusters but sometimes single propositions. For a thorough discussion of these the reader should refer to Tuggy 1992.) It is recognized that sometimes there is more than one type of pattern operating in a given unit (e.g., a repartee pattern as well as an individual intent pattern); when this is the case, both are referred to in the notes and both appear in the left-hand column of the display, but under the same heading in the box at the top of the column (¶ PTRN). To distinguish the paragraph-pattern relations from lower-level relational structure, the labels of the former are italicized in the displays. For both types of labels the most prominent constituent appears in uppercase letters. Paragraph pattern labels are connected by a vertical line drawn from the center of such labels.

(6) In some cases, a given proposition is given two relational labels, one above the other. In nearly all such cases the upper label relates to the preceding proposition and the lower label to the following proposition. For example, 2:12b is at the same time the CONCLUSION to the grounds in 12a and the CONTRAEXPECTATION to the concession in 12c. In a few places both labels of the double label relate to two preceding propositions or both to two succeeding propositions, the upper label relating to the first of them and the lower one to the second.

(7) Horizontal lines in the relational structure diagrams are drawn to the left of the proposition that is most prominent within a cluster of related propositions. If two or more propositions are considered equally prominent, the horizontal line to the left is connected to the center of the vertical line joining them. Vertical lines connect propositions or propositional clusters that are directly related to each other. The label of a less prominent proposition is slightly indented from the label of the more prominent proposition to which it is connected.

(8) In the thematic outline (pp. 16–27) and elsewhere in this work, the names of units above the paragraph level (e.g., part, subpart, division, subdivision, section) represent groupings of successive steps down in the hierarchy. For example, the unit 6:1–8:39 is called "subdivision"; and its constituents on the next lower level are called "sections." But note that 9:1–11:36 is called a "subdivision cluster" rather than a "subdivision." The term *cluster* denotes a unit whose constituents are not all of the same rank (i.e., at least one of its constituents is of lower rank than the others).

(9) The first person plural pronoun is to be taken as inclusive unless followed by *(exc)*. The second person pronoun is to be taken as plural unless followed by *(sg)*.

Use of a Semantic and Structural Analysis

To the translator who not only must determine the exegesis of a passage but also resolve a myriad of problems on how to translate it into a given receptor language, it may seem sheer drudgery to wade through the detailed arguments backing up the exegetical decisions of the SSA. After all, the SSA's purpose is to save the translator all this research. On the other hand, in some cases the decisions have been very difficult, and the material in the displays may not sound like other versions. Thus the translator is encouraged to study the notes, especially at those places where the display's rendering may seem questionable; the notes, in the interest of sound scholarship, present defenses of renderings that appear to be significantly different from the form of the original.

A translator may wish to compare a display with commentaries, versions, and other helps. Where there is obvious agreement, he can then move ahead with confidence. But where there are differences, the notes present the reasoning behind the rendering in the display. Then he can make his own informed decision on which interpretation he wishes to follow.

In some cases the notes present an alternate propositionalization which the translator might prefer; sometimes they present alternate suggestions for translation which might prove very helpful. For these additional reasons, then, the translator is encouraged to consult the notes consistently.

Finally, a few words of caution. This analysis represents the underlying semantic structure of a text, not what any specific translation in a given receptor language should look like. It is a source of information, *not* a model for translation. It seeks to represent the semantic content of the original in a way that the grammatical structure and the semantic structure match each other. (Concerning "mismatch or skewing between the semantic classification and the grammatical classification" see Beekman and Callow, p. 217.) Any translation that sounds just like the SSA rendering would be extremely dull, although in some languages it *will* be necessary to translate most abstract nouns in a form similar to that in the displays, and also all passive constructions as active as is almost always done in the displays. And certain figures of speech, such as metonymy, will have to be made nonfigurative as in the displays since they almost never occur in some receptor languages. *But the translator must always stay aware of the need to use the receptor-language forms in reformulating the semantic content.* This is why every time there is a figure of speech or a rhetorical question, there is, in the displays, a three-letter label in brackets identifying it. It is a signal saying to the translator, "Make sure you recognize the figure and translate it in the most appropriate way, not simply as the display has it."

Caution is also advised regarding the implicit information italicized in the propositions. If the translator were to include all the implicit information, the translation would sound overloaded or too interpretive; also the focus could be distorted. It is important to test the alternatives with speakers of the receptor language in order to determine what information they will and will not need, and how to include what they need in an appropriate way. (There are ways to present implicit information besides including it in the text.)

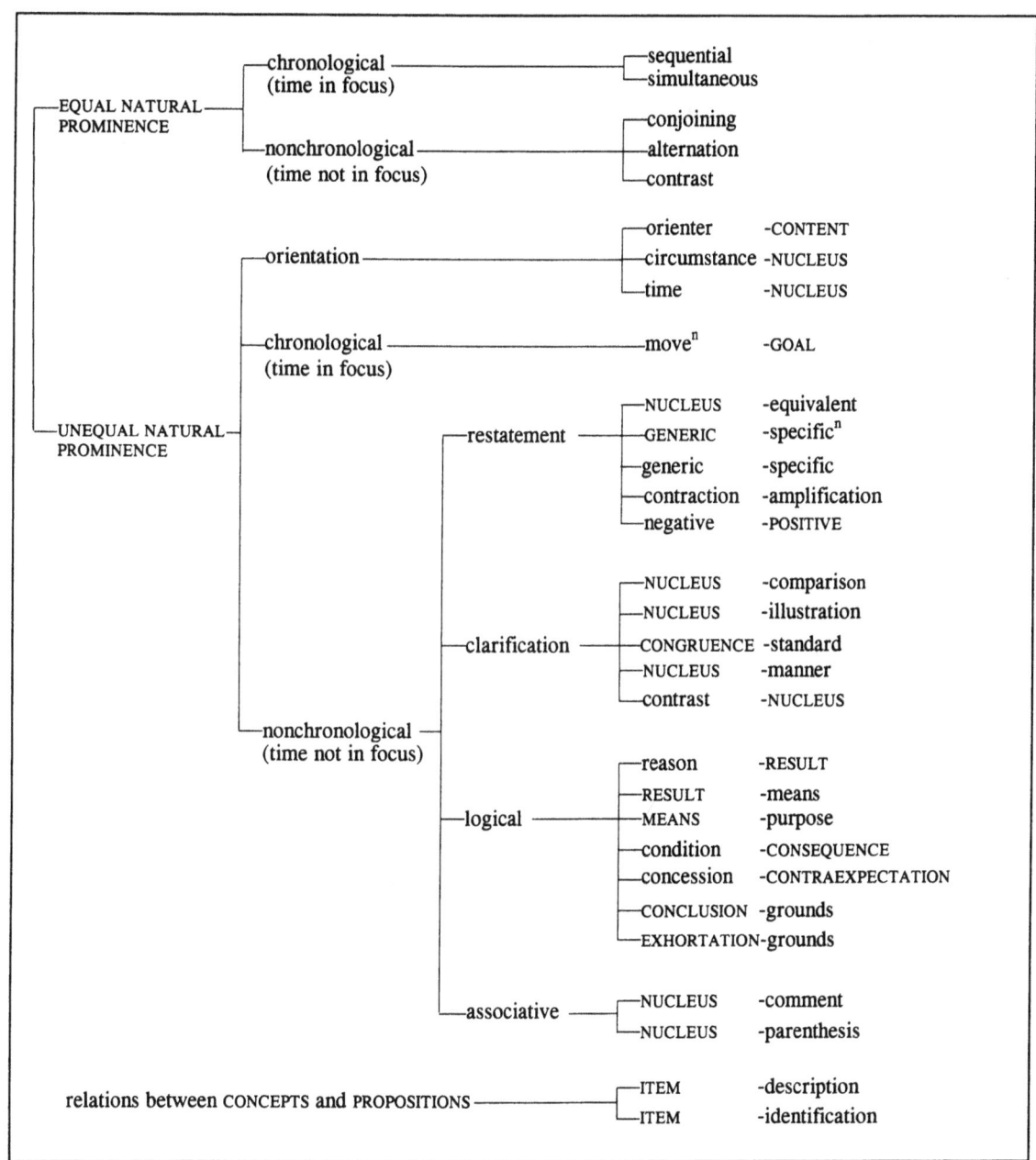

Chart of Communication Relations

Notes:
1. The relations are given in the chart in the usual order in which they are found in NT Greek. Where no natural prominence has been established and there is only contextual prominence, both relations are shown in lowercase letters (e.g., generic-specific).
2. In the displays an ITEM is shown as a gloss enclosed in single quote marks.

INTRODUCTION TO THE ANALYSIS OF ROMANS

The communication situation: Identification and status of the participants

The major participants in the Epistle to the Romans are identified at the beginning of the letter. Paul states that he is the writer (1:1) and that the letter is addressed to 'all God's beloved at Rome' (1:7). The Pauline authorship of the epistle has never been seriously questioned. Both the content and the style are typically Pauline, and church tradition has always been solidly behind Paul's being the author.

But some have questioned whether the epistle was actually destined for the church at Rome. These doubts have risen from two different considerations: First, certain manuscripts omit the words ἐν Ῥώμῃ 'in Rome' in 1:7 and 1:15. However, the evidence for the omission of these words is very weak. (The GNT editors give its inclusion an A rating, "certain," meaning that there is not much doubt in their minds.) It seems very likely that the words were deliberately omitted by some editor or copyist who felt that the letter was more general in application or that by omitting these words it could be commended as being general. (For a fuller discussion of the evidence supporting the inclusion of 'in Rome', see the notes on 1:7 and 1:15.)

The second consideration that could cause doubt about a Roman destination is that in quite a few manuscripts the 16:25–27 doxology appears at the end of chapter 14. These manuscripts seem to be based on Marcion's fourteen-chapter edition of the epistle dated c. 140 A.D. (Morris, pp. 21–24). Furthermore, one Vulgate manuscript contains summaries (breves) of sections of the epistle that give evidence of being based on a manuscript that lacked 15:1–16:24. Certain church fathers (Tertullian, Irenaeus, Cyprian) who would be expected to have commented on 15:1–16:24 make no quotations from them at all (ibid.:22). These and other considerations lead us to suspect that a fourteen-chapter version of Romans did exist. The question then is, What is its relation to the sixteen-chapter version, and how does this relate to its original destination?

Donfried, in his revised and expanded edition of *The Romans Debate* (p. 44), states, "There is a growing consensus, especially among continental NT scholars, that Romans 16 was not an original part of Paul's letter to Rome." Donfried takes issue with this view, and going on to discuss the major ideas concerning the purpose of the epistle, finds Marxsen's hypothesis (that it "was meant to deal with a specific set of problems in the church of Rome") the most plausible (p. 46). In the light of this purpose, Donfried concludes (p. 49) that

> it seems to follow quite well that Romans 16 was an original part of the letter to Rome, and the people whom Paul was greeting are persons he has met along his journeys who are now back in Rome after the death of Claudius.

(Marxsen himself did not come to this conclusion.)

With respect to the textual variations, Donfried (p. 50) suggests that the text originally ended at 16:23 (i.e., without the final doxology) and that Marcion shortened it for reasons of his own so that it ended at 14:23 and then added his own doxology. Donfried (ibid.) goes on to say:

> All further textual variations are then explained on the basis of a combination of this Marcionite edition of Romans with the primitive Pauline edition which had been preserved elsewhere.

Morris, in his excellent discussion on the status of chapter 16 (pp. 24–31), says, "It is not easy to escape the conclusion that Romans 16 is the intended and original conclusion of the letter."

Bruce (1991:176) is of the same opinion. He credits Harry Gamble's work in *The Textual History of the Letter to the Romans* with resolving the issue, stating that there "the problem of chapter 16 is dealt with . . . and answered—conclusively in my judgement—in favour of a Roman destination." One of the arguments concerning chapter 16 is that it seems strange for Paul to know twenty-six Christians in a city he has never visited. Proponents of this argument suggest that the letter containing chapter 16 went to Ephesus. That city is suggested because Priscilla and Aquila, mentioned in 16:3–4, are last heard of in Ephesus (Acts 18:19, 26). Lampe's reply (p. 219) to this argument, citing references to the frequency of travel between Rome and the east in that time is excellent; and he states in addition that "Nothing forces us to assume that Paul actually knew *all* of the 26 personally and that consequently all of them had been in the east for a while" (pp. 219–20). His whole discussion on the alleged problems of chapter 16 (pp. 217–21) is excellent.

Watson agrees: "it is . . . by no means certain that Paul knew personally all the individuals who are named in Rom. 16" (p. 208).

A very different approach to the destination of the epistle is given by Jervell. Though not doubting that the epistle was sent to Rome, he gives his thesis as follows: "The essential and primary content of Romans (1:18–11:36) is . . . the defense which Paul plans to give before the church in Jerusalem" (p. 56). He thinks the epistle "is primarily directed to Jerusalem, but also to Rome" (ibid.) because Paul needs the Roman congregation "for solidarity, support, and intercession on his behalf" (ibid.).

One difficulty with such a supposition is that Paul's mention of Jerusalem in 15:26 is only to show why he will be delayed in coming to Rome; there is no hint that he wants to do anything there except deliver the collected funds. Jervell says, "The reason for writing Romans is expressed in 15:30–32" (p. 57). One difficulty with such a statement is that in 15:30–32 Paul says nothing about "support and solidarity" with respect to his forthcoming trip to Jerusalem. Furthermore, if 15:30–32 expresses the reason for the epistle, then why all the previous fourteen chapters? He suggests that Paul wants to convey to the church in Jerusalem his belief that God still has a future for Israel. This, however, is but one small part of those fourteen chapters. Furthermore, there is no hint in the text that Paul plans or expects to be able to do this in Jerusalem. Jervell thinks that "In Romans Paul is absorbed by what he is going to say in Jerusalem" (p. 60), but Jervell's ideas are pure conjecture; there is no evidence for this from the text itself. He suggests that "the Roman congregation is supposed to fight with Paul against Jerusalem" and "help save him from the Jews" (p. 62). But Jerusalem is a long way from Rome, some 1,500 miles; and as Bruce (1991:192) notes, "There would . . . be no time for the Roman Christians to get in touch with Jerusalem between their receiving this letter and Paul's arrival in Jerusalem."

Wedderburn (p. 195, citing W. S. Campbell 1973–74) is correct in stating that "any view which saw in Romans a letter directed rather to the Jerusalem church failed to explain why it was ever sent to Rome." He refutes the suggestion that Romans was really a circular letter (so Manson and Jewett). Wedderburn says that there are too many specifics in the epistle to support such a suggestion, especially in chaps. 12–15. Morris (p. 10) concurs, pointing out the "very personal tone of some parts of the letter, for example, 1:8–15," adding that there is no evidence of the letter's having been sent anywhere except Rome.

The status of the Roman church

Jervell (pp. 54–55) laments that "attempts to understand Romans primarily on the basis of our knowledge of the Roman congregation lead us into a dead end." This statement, however, is certainly invalid in view of Wiefel's excellent article, originally published in German a year before Jervell's, but now available in English in Donfried's *The Romans Debate* along with Jervell's. Wiefel's research (pp. 86–101) has substantiated the following:

(1) Jews composed a significant part of the population at Rome (p. 87).

(2) The Romans considered the Jewish religion a foreign superstition and thus subject to scorn (p. 88).

(3) The Jews were "a diverse community of individually structured congregations whose esteemed officials [were] responsible for their religious and social functions" (p. 91); and this "loose structure . . . provided an essential prerequisite for the early penetration of Christianity in Rome" (p. 92).

(4) The edict by Claudius in A.D. 49 expelling all Jews from Rome "also meant the end of the first Christian congregation in Rome, which up until then had consisted of Jewish Christians" (p. 93). Therefore when that edict was, in effect, annulled by the death of Claudius in A.D. 54 and Christians were free to return, it resulted in a new congregation in Rome. But since synagogue assemblies were forbidden for some time, the Christians could gather only if they "had broken ties with the synagogue" (p. 94). This required the believers to set up a new organizational structure of house churches; and in these churches, Wiefel suggests (p. 96), the Jews were now only a minority. He also states, "It is safe to assume that quite a few of the returning Christians had been influenced by Paul's gospel of freedom from the law" (p. 94).

(5) There was "a strong anti-Jewish sentiment in Rome at the time of Nero and before. Positive statements [of Paul's] regarding all of Israel . . . must be seen against this background" (p. 100).

Lampe treats the composition of the church at Rome in detail (pp. 216–30). He calculates from the occurrences of the word συγγενής 'fellow countryman' in chapter 16 that probably 15 percent of those Paul mentions there are Jewish Christians (p. 225). He estimates that just over half of the individuals mentioned in chapter 16 were probably not born in Rome and that probably more than two-thirds "have an affinity to slave origins" (p. 228).

Bruce states (and other commentators agree) that "when Paul sent his letter to the Roman Christians, the majority of them were apparently Gentiles" (1991:180). This is clearly the meaning in 1:5–6 and especially 1:13: 'among you . . . as among the other Gentiles'. (Commentators also cite 11:13ff. and 15:15ff. as implying the same thing; but the latter passage is ambiguous on this point, and in the other Paul is addressing the Gentiles among his audience.) As to relations between the Jewish and Gentile Christians in this congregation, Bruce (1991:180) says, "It is implied in Romans 11:13–24 that the Gentile Christians tended to look down on their Jewish brethren as poor relations."

Many commentators note the conspicuous absence of ἐκκλησία 'church' in Romans in contrast to other epistles. Coupled with this, the mention in chapter 16 of groups meeting in the houses of various individuals is notable. In fact, "During the two first centuries the Christians of the city of Rome met separately in privately owned locations scattered around the capital city" (Lampe, p. 229). This statement is verified by historical records.

Dunn (p. lii) suggests that since Paul knew very few people of the Christian community in Rome, never having visited there, "there must have been at least several other house churches unknown personally to Paul." Stuhlmacher (1991a:241) makes an interesting inference from this, saying that "This meant that the letter to the Romans had to be passed around from one group to another." But his inference is perhaps unnecessary; the house churches may have met together from time to time.

Watson (p. 206) sees Paul as addressing "two congregations, separated by mutual hostility and suspicion over the question of the law, which he wishes to bring together into one congregation." In support of this idea he cites 15:7 ('Welcome one another'); he says, "The purpose of welcoming or receiving one another is 'common worship.'" But this is not what the word προσλαμβάνεσθε 'accept' implies. He takes ἐν ἑνὶ στόματι 'with one mouth' in 15:6 to mean "common worship"; but again this is poor exegesis. That phrase is part of the purpose cluster that relates to τὸ αὐτὸ φρονεῖν ἐν ἀλλήλους 'to live harmoniously with each other'. Watson (p. 209) takes 14:1–15:13 as another piece of evidence of two separate groups within the Roman church. But nothing in the text suggests that; all one can say for sure is that there were individuals who did not get along well with other individuals. He also says that the commands for greeting in chapter 16 are not addressed to individuals, and that Paul is "in effect requesting his readers in both groups to introduce themselves to one another" (p. 211). Such exegesis is totally unwarranted. Whether he greets individuals or groups, Paul always uses an imperative to ask the addressee(s) to greet that individual, never saying 'I greet X' (cf. Phil. 4:21, Col. 4:15, 2 Tim. 4:19, Tit. 3:15). Lampe's view (p. 230) that there were "at least seven separate groups" is the much more likely one.

Occasion and purpose of the letter

The question arises why the translator needs to know the occasion and purpose of Paul's letter to the Romans. One of the answers, in the words of Donfried (p. xliii), is that "if one does not know the original intention of a document one can hardly interpret its contemporary meaning with accuracy and precision." But more importantly for a translator, the communication situation is part of the meaning of any text. Any writer to a specific audience shares assumptions and background information with his audience, whether linguistic, cultural, social, political, or religious. This shared information molds what the writer says and—extremely important for a translator—what he does not say (because he assumes there is no need to say it). A writer also has certain attitudes toward his audience, and they are part of the communication situation meaning as well.

With that in mind, we turn to the epistle itself and find that much disagreement exists among commentators as to its occasion and purpose. Klein (p. 29) says that "this document has thus far revealed less of the secret of its occasion than has any other authentic letter of Paul." That is partly due to a long expository section (basically 1:16–11:32) that seems general enough to apply to any group of Christians, followed by certain hortatory sections (chaps. 12 and 13) that likewise seem, from a cursory glance, to be very general. Klein also points out that with respect to several unanswered questions about the epistle, "contradictory positions prevail which suggest that the basic methodology [for determining Paul's purpose] is unclear" (ibid.). This is true; and to fill the gap, I will offer suggestions toward a methodology of textual analysis (see p. 20) designed to give good, clear answers to many if not all of these questions.

Donfried (p. 102) states that although there is a plethora of ideas on the purpose of the epistle, "there are basically two major opposing viewpoints":

> (1) those scholars who believe that Paul directed this letter to deal with a specific, concrete situation in Rome; and (2) those interpreters who hold that it is directed primarily to a situation other than Rome.

We have already dealt with the second of these. Stuhlmacher (1991a:232) suggests that there is actually a third option, one that in a sense combines the first two, namely,

> that the message Paul intends to defend at Jerusalem is identical with the gospel he plans to preach at Rome, and from Rome all the way to Spain. Thus Romans is a synopsis of Paul's gospel as a whole, and in the course of history it became for subsequent generations his "testament."

Let us consider this last notion briefly. As Stuhlmacher (ibid.:231) notes, "Romans has been read by the church as the *doctrinae Christianae compendium* (Melancthon) and is still regarded as such." Although that idea was challenged by Baur in 1836, few took notice of his insights, and the notion of Romans as a compendium of the Christian religion held sway almost unchallenged at least until the publication of Nygren's commentary in 1944.

Manson has recently suggested a somewhat similar purpose for Romans. He suggests (p. 15) that the letter is "a manifesto setting forth [Paul's] deepest convictions on central issues, a manifesto calling for the widest publicity." Because of the previously mentioned textual problems, he thinks the letter was originally prepared to send to Ephesus, with a copy modified by many appended greetings sent to Rome. (The problems with these suppositions have already been discussed.) One of those sympathetic to Manson was Bornkamm. But although Bornkamm believes that chapter 16 belonged to a manuscript that was sent to Ephesus, his ideas on the portion that went to Rome are not much different from those of Melancthon. Manson concludes by saying (pp. 27–28),

> This great document, which summarizes and develops the most important themes and thoughts of the Pauline message and theology and which elevates his theology above the moment of definite situations and conflicts into the sphere of the eternally and universally valid, this letter to the Romans is the last will and testament of the Apostle Paul.

Donfried replies (p. 46) that although Romans did in effect become Paul's last will and testament, "this does not help us to understand why Paul should write a letter in the particular manner and style and send it to Rome. Why should the Romans be interested in such a last will and testament?" Furthermore, there are too many clues that this letter was addressing certain problems in Rome and was somehow intended to prepare the way for his intended visit there to dismiss it as being simply a general statement of Paul's theology.

We now turn to the various views of those who believe that the epistle expresses a vital relationship between Paul and the Roman church. In rebutting Klein (p. 39), who says, "Paul can consider an apostolic effort in Rome because he does not regard the local Christian community there as having an apostolic foundation," Donfried replies (p. 45) that "Klein's interesting suggestion has little exegetical support." He goes on to show that in 15:14–15 Paul states that he is very satisfied with their spiritual progress, and is writing what he does simply by way of reminder—

> hardly a situation which would indicate "that for Paul, Christianity in Rome still needed an apostolic foundation. . . ." Further, one would hardly expect Paul to do such a rebuilding job simply "in passing" (15:24) as he goes to Spain.

(See also Dunn, pp. lv–lvi.)

Bruce (1991:193) suggests that the main purpose of the epistle was to prepare the church for his visit. In view of the fact that Paul's driving ambition was "the evangelization of the Gentile world," if he could associate with his world vision a whole community like the Roman church, the unfinished task might be accomplished the sooner.... These hopes and visions embraced not only the advance of the Gentile mission but also the ingathering of Israel which, he was persuaded, would follow the completion of the Gentile mission. (ibid.)

The difficulty with this statement of purpose for the epistle is again that it is built on too much conjecture and not enough solid textual evidence. One could argue that in 15:14-29 Paul is writing a "letter of self-introduction to a church he hopes will undertake his support" (Greek consultant John Werner, personal communication). But to make the rather ambiguous words of the one clause ἐλπίζω . . . ὑφ' ὑμῶν προπεμφθῆναι 'I hope to be sent forward by you'—and that in a subordinate γάρ clause—*the* main purpose of the epistle is unwarranted, especially when balanced against fourteen and a half chapters of detailed exposition and exhortation. Paul gives no hint that he thinks his labors (or anyone else's) will cause "all Israel to be saved" (Rom. 11:26). He does not state overtly that he wants their support for anything other than a proposed visit to Spain. Furthermore, Bruce's thesis does not really account for the extended discussion of the relations between the 'weak' and the 'strong' in 14:1-15:13, or for the discussion on subjection to authorities in chapter 13, much less for the 1:16-11:28 expository section.

Kümmel's ideas are similar to those of Bruce. According to Kümmel, Paul wrote the epistle to build up good relations with the church in Rome because he wanted to establish Rome as a base for further operations, in Spain and elsewhere. The objections to Bruce's ideas apply to Kümmel's. As Klein notes (p. 33), "Apart from the casual remarks in 15:24, 28, there is no mention anywhere of the planned trip to Spain"; that is, its brief mention here is not thematic enough to establish this as the main purpose of the epistle. Nor, as Jervell notes (p. 57), "would it explain plausibly his extended remarks in the main section."

To come up with an adequate statement of purpose for the whole epistle, one needs to keep Stuhlmacher's statement (1991b:334) in mind: "If there is one central theme in the letter at all, then it must be evident for the reader on the basis of the text of the letter itself." And since the epistle does not contain a forthright statement such as "the purpose of this epistle is . . . ," it needs to come from a consideration of all the parts and their relation to one another, especially the hortatory passages, and not just of one exhortation (e.g., 15:30-31) and statement of goal (e.g., 1:15), especially one with no hint of seeking financial support.

The only expressions of purpose for the epistle which do justice to the whole text itself are those developed by Marxsen. As Donfried (p. 47) summarizes it, Marxsen's thesis is that

> the theology of Romans—especially the constant interplay between "Jew" and "Gentile"—reflects a concrete historical problem in the church of Rome.

At this point Karris (p. 127) raises a question: Why should we make the Pauline letter pattern so rigid that all Paul's letters have to be addressed to the specific situations of the churches or persons addressed? The answer is that we don't have to, but in all Paul's other letters he is clearly addressing specific needs and problems, and an adequate analysis of this epistle shows that it is not an exception to the rule. Donfried's first methodological principle (p. 103) is valid here:

> Any study of Romans should proceed on the initial assumption that this letter was written by Paul to deal with a concrete situation in Rome. The support for such an assumption is the fact that every other authentic Pauline writing, without exception, is addressed to the specific situations of the churches or persons involved. To argue that Romans is an exception to the Pauline pattern is certainly possible, but the burden of proof rests with those exegetes who wish to demonstrate that it is impossible, or at least not likely, that Romans addresses a concrete set of problems in the life of the Christians in Rome. This methodological principle is of great importance since so many recent studies begin with the opposite assumption and never even explore the historical data available concerning Jews and Christians in Rome; on the contrary, one must first begin with a review of the available historical data.

There are others besides Marxsen and Donfried who state that Romans was written to address a specific situation, for example, Minear, Wiefel, Wedderburn, Stuhlmacher, Aune, Morris, and Dunn. Some of their comments follow.

Minear (as summarized by Donfried, p. 106) gives two main purposes of Paul in writing to Rome:

(1) to communicate plans about his future apostolic work, and (2) to deal with "the difficulties which had been reported within the congregations in Rome."

Aune says (pp. 278–79),

> Romans is a speech of exhortation in written form which Paul addressed to Roman Christians to convince them (or remind them) of the truth of his version of the gospel . . . and to encourage a commitment to the kind of lifestyle which Paul considered consistent with his gospel.

This is good, but too general and does not identify the particular problems being addressed by Paul.

Stuhlmacher (1991a:239) agrees with Aune. He suggests that by the time Paul wrote the epistle he had quite a few Christian critics as well as friends at Rome, and that the influence of these "counter-missionaries" might make it impossible for Paul to have any ministry in Rome. The purpose of the epistle for him is thus to warn his recipients that they

> should pay no attention to the insinuations of those in Rome who oppose the gospel planted there, for Paul is entirely in agreement with it. . . . When the Apostle emphasizes in 1:16 that he is not ashamed of the gospel, he is signaling to friend and foe alike among his recipients that he intends to stick to his embattled cause in Rome as elsewhere.

While there is a good deal to commend such an interpretation, it does not begin to do justice to the major hortatory section in 14:1–15:13, nor to the extended discussion of the future of Israel in chapters 9–11.

At this point it would be helpful to review some of the major tenets of the method of discourse analysis used in the Semantic and Structural Analyses (referred to also in the General Introduction). We assume that any well-formed written discourse is composed of a hierarchy of constituent parts that are appropriately related to each other according to the genre of each of the units. In making an analysis one looks at each unit and determines from its surface forms what genre it belongs to (hortatory, expository, etc.). One then determines the constituent parts of the unit and then, according to whether these involve elements of solutionality, causality, or intentionality, determines the subtype. The theory also states that there is natural prominence and possibly marked prominence within the elements that make up any unit from the paragraph level on up.

Clearly there is in the Roman epistle a long expository division (1:16–11:36) followed by a generic hortatory division (12:1–15:13) and then several more specific hortatory parts (15:14–33, 16:1–16, 16:17–20). According to the theory, the theme for the book—and thus its purpose—should be drawn from the highest-level themes of all the major divisions of the book. In the case of the hortatory units this will mean including material from both the *APPEALS* and their *bases*. Since 1:16–11:36 is the *basis* for the *APPEAL* starting in 12:1, the theme for the whole book must reflect that. And the theme for the whole book must include material from all the high-level hortatory units in chapters 12–16, including the greetings in 16. And the resulting theme statement should tie in closely with what we know about the communication situation. Another pertinent feature of the theory is that motifs (indicated by certain recurring lexical items) are thematic and so need to be reflected in theme statements also.

The results of the analysis following these principles can be seen in the epistle's theme statement in the "Thematic Outline" (p. 24). It suggests that there is not one purpose but several in the epistle, and that these purposes are related. Paul does indeed explain what has hindered his visiting Rome thus far, and he explains his intention to see them and requests their prayers for his intervening time in Jerusalem (15:14–33). He asks them to greet various believers (16:3–16). He also asks them to be subject to civil authorities (13:1–7).

How does this last-mentioned matter relate to the communication situation? Dunn suggests (p. liv) that there was a "strong likelihood that in the years prior to 58 the collection of taxes was a sensitive matter within the public domain," and that the purpose of the 13:1–7 exhortation was to enable the Christians "to 'keep a low profile' on such a politically sensitive matter as public taxation" (ibid.).

Bruce (1991:185) goes a bit further. Since the arrival of the gospel had led to riots in Rome earlier,

> It was most important that Christians in the imperial capital should recognize their responsibility not to give any support by their way of life to this widespread imputation of disloyalty.

As to the section on Israel, again, as Bruce notes (1991:184), the exposition is very relevant to the communication situation:

> [In this passage, Paul] warns the Gentiles among his readers not to despise the Jews, whether the Jews in general or Jewish Christians in particular, because God has not written them off.

Gaston's comment (p. 326) is even more pertinent:

> God is faithful to his promises to Israel, . . . that all Israel will be saved, and . . . that all this has to do not with human doing or believing but with the grace and mercy of God. They should know this because they have been called into the people of God on exactly the same basis.

One question remains which most commentators do not seem to have grappled with adequately. (Gaston's comment points in the right direction.) Just how does all the expository material on justification by faith pertain to the communication situation and Paul's overall purpose? Part of the answer to this is that Paul is clarifying the gospel that he preaches; for, as Bruce (1991:182) points out, "Misrepresentations of [Paul's] preaching and his apostolic procedure were current and must have found their way to Rome."

But even more germane (and based on some of the tenets of the theory of semantic structure), there are two motif elements, 'all' and 'both Jews and Gentiles', which recur throughout the expository material. Although Paul makes several appeals in the latter part of the book, the longest of these, and thus presumably the most prominent, is in 14:1–15:13 regarding the relations between the 'strong' and the 'weak' Christians. (For the discussion defending the identification of the 'strong' with Gentile believers and the 'weak' with Jewish believers, see the notes on 14:1, 2b, 10a–b, and 20d–f.) If this analysis is valid—and most commentators agree that it is—then what Paul is saying in the long expository section is that there is one way of salvation for everyone. There is no difference between how Jews are saved and how Gentiles are saved. They are all on the same footing. And therefore neither group has grounds for antipathy towards the other. On the contrary, they all—both Jewish and Gentile believers—are to accept one another and act towards each other in ways that 'make for peace and mutual upbuilding' (14:19). Stuhlmacher's comment (1991b:341) on the relationship between Romans 1–11 and 12–16 is excellent. He gives two reasons why 12–16 is also related to the theme of the righteousness of God:

> First, and above all, because God in Christ does not just declare those who believe [i.e., both Jews and Gentiles] to be righteous on the basis of grace, but at the same time, in doing so, lays hold of them anew in obedience. The new life that the justified obtain is thus called, according to Rom. 6:15ff., a "slavery to righteousness" and finds its God-pleasing expression in the new way of life which the Christians lead. Second, chapters 12–16 belong inextricably to the letter to the Romans because the apostle nowhere (and certainly also not in Romans) expounds abstract theology, but always only concrete exhortation. Whether the Romans really believe in Christ as their redeemer and Lord will be evident, according to Paul, by how they (as Gentile and Jewish Christians) deal with one another and how they resolve the tensions among one another in Rome (cf. ch. 14).

Another subject should be considered here, one that has created a great problem for commentators who try to determine Paul's overall purpose. That is the relation between Paul's statements in 1:15 and 15:20. In 1:15 he says, "I am eager to preach the gospel also to you who are at Rome," and in 15:20, "It has always been my ambition to preach the gospel where Christ was not known" (NIV). Are these two statements contradictory? Klein (p. 32) says that they clearly are:

> Paul unmistakably makes known to us his intention to preach the gospel to the Romans; on the other hand, he states his principle of non-interference. If we at this point suggest restraint in interfering with the text, the above mentioned difficulty of interpretation will remain a major problem in attempting to clarify the circumstances of the origin of Paul's Epistle to the Romans.

Wedderburn (pp. 197-99) recognizes the conflict between the two statements and offers one possible solution—that the verb εὐαγγελίζεσθαι is used in a somewhat different sense in the two passages. This is clearly possible. Surely the good news about Christ and what he can do for us is not confined to initial salvation. Furthermore, Paul did more than just preach the gospel in his journeys, according to the record from Luke: "Paul and Barnabas remained in Antioch, teaching [διδάσκοντες] and preaching [εὐαγγελιζόμενοι] the word of the Lord" (Acts 15:35); and "he stayed [in Corinth] a year and six months, teaching [διδάσκων] the word of God among them" (Acts 18:11). So one can easily take the verb in Rom. 1:15 in a more generic sense, not just preaching to the unsaved.

Wedderburn (p. 199) has another good comment:

> It may be that Paul is guilty of an indiscretion in using this word in Rom. 1:15 and that he is not sticking to the letter of his principle laid down in 15:20; however, in all fairness it must be noted that he merely states what his ambition is in the latter verse and does not state that he utterly eschews any form of preaching where Christ is already named.

The analysis given here is based on the assumption that there is no discrepancy at all. In 1:15 there is no main verb with the adjective πρόθυμον 'eager'. English versions that supply a form of the verb 'to be' assume that it must be supplied in the present tense. But Stuhlmacher (1991a:237) points out that 1:15 is the conclusion of 1:13-14 and that it explains Paul's original plan, not what he is currently intending to do. He supports translating it as "Therefore for my part I was prepared to preach the gospel to you in Rome as well." Stuhlmacher's conclusion is that this verse in no way indicates that Paul is "still intending to come as a missionary to preach his gospel in Rome": what "he hopes to achieve there he has already told them in vv. 11-12," and preaching the gospel is clearly not implied.

Date of composition

Although it is impossible to pin down with certainty the exact date of writing, many scholars in recent years seem to have narrowed it down to within about one year. As Manson says (p. 4),

> It involves forward reckoning from the date of Gallio's proconsulship at Corinth and back reckoning from the date of the replacement of Felix by Festus in the procuratorship of Judaea.

Since Paul's trial before Gallio can hardly have taken place before the summer of A.D. 51, the intervening events would mean Paul's three months in Greece (where he wrote the epistle) could not have occurred before the winter of 54-55. Felix could not have taken over from Festus later than A.D. 61. Subtracting the time of Paul's imprisonment in Caesarea, the latest date for the epistle must be the winter of 58-59. Within that time frame, Barrett (p. 5) opts for an earlier date, the first three months of 55. Morris (pp. 6-7) also supports A.D. 55. Harrison (p. 4) tends towards early 57. Dunn (p. xliii) says "most probably late 55/early 56, or late 56/early 57," and Cranfield (p. 16) holds the same view. Bornkamm (p. 16) is certain that "the winter of A.D. 55/56" is correct. Bruce (1991:177) opts for "early in (probably) 57."

INTRODUCTION TO THE ANALYSIS OF ROMANS 23

THE CONSTITUENT ORGANIZATION OF ROMANS

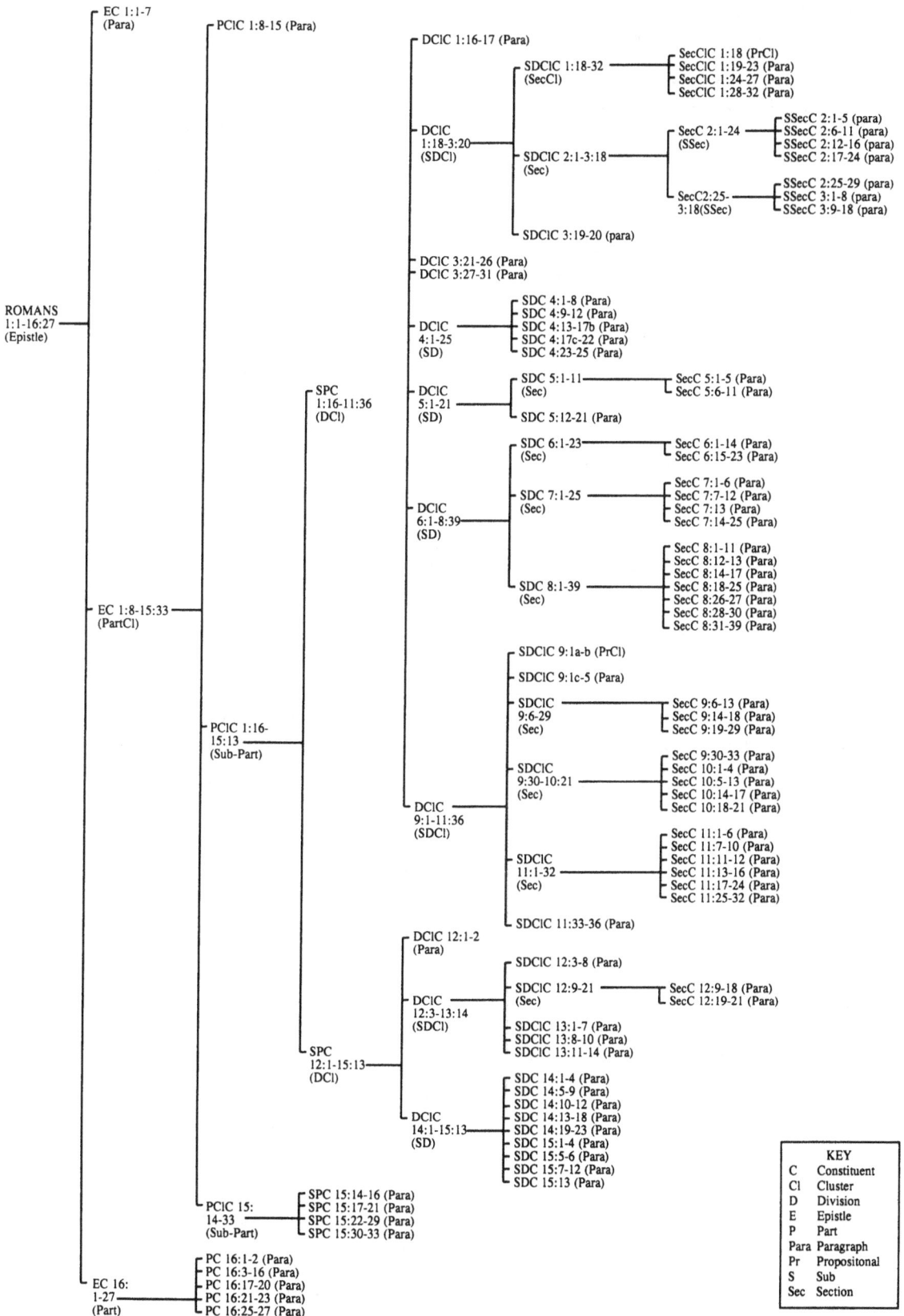

OVERVIEW: THEMATIC OUTLINE OF ROMANS

ROMANS 1:1–16:27 (Epistle)
Theme: I, Paul, an apostle appointed to proclaim the good news about Jesus Christ, am writing this letter to all you believers who are in Rome.

I thank God that people everywhere are talking about how you Roman believers are trusting Jesus Christ. I pray that God will permit me to visit you soon. I want you to know that I have longed to do that, but things have always prevented me. I was eager to proclaim the good news to you who live at Rome.

I very confidently proclaim the good news about what Christ has done. This good news states that everyone, whether Jew or non-Jew, has done evil and deserves to be condemned by God, but now God saves those who trust in Jesus Christ and declares their guilt is ended. Abraham illustrates that this way of being declared righteous is a gift, not earned. The implications of being declared righteous are that we have peace with God, we experience his grace, we rejoice even in suffering, we are saved from eternal punishment, we are freed from the control of sinful desires and compulsion to obey the Mosaic law to be saved, we can live as God's Spirit directs, and no one can prevail against us.

Though I grieve greatly that most Jews have rejected Christ, you non-Jews must not despise the Jews and must know that some day all the Jews will be saved.

Because of all these things, present yourselves to God to be like living sacrifices. Let God change your way of thinking and acting. Think about yourselves sensibly by considering the abilities God has given you. Love others sincerely in your actions toward them. Be subject to the civil authorities and pay all of them what they require. Accept those who doubt whether they are permitted to do certain things; specifically, anyone who thinks it is all right to eat all kinds of food must not despise those who don't, and those who don't think so must not condemn those who do.

Because of the work of proclaiming the gospel among the non-Jews in places where they have not heard about Christ, I have often been hindered from visiting you, but I hope to see you when I travel to Spain. But now I am about to go to Jerusalem. Pray that God will protect me from the unbelieving Jews there and that the believers will accept the money I take to them.

Finally, receive and help Phoebe. Greet many individual believers there. Note and avoid those who cause quarrels among you and those who cause people to turn away from God. Let us forever praise that One who alone is God and is truly wise. Several of the people here send their greetings.

EPISTLE CONSTITUENT 1:1–7 (Descriptive Paragraph: Opening of the epistle)
Theme: I, Paul, an apostle who was appointed to proclaim the good news about Jesus Christ, am writing this letter to all you believers who are in Rome. I pray that God will continue to act graciously toward you and grant you peace.

EPISTLE CONSTITUENT 1:8–15:33 (Hortatory Part Cluster: Body of the epistle)
Theme: I thank God that people everywhere are talking about how you Roman believers are trusting Jesus Christ. I pray that God will permit me to visit you soon. I want you to know that I have longed to do that, but things have always prevented me. I was eager to proclaim the good news to you who are living at Rome also.

I very confidently proclaim the good news about what Christ has done. This good news states that although everyone, whether Jew or non-Jew, has done evil and deserves to be condemned by God, now he saves those who trust in Jesus Christ and declares their guilt ended. Abraham illustrates that this way of being declared righteous is a gift, not earned. Because God has declared us righteous, we have peace with God, we experience his grace, we rejoice even in suffering, we will be saved from eternal punishment, we have been freed from being controlled by sinful desires and being required to obey the Mosaic law to be saved, we can live as God's Spirit directs, and no one can prevail against us.

Though I grieve greatly that most Jews have rejected Christ, you non-Jews must not despise the Jews, and you must know that some day all the Jews will be saved.

Because of all these things, present yourselves to God to be like living sacrifices. Let God change your thinking and acting. Think about yourselves sensibly by considering the abilities God has given you. Love others sincerely in your actions toward them. Be subject to the civil authorities and pay all of them what they require. Accept those who doubt whether they are permitted to do certain things; specifically, anyone who thinks it is all right to eat all kinds of food must not despise those who don't, and those who don't think so must not condemn those who do.

Because of the work of proclaiming the gospel among the non-Jews in places where they have not heard about Christ, I have often been hindered from visiting you, but I hope to see you when I travel to Spain. But now I am about to go to Jerusalem, and I urge you to pray that God will protect me from the unbelieving Jews in Judea and that the believers there will accept the money I take to them.

PART CLUSTER CONSTITUENT 1:8-15 (Emotive Paragraph: Introduction to the core)

Theme: I thank God that people everywhere are talking about how you Roman believers are trusting Jesus Christ. I pray that God will permit me to visit you soon. I want you to know that I have longed to do that, but things have always prevented me. I was eager to proclaim the good news to you who are living at Rome also.

PART CLUSTER CONSTITUENT 1:16-15:13 (Hortatory Subpart: Core of the epistle)

Theme: I very confidently proclaim the good news about what Christ has done. This good news states that although everyone, whether Jew or non-Jew, has done evil and deserves to be condemned by God, now God saves those who trust in Jesus Christ, and he declares their guilt ended. Abraham illustrates that this way of being declared righteous is a gift, not earned. Because God has declared us righteous, we have peace with God, we experience his grace, we rejoice even in suffering, we will be saved from eternal punishment, we have been freed from being controlled by sinful desires and from being compelled to obey the Mosaic law to be saved, we can live as God's Spirit directs, and no one can prevail against us.

Though I grieve greatly that most Jews have rejected Christ, this does not prove that God's promise has failed. God is saving many non-Jews to make the Jews seek salvation. Some day all the Jews will be saved.

Therefore present yourselves to God to be like living sacrifices. Let God change your way of thinking and acting. Think of yourselves sensibly by considering and then using the abilities God has given you. Love others sincerely in your actions toward them. Be subject to the civil authorities and pay all of them what they require. Accept those who doubt whether they are permitted to do certain things; specifically, anyone who thinks it is all right to eat all kinds of food must not despise those who don't, and those who don't think so must not condemn those who do.

SUBPART CONSTITUENT 1:16-11:36 (Expository Division Cluster: Basis of the appeals in 12:1-15:13)

Theme: I very confidently proclaim the good news about what Christ has done. This good news declares that although everyone, whether Jew or non-Jew, has done evil and deserves to be condemned, now God saves those who trust in Christ and he declares their guilt ended. So we cannot boast about achieving this by obeying the Mosaic law. Abraham, who was declared righteous because he believed God's promise, illustrates that being declared righteous is a gift, not earned, and he is thus a spiritual father to all who trust in God, Jews and non-Jews. Because God has declared us righteous, we have peace with God, we experience his grace, we rejoice even in suffering, and we will be saved from eternal punishment, we have been freed from being controlled by sinful desires and being compelled to obey the Mosaic law to be saved, we are compelled to live as God's Spirit directs, and no one can prevail against us.

Though I grieve greatly that most of the Jews have rejected Christ, this does not prove that God's promise has failed or that God's condemning them is unjust. God is saving many non-Jews to make the Jews jealous and seek salvation. But don't you non-Jews despise the Jews, because if you fall away from God, he won't spare you either. And you need to know that some day all the Jews will be saved.

DIVISION CLUSTER CONSTITUENT 1:16-17 (Expository Paragraph: Theme of 1:16-11:36)

Theme: Because it is the powerful means God uses to save everyone who trusts in Christ, whether they are Jews or non-Jews, I very confidently proclaim the good news about what Christ has done, since by it God reveals his way of declaring people righteous.

DIVISION CLUSTER CONSTITUENT 1:18-3:20 (Expository Subdivision Cluster: Difficulty solved by 3:21-26)

Theme: All people, no matter whether they are Jews or non-Jews, have done evil and so deserve to be condemned by God.

SUBDIVISION CLUSTER CONSTITUENT 1:18-32 (Expository Section Cluster: Claim$_1$ of 1:18-3:20)

Theme: God is making it clear that he is angry with godless and wicked non-Jewish people, whom he has allowed to become enslaved to their own evil desires and worthless thoughts.

SECTION CLUSTER CONSTITUENT 1:18 (Expository Propositional Cluster: Claim of 1:18-32)
Theme: God is making it clear that he is angry with godless and wicked non-Jewish people.
SECTION CLUSTER CONSTITUENT 1:19-23 (Expository Paragraph: Cause of 1:24-32)
Theme: Everyone can clearly know what God is like; therefore no one has a basis for saying, "We never knew about God."
SECTION CLUSTER CONSTITUENT 1:24-27 (Expository Paragraph: Effect$_1$ of 1:19-23)
Theme: So God let the non-Jewish peoples feel compelled to do disgraceful things, which resulted in their dishonoring their bodies sexually. He did this because they worshiped idols and things which were created instead of God. As a result of both men and women having unnatural sexual relations, they have been punished as they deserve.
SECTION CLUSTER CONSTITUENT 1:28-32 (Expository Paragraph: Effect$_2$ of 1:19-23)
Theme: The result of God's letting them become obsessed by their own depraved thoughts was that they themselves began to do all manner of evil things that God says are improper. They even approve of others doing such things.

SUBDIVISION CLUSTER CONSTITUENT 2:1-3:18 (Expository Section: Claim$_2$ of 1:18-3:20)
Theme: Any one of you Jews, who has all the advantages of being a Jew and disobeys God's law, will also be condemned by him; God will consider your circumcision worthless and will accept the non-Jews who obey his laws. They will declare that God is right in condemning you. God will not treat us Jews more favorably than he will treat non-Jews.

SECTION CONSTITUENT 2:1-24 (Expository Subsection: Claim$_1$ of 2:1- 3:18)
Theme: Since God will recompense each person, Jew or non-Jew, according to what he has done and condemn him for his sin, any one of you Jews who has all the advantages of being a Jew and insults God by disobeying the Mosaic law will also be condemned by God for doing evil.

SUBSECTION CONSTITUENT 2:1-5 (Expository Paragraph: Claim$_1$ of 2:1-24)
Theme: Any one of you who condemns non-Jews for doing evil will be condemned by God, since you also do the same evil things.
SUBSECTION CONSTITUENT 2:6-11 (Expository Paragraph: Justification of claim$_1$ of 2:1-24)
Theme: God will recompense each person according to what he has done, since he is not influenced by a person's status.
SUBSECTION CONSTITUENT 2:12-16 (Expository Paragraph: Justification of claim$_2$ of 2:1-24)
Theme: All non-Jews will be eternally separated from God for their sin and all Jews will be condemned for their sin, since it is only those who have continually obeyed the Mosaic law whom God will justify.
SUBSECTION CONSTITUENT 2:17-24 (Expository Paragraph: Claim$_2$ of 2:1-24)
Theme: It is disgusting that any one of you who has all the advantages of being a Jew would disobey God's law and, by doing so, insult God.

SECTION CONSTITUENT 2:25-3:18 (Expository Subsection: Claim$_2$ of 2:1-3:18)
Theme: If any of you disobey the Mosaic law, God will consider your circumcision worthless and will accept the non-Jews who obey his law; and they will declare that God is right in condemning you. Our being circumcised Jews does benefit us. God has certainly kept his promise to bless us. But it is certainly right for God to punish us. God will condemn those who claim I say that we should continue to do evil and that God will no longer punish us for doing so. God will not treat us Jews more favorably than he will treat non-Jews.

SUBSECTION CONSTITUENT 2:25-29 (Expository Paragraph: Claim$_1$ of 2:25-3:18)

Theme: God will consider non-Jews acceptable to him if they obey his law, and such non-Jews will declare God is right in condemning those who disobey his laws, because it is only those who are changed inwardly who are true Jews and acceptable to God.

SUBSECTION CONSTITUENT 3:1-8 (Expository Paragraph: Claim$_2$ of 2:25-3:18)

Theme: My reply to the objection that therefore there is no advantage in being a Jew or being circumcised is that there is, especially since God entrusted his promises to us. My reply to the objection that God has not kept his promise is that he certainly has, for his promises are always true. My reply to the objection that it is not right for God to punish us Jews is that it certainly is, because if God didn't judge us Jews he couldn't judge anyone. But to anyone who objects that if our doing evil results in people praising God we should continue doing evil and God should no longer condemn us, I would reply that God will justly condemn people who claim I say such things.

SUBSECTION CONSTITUENT 3:9-18 (Expository Paragraph: Claim$_3$ of 2:25-3:18)

Theme: My reply to a query whether God will treat Jews more favorably than non-Jews is no, since the Scriptures make clear that all people are condemned by God for their sin.

SUBDIVISION CLUSTER CONSTITUENT 3:19-20 (Expository Paragraph: Summary of 1:18-3:18)

Theme: In summary, no one is able to object to God's condemnation; everyone has been declared guilty by God.

DIVISION CLUSTER CONSTITUENT 3:21-26 (Expository Paragraph: Major principle of 1:16-11:36)

Theme: Now God declares righteous everyone, Jew or non-Jew, who trusts in what Jesus Christ has done for them. God presented Christ as the one who would atone for sins by shedding his blood on the cross.

DIVISION CLUSTER CONSTITUENT 3:27-31 (Expository Paragraph: Inferences drawn from 3:21-26)

Theme: Therefore we are prevented from boasting about being justified by obeying the Mosaic law. And God will accept non-Jews too on the same basis. And by saying that people are declared righteous by their trusting in Christ, we actually confirm, not nullify, the Mosaic law.

DIVISION CLUSTER CONSTITUENT 4:1-25 (Expository Subdivision: Exemplary evidence of 3:21-26)

Theme: We can draw conclusions from Abraham about how to be declared righteous. He could not boast about that because Scripture records that it was because he believed God's promise that he was declared righteous by God. This happiness of being declared righteous was a gift from God, not a reward. It is also for the non-Jews, because it was spoken about Abraham before he became a Jew by being circumcised, which was simply a sign of his previously being declared righteous by faith. Thus Abraham is a spiritual father to all, both Jews and non-Jews, who believe as he did, and what was written of him is an assurance to us who would also be declared righteous.

SUBDIVISION CONSTITUENT 4:1-8 (Expository Paragraph: Claim$_1$ of 4:1-25)

Theme: We can draw conclusions from Abraham about how to be declared righteous. He could not boast about that because Scripture records that it was because he believed what God promised that he was declared righteous. This being declared righteous was a gift from God, not a reward.

SUBDIVISION CONSTITUENT 4:9-12 (Expository Paragraph: Claim$_2$ of 4:1-25)

Theme: This happiness of being declared righteous is also for the non-Jews; remember that it was before Abraham was circumcised, when he was still in effect a non-Jew, that he was declared righteous. He later received circumcision simply as a sign of his being declared righteous by faith, with the result that he became a spiritual father of all who believe in God as he did, whether they are circumcised or not.

SUBDIVISION CONSTITUENT 4:13-17b (Expository Paragraph: Restatement$_1$ of claim$_1$ and claim$_2$ of 4:1-25)
Theme: It was because Abraham trusted in God that he was declared righteous by God and was promised many blessings by God. Therefore what God promised is guaranteed to all, both Jews and non-Jews, who believe as Abraham did.

SUBDIVISION CONSTITUENT 4:17c-22 (Expository Paragraph: Restatement of Claim$_1$ of 4:1-25)
Theme: It was because Abraham confidently believed God's promise to give him many descendants when there was no basis for his hoping that this would happen that he was declared righteous by God.

SUBDIVISION CONSTITUENT 4:23-25 (Expository Paragraph: Restatement$_2$ of claim$_1$ and claim$_2$ of 4:1-25)
Theme: The words about Abraham's being declared righteous by God were written also to assure us who believe in God, who would also be declared righteous.

DIVISION CLUSTER CONSTITUENT 5:1-21 (Expository Subdivision: Application$_1$ of 3:21-26)
Theme: Because God has declared us righteous, we have peace with God, we experience his grace, we rejoice even in suffering because we expect to receive God's glory, and we know we will be saved from eternal punishment. Although the sin of one man, Adam, led to all people dying and deserving punishment, Christ's one righteous act has led to many being acquitted and declared righteous and living eternally.

SUBDIVISION CONSTITUENT 5:1-11 (Expository Section: Nucleus$_1$ of 5:1-21)
Theme: Because God has declared us righteous, we have peace with God, we experience his acting graciously toward us, we rejoice because we expect to receive God's glory, we even rejoice in suffering because we know the results it brings, we know we shall be saved from God's punishing us eternally, and we boast of what God has done for us through Christ.

SECTION CONSTITUENT 5:1-5 (Expository Paragraph: Nucleus$_1$ of 5:1-11)
Theme: Because God has declared us righteous, we have peace with God, we experience his acting graciously toward us, we rejoice because we expect to receive God's glory, and we even rejoice in suffering because we know the results it brings.

SECTION CONSTITUENT 5:6-11 (Expository Paragraph: Nucleus$_2$ of 5:1-11)
Theme: Since Christ died for us ungodly people, he will certainly save us from God's eternal punishment, and so we boast of what he has done for us.

SUBDIVISION CONSTITUENT 5:12-21 (Expository Paragraph: Nucleus$_2$ of 5:1-21)
Theme: Although the sin of one man, Adam, led to all people dying and God declaring that they deserved to be punished, Christ's righteous act of obedience when he died led to many experiencing God's grace and being declared righteous and living eternally, and will result in their ruling with Christ.

DIVISION CLUSTER CONSTITUENT 6:1-8:39 (Expository Subdivision: Application$_2$ of 3:21-26)
Theme: We have been freed from being controlled by sinful desires and from being required to obey the Mosaic law to be saved. Now we are compelled to live as God's Spirit directs. In view of what God does for us through his Spirit, no one can prevail against us, and nothing can separate us from Christ's and God's loving us.

SUBDIVISION CONSTITUENT 6:1-23 (Expository Section: Claim$_1$ of 6:1-8:39)
Theme: If someone were to say that perhaps we should continue to sin in order that God may continue to act more graciously towards us, or because we are not obligated to obey the Mosaic law, I would reply that we have been freed from being controlled by sinful desires. Instead, we are to present ourselves to God to become slaves of righteous living.

SECTION CONSTITUENT 6:1-14 (Expository Paragraph: Claim$_1$ of 6:1-23)
Theme: If someone were to say that perhaps we should continue to sin in order that God may continue to act more graciously toward us, I would reply that we who ought to consider ourselves unresponsive to sinful desires should certainly not continue sinning. We must keep remembering that it is as though our former sinful nature has ceased to function and we have become unresponsive to sinful desires,

living a new way. Do not let the desire to commit sin control you. Instead, present yourselves to God to do righteous things.

SECTION CONSTITUENT 6:15-23 (Expository Paragraph: Claim$_2$ of 6:1-23)

Theme: If someone should conclude that perhaps we can sin now since we are not obligated to obey the Mosaic law, I would say certainly not; let your minds compel your bodies to act righteously.

SUBDIVISION CONSTITUENT 7:1-25 (Expository Section: Claim$_2$ of 6:1-8:39)

Theme: God has freed us from being required to obey the Mosaic law to be saved. The Mosaic law simply reveals that what we are doing is sinful. It is our desire, not the law, that causes us to sin and become spiritually dead. But Christ can free us from being controlled by what our bodies desire.

SECTION CONSTITUENT 7:1-6 (Expository Paragraph: Claim$_1$ of 7:1-25)

Theme: You know that a person is freed from being required to obey any law after he dies. Similarly, God has freed us from being required to obey the Mosaic law to be saved.

SECTION CONSTITUENT 7:7-12 (Expository Paragraph: Refutation of objection$_1$ to claim$_1$ of 7:1-25)

Theme: My reply to the objection that the law of Moses is evil because it causes us to sin is that the law is holy and good; what the law does is simply reveal that what we are doing is sinful.

SECTION CONSTITUENT 7:13 (Expository Paragraph: Refutation of objection$_2$ to claim$_1$ of 7:1-25)

Theme: My reply to the objection that God's law, being good, causes people to become spiritually dead is no, but instead that it is our desire to commit sin that causes us to sin and become spiritually dead.

SECTION CONSTITUENT 7:14-25 (Expository Paragraph: Claim$_2$ of 7:1-25)

Theme: The law is from God's Spirit, but you and I are influenced by our sinful nature. We often do not do the things we desire and do the things we detest, because of a desire to sin which permeates us and prevents us from doing good—unless Christ frees us from being controlled by these desires.

SUBDIVISION CONSTITUENT 8:1-39 (Expository Section: Claim$_3$ of 6:1-8:39)

Theme: God will not in any way condemn those who are united to Christ Jesus; we are compelled to live as God's Spirit directs, not as our sinful human nature directs. What we suffer now is not worth paying attention to as we consider the future splendor that God will reveal to us. The Spirit helps us as our spirits feel weak. And God works out all things in a way that produces good to us who love him. Therefore no one can prevail against us, and nothing can separate us from Christ's and God's loving us.

SECTION CONSTITUENT 8:1-11 (Expository Paragraph: Justification$_1$ for 8:31-39, justification for 8:12-13)

Theme: God will not in any way condemn those who are united to Christ Jesus, for God's Spirit has freed us from the inevitability of sinning and from spiritual death.

SECTION CONSTITUENT 8:12-13 (Expository Paragraph: Claim based on 8:1-11)

Theme: We are compelled to live as the Spirit directs, not as our sinful human nature directs, because if you do the latter you will be eternally separated from God, but if you cease doing the latter you will live eternally.

SECTION CONSTITUENT 8:14-17 (Expository Paragraph: Justification$_2$ for 8:31-39)

Theme: Since it is we who allow the Spirit of God to guide us, who are God's children, we will also inherit eternal blessing from God.

SECTION CONSTITUENT 8:18-25 (Expository Paragraph: Justification$_3$ for 8:31-39)

Theme: Since everything God has created is eagerly awaiting the time when he will reveal who are his true children, I consider that what we suffer now is not worth paying attention to.

SECTION CONSTITUENT 8:26–27 (Expository Paragraph: Justification$_4$ for 8:31–39)
Theme: The Spirit helps us as our spirits feel weak; the Spirit prays for us and God understands what the Spirit intends.
SECTION CONSTITUENT 8:28–30 (Expository Paragraph: Justification$_5$ for 8:31–39)
Theme: God works out all things in a way that produces good to us who love him. He does this because, having known that we would be saved and thus have the character of his Son, he chose us and declared us righteous, and he will surely give us future splendor.
SECTION CONSTITUENT 8:31–39 (Expository Paragraph: Claim based on 8:1–30)
Theme: We must conclude from these things that no one can prevail against us, and absolutely no one and nothing can separate us from Christ's and God's loving us.

DIVISION CLUSTER CONSTITUENT 9:1–11:36 (Expository Subdivision Cluster: Application$_3$ of 3:21–26)
Theme: I grieve greatly because most of the Jews have rejected Jesus as their promised deliverer, but this does not prove that God has failed to give many descendants to Abraham as he promised. Nor can we conclude that God is unjust in choosing the ones he wants to or that it is not right for God to condemn people. The Jews did not succeed in fulfilling what the Mosaic law requires; they tried to find a way to be declared righteous by doing things in order that God would accept them. To you Jews I say that God has certainly not rejected all of us, and that God is saving many non-Jews to make the Jews jealous and thus seek to be saved. To you non-Jews I say that I hope my work among you will accomplish just that. But don't despise the Jews that God has rejected and become proud, because just as God did not spare the Jews he will not spare you if you fall away from him. And I want you to know that all the Jews will some day be saved.

SUBDIVISION CLUSTER CONSTITUENT 9:1a–b (Expository Propositional Cluster: Problem in 9:1–11:36)
Theme: Most of my fellow Israelites have rejected Christ.
SUBDIVISION CLUSTER CONSTITUENT 9:1c–5 (Expressive Paragraph: Paul's reaction to the problem of the Jews' rejection of Christ)
Theme: I tell you very sincerely that I grieve greatly about this, and I would be willing to be separated from Christ if that would help them believe in Christ.
SUBDIVISION CLUSTER CONSTITUENT 9:6–29 (Expository Section: Wrong evaluation of the Jews' rejection of Christ)
Theme: This does not prove that God has failed in his promise to Abraham. Nor can we conclude that God is unjust in choosing the ones he wants to, or that it is not right for God to condemn people.

SECTION CONSTITUENT 9:6–13 (Expository Paragraph: Claim$_1$ of 9:6–29)
Theme: This does not prove that God has failed to do for Abraham what he promised, because, as Scripture illustrates, it is not all who are naturally descended from Jacob or Abraham whom God considers his children, but it is those who were born as a result of what God promised whom he considers his children.
SECTION CONSTITUENT 9:14–18 (Expository Paragraph: Claim$_2$ of 9:6–29)
Theme: As Scripture indicates, God's choosing people depends not on their wishes or efforts. But God helps whomever he wants to and he makes stubborn whomever he wants to. We cannot conclude that God is unjust in choosing the ones he wants to.
SECTION CONSTITUENT 9:19–29 (Expository Paragraph: Claim$_3$ of 9:6–29)
Theme: My reply to anyone's objection to this doctrine is that God has a right to carry out his purposes; he tolerated the people who caused him to be angry, in order that he might disclose how gloriously he acts toward those on whom he intends to have mercy.

SUBDIVISION CLUSTER CONSTITUENT 9:30–10:21 (Expository Section: Correct evaluation of the Jews' rejection of Christ)
Theme: The Jews did not succeed in fulfilling what the Mosaic law requires; they tried to find a way to be declared righteous by doing things in order that God would accept

them. *The Jews do not understand how to seek him correctly, which according to Scripture is that if anyone, Jew or non-Jew, confesses publicly that Jesus is Lord and believes inwardly that God raised him from the dead, he will be saved. People have been sent to preach about Christ to the Jews, but most Jews have not accepted the gospel. They certainly have heard it and should have understood it, because even the non-Jews, who were not searching for God, understood it.*

    SECTION CONSTITUENT 9:30-33 (Expository Paragraph: Claim of 9:30-10:21)
Theme: The non-Jews found the way by which God could declare them righteous. The Jews did not succeed in fulfilling what the Mosaic law requires; they tried to find a way to be declared righteous by doing things in order that God would accept them.
    SECTION CONSTITUENT 10:1-4 (Expressive Paragraph: Paul's feeling about the source of the problem of 9:1-11:36)
Theme: My deep desire and earnest prayer is that God would save the Jews, who do not understand how to seek him correctly.
    SECTION CONSTITUENT 10:5-13 (Expository Paragraph: Justification for the claim in 9:30-33)
Theme: The message of Scripture is that if anyone confesses publicly that Jesus is Lord and believes inwardly that God raised him from the dead, he will be saved, because God treats Jews and non-Jews alike.
    SECTION CONSTITUENT 10:14-17 (Expository Paragraph: Refutation of objection to the claim in 9:30-33)
Theme: My reply to the objection that the Jews cannot ask Christ to save them if God does not send someone to preach to them is that God has sent people to preach about Christ to them, but most of the Jews have not accepted the gospel. People are indeed believing in Christ and people are indeed hearing the message.
    SECTION CONSTITUENT 10:18-21 (Expository Paragraph: Responses to queries about the claim in 9:30-33)
Theme: In reply to a query of whether the Jews have heard or understood about Christ, I would say that, as is supported by Scripture, they have heard it and should have understood it, because even the non-Jews, who were not searching for God, understood it.

SUBDIVISION CLUSTER CONSTITUENT 11:1-32 (Expository Section: Solution to the problem of 9:1-11:36)
Theme: God has certainly not rejected all of us Jews, and God is saving many non-Jews to make the Jews jealous and thus seek to be saved. To you non-Jews I say that I hope my work among you will accomplish just that; but do not despise the Jews whom God has rejected and do not become proud, because just as God did not spare the Jews he will not spare you if you fall away from him. And I want you to know that all the Jews will some day be saved, as the Scriptures predict.

    SECTION CONSTITUENT 11:1-6 (Expository Paragraph: Query$_1$ about God's rejection of the Jews, and Paul's response)
Theme: My reply to a query whether God has rejected the Jews is that he has certainly not rejected all of us. I am evidence of that. Just as in the past, there is at the present time a small group of us Jews who have become believers.
    SECTION CONSTITUENT 11:7-10 (Expository Paragraph: General statement about the problem of God's rejection of the Jews)
Theme: The people of Israel as a whole did not find the way of being declared righteous, which is confirmed by the Scriptures, though those whom God had chosen did find it.
    SECTION CONSTITUENT 11:11-12 (Expository Paragraph: Query$_2$ about God's rejection of the Jews, and Paul's response)
Theme: My reply to a query whether the result of the Jews' unbelief is a permanent falling away from God is no, but that God is saving many non-Jews to make the Jews envious and thus to seek to be saved.

SECTION CONSTITUENT 11:13-16 (Expressive Paragraph: Statement to non-Jews of Paul's reaction to the problem of God's rejection of the Jews)
Theme: I highly esteem the work God has called me to do as an apostle among you non-Jews. I hope that my making my fellow Jews jealous will result in some of them being saved.
SECTION CONSTITUENT 11:17-24 (Hortatory Paragraph: Appeals to non-Jews)
Theme: You non-Jews must not despise the Jews whom God has rejected, and you must not become proud, but instead beware. God will not spare you if you fall away from him, and he will act kindly toward the Jews and be reunited to them if they trust in Christ.
SECTION CONSTITUENT 11:25-32 (Expository Paragraph: Solution to the problem of God's rejection of the Jews)
Theme: I want you to know that all the people of Israel will some day be saved, as the Scriptures predict. God still loves them because of their ancestors. It is God's purpose to act mercifully towards them as well as toward all Gentiles.
SUBDIVISION CLUSTER CONSTITUENT 11:33-36 (Expressive Paragraph: Doxology concluding 11:1-33)
Theme: I marvel at how great God's wisdom and knowledge are, and his decisions and actions toward us.

SUBPART CONSTITUENT 12:1-15:13 (Hortatory Division Cluster: Appeals of the epistle)
Theme: Present yourselves to God to be like living sacrifices, which is the appropriate way for you to serve him. Do not let anything non-Christian determine how you should act, but instead let God change your way of thinking. Specifically, think about yourselves sensibly, by considering and then using the abilities God has given you; love others sincerely in the ways you act towards them, and instead of avenging yourselves let God avenge you; be subject to the civil authorities and pay all of them what they require. Let your only continual obligation be to love one another. Accept those who doubt whether they are permitted to do certain things; specifically, anyone who thinks it is all right to eat all kinds of food must not despise those who don't, and those who don't think so must not condemn those who do.
DIVISION CLUSTER CONSTITUENT 12:1-2 (Hortatory Paragraph: Generic appeal of 12:1-15:13)
Theme: I appeal to you that, because of all the ways God has acted mercifully towards you, you present yourselves to God by making yourselves like living sacrifices, which is the appropriate way to serve him. Do not let anything non-Christian determine how you act, but instead let God change your way of thinking.
DIVISION CLUSTER CONSTITUENT 12:3-13:14 (Hortatory Subdivision Cluster: Specific appeal$_1$ of 12:1-15:13)
Theme: Think about yourselves sensibly, by considering the abilities God has given you; love others sincerely in the ways you act towards them and instead of avenging yourselves let God avenge you. Be subject to the civil authorities. Let your only continual obligation be to love one another.
SUBDIVISION CLUSTER CONSTITUENT 12:3-8 (Hortatory Paragraph: Specific appeal$_1$ of 12:3-13:14)
Theme: Do not think about yourselves more highly than you should. Instead, think about yourselves sensibly, considering your abilities that have been given to you by God because you trust in Christ. Let us do diligently and cheerfully the things God has given us ability to do.
SUBDIVISION CLUSTER CONSTITUENT 12:9-21 (Hortatory Section: Specific appeal$_2$ of 12:3-13:14)
Theme: Love others sincerely in the ways you act towards them. Instead of avenging yourselves, allow God to avenge you; and instead of being overcome by evil done to you, overcome these things by doing good deeds to those who do evil to you.
SECTION CONSTITUENT 12:9-18 (Hortatory Paragraph: Specific appeal$_1$ of 12:9-21)
Theme: Love others sincerely in the various ways you act toward them.

SECTION CONSTITUENT 12:19-21 (Hortatory Paragraph: Specific appeal$_2$ of 12:9-21)

Theme: Instead of avenging yourselves, allow God to avenge you; and instead of being overcome by evil done to you, overcome these things by doing good deeds to those who do evil to you, since this is what the Scriptures command.

SUBDIVISION CLUSTER CONSTITUENT 13:1-7 (Hortatory Paragraph: Specific appeal$_3$ of 12:3-13:14)

Theme: Every believer must be subject to civil authorities, because anyone who opposes them opposes what God has established and will bring on himself punishment from the authorities as God considers fitting. Do what is good and then they will commend you. Give to all the authorities what you are obligated to give them.

SUBDIVISION CLUSTER CONSTITUENT 13:8-10 (Hortatory Paragraph: Specific appeal$_4$ of 12:3-13:14)

Theme: Do not leave any debt unpaid. Your only continual obligation is to love one another, since doing so fulfills all that God's law requires.

SUBDIVISION CLUSTER CONSTITUENT 13:11-14 (Hortatory Paragraph: Generic appeal of 12:3-13:14)

Theme: Because it is time for us to be fully active, we must quit doing wicked deeds, we must do those things which will help us resist that which is evil, we must live properly, and we must be like Christ.

DIVISION CLUSTER CONSTITUENT 14:1-15:13 (Hortatory Subdivision: Specific appeal$_2$ of 12:1-15:13)

Theme: Accept those who doubt whether they are permitted to do certain things. Specifically, anyone who thinks it is all right to eat all kinds of food must not despise those who don't, and those who don't think so must not condemn those who do, because God has accepted them.

SUBDIVISION CONSTITUENT 14:1-4 (Hortatory Paragraph: Generic appeal of 14:1-15:13)

Theme: Accept those who doubt whether they are permitted to do certain things. Anyone who thinks it is all right to eat all kinds of food must not despise those who don't, and those who don't think so must not condemn those who do, because God has accepted them.

SUBDIVISION CONSTITUENT 14:5-9 (Hortatory Paragraph: Specific appeal$_1$ of 14:1-15:13)

Theme: Each person should be fully convinced about observing special days, thinking and deciding for himself. For doing such actions is not intrinsically wrong.

SUBDIVISION CONSTITUENT 14:10-12 (Hortatory Paragraph: Specific appeal$_2$ of 14:1-15:13)

Theme: You should neither condemn nor despise your fellow believers who believe differently about religious regulations, because it is God who will say whether he approves of what we have done.

SUBDIVISION CONSTITUENT 14:13-18 (Hortatory Paragraph: Specific appeal$_3$ of 14:1-15:13)

Theme: Instead of condemning each other, decide not to do anything that might lead your fellow believer to sin by following your example and which would then cause others to speak evil of you.

SUBDIVISION CONSTITUENT 14:19-23 (Hortatory Paragraph: Specific appeal$_4$ of 14:1-15:13)

Theme: Try to do what will help fellow believers to be at peace with each other and grow spiritually. Do not destroy what God has done in others' lives as a result of your eating certain things. Keep between yourself and God what you believe about eating such things, and don't try to force your views on others, because if those who are not certain if they should eat such things do eat them, they will be condemned by God and their own consciences.

SUBDIVISION CONSTITUENT 15:1-4 (Hortatory Paragraph: Specific appeal$_5$ of 14:1-15:13)
Theme: We should endure being irritated by the practices of those who are uncertain whether God will condemn them for doing certain things which the Mosaic law forbade, and do things which please our fellow Christians, since Christ has set us an example.
SUBDIVISION CONSTITUENT 15:5-6 (Expressive Paragraph: Specific prayer regarding 14:1-15:4)
Theme: May God enable you all to live harmoniously with each other.
SUBDIVISION CONSTITUENT 15:7-12 (Hortatory Paragraph: Restatement of 14:1-15:4)
Theme: Accept each other as Christ accepted you, remembering that what Christ has done was both to help the Jews and cause non-Jews to praise God.
SUBDIVISION CONSTITUENT 15:13 (Expressive Paragraph: Generic prayer concluding 14:1-15:13)
Theme: May God make you completely joyful and peaceful in order that you may have abundant hope.

PART CLUSTER CONSTITUENT 15:14-33 (Hortatory Subpart: Epilogue of the epistle)
Theme: Because of the work of proclaiming the gospel among the non-Jews in places where they have not heard about Christ, I have often been hindered from visiting you, but I hope to see you and be helped by you for my next journey. But now I am about to go to Jerusalem, and I urge you to pray that God will protect me from the unbelieving Jews in Judea and that the believers there will accept the money I take to them.

SUBPART CONSTITUENT 15:14-16 (Expository Paragraph: Introduction to 15:17-33)
Theme: I have written frankly to you in this letter because of what God has graciously commissioned me to do among the non-Jews.
SUBPART CONSTITUENT 15:17-21 (Emotive Paragraph: Description related to 15:22-29)
Theme: I am proud of my work for God, which I have now completed in this region by proclaiming the gospel in places where they have not heard about Christ.
SUBPART CONSTITUENT 15:22-29 (Descriptive Paragraph: Declaration based on 15:17-21 and basis for 15:30-33)
Theme: Because of this work, I have often been hindered from visiting you, but I hope to see you as I journey through your area and I hope that you will give me what I need for my next journey. But now I am about to go to Jerusalem to take funds to God's people there. So later I shall visit you in Rome and I know that Christ will bless us there.
SUBPART CONSTITUENT 15:30-33 (Hortatory Paragraph: Appeal of 15:14-33)
Theme: I urge you to pray fervently that God will protect me from the unbelieving Jews in Judea and that God's people there will accept the money I take to them and that I may be refreshed by visiting you. May God be with you all.

EPISTLE CONSTITUENT 16:1-27 (Hortatory Part: Closing of the epistle)
Theme: Finally, receive and help Phoebe. Greet many individuals among the believers there. Note those who cause quarrels among you and those who cause people to turn away from God, and avoid them. Several of the people here send their greetings. Let us forever praise that One who alone is God and is truly wise.

PART CONSTITUENT 16:1-2 (Hortatory Paragraph: Specific appeal of 16:1-27)
Theme: I am introducing and commending Phoebe to you, and I ask that you receive her as a fellow believer and give her whatever she needs.
PART CONSTITUENT 16:3-16 (Hortatory Paragraph: Greetings of 16:1-27)
Theme: Greet many individuals among the believers there. All the congregations in this area greet you.
PART CONSTITUENT 16:17-20 (Hortatory Paragraph: Generic appeal of 16:1-27)
Theme: Note those who are causing quarrels among you and those who cause people to turn away from God. Avoid them, since they only want to satisfy their own desires and deceive those who do not suspect their motives. If you avoid such people, God will soon crush Satan under your feet.
PART CONSTITUENT 16:21-23 (Descriptive Paragraph: Declaration of greetings)
Theme: Several of those who are with me send their greetings.
PART CONSTITUENT 16:25-27 (Expressive Paragraph: Doxology of 16:1-27)
Theme: Let us forever praise that One who alone is God, who alone is truly wise.

THE SEMANTIC UNITS OF THE EPISTLE TO THE ROMANS
ROMANS 1:1–16:27 (Epistle)

THEME: *(See the thematic outline in the Introduction.)*	
MACROSTRUCTURE	CONTENTS
opening	1:1-7 I, Paul, an apostle who was appointed to proclaim the good news about Jesus Christ, am writing this letter to all you believers who are in Rome. I pray that God will continue to act graciously toward you and grant you peace.
BODY	1:8-15:33 I thank God that people everywhere are talking about how you Roman believers are trusting Jesus Christ. I pray that God will permit me to visit you soon. I want you to know that I have longed to do that, but things have always prevented me. I was eager to proclaim the good news to you who are living at Rome also. I very confidently proclaim the good news about what Christ has done. This good news states that although everyone, whether Jew or non-Jew, has done evil and deserves to be condemned by God, now he saves those who trust in Jesus Christ and declares their guilt ended. Abraham illustrates that this way of being declared righteous is a gift, not earned. Because God has declared us righteous, we have peace with God, we experience his grace, we rejoice even in suffering, we will be saved from eternal punishment, we have been freed from being controlled by sinful desires and being required to obey the Mosaic law to be saved, we can live as God's Spirit directs, and no one can prevail against us. Though I grieve deeply that most Jews have rejected Christ, you non-Jews must not despise the Jews, and you must know that some day all the Jews will be saved. Because of all these things, present yourselves to God to be like living sacrifices. Let God change your thinking and acting. Think about yourselves sensibly by considering the abilities God has given you. Love others sincerely in your actions toward them. Be subject to the civil authorities and pay all of them what they require. Accept those who doubt whether they are permitted to do certain things; specifically, anyone who thinks it is all right to eat all kinds of food must not despise those who don't, and those who don't think so must not condemn those who do. Because of the work of proclaiming the gospel among the non-Jews in places where they have not heard about Christ, I have often been hindered from visiting you, but I hope to see you when I travel to Spain. But now I am about to go to Jerusalem, and I urge you to pray that God will protect me from the unbelieving Jews in Judea and that the believers there will accept the money I take to them.
closing	16:1-27 Finally, receive and help Phoebe. Greet many individuals among the believers there. Note those who cause quarrels among you and those who cause people to turn away from God, and avoid them. Several of the people here send their greetings. Let us forever praise that One who alone is God and is truly wise.

The structural coherence of the epistle as a whole is seen in the fact that it contains the standard epistolary features: an *opening* (1:1-7) consisting of the author's name, the name of the recipients, and a salutation; a BODY (1:8-15:33); a *closing* (16:1-27) consisting of greetings, a final exhortation, and a benediction.

Within the CORE of the BODY, features typical of the hortatory genre are seen: a section of building rapport with the audience (1:8-15); an extended expository *basis* (1:16-11:36) for the APPEALS that follow it; and the APPEALS themselves (12:1-15:33). Other features of coherence are Paul's references to his intended visit (1:11-12; 15:23-24) and the emphasis on 'all', including both Jews and Gentiles (explicit in 1:7, 8, 16; 2:9-10; 3:19, 23, 29-30; 4:16; 15:8-9; and implicit throughout much of chaps. 11 and 14).

Although many have said, or assumed, that coherence within the epistle is mainly shown by the concept of righteousness by faith, this is hardly true. This topic occurs only in certain places in the expository section. Rather, it is the overall chiastic structure that best demonstrates coherence. There is a sandwiching of themes at the beginning and end of the book:

  A *Opening* (1:1-7): Greets the Romans in general
    B *Introduction* (1:8-15): Desires to see the Romans
    B' *Conclusion* (15:14-33): Expresses specific plans to see the Romans
  A' *Closing* (16:1-13): Greets specific Romans

EPISTLE CONSTITUENT 1:1–7
(Descriptive Paragraph: Opening of the epistle)

THEME: I, Paul, an apostle who was appointed to proclaim the good news about Jesus Christ, am writing this letter to all you believers who are in Rome. I pray that God will continue to act graciously toward you and grant you peace.

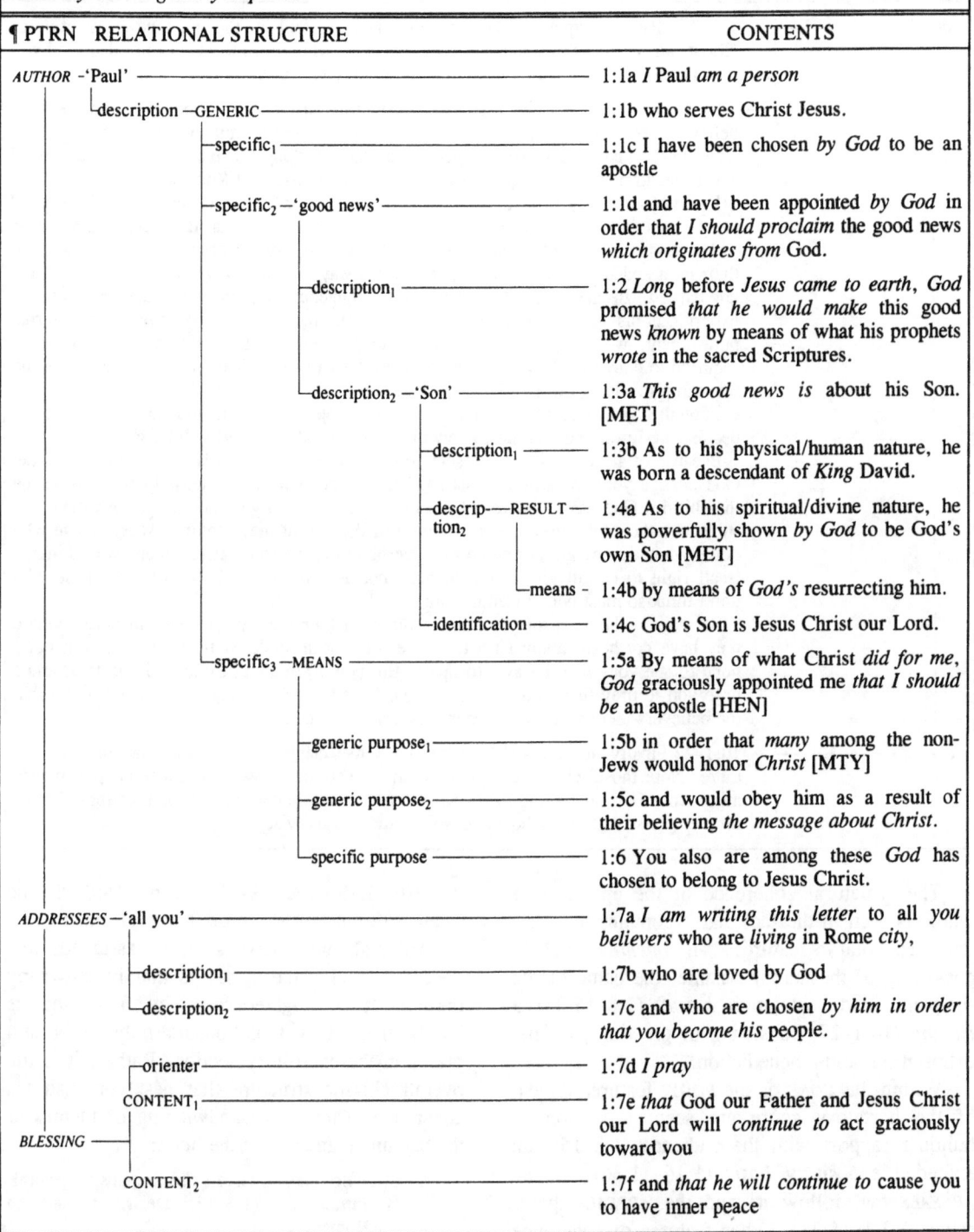

INTENT AND PARAGRAPH PATTERN

The purpose of the opening of an epistle, which normally includes a statement of the identity of the writer and his addressees, is to establish rapport between the writer and his intended audience. The opening of the Epistle to the Romans contains the three elements common to letters of the time: the name of and information about the author (vv. 1-6), the name of and description of the addressees (7a-c), and a wish for God's blessing on the addressees (7d-f).

How this structure fits the usual types and subtypes of paragraph patterns set forth by semantic theory is an open question. The best possibility seems to be to consider this a descriptive paragraph, the first two elements providing the description and the final element a declaration.

NOTES

1:1a *I* Paul *am a person* In composing a letter, a Greek writer of ancient times characteristically would begin by stating his name (as well as that of the recipients). Neither a first person pronoun nor a verb expressing the implied action would be used, as is the case here. Since the rest of the verse supplies three descriptions or identifications of Paul, only the copulative verb 'am' is supplied here.

1:1b-d These propositions comprise a description of Paul: a generic description followed by specifics. The concept of a servant of Christ in 1b is spelled out by the specific ways in which Paul serves him. These are Paul's credentials, establishing his right to address an audience he has not visited before. The descriptions of Paul in 1b-d were not meant to be taken as equal; if they had been, they would probably have been connected by καί 'and'.

1:1b who serves Christ Jesus The Greek is δοῦλος Χριστοῦ Ἰησοῦ 'a servant of Christ Jesus'. By rendering δοῦλος as 'one who serves' the relationship implied by the objective genitive Χριστοῦ Ἰησοῦ is made clear. Of course, Paul was not literally a slave of Christ in the way Onesimus was of Philemon. Yet Paul frequently uses this term to describe his service for Christ. If it is considered a live metaphor, it could be spelled out as 'one who serves Christ Jesus as a slave serves his master'. But it is not spelled out in the display because it is not certain that it is a live metaphor, and because spelling out the metaphor in a translation is liable to distort Paul's focus. Moreover, many languages do not have a word for 'slave'. But in languages with an appropriate word, it should probably be rendered 'I Paul, a servant/slave of Christ Jesus'.

Although the Textus Receptus has the names in the order Jesus Christ, the manuscript evidence here heavily supports the order followed in the display text: the GNT fourth edition lists it with a B rating ("almost certain"). The more common NT order of the names is Jesus Christ, but that is reversed here. (Paul uses the expression 'Christ Jesus' by itself seventy-three times and 'Jesus Christ' eighteen times; in addition there are twenty-four cases where the Greek manuscripts are divided.) Conzelmann (p. 20) states, "The word order 'Christ Jesus' is found only in the genitive and after the preposition ἐν, 'in,' but not when the Kyrios [Lord] title is also used. There is no difference of meaning between 'Jesus Christ' and 'Christ Jesus.'" It is not clear what semantic significance the word order has, if any, unless the difference in order somehow indicates prominence of the name versus function as Messiah.

1:1c I have been chosen *by God* to be an apostle The word κλητός in the phrase κλητὸς ἀπόστολος 'a called apostle' is used in a secondary sense. Louw and Nida (33.312) define the verb 'call' as "to urgently invite someone to accept responsibilities for a particular task." Since in English 'call' has a different primary sense, the display uses "chosen" (also LB; CEV has "God chose me"). The sense here is either that Paul was chosen to be an apostle or that he became in effect an apostle immediately at the time of his choosing. The agent is supplied ('by God') to satisfy the case frame to conform with v. 6.

1:1d and have been appointed *by God* The agent of the participle ἀφωρισμένος 'set apart, appointed' could be God (see the same word in Gal. 1:15 juxtaposed to 'from my mother's womb'), or it could be Christ, if Paul was thinking of the time of his conversion. The agent is not in focus here, and should not be expressed unless the receptor language requires it.

in order that *I should proclaim* the good news *which originates from* God The verb 'preach/proclaim' is implied (cf. TEV, JB, LB, CEV). The genitive θεοῦ 'of God' could mean 'about God', but the good news is more specifically about Christ, as 1:3a shows. Therefore it seems best to regard θεοῦ as a genitive of source, 'from God'.

1:2 Here begins a long somewhat parenthetical comment on the gospel.

Long* before *Jesus came to earth The verb προεπηγγείλατο 'before promised' raises the question of before what. Something similar to 'before the coming of Christ' should be understood. The word 'long' is supplied to convey the idea that a long time had elapsed since these prophecies were written. An alternative is simply 'long ago'.

God* promised *that he would make this good news known The word 'promise' expresses a communicative act; therefore, semantically, it requires a full proposition as its content. Alternatives to 'make known' might be 'to give us', 'to tell us'.

Since 'good news' occurs in 1d, it is supplied in 2a (and also in 3a).

by means of what his prophets *wrote* The preposition διά in the phrase διὰ τῶν προφητῶν 'through the prophets' is expressing means. This requires a full proposition semantically, and therefore the verb 'wrote' is supplied. CEV has "by what his prophet said."

the sacred Scriptures The Greek is γραφαῖς ἁγίαις 'writings holy'. For most English speakers the word 'Scriptures' connotes 'holy', and to say 'holy' here would be redundant. But in other cultures 'writings' would not connote 'holy writings'. Therefore ἁγίαις is rendered here as 'sacred'.

1:3a his Son 'Son' here is a metaphor, although commentators never seem to note that. Christ is one whose nature is like God's as a son's nature is like that of his father. In Heb. 3:6 one of the metaphor's points of similarity (faithfulness) is made specific. The sense of the figure here in Rom. 1:3 is that Christ is one who has the same essence as God. It might also be one who has the same rights as God or perhaps one who completely obeys God. The figure is considered a dead metaphor in most Western cultures, but in many other cultures it will be taken literally. In such cases a simile may be called for, such as 'one who was to God as a son is to his father' or 'the one who has the attributes of God as a son has the attributes of his father.

1:3b As to his physical/human nature, he was born a descendant of *King* David In the phrase ἐκ σπέρματος Δαυὶδ κατὰ σάρκα 'from seed (of) David according to flesh' the word σπέρμα 'seed' is a dead metaphor signifying 'descendants'. 'King' has been supplied as crucial information which the writer would expect his audience to know about David. Paul uses 'flesh' in many senses, but here it means 'physical descent, human nature' (BAGD, p. 744.4).

1:4a As to his spiritual/divine nature, he was powerfully shown *by God* to be God's own Son The participle ὁρισθέντος could mean 'appointed, designated', but this would be totally contrary to the theology of Paul's other writings. Therefore the sense 'declared, shown' is preferred by the great majority of commentators and versions.

The phrase ἐν δυνάμει 'in power' could go with either 'Son of God' or 'declared'. However, it is the latter that makes more sense: 'the demonstration (by his resurrection) was a powerful one'. This is better than 'he was shown to be a powerful Son of God', for the resurrection was by God's power, not Jesus' power. This is the interpretation of the majority of commentators.

There are several possible interpretations of κατὰ πνεῦμα ἁγιωσύνης 'according to spirit of holiness'. It could mean 'by the Holy Spirit'. Supporting this view is the claim that 'spirit of holiness' is an exact reflection in Greek of the Hebrew for 'Holy Spirit'. Against this view is the fact that Paul never uses such a term elsewhere to refer to the Holy Spirit, and this would be a unique sense for κατά. Another view is that it means Christ's human spirit. Supporting this is the immediately preceding reference to 'the flesh', suggesting 'spirit' as its counterpart here; however, no writer refers to Jesus' human spirit as 'spirit of holiness' or anything similar (cf. Mark 2:8, Luke 1:30, 23:46, Rom. 8:9). A third interpretation is 'his spiritual/divine nature', as in the display. It is supported by the majority of commentators, and also by the fact that a parallelism is involved: κατὰ σάρκα 'according to flesh' is followed by a clear reference to his human nature and descent (from David); that is followed in turn by another κατά and a reference to what Christ was shown to be by God's power. To balance the parallelism a reference to his divine or holy nature is required. LB has "with the holy nature of God himself."

For 'Son' see the note on 3a.

1:4b by means of *God's* resurrecting him The abstract noun in the phrase ἐξ ἀναστάσεως "from resurrection" could be made into a full intransitive clause as in NEB's "he rose from the dead," but in conjunction with the reference to God's power it is better to take it in a more clearly transitive sense and supply 'God' as the implied agent who raised Christ from the dead. Several English versions use a transitive verb here (e.g., TEV, JBP, LB, CEV, REB).

1:4c our Note that throughout this analysis all first person plural pronouns are considered to be inclusive (i.e., referring to Paul and his readers) unless otherwise indicated.

1:5–6 These verses present the third of Paul's specific statements about his commissioning as a servant of Christ. The first one (1c) was conveyed by an adjective, the second (1d) by a participle, and this third one by a finite verb in a relative clause.

1:5a By means of what Christ *did for me* Commentators are divided as to whether the phrase δι' οὗ 'through whom' refers to Christ as the source or agent. But if it were the source, ἀφ' οὗ 'from whom' would more likely have been used here. Furthermore, to have said his apostleship was from Christ would seem contradictory since Paul indicates elsewhere that it was God who had appointed him (e.g., 1 Tim. 1:1). Therefore 5a is taken as an abbreviated means proposition probably referring obliquely to Paul's conversion experience, and thus 'did for me' fills out the proposition. In languages that lack a generic term for 'do' it may be necessary to supply a specific verb such as 'by means of Christ's revealing himself to me (or, saving me)'.

graciously appointed me *that I should be* **an apostle** The Greek is ἐλάβομεν χάριν καὶ ἀποστολήν 'we received grace and apostleship'. Since the context speaks of promoting faith among all the (Gentile) nations, it seems best to follow the great majority of commentators and take ἐλάβομεν 'we received' as an editorial 'we' referring to Paul himself. It is so taken by TEV, NEB, NCV, and CEV.

With regard to the words χάριν καὶ ἀποστολήν 'grace and apostleship, 'grace' is not used here in the common Pauline sense of 'undeserved favor of granting salvation' because salvation is not in view. Since it is used in conjunction with the immediately following words 'and apostleship', the two terms almost certainly form a type of hendiadys in which the two nouns convey one semantic concept, the one modified by the other. Thus the sense is 'the grace of being an apostle', a mismatched way of saying 'God graciously made/appointed me to be an apostle'. CEV has "Jesus was kind to me and chose me to be an apostle."

In some languages this may have to be rendered 'that I should represent him as an apostle' to help make clear the denotation of 'apostle' as one who represents another.

1:5b among the non-Jews The word ἔθνη can mean 'nation' or 'ethnic group', but in Romans (with one third of all of the occurrences of this word in the NT) the sense is almost always 'non-Jews'. The attempt to break down barriers between Jewish and non-Jewish believers is part of the central theme of the book. The word 'Gentiles' is not used in SSAs because it is a technical term for which there is not likely to be an equivalent in most languages.

many . . . **would honor** *Christ* As most commentators suggest, the Greek expression ὑπὲρ τοῦ ὀνόματος αὐτοῦ 'on behalf of his name' means 'in order that the name (of Jesus) would be honored'. JB has "in honor of his name." It is an idiomatic expression involving a metonymy, the word 'name' standing for the person, specifically for the person's fame or reputation.

1:5c and would obey him as a result of their believing *the message about Christ* The words ὑπακοὴν πίστεως 'obedience of faith' could mean (1) obedience to the faith (= the body of Christian truth), or (2) obedience which results from faith, or (3) obedience which consists of faith. The first alternative is fairly well ruled out by the lack of a definite article before 'faith'. The difficulty with the third alternative is that obedience and faith, while they have much in common, are not really the same concept. Therefore the second alternative is chosen here, taking the genitive as representing a result-reason relationship. The question then arises, What term should serve as the implied content of πίστις? It could be 'Jesus Christ' or 'the gospel'; both have been mentioned already in the opening verses, and it is hard to say which, if either, is more in focus. The display thus includes both: 'believing the message about Christ'. An alternative would be 'trusting in what Christ has done'.

1:6 You also This verse begins with ἐν οἷς ἐστε καὶ ὑμεῖς 'among whom are also you', which phrase is related to the statements concerning the non-Jews in 1:5b–c. It is also related, by means of the pronoun ὑμεῖς 'you(pl)', to the blessing

Paul is about to invoke on them in v. 7. Thus it is a sort of tail-head linkage between v. 7 and vv. 1–6.

The co-occurrence of the second person plural pronoun ὑμεῖς and the correspondingly inflected verb 'to be' gives the sense of 'you yourselves'.

chosen to belong to Jesus Christ The construction κλητοὶ Ἰησοῦ Χριστοῦ 'called of Jesus Christ' could mean 'called by Jesus Christ' except that in the NT 'calling' is always ascribed to God the Father. Therefore some verb needs to be supplied; and since the genitive here suggests possession, 'to belong to' is probably the best. This is the interpretation of the overwhelming majority of commentators, and it is rendered accordingly in RSV, TEV, NIV, JB, JBP, etc. For the rendering of κλητοί as 'chosen', see the note on 1c.

1:7a *I am writing this letter* Since v. 7 names the letter's recipients, and a semantic event expressing the relationship between the participants is necessary to complete the case frame, 'I am writing this letter' is supplied. 'I am sending this letter' could be used equally well. Alternatives are "This letter is to" (CEV) and "I send greetings to" (REB).

to all *you believers* **who are** *living* **in Rome** *city* By supplying 'you believers' it is made clear that Paul is not writing to all the people of Rome. In some languages it may be necessary to supply 'living' between 'who are' and 'in Rome' in order not to imply that they just happened to be there temporarily. The generic term 'city' supplies situational information that Paul expected his audience to know. A small number of manuscripts omit the words 'in Rome' here and in 1:15 (see p. 5). Metzger, in supporting the GNT here, says the omission was "probably, as a deliberate excision, made in order to show that the letter is of general, not local, application" (p. 446). Morris comments that "the evidence of the overwhelming bulk of the MSS must be accepted as giving us the true reading" (p. 3). Its inclusion is given an A rating ("certain") in the fourth edition GNT.

The word 'all' here (and also in v. 8 and v. 16) is thematic. It is probably meant to signify 'all of you, both those who are Jews and those who are non-Jews'.

1:7c chosen *by him in order that you become his* **people** The phrase κλητοῖς ἁγίοις 'called holy (ones)' is the identical construction as in 1:1c ('called apostle') except that the second word here is an adjective, though with a nominal use. The words 'in order that you would become' convey the relationship between 'chosen' and 'saints', and they are so rendered by modern versions.

The word 'saint' is not used in the SSAs because in much of the English- and Spanish-speaking world it has a specialized sense contrary to Paul's meaning. Though 'saint' more literally means 'those dedicated/consecrated (to God)', it is roughly equivalent to 'believers/Christians'.

1:7d–f *I pray that* Typical of Paul's salutations, there is no verb in the Greek here. Since the whole utterance is expressing a desire or wish by Paul, and since some languages do not have an optative mood ('May . . .'), it is expressed here as 'I pray that', as in CEV.

act graciously Since 'grace' expresses an event concept, it is rendered 'act graciously' in the sense of bestowing undeserved kindness. NCV has "show you kindness"; CEV, "will be kind to you."

cause you to have inner peace The word εἰρήνη 'peace' here expresses an inward peace, not an absence of hostile actions toward or from others.

BOUNDARIES AND COHERENCE

The relational coherence of the 1:1–7 paragraph is seen in the fact that the writer gives his name, the name of the addressees, and a greeting in the form of a blessing, all without verbs. (This is the standard pattern of the time.) Within the paragraph there is a subordinate propositional cluster with three main theses, each of which is introduced by a relative pronoun or phrase: ὅ 'which' (v. 2); δι' οὗ 'through whom' (5a); and ἐν οἷς 'among whom' (v. 6).

This paragraph is clearly separated from the following unit, which is introduced by πρῶτον 'first' and the epistle's first finite verb (πρῶτον introduces the writer's first topic).

Internal coherence is shown by the occurrence of Χριστοῦ Ἰησοῦ 'Christ Jesus' (1:1b) and the same terms reversed (1:4c, 1:7e) and by ἀπόστολος 'apostle' (1:1c) and ἀποστολή 'apostleship' (1:5a).

PROMINENCE AND THEME

The theme of 1:1–7 is drawn, first of all, from the naturally prominent elements of the most naturally prominent propositions of the paragraph's three parts. In addition, the theme includes material from the description of Paul in 1b–d since the identification of himself as an apostle in 1c to establish his credentials to a group he has not yet visited is extremely crucial to Paul's whole purpose. Moreover, the mention of the good news in 1d is thematic in that it recurs in two key verses in the units that follow, namely in 1:15 and 16.

EPISTLE CONSTITUENT 1:8–15:33 (Hortatory Part Cluster: Body of the epistle)

THEME: (See the thematic outline in the Introduction.)	
MACROSTRUCTURE	CONTENTS
introduction	1:8–15 I thank God that people everywhere are talking about how you Roman believers are trusting Jesus Christ. I pray that God will permit me to visit you soon. I want you to know that I have longed to do that, but things have always prevented me. I was eager to proclaim the good news to you who are living at Rome also.
CORE	1:16–15:13 I very confidently proclaim the good news about what Christ has done. This good news states that although everyone, whether Jew or non-Jew, has done evil and deserves to be condemned by God, now God saves those who trust in Jesus Christ and declares their guilt ended. Abraham illustrates that this way of being declared righteous is a gift, not earned. Because God has declared us righteous, we have peace with God, we experience his grace, we rejoice even in suffering, we will be saved from eternal punishment, we have been freed from being controlled by sinful desires and being required to obey the Mosaic law to be saved, we can live as God's Spirit directs, and no one can prevail against us. Though I grieve deeply that most Jews have rejected Christ, this does not prove that God's promise has failed. God is saving many non-Jews to make the Jews seek salvation. Some day all the Jews will be saved. Because of all these things, present yourselves to God to be like living sacrifices. Let God change your thinking and acting. Think about yourselves sensibly by considering the abilities God has given you. Love others sincerely in your actions toward them. Be subject to the civil authorities and pay all of them what they require. Accept those who doubt whether they are permitted to do certain things; specifically, anyone who thinks it is all right to eat all kinds of food must not despise those who don't, and those who don't think so must not condemn those who do.
epilogue	15:14–33 Because of the work of proclaiming the gospel among the non-Jews in places where they have not heard about Christ, I have often been hindered from visiting you, but I hope to see you and be helped by you for my next journey. But now I am about to go to Jerusalem, and I urge you to pray that God will protect me from the unbelieving Jews in Judea and that the believers there will accept the money I take to them.

INTENT AND MACROSTRUCTURE

The 1:8–15:33 unit is the BODY of the epistle. It consists of three parts. The first (1:8–15) and the last (15:14–33) have personal notes concerning Paul and his hoped for visit to Rome. The middle part is the long expository-hortatory CORE containing Paul's APPEALS to the believers at Rome and the basis for them. The whole unit is thus hortatory.

BOUNDARIES AND COHERENCE

The coherence of the 1:8–15:33 BODY consists mainly in its sandwich structure: the central basis-APPEALS unit (1:16–15:13) comprising the CORE is bounded by two units, the introduction and epilogue, which deal with Paul's proposed visit to Rome. The start of the next unit at 16:1 is signaled by a switch from comments addressed to the congregation as a whole to mention of specific individuals.

PROMINENCE AND THEME

The 1:8–15:33 theme comprises the entire themes of the BODY's three parts. But although the material regarding Paul's proposed visit expresses one of the epistle's main purposes, the middle part (1:16–15:13), being far longer than the other two and with much more hortatory material, is considered more thematic.

PART CLUSTER CONSTITUENT 1:8–15
(Emotive Paragraph: Introduction to the core)

THEME: I thank God that people everywhere are talking about how you Roman believers are trusting Jesus Christ. I pray that God will permit me to visit you soon. I want you to know that I have longed to do that, but things have always prevented me. I was eager to proclaim the good news to you who are living at Rome also.

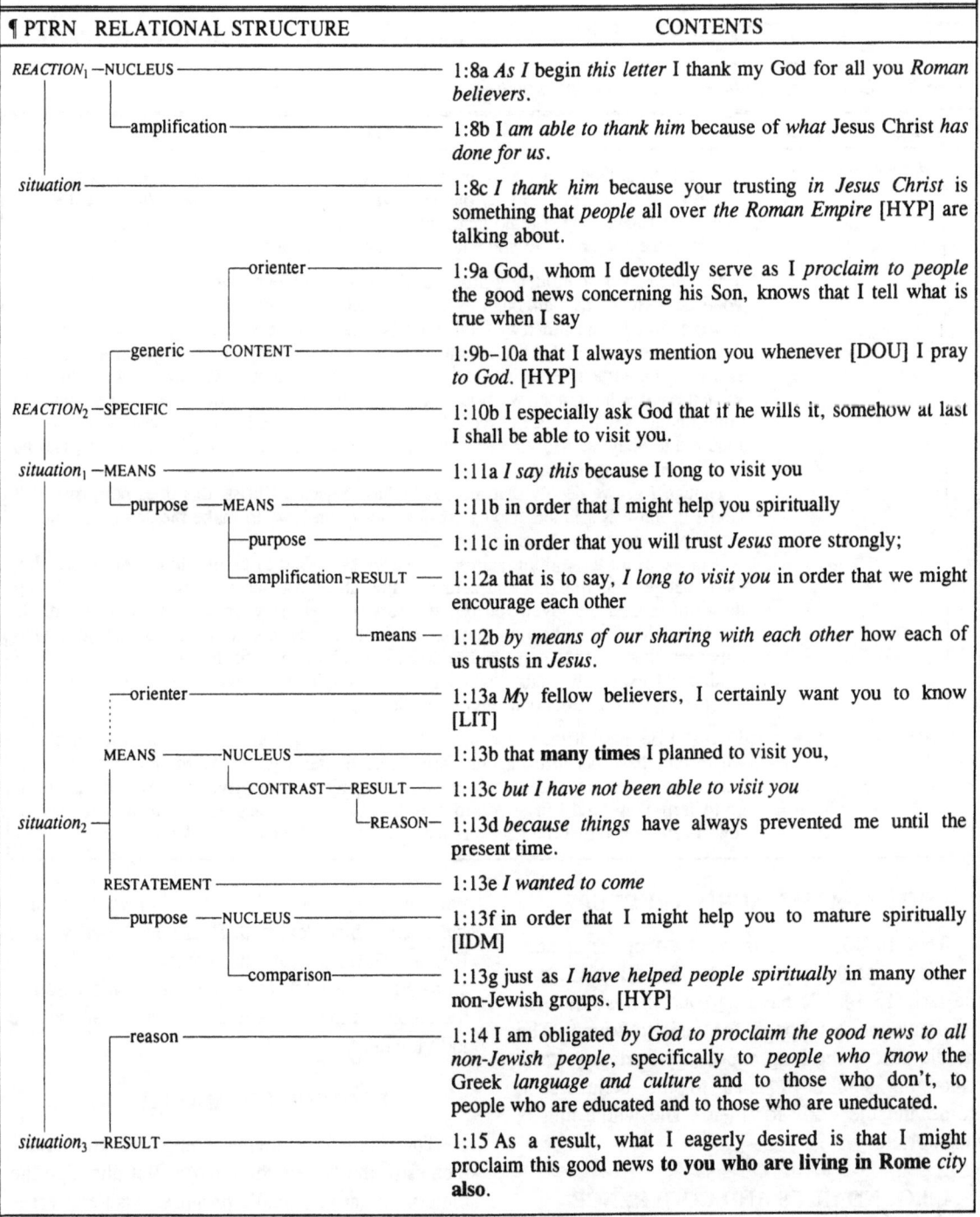

¶ PTRN RELATIONAL STRUCTURE	CONTENTS
REACTION₁ — NUCLEUS	1:8a As I begin *this letter* I thank my God for all you *Roman believers*.
— amplification	1:8b *I am able to thank him* because of *what* Jesus Christ *has done for us*.
situation	1:8c *I thank him* because your trusting *in Jesus Christ* is something that *people* all over *the Roman Empire* [HYP] are talking about.
— orienter	1:9a God, whom I devoutly serve as I *proclaim to people the good news concerning his Son*, knows that I tell what is true when I say
generic — CONTENT	1:9b–10a that I always mention you whenever [DOU] I pray *to God*. [HYP]
REACTION₂ — SPECIFIC	1:10b I especially ask God that if he wills it, somehow at last I shall be able to visit you.
situation₁ — MEANS	1:11a *I say this* because I long to visit you
— purpose — MEANS	1:11b in order that I might help you spiritually
— purpose	1:11c in order that you will trust *Jesus* more strongly;
— amplification — RESULT	1:12a that is to say, *I long to visit you* in order that we might encourage each other
— means	1:12b *by means of our sharing with each other* how each of us trusts in *Jesus*.
— orienter	1:13a *My* fellow believers, I certainly want you to know [LIT]
MEANS — NUCLEUS	1:13b that **many times** I planned to visit you,
— CONTRAST — RESULT	1:13c *but I have not been able to visit you*
— REASON	1:13d *because things* have always prevented me until the present time.
situation₂	
RESTATEMENT	1:13e *I wanted to come*
— purpose — NUCLEUS	1:13f in order that I might help you to mature spiritually [IDM]
— comparison	1:13g just as *I have helped people spiritually* in many other non-Jewish groups. [HYP]
— reason	1:14 I am obligated *by God to proclaim the good news* to all *non-Jewish people*, specifically to *people who know* the Greek *language and culture* and to those who don't, to people who are educated and to those who are uneducated.
situation₃ — RESULT	1:15 As a result, what I eagerly desired is that I might proclaim this good news **to you who are living in Rome** *city* **also**.

INTENT AND PARAGRAPH PATTERN

The 1:8-15 paragraph has a number of first person singular references to Paul and second person plural references to the Roman addressees. In 8c Paul expresses the *situation* and in 8a-b he gives the first part of his REACTION. Furthermore, in vv. 8-9 Paul states a number of things calculated to build rapport with his audience. Both are evidence that the paragraph falls into the emotive category. Within the second part of his REACTION in vv. 9-15, Paul expresses (in 9a-10b) a generic REACTION and a specific REACTION in the form of a prayer asking God to enable him to visit the Roman believers. This is followed by his delineation (in 11-15) of three *situations* that gave rise to this specific REACTION.

Although v. 9 begins with γάρ 'for', it does not seem to provide a situation or a reason supportive of v. 8. (Verse 9 is not introduced by any connector representing γάρ in TEV, NIV, JB, NEB, LB, JBP, or CEV.) It is considered, rather, to introduce a second REACTION (his constant prayers for them) motivated by three *situations*. The expressions ἐπιποθῶ 'I long' and τὸ κατ' ἐμὲ πρόθυμον 'my eager desire' are strong emotional elements, supporting the view that this whole paragraph is an emotive one.

NOTES

1:8a *As I begin this letter* The word πρῶτον 'first' could mean first in importance, but what follows hardly seems to be such. Therefore it is taken as 'the first thing I want to talk about in this letter'. NCV has "First I want to say that."

Since Paul does not possess God, some verb such as 'serve' or 'worship' may need to be supplied in some languages in order to express the role relationship implied by the words 'my God'. 'God whom I serve devotedly' captures the sense quite well.

1:8b I *am able to thank him* **because of** *what Jesus Christ has done for us* This prepositional phrase διὰ Ἰησοῦ Χριστοῦ 'through Jesus Christ' is the only occurrence of such a construction with Paul's thanksgivings. The preposition διά could mean that Christ is the intermediary who presents Paul's thanks to God, giving the sense of 'by thanking Jesus Christ, who presents my thanks to God the Father'. This seems rather strained, but is the interpretation followed by most commentators. The other alternative is the one chosen for the display—that Jesus Christ is the one who makes it possible for Paul to give thanks for them (by what Christ has done). This interpretation fits the overall theme of the letter better (so Cranfield).

1:8c *your trusting in Jesus Christ* **is something that** *people* **all over** *the Roman Empire* **are talking about** The display attempts to show the prominence of the forefronted phrase ἡ πίστις ὑμῶν 'your faith' by similarly forefronting it.

The phrase ἐν ὅλῳ τῷ κόσμῳ 'in the whole world' is hyperbole and means 'all over the known world', specifically, 'all over the Roman Empire'.

1:9a **devotedly** The phrase ἐν τῷ πνεύματί μου 'in the spirit of me' is an idiomatic expression. It means 'not just with my body', 'not superficially', hence 'devotedly'. TEV has "with all my heart."

as I *proclaim* **... the good news** In the phrase ἐν τῷ εὐαγγελίῳ 'in the gospel', 'in' is not used in its primary (i.e., locative) sense; therefore a verb such as 'proclaim/preach' is to be understood (cf. Barrett, Shedd). As to the relationship of such a proposition to the verb 'serve', it could be considered to express circumstance, 'while/as I proclaim' (so CEV). Alternatively, the proclaiming could be taken as the specific way in which Paul serves, or even as the means of his serving (so REB). There is little difference in sense.

1:9b-10a whenever The expression ἀδιαλείπτως ... πάντοτε 'unceasingly ... always' can be taken as a doublet. It is also somewhat hyperbolic and means 'each time I pray'. The one propositional cluster covers part of two verses in the Greek.

1:10b that if he wills it, somehow at last I shall be able The expression εἴ πως ἤδη ποτέ 'if somehow now sometime' indicates a desire coupled with a lot of uncertainty. The 'now sometime' means 'at long last, after several unsuccessful previous attempts'. The whole temporal phrase is forefronted, which gives it prominence. The forefronting in the display reflects this prominence.

The words εὐοδωθήσομαι ἐν τῷ θελήματι τοῦ θεοῦ 'I may succeed in the will of God' are represented somewhat literally in the display by 'if he wills it, ... I shall be able'. Perhaps the sense of the phrase could be conveyed as well by 'God may grant that'. CEV has "I ask God to make it possible." But, as Morris points out, there seems to be a clear respect for and emphasis on God's will being done in the proposed visit.

1:11b that I might help you spiritually The words χάρισμα ὑμῖν πνευματικόν 'gift to you spiritual' could mean 'gift bestowed by the Holy Spirit', as in Rom. 12:6-8 or 1 Corinthians 12. But the Romans 12 passage seems to indicate that Paul recognized they already had such gifts, and he does not discuss the subject further. Therefore that interpretation is not followed here. The one adopted here is suggested by Morris, Whedon, and others.

1:11c in order that you will trust *Jesus* more strongly It is hard in English to express the passive verb στηριχθῆναι 'be established' nonfiguratively. It carries the idea 'be strengthened, be made fixed, stand firm'.

1:12a that is to say Most commentators agree that τοῦτο δέ ἐστιν 'and this is' introduces some sort of restatement of the content of 11b-c. But since v. 12 talks of a mutual benefit and v. 11 mentions only benefit to the Romans, it is more of an amplification than a restatement. NEB has 'or rather'.

1:12b *by means of our sharing with each other how each of us trusts in Jesus* The Greek is διὰ τῆς ἐν ἀλλήλοις πίστεως ὑμῶν τε καὶ ἐμοῦ, literally 'through the in each other faith yours both and mine'. When Paul speaks of their mutual encouragement by each other's faith, he implies they will share not the content of their faith but the results of their faith in Jesus. The preposition διά is taken as expressing means. Note that throughout this analysis all first person plural pronouns are considered inclusive (i.e., referring to Paul and his readers) unless otherwise indicated.

1:13a fellow believers The word ἀδελφοί 'brothers' is a kinship term that Paul uses extensively in an extended sense to refer to fellow believers, fellow Christians. When used in this sense, it is represented in the displays as 'fellow believers'.

I certainly want you to know The use of a litotes here, οὐ θέλω δὲ ὑμᾶς ἀγνοεῖν 'I do not wish you to be ignorant', emphasizes that Paul wants them to know something. This particular figure is used by Paul a number of times and is rendered "I want you to know" in nearly all modern versions.

1:13b many times The adverb πολλάκις 'often' is forefronted, giving it more emphasis. In the display this emphasis is indicated by bold type.

1:13d *because things* have always prevented me The words καὶ ἐκωλύθην 'and I was prevented' clearly express the reason for the nonfulfillment of Paul's desire; therefore 13d is considered to convey a REASON relation. The Greek verb is in the passive voice. This is changed to active in the display and the generic 'things' supplied as its subject. The verb 'prevented' seems to suggest some forces that Paul considered hostile to his desires, but obviously no specific agent is in focus—an agent should be avoided if possible. In some languages, it will be necessary to complement 'prevented' with something like 'from coming to you'.

1:13e *I wanted to come* This proposition, which is based on 13b, is supplied simply because of the requirements of English grammar.

1:13f I might help you to mature spiritually The clause τινὰ καρπὸν σχῶ 'some fruit I might bear' is a dead metaphor in Greek (as in English) referring to the results of Paul's labors. Some have taken it to mean more converts (e.g., CEV), but it is better to take it more broadly: 'see some more spiritual growth among you'. NCV has "help you grow spiritually."

1:14 I am obligated *by God to proclaim the good news to all non-Jewish people*, specifically to *people who know* the Greek *language and culture* and to those who don't, to people who are educated and to those who are uneducated A 'debtor' (ὀφειλέτης) is one who is obligated to do something for someone. In view of the thrust of the following context, the obligation here is to 'proclaim the gospel to', so that phrase is supplied, borrowed from v. 15 (so Barnes, Hodge, Morris, Murray).

The terms 'Greeks' and 'barbarians' originally signified the cultured Greeks and uncultured foreigners, respectively; but by Paul's time the second term simply meant non-Greek peoples. Louw and Nida (11.95) suggest that the contrast in Ἕλλησίν τε καὶ βαρβάροις 'to Greeks and to barbarians' is best expressed by "the civilized and the uncivilized." The contrast appears to be a cultural one. As to ἀνοήτοις 'to foolish (ones)', Paul does not mean those who are truly foolish, but rather those who are considered to belong to this class due to their background. What he means is the educated and the uneducated. Both of these indirect object phrases are forefronted, which gives them prominence. Together they express the universality of obligation Paul feels, which the supplied words 'to all non-Jewish people' are intended to bring out.

1:15 what I eagerly desired is that I might proclaim . . . to you . . . also There are two difficulties with the phrase τὸ κατ' ἐμὲ πρόθυμον 'the according to me eagerness': (1) how to interpret it grammatically, and (2) whether it includes the sense of 'as far as I am concerned' in addition to the 'eager' denotation. (The solution to the first problem does not really affect the second.) Most commentators agree that the phrase does have this additional sense, which is reinforced in that everything else in the whole clause precedes the verb. The display tries to capture this with a cleft construction in the first part of the proposition and bold type in the latter part.

The main grammatical problem, however, is that there is no main verb in the verse. Commentators (e.g., Cranfield), in discussing the rather unusual Greek construction here, have assumed that the verb 'to be' needs to be supplied, and most versions do just that, but in the present tense (e.g., CEV has "I am eager"). Käsemann, on the other hand, adds ἐγένετο 'became'. As the context indicates, the past (or past perfect) tense is much more appropriate; it also avoids conflict with Paul's statement in 15:20. Dunn states, "The conviction of what he personally *had been* called to do dominates vv 13-15 [emphasis added]."

BOUNDARIES AND COHERENCE

Verses 1:8-15 are considered an *introduction* that sets the stage for Paul's long expository presentation by building rapport with his intended audience. This rapport is achieved by a series of 'I' and 'you(pl)' statements that express positive comments about the Roman believers. Seventeen overt first person singular references and thirteen second person plural references are found in these verses. (Except for 'I' in 1:16, no further such references occur until 3:5.)

Relational coherence is seen in the three 'I-you(pl)' statements of Paul's reactions to various situations involving the Roman believers: their faith (8c); his desire to visit them for mutual encouragement (11-12); the previous frustration of his plans to visit them (13).

There is some question as to whether 1:8-15 should be considered two units (i.e., 8-12 and 13-15), as proposed by some (e.g., Thomson and Davidson, Best). In favor of this is the occurrence of a vocative in v. 13. Against it is the reference to the gospel in vv. 9 and 15, and especially references to Paul's visit to them in vv. 10, 11, 13, and 15. This is in addition to the frequency of first person singular and second person plural pronouns in vv. 8-15.

The major boundary problem is whether the *introduction* continues through 1:17 or ends at 1:15. Verse 16 begins with γάρ 'for', which suggests that it supplies a reason for his eagerness to proclaim the gospel at Rome. However, semantically, it is rather poor to suggest that the reason for Paul's eagerness to preach the gospel was that he was proud of it (literally, 'not ashamed of it'). It seems better to assume, as do many commentators, that γάρ in 1:16 is signaling a tail-head linkage to a brief transition paragraph (1:16-17) in which Paul states the theme for all of 1:18-11:36. The tail-head linkage hinges on εὐαγγελίσασθαι 'to preach/announce the gospel/ good news' and its close cognate εὐαγγέλιον 'gospel' in v. 16. Hence in the display v. 16 begins 'That leads me to say that . . .'.

PROMINENCE AND THEME

The 1:8-15 theme is drawn from the naturally prominent propositions of the *situation* and both REACTIONS. Within the second REACTION, the SPECIFIC (the fact that in his prayers he is making a request to God) is more thematic because it is developed extensively throughout the rest of the paragraph. The theme also includes the three most naturally prominent propositions of vv. 11-15: the MEANS in 11a, the CONTRAST in 13c-d, and the RESULT in 15.

PART CLUSTER CONSTITUENT 1:16–15:13
(Hortatory Subpart: Core of the epistle)

THEME: *(See the thematic outline in the Introduction.)*	
MACROSTRUCTURE	CONTENTS
basis	1:16–11:36 I very confidently proclaim the good news about what Christ has done. This good news declares that although everyone, whether Jew or non-Jew, has done evil and deserves to be condemned, now God saves those who trust in Christ and he declares their guilt ended. So we cannot boast about achieving this by obeying the Mosaic law. Abraham, who was declared righteous because he believed God's promise, illustrates that being declared righteous is a gift, not earned, and he is thus a spiritual father to all who trust in God, Jews and non-Jews. Because God has declared us righteous, we have peace with God, we experience his grace, we rejoice even in suffering, and we will be saved from eternal punishment. We have been freed from being controlled by sinful desires and being compelled to obey the Mosaic law to be saved. Now we are compelled to live as God's Spirit directs, and it does not matter if anything opposes us. Though I grieve deeply that most of the Jews have rejected Christ, this does not prove that God's promise has failed or that God's condemning them is unjust. God is saving many non-Jews to make the Jews jealous and seek salvation. But don't you non-Jews despise the Jews, because if you fall away from God he won't spare you either. And you need to know that some day all the Jews will be saved.
APPEALS	12:1–15:13 Present yourselves to God to be like living sacrifices, which is the appropriate way for you to serve him. Do not let anything non-Christian determine how you should act, but instead let God change your way of thinking. Specifically, think about yourselves sensibly, by considering and then using the abilities God has given you; love others sincerely in the ways you act towards them, and instead of avenging yourselves let God avenge you; be subject to the civil authorities and pay all of them what they require. Let your only continual obligation be to love one another. Accept those who doubt whether they are permitted to do certain things; specifically, anyone who thinks it is all right to eat all kinds of food must not despise those who don't, and those who don't think so must not condemn those who do.

INTENT AND MACROSTRUCTURE

The 1:16–15:13 subpart is the CORE of the epistle. It is composed of the expository *basis* (1:16–11:36) and the hortatory APPEALS (12:1–15:13). Since the latter is the naturally prominent constituent and is hortatory, the entire subpart is therefore hortatory.

BOUNDARIES AND COHERENCE

The 1:16–15:13 CORE of the epistle contains all the expository material concerning the doctrine of justification by faith and its applications to Paul's intended audience, both Jews and Gentiles and, with one brief exception (16:17–20), all of the exhortations arising from them. Its closure is signaled in 15:13 by a generic prayer for the Roman believers. Within this closing prayer there is a reference to the power of the Holy Spirit; it echoes the very first verse of the unit (1:16) with its reference to the power of God.

The beginning of the next unit is marked by a reference to Paul's writing boldly on certain points. This refers to the CORE's contents.

PROMINENCE AND THEME

The theme for the 1:16–15:13 unit is drawn from the themes of its two constituents. Some less thematic parts of the 1:16–11:36 theme are omitted because they are implications not central to the main argument. Also omitted are the less thematic parts of the 12:1–15:13 theme—a comment on 'living sacrifice' and the negative exhortation in 12:2—because in a negative-positive set the positive is more thematic, and because the positive is developed far more in the rest of the unit.

SUBPART CONSTITUENT 1:16–11:36
(Expository Division Cluster: Basis of the appeals in 12:1–15:13)

THEME: (See the thematic outline in the Introduction.)	
MACROSTRUCTURE	CONTENTS
THEME	1:16–17 Because it is the powerful means God uses to save everyone who trusts in Christ, whether they are Jews or non-Jews, I very confidently proclaim the good news about what Christ has done, since by it God reveals his way of declaring people righteous.
difficulty solved by 3:21–26	1:18–3:20 All people, no matter whether they are Jews or non-Jews, have done evil and so deserve to be condemned by God.
MAJOR PRINCIPLE	3:21–26 Now God declares righteous everyone, Jew or non-Jew, who trusts in what Jesus Christ has done for them. God presented Christ as the one who would atone for sins by shedding his blood on the cross.
inferences	3:27–31 Therefore we are prevented from boasting about being justified by obeying the Mosaic law. And God will accept non-Jews too on the same basis. And by saying that people are declared righteous by their trusting in Christ, we actually confirm, not nullify, the law.
exemplary evidence	4:1–25 We can draw conclusions from Abraham about how to be declared righteous. Scripture records that it was because he believed God's promise that he was declared righteous by God. This happiness of being declared righteous was a gift from God, not a reward. It is also for the non-Jews, because it was spoken about Abraham before he became a Jew by being circumcised, which was simply a sign of his previously being declared righteous by faith. Thus Abraham is a spiritual father to all, both Jews and non-Jews, who believe as he did, and what was written of him is an assurance to us who would also be declared righteous.
application$_1$	5:1–21 Because God has declared us righteous, we have peace with God, we experience his grace, we rejoice even in suffering because we expect to receive God's glory, and we know we will be saved from eternal punishment. Although the sin of one man, Adam, led to all people dying and deserving punishment, Christ's one righteous act has led to many being acquitted and declared righteous and living eternally.
application$_2$	6:1–8:39 We have been freed from being controlled by sinful desires and from being required to obey the Mosaic law to be saved. Now we are compelled to live as God's Spirit directs. In view of what God does for us through his Spirit, no one can prevail against us, and nothing can separate us from Christ's and God's loving us.
application$_3$ for Jews	9:1–11:36 I grieve greatly because most of the Jews have rejected Jesus as their promised deliverer, but this does not prove that God has failed to give many descendants to Abraham as he promised. Nor can we conclude that God is unjust in choosing the ones he wants to or that it is not right for God to condemn people because no one has resisted what God has willed. The Jews did not succeed in fulfilling what the Mosaic law requires; they tried to find a way to be declared righteous not by trusting in what Christ did but by doing things in order that God would accept them. To you Jews I say that God has certainly not rejected all of us, and that God is saving many non-Jews to make the Jews jealous and thus seek to be saved. To you non-Jews I say that I hope my work among you will accomplish just that. But don't despise the Jews that God has rejected and become proud, because just as God did not spare the Jews he will not spare you if you fall away from him. And I want you to know that all the Jews will some day be saved.

INTENT AND MACROSTRUCTURE

The 1:16–11:36 unit is a long *basis* for the epistle's main APPEALS, which follow it. Although there are small portions of some of the constituents that are hortatory in nature (e.g., 11:17–24), most of the constituents are completely expository, and thus the unit as a whole is considered expository.

The unit consists of an introductory theme statement (1:16–17) regarding the gospel's application to everyone; a statement of the problem of universal guilt for sin (1:18–3:20); a statement of the central principle of God's solution to the problem, namely justification by faith in the atoning work of Christ (3:21-26); inferences drawn from the principle (3:27-31); exemplary evidence for the principle, Abraham (4:1-25); and three applications of the principle to the daily life of the believers at Rome (5:1-21; 6:1-8:39; 9:1-11:36).

BOUNDARIES AND COHERENCE

The coherence of the long 1:16-11:36 exposition consists in the fact that it centers on justification by faith as the one way of salvation for all, both Jews and non-Jews. It covers the universal need for salvation in 1:16-3:20, the presentation of that way of salvation in 3:21-26, and then a succession of units which give inferences, exemplary evidence, applications of that doctrine to everyday life, with implications for the Jews in particular.

The unit's closure is marked by the doxology in 11:33-36. The beginning of the following hortatory section in 12:1 is marked by παρακαλῶ οὖν ὑμᾶς, ἀδελφοί 'I appeal to you, therefore, brethren'.

There is a chiastic structure within this long expository passage of Rom. 1:16-11:36:

A 1:18-32 God hardened the minds of the wicked.
  B 2:2-16 There is no excuse for anyone.
    C 2:17-3:20 Jews cannot boast that they have the Mosaic law; having it is not enough.
      D 3:21-31 Righteousness is by faith, apart from the Mosaic law.
        E 4:1-25 Abraham received what God promised by faith, illustrating that those who believe will inherit, not those who rely on ancestry.
          F 5:1-21 We are right with God through faith in Christ, though we were ruled by sinful desires inherited from Adam before.
            G 6:1-7:6 Consider yourselves dead to sin but alive to God in Christ.
            G' 7:7-15 I serve the law of God with my mind, but the law of sin with my natural desires.
          F' 8:1-39 The Spirit of life has set us free from the power of sin and of death.
        E' 9:1-33 Israel is excluded because God's promise applied only to those who believe.
      D' 10:1-13 Righteousness comes by faith to all who believe, not by obeying the Mosaic law.
  B' 10:14-21 The people of Israel have no excuse: the gospel has been preached to all, including them.
A' 11:1-10 God hardened the minds of those who do not believe but saves those who do believe.
    C' 11:11-32 Gentiles cannot boast in their present favored position: it is only because they believe that God has accepted them.

PROMINENCE AND THEME

The theme statement of the 1:16-11:36 unit is drawn from the theme statements of its constituents, reworded and somewhat condensed and rearranged grammatically. From the 1:16-17 THEME only the independent clause, being naturally prominent, is included. From the 3:27-31 *inferences* only the first sentence is included because the second sentence is considered a somewhat incidental implication of justification by faith, not really central to the main argument. From the 4:1-25 *exemplary evidence* the statement in CLAIM₂ about righteousness being for the non-Jews is omitted because it is summarized in the statement "both Jews and non-Jews" which concludes that unit; the restatements within 4:1-25 are likewise omitted because they are redundant. From the first *application* (5:1-21) only parts of the first NUCLEUS (5:1-11) are included because nearly all of the second one consists of a restatement and illustration of the first. From the second *application* (6:1-8:39) the last clause is omitted because it does not cohere well without the less prominent reason clause that supports it.

DIVISION CLUSTER CONSTITUENT 1:16–17
(Expository Paragraph: Theme of 1:16–11:36)

THEME: Because it is the powerful means God uses to save everyone who trusts in Christ, whether they are Jews or non-Jews, I very confidently proclaim the good news about what Christ has done, since by it God reveals his way of declaring people righteous.

¶ PTRN	RELATIONAL STRUCTURE	CONTENTS
CLAIM	RESULT	1:16a That leads me to say that I very confidently proclaim [LIT] the good news *about what Christ has done*,
	REASON GENERIC	1:16b because this good news is the powerful *means* God uses to save all people who trust *in Christ*.
	specific	1:16c Specifically, first *God saves* the Jews *who heeded the good news*, and *then he saves* non-Jews.
justification	CONCLUSION	1:17a By means of this good news God reveals *how he is able to declare* that people are righteous (*or*, no longer guilty for having sinned); and his doing this is entirely because [IDM] they trust *in Christ*.
	evidential grounds	1:17b *This is confirmed* by means of what *a prophet long ago* wrote that God said, "Those *who are declared* righteous *by me* because they trust *in me* shall live *forever*."

INTENT AND PARAGRAPH PATTERN

The 1:16–17 unit is difficult to classify as to its paragraph pattern. Although the verb phrase οὐ ἐπαισχύνομαι 'I am not ashamed' does lend an emotive element to the paragraph, what seems to be happening is that the emotive elements of the rapport-building *introduction* (1:8–15) have spilled over into the first clause of 1:16–17. Therefore it seems better to say that the initial γάρ in 16b introduces the reason for Paul's 'confident proclamation' and not the content of what he is 'not ashamed of'. Although 16a could be considered as stating Paul's REACTION to the *situation* (16b–17) which led up to it, it seems better also to take 16a-b as expressing a CLAIM for which the γάρ in 17a introduces its *justification*. Another alternative would be to consider the γάρ in v. 17 as introducing an amplification on the subject of 16b's 'good news', but this would mean having a unit without the two usual constituent elements of a paragraph. The interpretation taken here is supported by Murray, who says, "In verse 17 we are given the reason why the gospel is the power of God unto salvation. And the reason is that in the gospel 'is revealed a righteousness of God.'" Erdman and Hodge agree.

NOTES

1:16a That leads me to say that I very confidently proclaim the good news *about what Christ has done* Although a reason-RESULT relationship can be seen across the boundary between 1:15 and 1:16, nevertheless the units in which 15 and 16 occur are not appropriately related by reason-RESULT on a higher level. The clause-initial γάρ, which ordinarily indicates subordination, here relates a tail-head construction in which 'proclaim the good news' (v. 15) is the tail and 'good news' (v. 16) is the head. This is expressed in the display by 'That leads me to say that'. It would not be wrong, however, for a translator to use a connective marking reason here.

The clause οὐ γὰρ ἐπαισχύνομαι τὸ εὐαγγέλιον, literally 'for not I ashamed of the gospel', is Paul's evaluation of the following content, but the content—summarized in 16a simply as 'about what Christ as done'—is far more prominent than the evaluation in that it is explicated in 16b–17 and then greatly expanded for the next eight chapters.

Some commentators suggest that in the Greco-Roman world there were many who did indeed look down on this implausible message about an obscure carpenter's son who was crucified, and that Paul is contrasting himself with them. But this sense would require the free pronoun ἐγώ to be stated. Furthermore, there is nothing in the context to support the idea that he is distancing himself from such critics. Since Paul spends the next seven and a half chapters extolling the virtues of the gospel, it seems best to follow many commentators and take the expression as a litotes meaning 'I am very proud of'. But Paul's meaning here is a bit different from the ordinary negative sense of 'proud' in English. What he means is 'knowing how God's saving power attends its proclamation, I very confidently proclaim it everywhere I can!'

Stuhlmacher points out (p. 336) that "this expression . . . belongs to the language of the early Christian confession. It corresponds to 'I acknowledge (the gospel)', a declaration to be uttered in a difficult situation." An alternative to the rendering in the display, assuming the correctness of Stuhlmacher's statement, would be 'I declare my allegiance to'.

The term 'gospel' means 'good news' and will always be thus represented in this study. But in its first mention, at least, the good news may need to be defined by adding 'about Jesus' or 'about Christ'. The words τοῦ Χριστοῦ 'about Christ' are, in fact, in the majority text. In some cases, perhaps in the early mention of the term, it may be necessary to render it 'the good news about what Christ has done'.

With respect to the definite article before 'gospel', Stuhlmacher says, "From Paul's perspective . . . there is only one way of salvation and only one single gospel" (p. 337).

1:16b is the powerful *means* God uses to save The Greek is δύναμις θεοῦ ἐστιν εἰς σωτηρίαν 'it (i.e., the gospel) is the power of God unto salvation'. This is somewhat figurative; Paul does not mean that the gospel is literally power, but rather it is the means by which God utilizes his power to save people. The word εἰς 'unto' before σωτηρίαν 'salvation' also signals the means-result relationship.

Semantically, the word 'power' refers to an attributive concept. The question is, What does that attributive modify? The solution given in the display is to supply the word 'means', which nominalizes a relationship, not an Event or Thing concept. For some languages this may be impossible to express. In such cases it may be necessary to render it as 'by means of people believing the gospel, God powerfully saves', or 'God powerfully causes people who believe the gospel to be saved', making 'powerfully' an attribute of the verb 'save' (in the Greek it is a noun, σωτηρία 'salvation'). Another possibility is to supply a different verb to express the means relationship: 'by means of people proclaiming the gospel, God powerfully saves' (so Dunn, Nygren).

all people who trust *in Christ* The word 'believing' in the participial phrase τῷ πιστεύοντι 'to the one believing' is rendered as 'trust' here because it has the sense of "to believe to the extent of complete trust and reliance" (Louw and Nida 31.85). It is not simply an assent to the truth of something. For some languages, a fuller content of 'trust' (here and elsewhere in the epistle) may be required, something like 'in what Christ has done for us'.

1:16c first *God saves* Most commentators suggest that the phrase Ἰουδαίῳ πρῶτον 'to the Jew first' means priority in time, and that is how it is rendered in the display. A few suggest that it means the Jews have a higher priority, but this seems contrary to the whole thrust of the epistle in promoting oneness between Jewish and Gentile believers.

1:17a This verse expresses a *justification* for the CLAIM in v. 16. See the Intent and Paragraph Pattern note.

By means of this good news The phrase ἐν αὐτῷ 'in it' means 'in the gospel'; hence the pronoun is here rendered 'this good news'.

God reveals *how he is able to declare* that people are righteous (*or,* no longer guilty for having sinned) The construction δικαιοσύνη θεοῦ 'righteousness of God' is taken here as indicating that God is the source of righteousness. This interpretation is supported by the reference to faith and by the fact that in the long expository section of this epistle, especially 3:24–26, Paul is not focusing on an attribute of God but on the way a person can have a right standing before God. But since the noun δικαιοσύνη expresses the attribute 'righteous' and God is the agent, some verb needs to be supplied to satisfy the case frame. There are two possibilities: (1) to make righteous, or (2) to declare righteous. The use of the verb δικαιόω by extrabiblical writers at the time of the NT suggests that the sense here is 'to justify, to vindicate, to treat as just' (BAGD, p. 197.2), hence 'to declare people righteous', as in the display. (For further discussion of 'righteousness', see the note on 3:21a.)

There is still a problem with rendering δικαιόω as 'declare righteous': how can God declare us to be what we are not? Is Paul saying that God says we are righteous when he goes to such great length in these first two chapters to show we are *not* righteous? To avoid this contradiction, the alternative 'declare that our guilt for sin is ended' is a good alternative. Something similar may be called for elsewhere in the epistle where this same phrase occurs (see the note on 3:21b).

In the Greek, 'righteousness of God' precedes the verb 'is revealed'. This fronting is a means of topicalization, giving prominence to the topic that will be developed in the following chapters.

entirely because they trust *in Christ* When the noun 'faith' is rendered as a verb, an object or content of the verb must be supplied (e.g., 'in Christ' or 'in what Christ has done for them') to satisfy the case frame.

The phrase ἐκ πίστεως εἰς πίστιν 'from faith unto faith' is variously understood. The interpretation chosen here, which is well supported in the commentaries, is that the expression is an idiom meaning 'by faith from the beginning to the end'. NCV renders the expression "begins and ends with faith" (see also REB). As Morris comments, the other interpretations are probably straining to see more than is justified.

1:17b *This is confirmed* **by means of what** *a prophet long ago* **wrote** *that God said* The expression καθὼς γέγραπται 'as it is written', which occurs six times in Romans, introduces an OT quotation cited in support of some argument. 'This is confirmed by' is the sense of the conjunction.

To avoid wrong meaning a generic agent of the passive 'is written' is supplied, as well as the implied time. The words 'that God said' are necessary in order to clarify that the speaker of the original was God; if this is not made clear, readers may think that the pronoun 'me' in the next clause refers to the prophet who is quoted.

"Those *who are declared* **righteous** *by me* **because they trust** *in me* **shall live** *forever*" In this quotation from Hab. 2:4, the expression ὁ δὲ δίκαιος ἐκ πίστεως ζήσεται 'but the righteous (one) by faith shall live' could mean 'he that is righteous shall live by faith' or 'he that is righteous by faith shall live'. The latter is supported by the fact that the immediate context is talking about being declared righteous, not living righteously. Furthermore, πίστις 'faith' and πιστεύω 'believe' occur thirty-four times in the first four chapters, while forms related to the noun ζωή 'life' occur only three times. As Morris notes, "The inference is that at this stage of the epistle Paul is concerned with the fact that it is by faith that God saves people rather than with how they live." Finally, several times in the early chapters of the epistle Paul connects righteousness with faith—he never connects righteousness with living by faith.

The phrase ὁ δίκαιος 'the just' is singular but carries the generic sense 'everyone declared righteous'. To avoid wrong meaning it is rendered by the plural 'those who' in the display. Obviously Paul is using the noun δικαιοσύνη 'righteousness' in 17a and the adjective δίκαιος 'righteous' in 17b to convey the same sense. The fact that they are rendered quite differently in the display is not intended to suggest they should be translated differently in each place.

The words ἐκ πίστεως 'out of faith' express cause: 'on account of faith'. Following the rules of propositionalization, this is rendered 'because they trusted'. The verb 'trust' requires an object or content; 'in me' is therefore supplied.

The word 'forever' is implied; Paul is not talking about physical life. BAGD (p. 336.2aβ) classify 'live' here under 'have eternal life'.

BOUNDARIES AND COHERENCE

The coherence of the 1:16–17 paragraph is seen in the references to the gospel (τὸ εὐαγγέλιον in v. 16, ἐν αὐτῷ 'in it' in v. 17); righteousness (δικαιοσύνη 'righteousness' and δίκαιος 'righteous' in v. 17); and faith (πιστεύοντι 'the one believing' in v. 16, ἐκ πίστεως εἰς πίστιν 'from faith to faith', and ἐκ πίστεως 'by faith' in v. 17). Verse 18 is considered to start a new unit dealing with all manner of wickedness, examples of which are given in almost every verse from 1:18 to 3:18.

PROMINENCE AND THEME

Following the principles of natural prominence the theme of 1:16–17 is drawn from the RESULT and REASON propositions of the *CLAIM* and the CONCLUSION proposition of the *justification*. The theme also includes the words 'Jews or non-Jews' from 16c based on the principle of marked prominence. These words are thematic due to their recurrent use in the early part of the epistle. (They occur overtly here and in 2:9 and 3:9.) They thus constitute a motif that is crucial to the overall intent of the epistle.

DIVISION CLUSTER CONSTITUENT 1:18–3:20
(Expository Subdivision Cluster: Difficulty solved by 3:21–26)

THEME: All people, no matter whether they are Jews or non-Jews, have done evil and so deserve to be condemned by God.

MACROSTRUCTURE	CONTENTS
CLAIM₁	1:18–32 God is making it clear that he is angry with godless and wicked non-Jewish people, whom he has allowed to become enslaved to their own evil desires and worthless thoughts.
CLAIM₂	2:1–3:18 Anyone of you Jews, who has all the advantages of being a Jew and disobeys God's law, will also be condemned by him; God will consider your circumcision worthless and will accept the non-Jews who obey his laws. They will declare that God is right in condemning you. God will not treat us Jews more favorably than he will treat non-Jews.
summary	3:19–20 In summary, no one is able to object to God's condemnation; everyone has been declared guilty by God.

INTENT AND MACROSTRUCTURE

The 1:18–3:20 unit, which states the *difficulty* posed by universal sin, contains two CLAIMS and a final *summary*. It is thus expository. The first CLAIM deals with the Gentiles; the second, with the Jews.

BOUNDARIES AND COHERENCE

Concerning the final boundary of the 1:18–3:20 unit, there are at least three indicators of a break between 3:20 and 3:21. First, 3:21 begins with 'but now apart from the Mosaic law', whereas the previous section is full of references to keeping the law (2:12, 13, 14, 15, 17, 18, 20, 23, 25, 26, 27). Second, 3:19–20 contains a summary restatement of what precedes in this subdivision cluster. Third, 1:18–3:20 is more or less a catalogue of transgressions by Jews and Gentiles to show that all stand condemned, whereas 3:21 introduces God's solution to the problem of sin. It is this topic of wickedness which provides coherence to the whole unit.

Relational coherence is shown in that the subdivision cluster consists of two central CLAIMS concerning God's indictment of the whole world, one relating to the Gentiles and the other to the Jews.

PROMINENCE AND THEME

The theme for the 1:18–3:20 unit is a condensation of the themes of its two most prominent constituents, the first stating God's anger with all Gentiles for their sin and the second one stating God's condemnation of the Jews for their sin. The nonthematic descriptive comments, the grounds for the conclusions, and the summary, being less thematic, are omitted from the overall theme.

SUBDIVISION CLUSTER CONSTITUENT 1:18–32
(Expository Section Cluster: Claim₁ of 1:18–3:20)

THEME: God is making it clear that he is angry with godless and wicked non-Jewish people, whom he has allowed to become enslaved to their own evil desires and worthless thoughts.

MACROSTRUCTURE	CONTENTS
CLAIM	1:18a–c God is making it clear that he is angry with godless and wicked non-Jewish people.
cause	1:19–23 Everyone can clearly know what God is like; therefore no one has a basis for saying, "We never knew about God."
EFFECT₁	1:24–27 So God let the non-Jewish peoples feel compelled to do disgraceful things, which resulted in their dishonoring their bodies sexually. He did this because they worshiped idols and things which were created instead of God. As a result of both men and women having unnatural sexual relations, they have been punished as they deserve.
justification EFFECT₂	1:28–32 The result of God's letting them become obsessed by their own depraved thoughts was that they themselves began to do all manner of evil things that God says are improper. They even approve of others doing such things.

INTENT AND MACROSTRUCTURE

The 1:18–32 unit is an expository section cluster of the volitionality subtype. It consists of two parts, a CLAIM about God's anger with the Gentiles (v. 18) and its *justification*. The *justification* in turn consists of three parts: the *cause* (vv. 19–23), namely the Gentiles' foolish thoughts about God, and two EFFECTS. The first of these EFFECTS (vv. 24–27) is introduced in v. 24 by διό 'wherefore'; the second (vv. 28–32) is coordinate with it, being introduced in v. 28 with καί 'and'.

BOUNDARIES AND COHERENCE

Relational coherence in the 1:18–32 unit consists of its stating God's anger with sin and the specifics of the sin which provoked that anger. Several causes of the anger are mentioned: rejection of what can be clearly known about God through nature; impure actions, specifically unnatural sexual behavior; and a long list of other improper actions. Additional coherence is provided by the expression παρέδωκεν αὐτοὺς ὁ θεός 'God gave them over', which occurs in vv. 24, 26, and 28. There is also pronominal coherence: all the pronouns are third person plural except for the one referring to God. There is no reference to the Jews; the third person plural pronouns refer to the Gentiles.

A chiastic structure might also be postulated for this unit:

  A 18a: wrath of God
    B 18b: godless and wicked Gentiles
    B' 19–31: catalog of wickedness
  A' 32a: deserve to be caused to die

The boundary at 2:1 is indicated by a switch to second person singular, a vocative 'O man', a switch to addressing the Jews in his audience, and the conjunction διό 'therefore'.

PROMINENCE AND THEME

The 1:18–32 theme statement is drawn from the first part of the main proposition of the v. 18 CLAIM plus a very brief condensation of the EFFECT elements of the *justification* in vv. 24–32.

SECTION CLUSTER CONSTITUENT 1:18
(Expository Propositional Cluster: Claim of 1:18–32)

THEME: God is making it clear that he is angry with godless and wicked non-Jewish people.

RELATIONAL STRUCTURE	CONTENTS
'people' ────────────	1:18a From *where he rules in* heaven God is making it clear to all godless and wicked *non-Jewish* people that he is angry with them *and that they deserve to be punished by him.* [MTY]
└─description ─ RESULT ─	1:18b They suppress what they know to be true *about God*
└─means ───────	1:18c by means of *their behaving* unrighteously.

INTENT AND PARAGRAPH PATTERN

Verse 1:18 is a CLAIM in a unit that is expository and thus is itself expository. Due to its being only a propositional cluster, *not* a paragraph, there is no paragraph pattern. For the same reason, there is no discussion of boundaries and coherence or prominence and theme.

NOTES

1:18a From *where he rules in* heaven God is making it clear . . . that he is angry . . . *and that they deserve to be punished by him* The word οὐρανοῦ 'heaven' could be considered a metonymy for 'God', but since the agent of 'is angry' is overtly expressed, it must be adding some additional meaning. Several commentators suggest that 'heaven' implies the place of God's rule and judgment, hence 'from where he rules in heaven'. The phrase ὀργὴ θεοῦ 'wrath of God' may legitimately be considered a metonymy. It stands not only for the anger but also for the effect or outcome of God's anger: 'that they deserve to be punished' is implied.

all godless and wicked *non-Jewish* people The phrase ἀσέβειαν καὶ ἀδικίαν 'godlessness and wickedness' is rendered in the display as 'godless and wicked'. There is not much difference between the noun and adjective forms. It is not a doublet. Moore (1993:39) agrees.

The word 'non-Jewish' is supplied because the description from here to the end of the chapter deals with Gentiles. The mention of images in v. 23 makes this clear; by Paul's time the Jews no longer worshiped idols. The point is not that Paul does not consider Jews to be sinners, but that he wishes to show first that the non-Jews all stand condemned by their sin. Proving that point is not too difficult, and by doing so he wins the approval of the Jews among his intended audience. Then, while they may be feeling quite smug, he will prove that they, too, are equally under God's condemnation for their sin.

1:18b suppress The verb κατέχω is explained by Louw and Nida (13.150) as "to prevent someone from doing something by restraining or hindering," and in this passage specifically "keep [the truth] from being known." Morris says they "do what they can to oppose it."

what they know to be true *about God* Most commentators take 'truth' to mean 'what they know about God' (Hodge, Morris, Bruce 1963). It is defined as such in v. 25.

1:18c by means of The preposition in the phrase ἐν ἀδικίᾳ 'in unrighteousness' could be taken as expressing circumstance, but the great majority of commentators take it as instrumental, expressing the means (a frequent Pauline usage, especially in Romans). The proposition could also be considered in a reason relation with 18b: the reason-result relationship would indicate that the result was not intended or premeditated. Either alternative is possible.

One might ask how unrighteous behavior suppresses the truth about God. Suppressing its effect is what is intended. But does Paul have in mind its effect on that individual or on others? Probably both.

SECTION CLUSTER CONSTITUENT 1:19–23
(Expository Paragraph: Cause of 1:24–32)

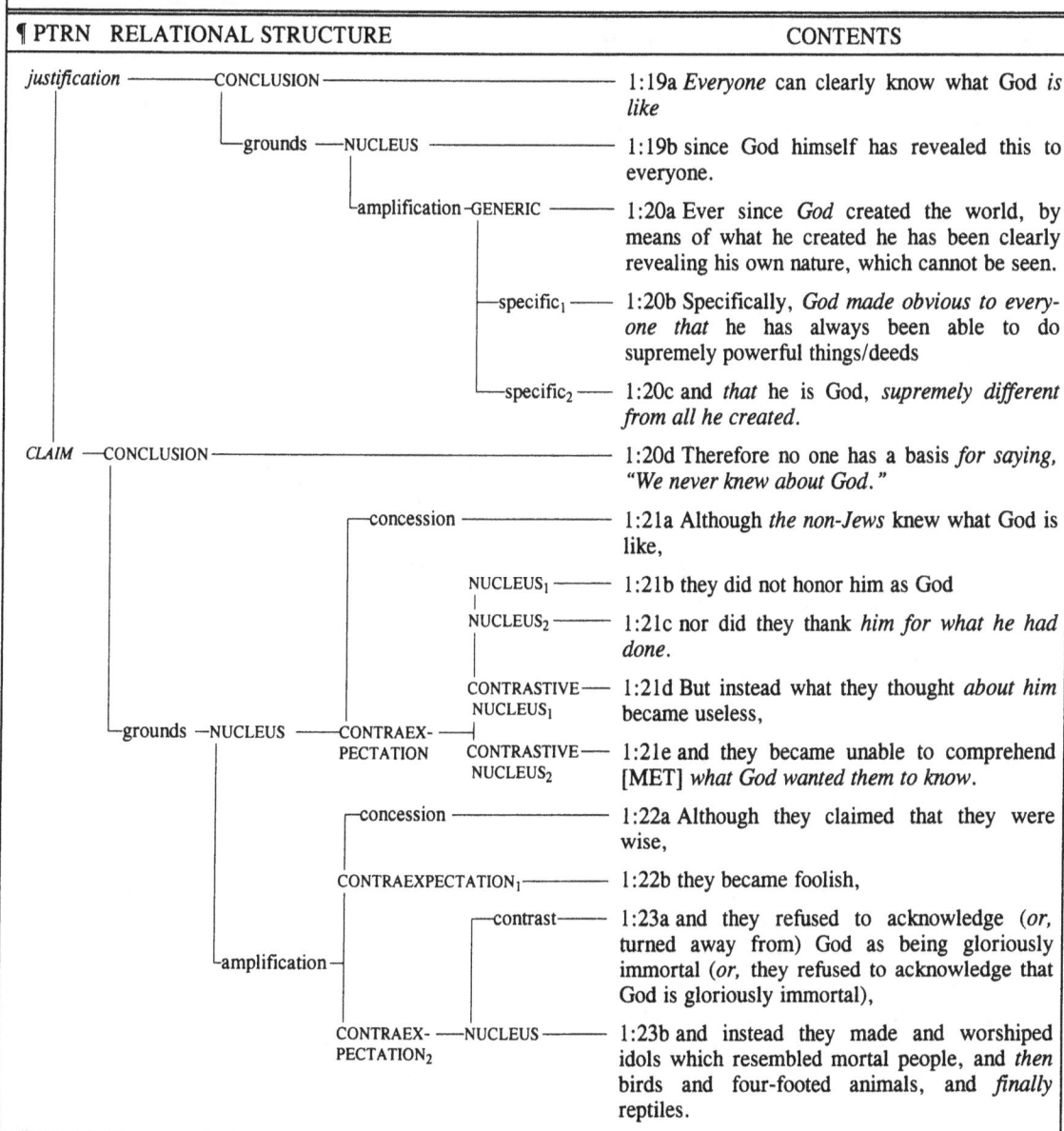

THEME: Everyone can clearly know what God is like; therefore no one has a basis for saying, "We never knew about God."

INTENT AND PARAGRAPH PATTERN

In 1:19–23 Paul continues his argument to show that all non-Jewish peoples stand condemned by God for their sin; the paragraph is clearly expository. The 20d statement about the Gentiles being without excuse is a CLAIM. This CLAIM is preceded by its *justification* in 19–20c, namely that God has revealed himself through his creation.

NOTES

1:19a The conjunction διότι, usually causal, here introduces the whole of 19–32 as being a *justification* of the CLAIM in v. 18 about God's being angry with people.

know what God *is* like In the display the grammatical categories of τὸ γνωστὸν τοῦ θεοῦ 'the known of God' are changed to make them more straightforward.

1:19b God himself has revealed this to everyone The subject of the clause ('God') and the indirect object ('to them') are both given some prominence by their position before the verb. Though it is difficult to express this in an English translation, the fact that the primary emphasis is on the agent is indicated in the display by 'God himself'.

1:20a Ever since *God* created the world, by means of what he created he has been clearly revealing his own nature, which cannot be seen The phrase τὰ ἀόρατα αὐτοῦ 'the invisible things of him' means 'his nature, which cannot be seen'.

In the Greek, all the elements in this clause except 'his everlasting power' and 'divine nature' precede the verb and thus have some marked prominence. It is difficult to capture this in English, but an attempt is made here through the use of 'ever since', 'his own nature', and the forefronting of 'by means of what he created'.

1:20b–c Specifically, *God made obvious to everyone that* he has always been able to do supremely powerful things/deeds and *that* he is God, *supremely different from all he created* The phrase ἥ ἀΐδιος αὐτοῦ δύναμις 'his everlasting power' is here rendered 'he has always been able to do supremely powerful things/deeds'. The term θειότης 'divine nature' means that he is God, wholly other from his creation. NCV renders it well: "all the things that make him God."

1:20d no one has a basis *for saying, "We never knew about God"* In the phrase εἰς τὸ εἶναι αὐτοὺς ἀναπολογήτους 'unto their being without excuse', 'excuse' implies stating a basis for doing or not doing something. Based on the context (cf. 19a), the following would seem to be the best content to supply: 'for saying "We never knew about God" (or, "We never knew that God existed")' (so Whedon, Hodge, Cranfield). Another possibility, which fits the context well, is 'for not worshiping God'. A less likely alternative is that of NCV, "no excuse for the bad things they do"; REB similarly has "Their conduct, therefore, is indefensible."

1:21a *the non-Jews* 'Non-Jews' is supplied to identify 'they' since this whole section deals with the condition of the Gentiles.

1:21a–b This could be viewed as a chiastic structure involving the two verb forms and their objects (the verbs form the outer elements, and 'God' the central elements):

A γνόντες 'knowing'
   A' τὸν θεὸν 'God'
   B' οὐχ ὡς θεὸν 'not as God'
B ἐδόξασαν 'glorified'

But since such a chiasm would not seem to convey any clear function, it is better to consider that ὡς θεὸν 'as God', by preceding the verb ἐδόξασαν 'they glorified', is being made prominent.

The text does not indicate who the excuses might be offered to, if anyone. Therefore this is not specified in the display. In some languages it might be necessary to say 'basis for saying to God, "We(exc) never knew about you" '.

1:21c thank *him for what he had done* A referent is required here, semantically, to identify the object of the thankfulness; thus a generic expression is supplied in italics.

1:21d what they thought *about him* became useless The Greek is ἐματαιώθησαν ἐν τοῖς διαλογισμοῖς αὐτῶν 'became futile in the reasonings of them'. The context implies a futility, not necessarily of their thinking in general, but more specifically of their thinking about God. LB has "they began to think up silly ideas of what God was like and what he wanted them to do," which is very free but captures the sense well.

1:21e they became unable to comprehend *what God wanted them to know* The phrase ἐσκοτίσθη ἡ ἀσύνετος αὐτῶν καρδία 'their senseless heart was darkened' contains two dead figures: 'darkened' and 'heart'. 'Darkened' implies 'unable to see the light', hence 'unable to comprehend the truth'. As a cognitive event, 'comprehend' requires that some content be supplied as the object. In the display the generic 'what God wanted them to know' has been supplied. A good alternative would be 'the truth' (so Barnes).

As to 'heart', the center of the rational and spiritual faculties, its meaning is encompassed by 'comprehend'.

1:22 There is no conjunction in the Greek to introduce this verse. But the sense of vv. 22–23 seems to be to elaborate on the 'futile thinking' of 21d, and the 'minds became darkened' of 21e. Therefore, an amplification relation is posited here.

1:23a–b they refused . . . and instead The Greek is ἤλλαξαν . . . ἐν 'they exchanged . . . into', a very unusual expression. Several commentators suggest it is a Hebraism. It is considered here to be a somewhat figurative way of expressing contrast: instead of doing X they began to do Y. Because the context is focusing on a downhill spiral of evil actions, the second part of the contrast (in 23b) is considered more prominent.

1:23b people, and *then* birds and four-footed animals, and *finally* reptiles The downhill progression of idolatry here is represented by supplying the words 'then' and 'finally'.

BOUNDARIES AND COHERENCE

The boundary at 1:24 is clearly marked by the start of a new sentence in which 'God' is the subject of the main clause, by the first of three occurrences of παρέδωκεν 'he gave them over', and by the beginning of an extensive discussion of sexual sins. The paragraph's coherence is provided by a series of references to the greatness of God, his divine attributes, and his creation.

PROMINENCE AND THEME

The theme of 1:19–23 is drawn from the naturally prominent CONCLUSIONS in the *justification* and CLAIM.

SECTION CLUSTER CONSTITUENT 1:24–27
(Expository Paragraph: Effect₁ of 1:19–23)

THEME: So God let the non-Jewish peoples feel compelled to do disgraceful things, which resulted in their dishonoring their bodies sexually. He did this because they worshiped idols and things which were created instead of God. As a result of both men and women having unnatural sexual relations, they have been punished as they deserve.

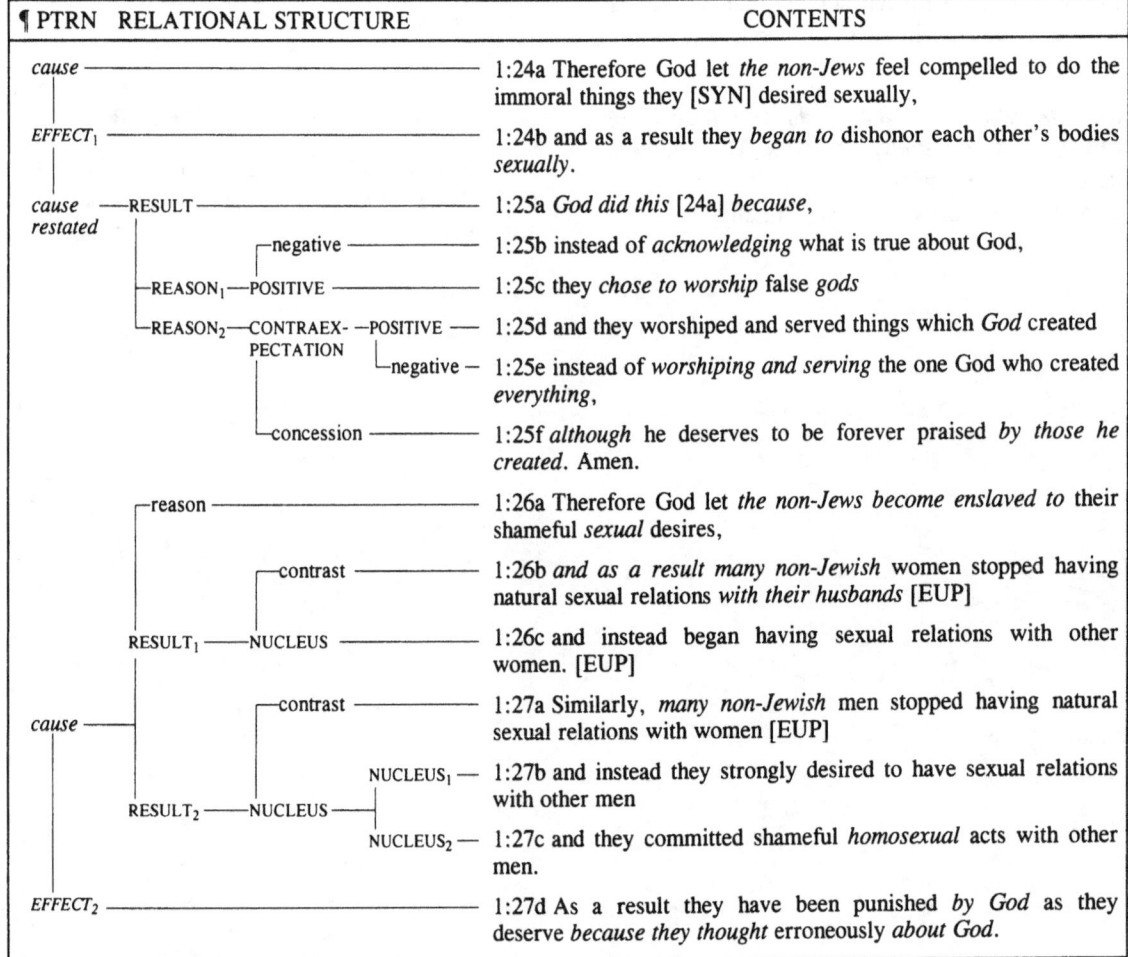

INTENT AND PARAGRAPH PATTERN

Paul in 1:24–27 presents the first set of the results of the Gentiles' rejection of their knowledge of God. The paragraph is expository, of the causality subtype. Though there are two *cause-EFFECT* clusters within the unit, the coherence provided by references to sexual sin in both clusters is the basis for considering it one paragraph.

NOTES

1:24a God let *the non-Jews* feel compelled to do the immoral things they desired sexually The verb παραδίδωμι 'to hand over' has the sense of 'abandoned' here (BAGD, p. 615.1b). But as some commentators note, it is difficult to assign a purposive relationship between the handing over and the sexual degradation, which is better taken as the outcome. Thus the verb is here rendered 'God let/allowed them', following LB, NCV, and CEV; and the sense of 'turning over to the custody of others' is conveyed by the words 'to feel compelled'.

Commentators take the preposition 'in' in the phrase ἐν ταῖς ἐπιθυμίας τῶν καρδιῶν αὐτῶν 'in the desires of their hearts' in a number of ways. BAGD (p. 261.3a) take it as expressing cause or reason, but it does not seem correct to say 'God allowed them to do sexually immoral things because they desired them'. Several commentators suggest that the ἐν introduces a description of the state of the people, and this is how it is handled in the display. An alternative way of expressing it would be 'God let non-Jews who desired inwardly (to do such things) feel compelled to do sexually immoral deeds'.

The word ἐπιθυμία 'desire' usually has a bad sense; here it is more specifically evil sexual desire (so Dunn, Barrett).

The word 'hearts' is a dead figure, a synecdoche in which the part stands for the whole. It is rendered by 'they' in the display.

The noun in the phrase εἰς ἀκαθαρσίαν 'to uncleanness' refers to immoral behavior. In English this requires that a generic verb and a generic noun be supplied, for example, 'perform/do' followed by 'things/deeds/acts'.

1:24b and as a result they *began to* **dishonor each other's bodies** *sexually* The infinitive phrase τοῦ ἀτιμάζεσθαι 'to be dishonored' that follows ἀκαθαρσία 'uncleanness' could be taken as denoting what kind of event characterized the 'uncleanness'. But since 'uncleanness' is rendered as an event ('to do immoral things'), it is better to take the dishonoring as a result (as do Barrett, Murray, Morris, Shedd, and also BAGD, p. 120). The same construction is used by Paul twelve other times (and forty-four times by Luke) to indicate result.

1:25b–c instead of *acknowledging* **what is true about God, they** *chose to worship* **false** *gods* The Greek is μετήλλαξαν τὴν ἀλήθειαν τοῦ θεοῦ ἐν τῷ ψεύδει, literally 'exchanged the truth of God into the lie'. The verbs supplied in the display represent what is really involved in the exchange process: the exchange means that instead of doing one thing they did something else.

There are several interpretations of 'truth of God'. It could mean 'the true God'; but if Paul had meant that, he would most likely have used a completely different construction. It could mean 'the truth about God' (LB, CEV) or 'the truth God has made known (about himself)'. There is not too much difference between these two, but the latter is probably more specific than necessary.

The final phrase, 'the lie', has the definite article and means more than just any lie. As the majority of commentators suggest, Paul is calling idolatry 'the lie' or, more fully, 'the notion that idols are real gods—which is a lie'. This has been rendered in the display as 'chose to worship false gods'.

1:25f *although* **he deserves to be forever praised** *by those he created***. Amen.** The Greek is ὅς ἐστιν εὐλογητὸς εἰς τοὺς αἰῶνας ἀμήν 'who is praised unto the ages; amen'. In form, this is a relative clause, and at first glance it appears to be a doxology. Although, semantically speaking, it has emotive elements, it serves as a concession to 25d–e: 'in spite of the fact that he deserves to be praised forever, they worshiped and served his creation'. The passive 'is praised' may require an agent to be expressed: 'by those he created' or even 'by us'. The 'amen' is rightly the congregation's response, giving their approval to some utterance, and may be rendered 'may it be so'.

1:26a For the rendering of παρέδωκεν as 'he let them become enslaved to', see the note on 24a.

1:26b–c stopped having natural sexual relations *with their husbands* **and instead began having sexual relations with other women** The expression μετήλλαξαν τὴν φυσικὴν χρῆσιν εἰς τὴν παρὰ φύσιν 'changed the natural use into the (one) against nature' is a euphemism for sexual relations between women. The words 'with their husbands' are included to make absolutely clear what Paul meant by 'natural'. The contrastive sense of 'changed' is rendered 'instead' (see the note on 23a–b).

1:27c committed shameful *homosexual* **acts** There is no conjunction or other form here to indicate the relationship of this proposition to the one preceding it. There is simply a participial phrase: ἄρσενες ἐν ἄρσεσιν τὴν ἀσχημοσύνην κατεργαζόμενοι 'males among males shameless deeds committing'. An identical participial construction is in 27d, joined with καί. Since present participles often present the same tense orientation as the finite verb they relate to, this is how the participles are taken here, that is, as indicating past tense to agree with the aorist tense of the verb in 27b. The supplied word 'homosexual' is implied by the phrase 'men among men', which may have been used euphemistically.

1:27d As a result One of the functions of καί is to introduce a result. Here it fits well as introducing the result of the actions described in 27b–c. It is implied that 27d is also the result of the actions in 26b–c.

have been punished *by God* as they deserve The Greek is ἀντιμισθίαν ἣν ἔδει . . . ἀπολαμβάνοντες, literally 'penalty which was necessary . . . receiving back', in which 'penalty' denotes punishment. The agent of the passive is supplied ('by God'), and the past tense is supplied for the same reason noted in 27c. In Greek, 'penalty', which is the object of 'receiving', is forefronted and thereby prominent. This could be represented in English by a cleft construction but at the expense of having to nominalize the event: 'the punishment which they deserve . . . is what they are already receiving back (from God)'. However, since the rendering in the display makes the verb 'receiving' unnecessary, it does not seem possible to retain this emphasis beyond what is signaled by 'already'.

because they thought* erroneously *about God Commentators agree that the word πλάνη 'error, delusion, deceit' must mean, in this context, 'their erroneous ideas about God'. Since 'error' expresses an attribute, the display has 'thinking erroneously about God'. According to BAGD (p. 665), the meaning here is "a false concept of God." A less likely alternative, chosen by a number of versions and supported by Louw and Nida (88.262), is to translate the word as 'perversion'. A number of German commentators also follow this interpretation: Michel has "aberration"; Käsemann, "error and dissoluteness."

BOUNDARIES AND COHERENCE

The next unit begins at 1:28, marked by a new coordinate sentence beginning with καί and by the start of a list of nonsexual sins. Coherence within 1:24–27 is provided by references to sexual sin in 24b and in 26–27. Furthermore, the existence of an inclusio or sandwich structure can be postulated, with God the expressed agent of the first proposition in 24a and the implied agent of the final proposition in 27d.

PROMINENCE AND THEME

The theme of 1:24–27 is drawn from the *cause* (24a) in the first *cause-EFFECT* cluster, a condensation of the EFFECT (24b) and two REASONS (25b–25e) in that cluster, and a condensation of the two RESULTS (26b–27c) in the second *cause-EFFECT* cluster plus the *EFFECT* itself (27d). Though 27d is introduced by καί, which by itself does not signal prominence, the fact that it clearly introduces the effect of the sins mentioned in 24a–27c gives it natural prominence.

SECTION CLUSTER CONSTITUENT 1:28-32
(Expository Paragraph: Effect₂ of 1:19-23)

THEME: The result of God's letting them become obsessed by their own depraved thoughts was that they themselves began to do all manner of evil things that God says are improper. They even approve of others doing such things.

¶ PTRN RELATIONAL STRUCTURE	CONTENTS
cause — reason	1:28a *Furthermore*, because they decided that knowing God was not worthwhile,
— RESULT	1:28b God allowed them to become obsessed by their own worthless/depraved thoughts,
NUCLEUS₁ — GENERIC	1:28c and as a result they began doing *evil* things that *God says* are improper.
— specific₁	1:29a They constantly/strongly desire to do all *kinds of* unrighteous deeds,
— specific₂	1:29b they constantly/strongly desire to do all *kinds of* evil things *to others*,
— specific₃	1:29c they constantly/strongly desire to possess things *which belong to others*,
— specific₄	1:29d and they constantly/strongly desire to harm *others* in various ways.
— specific₅	1:29e *Many non-Jews* are devoted to envying *other people*,
— specific₆	1:29f *many* are devoted to murdering *people*,
— specific₇	1:29g *many* are devoted to causing strife *between people*,
— specific₈	1:29h *many* are devoted to deceiving *others*,
EFFECT — specific₉	1:29i *many* are devoted to speaking hatefully *toward (or, maligning) others*,
— specific₁₀	1:29j *many* gossip *about others*,
— specific₁₁	1:30a *many* slander *others*,
— specific₁₂	1:30b *many* act especially hatefully toward God,
— specific₁₃	1:30c *many* speak or act in an insulting way *toward others*,
— specific₁₄	1:30d *many* treat *others* contemptuously,
— specific₁₅	1:30e *many* boast *about themselves to others*,
— specific₁₆	1:30f *many* invent new ways to do evil things/deeds,
— specific₁₇	1:30g *many non-Jewish children* disobey their parents,
— specific₁₈	1:31a *many non-Jews* act in other morally foolish ways,
— specific₁₉	1:31b *many* do not do what they promised *others they would do*,
— specific₂₀	1:31c *many* do not *even* love their own family members,
— specific₂₁	1:31d *and many* do not act mercifully *toward other people*.
— concession	1:32a Although they know that God has decreed that those who do such things deserve to be *caused to* die,
NUCLEUS₂ — CONTRAEXPECTATION — nucleus₁	1:32b they not only habitually do these *kinds of evil* things,
— NUCLEUS₂	1:32c they also approve of others who habitually do them.

INTENT AND PARAGRAPH PATTERN

The 1:28-32 paragraph concludes Paul's exposition of the universal guilt of the Gentiles for their sin. It is a paragraph of the causality subtype, giving *a cause* (28a-b) and its EFFECT (28c-32).

NOTES

1:28a they decided that knowing God was not worthwhile The construction οὐκ ἐδοκίμασαν τὸν θεὸν ἔχειν ἐν ἐπιγνώσει 'they did not approve of having God in knowledge' is a mismatched way of expressing the semantic concepts involved. The event signified by the noun ἐπίγνωσις is knowing or recognizing (BAGD, p. 291); to have God in knowledge thus means "to retain the knowledge of God" (NIV). However, one cannot decide not to know something he already knows. Therefore, to complete the thought a negative stative clause must be supplied in which 'knowledge of God' is the topic. In the display 'was not worthwhile' is used. Alternatives would be 'not important', 'insignificant', or even 'not relevant to their lives', following Dunn. The event signified by ἐδοκίμασαν is proving or testing; here, it means that people gave the idea of God's relevance to their lives consideration and then decided to reject it (i.e., they made a negative choice).

1:28b allowed them to become obsessed by See the note on 24a.

their own worthless/depraved thoughts The word νοῦς 'mind' represents the thinking faculty, hence 'thoughts'.

1:28c that *God says* are improper The Greek is τὰ μὴ καθήκοντα 'the things which are not proper', but since the people who do these things consider that there is nothing wrong with them, the sense must be 'not proper in God's estimation'.

1:29a They constantly/strongly desire to do all *kinds of* unrighteous deeds In Scripture the expression πεπληρωμένοι 'filled with' is often an idiom meaning 'fully controlled or dominated by'. But since one cannot be controlled by an action, it is rendered here as 'desire' modified by 'constantly' (i.e., habitually) or 'strongly' in order to make proper sense.

In the Textus Receptus there is an additional term, πορνεία 'fornication', preceding πονηρία 'wickedness'. It would seem that someone confused the two and the latter was added in some manuscripts. But since sexual sins were mentioned in vv. 24-27 and do not fit well in the list of vv. 29-31, the display follows the GNT and omits this word.

1:29-31 In the Greek each of these propositions is only one or two words, often only an abstract noun. This makes the list very striking and forceful; but since they all represent events, case roles require the inclusion of various implied agent and patient elements in many of them.

1:29e *Many non-Jews* are devoted to envying *other people* In the construction μεστοὺς φθόνου 'full of envy', the word 'full' (a different word from 'filled' in 29a) is figurative, a prominence device meaning 'habitually characterized by' or 'completely devoted to'. The term 'full of' applies to all the verbal nouns in 29f-i as well, so 'devoted to' is supplied in all those propositions. The word 'many' is used in all the propositions from 29e through 31d to indicate that not every Gentile was characterized by all of these sins. An alternative would be 'some of them'.

1:31a-d There is phonological word play in the four terms of v. 31, each of which begins with the alpha privative ἀ- 'without'. It will probably be impossible to capture this in most translations. NIV makes a good attempt by rendering them "senseless, faithless, heartless, ruthless." The Textus Receptus has an additional term here, ἀσπόνδους 'implacable, irreconcilable', but manuscript evidence for it is very weak.

1:32 Although they know This verse begins with the relative pronoun οἵτινες, but it clearly introduces a second and quite different result of God's having handed them over to improper conduct. Thus it is considered a propositional cluster coordinate with the one in 28c.

1:32a deserve to be *caused to* die The Greek is ἄξιοι θανάτου εἰσίν 'are worthy of death', clearly implying punishment, but commentators are divided as to whether physical or spiritual death is in view (or both). Probably the focus is on neither. Since punishment is in view, the sense is 'be put to death'.

BOUNDARIES AND COHERENCE

The closing boundary at 2:1 has already been discussed (see "Boundaries" under the 1:18-32 unit). The main feature of coherence in 1:28-32 is the long list of specific examples of 'improper' conduct (28c) and deictic reference to them in v. 32.

PROMINENCE AND THEME

The theme of 1:28–32 is drawn from the RESULT proposition of the *cause* and the two NUCLEI of the *EFFECT* (28c and 32c).

SUBDIVISION CLUSTER CONSTITUENT 2:1–3:18
(Expository Section: Claim₂ of 1:18–3:20)

THEME: Any one of you Jews, who has all the advantages of being a Jew and disobeys God's law, will also be condemned by him; God will consider your circumcision worthless and will accept the non-Jews who obey his laws. They will declare that God is right in condemning you. God will not treat us Jews more favorably than he will treat non-Jews.

MACROSTRUCTURE	CONTENTS
CLAIM₁	2:1–24 Since God will recompense each person, Jew or non-Jew, according to what he has done and condemn him for his sin, any one of you Jews who has all the advantages of being a Jew and insults God by disobeying the Mosaic law will also be condemned by God for doing evil.
CLAIM₂	2:25–3:18 If any of you disobey the Mosaic law, God will consider your circumcision worthless and will accept the non-Jews who obey his law; and they will declare that God is right in condemning you. Our being circumcised Jews does benefit us. God has certainly kept his promise to bless us. But it is certainly right for God to punish us. God will condemn those who claim I say that we should continue to do evil and that God will no longer punish us for doing so. God will not treat us Jews more favorably than he will treat non-Jews.

INTENT AND MACROSTRUCTURE

The 2:1–3:18 unit is considered expository since all its constituents are expository. It functions within a unit that is expository also.

The unit consists of two conjoined CLAIMS to the effect that all the world is under God's condemnation for their sins, with the focus here being on the Jews.

BOUNDARIES AND COHERENCE

The coherence of 2:1–3:18 is obvious. A basic theme in each of its two constituents is that the Jews have also sinned and are guilty before God and deserve his condemnation. Connected with this is the recurring theme that God judges all people in the same way regardless of whether they are Jews or non-Jews.

Paragraphs 2:25–29, 3:1–8, and 3:9–18 center around the matter of circumcision and other benefits of the Jews. While it is true that 2:25 begins with γάρ 'for', which on the surface would seem to indicate a close connection with the preceding unit rather than the starting point of a new subunit, γάρ also introduces 1:18, which begins an even higher-level unit. Thus, it is semantic considerations, not grammatical ones, that lead to viewing 2:25–3:18 as one unit.

The closing boundary of 2:1–3:18 is not entirely clear, since the unit might be considered to include 3:19–20. However, in this analysis, 3:19–20 is separated from what precedes it because it begins with οἴδαμεν δέ 'now we know', introducing a statement that would be agreed to by all those in his audience.

It is difficult to know whether 3:19–20 is a *summary* of the two CLAIMS in 1:18–3:20 or not (see the 1:18–3:20 display); and if not, how it does tie in. The first *evidence* in 3:19–20 has a close relationship to the quotation in 3:9–18; however, the two INFERENCES of 3:19–20 state what is essentially a summary of the CLAIMS within the 2:1–24 and 2:25–3:18 units, and it certainly functions as a summary of the whole 1:18–3:20 unit. At the same time, it may be that 3:20 functions not only as *evidence* for the 19c INFERENCE but also as a tail-head link with the beginning of the next unit. Thus 3:19-20 may be considered a multiple-functioning unit.

PROMINENCE AND THEME

The theme of 2:1-3:18 is drawn from the themes of the two constituent CLAIMS. Certain repetitious portions have been eliminated. The *justification* portions of 2:1-24 and 3:9-18 are eliminated as being less thematic than the CLAIMS. Paul's comment in 3:1-8 about those who claim that he preaches Christians should continue to do evil is also omitted as being less thematic than the rest.

SECTION CONSTITUENT 2:1-24
(Expository Subsection: Claim₁ of 2:1-3:18)

THEME: Since God will recompense each person, Jew or non-Jew, according to what he has done and condemn him for his sin, any one of you Jews who has all the advantages of being a Jew and insults God by disobeying the Mosaic law will also be condemned by God for doing evil.

MACROSTRUCTURE	CONTENTS
CLAIM₁	2:1-5 Any one of you who condemns non-Jews for doing evil will be condemned by God, since you also do the same evil things.
justification	2:6-11 God will recompense each person according to what he has done, since he is not influenced by a person's status.
justification	2:12-16 All non-Jews will be eternally separated from God for their sin and all Jews will be condemned for their sin, since it is only those who have continually obeyed the Mosaic law whom God will justify.
CLAIM₂	2:17-24 It is disgusting that any one of you who has all the advantages of being a Jew would disobey God's law and, by doing so, insult God.

INTENT AND MACROSTRUCTURE

The four paragraphs in the 2:1-24 expository subsection form a chiasm. In the first and fourth Paul states to the Jews in his audience two closely related specific CLAIMS regarding the condemnation they are under for their evildoing and disobedience of the Mosaic law. In the second and third paragraphs Paul makes more generic statements about God's impartiality in dealing with both Jews and non-Jews, statements which form the *justifications* for the two CLAIMS.

BOUNDARIES AND COHERENCE

A boundary has been posited between the 2:1-24 subsection and the one that follows on the basis of the chiastic structure of the four paragraphs of 2:1-24. Paragraphs 2:1-5 and 2:17-24 are alike in that Paul is addressing a representative Jewish person with second person singular forms, and both paragraphs deal with the hypocrisy of the Jews. The middle two paragraphs (2:6-11 and 2:12-16) are alike in that they have no second person singular forms and they both deal with the equality of Jews and non-Jews before God. Furthermore, 2:25 begins with περιτομή 'circumcision' forefronted, which topicalizes it as the main concept discussed in vv. 25-29.

PROMINENCE AND THEME

The 2:1-24 theme is a condensation of the themes of the four constituent paragraphs of the subsection. What is eliminated is the less thematic *justifications* in the themes of 2:1-5, 2:6-11, 2:12-16, and 2:17-24; the specific part of the CLAIM in the 2:6-11 unit; and also a certain amount of redundancy.

SECTION CONSTITUENT 2:1-5
(Expository Paragraph: Claim₁ of 2:1-24)

THEME: Any one of you who condemns non-Jews for doing evil will be condemned by God, since you also do the same evil things.

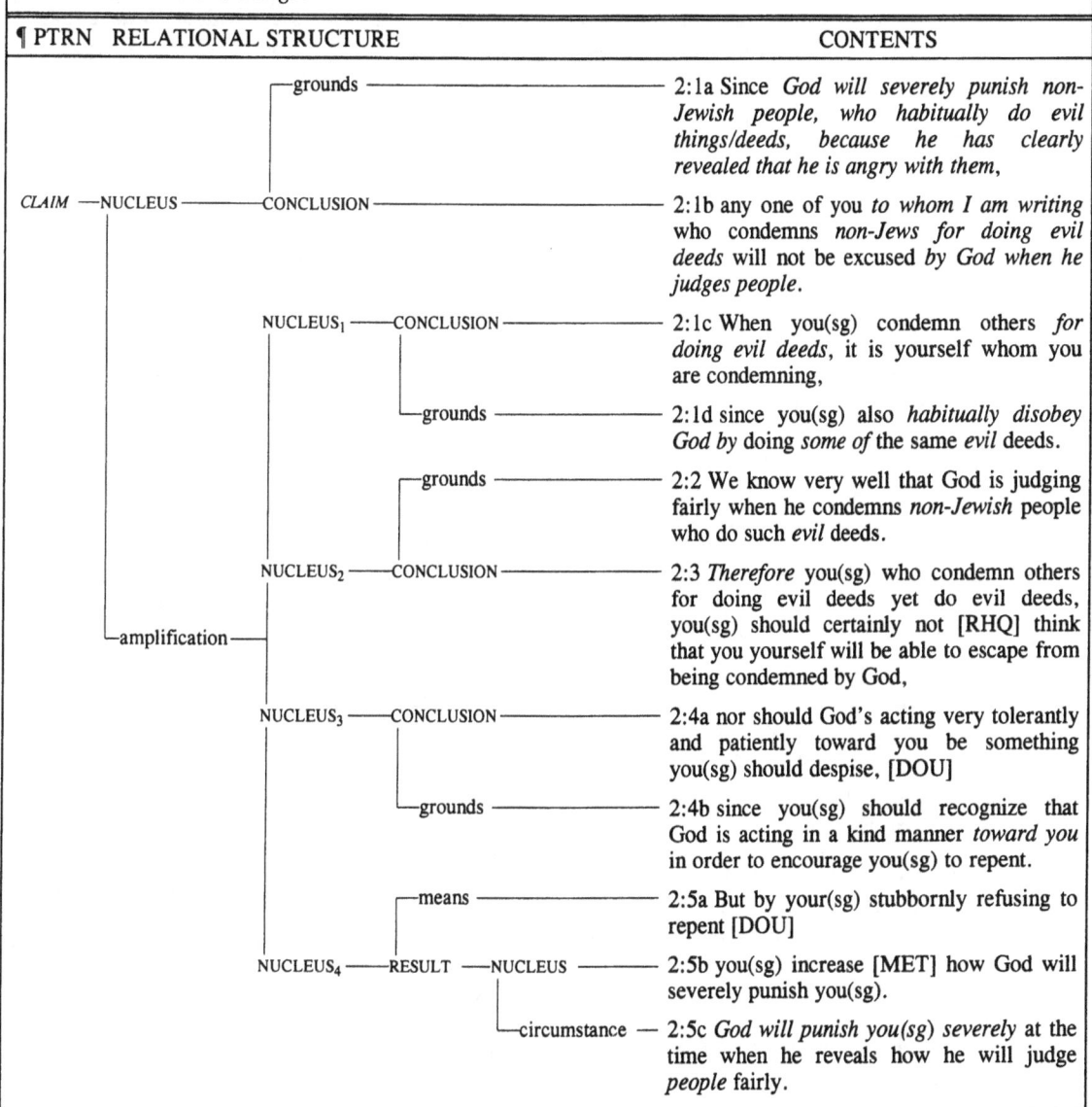

INTENT AND PARAGRAPH PATTERN

In 2:1-5 Paul continues his exposition of why the whole world is under God's wrath, both Jews and non-Jews. There does not seem to be a causality component between the two parts. Clearly 1c-5 is not a *justification* of 1a-b, but an amplification of it—a further development of the 1b CLAIM. The *justification* for the CLAIM in this paragraph follows in 2:6-11.

NOTES

2:1a This proposition is given as a summary of the previous section in order to provide the semantic content of διό 'therefore'. If the whole book, or even the first three chapters, were read through at one time, 1a would scarcely be necessary.

2:1b *any one of you to whom I am writing* The Greek is ὦ ἄνθρωπε 'O man', as though Paul were addressing a single individual, and he goes on to use a second person singular verb (εἶ 'thou art'), although he is addressing a group here, not one individual. The display attempts to spell out this mismatch by the rendering 'any one of you'. (In the displays 'you' always is to be taken as plural unless otherwise stated; here the second person component is represented by 'you' and the singular component by 'any one of'. The same device is used in v. 3 and several times in chapters 4–11.) Paul is at this point switching his attention specifically to the Jews at Rome. Though this is not shown in the display, the word 'Jews' could be inserted after 'any one of you' to make the referent clearer.

who condemns *non-Jews for doing evil deeds* The implied grounds for condemnation is summarized in the display.

will not be excused *by God when he judges people* The word ἀναπολόγητος means 'inexcusable', which implies the event of being excused; hence the agent of the excusing is supplied, as well as the implied time.

2:1c The conjunction γάρ here, which signals that what follows begins an amplification of 1a–b, is not expressed in the wording of the proposition. Several versions likewise omit the conjunction (e.g., TEV, JB, LB, NCV, CEV).

it is yourself whom you are condemning In the Greek, σεαυτόν 'yourself' is forefronted and thereby prominent. This prominence is represented by a cleft construction.

2:2–3 The argument here is in the form of a syllogism, in which an individual who agrees with the major premise in 2a then finds himself caught in his own logic:

Major premise:
  All people who do such evil deeds will be condemned by God.
Minor premise:
  You, O man, are one who does evil deeds.
Conclusion:
  Therefore you will be condemned.

NRSV makes the syllogism clearer by introducing v. 2 with "You say, 'We know that . . .'"

2:2 when he condemns *non-Jewish* **people who do such** *evil* **deeds** Since 'such (evil) deeds' refers to the deeds Paul listed in chapter 1 as characterizing the Gentiles, 'non-Jewish' is supplied here to eliminate confusion.

2:3 The grounds-CONCLUSION relationship between v. 2 and v. 3 is not signaled by any conjunction in the Greek, but from the point of view of semantics it is clearly there (see NIV).

you(sg) should certainly not think that you yourself will be able to escape from being condemned by God The rhetorical question in the Greek text here is equivalent to an emphatic negative statement. This force is conveyed by 'certainly not' in the display.

The second person singular free-standing pronoun form indicates prominence, which is shown in the display by 'you yourself'.

2:4a nor should God's acting very tolerantly and patiently toward you be something you(sg) should despise Paul here heaps up nouns which are all attributive: τοῦ πλούτου τῆς χρηστότητος αὐτοῦ καὶ τῆς ἀνοχῆς καὶ τῆς μακροθυμίας 'the riches of the kindness of him and the forbearance and the patience'. The word 'riches' functions as an intensifier of the attribute or event expressed by the following noun. (Paul uses 'riches' this way elsewhere as well, e.g., Rom. 9:23, Eph. 1:7, 2:7.) It is represented here by 'very'. The next three Greek nouns, although they are all grammatically objects of the verb 'despise', semantically are expressing attributes that modify the implied verb 'acts', whose agent 'God' is represented in Greek by the αὐτοῦ 'of him'. The final two of the three nouns are a doublet; they are almost exactly synonymous and are rendered by the one adverb, 'patiently', in the display. Moore (p. 39) considers them a near-synonymous doublet.

Though some versions (e.g., JBP, RSV) break this up into two rhetorical questions, there is only one in the Greek; and it has the force of calling the reader to pay special attention to a statement they ought to acknowledge as true.

2:4b This proposition is considered to be the grounds for 4a in view of the force of the present participle (a semantic consideration).

2:5a by your(sg) stubbornly refusing to repent The Greek is κατὰ δὲ τὴν σκληρότητά σου καὶ ἀμετανόητον καρδίαν 'but corresponding to the hardness of you(sg) and unrepentant heart'. 'Hardness' and 'unrepentant heart' are considered a doublet, being nearly synonymous. Moore (p. 40) considers them a figurative doublet. Both are figurative; they both signify stubborn refusal to repent. The word κατά is taken as expressing a propositional relationship of means.

2:5b you(sg) increase how God will severely punish you(sg) The Greek is θησαυρίζεις σεαυτῷ ὀργήν 'you(sg) store up for yourself anger'. The verb 'store up' can be considered a metaphor: As rich people cause their wealth to increase, so you cause God's anger to increase. The noun 'anger' is an experience-type event and at the same time a metonymy in which the cause, anger, stands for the effect, punishment.

BOUNDARIES AND COHERENCE

Lexical coherence in the 2:1-5 paragraph is provided by a long list of second person singular pronouns; in the 2:6-11 paragraph there are none.

In 2:1-5 there is a set of three emotionally charged rhetorical questions aimed at the Jews, and the vocative phrase ὦ ἄνθρωπε 'o man' occurs twice. There is a series of occurrences of the noun κρίμα 'judgment', cognate verbs κρίνω 'to judge' and κατακρίνω 'to condemn', and the cognate noun δικαιοκρισία 'righteous judgment'.

PROMINENCE AND THEME

The 2:1-5 theme is drawn (with some simplification and condensation) from the 1b CONCLUSION proposition of the CLAIM and enough of the 1c CONCLUSION and 1d grounds of the first NUCLEUS to provide relational coherence for the CLAIM.

SUBSECTION CONSTITUENT 2:6-11
(Expository Paragraph: Justification of claim₁ of 2:1-24)

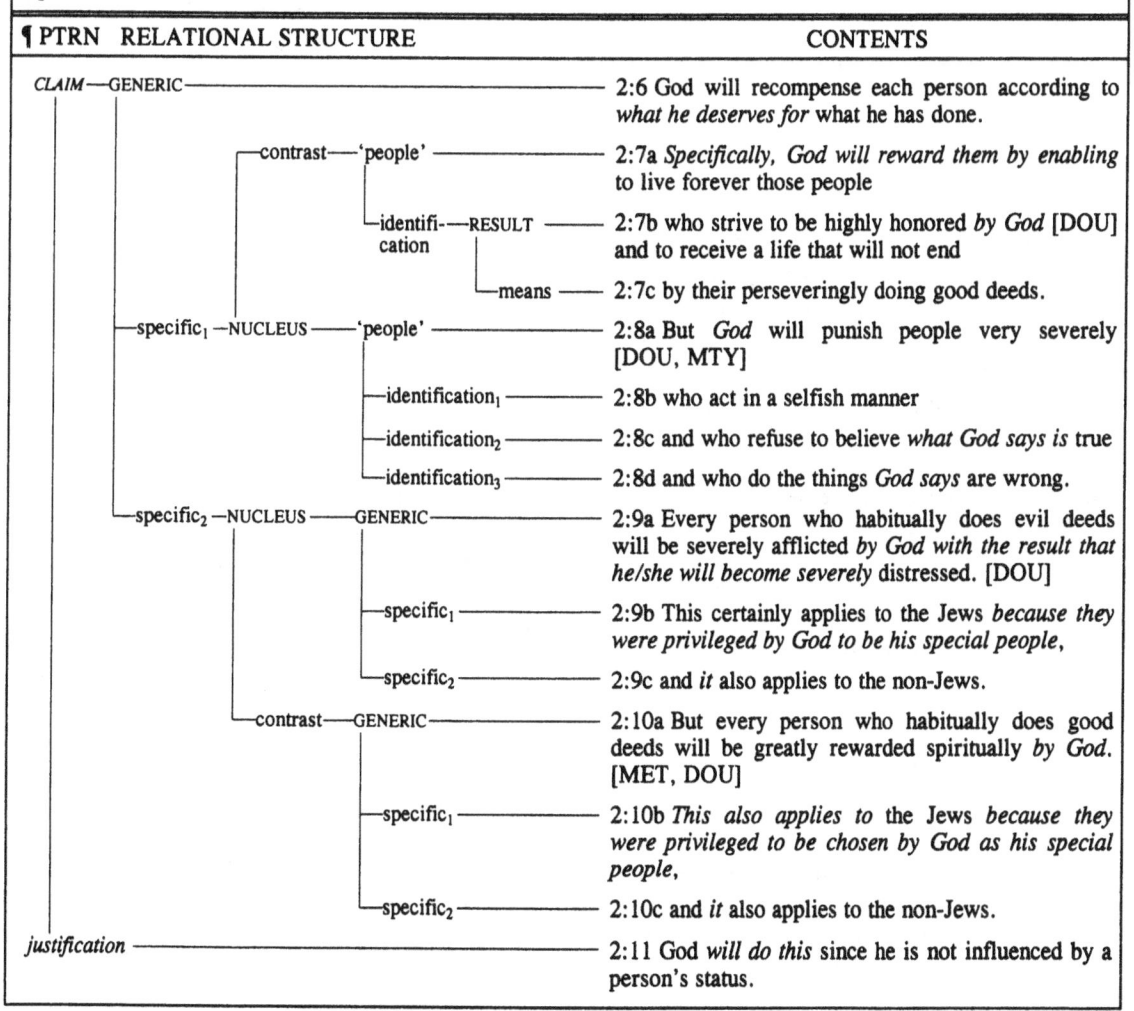

INTENT AND PARAGRAPH PATTERN

The 2:6-11 paragraph continues Paul's exposition of why both Jews and non-Jews are condemned. Here Paul discusses the equality of both groups in God's sight. There is a CLAIM consisting of a generic statement about God's rewarding people and two specific statements contrasting God's rewards for those who do evil deeds with the rewards of those who do good deeds. A *justification* of the CLAIM is in v. 11.

NOTES

2:6-11 There is a chiastic structure in these verses (as noted, e.g., by Käsemann):

A who will recompense each according to his deeds:
  B to those who do good,
    C life eternal;
      D but to those who do unrighteousness,
        E wrath and anger;
        E' affliction and anguish
      D' to those doing evil;
    C' but glory . . .
  B' to those doing good.
A' God shows no partiality.

In chiastic structures there can be prominence at the center element(s) and/or at the extreme ends. Here in the context of God's punishment of evildoers the prominence is at the center elements, where there is a piling up of morally negative actions plus God's punishment for them. The notion of the universality of God's rewards—expressed in the outermost elements of the chiasm—is also given prominence by virtue of the prominent phrase 'both Jews and non-Jews' that occurs in both 9b-c and 10b-c.

2:6 according to *what he deserves for* what he has done The Greek is κατὰ τὰ ἔργα αὐτοῦ 'according to the deeds of him'. The verb 'deserve' is implied (it is expressed in LB and JB).

2:7a *Specifically, God will reward* No verb is in the Greek; it is assumed to be ἀποδώσει 'will recompense', carried over from the previous verse.

2:7b who strive to be highly honored *by God* and to receive a life that will not end In the clause δόξαν καὶ τιμὴν καὶ ἀφθαρσίαν ζητοῦσιν 'glory and honor and immortality they seek', the three nouns represent states or events. The first two occur in conjunction many times in the NT as a doublet. They serve to intensify 'to honor'. The verb 'seek', which implies striving to obtain something, is almost impossible to render in English without using a verbal noun as the object of the verb; hence the object of 'receive' is rendered 'life'. The Greek word for 'immortality' means 'life that will not end', which is somewhat more quantitative than 'eternal life'.

2:7c by their perseveringly doing good deeds From a semantic point of view the first noun in the phrase καθ' ὑπομονὴν ἔργου ἀγαθοῦ (literally 'by the patience of good works') may be said to modify the event expressed by the second noun. CEV renders it "who has patiently done what is good," but the meaning of the first noun is closer to 'endurance' than 'patience' (Louw and Nida 25.174).

2:8a *God* will punish . . . *very severely* In the display a verb is supplied to render ὀργὴ καὶ θυμός 'wrath and anger'—the 'recompense' of v. 6 is assumed to be repeated. The words 'wrath and anger' are a doublet intensifying the one concept and, at the same time, a metonymy in which the cause stands for the effect (cf. v. 5); the straightforward phrase 'punish very severely' carries the sense well.

2:8b who act in a selfish manner The noun in the phrase ἐξ ἐριθείας 'from self-seeking' expresses a quality. It could be taken either as describing the people ('are selfish') or their actions ('act selfishly').

2:8c refuse to believe *what God says is* true The Greek is ἀπειθοῦσι τῇ ἀληθείᾳ 'disobey the truth'. Disobedience in the NT is always a conscious or deliberative act of an individual. It seems best, therefore, to follow BAGD (p. 82.3), who suggest the sense here is probably 'disbelieve', noting that "the supreme disobedience was a refusal to believe their gospel."

2:9a be severely afflicted *by God with the result that he/she will become severely* distressed The word καί 'and' conjoins θλῖψις 'affliction' and στενοχωρία 'anguish'. These words represent events, the second being the result of the first. Moore (p. 40) sees them as a near-synonymous doublet. The doublet signifies an intensification of one event.

2:9b This certainly applies to the Jews *because they were privileged by God to be his special*

people In the phrase Ἰουδαίου τε πρῶτον 'of Jew both firstly', 'firstly' may indicate either chronological order or pre-eminence. There does not seem to be any evidence elsewhere in Scripture of a temporal sequence in the judgment of racial groups; therefore the sense here must be 'especially, certainly' (so Hodge). The implied grounds for the judgment, which Paul would have expected his readers to know, is supplied (cf. 2:17-18, 3:2). This is the case both here and in 10b.

2:10a will be greatly rewarded spiritually *by God* The three nouns in δόξα δὲ καὶ τιμὴ καὶ εἰρήνη 'glory and honor and peace' are probably not meant to be taken one by one (see the note on 7b). This is simply a piling up of nouns to describe the richness of spiritual blessing awaiting the believer (so Morris). In the display the three nouns are not represented as distinct concepts but are covered as one in the words 'greatly rewarded spiritually'.

2:11 is not influenced by a person's status The word 'partiality' in οὐ ἔστιν προσωπολημψία 'not is partiality' is a complex term semantically, and the display attempts to unravel it. Partiality in this context means treating some people better than others because of their ethnic background or wealth or status, that is, 'not fairly'. 'God is without partiality' is thus rendered by 'is not influenced by a person's status'. An alternative that expresses it positively is 'he judges all people fairly, regardless of what ethnic group they belong to'.

BOUNDARIES AND COHERENCE

The coherence of 2:6-11 derives from its various references to rewards or retribution for deeds done.

The 2:12-16 paragraph begins with γάρ, and almost all English versions have a paragraph division at v. 12. The 2:12-16 paragraph has many references to the Mosaic law, while 2:6-11 has none.

PROMINENCE AND THEME

The theme of 2:6-11 is drawn from the 2:6 GENERIC statement of the *CLAIM* and from the *justification* in v. 11.

SUBSECTION CONSTITUENT 2:12-16
(Expository Paragraph: Justification of claim₂ of 2:1-24)

THEME: *All non-Jews will be eternally separated from God for their sin and all Jews will be condemned for their sin, since it is only those who have continually obeyed the Mosaic law whom God will justify.*

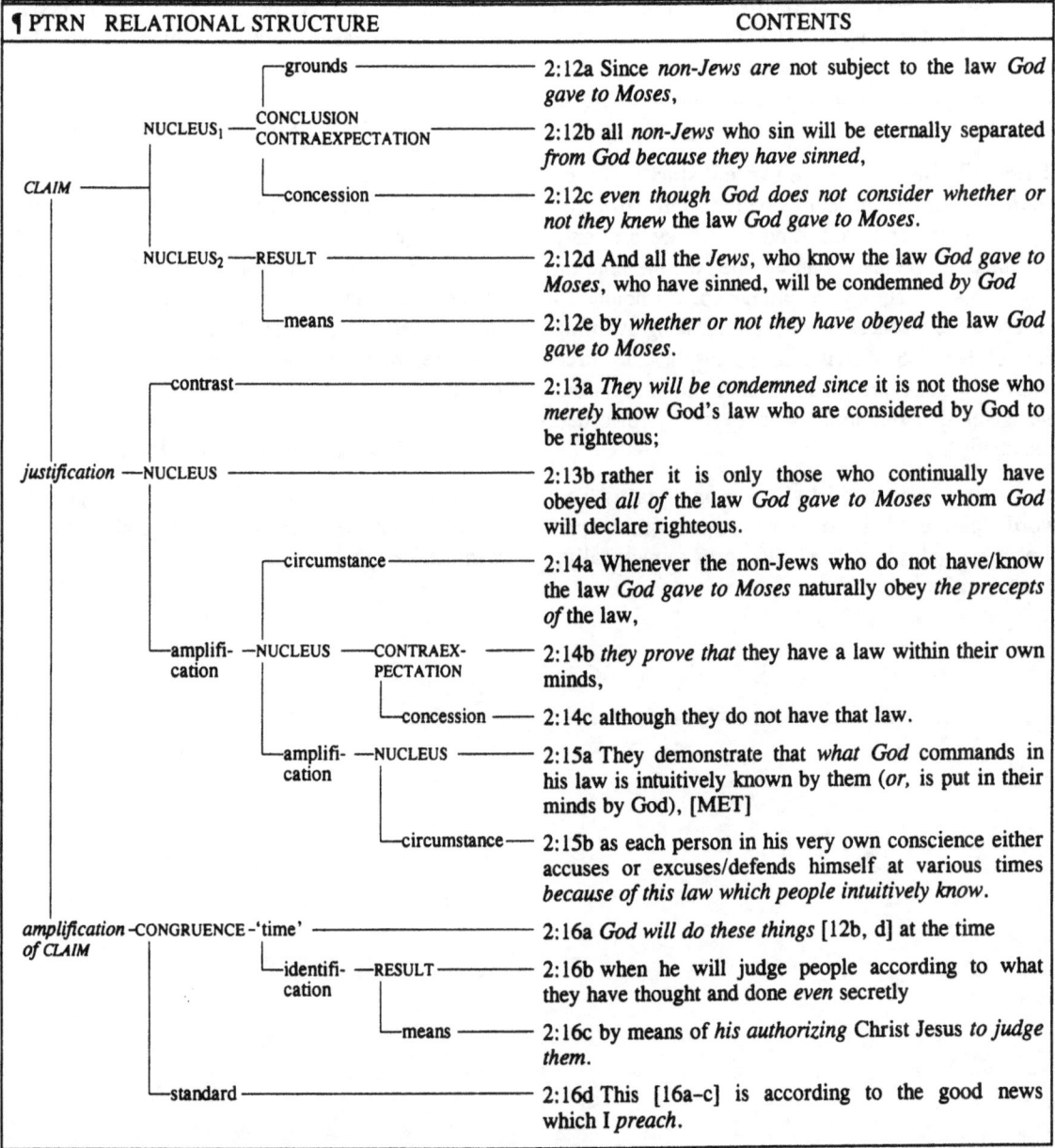

INTENT AND PARAGRAPH PATTERN

The 2:12-16 unit continues Paul's exposition of the condemnation of both Jews and non-Jews, here with respect to the Mosaic law. The paragraph comprises a CLAIM regarding both groups (v. 12) and the *justification* of that CLAIM (vv. 13-15) and concludes with a complex temporal phrase that seems to function as an *amplification* relating to v. 12.

NOTES

2:12a Since *non-Jews are* not subject to the law *God gave to Moses* Here there is a contrast to 'the (Jews) who know the law' in 12d: ὅσοι ἀνόμως 'all those who without law (12a) versus ὅσοι ἐν νόμῳ 'all those in law' (12d). The terms refer to Gentiles and Jews respectively. The law referred to is God's law, but more specifically the Mosaic law. In the displays this will be spelled out as 'the law God gave to Moses'. In many languages a shorter phrase may be possible.

2:12b will be eternally separated *from God because they have sinned* The word ἀπολοῦνται 'will perish' here refers to eternal, not physical death (BAGD, p. 95.2a) It could be rendered as 'die eternally', but these words do not collocate well in English. Some versions (TEV, NCV) use 'be lost', but this is an idiom using a secondary sense of 'lost' and is therefore avoided here. The display follows the sense of CEV's "be punished" (see also LB).

2:12c *even though God does not consider whether or not they knew* **the law** *God gave to Moses* According to Hodge, Haldane, and others, ἀνόμως 'without law' means 'without consideration of the Mosaic law'. Commentators and versions take this to mean 'without considering whether or not they had it', but it could also mean 'without considering whether or not they obeyed it'. In English the form '*without* + verb + *-ing*' is often shorthand for a concession.

2:12e by *whether or not they have obeyed* **the law** Here διὰ νόμου 'through law' must refer to obedience of the Mosaic law, not just possession or knowledge of it. The expression is a personification. As Morris says, "He is not saying that the law itself judges.... The law is the means God uses.... It means condemnation for those who have it and do not obey it."

2:13a *merely* **know** Paul uses the phrase οἱ ἀκροαταί 'the hearers' because the common people did not have copies of the Scriptures to read for themselves; scribes read it to them. But Paul is really contrasting those who know it and do nothing about it with those who obey it, not those who hear it with those who don't (or with those who read it). Translators who prefer to be more literal may need to say 'who hear God's law when it is read to them'. JBP renders it "familiarity with the Law."

A literal translation of 'those who know' could give the impression that Paul was opposed to hearing the Scriptures read. The word 'merely' is implied (cf. Beck, Goodspeed; CEV has "those who simply hear it"). In some languages it may be necessary to make the implied contrast explicit: 'know but don't obey'.

considered by God to be righteous The verb δικαιόω 'to justify' refers to "the act of clearing someone of transgression—'to acquit, to set free, to remove guilt'" (Louw and Nida 56.34). Paul uses the verb twenty-seven times, fifteen of which occur in Romans. Morris (p. 145) states, "The word is a forensic or legal term with the meaning 'acquit'. It is the normal word to use when the accused is declared 'not guilty'." As he points out, when a person is acquitted, he is *declared* to be righteous, not *made* righteous. The term is in opposition to κατάκριμα 'condemnation' (e.g., in Rom. 5:16): a condemned person is not 'made guilty' but 'declared guilty'. Louw and Nida (56.34) suggest that it may have to be rendered in some languages by an expression such as "say 'You are not guilty' or say 'You no longer have sin [= guilt for sin]'" (see the note on 1:17a).

2:13b those who continually have obeyed The contrast (13a with 13b) is not between those who know the law and those who do not, but between those who know and fully obey it and those who know and do not fully obey it.

all of **the law** *God gave to Moses* Paul is not here saying that people can be justified by obeying the law; in 3:20 and Gal. 3:10–12 it is clear that this is not possible. To avoid a seeming contradiction, the word 'all' is supplied: theoretically, God would justify anyone who unfailingly kept *all* the commandments.

In Greek there is no verb in 13a, but in 13b the verb is preceded by the subject, giving the subject prominence. The parallelism of the verse suggests that the subject would have been prominent in 13a as well. This is brought out in the display by cleft constructions.

declare righteous The Greek is δικαιόω 'to justify'. See the note on 3:21b.

2:14a Here γάρ introduces an amplification; that is, what follows is clearly related to, but is not a reason for, what precedes. Some versions render vv. 14–15 as parenthetical (e.g., NIV, NCV), but still on the subject of obedience to the law. In Greek both the subject and object precede the verb, but this is primarily a means of focusing on the subject, 'the non-Jews'.

2:14b *they prove that* **they have a law within their own minds** The question in regard to ἑαυτοῖς εἰσιν νόμος 'to themselves they are law' is whether the law that Paul speaks of is an unwritten set of standards, a cultural code of right and wrong, or whether it is the principles of the

Mosaic law. The lack of an article does not shed light on the question, since other occurrences of 'law' in vv. 12–14 that refer to Mosaic law have no article. The claim of some commentators that this must refer to Mosaic law is unconvincing. Paul is not building a case on how much the Gentiles have obeyed Mosaic law so much as on the fact that, Mosaic law or not, everyone has standards that they sometimes obey and sometimes fail to obey. The words 'they are a law' are metaphorical; a verb needs to be supplied to convey the sense, which is made clear in v. 15: 'prove that' corresponds to 'demonstrate that' in 15a.

2:15a *what God* **commands in his law is intuitively known by them** The phrase ἔργον τοῦ νόμου 'work of the law' requires some verb to express the implied relationship between the two nouns: 'works commanded in the law' or 'works required by the law' conveys the sense well. 'God' is supplied as agent in order not to personify 'the law' as the subject of 'commands'. Translators need to make sure that readers do not take this as meaning that *only* non-Jews have this understanding, not Jews. Words like 'even without knowing the Scriptures' (so Stuart) may have to be included.

2:15b as The Greek text here has no conjunction but instead a genitive absolute construction. Many versions omit any conjunction. Since the most likely function of a present participle following the main verb is attendant circumstance, and since that shows good relational coherence, such a relationship is posited in the display (following RSV).

each person in his very own conscience either accuses or excuses/defends himself The Greek is συμμαρτυρούσης αὐτῶν τῆς συνειδήσεως καὶ μεταξὺ ἀλλήλων τῶν λογισμῶν κατηγορούντων ἢ καὶ ἀπολογουμένων 'their conscience co-witnessing and between each other (their) thoughts accusing or even excusing'. Since there is little difference between conscience and thought, and since 'thoughts accusing' is a personification, the two are fully represented by 'each person in his own conscience'.

The plural possessive αὐτῶν 'their' precedes 'the conscience', which it modifies, making 'their' prominent. This prominence is shown by the words 'his very own conscience'. Because 'conscience' is singular, the sense is conveyed here by the distributing English construction 'each person excuses/defends himself'.

The nature of the accusing and excusing/defending needs to be made clear in the receptor language. It is a question of whether or not a person has lived up to the inner law.

There may be a chiastic structure in the second half of the verse:

A συμμαρτυρούσης 'witnessing'
 B αὐτῶν τῆς συνειδήσεως 'their conscience'
 B' καὶ μεταξὺ ἀλλήλων τῶν λογισμῶν 'and between each other the thoughts'
A' κατηγορούντων ἢ καὶ ἀπολογουμένων 'accusing or even excusing'

2:16a *God will do these things* **at the time** It is difficult to determine what part of the previous section this verse relates to. The first Greek phrase is ἐν ἡμέρᾳ 'on the day'. But the events described in v. 14 clearly do not occur on the day described in v. 16. But since the verse refers to judgment and the whole previous section deals with God's judgment of both Jews and Gentiles, a generic statement is given in the display.

2:16b according to what they have thought and done *even* **secretly** There seems to be no good reason not to assume that the term τὰ κρυπτά 'the hidden things' includes both thoughts and deeds. The word 'even' belongs to this phrase; that is, he will judge people not only for their known sins but even for those which are hidden. Paul does not mean that God will fail to condemn people for their open sins as well.

2:16c by means of *his authorizing* **Christ Jesus to judge them** The phrase διὰ Χριστοῦ Ἰησοῦ 'through Christ Jesus' is expressing the agent of a means proposition. The sense is that God the Father authorizes it, and Christ carries it out. LB has "at God's command Jesus Christ will judge. . . ." CEV translates it similarly: "when God has Jesus Christ judge. . . ." Interestingly, both these versions as well as JB, NIV, and NRSV follow the reading 'Jesus Christ', whereas the GNT has 'Christ Jesus' (with a C "difficulty in deciding" rating in the fourth edition; see the note on 1:1b).

2:16d This is according to the good news which I *preach* The phrase κατὰ τὸ εὐαγγέλιόν μου 'according to the gospel mine' precedes 'through Christ Jesus', which suggests that Paul's gospel included not just judgment, but judgment by Jesus Christ.

The genitive 'my' with 'gospel' means 'the gospel I preach' (so TEV) or 'which God revealed to me', not 'the gospel I possess'. This must be made specific in languages in which the ambiguity cannot be preserved.

BOUNDARIES AND COHERENCE

Lexical coherence in 2:12-16 is provided by nine instances of the word νόμος 'law' and two of ἀνόμως 'without law'. The start of the next paragraph is marked by a return to second person singular pronouns after the third person plural pronouns of this paragraph.

PROMINENCE AND THEME

The theme of 2:12-16 is drawn from the two NUCLEI of the v. 12 CLAIM and from the 13b NUCLEUS of the *justification*.

SUBSECTION CONSTITUENT 2:17-24
(Expository Paragraph: Claim₂ of 2:1-24)

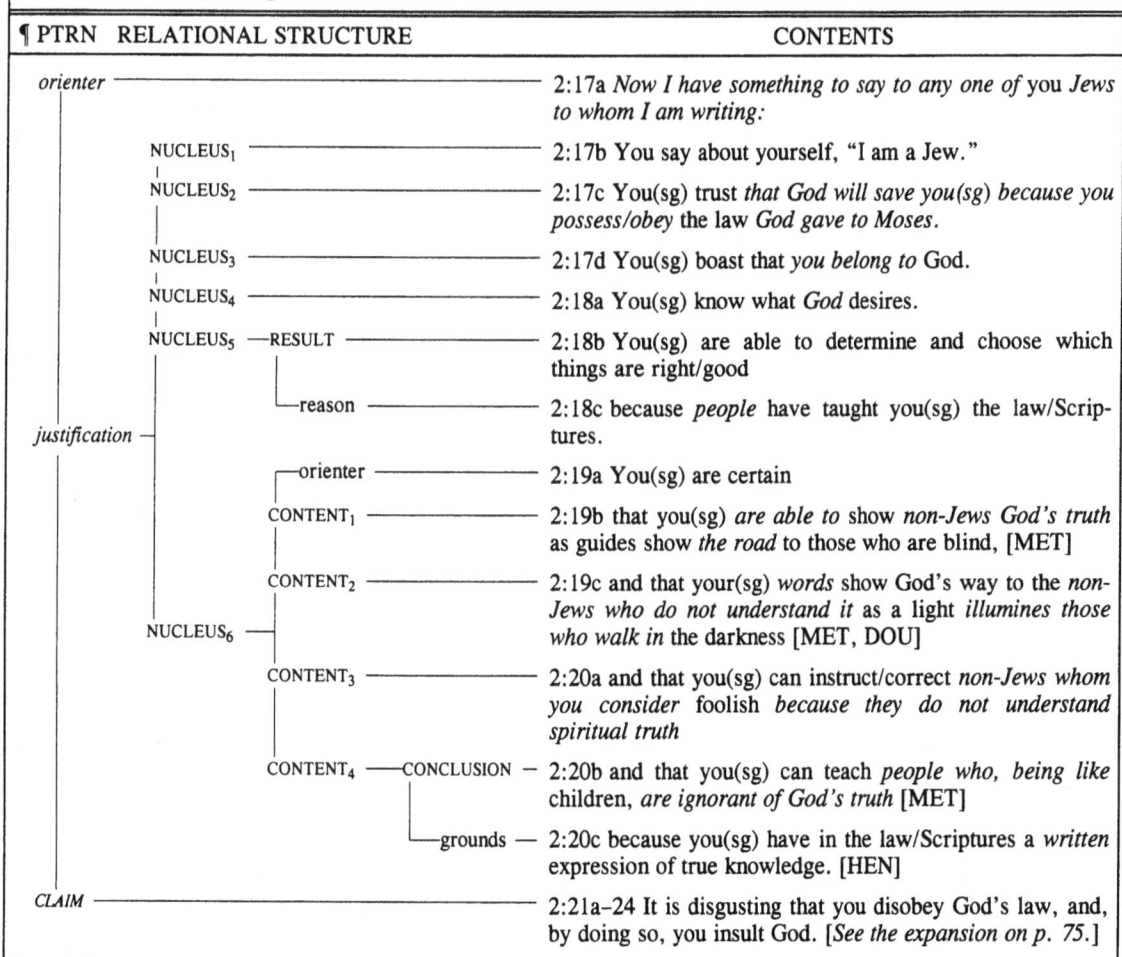

INTENT AND PARAGRAPH PATTERN

Although the 2:17-24 paragraph has emotive elements (Paul's switching to the second person singular in addressing the individual Jews in Rome and the swift series of five hard-hitting rhetorical questions in vv. 21-23 with their negative evaluations), the primary function of the paragraph is to prove that the Jews stand condemned as much as the non-Jews. That it is an expository paragraph is clear in that it presents a *justification* and a CLAIM.

NOTES

2:17:a *Now I have something to say to any one of you Jews to whom I am writing* The verse begins with εἰ δέ 'but if'. Textus Receptus has ἴδε 'see!' instead of εἰ δέ, but it is very poorly supported textually and does not make much sense.

Paul's argument continues, directed now to those of his audience who are Jews, as indicated by the words σὺ Ἰουδαῖος ἐπονομάζῃ 'you(sg) are named a Jew'. Many commentators say that the second person singular pronoun here signals the literary device known as diatribe: Paul writes as though he is addressing an imaginary questioner who proposes an objection. Paul probably thinks of the imaginary objector as representative of any and every Jew who believes he can be saved through the law, whether or not the specific accusations in vv. 21-23 apply to him. In some languages it might be necessary to introduce v. 17 with something like 'Now I address any Jewish person among you who believes he can be saved because he has the law God gave to Moses'. The use of the pronoun here, pointing to the fact that the Jews are again being directly addressed, in addition to the verbal affix gives prominence to the subject 'you'. The rendering in the display is an attempt to capture the prominence of the subject and yet avoid the wrong meaning that Paul is addressing one individual Jew.

2:17b **You say about yourself, "I am a Jew"** The fact that the 17-24 paragraph begins with εἰ 'if' presents three problems. First, it would be very difficult in some languages to render this as a succession of conditional clauses through 20c, before the apodosis in v. 21. Second, it is questionable whether there even is an apodosis. Many commentators and some versions (e.g., RSV, NIV) understand no apodosis. Third, as Newman and Nida point out, the εἰ + present indicative clauses here "are equivalent in force to an affirmative statement" and are so translated in TEV as well as in LB, JBP, NEB, and CEV. In the display they are rendered as statements.

The verb ἐπονομάζομαι means 'to call oneself'. In the display it is represented by the use of direct discourse.

2:17c **You(sg) trust** *that God will save you(sg) because you possess/obey* **the law** *God gave to Moses* The Greek is ἐπαναπαύῃ νόμῳ 'you(sg) rely on law'. It is difficult to be precise about the meaning of 'rely on'. Some commentators suggest 'rest their hopes on' (Morris, Dunn), but hopes for what? A more generic alternative to the words in the display is 'that God will act favorably toward you'. LB renders it as "think all is well between yourself and God because he gave his laws to you." It is not certain whether 'rely on the law' meant to rely on it in virtue of their possessing it or their obeying it; both alternatives are given in the display.

The 'law' needs to be identified as 'law of Moses' to distinguish it from some government law.

2:17d **You(sg) boast that** *you belong to* **God** The Greek is καυχᾶσαι ἐν θεῷ 'you(sg) boast in God'. A verb needs to be supplied as the content of 'boast'. The display supplies 'you belong to', which is fairly generic. Others have suggested 'boast about your knowledge of'. NCV has "brag that you are close to God"; NRSV has "boast of your relation to God."

2:18b **You(sg) are able to determine and choose which things are right/good** The Greek is δοκιμάζεις τὰ διαφέροντα 'you(sg) approve the things which excel'. Commentators are divided as to whether the verb 'approve' means 'to approve after testing' or 'to distinguish, by testing, between what is good and what is evil'. The display suggests that both are meant, by the use of the two verbs 'determine' and 'choose'.

2:18c the law/Scriptures The word νόμος 'law' could be taken to mean 'Scriptures' both here and in v. 20 because the sense is much wider than simply the commandments Moses received (so Hodge, Vine).

2:19b–c Paul uses two metaphors here, actually a figurative doublet (so Moore, p. 40): 'a guide to the blind' (19b) and 'a light to the ones in darkness' (19c). The rendering in the display is an attempt to spell out the metaphors. Commentators agree that it is the Gentiles who are the 'blind' and 'in darkness'.

Although 19b, 19c, 20a, and 20b are labeled as four separate nuclei, semantically they are saying the same thing in different ways. The last three could be labeled equivalents.

2:20a instruct/correct The noun παιδευτής means 'instructor' or 'corrector' (BAGD, p. 603). In this context either meaning is appropriate.

non-Jews whom you consider foolish because they do not understand spiritual truth The word ἄφρων means "foolish, senseless" (Louw and Nida 32:52). However, Paul is not suggesting that Jews are intelligent and Gentiles are not, but that Jews considered them so. The reason for this is given following suggestions by JBP, Denney, and Morris.

2:20b people who, being like children, are ignorant of God's truth Paul uses 'children' here as a metaphor in the sense of those who do not have much knowledge of the subject under discussion—hence 'ignorant of God's truth'. NCV renders it hyperbolically as "those who know nothing."

2:20c a written expression of true knowledge The Greek is τὴν μόρφωσιν τῆς γνώσεως καὶ τῆς ἀληθείας 'the embodiment of the knowledge and of the truth'. The word μόρφωσις means 'embodiment, formulation' (BAGD, p. 528.1) and in this context must refer to the written expression of divine truth. The words 'knowledge and truth' are a type of hendiadys in which the second item qualifies the first (so JBP).

EXPANSION OF THE *CLAIM* IN THE 2:17-24 DISPLAY

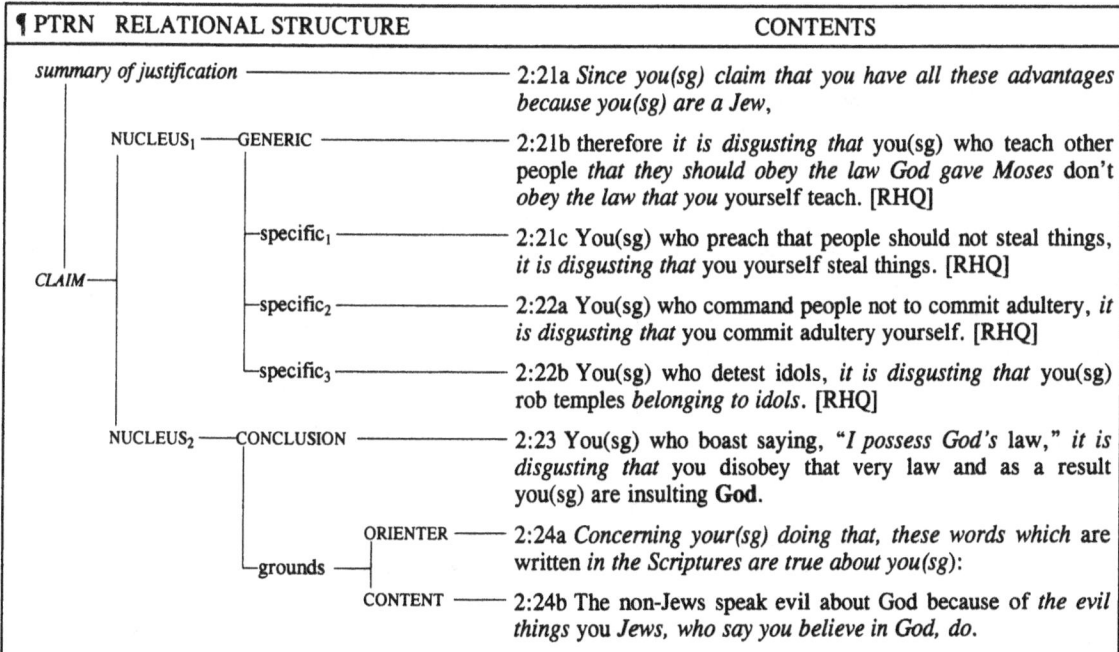

2:21-23 In these verses is a series of five yes/no rhetorical questions. Semantically, they are accusations. In English 'why do you (not) . . . ?' would capture the sense quite well (cf. TEV, JB, NCV).

2:21a Since you(sg) claim that you have all these advantages because you(sg) are a Jew The Greek word in this verse that relates it to what has come before is οὖν 'therefore'; the display provides a summary statement of what 'therefore' refers to.

2:21b it is disgusting that The yes/no rhetorical question in Greek is rendered nicely in CEV by "how can you . . . ?" and in NCV and TEV by "why don't you . . . ?" But these are still rhetorical questions. The function of the rhetorical question in vv. 21-23 is accusation, in other words, a negative evaluation. In the display this negative evaluation is given in the form of an orienter ('it is disgusting that') preceding each statement. In some languages it may be possible to use 'you should not' or 'you ought not to'.

that they should obey the law God gave Moses The Greek text has only ὁ διδάσκων ἕτερον 'who teach another'. As is clear from 21c-23, what Paul was condemning them for was failure to obey the very things they were teaching others. The words 'teach yourself' in the second part of 21b are in effect a metonymy: it stands for 'obey what you teach'. As Haldane says, "this implies that the Jews did not practice the precepts of their law." Thus 21b is rightly seen as a generic statement, 21c–22b being the specific statements of condemnation.

2:22b rob temples *belonging to idols* Some commentators think that ἱεροσυλεῖς 'you(sg) rob temples' is used in a metaphorical sense, that literal robbery is not in view, but rather acting sacrilegiously by withholding from God what he demands (cf. Mal. 3:8). But since history records that idol temples actually were plundered by Jews, there seems to be no good reason for avoiding a literal sense, especially in light of Acts 19:37. The question is, If the word is taken in its literal sense, just what is Paul condemning? One suggestion is the actual theft; another is the profiting from the sale of the stolen objects (and thereby actually encouraging idol worship by those who bought the stolen items). Some commentators suggest that the defilement was as bad as the theft itself.

2:23 boast saying, "*I possess God's* **law"** The word 'boast' in the clause ἐν νόμῳ καυχᾶσαι 'in law you(sg) boast' requires some content of the boast (see 2:17c). The generic 'I possess' works well here. TEV has "boast about having"; NCV has "brag about having."

The phrases ἐν νόμῳ 'in law' and διὰ τῆς παραβάσεως τοῦ νόμου 'through the transgression of the law' as well as the object τὸν θεόν 'God' are prominent by virtue of preceding the verb. The display attempts to capture the force of the first phrase by putting it in direct quotes, the second by forefronting the reason clause, and the third by bold type.

2:24a *Concerning your(sg) doing that, these words which* **are written . . .** *are true about you(sg)* See the note on 1:17b. As to how this quotation (from Isa. 52:5, Ezek. 36:22, or perhaps Ezek. 36:20ff.) relates to Paul's accusation, the fact that it precedes the words 'as it is written' suggests that what was written by Isaiah was now taking place in Paul's time; that is, the Jews were now doing what Isaiah had said long before. The phrases supplied in the display, 'concerning your doing that' and 'are true about you', are exactly what Paul wants to convey. In JBP the sense is communicated by stating the question as though it describes Paul's addressees, and then adding, "There is a verse of Scripture to that effect." Morris says, "Paul proves his accusation with a quotation." Thus γάρ is taken as introducing grounds for the CONCLUSION in v. 23.

BOUNDARIES AND COHERENCE

The coherence of the 2:17–24 paragraph derives from its being addressed to the Jews in the church at Rome and its topic, their breaking of the law. It is a list of charges against the Jews for breaking God's law in spite of the advantages that Paul says they claim to have. Although the following unit is introduced by γάρ, versions seem unanimous in starting a new paragraph at v. 25. This boundary is supported by the fact that vv. 25–29 deal wholly with circumcision, which is not mentioned in vv. 17–24.

PROMINENCE AND THEME

Part of the 2:17–24 theme is a brief summary of the statements of the *justification*; in other words, NUCLEI 2–6 (17c–20c) are all specific advantages of being a Jew (17b). Most of the theme, however, is drawn from condensations of the *CLAIM*'s two prominent statements (21b and 23).

SECTION CONSTITUENT 2:25–3:18
(Expository Subsection: Claim₂ of 2:1–3:18)

THEME: If any of you disobey the Mosaic law, God will consider your circumcision worthless and will accept the non-Jews who obey his law; and they will declare that God is right in condemning you. Our being circumcised Jews does benefit us. God has certainly kept his promise to bless us. But it is certainly right for God to punish us. God will condemn those who claim I say that we should continue to do evil and that God will no longer punish us for doing so. God will not treat us Jews more favorably than he will treat non-Jews.

MACROSTRUCTURE	CONTENTS
CLAIM₁	2:25–29 God will consider non-Jews acceptable to him if they obey his law, and such non-Jews will declare God is right in condemning those who disobey his laws, because it is only those who are changed inwardly who are true Jews and acceptable to God.
CLAIM₂	3:1–8 My reply to the objection that therefore there is no advantage in being a Jew or being circumcised is that there is, especially since God entrusted his promises to us. My reply to the objection that God has not kept his promise is that he certainly has, for his promises are always true. My reply to the objection that it is not right for God to punish us Jews is that it certainly is, because if God didn't judge us Jews he couldn't judge anyone. But to anyone who objects that if our doing evil results in people praising God we should continue doing evil and God should no longer condemn us, I would reply that God will justly condemn people who claim I say such things.
CLAIM₃	3:9–18 My reply to a query whether God will treat Jews more favorably than non-Jews is no, since the Scriptures make clear that all people are condemned by God for their sin.

INTENT AND MACROSTRUCTURE

The 2:25–3:18 unit is expository as are all its constituents. It consists of a CLAIM (2:25–29) regarding circumcision and two further CLAIMS (3:1–8 and 3:9–18), which are in effect the refutations of two possible objections arising from the first CLAIM.

BOUNDARIES AND COHERENCE

The boundary with the next unit is marked in 3:19 with the orienter οἴδαμεν δὲ ὅτι 'now we know that' introducing a summary statement referring to everyone, not just the Jews.

Coherence within the paragraph is provided by seven occurrences of περιτομή 'circumcision' in 2:25–3:1, four occurrences of ἀκροβυστία 'uncircumcision', three occurrences of Ἰουδαῖος 'Jew', plus three synonyms in the initial clauses of each constituent part: ὠφελεῖ 'profit' (2:25), περισσόν 'advantage' (3:1), and προεχόμεθα 'excel' (3:9).

PROMINENCE AND THEME

The theme of 2:25–3:18 is drawn from the themes of the three CLAIMS. The parts that suggest Paul is answering possible objections are omitted as are the *justification* portions of the CLAIMS since these are less thematic.

SUBSECTION CONSTITUENT 2:25–29
(Expository Paragraph: Claim₁ of 2:25–3:18)

THEME: God will consider non-Jews acceptable to him if they obey his law, and such non-Jews will declare God is right in condemning those who disobey his laws, because it is only those who are changed inwardly who are true Jews and acceptable to God.

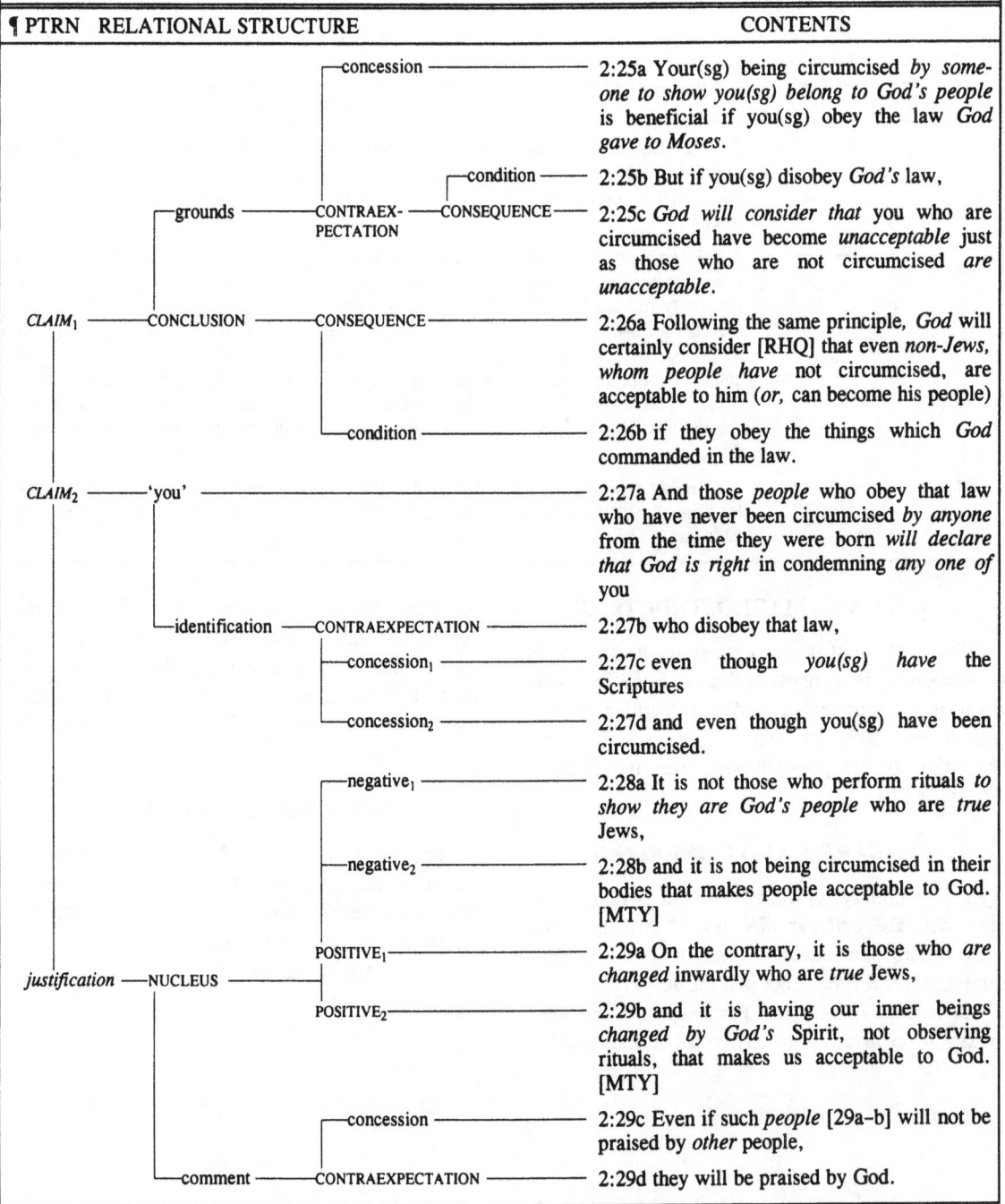

INTENT AND PARAGRAPH PATTERN

The 2:25–29 unit is another of the expository paragraphs discussing God's just condemnation of the Jews. Paul makes two parallel CLAIMS (vv. 26 and 27) joined by καί 'and' (27a). The second CLAIM is followed by a *justification* (introduced by γάρ) in vv. 28–29.

There is a question as to whether this should be considered one paragraph or two. Even though there are two CLAIMS with but one *justification*, NIV, JBP, and LB make vv. 28-29 a separate paragraph, ignoring γάρ in v. 28, but perhaps indicating that they thought of 28-29 as support for more than v. 27. The καί introducing v. 27 argues for a close connection between vv. 25-26 and vv. 27-29. Murray supports this decision: "The relation to what precedes, indicated by 'for' at the beginning of v. 28, is that the criteria of a *true* Jew and of *true* circumcision set forth in verses 28, 29, support and confirm what had been affirmed in the three preceding verses."

NOTES

2:25a circumcised . . . *to show you(sg) belong to God's people* Paul uses the word περιτομή 'circumcision' here to refer to the actual ritual of circumcision. The words 'to show you belong to God's people' are the very minimum of what Paul would count on his audience to know as far as the significance of the ritual to the Jews. JBP thus translates it as "that most intimate sign of belonging to God that we call circumcision."

2:25b if you(sg) disobey *God's* law The word νόμον 'law' precedes the verb for contrast with the other significant items mentioned in v. 25, especially 'transgressor of the law'.

2:25c *God will consider that* you who are circumcised have become *unacceptable* just as those who are not circumcised *are unacceptable* The Greek is ἡ περιτομή σου ἀκροβυστία γέγονεν 'the circumcision your(sg) uncircumcision is become'. There is an implied comparison here, the point of similarity being 'useless' or 'no better than'. But it seems strange to speak of an event that did not occur as being worthless. Therefore, since the Jews considered that circumcision was what made them acceptable to God, unacceptability is taken to be the point of similarity. TCNT renders the clause as "your circumcision is no better than uncircumcision."

2:26a *God* will certainly consider The Greek is λογισθήσεται 'will be estimated as'. In the display it is made clear that it is God who makes the estimation (so also TCNT). The force of the yes/no rhetorical question is captured by the emphatic positive statement.

even *non-Jews, whom people have* not circumcised, are acceptable to him (*or,* can become his people) The Greek is ἡ ἀκροβυστία αὐτοῦ εἰς περιτομήν, literally 'the uncircumcision of him unto circumcision', a metonymy in which the event stands for the recipients of the event. Circumcision was the rite seen either as making the Jews acceptable to God or making them his people; both these alternative renderings for 'circumcision' are thus given here.

The respective subjects of each clause as well as the other nonverb elements all precede the verbs. It is possible that prominence is shown by this, but it is more likely that this word order is intended to bring out the symmetry in Paul's argumentation. However, the first subject, at least, may be semantically highlighted; thus the display has 'even non-Jews'.

2:27a-b And those *people* who obey that law who have never been circumcised *by anyone from the time they were born will declare that God is right* in condemning *any one of* you who disobey that law The words κρινεῖ ἡ ἀκροβυστία 'will judge the uncircumcision' are taken as another rhetorical question by some commentators and versions. Others take it as a statement. The sense is the same either way; but if it is taken as a question in Greek and rendered as a statement, the word 'certainly' might be added to signify the emphatic positive sense.

Several commentators (Murray, Sanday and Headlam, Alford) have noted that the statement that the Gentiles will do the condemning is not to be taken literally; it is God who does the condemning. The words 'will declare that God is right' are supplied in the display as an attempt to keep the focus on the non-Jews as the overall agent of the propositional cluster, while making clear that God is the actual agent of the condemning. An alternative might be 'the uncircumcised by their example will force God to condemn'.

The words 'any one of you' in 27a are an attempt to capture some of the impact of the singular pronoun σύ here.

2:27c even though *you(sg) have* the Scriptures The great majority of commentators and versions agree that διά in the phrase διὰ γράμματος 'with letter' expresses attendant circumstance. However, as far as the semantic role in the context is concerned, the διά phrase is actually expressing a concession relation. Many commentators do in fact note that the sense of 'although' is clearly present. TEV, NIV, JB, and CEV all have 'even though'. A concession relationship is thus indicated in the display.

2:28a It is not those who perform rituals . . . who are *true* Jews The Greek is οὐ ὁ ἐν τῷ φανερῷ Ἰουδαῖός ἐστιν 'not he who in the open Jew he is'. The form, which is singular, has a plural, generic sense, and this is made explicit in the display. The phrase 'in the open' means 'outwardly' (BAGD, p. 852.2) or 'by external acts', hence 'perform rituals'. 'Jew' means 'a true Jew in God's sight'. It is another way of saying 'who are truly God's people'.

to show they are God's people The function of the outward rituals Paul refers to is supplied here because it is crucial to the right understanding of Paul's argument.

2:28b and it is not being circumcised in their bodies that makes people acceptable to God The Greek is οὐδὲ ἡ ἐν τῷ φανερῷ ἐν σαρκὶ περιτομή 'nor the in the open in flesh circumcision', which is really a restatement of 28a. The word 'circumcision' is a metonymy in which the event stands for the people on which it is performed (as in 26a), along with the result, acceptance by God. Paul assumed his readers had this knowledge.

2:29a *changed* **inwardly** The phrase ἐν τῷ κρυπτῷ 'in the secret' is used adverbially (see BAGD, p. 454.2b). NRSV, NEB, NIV, and JB all have 'inwardly'. In this verse Paul is treating circumcision as a metaphor: it is a ritual that changes a man externally, but what God wants is an inner change. Hence 'changed' is supplied as the point of similarity.

2:29b it is having our inner beings *changed by* **God's Spirit, not observing rituals, that makes us acceptable to God** The Greek is περιτομὴ καρδίας ἐν πνεύματι οὐ γράμματι, literally 'circumcision of heart in spirit not (in) letter'. Here 'heart' is a dead figure standing for one's inner being or nature. The metaphor is continued: as circumcision changes a male's outward appearance, so God's Spirit changes us inwardly. Hence 'changed' is again used in the display. Formerly many commentators took the phrase 'in spirit' to mean 'spiritually' in contrast with 'in letter' meaning 'literally', but this view is largely abandoned now. It could mean 'in (the human) spirit', but this would be virtually synonymous with 'of heart', an inexplicable redundancy. It seems best to take it as meaning 'by the Spirit' (thus Morris, Dunn, Hodge, Best, Murray, Harrison, and Michel).

2:29c-d Even if such *people* The antecedent of the singular οὗ 'whose' is the singular ὁ Ἰουδαῖος 'the Jew'. Its sense, however, is not singular but generic. The two propositions are separated by ἀλλά, which expresses a strong contrast; but it is difficult to know how to label the relationship. The sense is 'even if' (so LB). JB indicates the relationship with "A Jew like that may not be praised by men, but he will be praised by God."

Nearly all modern commentators agree that there is a play on words here: Ἰουδαῖος 'Jew' means 'descendant of Judah', and 'Judah' in Hebrew means 'praise'. To capture this play on words in translation is nearly impossible (a footnote might be appropriate); hence it is not represented in the display.

BOUNDARIES AND COHERENCE

The 2:25-29 paragraph is coherent in that it consists of a list of charges against the Jews for breaking God's law in spite of the advantages they claim to have. Also, the paragraph is dominated by the words περιτομή 'circumcision' (five times) and ἀκροβυστία 'uncircumcision' (four times), which do not occur in the preceding or following units except in the mouth of an objector in 3:1.

The boundary between 2:25-29 and the following unit is signaled in 3:1 by a pair of rhetorical questions stating hypothetical objections to what has preceded.

PROMINENCE AND THEME

The theme of 2:25-29 is drawn from the naturally prominent propositions of the *CLAIMS* (vv. 26 and 27) and of the *justification* (v. 29). To make the thought complete, the 25b condition is also included. In several places, especially 29a-b, the wording has been condensed to make the theme more concise.

SUBSECTION CONSTITUENT 3:1-8
(Expository Paragraph: Claim₂ of 2:25-3:18)

THEME: My reply to the objection that therefore there is no advantage in being a Jew or being circumcised is that there is, especially since God entrusted his promises to us. My reply to the objection that God has not kept his promise is that he certainly has, for his promises are always true. My reply to the objection that it is not right for God to punish us Jews is that it certainly is, because if God didn't judge us Jews he couldn't judge anyone. But to anyone who objects that if our doing evil results in people praising God we should continue doing evil and God should no longer condemn us, I would reply that God will justly condemn people who claim I say such things.

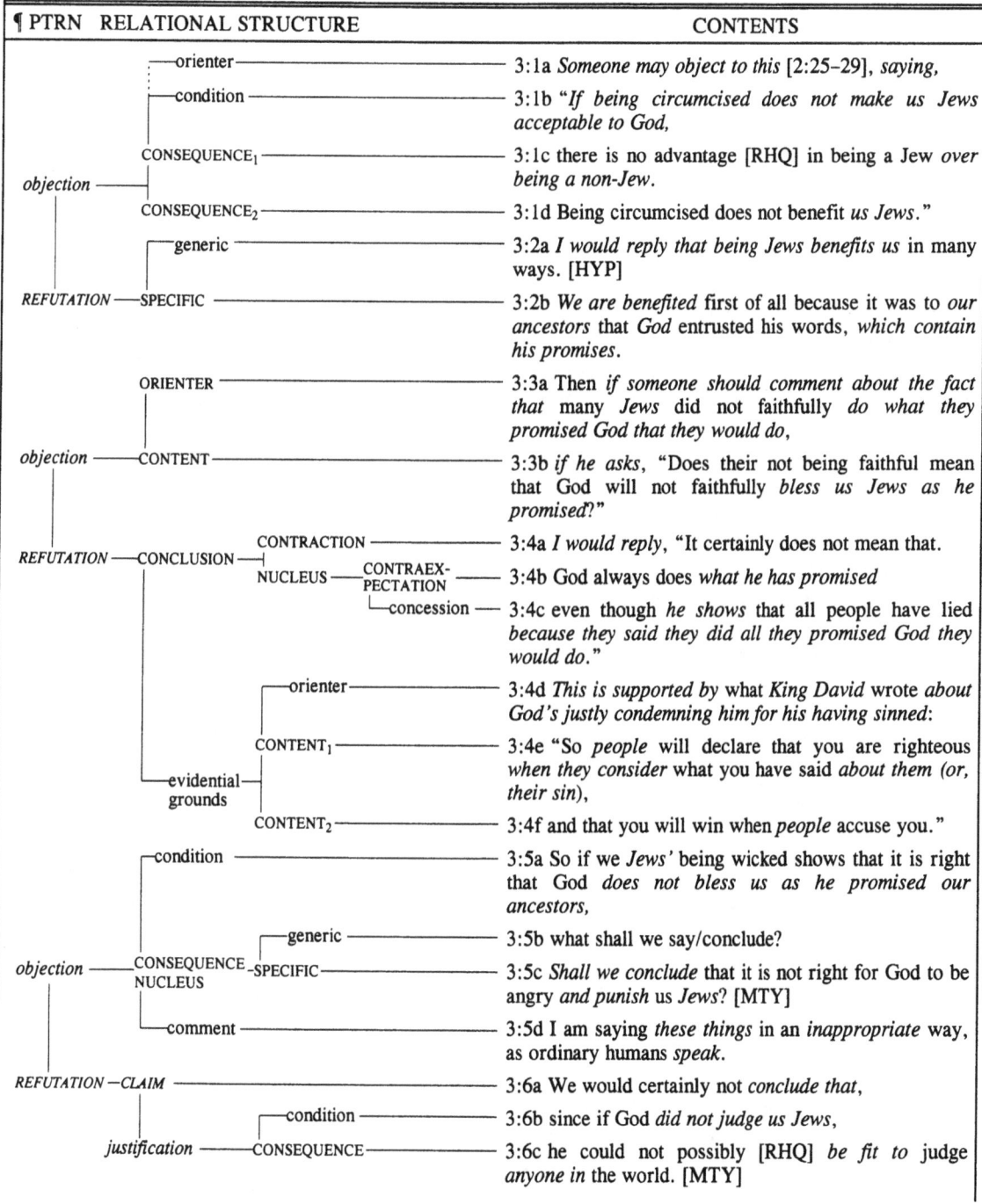

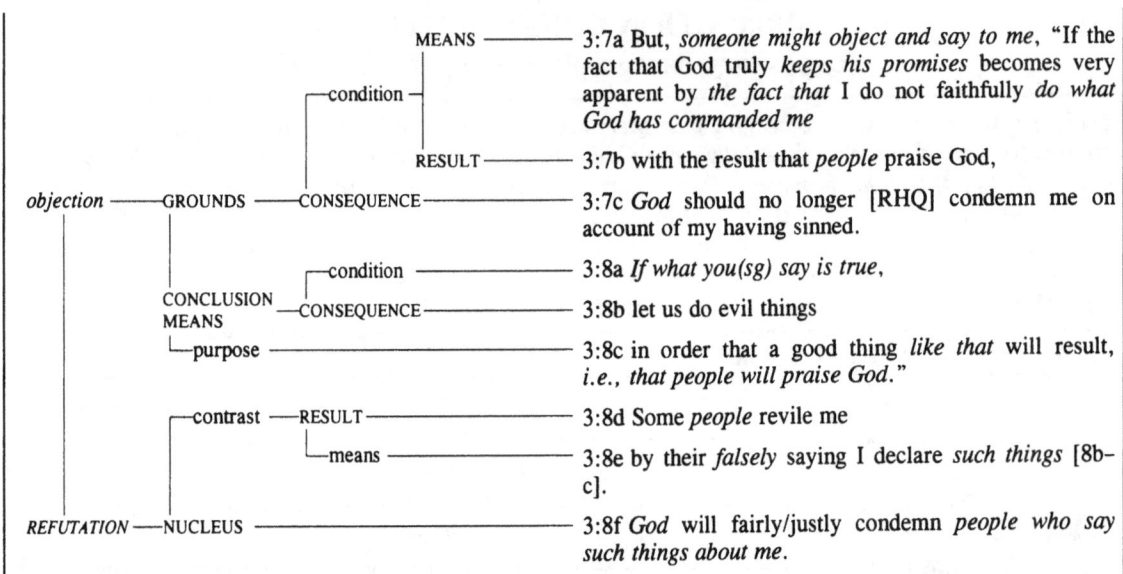

INTENT AND PARAGRAPH PATTERN

Here in the 3:1-8 paragraph, for the first time in the epistle, Paul resorts to the device of anticipating queries arising from his exposition thus far. He raises queries and objections that the Jews among his addressees might make, and he gives his replies. The paragraph is thus expository in nature.

There are two levels of paragraph pattern here: the repartee pattern, consisting of *objections* and their REFUTATIONS, and the other, within one of the REFUTATIONS (v. 6), consisting of a CLAIM and its *justification*.

As to the question of how many *objection*-REFUTATION units there are in this paragraph, three possibilities exist: (1) there are only two, vv. 1-2 and vv. 3-8; (2) there are three, vv. 1-2, vv. 3-6, and vv. 7-8; (3) there are four, vv. 1-2, vv. 3-4, vv. 5-6, and vv. 7-8. Against this last possibility, some would say, is the fact that the question in 3:5 expects a negative answer. In other words, the person asking the question is trying to show that the statement expressed in 5c is false. But that supposedly would be an impossible objection, coming from Jews. Therefore, following Hodge, vv. 6-8 should be taken as a second main point of the REFUTATION to the *objection* stated in v. 3. But following a similar line of argument, there is no way vv. 7-8 could express the content of *Paul's* thinking. Therefore in the display (following NIV) it is made explicit that vv. 7-8 are a separate *objection*-REFUTATION unit. However, it is admitted that to this objection all Paul says is "God will justly judge those who claim I say such things." Since this brings in a first person singular reference, it seems to be a REACTION, not a REFUTATION, which does not fit semantic theory well. What should go with a REACTION is a *situation*, but in vv. 7-8 clearly more than just that is expressed.

NOTES

3:1a-d *Someone may object to this, saying* This is the first of a set of questions in the epistle that Paul anticipates might be raised against his arguments. It is probably futile to try to decide whether the questions are real or hypothetical, that is, whether they are questions Paul has actually heard from others (or heard reported) or questions he suspects *might* be asked by others or Paul's own questions. The point is that Paul raises and then answers these questions, and the fact that he is doing so is made explicit in the display.

A number of commentators have speculated whether this abundance of such questions and answers suggests that the whole epistle ought to be classified as a diatribe, following the pattern of certain classical Greek scholars. Stuhlmacher rejects this notion; he comments (p. 240), "In every case the Apostle is alluding to criticisms and challenges from his Jewish Christian opponents."

In the display it is made explicit that Jews and non-Jews (i.e., Gentiles) are being compared. TEV makes it clear with "Do the Jews have any advantage over the Gentiles?"

us Jews To clarify that Paul himself was a Jew, 'us Jews' is made explicit. The singular form τοῦ Ἰουδαίου 'of the Jew' in 1c is used with a plural generic sense, hence the plural in 1b, 1d, etc. To capture the generic sense it may be necessary in some cases to say 'advantage in being Jewish'.

3:1b This clause is supplied to provide what is in effect the grounds for the conclusion (introduced by οὖν 'therefore') that Paul's critics would arrive at.

3:1c The phrase ἡ ὠφέλεια means 'the advantage', hence 'advantage' in the display. For some languages the translator may have to use something like 'be superior to'.

3:2a Paul's response is to the question in 1c. Thus 'being Jews' is the implied subject here, and 'benefit' is supplied as the verb to make a complete clause.

in many ways The Greek text has πολὺ κατὰ πάντα τρόπον 'much by every way'. Since in 2b Paul states only *one* way, 'every' is a hyperbole.

3:2b first of all The word πρῶτον 'first' here could mean either 'first of all' (as in LB, NIV), which is the most natural sense, or 'most importantly'. The main problem with 'first of all' is that Paul does not go on with other items in a list; but he uses it like this in other places (1:8, 1 Cor. 11:18), so we assume this is its use here (see the note on 1:8a).

In the display the third person plural pronoun ('they were entrusted') is identified as 'our ancestors'. It was to their ancestors, not the Jews in Paul's time, that the promises were given.

his words, *which contain his promises* Concerning τὰ λόγια τοῦ θεοῦ 'the sayings of God', many commentators point out that what is in view here is God's promises rather than the OT in its entirety (also BAGD, p. 476).

3:3–4 Here Paul answers another objection. The display follows the GNT's punctuation.

3:3a did not faithfully *do what they promised God that they would do* The word ἠπίστησαν 'disbelieved' could mean 'were unfaithful', and the rendering in the display is based on this. If it were taken in the other possible sense, 'disbelieved', an implied content, something like 'the promises of Scripture', would have to be supplied. In view of the preceding verb, 'entrusted', and the immediately following phrase, 'faithfulness of God', 'unfaithful' is most likely the correct sense here. But by itself, 'unfaithful' has an entirely different sense in English; it needs to modify some verb phrase similar to the one supplied in the display. According to most commentators, the word refers to the Jews' infidelity to what was entrusted to them, namely the covenant made with their ancestors. This sense is conveyed generically by 'do what they promised God that they would do'.

3:3b God will not faithfully *bless us Jews as he promised* The Greek is τὴν πίστιν τοῦ θεοῦ καταργήσει 'the faithfulness of God nullify'. Here 'faithfulness' is semantically an attribute, requiring an event for it to modify. Several commentators (e.g., Morris, Barnes, Sanday and Headlam, Haldane, Erdman) connect it with God's keeping his promises. NCV has "will that stop God from doing what he promised?"

In the Greek, both the subject 'their unbelief' and the object 'God's faithfulness' precede the verb 'destroy/nullify', but it is difficult in English to maintain the prominence signaled by this, especially after making a clause of each of the two nouns in order for the grammatical and semantic classes to match.

3:4b God always does *what he has promised* The imperative 'become' in γινέσθω δὲ ὁ θεὸς ἀληθής 'but let God become true' obviously cannot mean that God should change from being untruthful to truthful. In the display the concept of God's promise is maintained, and the imperative is rendered as equivalent to an indicative, as many commentators agree. The intensity signaled by the Greek imperative here is rendered by 'always' in the display. Another approach would give 'let it become apparent (to everyone) that (what) God (has promised) remains true', but this component of meaning is carried in 4c by the implied 'he shows'. LB has "God's words will always prove true."

It is apparent that this whole clause, along with the one in 4c, is an idiomatic expression. Since the context deals with faithfulness to promises, the display follows Morris, who suggests that 'true' stands for reliability: doing what was promised.

3:4c all people have lied There is a problem in knowing whether ψεύστης 'liar' is only a generic reference to lying or has to do with specific lies relevant to the context. Sanday and Headlam suggest that the lies are "in asserting that God's promises have not been fulfilled," but that does not seem to fit the immediate context, which refers to unfaithfulness. Some may prefer the more generic reference, omitting 4c's final italicized causal clause.

3:4d *This is supported by* This is the sense of the conjunction καθώς here and in many other places where it introduces a Scripture quotation (see the note on 1:17b).

King David wrote *about God's justly condemning him for his having sinned* It is important to know the original situational context of the quotation from Psa. 51:4 which follows in 4e–f to see how it fits as the evidential grounds. To this end 'King David' has been supplied as the agent of 'written', 'God' has been supplied as the referent for 'you', and 'justly condemning him for his having sinned' has been supplied as a brief, generic situational context.

3:4e *what you have said about them* (or, *their sin*) The Greek is ἐν τοῖς λόγοις σου 'in the sayings of you(sg)'. The context demands understanding not just God's words in general, but what God has to say about their sin.

3:5a *we Jews' being wicked* The receptor-language reader may need to be reminded that this whole section (2:17–3:18) is speaking about Jews and is addressed to Jews.

it is right that God does not bless us as he promised our ancestors The Greek is θεοῦ δικαιοσύνην 'God's righteousness', which must mean that God acts in a just or righteous manner. According to Dunn, it is a different way of stating 'God's faithfulness' (v. 3).

As in 3b, the subject and object precede the verb. The subject is probably prominent.

3:5c *and punish* See the note on 2:5b.

3:5d In almost all English versions this proposition appears in parentheses, indicating that it is taken to be a parenthetical comment. It should be noted that in the displays parentheses are never used in this way.

in an inappropriate way, as ordinary humans speak The Greek is κατὰ ἄνθρωπον 'according to man'. Paul is apologizing here for what sounds like a blasphemous idea, totally inappropriate for Paul as an apostle, or even as a Christian, to say.

3:6b *if God did not judge us Jews* The word ἐπεί 'otherwise' implies a contrary-to-fact proposition. Hodge's comment here is very helpful in understanding its force:

To the declaration that they were exposed to condemnation, the Jews pleaded the promise of God, which their unfaithfulness could not render of no effect, and the less so because their unrighteousness would serve to render the righteousness of God the more conspicuous. Paul says on this principle God cannot judge [anyone in] the world. The ground assumed by the Jews might be assumed by all mankind, and if valid in the one case it must be in all.

The display makes the sense clear with 'judge us Jews'.

3:6c *he could not possibly be fit to judge anyone in the world* These words convey the emphatic negative sense of the Greek rhetorical question introduced by πῶς 'how?'. The point is that God would not be qualified to carry out the final judgment on people equitably if he did not act fairly.

In the display 'anyone in the world' represents κόσμος 'world', a metonymy. In some languages this could be rendered 'the other people in the world'.

3:7a *But, someone might object* Here Paul answers still another possible objection. There is some manuscript evidence supporting εἰ γάρ 'for if' at the beginning of this verse but the fourth edition GNT supports εἰ δέ 'but if' with a B rating, meaning "almost certain." Metzger (p. 448) says εἰ γάρ is "a rather inept scribal substitution."

and say to me These word are included to make clear whom the 'you(sg)' in 8a refers to.

truly keeps his promises See the note on 3:4b. The forefronting of the subject, ἡ ἀλήθεια τοῦ θεοῦ 'the dependability of God', emphasizes it.

I do not faithfully do what God has commanded me The sense of ἐμῷ ψεύσματι 'my lie' is 'untruthfulness, unreliability', hence 'unfaithfulness' (BAGD, p. 892), as many commentators suggest. This is the only instance of ψεῦσμα in the NT. Since it is an abstract noun representing an attribute that modifies an action, some generic event needs to be supplied such as 'do what God has commanded'.

3:7c The rhetorical question here introduced by τί 'why' has the force of a strong negative evaluation, equivalent to 'God should not' or 'it is not right for God to'.

3:8 This verse (8a–c) is part of the *objection* introduced in v. 7, not Paul's reply. Morris says of this verse,

> wherever people have followed Paul in emphasizing that human merit has no part in bringing about our salvation and that we are saved by grace alone, some have drawn the conclusion that it does not matter whether we sin or not. It seems that the same conclusion was drawn by some of Paul's contemporaries.

3:8a *If what you(sg) say is true* This proposition expresses the implied condition for the CONSEQUENCE. It is probably referring to v. 7, but perhaps back to what Paul said earlier, even in 2:25–29. It introduces an additional CLAIM an objector might make. LB renders this implied condition as "If you follow through with that idea, you come to this."

3:8d–f It is difficult to determine whether the pronoun ἡμᾶς 'we' is the editorial 'we', referring to Paul alone, or whether it is literal, and if literal whether it refers to Paul and other Christians or Paul and other apostles. Commentators give little help. Since Paul's critics are in view, the pronoun here is taken as expressing the first person singular, as in LB, NEB, JBP, and TEV.

3:8f *people who say such things about me* There is a question here concerning the relative pronoun ὧν 'whose'. Does it refer to people who teach such wrong doctrinal conclusions, or to those who accuse Paul of teaching it? (It could even refer to the content of the argument.) But since ὧν normally requires an antecedent, and since the only one expressed is τινές 'some', the display has 'who say such things about me', not 'who teach such things'.

BOUNDARIES AND COHERENCE

The 3:1–8 paragraph contains a set of four *objection-REFUTATION* units. The *objections* are ones Paul anticipates Jews might make as an outcome of his exposition of the spiritual state of the Jews. These four sets provide relational coherence to the paragraph. Lexical coherence is seen in the references to truth (vv. 4 and 7) and falsehood (vv. 4 and 7).

The beginning of the following paragraph is signaled with the rhetorical question τί οὖν; 'what then?'.

PROMINENCE AND THEME

Since there are two levels of paragraph-pattern relations in some parts of the 3:1–8 paragraph, the theme is drawn from both levels, where pertinent. It includes material in somewhat condensed form from the naturally prominent propositions of each *objection* and *REFUTATION*. From within the first *objection* the theme draws from both the condition and the CONSEQUENCES for semantic completeness. From within the second *REFUTATION* it draws from both the CONTRACTION (4a) and NUCLEUS (4b). From within the third *REFUTATION* it draws from both the CLAIM and its *justification*. From within the fourth *objection* it includes part of the 7a-b condition since the argument would be incomplete without it.

SUBSECTION CONSTITUENT 3:9–18
(Expository Paragraph: Claim₃ of 2:25–3:18)

THEME: *My reply to a query whether God will treat Jews more favorably than non-Jews is no, since the Scriptures make clear that all people are condemned by God for their sin.*

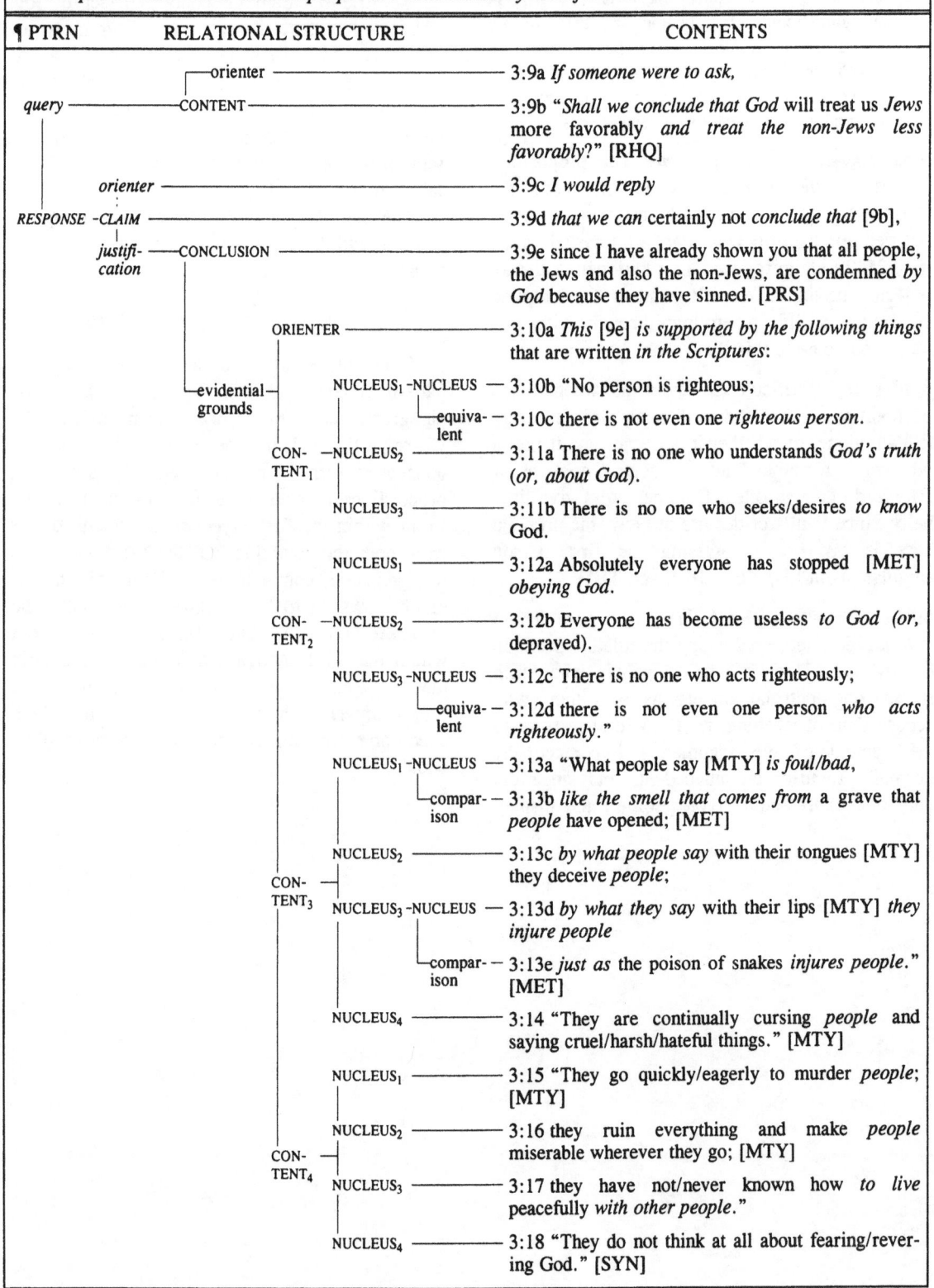

INTENT AND PARAGRAPH PATTERN

In the 3:9–18 paragraph, Paul uses the technique of giving an anticipated *query* and his *RESPONSE*. On the lower level the *RESPONSE* consists of a *CLAIM* in 9d with a *justification* following in which in 9e Paul's previous *CLAIMS* are referred to and in vv. 10–18 scriptural support for the *justification* is marshaled. Thus this is an expository unit.

NOTES

3:9a–c *If someone were to ask . . . I would reply* This rendering is similar to the NIV's. The Greek here is τί οὖν 'what therefore?' followed by a one-word question προεχόμεθα, 'do we excel?' (9b), and a two-word reply, οὐ πάντως 'not at all' (9d). Since Paul is asking the question and answering it himself, it can be considered rhetorical, but it is not clear whether this form is functioning only as an introduction to a new topic/conclusion or whether it is presenting a question someone might genuinely ask at this point. The display's rendering is based on the latter interpretation, hence the *query*-*RESPONSE* labels. The alternative would be to eliminate this outer layer of paragraph-pattern relations indicating repartee (answers to hypothetical or anticipated questions) and label it only as *CLAIM*-*justification*. In this case the propositionalization might read something like:

> 9a Therefore we should certainly not conclude that . . .
> 9b since I have already shown . . . [RHQ]

3:9b *that God will treat us Jews more favorably and treat the non-Jews less favorably* There is a great deal of uncertainty as to the meaning of the verb προεχόμεθα. Most commentators take the verb here as expressing middle voice, with an active sense of 'do we (Jews) excel?' Some assume a passive, with the sense of 'are we (Jews) surpassed?' It has been suggested that it refers to Paul and others who have been slandered (v. 8), with the sense of 'are we making excuses?' It has even been suggested that it refers to Christians in general, with the sense 'what then do we present as a defense?' All of the proposed solutions have their difficulties. Knox's translation "Well, then, has either side the advantage?" preserves the ambiguity and fits in well with the immediately following context. Perhaps this is as good as any. But the display follows the majority of recent commentators (such as Cranfield, Käsemann, Michel) with 'do we Jews have an advantage?' The reasons for this choice are that middle verbs are sometimes used with an active sense and this passage is still focusing on the Jews as his addressees. The objection that this contradicts 3:1 is answered by the fact that in 3:1 Paul is discussing how God has dealt with the Jews historically, while here he is discussing how they stand before God spiritually.

Having an advantage implies a comparison with another group. Therefore the words 'and treat non-Jews less favorably' are supplied to complete the comparison. CEV has "better off than the Gentiles."

3:9e *I have already shown you* Since Paul is referring to what he has written thus far in the epistle, the first person plural here is clearly an editorial 'we'. The display has 'I', as do TEV, RSV, CEV, and JBP.

The meaning of the verb προαιτιάομαι is usually determined from the meaning of its two constituents, since it is found nowhere else in the NT or the Septuagint or the Greek classics. Its literal sense is 'accuse beforehand' but the context gives it more the sense in the display. It is rendered similarly by TEV, LB, and JBP. For languages where 'show' is applicable only to transitive objects, 'proven' or 'made clear' are good alternatives.

the non-Jews The word Ἕλληνας 'Greeks' here is practically synonymous with 'Gentiles' and means 'everyone else in the world'. It is assigned the meaning 'Gentiles' by BAGD (p. 252.2a) and is so translated by TEV, NIV, LB, and CEV. NCV renders it as 'non-Jews'.

condemned *by God* **because they have sinned** The word 'under' in ὑφ' ἁμαρτίαν 'under sin' means 'under the control of' or 'ruled by'. This personification makes the notion of being unable to escape God's condemnation for sin more vivid.

3:10b–18 The OT quotations in 3:10b–18 include several doublets. They have all been retained as pairs because the repetition is a feature of prominence—it adds to the impact.

These verses form a catena, a connected series of biblical references on one theme. Cranfield says,

> The catena has been constructed with considerable care and artistry, so as to form a real new unity out of a multiplicity of excerpts. It

is arranged in three strophes, the first (vv. 10–12) consisting of two sets of three lines, the second (vv. 13–14) and third (vv. 15–18) each consisting of two sets of two lines.

The first strophe (vv. 10–12) deals with the universality of mankind under sin, answering to the πάντας of v. 9, the five occurrences of οὐκ ἔστιν, plus other words also, marking this. The second and third strophes (vv. 13–18) are distinctive in the use of body parts engaged in sin. Mentioned are λάρυγξ 'throat', γλῶσσα 'tongue', χείλη 'lips', στόμα 'mouth', πόδες 'feet', and ὀφθαλμοί 'eyes'. The idea that comes across is that not only are *all* men sinners but the *whole* of individual man is involved in sin. All are sinners and each one is completely sinful. But the question for translators is to what extent we should keep these body parts in literal form. Since this borders on live metaphor, we should probably strive to keep as many as possible.

Another thing to be careful about in all these quotations is the matter of exclusion-inclusion. Greek does not have a big problem with this, but some languages do. Unless God is seen as the speaker, the very fact that the main focus is the universality of sin means that no human can be excluded. There is no distinction between 'us' and 'them'. How then is αὐτῶν 'their' to be handled? It occurs all through vv. 13–18. One answer would be to use a word that means 'mankind in general'.

3:10–12 It can be argued that there is a great deal of hyperbole here: οὐδὲ εἷς 'not one' (v. 10), πάντες 'all' (v. 12), ἅμα 'together' (v. 12), οὐκ ἔστιν ἕως ἑνός 'there is not even one' (v. 12). On the other hand, Paul may be intending these words quite literally. At any rate, they are a means of adding impact to Paul's argument concerning the universality of sin and thus are translated literally in the display. (The OT quotations are from Psa. 14:1–3 and Psa. 53:1–3.)

3:10a See the note on 1:17b. The sense is carried well by JBP's "The Scriptures endorse the act plainly enough."

3:11a There is no one who understands *God's truth (or, about God)* Some such content as 'God's truth' or 'about God' is required after the verb 'to understand'.

3:11b There is no one who seeks/desires *to know* **God** Since 'seek' could imply that God was lost, the words 'to know' are supplied. In some languages 'seek' could be translated literally; in others it may be necessary to say 'desire to know'. CEV has "looks to God for help."

3:12a Absolutely everyone In the Greek, πάντες 'all' is forefronted, giving it additional prominence; 'absolutely' expresses this emphasis.

stopped *obeying God* If the verb ἐξέκλιναν 'turned aside' is translated literally (i.e., by retaining the metaphor), some such phrase as 'obeying God' must be supplied in order to identify that which people turned from. The verb 'stopped' likewise requires a complement.

3:12b has become useless *to God (or,* **depraved)** The verb ἀχρειόομαι means "become depraved, worthless" (BAGD, p. 128.2) or "go wrong, become perverse" (Louw and Nida 88.263). It is difficult to know which of the meanings is in view here. Two are given in the display. The rendering 'useless' is preferred to 'worthless' because 'worthless' could signify 'of no value whatsoever.' This is somewhat hyperbolic, so 'to God' is supplied. Haldane expresses this with "They are become unfit for that for which God made them."

3:13–17 In this passage, nearly every clause that contains a verb has major nonverbal elements preceding the verb, giving them prominence. Some of this word order, however, may be due to the poetic style and figurative language. In the display the prominence has been indicated by forefronting wherever possible.

3:13a What people say *is foul/bad* There is a metonymy here: the word 'throat' signifies speech.

3:13b *like the smell* Here the throat is compared metaphorically to an opened tomb (a quotation from Psa. 5:9). Spelled out, the metaphor signifies that as a tomb when opened emits a foul smell, so the throat of a sinner when the mouth opens emits bad language. The display supplies the missing parts of the metaphor.

3:13c *what people say* **with their tongues** 'Tongue' is a metonymy signifying speech. In many languages the words 'with their tongues' will need to be omitted because the expression will otherwise appear unnatural and redundant (and similarly in 13d).

3:13d *what they say* **with their lips** The word 'lips' is a metonymy that signifies speech.

3:13e *just as* **the poison of snakes** *injures people* In this quotation from Psa. 140:3 lips are compared to the poison of certain snakes. Spelled out, this metaphor signifies that as a snake's venom harms people physically, so sinful speech harms people spiritually.

3:14 The word 'mouth' here is another metonymy signifying speech. The quotation is from Psa. 10:7.

3:15–17 This passage is a quotation from Isa. 59:7–8.

3:15 go quickly/eagerly to murder *people* The first metonymy here is 'feet', in which the body part stands for the associated action. (Alternatively it could be considered a synecdoche, the part being used for the person as a whole.) Another metonymy here is 'shed blood', in which the means signifies the purpose: to murder people.

3:16 they ruin everything and make *people* **miserable wherever they go** There is a rather unusual type of metonymy here involving 'roads/ways', in which a place signifies the people who have passed there, causing ruin and misery as they go. The CEV rendering is, "Wherever they go, they leave ruin and destruction," which is close to the rendering in the display except for the abstract nouns.

3:17 how *to live* **peacefully** *with other people* The Greek is ὁδὸν εἰρήνης 'a way of peace'. An alternative to the rendering in the display is "to live in peace" (CEV, NCV).

3:18 fearing/revering God This verse is a quotation from Psa. 36:1. The phrase ἀπέναντι τῶν ὀφθαλμῶν 'before their eyes' is an idiom meaning 'in their thinking'. As in the display, 'eyes' might be taken as a synecdoche in which the part is used for the whole person. REB has "And reverence for God does not enter their thoughts."

BOUNDARIES AND COHERENCE

Relational coherence in the 3:9–18 paragraph lies in the fact that Paul is presenting an anticipated concluding query from the Jews among the Roman believers, then his own terse reply backed up with OT quotations as evidence. Lexical coherence is provided by words indicating the universality of sin: 'all' (vv. 9, 12); 'not one' (twice in v. 10, twice in v. 12, and once in v. 11); and a series of figures of speech involving body parts.

PROMINENCE AND THEME

The first part of the 3:9–18 theme is drawn from the CONTENT proposition of the *query*. Its second part is drawn from the *RESPONSE* and includes the 9d CLAIM and a condensation of the 9e *justification*. It also includes reference to the fact that vv. 10–18 are a long list of Scripture references to support the statement in 9e, which gives it enough prominence to be mentioned in the theme. It should be noted that Paul throughout the epistle cites Scripture to support his points. The fact that he can and does do so is often considered as thematic as the actual content of the quotations.

SUBDIVISION CLUSTER CONSTITUENT 3:19-20
(Expository Paragraph: Summary of 1:18-3:18)

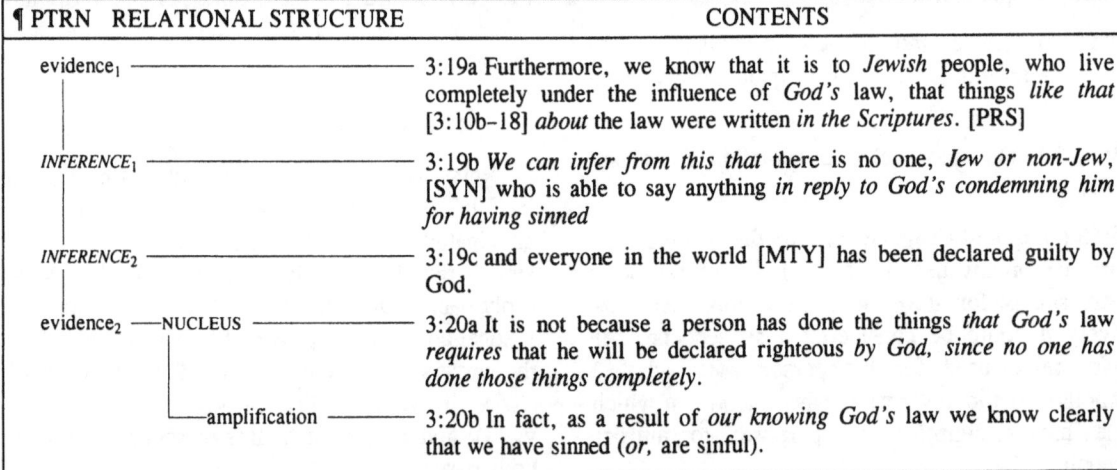

THEME: In summary, no one is able to object to God's condemnation; everyone has been declared guilty by God.

¶ PTRN RELATIONAL STRUCTURE	CONTENTS
evidence₁	3:19a Furthermore, we know that it is to *Jewish* people, who live completely under the influence of *God's* law, that things *like that* [3:10b-18] *about* the law were written *in the Scriptures*. [PRS]
INFERENCE₁	3:19b *We can infer from this that* there is no one, *Jew or non-Jew,* [SYN] who is able to say anything *in reply to God's condemning him for having sinned*
INFERENCE₂	3:19c and everyone in the world [MTY] has been declared guilty by God.
evidence₂ — NUCLEUS	3:20a It is not because a person has done the things *that God's* law *requires* that he will be declared righteous *by God, since no one has done those things completely*.
— amplification	3:20b In fact, as a result of *our knowing God's* law we know clearly that we have sinned (*or,* are sinful).

INTENT AND PARAGRAPH PATTERN

In 3:19-20, the declarative statements and their place within the total structure of the 1:18-3:20 subdivision cluster, which is an expository unit, make it clear that this too is an expository unit. The relationship between the major units of the paragraph is of a causality type of grounds-conclusion, and so the paragraph is of the *evidence-INFERENCE* subtype. Though it is obvious that 19a is referring to the Jews, the use of πᾶν 'every' in 19b shows that 19b refers to the condemnation of everyone, both Jew and Gentile. The final proof that the Jews are all guilty completes the proof that all mankind is guilty. A similar declaration follows immediately in 19c. Verse 20 gives a second *evidence* for these *INFERENCES*.

NOTES

3:19a Furthermore The word δέ here indicates a further point in Paul's argument. Some consider that Paul is here answering an anticipated objection to what was just stated; that is, some might say that these Scriptures just cited do not refer to the Jews but to Gentiles (cf. Erdman, Morris, Nygren). But if this had been Paul's intent, he would no doubt have introduced it with a question as elsewhere in the epistle. The words 'things like that' are supplied in the display to make it clear that, in making this statement, Paul is referring to the Scriptures just cited.

it is to *Jewish* people, who live completely under the influence of *God's* law The phrase τοῖς ἐν τῷ νόμῳ 'to those in the law' (the Jews, according to the great majority of commentators) is prominent by virtue of forefronting. This is indicated in the display by the cleft construction.

The phrase ἐν τῷ νόμῳ 'in the law' is somewhat similar to 'under the law' (cf. 6:14-15), and several versions (RSV, JBP, TEV, NIV, KJV) render it "under the law." But the sense here is more 'directed by', without the component of compulsion to obey that is signaled by ὑπὸ νόμον 'under law'.

things *like that* The GNT has ὅσα 'whatever things', but in the context the reference is clearly to the type of thing Paul has just cited from the OT.

about* the law were written *in the Scriptures The expression ὁ νόμος λέγει 'the law says' is a personification of the law, since the law and the written Scriptures cannot literally *speak* (see the note on 2:18c). The display does not supply an agent for the passive 'were written' because no agent is in focus here. In languages that lack a passive construction the translator should use whatever device is most natural.

3:19b there is no one, *Jew or non-Jew*, who is able to say anything The phrase πᾶν στόμα 'every mouth' precedes the verb and is thereby prominent. This emphasizes the universality of guilt before God. The word 'every' is a thematic motif throughout the epistle; in this summary paragraph it signifies specifically both Jews and non-Jews (so Hodge, Vine, Morris).

The words 'we know that' at the beginning of v. 19 introduce something which is known and believed by all concerned. If ἵνα were taken as introducing purpose (as some commentators take it), it would mean that the whole means-purpose construction (19a–b) would be something that everyone would subscribe to, but it is very difficult to see how the Jews would accept such a thought. Although ἵνα usually indicates purpose, it sometimes signals result. That is clearly the sense here. Paul has covered the guilt of the non-Jews in chapter 1, and in 3:19a he has shown the Jews that they are certainly included in the quotations stating universal guilt. Therefore πᾶν στόμα is without doubt to be taken as signaling 'Jews and non-Jews'.

The text has 'mouth', which is either a synecdoche meaning 'people' or a metonymy meaning the ability to speak. More specifically, the sense here is 'will be unable to say anything to God in their own defense'. REB has "no one may have anything to say in self-defence"; NCV, "This stops all excuses."

3:19c and The conjunction καί is considered to introduce a second *INFERENCE*. The first is that no one can say anything in his own defense; the second, that everyone is condemned and liable to judgment.

everyone in the world The word κόσμος 'world' is a metonymy signifying the people in the world.

3:20a It is not because a person has done the things *that God's* **law** *requires* The Greek is ἐξ ἔργων νόμου, literally 'from/by works of law'. Works are the things people do. The genitive 'of the law' needs an event to be supplied to convey its sense clearly, hence 'requires', as in the TEV. This phrase, being forefronted in the Greek, is prominent, hence the cleft construction in the display.

since no one has done those things completely There is a problem here in that 2:13 states that 'the doers of the law will be justified' whereas 3:20 says 'no one will be justified by keeping the law'. These statements seem contradictory. But Paul is stating a syllogism which might be summarized as follows:

Major premise: All who keep the law completely will be justified.
Minor premise: No one keeps the law completely.
Conclusion: No one will be justified.

The proposition in the display states the minor premise succinctly. Essentially it sums up what Paul already said in detail in 2:12–3:18.

3:20b In fact The conjunction γάρ usually signals reason or grounds, but here the proposition coheres much better as introducing an amplification for what precedes it.

as a result of *our knowing God's* **law** The phrase διὰ νόμου 'through/by the law' is a shortened form expressing a reason. The event 'our knowing' is implied. Many English translations personify 'law' here; for example, CEV has "All the law does is point out our sins."

BOUNDARIES AND COHERENCE

Lexical coherence in 3:19–20 is provided by four occurrences of νόμος 'law' and two of πᾶς 'all'. The boundary at 3:21 has already been discussed under the 1:18–3:20 unit. (See also the discussion of boundaries under 2:1–3:18.)

PROMINENCE AND THEME

The theme statement for the 3:19–20 paragraph is drawn from the two *INFERENCES* since they are naturally prominent.

DIVISION CLUSTER CONSTITUENT 3:21–26
(Expository Paragraph: Major principle of 1:16–11:36)

THEME: *Now God declares righteous everyone, Jew or non-Jew, who trusts in what Jesus Christ has done for them. God presented Christ as the one who would atone for sins by shedding his blood on the cross.*

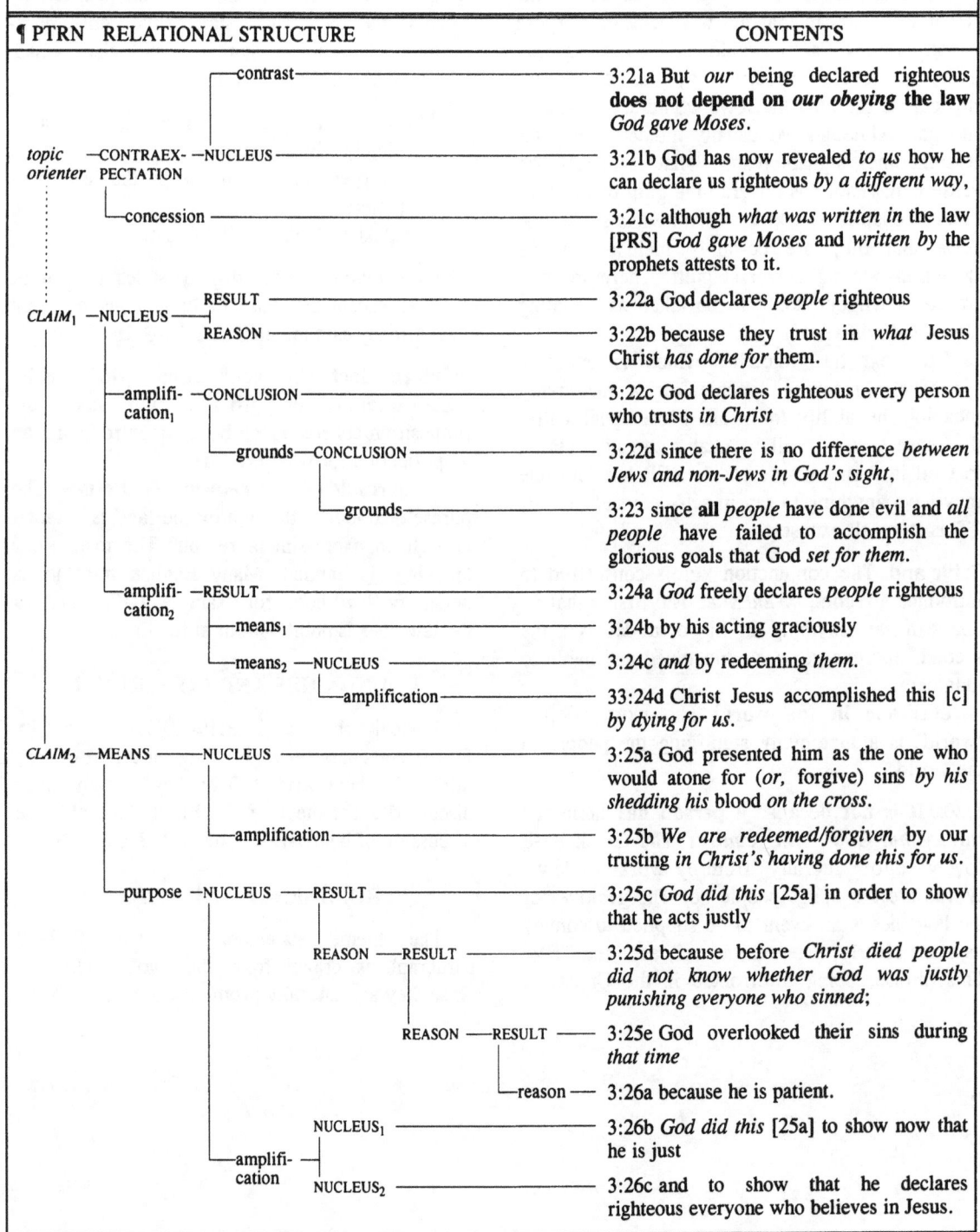

INTENT AND PARAGRAPH PATTERN

The 3:21-26 paragraph serves as the *MAJOR PRINCIPLE* of 1:16-11:36 (the expository section of the book) and is the central unit to which nearly all the first eleven chapters relate. The unit consists of two *CLAIMS*. It does not fit the usual pattern in which a *justification* supports a *CLAIM* because the *MAJOR PRINCIPLE* is itself supported by much of what follows, especially the discussion of Abraham in 4:1-25.

NOTES

3:21a *our* being declared righteous does not depend on *our obeying* the law *God gave Moses* A few commentators have tried to connect the phrase χωρὶς νόμου 'without law' with the verb 'has been manifested'; but if it were so connected, it would surely be closer to that verb. This phrase should be recognized as a shortened form of a means clause with a verb such as 'obey/keep' implicit, as in CEV's "and it isn't by obeying the Law of Moses." The majority of commentators are correct in connecting it with 'righteousness of God'. First person plural pronouns were needed in this paragraph to satisfy case frames. Translators could use 'people' and third person plural pronouns instead.

The phrase 'without law' is prominent by virtue of being forefronted; but since this phrase has been expanded to a full sentence in the display, it is hard to show this prominence other than by bold type.

3:21b now Commentators are somewhat divided as to whether the word νυνί 'now' (the first word in v. 21) has temporal or logical force. In view of the temporal component of the verb πεφανέρωται 'has been manifested' and the fact that in this paragraph Paul is presenting a whole new way of justification which contrasts with that of the law under the previous dispensation, there seems no reason to disagree with the majority of commentators who opt for the temporal sense here.

has revealed *to us* The perfect form of the verb πεφανέρωται 'has been manifested' indicates an action completed in the past but with continuing results in the present.

how he can declare us righteous This is the second of many occurrences in Romans of δικαιοσύνη 'righteousness' or δικαιοσύνη θεοῦ 'righteousness of God'. Many biblical scholars in previous centuries concluded that the phrase was referring to an attribute of God. But this is untenable, because, as Haldane notes (p. 130), "in what possible sense can it be said that God's righteousness or justice (as an essential attribute) is by faith in Christ?" It is then clear that the words express a genitive of source. Many have expounded on the notion that to Paul it does not mean 'made righteous by God', but rather 'be declared righteous' (see the note on 2:13). To translate in this way, however, may still fail to avoid the wrong meaning that 'God declares that we really are righteous' or 'God declares us innocent' (i.e., that we never did anything deserving punishment). To convey the idea that 'God declares us to be what we really are not' many translators find that the rendering 'God declares that our guilt (for sin) no longer exists' or 'God declares us freed from the guilt of sin' is the most satisfactory way of expressing justification.

by a different way These words are supplied to express the contrast indicated by χωρὶς νόμου 'without law' and the new way of righteousness to be presented in v. 22 (cf. LB).

3:21c although The present participle μαρτυρουμένη 'being witnessed' is taken as expressing a concession relation, as several modern versions bring out (RSV, JBP, REB, LB, C. B. Williams). This point is not discussed in the major commentaries, however.

what was written *in* the law *God gave Moses* The words in italics remove the personification of 'law' and specify what law Paul was referring to.

and *written by* the prophets The phrase τοῦ νόμου καὶ τῶν προφητῶν 'the law and the prophets' is used several times in the NT to refer to the two parts of the OT. LB renders it as "the Scriptures." If possible, it should be rendered as one phrase.

3:22a God declares *people* righteous In this paragraph there are a number of abstract nouns such as δικαιοσύνη 'righteousness'. Expressing them as full clauses requires the subjects and objects of the verbs to be supplied. In vv. 22-23 third person plural pronouns have been supplied, but in some languages it will be necessary to use first person plural pronouns.

3:22b because they trust in *what* Jesus Christ has done *for* them The Greek is διὰ πίστεως Ἰησοῦ Χριστοῦ 'through faith of Jesus Christ'. Some have taken the genitive as subjective, meaning 'the faithfulness of Jesus Christ'.

Though that is possible, the thrust of this whole section is to explicate the Scripture quoted in Rom. 1:17b, 'Those *who are declared* righteous *by me* because they trust *in me* shall live forever'. This, coupled with the occurrence of this same genitive construction in Gal. 2:16, where it is equated with 'believed in Christ Jesus', points to an objective genitive, as held by the great majority of commentators. Similar uses of this construction involving πίστις refer to Christ as the goal of faith (see Gal. 2:20, 3:22; Eph. 3:12; Phil. 3:9).

'Trusting in Jesus Christ' is expanded to 'trust in what Jesus Christ has done for them' because in many languages the verb 'believe' or 'trust in' requires a clause as its goal, and because believing in a person is a broad concept—even the demons believe in Jesus.

3:22c every person The fourth edition GNT has εἰς πάντας 'unto all' and lists no variants, but the Textus Receptus has an additional phrase καὶ ἐπὶ πάντας 'and upon all'. This seems to be a conflation of two readings: a couple of minor witnesses have only 'upon all'.

3:22d no difference *between Jews and non-Jews in God's sight* The clause 'there is no distinction' raises two questions: Between whom is the distinction, and distinction as to what? The context shows that the distinction is between Jews and Gentiles (JB has "Jew and pagan alike"). As to the second question, some commentators say the distinction is in respect to sin, and some say it is in the method of salvation. At least one (Shedd) suggests it is both, and he is probably right. The display attempts to preserve the ambiguity.

3:23 all The word πάντες 'all' occurs before the verb, emphasizing it. This emphasis is conveyed by bold type in the display.

have done evil The main problem here is the force of the aorist tense of the verb ἥμαρτον 'sinned'. Robertson calls this a gnomic or timeless aorist, expressive of what is true generally or at any time. Burton (p. 28) has an excellent treatment of the word:

> In Rom. 3:23, ἥμαρτον is evidently intended to sum up the aggregate of the evil deeds of men, of which the Apostle has been speaking in the preceding paragraphs (1:18– 3:20): It is therefore a collective historical aorist.... It must therefore be expressed in English by the perfect tense.... From the point of view from which the Apostle is speaking, the sin of each offender is simply a past fact, and the sin of all a series or aggregate of facts together constituting a past fact.

have failed to accomplish the glorious goals that God *set for them* The Greek is ὑστεροῦνται τῆς δόξης τοῦ θεοῦ, literally 'they come short of the glory of God'. There are about as many interpretations of this clause as there are commentators. Since the noun 'glory' very frequently represents what is semantically an attribute ('glorious'), and since the original sense of the verb here is 'to miss, fail to reach', the rendering in the display seems at least as good as any other.

3:24a *God* freely declares *people* righteous The problem of the Greek participle δικαιούμενοι 'being justified' here is that it seems to refer to πάντες 'all' in 23a, suggesting universalism: all have sinned, and all are declared righteous. The best solution seems to relate the participle to τοὺς πιστεύοντας 'those who believe' in 22b (so Sanday and Headlam, Murray, Michel, Denney) or else follow Morris and others who say that the meaning is that whoever is declared righteous is declared righteous this way. Either way, the participle is taken as introducing a somewhat parenthetical amplification of what precedes.

3:24b by his acting graciously The noun 'grace' in τῇ αὐτοῦ χάριτι 'by the of him grace' represents an event (see the note on 1:7d). The word 'of him' is in the emphatic position; it seems to point to the contrast between God's grace and man's works.

3:24c–d *and* There is no conjunction here in the Greek. But since both the dative clause of 24b and the διά 'through' construction of 24c seem semantically to represent coordinate means propositions, they are joined with 'and'.

by redeeming *them*. Christ Jesus accomplished this *by dying for them* The Greek is διὰ τῆς ἀπολυτρώσεως τῆς ἐν Χριστῷ Ἰησοῦ 'through the redemption which in Christ Jesus'. The majority of commentators take 'in' as expressing means, as done here; there appears to be no good reason to do otherwise. Since a means proposition requires a full clause, and since the τῆς construction following ἀπολυτρώσεως 'redemption' transfers to English as a relative construction (here an amplification), 24d is made a full sentence on its own.

The noun ἀπολύτρωσις 'redemption' comes from the verb ἀπολυτρόω, meaning to redeem someone by paying a price or to let someone go free on receiving a payment. The question is whether payment is in focus here or not. The use of the cognate words (λύτρον in Mark 10:45 and Matt. 20:28; ἀντίλυτρον in 1 Tim. 2:6; and λυτρόω in Tit. 2:14 and 1 Pet. 1:18) definitely conveys the notion of a ransom paid. But it is probably wise, following Sanday and Headlam, to note that it is pressing the metaphor too far to ask who paid the ransom and to whom.

3:25a God presented him The verb in the clause ὃν προέθετο ὁ θεός 'whom God set forth' means 'exhibited'. Käsemann renders it as "Him God has publicly set forth." Michel also emphasizes the public aspect. But that literal sense seems inappropriate here. The reason for using 'presented' in the display is to avoid the 'spectacle' connotation. Perhaps 'appointed' (JBP) or even 'sent' (CEV) would carry much of the meaning, but these words lack the open-to-the-public component of the verb which is reinforced by the two occurrences of the word ἔνδειξις 'showing forth' in vv. 25-26. It is also supported by the fact that προτίθεμαι 'set forth' was often used to express the exhibition of dead bodies.

the one who would atone for (*or*, forgive) sins The word ἱλαστήριον, whose meaning is given as "*that which expiates* or *propitiates*" (BAGD, p. 375) is used in the LXX in Exodus and Leviticus in reference to the cover, or lid, of the chest that contained the tablets inscribed with the Ten Commandments. On this lid, blood would be sprinkled to atone for the sins of the Israelites. The literal sense is obviously not meant here, though that is the meaning in Heb. 9:5 (the only other occurrence of the word in the NT). However, several of the concepts associated with what took place in the tabernacle (blood, God's glory, anger against sin) are indeed in this context as well.

Some commentators take ἱλαστήριον as meaning 'the place at which propitiation was made' or 'means of propitiation', even though this appears not to be supported by its use elsewhere. However, even those who insist on a literal OT sense here need to see the double metonymy: a place (the cover) standing for the event which occurred there (making atonement for sins by sprinkling blood), and then the event standing for the person who was the means by which the event was accomplished. NEB renders the phrase "a way to forgive sin"; REB, as "the means of expiating sin." For languages in which there is no word for 'atone for', it may be necessary to use 'forgive' (supplied as an alternative in the display).

There is a lot of discussion by commentators as to whether ἱλαστήριον refers to propitiation or expiation. *Webster's New Twentieth Century Dictionary* defines *expiate* (p. 645) as "to atone for; to make amends or reparation for (wrongdoing or guilt); to pay the penalty of," and *propitiate* (p. 1443) as "to cause to become favorably inclined; to win or regain the good will of; to appease or conciliate." Much of the discussion of this term by commentators is probably theologically motivated and not very helpful to translators. From the viewpoint of semantic theory, the question boils down to which of the following possibilities is the relationship between the concept of making atonement and the concept of appeasing God:

```
MEANS ─────────── he would atone for sin
  └─purpose─────── to appease God's anger

RESULT ─────────── he would appease God's anger
  └─means───────── by atoning for sin
```

For the display it is assumed MEANS-purpose is correct (i.e., atonement is more in focus than propitiation), but the atonement's implied purpose is not considered thematic enough to be supplied in italics in the display. Thomson and Davidson say,

> The idea is not that of conciliation of an angry God by sinful humanity, but of expiation of sin by a merciful God through the atoning death of his Son. It does not necessarily exclude, however, the reality of righteous wrath because of sin. Christ is therefore a means of satisfaction for sin, this expiation being effected by the death of Jesus.

by his shedding his* blood *on the cross The Greek is διὰ πίστεως ἐν τῷ αὐτοῦ αἵματι 'through faith in the of him blood'. Some have objected that Paul never refers elsewhere to faith in an object. But blood here is a metonymy standing for the event associated with it. This event is supplied in the display in italics. (NCV seems alone in making this event explicit with its rendering "the blood of Jesus' death.")

3:25b *We are redeemed/forgiven* There is a semantic gap between 'propitiation' and 'through faith' immediately following it. Most commentators and versions take 'through faith' as somewhat parenthetical. JBP joins the concepts of propitiation and blood: "a propitiation accomplished by the shedding of his blood," followed by the addition of "to be received and made effective in ourselves by faith." NEB's treatment is similar: "the means of expiating sin by his sacrificial death, effective through faith." However, while 'propitiation' would collocate well with 'blood', it would be redundant. Moreover, the very separation of 'propitiation' and 'by his blood' argues conclusively against their being taken together, while the similarity of 'through faith in his blood' and 'through faith in Jesus Christ' in v. 22 argues for putting these two together. Hodge, Cranfield, Barrett, Morris, and others suggest that words such as 'which is received, appropriated, accepted' be supplied (see also RSV, JBP, REB). These are fine, except that they make an abstract noun, 'propitiation' or 'expiation', the object of the supplied verb. To avoid this, 25b is made an amplification in the display and 'are redeemed/forgiven' is supplied. (Either word, 'redeemed' or 'forgiven', is contextually appropriate.) It can be argued that the agent of 'redeemed/forgiven' is God, and the agent of 'trusting' is 'we', which makes it hard to know how to translate this in languages that lack a passive. Perhaps it could be rendered 'God redeems us because we trust in Christ'.

by our trusting *in Christ's having done this for us* Though we are called to put faith in Christ, it is specifically by putting our trust in what Christ accomplished when he shed his blood that we are saved. That is exactly what Paul is stating here. An alternative to the rendering in the display is 'by trusting in *what he accomplished when he shed* his blood *when he died*'. (Paul uses 'blood' as a metonymy also in Eph. 1:7 ['redemption through his blood'] and Rom. 5:9 ['justified through his blood'].)

3:25c in order to show that The preposition εἰς can signify either purpose or result, but it is taken as purpose here because the restatement of the same concept in 26b is introduced by πρός, which clearly indicates purpose.

he acts justly The phrase here, τῆς δικαιοσύνης αὐτοῦ 'his righteousness', is like that in v. 21, but the majority of commentators take it as referring to an attribute of God, his justice or fairness, not the way he declares people righteous. The interpretation is forced by what Paul mentions in the rest of the verse. Morris explains Paul's argument thus:

> When God does not punish the sinner, that might well show him to be merciful or loving. But just? It would mean that God condones evil. Justice demands that the guilty be punished just as it demands that the innocent go free. So God might be accused of being unjust. Not any more, says Paul.

3:25d There is something implied here that is not supplied in the display, namely that God's justice demands that sin be punished. (Divine retribution for sin had not been made before Christ himself was punished in our place.) This whole proposition thus functions simultaneously as the implied statement for which 25e–26a supplies the reason and the implied reason for 25c.

3:25e God overlooked The preposition διά occurs here with a causal sense: 'because God overlooked'. The great majority of commentators and versions render it this way, and the causal sense coheres well relationally. However, 'because' is omitted here in the interests of a smooth reading. A succession of three *because*'s (in 25d, 25e, 26a) would not read well in English.

The noun πάρεσις, here rendered 'overlooked', expresses an event, 'let pass, pass by, disregard, ignore'.

3:26a because he is patient The Greek is ἐν τῇ ἀνοχῇ τοῦ θεοῦ 'in the forbearance of God'. The preposition could be temporal or causal. But since the temporal sense has already been expressed in the word προγεγονότων 'having occurred previously', in 25d–e, and since ἀνοχῇ is really a moral attribute, the temporal idea is inappropriate here and thus the causal sense preferred instead.

3:26b The preposition πρός 'for' is taken as introducing a purpose relation.

he is just The sense of δίκαιος here is more 'just' than 'righteous'; it refers to God as judge acting according to strict justice. In former times God appeared neither just nor justifying: Paul declares that now God shows he is both.

3:26c he declares righteous everyone who believes in Jesus The expression τὸν ἐκ πίστεως Ἰησοῦ 'the one out of faith in Jesus' is a strange and rare construction in the NT and also extrabiblically. But, as Morris notes, "The meaning of the expression here does not seem to be in doubt": the ἐκ signals 'characterized by'. The singular form has a generic sense; hence it is rendered 'everyone who' in the display. As previously, it may be necessary in some translations to spell out 'faith' as 'trusts in what Christ has done' (see the note on 22b).

There are several textual variants of Ἰησοῦ 'Jesus', but none with very strong manuscript support. (The word 'Christ' was obviously added by some copyist.)

BOUNDARIES AND COHERENCE

There is a good deal of disagreement among commentators as to the boundaries between 3:21 and 11:36. Some (e.g., Morris, Bruce 1985, Vine, Dunn, Harrison) suggest a unit 3:21- 5:21, its theme being justification. Some (Dodd, Nygren, Shedd) suggest 3:21-4:25 as a unit with that same theme, and 5:1-21 as a unit on the effects of justification. The vast majority of commentators, however, take 3:21-31 as a unit, with its theme being justification by faith. The weakness of all of these is the failure to recognize that everything from 3:27 to 11:36 (including even the paean of praise in 11:33-36) falls under the category of inferences drawn from, or illustrations of, the doctrine of justification by faith. Many of these succeeding units begin with οὖν or ἄρα (e.g., at 3:27, 4:1, 5:1, 6:1, 8:1), both of which can mean 'therefore'. But in each of these units it is not the illustration or inference which is more important; all these units hinge on and grow out of 3:21-26. In other words, the view maintained in this analysis is that Paul in this epistle states his *MAJOR PRINCIPLE* (3:21-26) and then uses one of these two conjunctions to introduce an inference that follows from it (or, in one case, exemplary evidence of it).

The coherence of 3:21-26 is shown by forms of the noun δικαιοσύνη 'righteousness' (in 21, 22, 25, and 26) and of the verb δικαιόω 'declare righteous' (in 24 and 26) and forms of πίστις 'faith' (in 22, 25, and 26).

The boundary between the 3:21-26 unit and the next is marked at v. 27 by οὖν 'therefore' and a rhetorical question.

PROMINENCE AND THEME

The theme of 3:21-26 is drawn from the 22a-b NUCLEUS of the first *CLAIM* plus the second *CLAIM*'s most prominent NUCLEUS, 25a. The phrase εἰς πάντας τοὺς πιστεύοντας 'unto all those who believe' is thematic since the word πάντας recurs throughout the first three chapters. The same idea is found in the notion 'there is no difference', which is rendered fully as 'there is no difference between Jews and non-Jews in God's sight'. The phrase 'Jews and non-Jews' recurs throughout the first three chapters (1:16; 2:10; 3:29) and is a critical part of the thrust of the whole epistle. For this reason the words 'everyone' and 'Jew or non-Jew' are included in the theme statement even though they do not occur in the more naturally prominent NUCLEUS (22a-b), but in the amplification in 22c-d.

DIVISION CLUSTER CONSTITUENT 3:27-31
(Expository Paragraph: Inferences drawn from 3:21-26)

THEME: Therefore we are prevented from boasting about being justified by obeying the Mosaic law. And God will accept non-Jews too on the same basis. And by saying that people are declared righteous by their trusting in Christ, we actually confirm, not nullify, the Mosaic law.

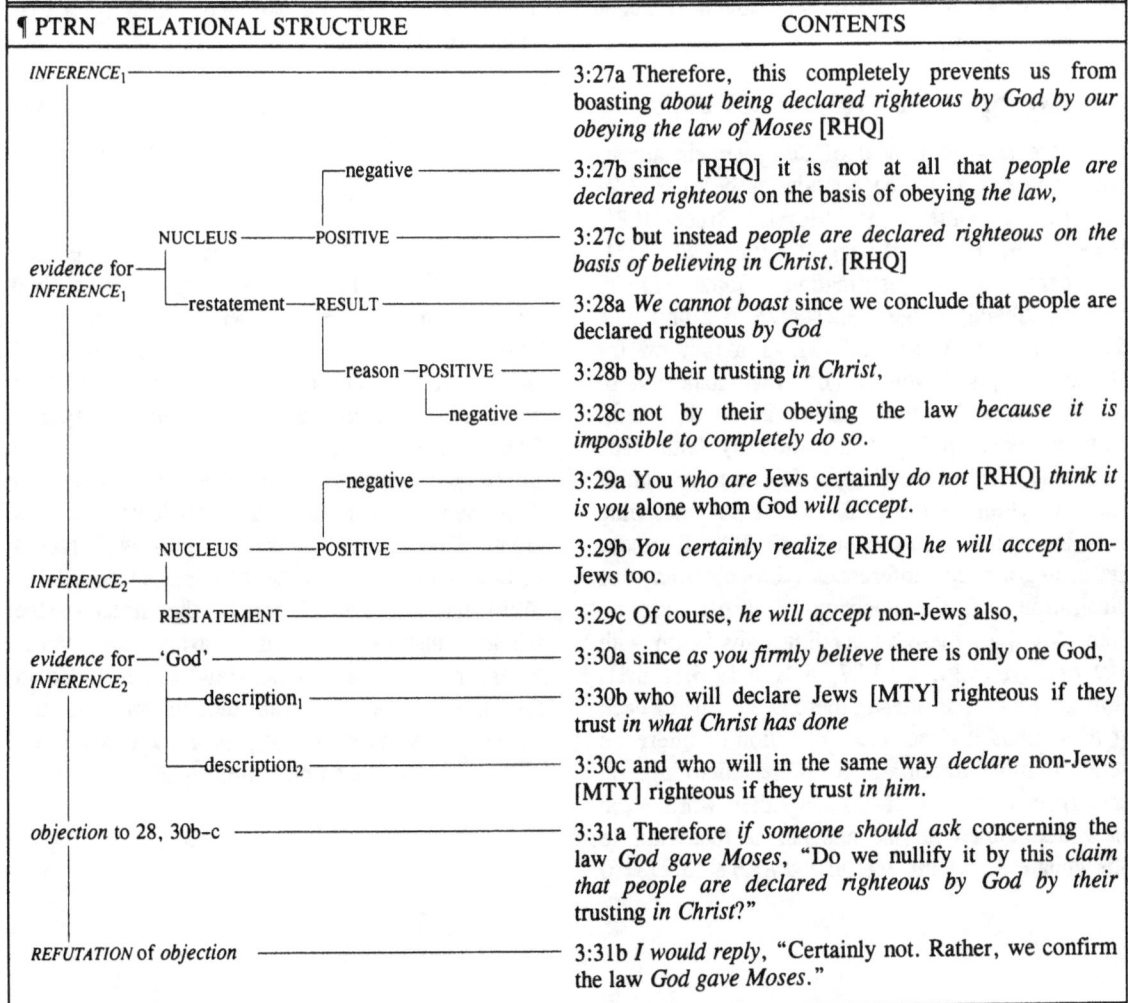

INTENT AND PARAGRAPH PATTERN

In the 3:27-31 paragraph Paul anticipates possible queries regarding his 3:21-26 exposition of the doctrine of justification by faith. (In later chapters Paul anticipates several more such possible queries or objections.) There are two INFERENCES, each with its own *evidence*, in this expository paragaph. The paragraph ends with an anticipated *objection* introduced by οὖν 'therefore' (v. 31a). This objection is to statements in 28 and 30b-c on the validity of faith over law for justification. This *objection* is refuted in 31b. The whole paragraph continues to build the case for justification by faith.

NOTES

3:27 The two rhetorical questions in 27a and 27b function both to introduce a new paragraph and to emphasize the declarative statements, hence the words 'completely' and 'at all' in the display.

3:27a boasting The word καύχησις 'boasting' implies a referent or content of the boasting; therefore 'about being declared righteous by God' is supplied. LB makes it specific: "Then what can we boast about doing to earn our salvation?" To avoid wrong meaning (e.g., we could boast of our imputed righteousness), the implied means is supplied: 'by obeying the law'. An alternative is 'by our own efforts'.

3:27b it is not at all that *people are declared righteous* **on the basis of obeying** *the law* The questions διὰ ποίου νόμου; 'through what law?' and τῶν ἔργων; 'of works?' are very elliptical. They are combined in one proposition here. The sense of the word 'law' is 'system' or 'means'. But system or means of what? The answer is supplied from the context: 'of being declared righteous'. Thus 'law' is rendered 'basis'. 'Works' is specified as 'obeying the law'. CEV has "because we obeyed some law"; NEB, REB, TEV, and NIV are similar.

3:28a The display follows the GNT, which has γάρ 'since' with a B rating ("almost certain"), not οὖν 'therefore'. The former has better external evidence; moreover, principles of relational coherence require this proposition to be supportive of 27b-c and not vice versa.

3:28b trusting *in Christ* As has been pointed out previously, the abstract noun πίστις 'faith' expresses an event, which in turn requires a content of 'believing' or 'trusting' as its object. In some languages, a phrase such as 'in what Christ has done' may be needed.

3:28c *because it is impossible to completely do so* The reason why people are not justified by obeying the law is supplied to keep readers from getting a wrong meaning (cf. Gal. 2:16).

3:29a You *who are* **Jews** *certainly* **do not think** *it is you* **alone whom God** *will accept* The initial ἤ 'or' introduces the new argument and is also a means of introducing the rhetorical questions that force the Jews in his audience to consider his arguments carefully. The rhetorical questions have the effect of emphatic statements. The emphasis is conveyed by the use of 'certainly'.

The genitive construction Ἰουδαίων ὁ θεός 'of Jews God' requires some expression of the relation between God and the Jews. It is not possession. Either 'saves' (as in LB) or 'accepts' fits well. The forefronting of 'of Jews' conveys emphasis, hence the cleft construction in the display: 'it is you . . . whom'.

Paul is here bringing out an implication of monotheism: if there is only one God, he has to be the God who accepts Gentiles too. Thus 'you who are Jews' makes explicit that this whole paragraph (3:27-31) is aimed at the Jews in Rome. The force of the argument is made clear in the display by making the elliptical sentences of v. 29 into full sentences (29a, b, c).

3:30a since *as you firmly believe* **there is only one God** Paul is here appealing to their strong belief in monotheism, as alluded to by the conjunction εἴπερ 'since, indeed, if after all'. Hence the words 'as you firmly believe' are supplied.

3:30b, c Jews, non-Jews The terms περιτομή 'circumcision' and ἀκροβυστία 'uncircumcision' are metonymies standing for the people (Jews and non-Jews) with whom the event was associated. Paul uses these terms frequently (e.g., Rom. 4:9, 12a, 15:8). They are rendered nonfiguratively in several versions (e.g., LB, TEV, CEV, NCV), as also in the display.

3:31a-b *if someone should ask* **concerning the law** *God gave Moses, . . . I would reply* In the display it is made clear that this is a hypothetical question, and that Paul is answering it.

The word νόμον 'law' is forefronted in 31a and 31c as a feature of topicalization: Paul is reintroducing the subject of the Mosaic law and commenting about it. This topicalization is represented in the display by the phrase 'concerning the law God gave Moses'.

31a *that people are declared righteous by God by their* **trusting** *in Christ* The article in τῆς πίστεως 'the faith' is shorthand; the meaning of τῆς πίστεως is 'this statement about justification by faith' (so Barnes and Morris).

BOUNDARIES AND COHERENCE

The lexical coherence of the 3:27-31 paragraph derives from the recurring words νόμος 'law' (twice in 27, once in 28, and twice in 31) and πίστις 'faith' (once in 27 and 28, twice in 30, and once in 31). The series of six rhetorical questions with Paul's replies also lends coherence. That 4:1 starts a new unit is clear from the new topic, Abraham, reinforced by a rhetorical question introducing Abraham as an illustration of justification by faith.

PROMINENCE AND THEME

The theme of 3:27-31 is drawn from the two *INFERENCES*, their *evidences*, and the *objection-REFUTATION*.

DIVISION CLUSTER CONSTITUENT 4:1-25
(Expository Subdivision: Exemplary evidence of 3:21-26)

THEME: *(See the thematic outline in the Introduction.)*	
MACROSTRUCTURE	CONTENTS
CLAIM$_1$	4:1-8 We can draw conclusions from Abraham about how to be declared righteous. He could not boast about that because Scripture records that it was because he believed what God promised that he was declared righteous. This being declared righteous was a gift from God, not a reward.
CLAIM$_2$	4:9-12 This happiness of being declared righteous is also for the non-Jews; remember that it was before Abraham was circumcised, when he was still in effect a non-Jew, that he was declared righteous. He later received circumcision simply as a sign of his being declared righteous by faith, with the result that he became a spiritual father of all who believe in God as he did, whether they are circumcised or not.
restatement$_1$ of CLAIM$_1$ and CLAIM$_2$	4:13-17b It was because Abraham trusted in God that he was declared righteous by God and was promised many blessings by God. Therefore what God promised is guaranteed to all, both Jews and non-Jews, who believe as Abraham did.
restatement of CLAIM$_1$	4:17c-22 It was because Abraham confidently believed God's promise to give him many descendants when there was no basis for his hoping that this would happen that he was declared righteous by God.
restatement$_2$ of CLAIM$_1$ and CLAIM$_2$	4:23-25 The words about Abraham's being declared righteous by God were written also to assure us who believe in God, who would also be declared righteous.

INTENT AND MACROSTRUCTURE

Though the 4:1-25 unit does contain a number of rhetorical questions, they are not of the emotive type. Paul here is giving exemplary evidence from the life of Abraham regarding the validity of the concept of justification by faith. It comprises two CLAIMS (1-8 and 9-12) and a set of three *restatements* of one or both of these CLAIMS.

BOUNDARIES AND COHERENCE

Chapter 4 focuses on Abraham, which provides its coherence. Abraham's name is mentioned seven times, and there are many more pronominal references to him. In addition πίστις 'faith' occurs eight times (and none in chap. 5 except for a recapitulation in 5:1) and its verbal cognate πιστεύω 'believe' five times; the noun δικαιοσύνη 'righteousness' occurs eight times and its cognate δικαιόω 'declare righteous' twice. The verb λογίζομαι 'reckon' occurs eleven times in chapter 4 and not at all in chapter 5.

The boundary between this and the next unit is marked at 5:1 by οὖν 'therefore' and a summary clause 'since we have been justified by faith'.

PROMINENCE AND THEME

The theme of 4:1-25 is drawn from the themes of its constituent paragraphs. Part of the first sentence of the 4:9-12 theme is condensed, and the reason part of the second sentence is omitted since it is less thematic than the result. The first two sentences of the 4:13-17b paragraph are omitted because they are repetitions of parts already included.

SUBDIVISION CONSTITUENT 4:1–8
(Expository Paragraph: Claim₁ of 4:1–25)

THEME: We can draw conclusions from Abraham about how to be declared righteous. He could not boast about that because Scripture records that it was because he believed what God promised that he was declared righteous. This being declared righteous was a gift from God, not a reward.

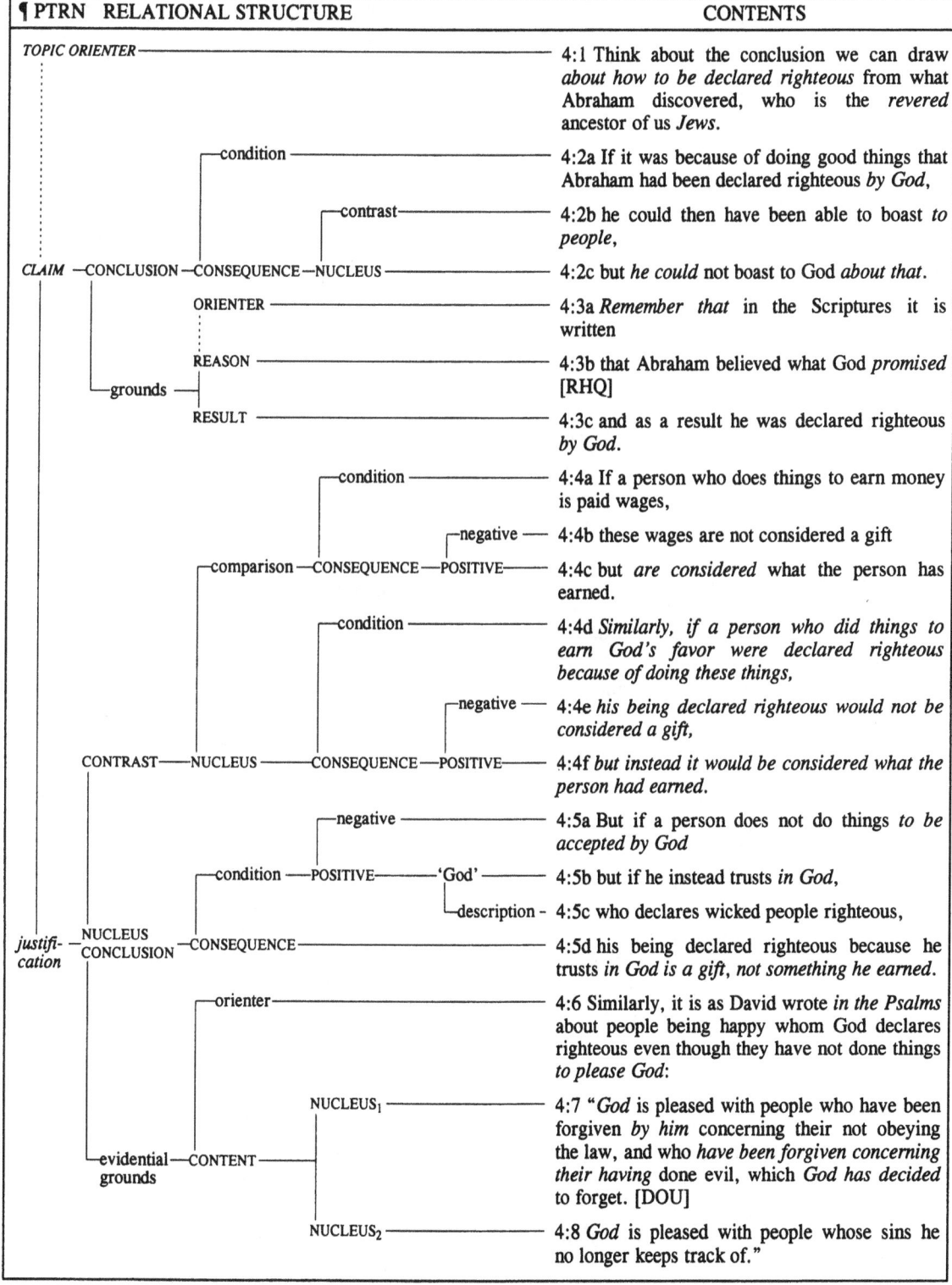

INTENT AND PARAGRAPH PATTERN

The absence of exhortations and first person singular references in the 4:1-8 paragraph is a clear indication that it is expository. The whole unit centers around Abraham, which provides its unity. The paragraph begins Paul's exposition of how the life of Abraham illustrates justification by faith, not works. First is a TOPIC ORIENTER to the effect that we can learn something about this topic by considering Abraham. Then there is a CLAIM in vv. 2-3 about Abraham's not being able to boast about his being declared righteous followed by a *justification* of this CLAIM in vv. 4-8.

NOTES

4:1 Think about... The rhetorical question 'What then shall we say?' is a means of introducing the 4:1-25 *exemplary evidence* that supports the 3:21-26 MAJOR PRINCIPLE. As previously noted, Paul uses οὖν to introduce major considerations relating to this principle. The rhetorical question calls the reader to give special attention to what follows. The scope of the conclusion the reader is to draw about Abraham is indicated by 'about how to be declared righteous', the topic of the whole chapter.

revered ancestor of us Jews The idea of 'revered' is connoted by the phrase 'our ancestor according to the flesh'; it is a clear implicature of Paul's argument. Thus it is supplied in the display.

There is a textual problem here that affects the understanding of the phrase κατὰ σάρκα 'according to the flesh'. Some manuscripts put 'Abraham our forefather' before the verb 'has found', leaving 'according to the flesh' to follow and relate to the verb. A couple of manuscripts omit the verb. But there is no reason that copyists would have added the verb at various places. So it must have been omitted accidentally due to the similarity of the preceding word. Those manuscripts that have 'Abraham our father' before the verb also have a word for 'father' that is different from the one in the GNT. The GNT has προπάτορα 'forefather', which occurs nowhere else in the NT. It appears that some copyist decided to use the more common πατήρ 'father' and for some reason move the verb as well. Semantically it makes much better sense to have 'our forefather' connected to 'according to the flesh' (i.e., 'human') than to the verb ('has found according to the flesh'). The phrase then means 'our human ancestor Abraham'; but since he was not the ancestor of the non-Jews to whom Paul was writing, the display renders the phrase more specifically, supplying 'Jews'.

4:2 There is a problem in relation to γάρ here and also in v. 3. Semantically, v. 2 does not seem to fit as the grounds of v. 1, whereas v. 3 does seem to fit as the grounds of v. 2. It is possible to consider v. 2 a comment brought to mind by the word 'boasting' in 3:27 (so Lenski), in which case v. 3 would be the evidential grounds for v. 1. However, if the rhetorical question in 4:1 is rendered as a statement functioning as a topic orienter, then the γάρ introducing v. 2 is most appropriately seen as following the rhetorical question and introducing the content of what they were to 'think about' (v. 1) regarding Abraham's justification.

4:2a because of doing good things The phrase ἐξ ἔργων 'by works' is an event that expresses a reason (cf. LB's "because of his good deeds" and TEV's "by the things he did"). The phrase is forefronted in Greek and is thereby prominent; in the display this prominence is conveyed by the cleft construction.

4:3a *Remember that* The rhetorical question here is to remind the readers of what was written in the Scriptures about Abraham in Gen. 15:6.

4:4-5 The interpretation given here rests on the recognition of the relationship between v. 4 and v. 5: v. 4 is an illustration; v. 5 applies the illustration to the spiritual realm. Note that a participle and a verb in v. 5 are exactly the same as a participle and a verb in v. 4 (ἐργαζομένῳ 'works' and λογίζεται 'is considered/reckoned'). Both v. 4 and v. 5 have contrastive negative and positive clauses: οὐ κατὰ χάριν 'not according to grace' and ἀλλὰ κατὰ ὀφείλημα 'but according to obligation' (in v. 4); τῷ μὴ ἐργαζομένῳ 'to him not working' and πιστεύοντι δέ 'but believing' (in v. 5). However, there are no κατά phrases in v. 5 corresponding with those in v. 4. Verse 4 *is* completely illustrative, but the point it illustrates is not stated. Verse 5 is not the point of v. 4; rather, it is a nonfigurative statement that contrasts with the implied topic of v. 4. Thus this topic is supplied in 4d-f. (LB recognizes the problem and states the point of the illustration but omits the illustrative part itself.) In v. 5 the phrase ἡ πίστις αὐτοῦ 'his faith' is grammatically the subject of the verb λογίζεται 'is considered'.

But God is the one who does the reckoning. Furthermore, the contrastive balance of these two verses demands that οὐ κατὰ ὀφείλημα ἀλλὰ κατὰ χάριν 'not according to debt but instead according to grace' be carried over (i.e., with the nouns switched in position) from v. 4. This implicature of the argument is therefore also supplied in italics in 5d. Hodge says, "If Adam had remained faithful and rendered perfect obedience, the promised reward would have been due him as a matter of justice; the withholding of it would have been an act of injustice." The phrase ἡ πίστις αὐτοῦ εἰς δικαιοσύνην 'his faith unto righteousness' is the subject of the verb λογίζεται 'is considered' and should not be split up. Since in this context it is righteousness that is the gift, not faith, and since in semantic relationships result is more prominent than reason, the rendering in the display is 'his being declared to be righteous (result) because he trusts in God (reason)'.

The word 'work' in these verses is used with two different senses: in the illustration it is literal; in its second occurrence it refers to performing religious acts to gain favor with God. The parallelism in the two verses hinges on this play on words. Hence, in an effort to maintain some of the word play, the first occurrence is rendered 'does things to earn money' and the second 'does things to be accepted by God'.

The indirect object phrase in the first clause of each of these verses is forefronted, which is a feature of topicalization.

4:6 David wrote *in the Psalms* Paul would expect his readers to identify David as the Psalmist, King David. LB has "King David spoke of this." CEV identifies the writings as "In the Scriptures."

being happy The word μακαρισμός 'blessing' here (and in v. 9) is not the same as the related μακάριος in vv. 7-8 or μακαριότης, the usual word for blessedness. Rather, the word here refers more to the happiness and joy of a person who is blessed by God. Several versions render it "happiness" (e.g., REB, TEV, LB).

God In the Greek the word 'God' is emphasized by occurring before the verb.

even though they have not done things *to please God* In the phrase χωρὶς ἔργων 'without works' the implied purpose of 'works' is 'to gain God's favor'. Therefore 'to please God' is supplied in the display.

4:7 *God* **is pleased with** It is difficult to render μακάριος satisfactorily. It means 'in a state resulting from being blessed by God', but how to describe that state? It clearly does not mean 'happy'. (The same word occurs in the Beatitudes of Matt. 5:3-11 of situations that are not causes of happiness.) BAGD (p. 486) give 'fortunate' as one of the primary meanings, but in English this carries too much a sense of good luck. Also, a proper understanding of the word is affected by whether God is in focus or not. Does the word mean simply a state that the righteous experience, or how God feels toward them? It is probably true that God is really not in focus here, but for the reasons just stated it is rendered as 'God is pleased with' in the two places in Romans where Paul uses the word (cf. 14:22). In languages where an appropriate term not mentioning God is available, that would probably be preferable.

concerning their having **done evil, which** *God* **has decided to forget** The verb ἐπεκαλύφθησαν 'covered' is used here in a figurative sense. It means 'to have been put out of sight', hence 'forgotten' (so CEV). There is very little difference in meaning between 'lawlessnesses were forgiven', 'sins were covered over', and (in v. 8) 'sins are not reckoned'. These three expressions form a triplet (i.e., three synonyms). The three are kept in the display due to the poetic nature of the OT passage being quoted in vv. 7-8 (from Psa. 32:1-2). In translating them as three separate expressions, the translator should make certain not to convey the sense that three different concepts are in view. The first two, especially, refer to the same thing.

4:8 no longer keeps track of It is recognized that this is a somewhat idiomatic expression, but it seems the best available, and LB's "no longer counted against him" is also very good.

BOUNDARIES AND COHERENCE

The opening of the 4:1-8 unit is marked by a rhetorical question and the first mention of Abraham. This paragraph comprises a TOPIC ORIENTER in v. 1 inviting consideration of Abraham, a CLAIM in vv. 2-3 about Abraham not being entitled to boast about his having been declared righteous, and the *justification* for this CLAIM in vv. 4-8 to the effect that justification is a gift, not a reward.

In addition to the lexical coherence found throughout chapter 4, coherence in this paragraph is also achieved by three occurrences of the word μακάριος 'blessed' or μακαρισμός 'blessedness' (the word occurs in v. 9, but only in a recapitulation leading to the new topic) and two of the noun ἔργον 'work' and two of the verb ἐργάζομαι 'work'. (Neither ἔργον nor ἐργάζομαι is found in the paragraph that follows.)

The boundary of the next paragraph, which starts at 4:9, is marked by a rhetorical question regarding the time of Abraham's circumcision. That is followed by a discussion concerning circumcision, which is not in focus in 4:1-8.

PROMINENCE AND THEME

The *TOPIC ORIENTER* in 4:1 is prominent by virtue of its being in the form of a rhetorical question; therefore much of it is included in the 4:1-8 theme. All of 4:3 is also included, the ORIENTER because of its prominence in being a rhetorical question, and the REASON and RESULT propositions because they are both essential to the argument and are joined by καί, indicating equivalence (one is not subordinate to the other). A condensation of the most naturally prominent proposition of the 5d NUCLEUS of the *justification* is also included in the theme.

ROMANS 4:9–12

SUBDIVISION CONSTITUENT 4:9–12
(Expository Paragraph: Claim₂ of 4:1–25)

THEME: *This happiness of being declared righteous is also for the non-Jews; remember that it was before Abraham was circumcised, when he was still in effect a non-Jew, that he was declared righteous. He later received circumcision simply as a sign of his being declared righteous by faith, with the result that he became a spiritual father of all who believe in God as he did, whether they are circumcised or not.*

¶ PTRN   RELATIONAL STRUCTURE   CONTENTS

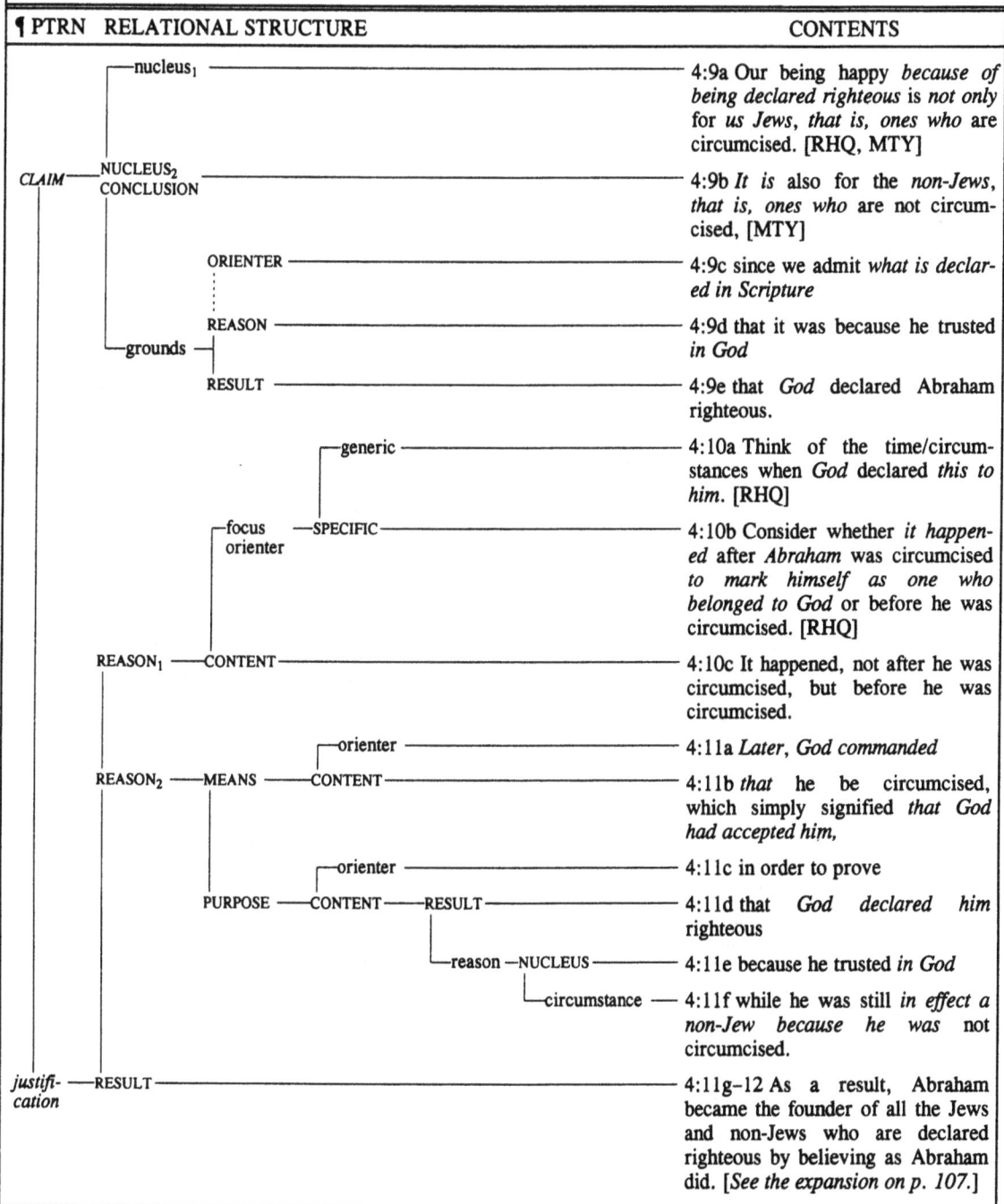

CLAIM
—nucleus₁ — 4:9a Our being happy *because of being declared righteous* is *not only* for *us Jews, that is, ones who* are circumcised. [RHQ, MTY]

NUCLEUS₂ CONCLUSION — 4:9b *It is also* for the *non-Jews, that is, ones who* are not circumcised, [MTY]

grounds
 ORIENTER — 4:9c since we admit *what is declared in Scripture*
 REASON — 4:9d that it was because he trusted *in God*
 RESULT — 4:9e that *God* declared Abraham righteous.

REASON₁ —CONTENT
 focus orienter
  generic — 4:10a Think of the time/circumstances when *God* declared *this* to him. [RHQ]
  SPECIFIC — 4:10b Consider whether *it happened* after Abraham was circumcised *to mark himself as one who belonged to God* or before he was circumcised. [RHQ]
 CONTENT — 4:10c It happened, not after he was circumcised, but before he was circumcised.

REASON₂ —MEANS
 orienter — 4:11a *Later, God* commanded
 CONTENT — 4:11b *that* he be circumcised, which simply signified *that God had accepted him,*

PURPOSE —CONTENT
 orienter — 4:11c in order to prove
 RESULT — 4:11d that *God* declared *him* righteous
 reason —NUCLEUS — 4:11e because he trusted *in God*
  circumstance — 4:11f while he was still *in effect a non-Jew because he was* not circumcised.

justification —RESULT — 4:11g–12 As a result, Abraham became the founder of all the Jews and non-Jews who are declared righteous by believing as Abraham did. [See the expansion on p. 107.]

INTENT AND PARAGRAPH PATTERN

The 4:9–12 expository paragraph is considered to be of the volitionality subtype since it lacks any feature of solutionality or causality. It consists of one CLAIM (v. 9)—namely, that justification is for the non-Jews also—and its *justification* (vv. 10–12), based on the life of Abraham.

NOTES

4:9a–c If the grammatical structure of 9a-b is taken literally (i.e., as a question with two possible answers), 'for' is not a good rendering of γάρ in 9c. But since the rhetorical question, based on a consideration of its real semantic function, is here reduced to two statements, one concerning the Jews (with an implied 'not only') and one concerning the non-Jews, 'for' fits well as introducing the grounds for the second statement.

4:9a Our being happy *because of being declared righteous* The reason for the happiness is repeated from v. 6.

not only **for** *us* **Jews** The words 'not only' are implied. 'Only' is also made explicit in the RSV, TEV, NIV, JB, LB, and JBP. The Greek is ἐπὶ τὴν περιτομήν 'on the circumcision'. (In 9b it is ἐπὶ τὴν ἀκροβυστίαν 'on the uncircumcision'.) The words 'circumcision' and 'uncircumcision' are metonymies meaning 'the Jews' and 'the non-Jews'.

4:9c since we admit *what is declared in Scripture* It is difficult to know how to interpret λέγομεν 'we say'. It could mean 'I have already cited', but that has the difficulty of an editorial 'we' and an incorrect tense. Barnes and Murray suggest the sense 'we admit', which is undoubtedly correct. The problem then is whether or not to recognize what follows as from Scripture. It is a condensation of the quotation in v. 3 and a clear reference to the same Scripture, though not so exactly quoted; 'what is declared in Scripture' is implied. CEV renders it "the Scriptures say."

4:9d trusted *in* **God** From the OT context we can see that the implied object of 'trusted' is 'that God would give him what he had promised', but that is not in focus here. Therefore, the broader 'in God' is supplied. CEV has "faith in him."

4:10 The two rhetorical questions here function to get the readers to consider the situation of Abraham's circumcision and its implications, hence 'Think of' (10a) and 'Consider whether' (10b).

The first of the two questions is introduced by πῶς 'how', which here means 'under what circumstances?' In this context it is asking 'when in Abraham's life?' TEV has "When did this take place?"; CEV, "But when did this happen?"; REB, "In what circumstances?"

4:10b *to mark himself as one who belonged to God* Since the purpose of circumcision is crucial to the discussion, and since Paul expected his readers to know the purpose, it is supplied here. LB has "before he became a Jew—before he went through the Jewish initiation ceremony of circumcision," which is lengthy but excellent. Abraham was presumably the agent of his own circumcision; therefore, in translating into languages that lack a passive construction, it would be valid to say he circumcised himself.

4:10c Paul's main point here regarding the time of Abraham's circumcision as it relates to his whole argument on justification is that since Abraham's circumcision occurred after he was declared righteous, it was not circumcision that made him righteous in God's sight.

4:11a–b Later 'Later' is implied here. The word is explicit in TEV, JB, LB, NEB, and JBP. JBP even has 'afterwards' italicized for emphasis.

God commanded that **he be circumcised** The Greek is σημεῖον ἔλαβεν περιτομῆς 'a sign he received of circumcision', but what Abraham received from God was not the event of circumcision but God's command to be circumcised. The display specifies this.

simply signified *that God had accepted him* In the Greek the word σημεῖον 'sign' precedes the verb, which seems to focus on circumcision as the symbol, not the real thing; the real thing was his being declared righteous. This focus is represented in the display by 'simply'. JB has "only as a sign."

Here 'sign' is represented by a verb since it expresses an event. Satisfaction of the case frame then requires an object of 'signify'; hence 'that God accepted him' is supplied. Hodge says circumcision was "to confirm to him the fact that he was regarded and treated by God as righteous." NCV has "to show that he was right with God."

4:11c to prove The word σφραγίδα 'seal' is a metaphor, but a dead metaphor, since it is frequently used both in biblical and extrabiblical literature this way. A seal is something applied to an object to guarantee or prove that the object has not been tampered with. It is rendered here as a verb, 'prove'. CEV has "to show that." The phrase σφραγῖδα τῆς δικαιοσύνης τῆς πίστεως 'seal of the righteousness of the faith' is in apposition to 'sign' in 11b, but since 'seal' represents an event concept stating the purpose of the 'sign', 11c-d is labeled as in a purpose relationship with 11b.

4:11d–e righteous because he trusted The genitive phrases 'of the righteousness' and 'of the faith', since they represent events, are rendered in separate propositions in the display and assigned appropriate interpropositional relationships (cf. Hodge).

in God The noun πίστις 'faith' represents an event which may require some cognitive content of the event to be expressed. The display supplies the words 'in God' in 11e (and 'in God's promise' in 11h), which is only suggestive.

4:11f still *in effect a non-Jew because he was not circumcised* The supplied words are crucial to the argument as to how the timing of Abraham's circumcision proved that righteousness by faith was also for non-Jews. Abraham "believed and was justified before the rite of circumcision (the mark of Jews) was instituted" (*NIV Study Bible*, p. 1711). As Barrett puts it, "In terms of religion . . . he was a Gentile when God counted his faith as righteousness."

EXPANSION OF THE 4:11g–12 RESULT IN THE 4:9–12 DISPLAY

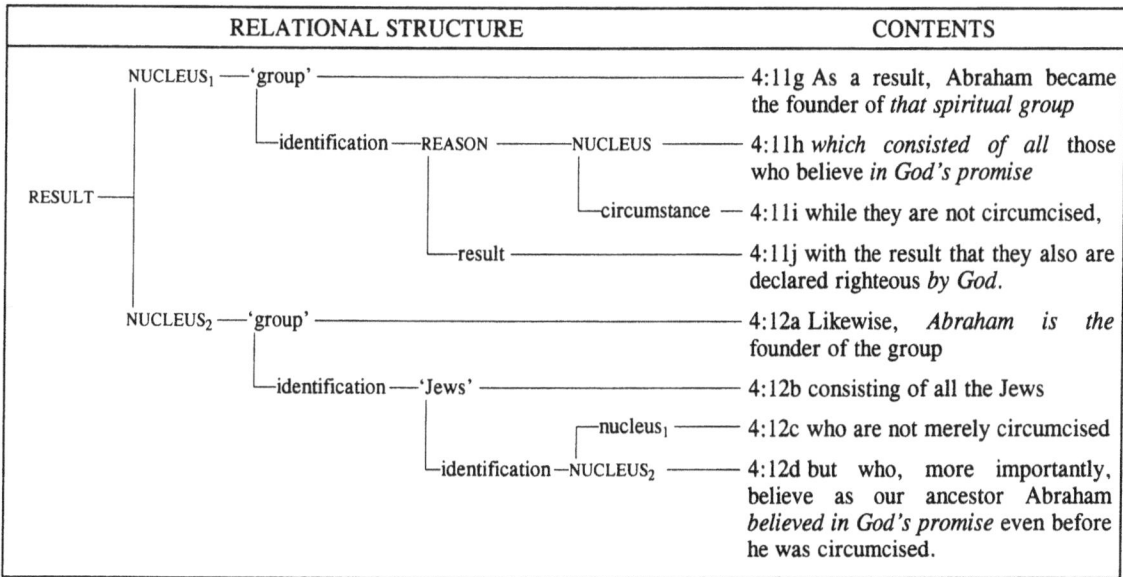

4:11g founder Here πατήρ 'father' is used figuratively to denote one individual who is the founder of a group or class of people (BAGD, p. 635.2f). As a dead metaphor, it is rendered 'founder' instead of 'father' (also in 12a).

4:11i while they are not circumcised The phrase δι' ἀκροβυστίας is taken to mean 'while they are not circumcised' following BAGD (p. 180.AIII1c) and REB. This, according to BAGD, is an example of διά with the genitive expressing attendant circumstance.

4:12d who, more importantly As is usually the case, οὐ μόνον ἀλλὰ καί signals that the part introduced by ἀλλὰ καί is more significant in the context than the part qualified by οὐ μόνον.

***who . . . believe as our ancestor Abraham believed in God's promise* even before he was circumcised** The Greek is τοῖς στοιχοῦσιν τοῖς ἴχνεσιν τῆς ἐν ἀκροβυστίᾳ πίστεως τοῦ πατρὸς ἡμῶν Ἀβραάμ 'to those walking in the footprints of the in uncircumcision faith of our father Abraham'. 'To walk in the footprints of' is an idiom meaning 'to follow the example of', thus 'to do as someone else did'. In the context, what Abraham did was to believe God's promise, so this is specified in the display, and an attempt is made to capture the overall meaning.

BOUNDARIES AND COHERENCE

The opening of the 4:9–12 paragraph is marked by another rhetorical question (actually a set of them) and the conjunction οὖν 'therefore', which is not introducing a conclusion so much as a new aspect of the discussion. Here the topic is circumcision: lexical coherence is manifested by six occurrences of the word περιτομή 'circumcision' and six of ἀκροβυστία 'uncircumcision'. These words do not occur in the rest of the chapter. The word πατήρ 'father' occurs three times in this short paragraph, then not again until v. 16.

The start of a new unit at v. 13 (supported by all the modern versions) is marked by γάρ, which marks a switch to the subject of God's promise to Abraham.

PROMINENCE AND THEME

Much of 9a is included in the theme of 4:9–12 because it is prominent, being in the form of a rhetorical question. The theme also includes 9b, the CLAIM of the paragraph. The time element of the *justification* is prominent due to its being referred to by two rhetorical questions in 10a-b. In light of this, it is not only included in the theme but is expressed as a cleft construction introduced by "remember that" for the sake of greater emphasis. The theme also includes a brief condensation of the v. 11 and v. 12 NUCLEI of the RESULT propositional clusters within the *justification*. The two supporting REASON propositions (v. 10 and v. 11) are also included in condensed form. The PURPOSE propositions (11c-d) are included as well as the MEANS (11a-b) because of the prominence of the forefronted noun which expresses the MEANS. Most of 11f is also included in the theme because it is an essential implicature of the argument here.

SUBDIVISION CONSTITUENT 4:13–17b
(Expository Paragraph: Restatement₁ of claim₁ and claim₂ of 4:1–25)

THEME: It was because Abraham trusted in God that he was declared righteous by God and was promised many blessings by God. Therefore what God promised is guaranteed to all, both Jews and non-Jews, who believe as Abraham did.

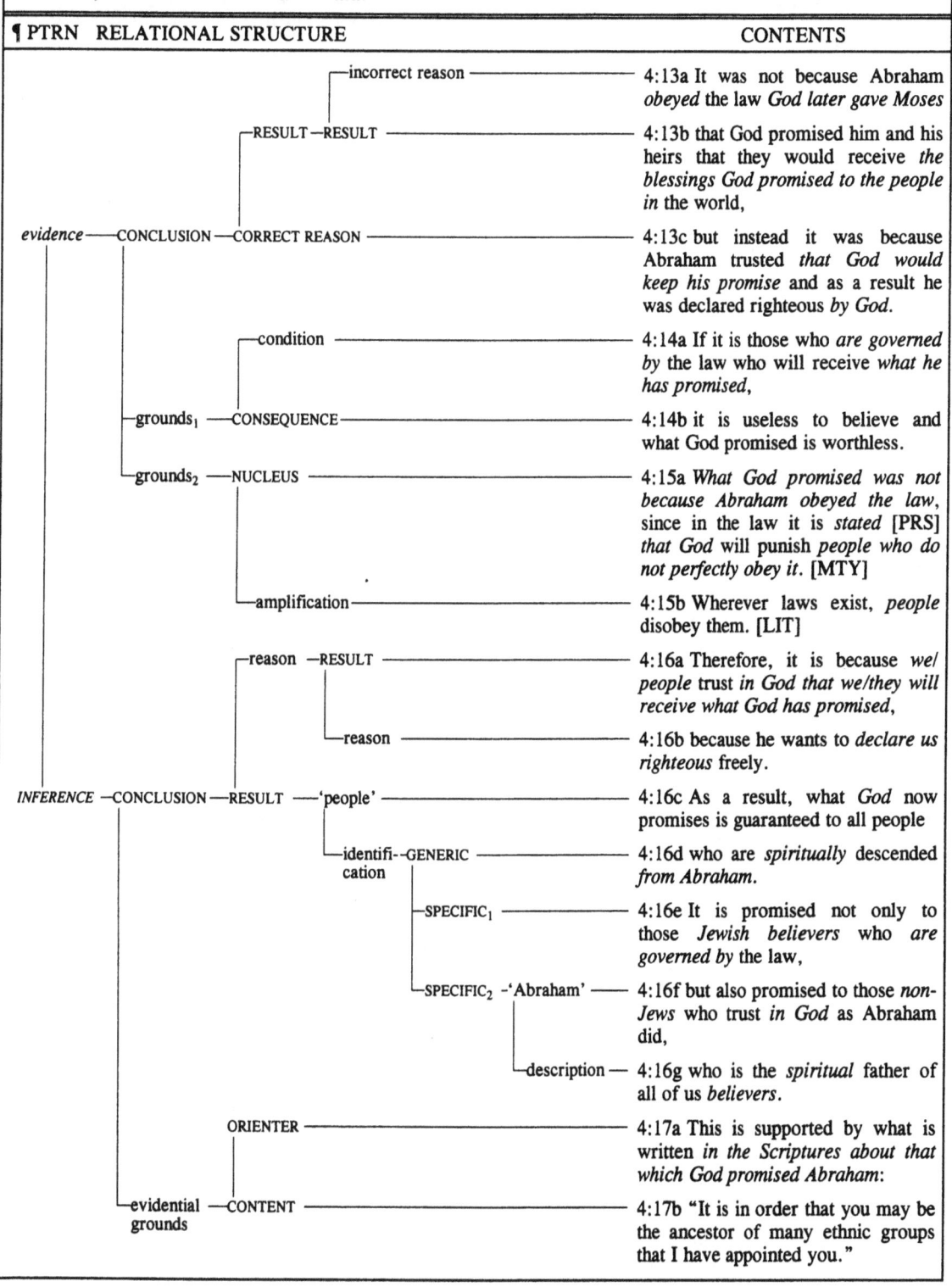

INTENT AND PARAGRAPH PATTERN

The 4:13-17b paragraph, a restatement of the *CLAIMS* in the two previous paragraphs, continues in the expository mode. Considered to be of the causality subtype, it is in the form of some deductive reasoning by Paul:

> X is true for Abraham.
> We are spiritually descended from Abraham.
> Therefore X is true for us.

In vv. 13-15 Paul states that it was on account of his faith that Abraham was justified. From this he concludes in vv. 16-17b that what was promised is guaranteed to all who believe as Abraham did. In the display vv. 13-15 are labeled as the *evidence* that leads to Paul's *INFERENCE* stated in 16-17b.

NOTES

4:13a It was not because Abraham *obeyed* the law The phrase οὐ διὰ νόμου 'not through law' has special prominence in that it is the first phrase in the sentence. This prominence is conveyed in the display by the use of a forefronted cleft construction. Commentators (e.g., Hodge, Barnes, Murray) suggest that obedience of the law is implied by this phrase; and since the causal relation requires a verb to be expressed, 'obeyed' is the one supplied in the display. CEV, LB, and TEV render it similarly.

God later gave Moses It is felt that to avoid wrong meaning the word νόμος 'law' needs qualification, but contrary to the usual pattern of supplying 'that God gave Moses', 'later' is given also, since the law was given to Moses hundreds of years after Abraham's time.

4:13b God promised him In the construction ἡ ἐπαγγελία τῷ Ἀβραάμ 'the promise (was) to Abraham' there is no verb, but in the display 'promise' is rendered as a verb.

that they would receive *the blessings God promised to the people in* the world The Greek is τὸ κληρονόμον αὐτὸν εἶναι κόσμου 'the heir him to be of the world'. An heir is one who receives what has been promised to him. Abraham was not promised that he and his descendants would inherit the world. Nor did they literally inherit or receive the world. Abraham is an example of faith to those who followed him, and the phrase should be understood as 'receive the blessings God promised to the world', which is what God *did* promise Abraham (Gen. 12:7).

What Abraham was promised with respect to 'the world' was that "all the people on the earth will be blessed through you" (NCV, Gen. 12:3; see also Gen. 18:18, 22:17-18). Although Dunn admits that 'heir of the world' is "an odd rendering of the promises of Gen 12:2-3 and 15:5," he goes on to say, "But in fact this was how the promise to Abraham was regularly understood. Indeed it had become almost a commonplace of Jewish teaching that the covenant promised that Abraham's seed would 'inherit the earth'." Dunn does not document this claim, however, or state what was understood by 'inherit the earth'. Morris also recognizes that the phrase "is not a particularly easy expression," but seems to lean toward the interpretation given here: "It could be understood as an enthusiastic description of great national prosperity, but we expect something in the way of spiritual blessing here. Perhaps material blessing is used as a symbol of spiritual blessing."

As to the meaning of 'earth' here, Hodge has a lengthy presentation of four views. One is that it refers to the land of Israel only. But there does not seem to be any other reference where the word has that meaning. A second notion is that it refers to God's promise to give Abraham innumerable descendants, in which case they might be said to possess the world. The third view is much like that given above. The fourth view (his view) is that "it refers to the actual possession of the world by the spiritual seed of Abraham, and Christ their head." But the *ungodly* have always possessed much of the world, and that situation does not seem likely to change until the Millennium, which is hardly in focus here.

One possible alternative to 'people in the world' is 'people all over the world'.

4:14a *are governed by* Some verb needs to be supplied in the expression οἱ ἐκ νόμου 'those out of law' such as 'adhere to', 'live by', 'are governed by'. An alternative is to supply 'obey' as in the TEV and CEV.

what he has promised The event inherent in κληρονόμοι 'heirs' is 'receive what he has promised' as in 13b. It also fits well here.

4:14b is useless The sense of the verb κεκένωται is 'made of no effect' (BAGD, p. 428.2). REB has "is pointless." NCV renders both κεκένωται and 14b's second verb (κατήργηται) as "is worthless".

4:15a This proposition is best seen as supplying the grounds for v. 13; it does not fit well as a grounds for v. 14.

in the law it is *stated that God* **will punish** As in 2:5 and 3:8, 'anger' is a metonymy for 'punishment' (REB has "retribution"). There is also a personification here: 'the law brings God's punishment', which in the display is rendered nonfiguratively. The implied object of 'punish' is 'those who do not fully obey it', which is implied by Paul's statement in 2:13.

In the Greek the subject ('law') and object ὀργή ('wrath') both precede the verb, either as a feature of emphasis or of lessening the focus on the verb.

4:15b Wherever laws exist, *people* **disobey them** Taken literally, this statement does not seem to fit into the argument. The Textus Receptus has γάρ 'for' here; however, the GNT fourth edition has δέ 'but/and' with a B rating of "almost certain." The display follows the GNT reading, meaning that there is no logical connector and the statement seems to be no more than a parenthetical comment. One suggestion is to supply the word 'only', as Knox does; NLT has "(The only way to avoid breaking the law is to have no law to break!)." Another is to assume a litotes, giving the sense of 'there is disobedience of the law wherever laws exist' (see Lenski, Shedd). This is the solution adopted here. It gives a sense nearly the same as supplying 'only' and allows 15b to be labeled as an amplification of 15a.

4:16a Therefore, it is because *we/people* **trust** *in God that we/they will receive what God has promised* The Greek is διὰ τοῦτο ἐκ πίστεως 'on account of this out of faith', with no subject or verb. The most logical subject to supply is either 'the inheritance' or 'the promise'. Commentators are divided as to which is correct. Semantically, the answer is both, hence 'receiving what God has promised', carried over from both v. 13 and v. 14. Most of the versions supply "promise" (e.g., NCV, REB, TEV, NIV; also Barnes, Vine, Dunn).

4:16b *declare us righteous* **freely** In the Greek there is no subject or verb. Several versions (e.g., RSV, TEV) make 'promise' the subject. But κατὰ χάριν 'according to grace' is well taken as an adverbial modifier of some unexpressed event: 'graciously/freely'. Since the wider context speaks of justification, 'declare us righteous' is supplied as the event. An alternative is 'he fulfills what he promised', but that would be redundant with 16a.

4:16c As a result A result construction introduced by εἰς is usually of less prominence than the reason proposition to which it relates. But here the result proposition is more prominent in that it is the theme of the argument, hence the new sentence beginning with these words.

is guaranteed In view of the indirect object 'to all the people' following βέβαιος 'firm', βέβαιος is appropriately rendered here by a verb such as 'is guaranteed' (so RSV, TEV, and NIV).

4:16d who are *spiritually* **descended** *from Abraham* The word σπέρμα 'seed' is a dead metaphor meaning 'descendants'. Here Paul means the descendants of Abraham. The rest of the verse makes it clear he must mean spiritual descendants, not physical ones, so this is specified in the display.

4:16e to those *Jewish believers* In οὐ τῷ ἐκ τοῦ νόμου μόνον 'not to him who (is) of the law alone', the pronominal form is singular, referring to 'seed' in 16d, but the sense is plural. The words 'Jewish believers' are supplied to avoid any ambiguity as to the referent.

are governed by **the law** See the note on 14a.

4:16f to those *non-Jews* **who trust** *in God as Abraham did* In τῷ ἐκ πίστεως Ἀβραάμ 'to him who (is) out of faith of Abraham', it is the Gentiles who are being referred to, as the *NIV Study Bible* footnote (p. 1711) brings out. (The English versions do not make this clear.)

The phrase 'faith of Abraham' is a nominalized form meaning 'who trust (in God) as Abraham did'.

4:16g us *believers* The word 'believers' is supplied to make the referent of 'us' clear.

4:17a This is supported by what is written See the note on 1:17.

about that which God promised Abraham These words are supplied to identify the first and second person singular pronominal referents in the quotation that follows.

4:17b It is in order that you may be the ancestor of many ethnic groups The object phrase πατέρα πολλῶν ἐθνῶν 'father of many nations' (a quotation from Gen. 17:5) precedes the verb, which gives it prominence. The display conveys this prominence by means of the cleft construction.

For 'ethnic groups' see the note on 1:5b.

BOUNDARIES AND COHERENCE

The 4:13-17b paragraph begins with γάρ and vv. 13-15 function as *evidence* for the INFERENCE that follows in vv. 16-17b. There is a problem as to whether vv. 13-25 constitute one paragraph or should be divided into two (or three). NIV, JB, NCV, CEV, and JBP have a paragraph break before v. 18, but grammatically there is no break: v. 18 begins with a relative pronoun which obviously refers to the subject of the verb ἐπίστευσεν 'believed' in 17c. However, there is a clear semantic break at 17c; it seems to be signaled by the perplexing construction that begins 17c (see the note on 17c). Propositions 17c-d, and the rest of the material through v. 22, have no relevance to 17a-b as providing the scriptural basis for the conclusion in 16c-d, that what God promised is guaranteed to all who are Abraham's spiritual descendants. Therefore in this analysis the boundary is taken to be between 17b and 17c.

PROMINENCE AND THEME

Based on the usual theoretical considerations, the theme of 4:13-17b is drawn from both the *evidence* and INFERENCE of the paragraph. Within the former, the CORRECT REASON proposition (13c) is included because of marked prominence. The cleft construction in the theme shows this prominence. The content of 13b is included in the theme in somewhat condensed form, the blessings promised by God to those who believe being the main point in common between the 13-15 *evidence* and the 16-17b INFERENCE. Finally, the 16c RESULT proposition of the INFERENCE is included plus a condensation of the two SPECIFIC identification propositions, 16e-f, which relate to 16c.

SUBDIVISION CONSTITUENT 4:17c–22
(Expository Paragraph: Restatement of claim₁ of 4:1–25)

THEME: It was because Abraham confidently believed God's promise to give him many descendants when there was no basis for his hoping that this would happen that he was declared righteous by God.

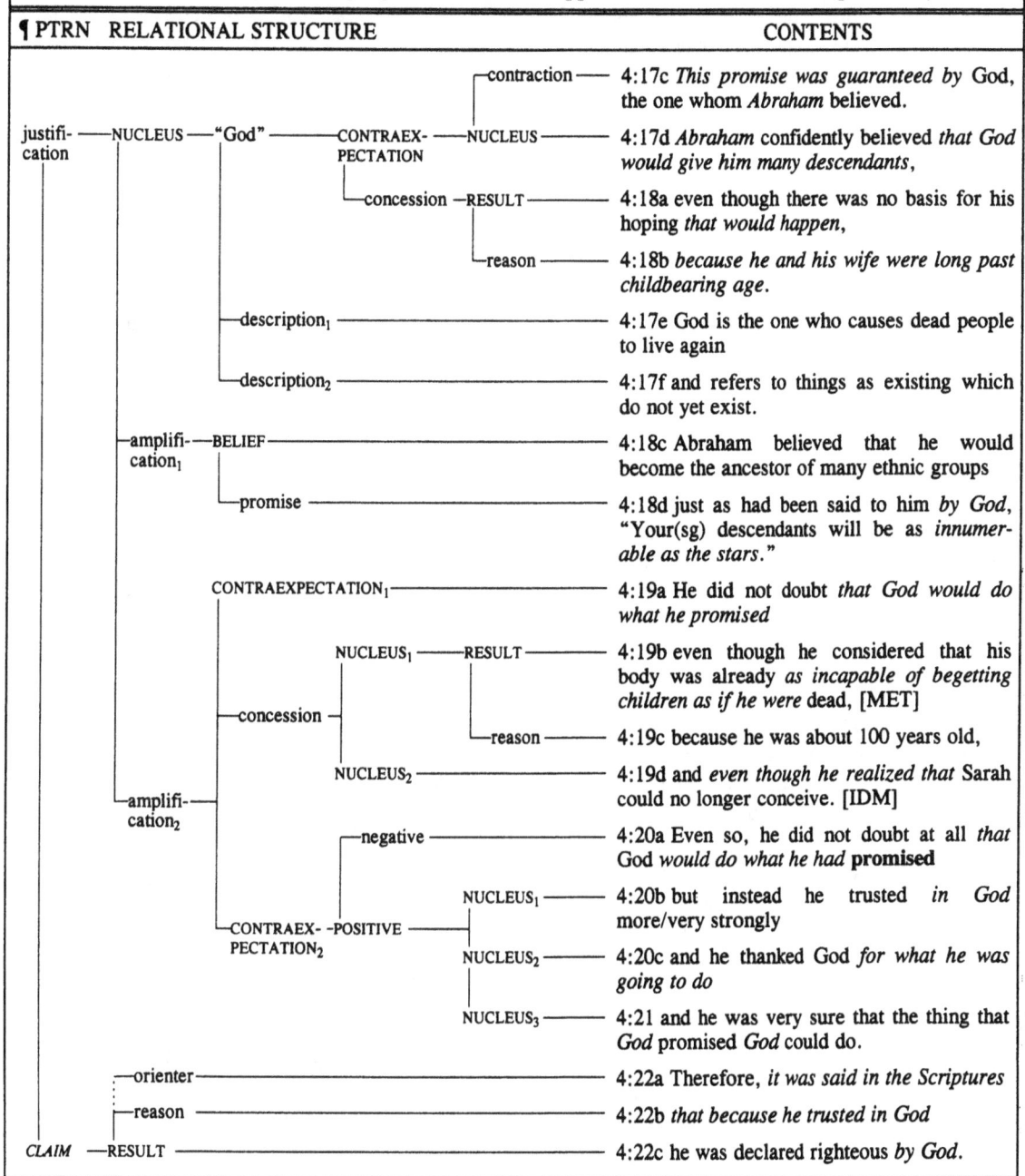

INTENT AND PARAGRAPH PATTERN

The 4:17c–22 paragraph is a *restatement* of 4:1–8, the first CLAIM of the 4:1–25 unit; and since 4:1–8 is expository, the 4:17c–22 paragraph is also expository. It is made up of an extended *justification* (17c–21) preceding a CLAIM (v. 22). A feature of volitionality seems to be involved: the cause of Abraham's being justified was his trust in God when there was no basis for it.

NOTES

4:17c *This promise was guaranteed by* **God, the one whom** *Abraham* **believed** Commentators disagree about which clause the words κατέναντι οὗ ἐπίστευσεν θεοῦ 'before whom he trusted God' are connected with. The preposition κατέναντι takes the genitive case; and since the subject of 'believed/trusted' is 'Abraham', the phrase must be equivalent to κατέναντι (τοῦ) θεοῦ ᾧ ἐπίστευσεν 'before (the) God in whom he believed' (cf. BDF, p. 154; Robertson, p. 717; BAGD, p. 421.2b). But the use of the genitive οὗ ἐπίστευσεν 'whom he believed' preceding 'God' emphasizes this description of God. This emphasis is shown in the display by 'God, the one whom'. The sense of 'before' is maintained by translating as 'God's promise was guaranteed', which is the main proposition in v. 16. The vast majority of commentators support this.

4:17-18 The display here reverses the order of propositions, placing 18a–b before 17e–f to maintain the flow of relationships. First of all, there is the necessity of stating the implied content of what Abraham believed (borrowed from 18c) in order to understand 18a. Then 17d connects much more naturally with the 18a concessive clause immediately following it in the display. (It may look like a misprint to have 4:18b followed by 4:17e in the display, but it is done like this so that readers will know where the Greek phraseology so represented is actually found in the GNT.)

4:18a even though there was no basis for his hoping *that would happen* The Greek is παρ' ἐλπίδα ἐπ' ἐλπίδι ἐπίστευσεν 'beyond hope on hope he believed'. The expression here is idiomatic and is a play on the word 'hope'; 'in hope' means 'confidently' (cf. Hodge, Murray), and 'against hope' means to hope when there is no circumstantial basis for hoping. The words 'that would happen' are supplied because the event of hoping requires some cognitive content. JB's rendering, "Though it seemed Abraham's hope could not be fulfilled," is excellent.

4:18b *because he and his wife were long past childbearing age* The circumstantial reason underlying 'against hope', which Paul would expect his readers to know from the Genesis account, is supplied.

4:17f refers to things as existing which do not yet exist The Greek is καλοῦντος τὰ μὴ ὄντα ὡς ὄντα 'calling the things not being as being'. Some commentators take this to mean 'call into existence'. But 'as being' can hardly mean 'into existence'. Moreover, the whole focus of the passage is on Abraham's faith in the promise before it was fulfilled, not on the fulfillment of the promise itself. In this passage, 'the things' refers to the yet unborn children of Abraham. The word 'call' means 'summon' in some contexts, but it is used just as frequently in the sense 'address as, name, refer to as'. This latter interpretation, which is supported by many commentators and versions, is the one chosen in the display.

4:18d "Your(sg) descendants will be as *innumerable as the stars*" The Greek is οὕτως ἔσται τὸ σπέρμα σου 'thus will be the seed of you(sg)'. For 'thus' to make sense, the reader must know the situational context in Gen. 15:5. Paul assumed his readers had this knowledge. But for modern readers who do not, 'thus' can be spelled out in a longer form (e.g., 'when God told him to look up and try to count the stars'), but not as part of the quotation itself. A shorter solution is to leave out any situational meaning (referring to the stars) and translate as in CEV, "a lot of descendants," or NCV, "too many to count."

4:19a He did not doubt The Greek is μὴ ἀσθενήσας τῇ πίστει 'not weakening in faith'. To weaken in faith' is to believe something less strongly or to doubt.

that God would do what he promised Rendering 'weak in faith' as a verb requires that some cognitive content or object of 'doubt' be supplied.

4:19b *incapable of begetting children* The Greek κατενόησεν τὸ ἑαυτοῦ σῶμα ἤδη νενεκρωμένον 'he considered his own body already to have died' is a metaphor, the point of similarity being inability to beget children. Moffatt has "The utter impotence of his own body."

There are two textual problems here. Quite a number of manuscripts have the negative with the verb. This would give the sense 'he was so strong in faith that he did not pay any attention to . . .' (cf. KJV, LB). However, the presence of καί 'and' to introduce the coordinate concession in 19d rules out the negative in 19b. If Paul had meant 'considered neither . . . nor . . .', he would have had to use a negative conjunction with each proposition.

The second problem is whether the word ἤδη 'already' belongs in the text. The great preponderance of manuscript evidence is for its inclusion, but it is possible that some eager copyist might have inserted it to add more flavor to the text. The sense is little affected either way.

4:19d *he realized that* **Sarah could no longer conceive** The words τὴν νέκρωσιν τῆς μήτρας Σάρρας 'the death of the womb of Sarah' are considered an idiom. Thus no attempt is made to retain the image in the display rendering. Instead, the sense is rendered nonfiguratively as in the NCV, TEV, CEV, which have "could not have children." The verb 'he realized' is repeated from 19b ('he considered').

4:20a doubt The main verb here is διεκρίθη. It most frequently means 'judge', but sometimes 'dispute, doubt' (BAGD, p. 185.2b, has 'doubt'). The latter sense underlies the rendering here.

Commentators (e.g., Hodge, Denney, Lightfoot, Morris; also Moulton, p. 242) take the phrase τῇ ἀπιστίᾳ 'by unbelief' as a causal dative, 'because he did not trust in (believe) God'. It will be noted that this phrase is not rendered as such in the display. There are two phrases in the Greek that refer to the same concept: a verb phrase οὐ διεκρίθη 'he did not doubt' and τῇ ἀπιστίᾳ 'in unbelief'. They could be viewed as an intensification of the one concept (as in the display). The other possibility is to try to distinguish them, but this would create an awkward and ambiguous rendering: 'he did not doubt [effect] . . . because he did not trust (in God) [cause]'. In the display the cause-effect sense is conveyed by 'he did not doubt at all'.

God *would do what he had* **promised** The phrase εἰς τὴν ἐπαγγελίαν τοῦ θεοῦ 'against the promise of God' is forefronted in Greek, but this prominence is hard to convey in English due to its being rendered as a full clause, the object of 'doubt'. Hence the verb 'promised' is simply made bold in the display.

4:20b he trusted *in God* **more/very strongly** The expression ἐνεδυναμώθη τῇ πίστει 'was empowered in faith' is a mismatched way of saying 'his faith was strengthened' or 'his faith grew stronger'.

4:20c and he thanked God *for what he was going to do* The expression δοὺς δόξαν τῷ θεῷ 'giving glory to God' is equivalent to 'praising God', since glory is not a tangible object that can be given (cf. TEV, Goodspeed, TCNT, NCV, Berkeley). It is here rendered 'thanked', as in 1:21. This in turn semantically requires an identification of what Abraham was thankful for. Many commentators (e.g., Harrison, Alford, Hodge, Haldane, Barnes, Thomson and Davidson) suggest something like 'confidence in God's ability to fulfill this promise'. However, just as 'for what he had done' was supplied in 1:21, here the generic 'for what he was going to do' is supplied. There does not seem to be strong support for this in the commentaries, but LB has "he praised God for this blessing even before it happened" and Erdman has "he praised God for the miracle which was to be performed." Without assuming such a focus of his praise, it is difficult to see how 'giving glory to God' coheres at all with the context.

4:21 The words ὃ ἐπήγγελται 'what he had promised' precede the verb and are thereby in focus. This focus is indicated in the display by forefronting.

4:22 The Greek is elliptical here and certain phrases are accordingly supplied. That Paul is citing the Scriptures (Gen. 15:6) is made explicit in the display.

BOUNDARIES AND COHERENCE

Proposition 4:17d is clearly the *justification* for the CLAIM in 4:22 (which is a restatement of 4:3c) that Abraham was justified by his faith. In other words, 17c–22 is discussing a topic different from that of the preceding paragraph. It has its own CLAIM and *justification* quite different from those in 13–17b.

There is some lexical evidence for the unity of 13–22: the noun ἐπαγγελία 'promise' is found in both 13–17b and 17c–22 (and the cognate verb ἐπαγγέλλομαι in v. 21); πίστις 'faith' is found four times in 13–17b and twice in 17c–22 (and the cognate verb πιστεύω once in 13–17b and twice in 17c–22). However, 17c–22 has many lexemes dealing with life and death which are absent in 13–17b: ζῳοποιοῦντος 'life-giving' (v. 17); νεκρούς 'dead' (v. 17); καλοῦντος ὡς ὄντα 'calling as being' (v. 17); παρ' ἐλπίδα 'beyond hope' (v. 18); νενεκρωμένον 'having died' (v. 19); νέκρωσιν 'death' (v. 19). Therefore, in view of both the semantic and lexical evidence a new paragraph is begun at 17c in the display. Regarding the boundary before v. 23, see "Boundaries and Coherence" for the 4:23–25 paragraph. (LB, NEB, and JBP also have a paragraph break before v. 23.)

PROMINENCE AND THEME

The theme of 4:17c–22 is drawn from the 17d–18a NUCLEUS of the *justification* and from the 22c RESULT of the *CLAIM*. The 18a concession is also included in the theme since it has features of marked prominence: the forefronted παρ' ἐλπίδα 'beyond hope' is prominent, and the topic itself ('when there was no basis for hope') is thematic, being developed extensively in the rest of the paragraph.

SUBDIVISION CONSTITUENT 4:23–25
(Expository Paragraph: Restatement₂ of claim₁ and claim₂ of 4:1–25)

THEME: *The words about Abraham's being declared righteous by God were written also to assure us who believe in God, who would also be declared righteous.*

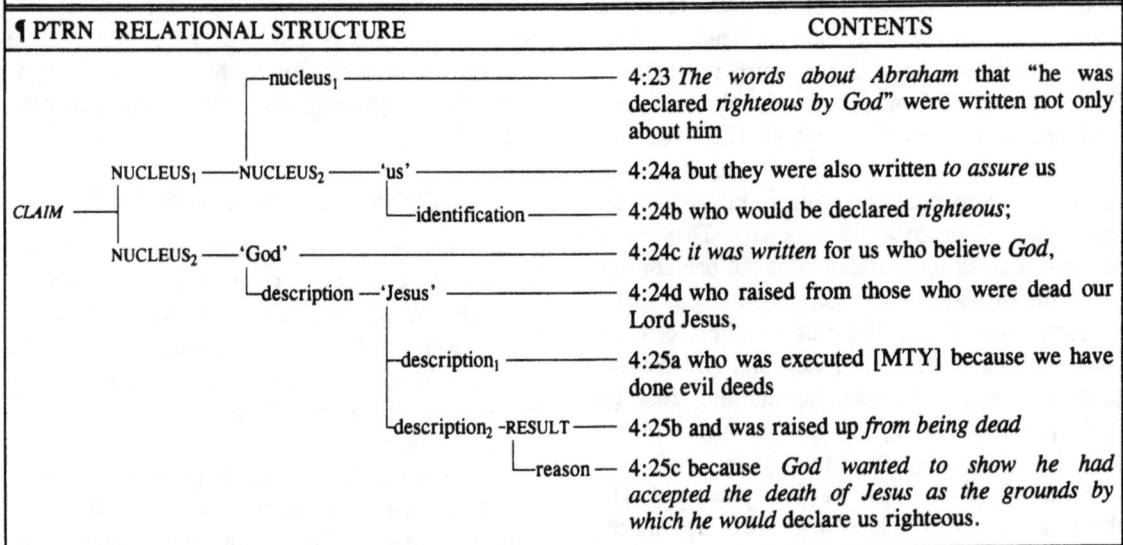

INTENT AND PARAGRAPH PATTERN

The 4:23–25 paragraph closes the 4:1–25 subdivision; it functions to summarize and close it off. Like the preceding paragraphs in 4:1–25, 4:23–25 is expository, consisting of one *CLAIM*. It does not contain two elements as is characteristic of most paragraphs.

NOTES

4:23–24 The phrases δι' αὐτόν 'on account of him' (v. 23) and δι' ἡμᾶς 'on account of us' (v. 24a) are parallel in form, indicating contrast, but they do not have the same sense, notwithstanding attempts by most English versions to use the same English representation. The one in v. 23 means 'about him'; and the one in 24a, 'for our sakes'. The latter is rendered 'to assure us' in the display (so LB).

In the Greek there is no content of the declaring; it is simply ἐλογίσθη 'he was declared' (v. 23) and μέλλει λογίζεσθαι 'about to be declared' (v. 24b). The words 'righteous by God' must be supplied to make a complete clause (as in TEV and JBP).

4:25a executed The word παρεδόθη 'handed over' implies that one individual was put into the custody of another. By extension, it means 'handed him over for the outcome' of the custody, such as trial, imprisonment, or, as here, execution. (NRSV has "handed over to death.") The word thus is a metonymy, the cause standing for the effect. Since nothing is gained by translating this literally, it is rendered 'executed' in the display.

4:25c because *God wanted to show he had accepted the death of Jesus as the grounds by which he would* **declare us righteous** The Greek is διὰ τὴν δικαίωσιν ἡμῶν 'on account of the justification of us'. Most commentators and versions take διά as expressing purpose, and translate it 'for our justification'. There are, however, insuperable difficulties to this. First, there is no indication that διά ever signals purpose. Neither BAGD nor Louw and Nida give διά such a meaning. BAGD (p. 181.BII1) say its meaning here is 'because'; Käsemann says it signals what follows as the *"basis."* Second, there is no support anywhere else in the NT for the resurrection's being the means of our justification. Furthermore, if Paul had meant 'with a view to, to accomplish', he would most certainly have used εἰς 'unto'. If we take the sense of the preposition to be the same in both of the διά phrases (διὰ τὰ παραπτώματα 'on account of our offenses' in 25a and διὰ τὴν δικαίωσιν ἡμῶν 'on account of our justification' in 25c), we get the meaning 'he was raised because we had been justified'. But in what sense can we say this was true? Was not our justification declared on the grounds of (our trust in) the substitutionary atonement of Christ? Surely it was. But on what grounds are we assured that the sacrifice of Christ was accepted as payment in full to achieve our being declared righteous? The answer is given by Paul here: Christ was raised because his work to secure our justification was complete and because God wanted to prove it to us (cf. Erdman, Bruce 1963, Harrison). Taylor (p. 298) argues that διά plus accusative almost invariably has a causal sense. He cites 4:25 as the only other possible example in addition to 3:25 with a meaning of 'with a view to', noting that other examples of 'with a view to' are extremely rare in Classical Greek, nonexistent in the LXX, and not mentioned by Moulton and Milligan in their *Vocabulary of the Greek New Testament*. And if one concedes that 'because + want to' indicates intention in almost the same way that purpose does, one can say that the propositionalization here still indicates purpose.

BOUNDARIES AND COHERENCE

There are a number of reasons for making 4:23–25 a separate paragraph. First, there is little lexical cohesion with what precedes it. Second, it is not only a *restatement* of the CLAIMS in vv. 1–12, but it also functions as a summary statement for all of chapter 4, which deals with implications of Abraham's being justified by faith. Third, v. 25 seems to serve as a transition to a new topic.

PROMINENCE AND THEME

The theme of 4:23–25 is drawn from the two v. 24 NUCLEI plus enough of v. 23 to specify the pronominal 'they' of 24a.

DIVISION CLUSTER CONSTITUENT 5:1-21
(Expository Subdivision: Application₁ of 3:21-26)

> *THEME: Because God has declared us righteous, we have peace with God, we experience his grace, we rejoice even in suffering because we expect to receive God's glory, and we know we will be saved from eternal punishment. Although the sin of one man, Adam, led to all people dying and deserving punishment, Christ's one righteous act has led to many being acquitted and declared righteous and living eternally.*

MACROSTRUCTURE	CONTENTS
NUCLEUS₁	5:1-11 Because God has declared us righteous, we have peace with God, we experience his acting graciously toward us, we rejoice because we expect to receive God's glory, we even rejoice in suffering because we know the results it brings, we know we shall be saved from God's punishing us eternally, and we boast of what God has done for us through Christ.
NUCLEUS₂	5:12-21 Although the sin of one man, Adam, led to all people dying and God declaring that they deserved to be punished, Christ's righteous act of obedience when he died led to many experiencing God's grace and being declared righteous and living eternally, and will result in their ruling with Christ.

INTENT AND MACROSTRUCTURE

The 5:1-21 unit is expository, presenting the first of a set of applications of the doctrine of justification by faith set forth in 3:21-26. The indicative verbs in the main clauses of 5:1-21 show its expository nature as does the fact that at the paragraph level the two constituents present *CLAIMS* with their *justifications*. The unit's two constituents seem to be equal; neither one is subordinate to the other.

BOUNDARIES AND COHERENCE

While there are clearly two units in 5:1-21 and some commentators do not see any coherence between the two, there is some lexical coherence provided by occurrences of ἀποθνῄσκω 'die' and θάνατος 'death' in both units. Coherence is exhibited by references to death in either a nominal or verbal form, in vv. 6, 7 (twice), 8, 10, 12 (twice), 14, 15, 17, and 21, and to χάρις 'grace' in 2, 15 (twice), 17, 20, and 21 ('grace' occurs only once in chap. 4). The most obvious feature of coherence is the chiastic structure involving the words 'through the Lord Jesus Christ' in the first and last verses of Romans 5:

διὰ τοῦ κυρίου ἡμῶν Ἰησοῦ Χριστοῦ (1)	through our Lord Jesus Christ
διὰ Ἰησοῦ Χριστοῦ τοῦ κυρίου ἡμῶν (21)	through Jesus Christ our Lord

This phrase or some variant of it including 'through him' also occurs in vv. 2, 9, 11, 17.

The final boundary of 5:1-21 is marked at 6:1 by οὖν 'therefore' and the rhetorical question 'what shall we say?', which introduces another implication of justification, the believer's deliverance from bondage to sin. The start of the next unit is marked by a series of rhetorical questions (four in the first three verses of chap. 6) and by a change of topic from the universal application of justification to the question of continuing to sin.

PROMINENCE AND THEME

The theme of 5:1-21 is drawn from the themes of its two constituents since they are considered equally prominent. The portions about rejoicing in 5:1-11 are combined to avoid repetition, and the concession statement about Adam in 5:12-21 is omitted as being less thematic than the contraexpectation.

SUBDIVISION CONSTITUENT 5:1-11
(Expository Section: Nucleus₁ of 5:1-21

THEME: Because God has declared us righteous, we have peace with God, we experience his acting graciously toward us, we rejoice because we expect to receive God's glory, we even rejoice in suffering because we know the results it brings, we know we shall be saved from God's punishing us eternally, and we boast of what God has done for us through Christ.

MACROSTRUCTURE	CONTENTS
NUCLEUS₁	5:1-5 Because God has declared us righteous, we have peace with God, we experience his acting graciously toward us, we rejoice because we expect to receive God's glory, and we even rejoice in suffering because we know the results it brings.
NUCLEUS₂	5:6-11 Since Christ died for us ungodly people, he will certainly save us from God's eternal punishment, and so we boast of what he has done for us.

INTENT AND MACROSTRUCTURE

The 5:1-11 section continues in the expository mode, with indicative verbs, as Paul develops one of the implications of the doctrine of justification. The unit consists of two NUCLEI, each on a different theme but of equal prominence. These two constituents contain *CLAIMS* and their *justifications*, though they have other elements as well.

BOUNDARIES AND COHERENCE

The closing boundary at 5:12 is marked by διὰ τοῦτο 'therefore', introductory not to a consequence of 5:1-11, but to another implication of justification by faith. It is also marked by a switch from 'we' to third person. The 5:12-21 unit is quite distinct from 5:1-11 in that it contains a set of contrasts between two representative men: Adam and Christ. Cohesion in 5:1-11 derives from the long list of believers' spiritual benefits.

PROMINENCE AND THEME

The theme of 5:1-11 is drawn from the themes of its two constituents. The *justification* part of the second (vv. 6-8) is omitted since it is less thematic than the *CLAIM*.

SECTION CONSTITUENT 5:1–5
(Expository paragraph: Nucleus₁ of 5:1–11)

THEME: Because God has declared us righteous, we have peace with God, we experience his acting graciously toward us, we rejoice because we expect to receive God's glory, and we even rejoice in suffering because we know the results it brings.

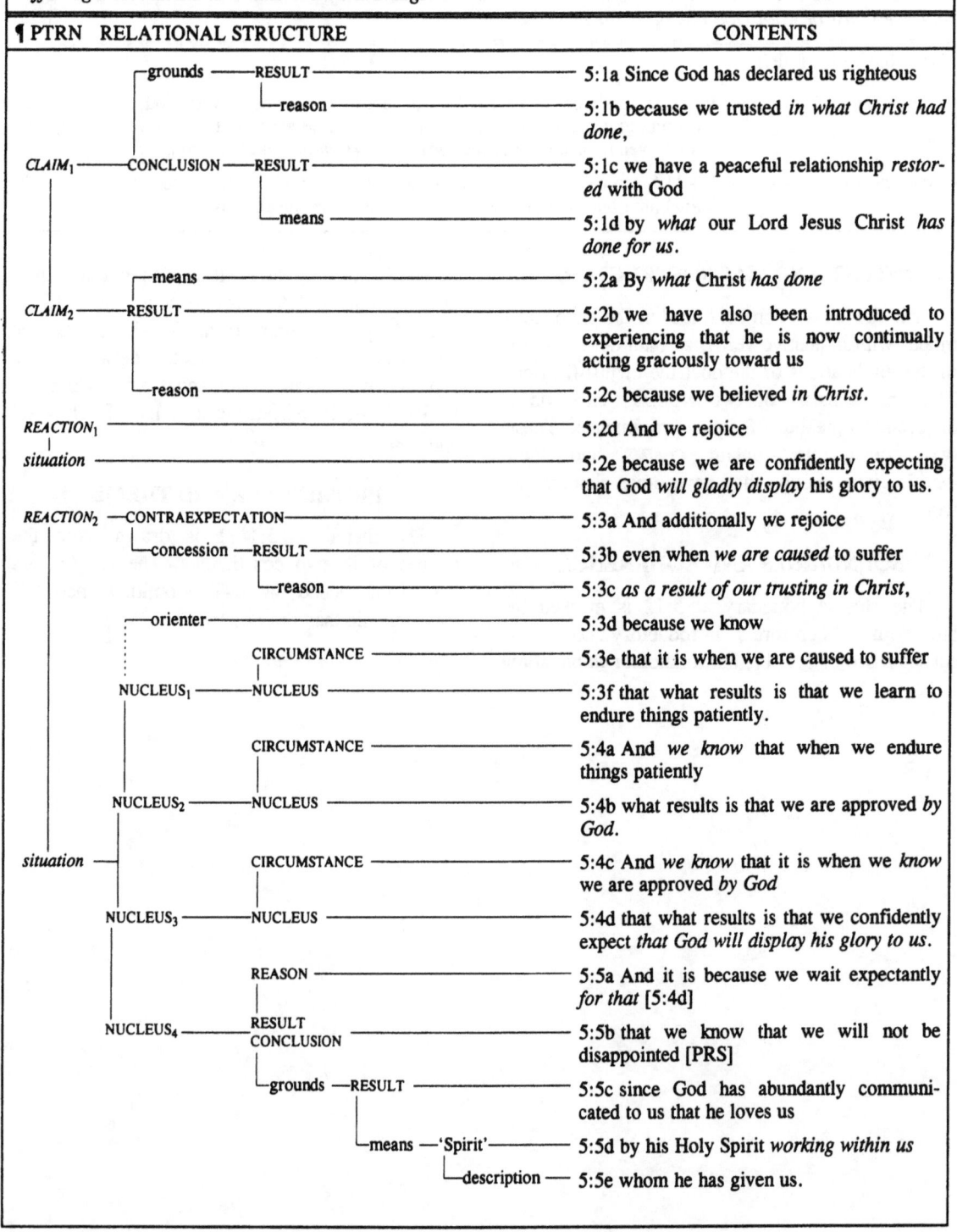

INTENT AND PARAGRAPH PATTERN

The 5:1-5 paragraph has been analyzed as consisting of two *CLAIMS* followed by two *situation-REACTION* units. It does have emotive elements, but because it is in the middle of an expository unit it is considered to be an expository paragraph.

NOTES

5:1b because we trusted *in what Christ had done* The phrase ἐκ πίστεως 'out of faith' is taken as expressing reason. Making it into a full proposition calls for some content of 'trust/believe' to be supplied (see 3:26, 30).

5:1c we have a peaceful relationship *restored* The fourth edition GNT has ἔχομεν 'we have' with an A rating ("certain"). Though the manuscript evidence for ἔχωμεν 'let us have' is strong, the fact that as far back as the first century people no longer made a difference between o and ω means that the context must determine the sense. Here, in the middle of a long expository passage and with no contiguous imperatives, the sense must be 'we have'.

The position of εἰρήνην 'peace' before the verb emphasizes it. Semantically, 'peace' is a quality, not a thing, so it is represented in the display by 'peaceful relationship'. An alternative would be the English idiom 'at peace with'. Since the phrase 'to have peace with' implies a previous state of hostility, the word 'restored' is supplied.

5:1d by *what* our Lord Jesus Christ *has done for us* Since διά 'by' requires a verb to express the means event, 'has done for us' is supplied here (and also in 2a). LB does likewise.

5:2b we have also been introduced to experiencing that he is now continually acting graciously toward us The first καί 'and' in v. 2 could go with δι' οὗ, which would give 'it is also through him . . .'; or it could go with τὴν προσαγωγήν, which would give 'we have access also'. Commentators are silent on this point, and no modern English translations include the word at all. But in view of the καί later in v. 2 (2d, 'And we rejoice'), it is best to take it as introducing an additional benefit of justification (peace having been the first).

The expression τὴν προσαγωγὴν ἐσχήκαμεν εἰς τὴν χάριν 'the access we have received into the grace' is problematic. First, the noun 'grace' here represents an event (see the note on 3:24b).

Then, as to προσαγωγήν, commentators disagree on whether it means 'access' or 'introduction'. (In any case, having an introduction to an important person does lead to access to him.) But note that these words are followed by the phrase ἐν ἑστήκαμεν 'in which we now stand', describing our current state of experiencing God's gracious help. If the sense of προσαγωγήν were 'access,' this phrase would be redundant; therefore it seems best to take it as 'introduction', pointing to Christ as introducer (so Lightfoot, Harrison, Morris, Sanday and Headlam; also CEV).

The phrase ἐν ἑστήκαμεν 'in which we stand' is difficult to translate because it is figurative, denoting our present experience as a result of a past action (the verb is in the perfect tense). In the display 'experiencing that he is now continually acting . . .' conveys the sense. NCV captures the same sense with "that we now enjoy."

5:2c because we believed The words τῇ πίστει 'in faith', which are included in the GNT with a C rating ("difficulty in deciding"), are omitted in some good manuscripts. The sense is not affected much either way, since Paul has just finished an exposition connecting faith with grace. Probably the best explanation is that, being extraneous, it was deliberately omitted by some copyist.

5:2e because we are confidently expecting The Greek is ἐπ' ἐλπίδι 'on hope'. The preposition ἐπί with the dative introduces the basis for something (BAGD, p. 287.II1bγ), hence 'because'.

In the NT the noun ἐλπίς 'hope' denotes an attitude of confident expectation in regard to some future event. It is rendered 'confidently expecting' since 'hope' in English does not convey absolute confidence.

God *will gladly display* his glory The phrase τῆς δόξης τοῦ θεοῦ 'of the glory of God' implies some event word to express the relation of 'glory' to 'hope'. The phrase refers either to God's glorious nature and attributes (in which the sense would be 'that God will display/reveal his glory') or the glorious nature that God will give to or bestow on believers. Some commentators mention both and make no attempt to distinguish between them; contextually there is no way to know which Paul had in mind or if, in fact, he did have one or the other in mind.

5:3a And additionally The initial οὐ μόνον δέ, ἀλλὰ καί 'and not only, but also' is, on the surface, elliptical. It seems to require 'do we rejoice in the hope of God's glory' to go with 'not only'. But this would be redundant. The display captures the sense better with 'and additionally'. The strong adversative ἀλλά introduces something contrary to expectation. The following would express it more fully: 'we not only rejoice as we contemplate the glorious things that God has prepared for us in heaven, but, unexpectedly, we rejoice also during afflictions'.

5:3b even when A number of commentators have held that the preposition in the phrase ἐν ταῖς θλίψεσιν 'in afflictions' is expressing grounds or reason, but there appears no reason contextually to support such a masochistic interpretation. The circumstance relationship makes more sense.

we are caused **to suffer** Semantically, the noun θλῖψις 'affliction' refers to an event, hence the intransitive 'suffer, be distressed'. If a transitive verb such as 'afflict' must be used, then there is the problem of what the agent should be, things or people? Either could be causing the afflictions.

5:3c *as a result of our trusting in Christ* Many commentators suggest that the afflictions Paul refers to are those we endure because of our faith in and service for Christ. While this is probably true, they are not necessarily confined to such afflictions. The implication in italics in 3c should be included in a translation only if the readers would not at all associate sufferings with what believers endure for Christ's sake.

5:3e it is when we are caused to suffer The problem here is how to avoid the personification in ἡ θλῖψις ὑπομονὴν κατεργάζεται 'affliction works patience', in which the two events or experiences are represented with nouns. A good solution is to treat the event represented by the subject as the circumstance: 'when we are afflicted'.

The subject 'affliction' is forefronted in the Greek; the emphasis thus expressed is conveyed in the display by a cleft construction, 'it is when . . .'. The object of the verb also precedes the verb, but this is a case in which the forefronting of the subject for emphasis draws the object with it; thus only the subject is included in the cleft construction.

5:3f that what results The verb κατεργάζεται 'produces/creates' is somewhat figurative in that there is no animate agent that does the producing. In the display the sense is expressed nonfiguratively as 'what results'.

5:4a–d The Greek verbs in v. 4 are elided. It is presumed that κατεργάζεται 'produces/creates' from 3f is to be understood and that, if present, would again occur last in each clause, giving prominence to the subject and object. This is the reason the propositionalizations here correspond to those in 3e–f.

5:4b approved *by God* The Greek is δοκιμή 'approved', that is, "the quality of being approved" (BAGD, p. 202.1). Here the one giving the approval is God.

5:4d we confidently expect *that God will display his glory to us* The noun ἐλπίς 'hope', that is, 'confident expectation' (as in 2e), semantically requires that some cognitive content be supplied (an object or content for its case frame). The clause supplied here is repeated from 2e.

5:5a–b For the propositionalization here, see the notes on 5:3e–f.

wait expectantly The personification of ἐλπίς 'hope' that is in the Greek is avoided as it was in vv. 3–4.

not be disappointed The word καταισχύνει has more the sense of 'be disappointed' than 'be put to shame' (BAGD, p. 410.3a), but specifically it means to be humiliated because the source of one's faith has been shown to be inadequate.

5:5c God has abundantly communicated to us The literal meaning of ἐκκέχυται is 'has been poured out', but here as in several other NT references the sense is figurative: 'having come down abundantly from heaven to refresh people spiritually as rain comes down to refresh growing plants'. In order to make the clause 'that he loves us' fit as the object of the verb, it is rendered 'has abundantly communicated to us'.

that he loves us The phrase 'love of God' involves a subjective genitive: God's love toward us. Here it is made a full clause.

5:5d by his Holy Spirit *working within us* The word διά 'through/by' expresses means and requires a full proposition to express it. Therefore the phrase 'working within us' has been supplied to complete the clause. Alternatives would be 'by what the Holy Spirit has done' or more specifically 'by the Holy Spirit's assuring us that God does love us'.

BOUNDARIES AND COHERENCE

The main feature of coherence within the 5:1-5 paragraph is the progression of the outcomes of the 3e, 4a, 4c CIRCUMSTANCES and the 5a REASON, with certain of the elements being repeated in the progression. The paragraph lists several benefits of justification by faith, all joined by καί 'and'. The boundary at v. 6 is marked by a new topic involving several references to Christ's death.

PROMINENCE AND THEME

The theme of 5:1-5 is drawn from the naturally prominent propositions of the *CLAIMS*, *REACTIONS*, and *situations*. The 3b concession of the second *REACTION* (3a) is also included in the theme, not that it is naturally prominent but because it is necessary to complete the thought and is the starting point for the progressive series of situations elaborated in 3d-5e.

SECTION CONSTITUENT 5:6–11
(Expository Paragraph: Nucleus₂ of 5:1–11)

THEME: *Since Christ died for us ungodly people, he will certainly save us from God's eternal punishment, and so we boast of what he has done for us.*

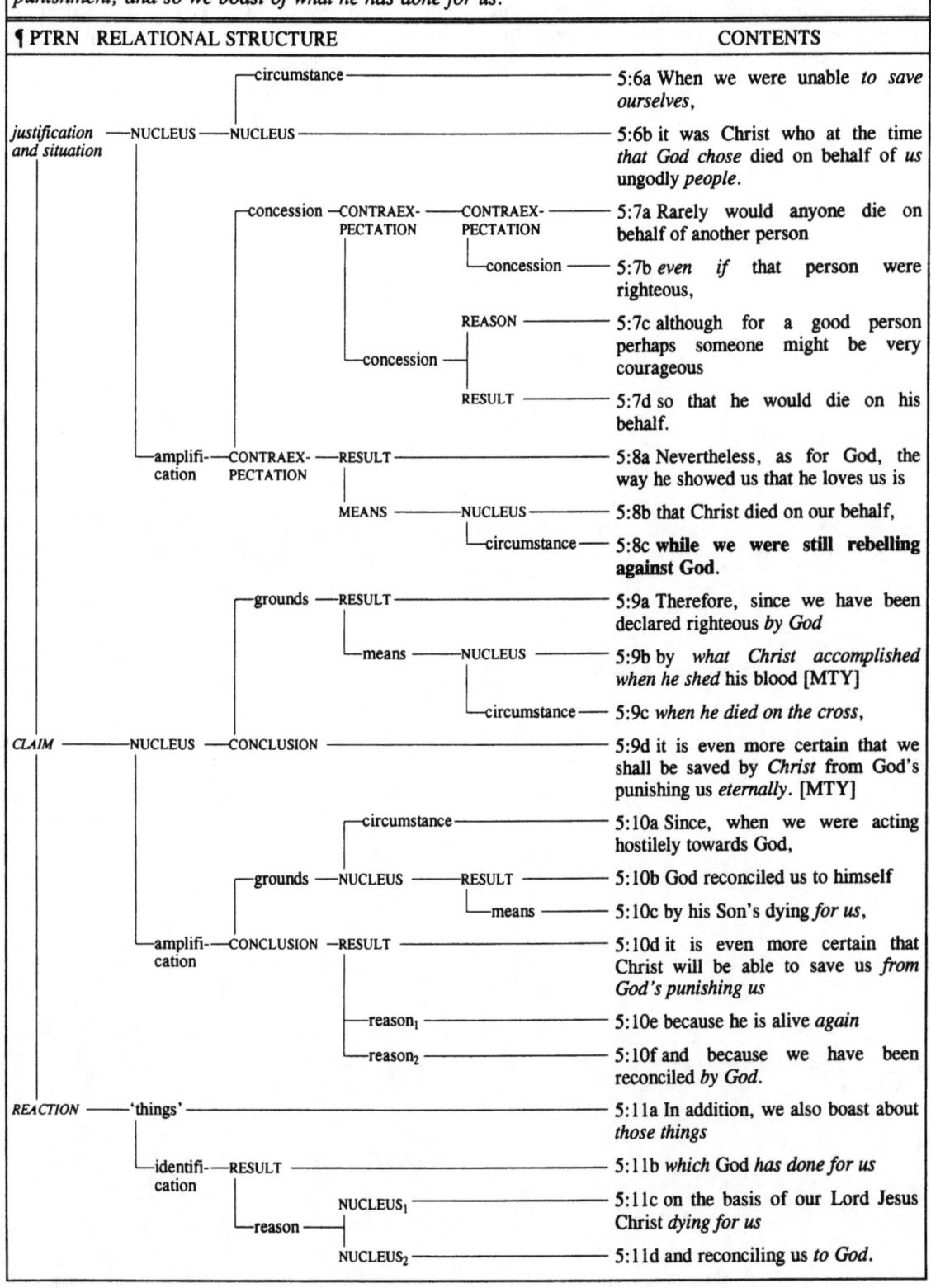

INTENT AND PARAGRAPH PATTERN

The 5:6-11 unit is best seen as continuing in the expository mode: Paul explicates the implications of what Christ has done for us using indicative verbs. In 5:9-10 he clearly makes another CLAIM. But there are expressive elements as well. The first part of the paragraph (5:6-8) is both a *justification* for the CLAIM and also a *situation* leading to the CLAIM and to the emotive REACTION in 5:11.

NOTES

5:6a There is a difficult textual problem here, but fortunately the meaning is exactly the same regardless of the solution. The introductory words here, of which there are several variants, introduce a new paragraph that extends through v. 11. The fourth edition GNT has ἔτι γάρ 'for (when)... still' for these introductory words, but with a C rating, indicating a fairly high degree of doubt.

When we were unable *to save ourselves* The genitive absolute ὄντων ἡμῶν ἀσθενῶν 'we being weak' expresses a circumstantial relation. The adjective 'weak' means 'without strength or power' and, in the context, means 'without ability to help ourselves spiritually' or 'without ability to provide our own justification/salvation'. NCV has "unable to help ourselves."

5:6b it was Christ who at the time *that God chose* **died** There is an unusual separation of the subject ('Christ') from the verb ('died'), the former being the first word in the verse and the latter the last word. The resulting prominence is indicated in the display by the cleft construction.

The phrase κατὰ καιρόν 'according to time' is a somewhat idiomatic expression meaning 'at the right time'. This in turn means "at the appointed time" (REB) or "at the time that God chose" (TEV).

on behalf of *us* **ungodly** *people* The pronoun 'us' is supplied to avoid the implication that Paul was referring to some group of which he was not a member.

5:7a Here γάρ introduces a further amplification of the subject of Christ's dying for the ungodly.

on behalf of another The preposition ὑπέρ probably means 'for the sake of, on behalf of' although some commentators (Hodge, Lenski, Shedd, Stuart, Morris) see here the more specific sense of 'in place of'.

5:7b *even if . . .* **righteous** The phrases 'righteous (person)' and 'good person' are taken by the majority of commentators to refer to two kinds of persons; and of the two, a 'good person', because of his actions, is held in higher esteem than a 'righteous person'.

5:7c although for a good person Here γάρ does not carry its usual sense of introducing a reason, explanation, or amplification; rather, as required by the context, it carries a concessive sense (so Stuart, CEV, NIV, JB, REB). BAGD (p. 152.4) render it 'but'. The words 'on behalf of a good person' are emphasized in the Greek by being forefronted. They are likewise forefronted in the display.

5:8c while we were still rebelling against God Here ὅτι has the function of introducing a forefronted participial phrase. This emphasis indicates an unexpected contrast; the sense is 'in that' (BAGD, p. 589.1c). The prominence is shown in the display by bold type.

The word ἁμαρτωλῶν 'sinners' that is part of the genitive absolute refers to people who are still in a state of rebellion against God (cf. BAGD, p. 44.2) as manifested by sinning. It is not just 'people who were sinning'.

5:9b by *what Christ accomplished when he shed his blood* Here ἐν is taken as expressing means (BAGD, p. 260.III1a). A means proposition requires a full clause, and the full clause implied by 'blood' is 'Christ's shedding his blood'. NCV has "the blood of Christ's death"; TCNT has "the shedding of his blood." Although 'blood' is a metonymy standing for Christ's death, the figure of blood being shed for atonement is so prevalent throughout Scripture that the word ought not be dropped in spelling out the figure in 9b-c. One could argue that we are justified not by Christ's shed blood but by our trust in its efficacy, but since this is a matter of theological interpretation it is not made specific in the display. Instead a more neutral interpretation is adopted: 'by what Christ accomplished when he shed his blood'.

5:9c *when he died on the cross* The blood referred to is the blood Christ shed during the crucifixion, hence 'when he died on the cross'.

5:9d from God's punishing us *eternally* The word ὀργή 'anger/wrath' is a metonymy in which the cause stands for the effect. Here 'anger' stands for the judgment or punishment for sin that God's wrath will bring about. REB has "final retribution." Since commentators say that this retribution is eschatological, not suffering for sin which people may experience during their present lifetime or suffering during the Great Tribulation, the word 'eternally' is supplied to avoid wrong meaning.

5:10a acting hostilely towards God The phrase ἐχθροὶ ὄντες 'we being enemies' is figurative, since most people in their unregenerate state do not consider God their enemy, nor does God consider us enemies. It is therefore somewhat hyperbolic to refer to our hostile acts towards him as making us his enemies. In the display this hostility is expressed as being on the one side only; the sense might be better conveyed by the idiom 'we were not on speaking terms'.

5:10d Christ will be able to save us *from God's punishing us* Since 10b speaks of our reconciliation as accomplished, the question arises as to what 'we shall be saved' in 10d refers to. The future tense indicates an eschatological interpretation. So the words 'from God's punishing us' are supplied based on the reference in v. 9 to being saved from God's wrath. In translating, this idea may have to be included to make the sense clear.

5:10e he is alive *again* The phrase ἐν τῇ ζωῇ αὐτοῦ 'in his life' refers to Christ's post-resurrection life; 'again' is implied. Denney says the ἐν 'in' is instrumental: "The Living Lord, in virtue of His life, will save us." This is tantamount to giving it causal force. Hodge does the same thing in stating the content of 10d-e as "the fact that he lives will certainly secure our final salvation."

5:11a-b In addition, we also boast about *those things which* God *has done for us* The words οὐ μόνον δέ, ἀλλὰ καί 'and not only but also' suggest the ellipsis of some clause to accompany 'not only'. Commentators are divided as to which clause is omitted, whether one that refers to reconciliation or one that refers to salvation. The latter is more likely; but in any case the sense is an additional implication of justification, specifically a reaction to it, hence 'In addition' in the display.

Following the participle καυχώμενοι 'boasting', ἐν introduces the substance of the boast. Rejoicing about a person requires that some event or quality be attributed to that person; thus the generic clause 'has done for us' is supplied here. LB has "rejoice in our wonderful new relationship with God."

5:11c on the basis of our Lord Jesus Christ *dying for us* The phrase 'through our Lord Jesus Christ' requires a full proposition since it expresses a reason relationship. The basis for the blessings God has given us is Christ's death for us.

5:11d and reconciling us *to God* The Greek is δι' οὗ νῦν τὴν καταλλαγὴν ἐλάβομεν 'through whom now we have received reconciliation'. By making the noun 'reconciliation' into a full clause the need for any representation of the verb 'received' is eliminated.

BOUNDARIES AND COHERENCE

Lexical coherence within the 5:6–11 paragraph is provided by expressions of the death of Christ (vv. 6, 8, 10) and two occurrences of the verb καταλλάσσω 'reconcile' in v. 10 and one of the cognate noun καταλλαγή 'reconciliation' in v. 11.

For the boundary with the following unit, see "Boundaries and Coherence" for 5:1–11.

PROMINENCE AND THEME

The theme of 5:6–11 is drawn from the most naturally prominent propositions of the *justification and situation* (6b), the CLAIM (9d), and the REACTION (11a).

SUBDIVISION CONSTITUENT 5:12–21
(Expository Paragraph: Nucleus₂ of 5:1–21)

THEME: *Although the sin of one man, Adam, led to all people dying and God declaring that they deserved to be punished, Christ's righteous act of obedience when he died led to many experiencing God's grace and being declared righteous and living eternally, and will result in their ruling with Christ.*

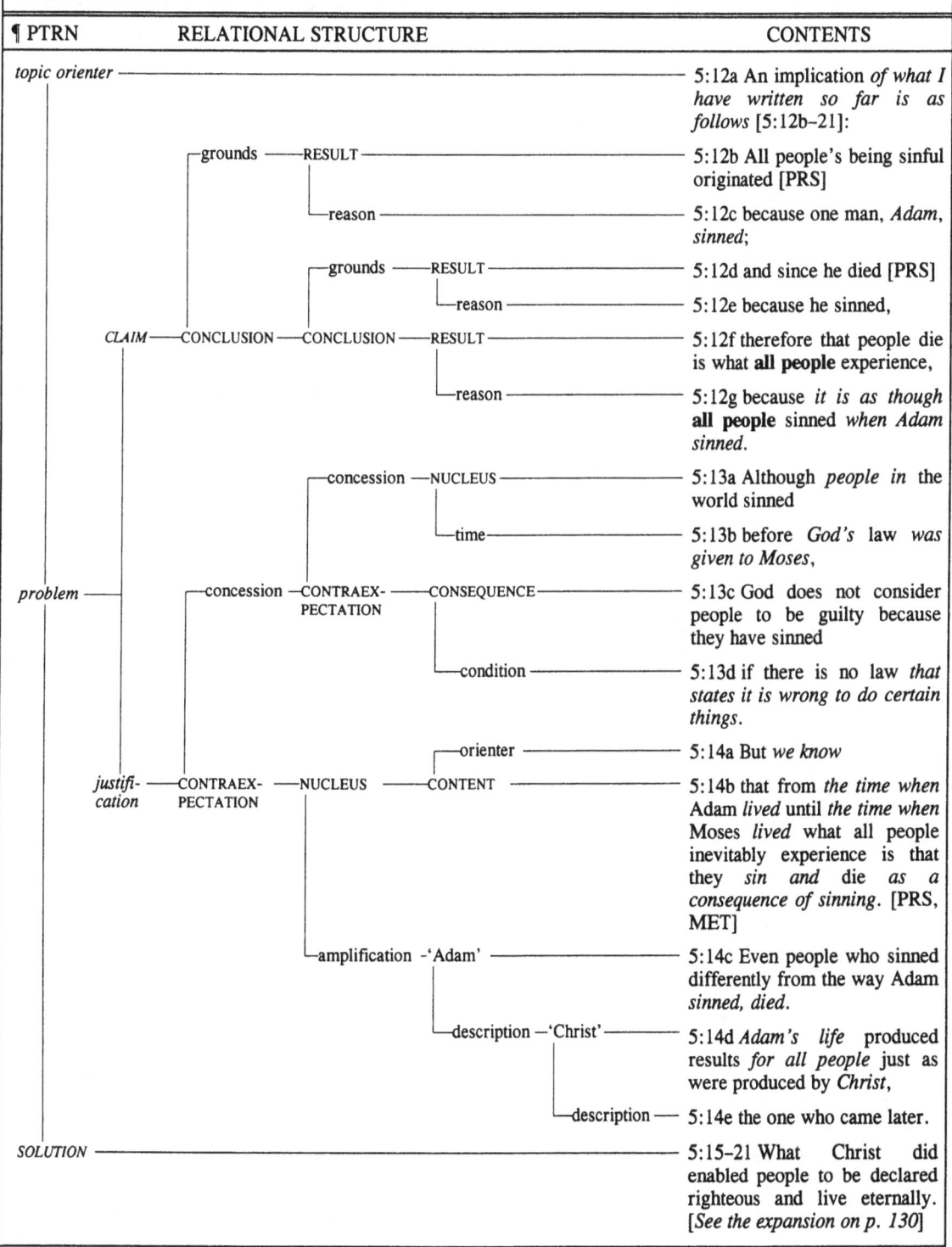

INTENT AND PARAGRAPH PATTERN

That 5:12-21 is an expository paragraph is clear from the indicative verbs in all the main clauses and the absence of any first person references. It presents the implications for the believer of the doctrine of justification by faith. But there are difficulties in determining the relations of its subunits. Clearly it starts with a *CLAIM* (v. 12) and its *justification* (vv. 13-14). Then there seems to be a further set of *CLAIMS*. Although vv. 17 and 19 each begin with γάρ, usually an indicator of a subordinate unit, these two verses do not cohere as *justifications* for the vv. 15-16 propositions. Furthermore, vv. 12-14 present spiritual death because of sin, whereas vv. 15-21 speak of life because of what Christ has done. Therefore 12-14 are seen as a *problem* and 15-21 the *SOLUTION*.

NOTES

5:12a The words διὰ τοῦτο 'therefore' introduce another implication of the doctrine of justification, not just of vv. 1-11 (so Dunn, Denney, Hodge), hence 'an implication of what I have written so far is . . .' in 12a. REB's rhetorical question "What does this imply?" carries the same sense.

The main difficulty in this verse is that Paul starts a comparison beginning with ὥσπερ 'just as' but never completes the sentence. Some versions (NIV, RSV) indicate the unfinished sentence with a dash at the end of v. 12. But as most commentators note, Paul does complete the thought in v. 18, the first part of which is almost a restatement of 12a. One could include the thought from 18b here to remove the ellipsis and complete the comparison. Some of the more recent translations (e.g., CEV, REB, NCV) make a full sentence here, ignoring the ὥσπερ in the text, and that is the solution taken here. To do otherwise would be to state the author's main point before *he* does. Since the SSAs use complete sentences in propositionalizing, even where the author did not, a brief sentence is supplied here as a topic orienter.

5:12b All people's being sinful originated The expression 'sin came into the world' is a personification (Robertson, Dunn, Hodge, Sanday and Headlam). It refers to the origin of sin and the fact that all people are sinful.

5:12c because one man, *Adam,* **sinned** The phrase 'through one man' expresses means, which requires a full clause. Therefore 'sinned' is supplied. The identity of the one man is supplied in the display (also in CEV and LB). Paul evidently assumed his readers would make that identification.

5:12d-e since he died because he sinned The phrase 'and death through sin' is a personification as well as being elliptical. The main question here is whether the implied subject of the event 'to die' is 'Adam' or 'all people'. It must be the former, since Paul states the latter in 12f-g.

5:12f that people die is what all people experience The clause εἰς πάντας ἀνθρώπους ὁ θάνατος διῆλθεν 'unto all men death spread' is a figurative way of saying that death is now a universal experience. The phrases 'unto all men' and 'death' are forefronted in the Greek. The cleft construction and bold type in the display convey the emphasis thus indicated.

5:12g *it is as though* **all people** *sinned when Adam sinned* The meaning of ἐφ' ᾧ has been much debated, but parallels in 2 Cor. 5:4 and Phil. 3:12 and 4:10 as well as many occurrences in extrabiblical literature make the reason relation quite certain (see Moulton 1:107 and BAGD, p. 287.II1bγ). The words 'all people' are in bold to indicate the emphasis shown by forefronting in the Greek.

Another classic debate on this proposition is whether the verb refers to (1) actual sins by everyone, (2) all people's sinning through Adam as their representative, or (3) the fact that all inherit the tendency to sin because of their descent from Adam, who sinned first. (Much of the discussion is heavily influenced by theology.) There are two strong reasons for rejecting the first interpretation. One is that the verb tense is aorist, indicating a one-time action—if Paul had meant 'habitually sin', he would have used the present tense or possibly the imperfect. The other is that the context revolves around the contrastive effects of the actions of only two individuals, Adam and Christ. The third interpretation is subject to the same criticism as the first. Furthermore, as Hodge notes, if v. 12 is simply stating that all people are sinners, then the statement in vv. 13-14, which is introduced by γάρ, supplies the justification for v. 12 and must mean that all people prior to Moses were sinners. But that is a statement no one questions, and it is extraneous to Paul's argument. For the display, therefore, interpretation 2 is taken as the correct one. But though the aorist tense requires a once-for-all action in the past to be understood, it is not literally true that all people sinned at some specific point of time, hence the rendering 'it is as though all people sinned when Adam sinned'. Those who wish to read more extensive treatments of the verse are referred to Cranfield (seven pages), Morris (three pages) and Hodge (seven pages).

5:13 There is a question on how this verse fits into Paul's argument. The only viable solution seems to be Hodge's, which is followed here, that even though there was no law and there was consequent disobedience (v. 13), people still died (v. 14). Therefore v. 13 is considered to be in a concession relationship with v. 14.

5:13a *people in* **the world sinned** The mismatch between semantics and grammar involving the abstract noun ἁμαρτία 'sin' in the clause 'sin was in the world' is removed in the display.

5:13b before *God's* **law** *was given to Moses* The Greek is simply ἄχρι νόμου 'until the law'. The word 'God's' is supplied to avoid ambiguity.

Some verb is required to complete the clause introduced by 'until' (rendered 'before' in the display). Most English versions supply 'was given' (RSV, NIV, JB, C. B. Williams, Beck). The verb 'give' then requires a recipient; in the display 'to Moses' is supplied, making the recipient specific.

5:13c God does not consider people to be guilty because they have sinned Theologians and commentators have given various interpretations to the clause ἁμαρτία οὐκ ἐλλογεῖται 'sin is not counted'. Some suggest that it implies an unwritten law in human hearts which people disobey; others, that there is sin where there is no law even though the sin may not be called such; and still others, that there are no sins where there is no law forbidding them and therefore no punishment is called for.

This third sense is totally foreign to Paul's discussion of the universality of sin both here and in chapters 1-3. The second view at first seems to suggest that Paul is talking out of both sides of his mouth—that he doesn't mean what he says. While the first sense is possible, it makes the reader who believes in the universality of guilt for sin search for some loophole to avoid what Paul seems to be saying.

The solution proposed here is that since ἁμαρτία is singular, not plural, it has the sense of guilt for sin, not sins. This is frequently its sense (e.g., in 4:8), here reinforced by the verb ἐλλογέω 'to charge to one's account' and thus 'to consider/reckon as guilty for having committed a breach of law'. The sense here is therefore that where there is no law, people do sin and thus stand condemned by God, but the guilt incurred is not for having broken specific laws. NCV has "God does not judge people guilty of sin if. . . ."

5:13d no law *that states it is wrong to do certain things* To complete the argument the sense must be understood as 'no law commanding or forbidding certain things'. Conybeare and Howson (p. 510) have "when there is no law [forbidding it]."

5:14b what all people inevitably experience is that they *sin* **and** *die as a consequence* The clause ἐβασίλευσεν ὁ θάνατος 'death reigned' involves both a metaphor and personification. The sense of the metaphor is that death is in complete control of everyone as a king is in control of his subjects. The personification is removed; the sense is conveyed in the display with 'what all people inevitably experience'. While the mention of death here may seem out of context (the topic under discussion being the universality of sin), the universality of death as proof of the universality of sin *was* mentioned in v. 12, and this idea is conveyed by 'sin and die as a consequence'. It could also be expressed as 'die because they have all sinned'.

The phrase 'from Adam to Moses' is a short way of saying 'from the time Adam lived to the time Moses lived' (cf. TEV, NEB, CEV).

5:14c Even people who sinned differently from the way Adam *sinned, died* The words 'death reigned' are presumed to be implied, repeated from 14b, hence 'died' in the display.

The negative in the verb phrase μὴ ἁμαρτήσαντας ἐπὶ τῷ ὁμοιώματι τῆς παραβάσεως Ἀδάμ 'not having sinned in the likeness of the transgression of Adam' goes with the latter part of the phrase, not with the verb 'sinned'. Hodge says the sense is "Death reigned over a class of persons who had not sinned as Adam had," but this interpretation is rejected here. Hodge misses the problem of the misplacement of the negative, and also misses the main point of the argument. The nouns 'likeness' and 'transgression' together are a mismatched way of saying 'as Adam transgressed'.

5:14d *Adam's life* **produced results** *for all people* **just as were produced by** *Christ* The Greek is ὅς ἐστιν τύπος 'who (Adam) is a type'. For one person to be a type of another means that their lives correspond in some way. In this context the sense is that the effects of the one's life were similar in some respect to the effects produced by the other's (so Barnes, Harrison, Dunn), and more specifically that the effects of each life reached all the rest of mankind.

EXPANSION OF *SOLUTION* IN THE 5:12–21 DISPLAY

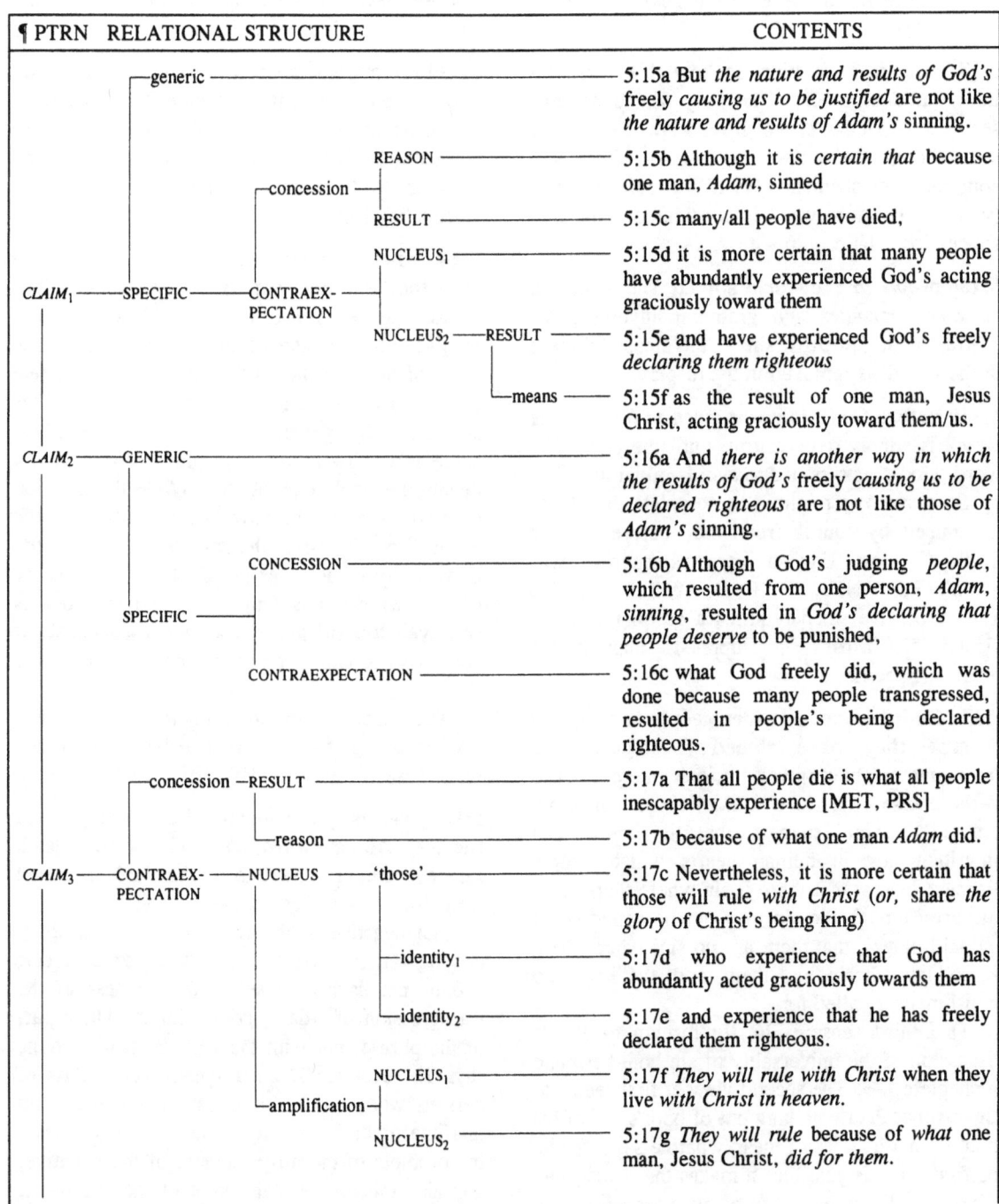

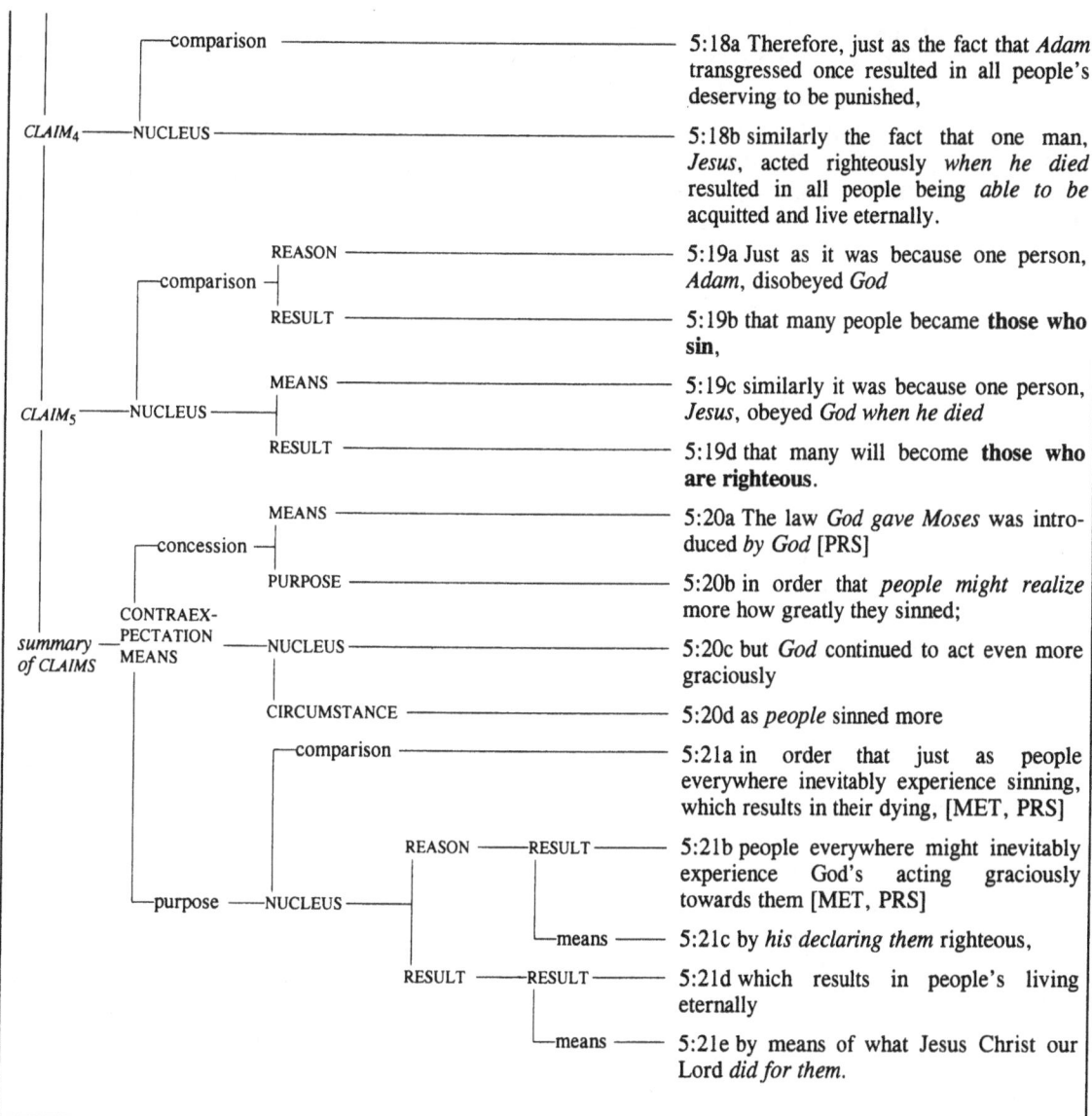

5:15a *the nature and results of God's* **freely causing us to be justified** **are not like** *the nature and results of Adam's* **sinning** Paul here contrasts two things: χάρισμα 'free gift' and παράπτωμα 'trespass'. The free gift is justification (see 3:24, also 5:16-21).

The trespass referred to here is Adam's; this is made specific in the display to satisfy the case frame. Since 'justification' and 'trespass' have almost nothing in common semantically, the display makes specific that aspect of each that can be contrasted: the nature and results.

5:15b Here γάρ introduces a specification or explanation of 15a, not the reason why the free gift differs from the trespass.

Although In 5:15b-f the context suggests a concession-CONTRAEXPECTATION relation. This is shown by the bad news in 15b-c and the good news in 15d-g. It is similarly rendered by NCV, CEV, TEV.

because one man, Adam, sinned The dative in τῷ τοῦ ἑνὸς παραπτώματι 'by the transgression of the one' is taken as expressing reason.

5:15c-f many/all people have died The words οἱ πολλοί 'the many' in 15c can rightly be taken to mean 'all people', because in the context Paul says the effects of sin have spread to all mankind (cf. the use of πάντας ἀνθρώπους in vv. 12, 18). But the main reason Paul uses 'many' here is that 'many' is appropriate in the other half of the comparison (15d), and using the same word in 15c balances the comparison. (For rhetorical effect Paul frequently uses the same word in two halves of a balanced construction when the meaning is not identical in each half.)

In both parts of the v. 15 comparison, all the nonverb elements are prominent by virtue of being forefronted. To convey this prominence, cleft constructions are used beginning in 15b. This, in English, requires gerund phrases in 15d and 15e as objects of the verb 'experienced'.

5:15d it is more certain Although most versions connect πολλῷ μᾶλλον 'by much rather' with 'grace' (TEV, e.g., has "but God's grace is much greater"), the great majority of commentators support the sense of greater certainty given here, applying it to the verb ἐπερίσσευσεν 'abounded' and everything else in 15d–f. BAGD (p. 489.2b) also give this sense. This interpretation is based on the fact that μᾶλλον is an adverb and could not modify a noun such as 'grace'.

many people have abundantly experienced God's acting graciously toward them The Greek is ἡ χάρις τοῦ θεοῦ . . . εἰς τοὺς πολλοὺς ἐπερίσσευσεν 'the grace of God . . . unto the many abounded'. To reduce this to its semantic propositions requires a fair amount of unscrambling. The noun phrase 'grace of God' is expressing the event 'God has acted graciously'; 'abounded to' is a verb with an adverbial sense, 'abundantly'. This would give 'God has abundantly acted graciously toward many people'. But in the display it is rendered 'many people have abundantly experienced' (i.e., experienced God's grace) in order to maintain the parallelism of the subjects ('many people' in 15c and 15g) and also to maintain the prominence previously noted.

5:15e and . . . God's freely *declaring them righteous* The Greek is καὶ ἡ δωρεά 'and the gift'. But as Morris says (p. 215), the word 'gift' signifies a free gift and in the NT is used only with God's good gifts to mankind. The word 'gift' here functions as a modifier, semantically speaking, hence 'freely'; 'declaring us righteous' is supplied as the implied event that it modifies (see the note on 5:15a).

5:15f the result of one man, Jesus Christ, acting graciously toward them/us The phrase ἐν χάριτι 'in grace' is taken here as expressing means. 'Grace', grammatically a noun but semantically an event, is represented in the display by 'acting graciously toward us'.

5:16a Semantically, 16a is almost identical with 15a; it simply introduces another comparison, again a contrastive one.

there is another way These words are supplied to bring out the relation of v. 16 to v. 15. (For 'results of', 'causing us to be declared righteous', and 'Adam', see the note on 15a.)

5:16b As in 15b, γάρ introduces a specification of the way the actions of Adam and Christ contrast.

God's judging *people* The noun κρίμα 'judgment' here signifies an event, that of judging. It might be a metonymy in which the result of the judging process is really what is in view, namely the guilty verdict (cf. BAGD, p. 450.4a). REB has "the judicial action . . . resulted in a verdict of condemnation."

which resulted from one person, *Adam, sinning* The Greek is the elliptical ἐξ ἑνός 'from one'. The identification of 'one', Adam, and the event of sinning are carried over from vv. 14–15.

resulted in *God's declaring that people deserve* to be punished The Greek has only εἰς κατάκριμα 'unto condemnation'. Satisfaction of the case frame requires the subject of the condemning ('God') and the object of the condemning ('people') to be supplied to complete the proposition. Commentators (e.g., Morris, Dunn) note that κατάκριμα is a strong word almost equivalent to 'punishment' (see also BAGD, p. 412), hence 'deserve to be punished'. CEV has "led to punishment."

5:16c what God freely did, which was done because many people transgressed, resulted in people's being declared righteous The nouns χάρισμα 'free gift', παραπτωμάτων 'offenses', and δικαίωμα 'justification' all represent events. The appropriate subjects and objects are supplied to satisfy the case frame.

5:17a Here γάρ introduces another CLAIM following the one made in v. 16.

The words ὁ θάνατος ἐβασίλευσεν 'death reigned' are a personification as well as a metaphor (see the note on 5:14b). CEV renders it "ruled like a king." The sense is that death is in absolute control of all people; it is the universal experience of everyone, hence 'is what all people inescapably experience'.

5:17c–g Note that it may be necessary in some languages to change all the third person plural pronouns to first person plural to avoid the connotation that Paul is not included among those referred to. CEV uses the first person plural here.

5:17c those will rule *with Christ* (*or*, share *the glory* of Christ's being king) The Greek is βασιλεύσουσιν 'will reign'. It is not clear whether it was intended literally or figuratively, in the sense of having achieved ultimate victory over everything ranged against us, including death itself. It could also mean, as several commentators take it, 'share the glory of Christ's being king'. The display presents both alternatives.

5:17d God has abundantly acted graciously towards them The two nouns in the phrase περισσείαν τῆς χάριτος 'abundance of grace' represent the attribute 'abundantly' and the event 'God acts graciously' (cf. 15a).

5:17e he has freely declared them righteous The two nouns in the phrase δωρεᾶς τῆς δικαιοσύνης 'gift of righteousness' represent an attribute modifying an event: 'freely declares (them) righteous' (cf. 15e).

5:17f when they live *with Christ in heaven* The phrase ἐν ζωῇ 'in life' is taken to refer to a future state due to the future tense of the verb 'will reign'. Thus the rendering 'with Christ in heaven' is not only implied but necessary to avoid confusion as to what life Paul means.

5:18a Therefore This verse begins with ἄρα οὖν, usually translated 'therefore'. But here it introduces a new CLAIM, which, though related to the previous ones, is somewhat different from the ones in v. 15-17: having new elements makes the CLAIM different from the preceding ones. The context would not support its introducing a CONCLUSION of the preceding argument. This means that the CLAIM in v. 17 is not subordinate to the one in v. 18, but only that there is a similarity in the two verses that contrast one man, Adam, with another, Christ.

the fact that *Adam* transgressed once resulted in all people's deserving to be punished Commentators are divided as to whether δι᾽ ἑνὸς παραπτώματος means 'through one trespass' or 'through one man's trespass'. Grammatically it is 'one trespass'; but semantically it refers to the one sin (eating the forbidden fruit) of the one man Adam. In some translations it may have to be made specific in some way. Furthermore, the translator must make sure the readers do not assume that Adam committed only one sin during his life. It may be necessary to say 'Adam's very first transgression'. For 'deserving to be punished', see the note on 16b.

5:18b one man, *Jesus*, acted righteously *when he died* The phrase ἑνὸς δικαιώματος 'one righteous act', which follows the contrasts in vv. 15-17, clearly refers to an act by Christ. Grammatically parallel to the phrase 'one trespass' in 18a, it means 'one righteous act', not 'one man's act of righteousness'. Semantically, the reference is to the one supreme righteous act of the one man Christ. As commentators note, that act is his substitutionary death; hence the words 'when he died' are supplied to make clear what Paul intended and to avoid ambiguity as to which act is referred to or the wrong notion that Christ performed only one righteous act during his life.

***all people* being *able to be* acquitted and live eternally** The words 'able to be' are supplied to keep Paul's exposition of his main theme in 3:22 consistent, free from self-contradiction. As an alternative, 'all people' could be qualified as 'all people who believe in Christ' or 'all people who accept this'.

In the phrase δικαίωσιν ζωῆς 'justification of life', 'life' has often been taken to be the result of 'justification'. Sometimes 'life' is taken as the definition of 'justification'. But Paul never equates the two elsewhere. On the other hand, eternal life as the outcome of being justified is expressed in v. 17 and implied by contrast with death, which is presented as the outcome of Adam's trespass in vv. 12 and 15.

5:19a Here γάρ introduces a new CLAIM. It is related to the one made in v. 18, and is not a reason for it.

5:19b, d many people became those who sin . . . those who are righteous As he does here with οἱ πολλοί 'the many', Paul often uses the same words with different senses in parallel structures for rhetorical effect (cf. v. 18). In 19b the sense is equivalent to 'all men' in v. 12; in 19d the same phrase is to be taken literally as 'many', not 'all'.

The words ἁμαρτωλοί 'sinners' in 19b and δίκαιοι 'righteous' in 19d are in emphatic position. The emphasis thus conveyed is shown in the display by bold type.

The two occurrences of the verb καθίστημι 'to be caused to become' (BAGD, p. 390.3) mean 'to be constituted as' in the sense of 'become members of that class known as'.

5:19c because one person, *Jesus*, obeyed *God when he died* Christ's whole life was one of obedience to his Father, but here in an amplification of v. 18 the 'one act' being referred to is his 'obedience unto death' (cf. Phil. 2:8). The translator should be sure to avoid the wrong meaning that Jesus performed only one righteous deed during his life.

For 'when he died', see the note on 18b.

5:20a The conjunction δέ occurs here. It indicates the switch to a brief mention of νόμος 'law'. In almost no English translation is it represented, since vv. 20–21 are a summary statement concluding the whole chapter. In 20c there is a second δέ, which is clearly adversative.

The law *God gave Moses* **was introduced** *by God* The Greek is νόμος παρεισῆλθεν 'the law entered', a personification. It is rendered nonfiguratively in the display (cf. TEV). The 'law' is specified as the law of Moses to remove any ambiguity as to which law was in view. LB has "the Ten Commandments."

5:20b in order that *people might realize* **more how greatly they sinned** The Greek is ἵνα πλεονάσῃ τὸ παράπτωμα 'in order that the transgression would increase'. The first problem commentators wrestle with here is whether ἵνα truly expresses purpose or simply the result/effect. But as several commentators point out (Morris, Sanday and Headlam, Harrison), Paul states in this epistle (3:19–20) and elsewhere (Gal. 3:19) that the purpose of the Mosaic law was to bring about an awareness of sin; hence 'that people might realize' is supplied in the display. LB renders it very nicely by "so that all could see the extent of their failure to obey God's laws."

The other problem is the sense of 'abounded'. Most commentators agree that 'abounding' does not refer to increase in number of sins, but in their heinousness in the sight of God.

The singular subject 'transgression' balances ἡ χάρις 'the grace', which is the singular subject later in the verse. Semantically, however, the sense is 'transgressions'.

5:20c–d *God* **continued to act even more graciously as** *people* **sinned more** The clauses ἐπλεόνασεν ἡ ἁμαρτία 'sin abounded' and ὑπερεπερίσσευσεν ἡ χάρις 'grace overabounded' could be considered personifications. In the display they are rendered nonfiguratively, the events being expressed by verbs and the appropriate subjects supplied.

5:21a–b In v. 21 the verb βασιλεύω 'to reign' occurs twice. The idea of universality being conveyed by the figures of speech here is expressed as 'people everywhere inevitably experience'. See the discussion on 14b and 17a.

which results in their dying Most commentators try to handle the phrase ἐν τῷ θανάτῳ 'in death' with eloquence by maintaining the personification, but they fail to deal adequately with ἐν 'in'. The rendering in the display removes the personification of which 'in' is a part. Then the relation signaled by ἐν is taken as result: 'which results in their dying'. This seems most appropriate to what Paul has already stated.

5:21c by *his declaring them* **righteous** The phrase διὰ δικαιοσύνης 'through righteousness' represents an event, either 'by their living righteously' or 'by God's declaring them righteous'. The whole previous context suggests the latter, as does the phrase 'unto eternal life' which immediately follows.

5:21e See the note on 5:1d.

BOUNDARIES AND COHERENCE

The relational coherence of the 5:12–21 paragraph consists of its having two basic parts: one, the *problem* (12b–14) of the universality of spiritual death brought on by Adam and, two, the SOLUTION (vv. 15–21). The latter consists of a series of five CLAIMS and a *summary*: the CLAIMS (15–19) contrast the sin of Adam with the greater righteous act of Christ and its universal effects; the *summary* (20–21) contrasts the sin of people with the greater grace of God.

There are several bits of lexical coherence in the paragraph. For one, παράπτωμα 'trespass' occurs six times (and not again until chap. 11). Also, there are eight references to Adam, either by name or by the expressions 'one' or 'one man' (the word 'one' occurs twelve times here and not again until chap. 9). There are four references to Christ either by 'one' or 'one man'.

For the boundary at 6:1, see "Boundaries and Coherence" under 5:1–21.

PROMINENCE AND THEME

The 5:12–21 paragraph consists of a series of contrasts between the effects on humankind arising from what one man, Adam, did, and what another man, Jesus Christ, did. The contrasts are indicated by use of the recurring word 'one' to refer to these two individuals, which device makes the set of contrasts prominent.

The first part of the theme is taken from the naturally prominent CONCLUSION (12f) of the CLAIM within the *problem*. The rest of the theme is from the set of five CLAIMS in the SOLUTION (vv. 15–21), but greatly condensed to eliminate the repetition in them. The material from the *summary* at the end of the paragraph is not included in the theme because it serves primarily as a boundary for the unit and does not contain any new material. Nor is the material in vv. 13–14, the *justification* of the 12f CLAIM, included, since it is largely amplificatory and contains very little new information.

DIVISION CLUSTER CONSTITUENT 6:1–8:39
(Expository Subdivision: Application₂ of 3:21–26)

THEME: We have been freed from being controlled by sinful desires and from being required to obey the Mosaic law to be saved. Now we are compelled to live as God's Spirit directs. In view of what God does for us through his Spirit, no one can prevail against us, and nothing can separate us from Christ's and God's loving us.

MACROSTRUCTURE	CONTENTS
CLAIM$_1$	6:1–23 If someone were to say that perhaps we should continue to sin in order that God may continue to act more graciously towards us, or because we are not obligated to obey the Mosaic law, I would reply that we have been freed from being controlled by sinful desires. Instead, we are to present ourselves to God to become slaves of righteous living.
CLAIM$_2$	7:1–25 God has freed us from being required to obey the Mosaic law to be saved. The Mosaic law simply reveals that what we are doing is sinful. It is our desire, not the law, that causes us to sin and become spiritually dead. But Christ can free us from being controlled by what our bodies desire.
CLAIM$_3$	8:1–39 God will not in any way condemn those who are united to Christ Jesus; we are compelled to live as God's Spirit directs, not as our sinful human nature directs. What we suffer now is not worth paying attention to as we consider the future splendor that God will reveal to us. The Spirit helps us as our spirits feel weak. And God works out all things in a way that produces good to us who love him. Therefore no one can prevail against us, and nothing can separate us from Christ's and God's loving us.

INTENT AND MACROSTRUCTURE

All the constituent paragraphs within the 6:1–8:39 unit are expository. The unit, therefore, is considered expository. It is a further application (or set of applications) of justification by faith to the everyday life of the believer. The three sections of the unit present equally prominent CLAIMS.

BOUNDARIES AND COHERENCE

It seems best to follow a host of commentators here (e.g., Dunn, Harrison, Morris) and consider 6:1–8:39 as one unit. It is difficult, however, to do so on the basis of lexical coherence. (One can say only that throughout this subdivision there is a heavy use of the second person plural pronoun in contrast to the first person singular starting with chap. 9.) Rather, its coherence derives from the fact that it deals with the practical implications of the doctrine of justification by faith for the daily spiritual life of all believers.

This unit ends, in 8:39, with 'in Christ Jesus our Lord', paralleling the ending of the previous unit ('through Jesus Christ our Lord'). In the unit that follows (9:1–11:36) the focus shifts from the implications of justification for believers in general to its implications for the Jews in particular.

PROMINENCE AND THEME

Because the constituents of 6:1–8:39 are considered equal, the theme is drawn equally from them. The theme consists of a brief condensation of the two CLAIMS of 6:1–23, the two CLAIMS of 7:1–25, and a very brief condensation of the content of the 8:1–39 *justifications* and CLAIM.

SUBDIVISION CONSTITUENT 6:1–23
(Expository Section: Claim₁ of 6:1–8:39)

THEME: If someone were to say that perhaps we should continue to sin in order that God may continue to act more graciously towards us, or because we are not obligated to obey the Mosaic law, I would reply that we have been freed from being controlled by sinful desires. Instead, we are to present ourselves to God to become slaves of righteous living.

MACROSTRUCTURE	CONTENTS
CLAIM₁	6:1–14 If someone were to say that perhaps we should continue to sin in order that God may continue to act more graciously toward us, I would reply that we who ought to consider ourselves unresponsive to sinful desires should certainly not continue sinning. We must keep remembering that it is as though our former sinful nature has ceased to function and we have become unresponsive to sinful desires, living a new way. Do not let the desire to commit sin control you. Instead, present yourselves to God to do righteous things.
CLAIM₂	6:15–23 If someone should conclude that perhaps we can sin now since we are not obligated to obey the Mosaic law, I would say certainly not; let your minds compel your bodies to act righteously.

INTENT AND MACROSTRUCTURE

Both constituents of the 6:1–23 unit are expository; thus the whole unit is expository. Both present hypothetical *objections* to the doctrine of justification by faith set forth in 3:21–26 and Paul's REFUTATIONS of the these *objections*. The two paragraphs are considered equal, neither being subordinate to the other.

BOUNDARIES AND COHERENCE

The great majority of commentators recognize 6:1–23 as one unit consisting of two *objection-REFUTATION* subunits, as is done here. (Morris and Harrison, who take 6:1–14 as one unit and 6:15–7:6 as the next, are exceptions.) Paul in 6:1–23 anticipates an erroneous conclusion that might be drawn from what he has presented, and then he refutes it.

Lexical coherence within 6:1–23 is provided by words in the semantic domain of slavery: δοῦλος 'slave' three times (vv. 16, 17, 20); the verbs δουλόω 'to enslave' twice (vv. 18, 22); δουλεύω 'be a slave' once (v. 6); κυριεύω 'lord it over' twice (vv. 9, 14); ἐλευθερόω 'set free' twice (vv. 18, 22); and βασιλεύω 'reign' once (v. 12).

In v. 23 the final boundary marker is once again the phrase 'in Christ Jesus our Lord'. The opening of the next unit (beginning in 7:1) is marked with a vocative ἀδελφοί 'brethren' and a rhetorical question.

PROMINENCE AND THEME

Since the constituent paragraphs of 6:1–23 are considered coordinate, the theme is drawn from the themes of both of them. They are condensed to eliminate nonthematic material such as orienters and repetitive material.

SECTION CONSTITUENT 6:1-14
(Expository Paragraph: Claim₁ of 6:1-23)

> *THEME: If someone were to say that perhaps we should continue to sin in order that God may continue to act more graciously toward us, I would reply that we who ought to consider ourselves unresponsive to sinful desires should certainly not continue sinning. We must keep remembering that it is as though our former sinful nature has ceased to function and we have become unresponsive to sinful desires, living a new way. Do not let the desire to commit sin control you. Instead, present yourselves to God to do righteous things.*

¶ PTRN	CONTENTS
objection	6:1a-e If . . . perhaps . . . [*See the expansion below.*]
REFUTATION — basis₁	6:2-5 We who ought to consider ourselves unresponsive to sinful desires should certainly not continue sinning. [*See the expansion on p. 139.*]
basis₂	6:6-8 We must keep remembering that it is as though our former sinful nature was caused to cease to function when Christ was crucified. [*See the expansion on p. 142.*]
APPEAL₁	6:9-11 You must consider that it is as though you have become unresponsive to sinful desires and now are living a new way. [*See the expansion on p. 144.*]
APPEAL₂	6:12-14 Do not let the desire to commit sin control you; instead present yourselves to God to do righteous things. [*See the expansion on p. 145.*]

INTENT AND PARAGRAPH PATTERN

At this point in his discourse Paul begins to anticipate some possible objections and to give counterarguments. This style has often been equated, rightly or wrongly, with the diatribe form of argumentation. In effect, Paul is stating in 6:1-14 an anticipated criticism of what he has just said about justification by faith. There are therefore two levels of paragraph-pattern relations: On the higher level are an *objection* and a *REFUTATION* (or they might be called *query* and *RESPONSE*). For this reason, and because the whole of 1:18-11:36 is expository, the 6:1-14 unit is considered expository, of the solutionality subtype. The fact that at the lower level there are a number of exhortations (e.g., in 11a, 12a, 13a-b, 13e) does not make it hortatory because these are lower-level relations within the higher-level *REFUTATION*. Paul's main thrust in 6:1-14 is to answer an anticipated objection. The fact that in doing so he feels it necessary to make several exhortations (so as not to have to deal with them later) is recognized, but since this is the lesser of Paul's purposes here, the paragraph is still considered expository. At the lower level Paul's *REFUTATION* consists of two *APPEALS* (9-11, 12-14) preceded by two *bases* (2-5, 6-8).

EXPANSION OF THE *OBJECTION* IN THE 6:1-14 DISPLAY

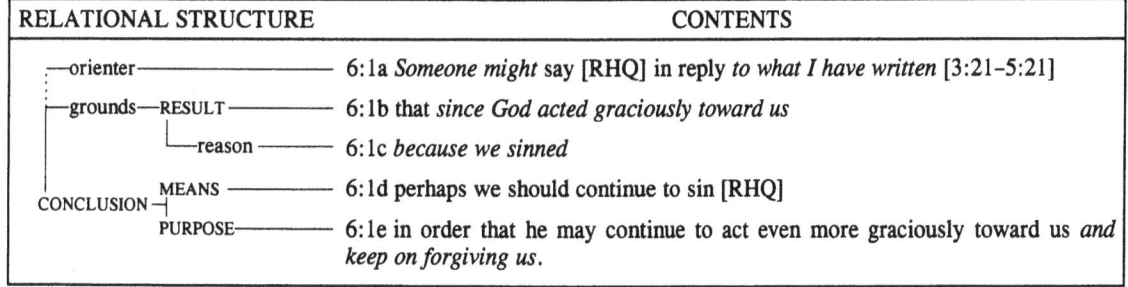

RELATIONAL STRUCTURE	CONTENTS
orienter	6:1a *Someone might* say [RHQ] in reply *to what I have written* [3:21-5:21]
grounds — RESULT	6:1b that *since God acted graciously toward us*
reason	6:1c *because we sinned*
CONCLUSION — MEANS	6:1d *perhaps we should continue to sin* [RHQ]
PURPOSE	6:1e *in order that he may continue to act even more graciously toward us and keep on forgiving us.*

NOTES

6:1a Someone might say The rhetorical question at the beginning of this verse is the first of a series of rhetorical questions, the others being in 6:15, 7:7, 8:31, and 9:14. Each such question is used by Paul to introduce a hypothetical (and wrong) objection to what he has stated thus far, which in turn leads into an answer to such an objection. The hypothetical objection is also worded as a question and can be considered rhetorical, giving two rhetorical questions in sequence in v. 1. In the display the two are collapsed into one statement. (All rhetorical questions are rendered by nonquestions in the displays.) The first of the rhetorical questions is rendered as the orienter introducing the objection; and the second, the objection itself.

Alternatively, either or both of these questions may be rendered as question forms. If the translator prefers a more literal translation of τί οὖν ἐροῦμεν 'What therefore shall we say?', in many languages the implicit referent may have to be made explicit: 'about our being declared righteous by God', which is the topic of the whole previous section.

in reply *to what I have written* These words convey the sense of οὖν 'therefore', which is taken as introducing a conclusion Paul anticipates could be drawn (or perhaps knows has been drawn) from his whole presentation of justification of faith.

6:1b–c *since God acted graciously toward us because we sinned* The second question in the Greek text presents a wrong inference from the preceding exposition. From the point of view of paragraph pattern theory, a grounds for this inference is implied and therefore supplied in 1b–c. This alternative is chosen for the display. There is another alternative, though with little difference in meaning, namely, to consider 1b–c of the first alternative simply the semantic content of 'therefore' by itself, keeping it as Paul's words instead of the words of an objector. This would give:

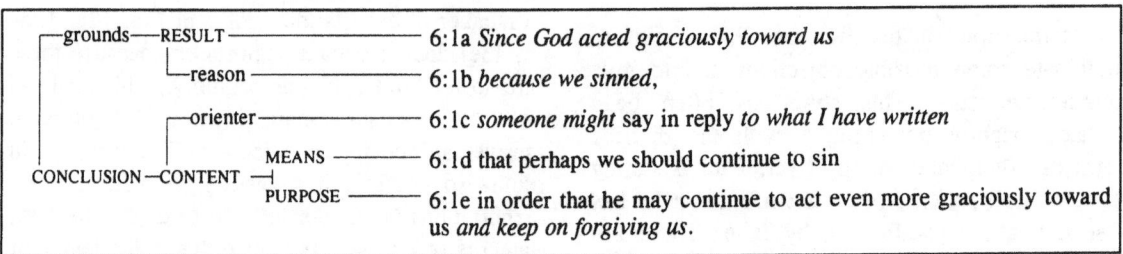

6:1d perhaps Paul worded the hypothetical objection in the form of a question. The answer was, to Paul, a foregone conclusion. The objector, however, is raising this as a possible conclusion and this possibility is shown in the display by 'perhaps'. Alternatively, it could be rendered as a yes-no question, retaining the literal form of the original.

6:1e *and keep on forgiving us* This phrase is the implied result of God's grace abounding: if we keep sinning, God will keep forgiving us.

EXPANSION OF *BASIS*₁ IN THE 6:1-14 DISPLAY

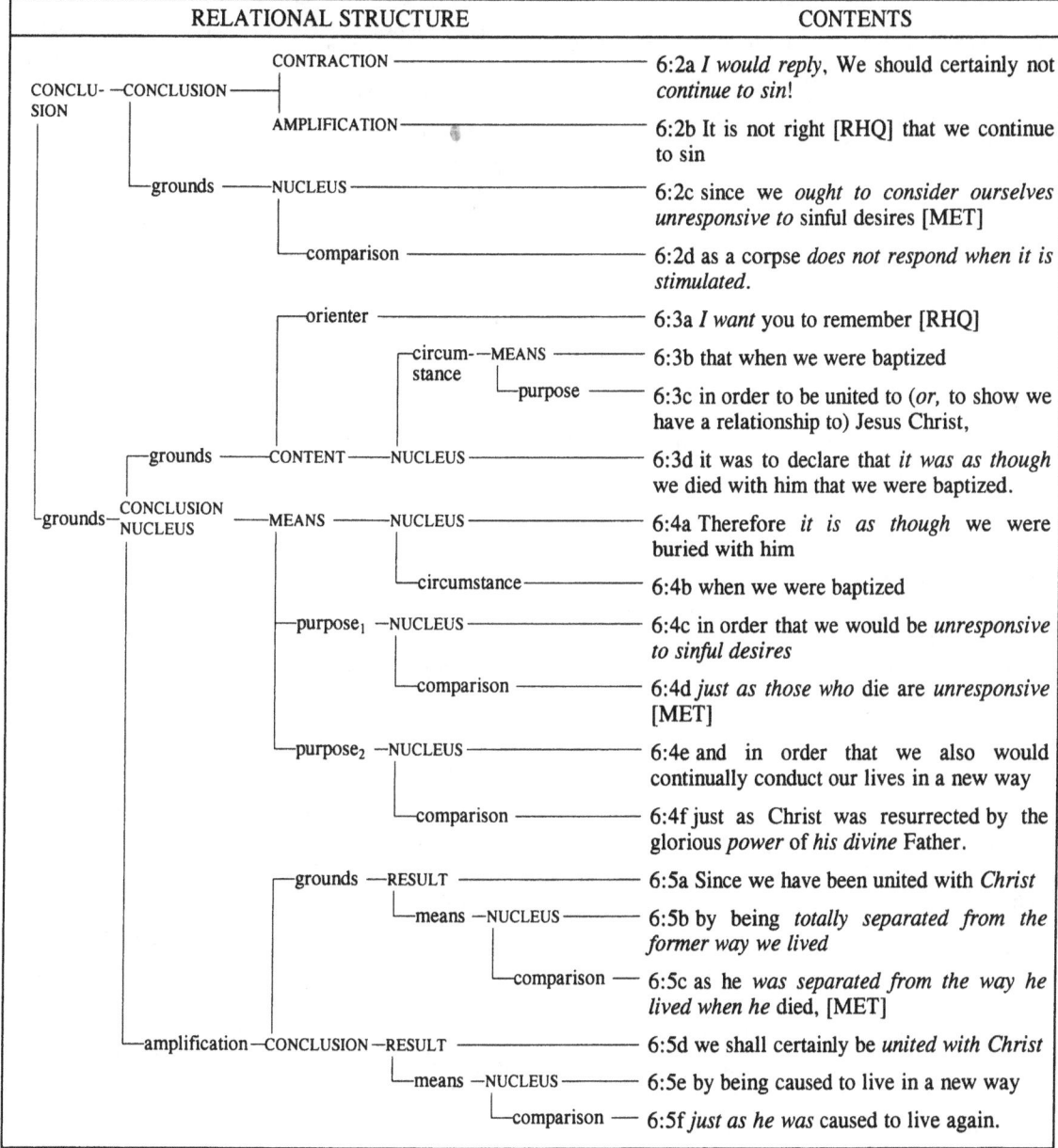

6:2a I would reply The fact that Paul is replying to a presumably hypothetical objection is made clear by including the orienter words 'I would reply'.

certainly not The phrase μὴ γένοιτο is simply an emphatic negative reply. It might be represented in English by such abbreviated idiomatic expressions as 'Absolutely not!', 'By no means!', 'Heavens, no!', 'No way!' (cf. 3:4, 6), but in some languages a full sentence may be necessary.

6:2b It is not right The rhetorical question here has the force of an emphatic negative, which in effect duplicates the negative preceding it. Alternatively, a reworded rhetorical question could be used: 'Should we . . . ?' or 'Do you think that we . . . ?' But translators should follow the natural patterns for emphatic negatives in the receptor language.

continue to sin These words are a straightforward rendering of ζήσομεν ἐν αὐτῇ 'shall live in it (i.e., in sin)'. This is not meant to imply that Paul was teaching sinless perfection for believers;

the sense is 'not continue to keep on deliberately/habitually sinning'.

6:2c–d *ought to consider ourselves unresponsive to* The point of similarity in the metaphor ἀπεθάνομεν τῇ ἁμαρτίᾳ 'we died to sin' is insensitivity or inability to be influenced. Here it is rendered 'unresponsive to'. Some suggest 'freedom from the power of', which, though similar, is a personification.

Even after spelling out the metaphor, a problem remains: Christians do not become insensitive to sin at conversion. Paul is using hyperbole here; what he is saying is, as expressed in the display, 'we ought to consider . . .' A somewhat more literal translation in which the point of similarity is not spelled out would be: 'It is as though we died'.

6:2c sinful desires The sense of ἁμαρτία 'sin' here (and subsequently in chaps. 6 and 7) is somewhat different from its sense in v. 1. What we are to become insensitive to is not the specific sinful acts, but the desire to sin. As noted by BAGD (p. 43.3), in many of these passages Paul's use of the word amounts to personification. It is difficult to express the idea in the display without nominalizing the word, hence 'sinful desires'.

6:2d corpse In some languages it is possible to say 'dead person', and in others it is necessary to use a word for 'corpse'.

6:3a *I want* **you to remember** In Romans Paul frequently uses the rhetorical question 'Do you not know . . . ?' to emphasize, not something they necessarily know, but something he wants them to keep in mind, whether they know it already or not.

The conjunction ἤ 'or' is used a number of times by Paul (and once by Matthew) to introduce a rhetorical question. From the viewpoint of semantics, the question here introduces the grounds for the statement in 2b, and the use of ἤ grammatically prohibits the use of γάρ, the usual introducer of grounds.

6:3c in order to be united to (*or,* **to show we have a relationship to**) **Jesus Christ** The phrase εἰς Χριστὸν Ἰησοῦν 'into Christ Jesus' is taken by most commentators as expressing 'into union with Christ' (cf. Hodge, Sanday and Headlam, Alford, Denney, Nygren, Morris, Harrison, Murray, Haldane). But does 'into' mean 'in order to be united to' or 'in order to show we are united to'? That is, does baptism place us in the body of Christ or is it an outward symbol of an internal transformation? Here one's theology must decide. The first alternative in the display follows the former; the second follows the latter.

6:3d *it was as though* **we died with him** The phrase εἰς τὸν θάνατον αὐτοῦ 'into his death' is, in the Greek, emphasized by being forefronted; this is indicated in the display by the reversal of order in the cleft construction. The phrase itself is puzzling, and commentators do not shed much light on it. The display retains the ambiguity. If the alternative in the note for 6:3c were followed, it would give 'it symbolizes that it was as though we died with him'. Some commentators (e.g., Hodge, Cranfield) take the meaning to be 'to testify that we have appropriated the benefits of his death', which has much to commend it.

6:4a *it is as though* **we were buried with him** In this metaphor, it is impossible to make the point of similarity explicit and still preserve theological neutrality. Hence the metaphor is rendered as a simile and not fully spelled out.

6:4c *unresponsive to sinful desires* The phrase here, εἰς τὸν θάνατον 'into death', contrasts with 'into his death' in 3d. In the context of not continuing to sin (2b) and a new life (4e), the word 'death' has the same metaphorical sense as in 2c, namely, being insensitive or unresponsive to sinful desires.

6:4e conduct our lives in a new way The clause ἐν καινότητι ζωῆς περιπατήσωμεν 'in newness of life we might walk' exhibits several semantic mismatches. The noun 'newness' expresses an attribute; 'life', an event. 'Walk' is a dead metaphor (used frequently by Paul and John to express the idea 'to live, to conduct oneself'). But since 'life' and 'walk' both refer to 'way of life', 'walk' is rendered here by 'conduct our lives'. Another possibility would be 'experience that we are living'. The use of the free pronoun 'we' with 'also' and the forefronting of the phrase 'in newness of life' give emphasis to both of these.

6:4f Christ was resurrected The verb phrase ἠγέρθη ἐκ νεκρῶν 'was raised from the dead', which is rendered here as 'was resurrected', may have to be rendered more fully in some languages, for example, 'was caused to live again after he died'.

the glorious *power* **of** *his divine* **Father** The phrase διὰ τῆς δόξης τοῦ πατρός 'through the glory of the father' is expressing means or instrument. The word 'glory' is, semantically, an attribute modifying the implied concept 'power' (cf. BAGD, p. 203.1a). In REB, TEV, and LB it is rendered in keeping with this. In many languages, kinship terms are obligatorily possessed, hence 'his'. Other possible alternatives for the meaning of the phrase are 'by his powerful/glorious Father' and 'by his Father acting powerfully'.

The word 'divine' is supplied because the primary sense of πατήρ is 'human father'. This is a figurative usage here, and in some languages it will not be possible to use the ordinary word for 'father' without qualification. This is the reciprocal of the problem involving 'Son of God' (see the note on 1:2).

6:5a Since An amplification of the statement in 4a is introduced here by γάρ; εἰ 'if' has a causal force expressing factual grounds and is rendered by 'since'.

6:5b–c by being *totally separated from the former way we lived,* **as he** *was separated from the way he lived when he* **died** The phrase τῷ ὁμοιώματι τοῦ θανάτου αὐτοῦ 'in the likeness of his death' expresses a comparison in a mismatched way, that is, by the noun 'likeness'. But in what way can it be said that we died as he died? The theme of the paragraph is separation from sin, and the metaphor of death is used to indicate the finality of the separation.

6:5d we shall certainly be In using the future tense of the verb ἐσόμεθα 'we shall be', does Paul refer to an ultimate union with Christ at the time of our final resurrection or to the new life we receive at the time of conversion? Commentators are divided. The problem with an eschatological interpretation is that the only resurrection in focus in this passage is the metaphorical one in v. 4: a rising to a new life here and now. In the context, a reference to a future resurrection would be irrelevant as a grounds for the conclusion that we should not continue in sin (2b) unless Paul had specifically made the point 'since you will someday be physically raised to a new life in a new body, you should act as though that new life were in effect now'. This he does not do in this paragraph. The display therefore retains the future tense, but spells out the metaphor in such a way that it could be taken to refer to the present new life Paul is dealing with in this passage.

united with Christ There is an ellipsis of 'united to Christ', which should be understood as carried over from 5a.

6:5f *just as he was* There is an ellipsis of the words 'in the likeness of', represented here by 'just as he was'.

142 A SEMANTIC AND STRUCTURAL ANALYSIS OF ROMANS

EXPANSION OF *BASIS*₂ IN THE 6:1-14 DISPLAY

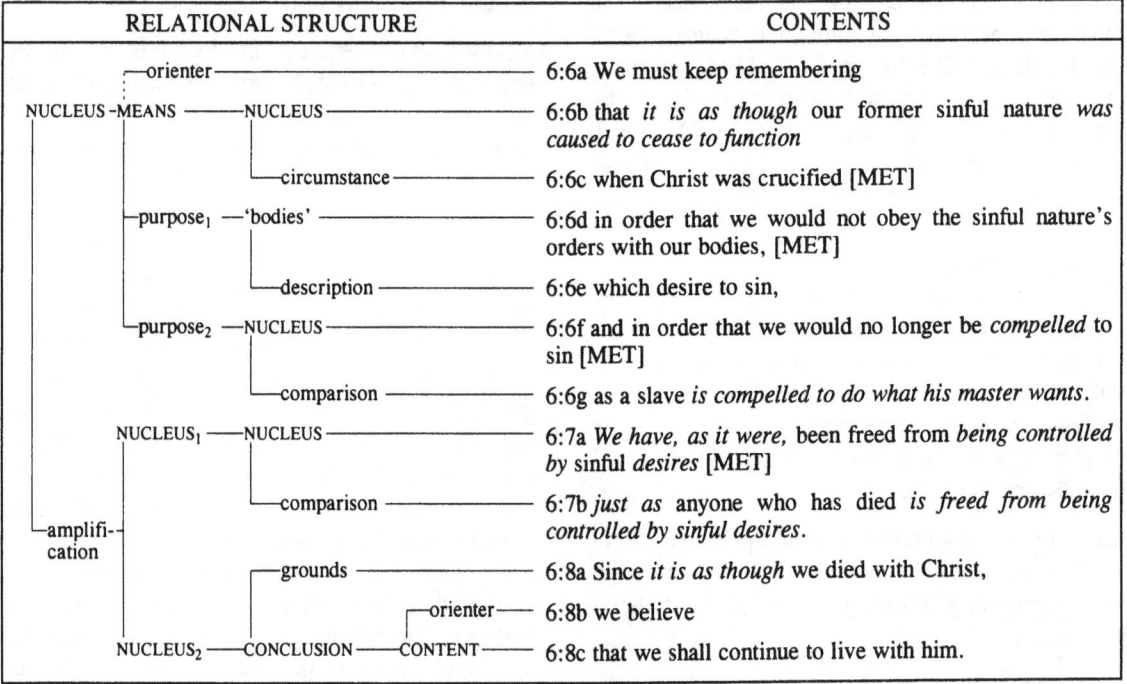

6:6a We must keep remembering The participial phrase τοῦτο γινώσκοντες 'knowing this' has been taken by some as introducing the grounds for the argument in the previous verse. But semantically the argument in vv. 6-7 does not serve as a grounds for v. 5; and the occurrence of τοῦτο, which is explicated by the ὅτι content clause that follows, also rules against such a relationship. In all the cases where τοῦτο is followed by γινώσκω (cf. Luke 12:39, 2 Pet. 1:20 and 3:3 [this last also having the verb in its participial form]), there is only a cataphoric reference, never a logical relationship to what precedes. John uses ἐν τούτῳ, always cataphorically, in a similar way nine times, all but one being in 1 John. Rom. 6:6a is therefore taken as introducing a second *basis* supporting the APPEALS of 9-11 and 12-14.

As in 6:3a, 'know' refers not so much to what they already know, but what Paul wants them to keep in mind. JBP has "Let us never forget," similar to the rendering in the display.

6:6b *it is as though* our former sinful nature *was caused to cease to function* The phrase ὁ παλαιὸς ἡμῶν ἄνθρωπος 'our old man' refers to the nature we had before we became Christians: 'sinful' is clearly implied. The reference to crucifixion is metaphorical; the point of similarity is 'caused to cease to function'. The rendering in the display is based on Paul's statement in Eph. 4:22 that the old sinful nature still needs to be dealt with.

6:6d-e in order that we would not obey the sinful nature's orders with our bodies, which desire to sin The Greek is ἵνα καταργηθῇ τὸ σῶμα τῆς ἁμαρτίας 'in order that the body of sin might be made ineffective'. Commentators disagree as to the meaning of 'the body of sin'. Some consider it our bodies as controlled by sin (thus RSV and JB, "our sinful bodies"); others, our sinful nature as the cause of sinful acts by our bodies (taking it as a metonymy); still others, a personification of sin (i.e., our sinful desires). Determining the correct sense hinges a fair bit on the sense given to the verb, which Paul sometimes uses in the sense of 'make ineffective' (cf. 3:3, 3:31, 4:14) and sometimes in the sense of 'abolish, do away with'. Since this verb spells out the purpose of the metaphorical statement in 6b-c (in conjunction with the additional purpose statement in 6f 'in order that we would no longer be compelled to sin'), it is clear that Paul is not referring to a present or future doing away with the body. Paul does not elsewhere use the expression 'body of sin'; but since he does use 'body' in v. 12 in its literal sense, and elsewhere uses σάρξ to refer to the sinful nature, the expression 'body of sin' here is almost certainly not referring to human nature but rather to the body in some way. It seems best to take it as expressing a characteristic of the human body, hence 'bodies which desire to sin' in the display. (LB has "sin loving bodies.") The verb 'made ineffective' combined with this phrase gives the sense 'in order that our bodies which desire to sin would not be able to cause that to happen'.

6:6f *compelled* **to sin** The point of similarity in the metaphor δουλεύειν τῇ ἁμαρτίᾳ 'to serve sin' is 'compelled, forced to do something'. It is taken as a live metaphor because Paul continues the figure in vv. 7, 15-18, 20-23. In the display the parts of the metaphor are spelled out and the personification of sin is rendered nonfiguratively. (Note that there is no agent of 'compelled' given in the display for 6f.)

6:7a Here γάρ introduces an amplification of the metaphor in v. 6, not the reason or grounds for it.

We have, as it were, **been freed from** *being controlled by* **sinful** *desires* There is a double metaphor here: ὁ ἀποθανών 'he that died' and δεδικαίωται 'has been set free'. The usual Pauline sense of the verb δικαιόω is 'justified, declared righteous'; but here it means 'set free' (BAGD, p. 197.3c; Louw and Nida 37.138). As for ὁ ἀποθανών 'he that has died', most commentators take it to refer to physical death as illustrative of the principle of being set free from earthly claims. A few take it to refer to our mystical death with Christ. Or it could be taken in almost a proverbial sense to mean physical death (i.e., 'a corpse can no longer be made anyone's slave'), except that Paul adds ἀπὸ τῆς ἁμαρτίας 'from sin'. The nature of the statement here suggests that Paul is making a universally true statement and is using that as the figurative part of his metaphor referring to believers being freed from control by desires to sin. That metaphorical interpretation is the one chosen here. If one prefers the mystical interpretation, 7a would read 'by, as it were, our dying with Christ'. The phrase 'from sin' is rendered as 'from being controlled by sinful desires' since Paul uses ἁμαρτία frequently in this sense in this passage. Some commentators have suggested that the sense here is guilt for sin, or perhaps *both* the guilt and power of sin, since the word δεδικαίωται occurs too. Though it is possible that Paul is using a play on words, the idea of justification is totally out of context here; moreover, the verb δικαιόω is used elsewhere in the NT in the sense of 'set free' (Acts 13:38-39, 1 Cor. 6:11).

6:8a Since *it is as though* **we died with Christ** Here εἰ is used in a causal, not a conditional, sense (BAGD, p. 219.III).

The mystical sense of ἀπεθάνομεν σὺν Χριστῷ 'we died with Christ' is brought out in the display by 'it is as though'.

6:8c we shall continue to live with him Most commentators take the future tense of συζήσομεν αὐτῷ 'we shall live with him' to refer to what begins now during our Christian life and continues after death, but some (Dodd, Lenski, Haldane) say the reference is exclusively eschatological. The context, however, concerns our present life, not our future existence; therefore, the display follows the majority view and tries to capture both present and future.

EXPANSION OF *APPEAL*₁ IN THE 6:1-14 DISPLAY

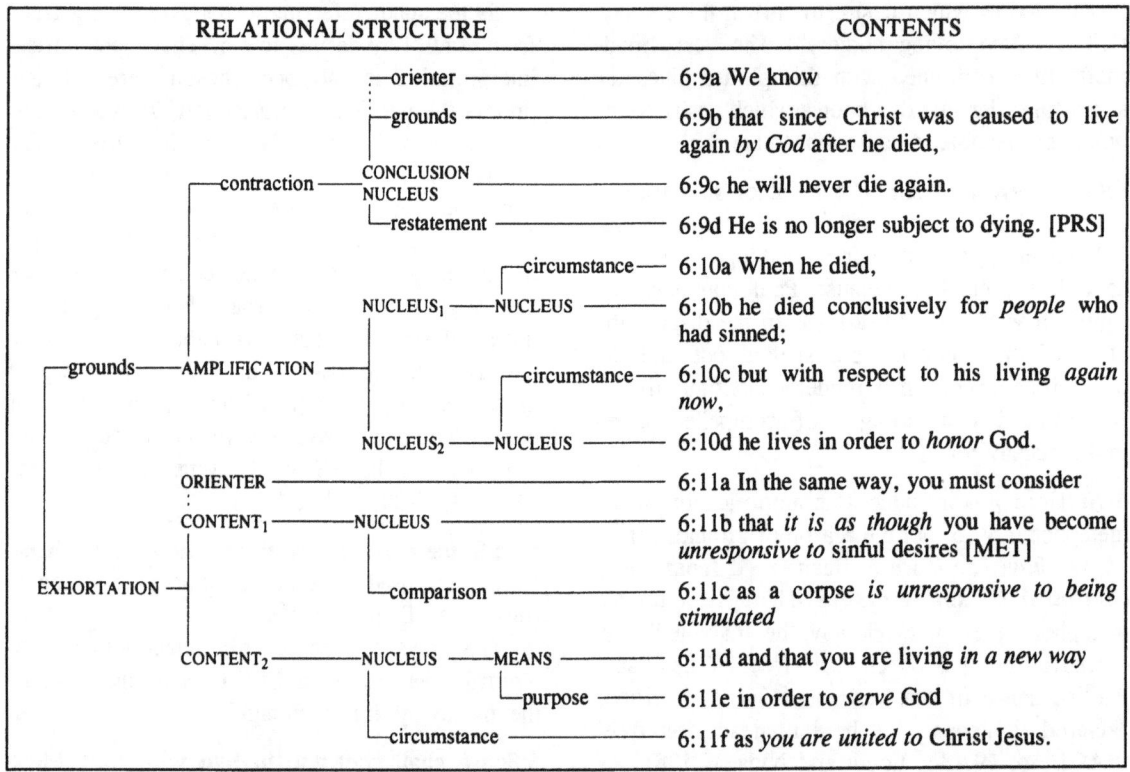

6:9a We know As with the participle γινώσκοντες 'knowing' in 6a, the participle εἰδότες 'knowing' here is best seen not as having causal force referring to what immediately preceded it (since it does not cohere relationally with causative force), but simply as an orienter to a grounds for the v. 11 EXHORTATION.

6:9d is no longer subject to dying The personification in θάνατος αὐτοῦ οὐκέτι κυριεύει 'death no longer lords it over him' is rendered nonfiguratively. A good alternative is 'he will never have to (or, be forced to) die again'.

6:10a Here γάρ introduces an AMPLIFICATION of the subject of Christ's death, which was introduced in v. 9.

6:10b conclusively The word ἐφάπαξ means 'once for all' (BAGD, p. 330.2), which is somewhat ambiguous in English. The sense is 'once, never to occur again', that is, 'unrepeatedly' or 'once, which was sufficient for all time', carrying also the sense of 'definitively, uniquely'. Louw and Nida (60.68) suggest "once and not again."

for *people* who had sinned In τῇ ἁμαρτίᾳ ἀπέθανεν 'to sin he died', the phrase 'to sin' is made prominent by forefronting. This dative construction has several possible interpretations. But note that the identical construction in v. 2 has 'we' as the subject, not 'Christ', so the interpretation applicable there cannot possibly be applicable here. Some (e.g., Barnes, Haldane, Cranfield) suggest 'for the removal of the guilt of sin'; others (e.g., Hodge, Denney, Sanday and Headlam, Lenski, Lightfoot) take it to mean 'death freed Christ from having to bear further the guilt of sin'. Still others suggest 'Christ at his death ceased from being any longer under the power of death'. Barrett suggests 'Christ died sinless' (i.e., died rather than sin). None of these are very appealing because they suggest specific meanings not in focus here. Therefore, following Morris and Alford, it is best not to read very much into the dative expression or be dogmatic. The display shows a generic referential relation.

6:10c *again now* The verb ζῇ 'he lives' is in the present tense and refers to Christ's post-resurrection life; hence 'again now' is implied.

6:10d to *honor* God The dative construction τῷ θεῷ 'to God' balances 'to sin' in 10b. Paul frequently uses such grammatical and lexical parallelisms in which the sense is not the same between the parts. The semantic difference between 'to sin' in 10b and 'to God' here is clear.

The former explicitly signals an event whereas 'to God' does not. Some verb is required here in 10d because purpose must be expressed by an event verb. The display has 'to honor' (supported by Barnes, Stuart) because, in the context, living a life free from submission to the power of sin honors God. Possible alternatives are 'to serve' (Best) and 'be devoted to'.

6:11a-b you must consider that *it is as though* Here the verb λογίζεσθε 'consider' means 'look upon it as' or 'take it to be true that'. The words 'it is as though' are supplied because 'consider' by itself has such a broad area of meaning.

6:11b *unresponsive* The metaphorical phrase 'dead to sin' is treated the same way as the identical phrase in v. 2. The point of similarity is unresponsiveness to a stimulus.

6:11d living *in a new way* The phrase ζῶντας τῷ θεῷ 'living to God' comes after the metaphor that refers to death and is a contrast to it. It alludes to the believer's new life.

6:11e to *serve* **God** The phrase 'to God' is the same as in 10e; but since our relation to God is somewhat different from Christ's, the implied verb is taken to be 'serve' (so Morris, Norlie). The verb 'honor' could be used if concordance with 10d is desired.

6:11f as *you are united to* The prepositional phrase ἐν Χριστῷ Ἰησοῦ 'in Christ Jesus', estimated to occur as often as two hundred times in the NT, signifies believers' unity with Christ (cf. TEV, REB). Because 'united to' is somewhat figurative, a good alternative would be 'because of your relationship with'.

The Textus Receptus appends τῷ κυρίῳ ἡμῶν 'our Lord', perhaps for liturgical reasons. Among the best manuscripts, almost none have these words. There is no good reason to account for its deletion if 'our Lord' had been in the original text.

EXPANSION OF *APPEAL₂* IN 6:1-14 DISPLAY

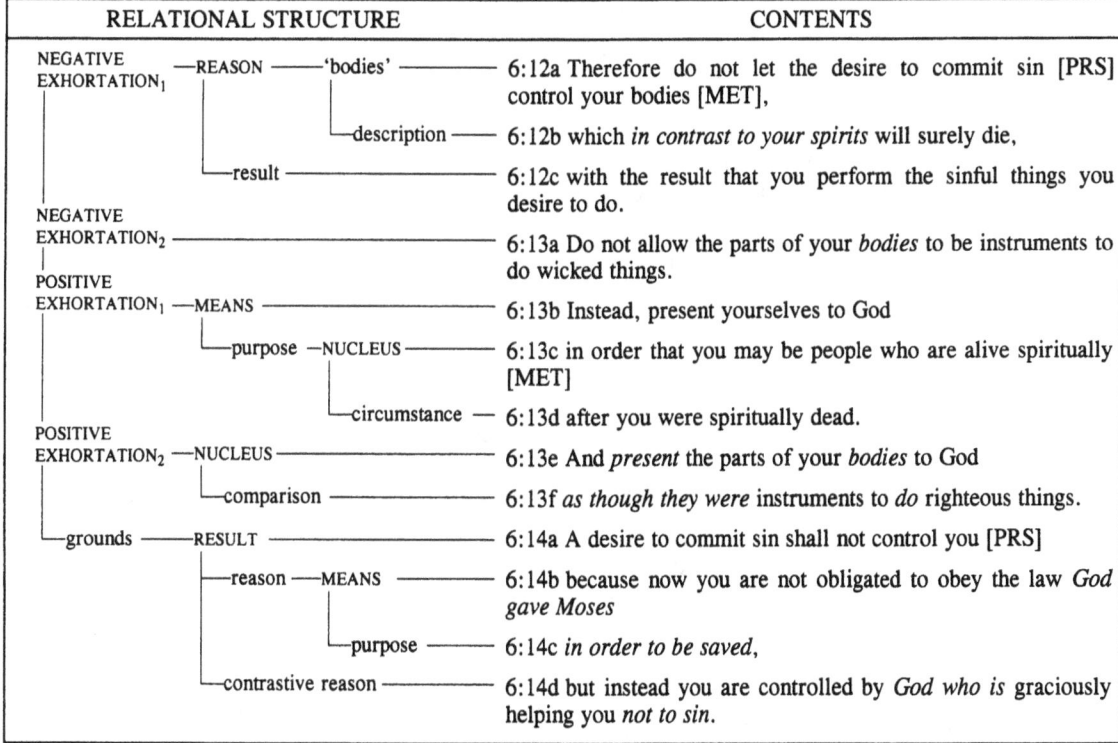

6:12a do not let the desire to commit sin control your bodies In the clause μὴ βασιλευέτω ἡ ἁμαρτία 'do not let sin reign', 'sin' is a personification. It refers to 'the desire to sin', not actual sinful acts. Although to render it with the phrase 'the desire to commit sin' as the subject of the verb 'control' does not entirely remove the personification, it is almost impossible to express the sense in any other way.

In the 'reigns' metaphor (cf. 5:14), the point of similarity is absolute control: sin is like a king who is in absolute control of the people he rules. Note that there is a reciprocal relationship between βασιλευέτω 'reign' in 12a and ὑπακούειν 'obey' in 12c. In some languages this relationship will force the translator to make 12c a restatement of 12a, and begin 12c with '*that is*, making you perform.'

6:12b which *in contrast to your spirits* will surely die The question arises, Why does Paul mention the word 'mortal'? Murray provides insight: "the mortality of the body underlies the folly of yielding to its lust; the life of the believer is incorruptible and immortal." In a similar vein, Morris comments, "It is stupid to allow that which will die to have the supreme position." The display attempts to convey this implied contrast.

The phrase ἐν τῷ θνητῷ ὑμῶν σώματι 'in your(pl) mortal body' is a curious Semitism, with the singular 'body' modified by the plural 'your'. On this basis, 'body' could be taken as a synecdoche representing the person as a whole (corresponding to 'yourselves' in 13b). In the display, however, it is rendered literally. The word θνητῷ 'mortal' is rendered as 'which will surely die'.

6:12c the sinful things you desire to do The phrase ταῖς ἐπιθυμίαις αὐτοῦ 'its desires' represents an event and is rendered accordingly.

These words seem to have been replaced in several, mostly Western, texts by αὐτῇ 'it' (influenced perhaps by the occurrence of the word 'sin' several times in the following verses). The Textus Receptus follows several texts which combine the two, giving αὐτῇ ἐν ταῖς ἐπιθυμίαις αὐτοῦ 'it in its desires'. But the fourth edition GNT has ταῖς ἐπιθυμίαις αὐτοῦ with a B rating indicating "almost certain," and the display follows this reading.

6:13a Do not allow This clause begins with μηδέ 'neither'; semantically it introduces an additional command.

the parts of your *bodies* The phrase τὰ μέλη ὑμῶν 'your members' refers to the parts of the body. In languages without such a generic term, it may have to be translated 'your hands and feet' or some equivalent expression that represents all the body parts.

instruments The word ὅπλα 'instruments' can also mean 'weapons'. Some commentators take it that way, and that is its sense in the rest of its NT occurrences. But semantically it is very strained to equate 'weapons (of destruction in war)' with body parts. Moreover, there is nothing in the context pointing to warfare. Therefore it is best to take it as a sort of synecdoche, the species (weapons) standing for the genus (instruments). In some languages it may be impossible to find a term which can express this extended sense of 'instruments'. In such cases the clause could be expressed as 'Do not use the parts of your body in order to do wicked things'.

to do wicked things In the phrase ὅπλα ἀδικίας τῇ ἁμαρτίᾳ 'instruments of unrighteousness to sin', 'to sin' complements the verb 'present' in the same way that 'God' complements 'present' in 13e. Sin is personified, but the rendering here is nonfigurative. 'Unrighteousness' and 'sin' basically refer to the same concept, and the two nouns are therefore represented only once in the display as 'wicked things'.

6:13b *present yourselves* The aorist form of the imperative suggests a once-for-all-time action, not one that is to be constantly repeated.

6:13c–d people who are alive spiritually after you were spiritually dead Note that ἐκ νεκρῶν ζῶντας 'from dead living' is metaphorical. Fully spelled out it would be something like the following:

> . . . in order that you may be people who are spiritually alive
>   after you were spiritually dead,
> just as people who have been resurrected live again
>   after they have died.

6:13e And *present* the parts of your *bodies* to God It is possible to see 13e as an amplification of 13b. However, καί 'and' here is taken as introducing another act, a specific act—presenting our bodies' parts to God for his use—in addition to the "generic" presentation of ourselves to God in 13b. Note that 'present' is repeated from 13b to remove the ellipsis.

6:13f to *do* righteous things In the phrase ὅπλα δικαιοσύνης 'instruments of righteousness', the second word is semantically an attribute, hence 'righteous things'. The implied event connecting 'instruments' and 'righteousness' is 'do/perform'.

6:14a Here γάρ introduces what is semantically grounds for the exhortations of vv. 12–13.

a desire to commit sin shall not control you The word ἁμαρτία here means 'sinful desire'. It is a personification and is rendered as such in the display. An alternative would be 'you will not be subject to a desire to sin' (cf. 'be subject to dying' in 6:9d).

6:14b not obligated to obey the law *God gave Moses* The preposition ὑπό 'under' is rendered as in 3:19a, 'obligated to obey'. The law (νόμος) is identified as 'the law God gave Moses' to avoid ambiguity.

6:14c *in order to be saved* This proposition is implicit (cf. Hodge, Barnes, Morris) and is supplied to avoid the implication that Christians are free from obligation to obey any law, governmental or spiritual. It is true that the purpose is not in focus and should not be included if it can be avoided without conveying wrong meaning. The context favors the sense of 'which enslaves us' as an identification of the law, but that would not only be metaphorical but also redundant with 14b, and would still not avoid the potential wrong meaning. Other alternatives might be 'law which could not help us' and 'law which condemned us'.

6:14d controlled by Paul uses the preposition ὑπό 'under' here, as he frequently does, to maintain a grammatical and lexical parallelism while he intends to convey something else semantically. It cannot mean 'obligated to obey' as in 14b, but it could mean 'controlled by' in both phrases. CEV has "ruled by."

God who is **graciously helping you** In some translations 'you(pl)' may have to be changed to 'us(inc)' to avoid the implication that Paul was under law and not under grace.

not to sin These words are supplied to make the force of Paul's argument clear. The reason we don't have to be controlled by our sinful desires, Paul says, is that we have God's gracious help to keep us from giving in to them.

BOUNDARIES AND COHERENCE

The 6:1-14 paragraph is relationally coherent in that it consists of an *objection* and REFUTATION. The latter contains two *bases* and two APPEALS.

The paragraph's lexical coherence is provided primarily by items from the semantic domain of death and resurrection: θάνατος 'death' in vv. 3, 4, 5; ἀποθνῄσκω 'die' in vv. 2, 7, 8, 9, 10 (twice); νεκρός 'dead' in vv. 4, 11, 13; the verb ζῶ 'live' in vv. 2, 8, 10 (twice), 11, 13; ζωή 'life' in v. 4; συνθάπτω 'bury with' in v. 4; ἀνάστασις 'resurrection' in v. 5; and ἐγείρω 'raise' in vv. 4 and 9. In addition, there is a sandwich structure with the terms ἁμαρτία 'sin' and χάρις 'grace', which occur in both the first and final verses of the paragraph.

The boundary with the next unit, which begins in 6:15, is marked by a new anticipated *objection* and its REFUTATION and another CONCLUSION which Paul states might be drawn from his exposition of justification.

PROMINENCE AND THEME

The theme of the 6:1-14 paragraph, which consists of an *objection* and Paul's REFUTATION, is drawn from both these subunits. From the *objection* are included the MEANS (1d) and the PURPOSE (1e) propositions of the naturally prominent CONCLUSION, because the thought would not be complete without both. From the REFUTATION are included the NUCLEI of the two *bases* (including the orienters) and the main EXHORTATIONS of the second APPEAL (the two APPEALS having a good deal of sameness of semantic content).

SECTION CONSTITUENT 6:15–23
(Expository Paragraph: Claim₂ of 6:1–23)

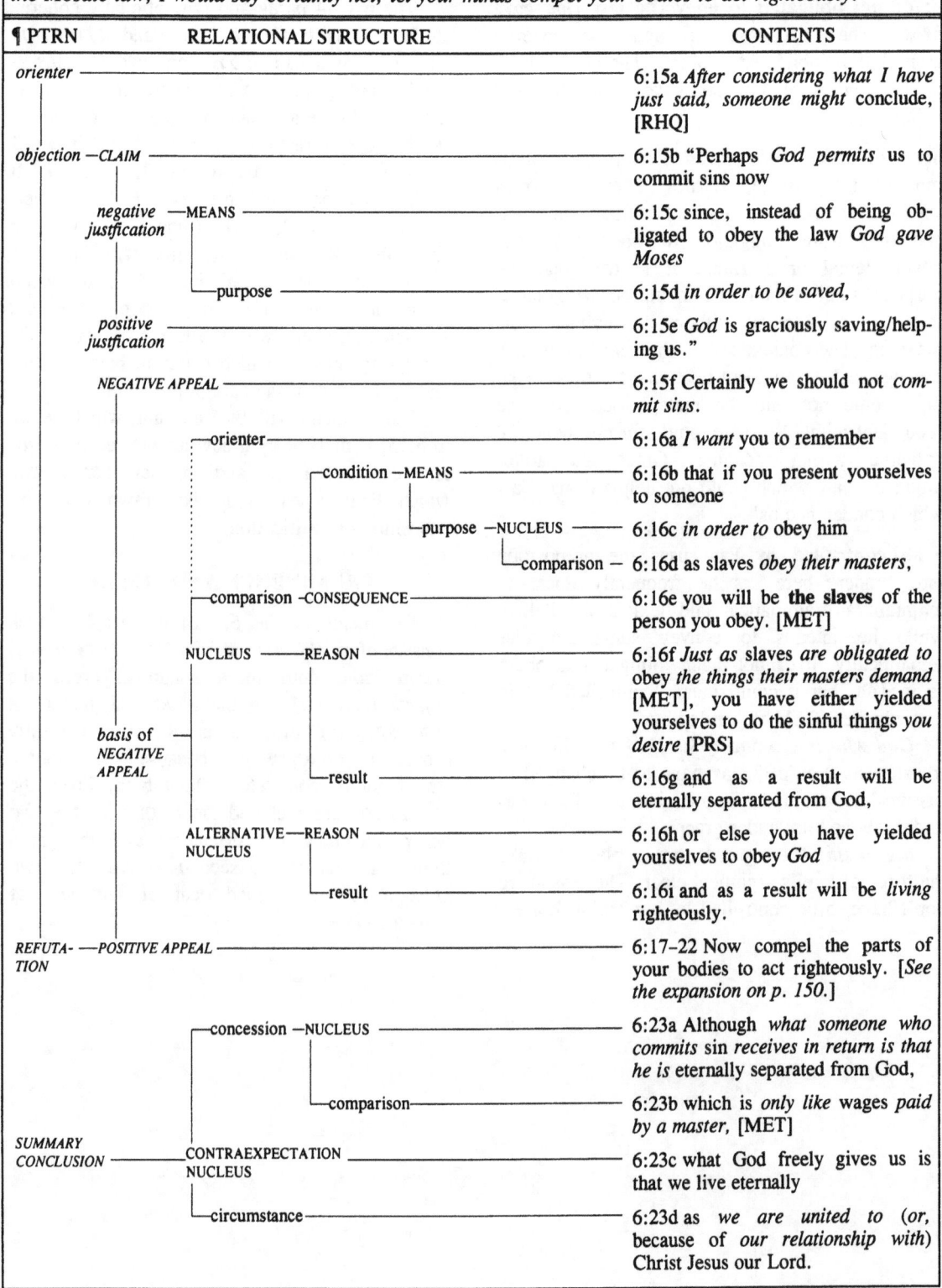

INTENT AND PARAGRAPH PATTERN

In 6:15-23, Paul states another anticipated criticism of his development of the doctrine of justification by faith, and then he refutes it. Thus 6:15-23 can be considered an expository paragraph. It is true that it has one imperative verb (19f). But, as in the 6:1-14 unit, Paul's primary intent in 6:15-23 is not to change behavior, in which case this would be a hortatory paragraph. Rather, it is to change wrong thinking; hence it is expository. The fact that both 6:1-14 and 6:15-23 are parts of the 1:16-11:36 division cluster, which is expository, supports the view that Paul's primary intent here is to influence thinking, not behavior. It is considered that the *objection-REFUTATION* pattern is paramount here (as explained under "Intent and Paragraph Pattern" for 6:1-14). Therefore this is expository discourse of the solutionality subtype.

The lower-level paragraph pattern in the *REFUTATION* consists of a *NEGATIVE APPEAL* (15f) and its *basis* (16) and a *POSITIVE APPEAL* (19) and its *bases* (17-18 and 20-22). In v. 23 is the *CONCLUSION*, a summary statement using metaphorical language. It marks the break between the *objection-REFUTATION* paragraphs of chapter 6 and the strictly expository material at the start of chapter 7, which states another implication of the doctrine of justification by faith.

NOTES

6:15a *After considering what I have just said, someone might* **conclude** The rhetorical question τί οὖν 'What therefore?' introduces what is in essence a hypothetical question, as in 6:1. It could be considered a conclusion to Paul's argument thus far, as is brought out in the display text.

6:15b Perhaps *God permits* **us to commit sins** Concerning 'perhaps' see the note on 1d. The aorist tense of the verb ἁμαρτήσωμεν 'shall we sin?' points to specific acts of sin.

6:15c-d See the notes on 14b and 14c. LB has "for our salvation does not depend on keeping the law."

6:16a *I want* **you to remember** The purpose of the Greek rhetorical question 'Do you not know . . . ?' is to make the readers think about and remember the point. It is rendered as a statement in the display. JPB renders it "just think what it would mean."

6:16c-d *in order to* **obey him as slaves** From a semantic point of view, the words 'unto obedience' in the phrase δούλους εἰς ὑπακοήν 'slaves unto obedience' represent 'in order to obey him'. The metaphorical 'slaves' is spelled out in 16d: 'as slaves obey their masters'. An alternative might be 'by being his slaves' or 'while you are his slaves'.

6:16e the slaves The word δούλους 'slaves' is forefronted in the Greek, which gives it emphasis. This emphasis is indicated in the display by bold type.

6:16f *Just as* **slaves** *are obligated to* **obey** *the things their masters demand* Here the general principle in 16b-e is applied to spiritual life. Both 16f and 16h are elliptical: 'you are the slaves' is carried over from 16e. This is a metaphor, the point of similarity being 'under obligation'. Because the metaphor about slavery continues over several verses, it is a live metaphor, and the topic and grounds of comparison are spelled out in this verse. It is represented in the display as a simile.

do the sinful things Here ἁμαρτίας 'of sin' is a personification signifying the desire to sin.

6:16g and as a result will be eternally separated from God The result phrase εἰς θάνατον 'unto death' refers to spiritual death (so NCV) or eternal death, not physical death. This phrase is omitted in a few texts, and it is not referred to by the church fathers. However, the likelihood of Paul's using it to parallel εἰς δικαιοσύνην 'unto righteousness' in 16i is so strong that the omission must be considered accidental, not deliberate. Since 'dying spiritually' is collocationally very difficult (as is 'dying eternally'), and since Paul says elsewhere that prior to conversion people are already dead spiritually (cf. Eph. 2:1), the term θάνατος in Romans referring to eternal death is often rendered in the displays as 'be eternally separated from God'.

6:16h obey *God* The word ὑπακοῆς 'of obedience' conveys an event. The word 'God' is supplied to complete the comparison in the metaphor and satisfy case frames (cf. NCV, JBP).

6:16i and as a result will be *living* **righteously** Some have taken the phrase εἰς δικαιοσύνην 'unto righteousness' as 'being declared righteous'. But in this section Paul is talking about the need for righteous living as the outcome or implication of being declared righteous, not about justification per se.

EXPANSION OF *POSITIVE APPEAL* (6:17-22) IN THE 6:15-23 DISPLAY

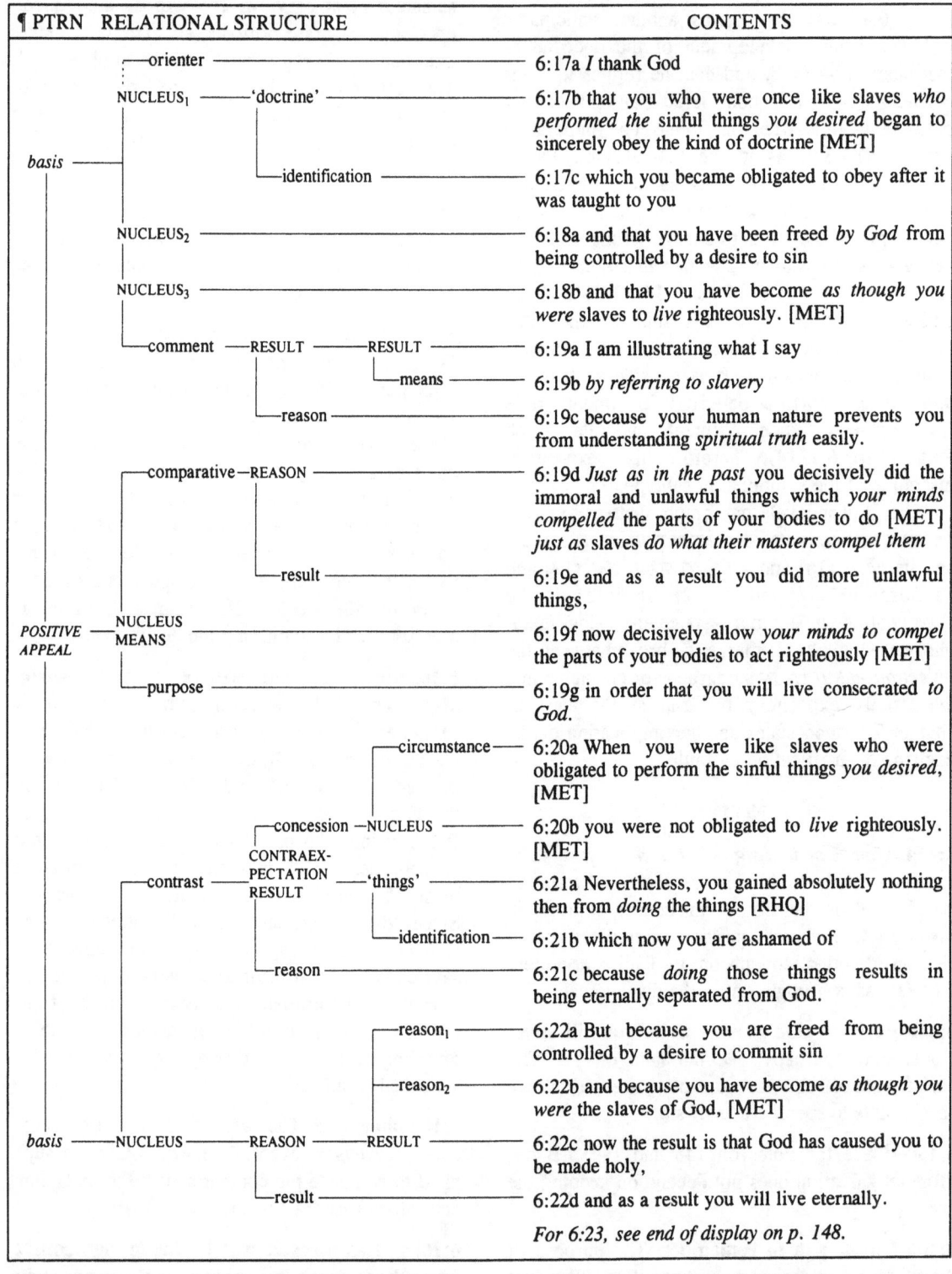

For 6:23, see end of display on p. 148.

6:17a *I thank God* With the standard expression χάρις τῷ θεῷ 'thanks to God' Paul expresses his own thanks (so CEV). It is not a first person plural statement or a second person plural imperative.

6:17b like slaves *who performed the* sinful things The Greek here is δοῦλοι τῆς ἁμαρτίας 'slaves of sin'. See the note on 16f.

began to sincerely obey the kind of doctrine The aorist tense of the verb 'obey' points to a definite time in their experience rather than the present state. It is taken as inceptive in force, hence 'began to'. The expression ἐκ καρδίας 'out of heart' is an idiom meaning 'sincerely'. The word διδαχή means 'teaching', but specifically 'teaching of spiritual truth', hence 'doctrine'.

6:17c became obligated to obey after it was taught to you The clause εἰς ὃν παρεδόθητε 'unto which you were delivered' seems a curious way of stating 'which was delivered to you' (i.e., taught to you), if indeed that is what was intended. But several commentators suggest that Paul here continues the figure of slavery: Christian teaching is the new master. The rendering in the display follows the latter interpretation.

6:18a from being controlled by a desire to sin The phrase ἐλευθερωθέντες ἀπὸ τῆς ἁμαρτίας 'having been liberated from sin' could refer to liberation from the guilt of sin, but in this context it must be taken as liberation from the power of sin, or the compulsion to sin.

6:18b *as though you were* slaves to *live* righteously The words ἐδουλώθητε τῇ δικαιοσύνῃ 'were enslaved to righteousness' continue the metaphor. This is indicated in the display by the words 'as though you were' rather than by spelling out the figure. If the metaphor were spelled out completely, it could be expressed as 'obligated to live righteously as a slave is obligated to obey his master'. 'Righteousness' in this context refers to righteous living, not imputed righteousness.

6:19a-b I am illustrating what I say *by referring to slavery* The words ἀνθρώπινον λέγω 'I speak humanly' are somewhat parenthetical. Paul is referring to the human institution of slavery as an illustration of the truth he is presenting. Cranfield says, "Paul is clearly aware of the fact that the figure of slavery is inadequate, unworthy and misleading as a way of speaking about the believer's relation to δικαιοσύνῃ . . . that is why he apologizes for the all too human nature of his language, as soon as he has made the statement that they have been enslaved to righteousness." In the display 19a-c are labeled as comment. LB expresses the sense fully: "I speak this way, using the illustration of slaves and masters."

6:19c human nature The word σάρξ is not taken as 'sinful human nature' here because Paul has not used it in that sense yet in this epistle, and there is no contextual reason to do so. It is simply 'human nature'.

prevents you from understanding *spiritual truth* easily The word ἀσθένεια 'weakness' is not used in the primary sense of physical weakness here, but, as Morris suggests, the inability to exercise spiritual discernment. JBP renders the clause in wholly positive terms with "human nature grasps truth more readily that way."

6:19d Here γάρ marks the transition from the comment (19a-c) to the beginning of the APPEAL itself.

decisively The verb in παρεστήσατε τὰ μέλη ὑμῶν δοῦλα 'you presented your members slaves' is in the aorist tense, which points to a decisive past action, hence 'wholeheartedly' or 'decisively'.

compelled The metaphor 'presented as slaves' is spelled out fully in the display.

6:19e and as a result you did more unlawful things Most English versions take the phrase εἰς τὴν ἀνομίαν 'unto iniquity' as simply an intensifier of the preceding word, 'iniquity', thus 'greater and greater iniquity'. But the parallel with εἰς ἁγιασμόν 'unto sanctification' in 19f suggests either a purpose or result relationship here. Since purpose involves intentionality, the result relationship is better here.

6:19g in order that you will live consecrated *to God* The phrase εἰς ἁγιασμόν 'unto sanctification' could express either purpose or result. Most versions take it as expressing purpose, and that is the interpretation chosen here. The noun ἁγιασμός refers here in this context more to a holy manner of living than to a state.

6:20a Here γάρ introduces the *basis* for the APPEAL stated in 19f. But since the basis is of the sort that does not lend itself to a conjunction, γάρ is not represented in the display.

like slaves See the note on 6:16f for the rendering of the metaphorical δοῦλοι τῆς ἁμαρτίας 'slaves of sin'.

6:20b not obligated to *live* righteously The word ἐλεύθεροι 'free' is metaphorical, the point of similarity being 'not under obligation'. Spelled out more fully, it would be, 'as a free person is not obligated to obey any master'. The phrase τῇ δικαιοσύνῃ 'to righteousness' refers to righteous living.

6:21a Nevertheless The conjunction οὖν is used here in a fairly rare adversative sense (cf. RSV, JBP, CEV).

you gained absolutely nothing then from *doing* the things Commentators are divided, as are versions, on whether the question ends with τότε 'then' or with ἐπαισχύνεσθε 'you are ashamed'. But when the rhetorical question is rendered according to its semantic force as an emphatic negative statement, the dispute is academic. The thought continues with good relational coherence to the end of the verse. The word 'doing' is supplied simply to fill in an ellipsis here (and in 21c).

6:21b now The word 'now' is emphasized in contrast to 'then' by being forefronted; in the display it is also forefronted to indicate this.

6:21c results in The noun τέλος 'end' means 'outcome' or 'result' (here and in 22d) and is rendered in the display by the verb 'results in'.

being eternally separated from God The word θάνατος means 'death'. In this context its primary meaning is not physical death, but rather eternal death. But to render it as 'die eternally' would be awkward, almost a contradiction in terms, hence the rendering in the display. See the note on 16g.

6:22a For 'freed from sin' see the note on 18a.

6:22b because you have become *as though you were* the slaves of God Both aorist participles here precede the main verb and are taken as introducing the reason for the RESULT in 22c.

The phrase δουλωθέντες τῷ θεῷ 'enslaved to God' continues the metaphor. That there is a comparison is indicated by 'as though you were'. If it were fully spelled out, it would be 'obligated to serve God as a slave is obligated to serve his master'.

6:22c the result is that God has caused you to be made holy The Greek is ἔχετε τὸν καρπὸν ὑμῶν εἰς ἁγιασμόν 'you have your fruit unto sanctification'. The word 'fruit' here is considered a dead metaphor meaning 'results' or 'outcome', hence 'the result is'. 'Sanctification' is an event concept, hence 'causing you to be made holy' or 'consecrating you to himself'.

6:23a–b Here γάρ is best seen as introducing a summary conclusion of the present topic. Murray says, "This is the triumphant conclusion to chapter 6 and should be compared in this respect to 5:21 as the triumphant conclusion to chapter 5." His view is supported by Harrison and Denney. Cranfield tries to have it both ways, saying it "provides both clarification of vv. 21–22 and also a solemn conclusion to the section as a whole." It is true that v. 23 could be considered an amplification of v. 22, and it is also true that v. 23 is not a *summary exhortation*, whereas what immediately precedes it (v. 15–22) is clearly hortatory on the lower level. However, as previously stated, on the highest level the paragraph is an *objection-REFUTATION* expository unit. Verse 23 could be seen as a conclusion to the whole chapter, not just as an internal part of the 6:15–23 paragraph. However, v. 23 discusses spiritual death as a result of sin, and this concept is mentioned in vv. 16 and 21, not in vv. 1–14. An alternate to the present diagram would be to take 6:23 as functioning on a section level as the conclusion to the chapter, not as an integral part of 6:15–23.

what someone who commits sin *receives* . . . is . . . only like wages *paid by a master* The phrase ὀψώνια τῆς ἁμαρτίας 'wages of sin' is a live metaphor. 'Sin' is a metonymy and stands for the person who commits the sin (an event). Wages usually are a soldier's food ration but could also refer to wages in general—there is no reason to insist that Paul suddenly shifts from the symbolism of slavery to the military. The point of similarity here is reward or compensation, what someone receives in return for services rendered.

6:23d Here ἐν is taken as introducing a circumstance proposition: 'as we are united to'. It might also be rendered as 'because of our relationship with' (see the note on 6:11f).

BOUNDARIES AND COHERENCE

Like the previous paragraph, 6:15–23 consists of an *objection* and REFUTATION. Within the REFUTATION are a NEGATIVE APPEAL, supported by an illustrative *basis* referring to slavery, and a POSITIVE APPEAL with two supporting *bases*, both of which also refer to slavery. The paragraph ends with a CONCLUSION, which again refers metaphorically to slavery. This structure provides the paragraph its relational coherence.

Lexical coherence is seen in the words in the semantic domain of slavery: δοῦλος 'slave' in vv. 16 (twice), 17, 19 (twice, the adjective), and 20; δουλόω 'enslave' in vv. 18 and 22; ὑπακοή 'obedience' twice in v. 16; ἐλευθερόω 'set free' in vv. 18 and 22; and ἐλεύθερος 'free' in v. 20.

The boundaries of the paragraph have already been discussed (see the discussion on p. 136 of boundaries for 6:1–23).

PROMINENCE AND THEME

The theme of 6:15–23 is drawn from the naturally prominent elements of the *objection* and *REFUTATION*. This requires some of the *orienter* in 15a to be stated as well as the CLAIM and *negative justification* in 15b–c. From within the *REFUTATION* are included the 15f NEGATIVE APPEAL and a condensed version of the 19f POSITIVE APPEAL.

SUBDIVISION CONSTITUENT 7:1–25
(Expository Section: Claim₂ of 6:1–8:39)

> *THEME: God has freed us from being required to obey the Mosaic law to be saved. The Mosaic law simply reveals that what we are doing is sinful. It is our desire, not the law, that causes us to sin and become spiritually dead. But Christ can free us from being controlled by what our bodies desire.*

MACROSTRUCTURE	CONTENTS
CLAIM₁	7:1–6 You know that a person is freed from being required to obey any law after he dies. Similarly, God has freed us from being required to obey the Mosaic law to be saved.
refutation of *objection*₁ to CLAIM₁	7:7–12 My reply to the objection that the law of Moses is evil because it causes us to sin is that the law is holy and good; what the law does is simply reveal that what we are doing is sinful.
refutation of *objection*₂ to CLAIM₁	7:13 My reply to the objection that God's law, being good, causes people to become spiritually dead is no, but instead that it is our desire to commit sin that causes us to sin and become spiritually dead.
CLAIM₂	7:14–25 The law is from God's Spirit, but you and I are influenced by our sinful nature. We often do not do the things we desire and do the things we detest, because of a desire to sin which permeates us and prevents us from doing good—unless Christ frees us from being controlled by these desires.

INTENT AND MACROSTRUCTURE

The 7:1–25 unit consists of four paragraphs: a CLAIM (1–6), two *refutations* (7–12 and 13) of hypothetical *objections* to the CLAIM, and a second CLAIM that is an illustration from Paul's own experience (14–25). Another in the series of applications of the doctrine of justification by faith, the unit is clearly expository and of the solutionality subtype, due to the *objection-REFUTATION* elements.

BOUNDARIES AND COHERENCE

Lexical coherence is shown by the recurring words νόμος 'law' (twenty-two times, more than in any other NT chapter) and ἐντολή 'commandment' (six times). (There is only one other occurrence of ἐντολή in Romans.) But the chief evidence for lexical coherence is the use of first person singular pronouns: eight occurrences of the free subject pronoun, fourteen of 'me', four of 'my', and twenty-six of the pronoun in verb endings.

The final boundary of 7:1–25 is marked by the phrase 'Jesus Christ our Lord' (as are the units ending at 5:21 and 6:23).

The next unit begins at 8:1 with ἄρα 'so, then, consequently' and a change in topic from 'the law of sin' to 'the law of the Spirit'. While in chapter 7 the first person singular pronoun occurs frequently, it is entirely absent in 8:1–39, except in a couple of speech orienters.

PROMINENCE AND THEME

The theme of 7:1–25 is drawn from the theme of the unit's first CLAIM (omitting the nonthematic illustrative portion), the *refutation* parts of 7–12 and 13 (the *objections* being less thematic), and the main statement of the second CLAIM.

SECTION CONSTITUENT 7:1-6
(Expository Paragraph: Claim₁ of 7:1-25)

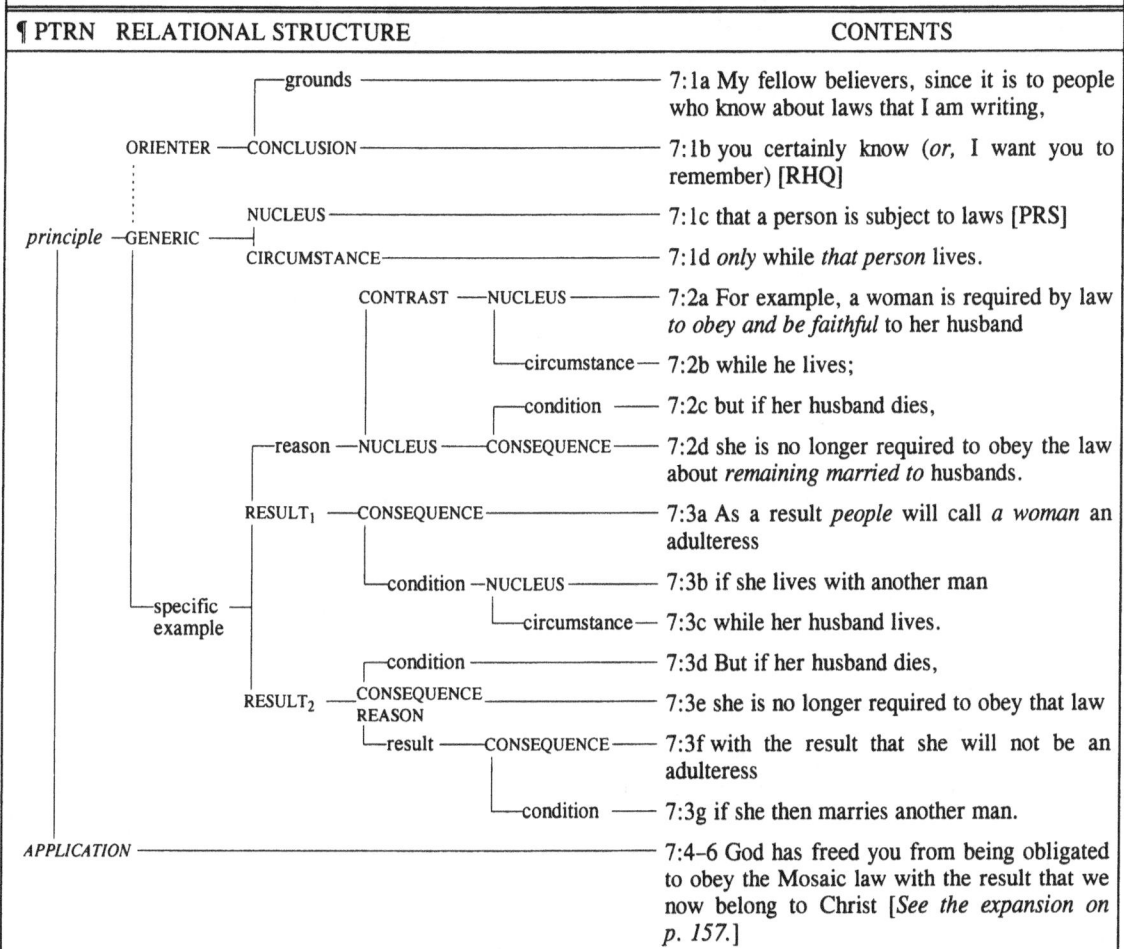

INTENT AND PARAGRAPH PATTERN

Paul in 7:1-6 is continuing his exposition of the implications of the doctrine of justification by faith. The *principle* (about being freed from laws after death) is expounded in vv. 1-3, and the APPLICATION of it is made in vv. 4-6.

NOTES

7:1a to people who know about laws The phrase γινώσκουσιν γὰρ νόμον 'to ones knowing law' is emphasized in the Greek by being forefronted; it is likewise forefronted in the display. The word νόμος 'law' here could refer to the Mosaic law or Roman law or law in general. The lack of the definite article preceding 'laws' indicates that it means law in general. But, as many commentators note, in this context the question as to the referent is irrelevant, so the display does not define it. TEV renders it generically: "know about law." CEV similarly has "understand enough about law." Goodspeed has "know what law is."

I am writing The Greek text has λαλῶ 'I speak', but it is rendered 'I am writing' here since Paul is writing to his audience, not speaking to them. (The fact that Paul is using an amanuensis is irrelevant.)

7:1b you certainly know The Greek rhetorical question here can be considered semantically equivalent to an emphatic positive statement, 'you certainly know' or, as in 6:3 and 6:16, an introducer of something the readers need to keep in mind.

7:1c a person is subject to laws The expression ὁ νόμος κυριεύει τοῦ ἀνθρώπου 'the law lords it over a man' is a personification of 'law', here rendered nonfiguratively (cf. 6:9d) as in REB.

7:1d *only* The word 'only' is clearly implied and necessary to the correct understanding of the proposition. Almost all modern English versions supply it in some way (as does Käsemann).

7:2a For example Here γάρ introduces, not a reason for v. 1, but an example to illustrate it. Most modern versions have 'For example' or its equivalent.

a woman is required by law *to obey and be faithful* **to her husband** The subject of the Greek clause is ὕπανδρος 'a married woman'; it is forefronted, signaling topicalization (not emphasis). Since the idea in the word 'married' is conveyed by the words 'her husband' which follow, it is omitted in the display. The verb δέδεται 'bound, tied' is a dead figure and is used in the extended sense of 'forced, obligated, required'. Some verb is called for to follow 'required'. In the larger context, 'obey' would be suitable; but in the immediate context dealing with adultery, 'be faithful to' is implied. In the display both are supplied. An alternative would be "stay married to" (NCV), but the context deals with not being an adulteress, and 'be faithful to' carries that connotation, whereas 'stay married to' does not.

7:2b while he lives As in nearly all English versions, the participle ζῶντι 'living' is taken as a full proposition expressing circumstance (see also 3c).

7:2d no longer required to obey the law The clause κατήργηται ἀπὸ τοῦ νόμου 'she is released from the law' is the opposite of 'bound' in 2a.

about *remaining married to* **husbands** The genitive in the phrase νόμου τοῦ ἀνδρός 'law of the husband' is taken as a genitive of reference, 'the law about husbands' or, more specifically in this context, 'the law about remaining married to husbands'.

7:3a *a woman* The free subject of the main clause is elided and presumed to be carried over from 2a.

7:3b lives with The verb γένηται 'she becomes' is followed by 'another husband's' (involving a dative of the possessor). It is rather unusual both grammatically and lexically. It is given the sense 'belong to' by BAGD (p. 160.II3), unique among its many occurrences in the NT, and means 'marries', 'is joined to', or more probably 'lives with, cohabits with' (cf. RSV, TEV). The CEV rendering is very colloquial: "goes off with."

7:3c while her husband lives The genitive absolute construction ζῶντος τοῦ ἀνδρός 'while her husband is living' appears at the beginning of the sentence by grammatical necessity but semantically is subordinate to the 'if' clause that follows the main verb.

7:3e no longer required to obey The expression ἐλευθέρα ἀπό 'free from' is rendered just as κατήργηται in 2d was.

that law In some languages, further specification of τοῦ νόμου 'that law' may be needed (e.g., 'that law about husbands' or 'about being faithful to her husband').

ROMANS 7:1-6

EXPANSION OF THE *APPLICATION* IN THE 7:1-6 DISPLAY

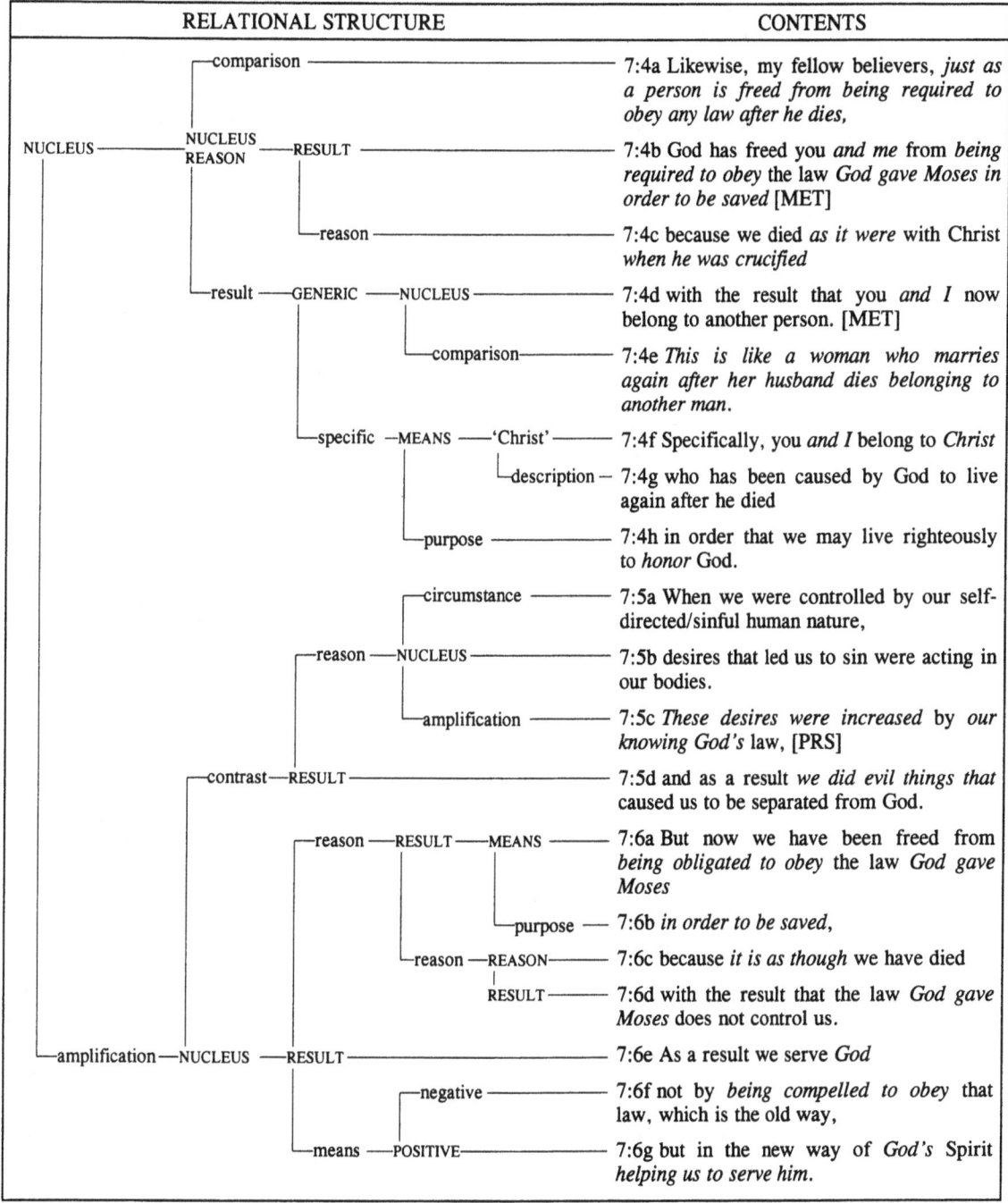

7:4a *just as a person is freed from . . . law* The expression ἐθανατώθητε τῷ νόμῳ 'you have been put to death to the law' is a metaphor based on the illustration in vv. 1-3. The point of similarity is 'freed from further obligation to obey' and is made explicit in the display.

7:4b *freed you and me from being required to obey* The Greek has the second person plural pronoun here, but 'and me' is added to avoid a wrong inference that Paul does not include himself as free. Commentators are fairly well agreed that the sense of ἐθανατώθητε τῷ νόμῳ 'dead to the law' is 'be freed from' (see also NCV). This is a continuation of the figure of death from the preceding verses.

the law *God gave Moses* The reference is clearly to the law of Moses and specified as such to remove ambiguity.

to be saved Believers are not discharged from obligation to obey governmental laws. Furthermore, believers are not free from obligation to obey the Ten Commandments. What we are freed from is the obligation to obey them as the means of obtaining eternal life. Thus the words 'to be saved' are included to avoid wrong meaning (cf. 6:14c). Morris states that the law "is not for them an option as a way of salvation."

7:4c *because* we died *as it were* with Christ when he was crucified The phrase διὰ τοῦ σώματος τοῦ Χριστοῦ 'through the body of Christ' presents a number of problems. Is 'body' a metonymy referring to Christ's death? Or does it refer to the body of Christ in the sense of all believers, those belonging to and under the direction of Christ? Or does it refer to both? Commentators are divided; the majority, however, follow the interpretation chosen for the display. It should be noted that the word σῶμα immediately followed by 'of Christ' or 'of the Lord' always refers to the physical body of Christ (or by metonymy to his death), never to believers as his body. But the main argument against taking 'body' here as referring to all believers is that it does not fit the context. As Morris says, "How does church membership put the believer to death?"

Another question is, Granted that διά is introducing a reason proposition, what verbal idea is to be supplied? There are several possibilities: (1) 'sacrificing' (because of Christ's sacrificing his body for us, i.e., his crucifixion); (2) 'union with' (because of our union with Christ who was crucified for us); (3) 'our dying with Christ' when he was crucified for us. In the context of death's setting us free from the law's demands, interpretation 3 seems the best and is the one chosen here.

7:4d with the result that you *and I* now belong to another person The phrase εἰς τὸ γενέσθαι ὑμᾶς ἑτέρῳ 'so that you might become to another' represents a result clause. Its grammatical form suggests that it is not more prominent than the clause containing the fully inflected verb (4b). The verb γίνομαι 'become' means 'belong to', which is an expression often used in the LXX to refer to the relation of a woman to her husband. The use here is metaphorical and is based on the same verb used in the marriage illustration in vv. 2-3.

7:4e like a woman who marries again after her husband dies A metaphor should not be pressed for similarity between the image and the topic at all points. The obvious point of similarity between the woman in this illustration and believers is 'belonging to a new person'. Paul probably did not mean us to ask whom believers belonged to before we were 'joined to another'.

7:4h in order that we may live righteously to honor God Some have suggested that ἵνα καρποφορήσωμεν τῷ θεῷ 'that we may bear fruit to God' is a live metaphor continuing the marriage metaphor. But no form of the word καρπός 'fruit' is ever used to refer to human offspring, and where believers are described as 'the bride of Christ' there is never any reference to offspring. The context deals with living righteously; hence 'fruit' is treated as a dead metaphor meaning righteous living. The phrase 'to God' is taken as a shortened form of a purpose proposition with some verb such as 'honor' or 'please' being implied (see the note on 6:11e).

7:5a Here γάρ introduces an amplification or further development of v. 4, not a reason or grounds for it.

self-directed/sinful human nature This is the first occurrence in Romans of σάρξ 'flesh' to refer to the sinfully oriented human nature. The majority of commentators take the phrase 'in the flesh' as equivalent to 'unconverted' (also BAGD, p. 744.7), but this is probably due more to theological conviction than to solid textual evidence. Paul uses σάρξ in different senses in different places, and even refers to himself as living 'in the flesh' (ἐν σαρκί) in Gal. 2:20 and Phil. 1:22 with no negative connotation at all. Commentators agree that ἐν means 'under the influence/control of', and the rendering in the display is in accord with this. At the same time, however, they avoid the theological question of whether or not 'controlled by our sinful human nature' of necessity refers to an unregenerate state. (The use of the present tense in vv. 14-24 makes the notion that the whole chapter is dealing with a preconversion state very hard to defend.) The rendering in the display is similar to NIV's.

There is also the question as to whether 'sinful' is clearly implied. Hodge says it refers to one's nature "considered apart from the Divine influence." This is somewhat ambiguous. Dunn is also ambivalent: "a kind of living dominated or characterized by the weakness and appetites of this life." Murray is clearly on the negative side, giving as his definition "human nature as controlled and directed by sin." But this seems to put the inevitable results of living ἐν σαρκί into the basic, more neutral sense of the word. Newman and Nida say, in the same vein, "life lived according to one's own human nature." In this analysis the sense suggested is 'when we live just as we ourselves want to' or 'when we live just as most people desire to live'. Other alternatives are TEV's "lived according to our human nature" and REB's "lived on the level of mere human nature."

7:5b desires that led us to sin The genitive phrase παθήματα τῶν ἁμαρτιῶν 'desires of sins' is easily translated as 'sinful passions' in English but difficult to render in semantic propositions. Only here and in Gal. 5:24 does παθήματα have the negative sense of 'passions, desires'. The relationship of desires to sins is best taken as 'desires which lead to' or 'which result in' (BDF, pp. 166–67, Dunn, Murray, Meyer, Phillipi, Gifford); and since the plural 'sins' is an event concept, the relation is represented in the display by 'desires which led us to sin'. But in some languages it will have to be expressed by 'do sinful things.'

in our bodies The phrase ἐν τοῖς μέλεσιν ἡμῶν 'in our members' refers to the parts of the body; but as most English versions translate and as commentaries note, it is a part-whole type of synecdoche.

7:5c *were increased* by *our knowing God's law* The phrase διὰ τοῦ νόμου 'through the law' expresses a means proposition, and therefore some such event as 'stimulated', 'excited', 'kindled', 'aroused' needs to be supplied. All of these ideas, however, continue the figure of personification, which is removed in the rendering here.

7:5d and as a result *we did evil things that caused us to be separated from God* The word 'fruit-bearing' in the result phrase εἰς τὸ καρποφορῆσαι τῷ θανάτῳ 'unto the fruit-bearing to death' is the same word as in 4h. But there it refers to living righteously, and here it refers to evil deeds leading to or resulting in death. It is a dead figure and is therefore rendered nonfiguratively.

The words 'to death' are a personification that means "the consequence or end secured by our sins" (Hodge). The concept of spiritual death is rendered as in 6:16 and 23.

7:6a we have been freed In keeping with the larger context, κατηργήθημεν ἀπὸ τοῦ νόμου 'discharged from the law' means 'set free from obligations to obey the law'.

7:6b *in order to be saved* See the note on 4b.

7:6c *it is as though* we have died The GNT has ἀποθανόντες 'we having died'. This is much more strongly supported than τοῦ θανάτου 'of death', which is supported by several Western manuscripts. The KJV seems to be based on a reading for which there is no manuscript evidence: ἀποθανάντος 'it (the law) having died'. These variants are not even mentioned in the fourth edition GNT. The force of the aorist participle following the main verb is taken as expressing reason or grounds. Since 'we have died' is a figure, the display has 'it is as though'.

7:6d the law *God gave Moses* does not control us The relative pronoun 'which' in ἐν ᾧ κατειχόμεθα 'in which we were restrained' is somewhat ambiguous. It has been taken by some to refer to the sinful nature; but since Paul is here talking about our being set free from bondage to the law, 'law' is the referent of 'which'. The concept of 'restrained' is rendered 'control'.

7:6e serve *God* An object of the infinitive δουλεύειν 'to serve' is required semantically.

7:6f not by *being compelled to obey* that law The Greek is οὐ παλαιότητι γράμματος 'not in oldness of letter'. The word 'letter' here refers to the Mosaic law, as commentators agree (also BAGD, p. 165.2c). This dative case phrase, like the one in 6g, represents a semantic proposition the implied verb of which is supplied from the context ('being compelled to obey'). CEV renders it "by obeying the written law."

In the Greek text this phrase occurs at the end of v. 6, propositions 6f and 6g being in reverse order here to make the positive one follow the negative one. Translators should follow the receptor-language pattern in rendering such positive-negative sets.

7:6g in the new way of *God's* Spirit *helping us* In the phrase ἐν καινότητι πνεύματος 'in newness of Spirit' the first noun expresses a quality semantically and is rendered 'in a new way'. The genitive 'of Spirit' is variously interpreted by commentators as referring to (1) the Holy Spirit, who brings about or enables newness; or (2) the manner of spiritual life or obedience or service which is new; or even (3) the human spirit renewed by Christ (thus Lenski). Interpretation 2 is not a good option since Paul would certainly have used the adjective πνευματική for this meaning. Interpretation 1 seems the best and is the one chosen here. An alternative would be 'which the Spirit effects'.

BOUNDARIES AND COHERENCE

The 7:1-6 paragraph starts with a rhetorical question. (The start of the next unit is marked by two rhetorical questions.)

This paragraph is relationally coherent in that it consists of a generic *principle* about people being subject to laws only while they are alive and its *APPLICATION* about believers being freed from having to obey the Mosaic law by their having died with Christ.

Lexical coherence is shown by three occurrences of the verb ἀποθνῄσκω 'die' and words in the semantic domain of marriage: ἀνήρ 'husband' (eight times) and μοιχαλίς 'adulteress' (twice).

PROMINENCE AND THEME

The theme of 7:1-6 is drawn from the prominent propositions of the *principle* (vv. 1-3) and of the *APPLICATION* (vv. 4-6). Both the NUCLEUS and CIRCUMSTANCE are included from 1c-d because the whole argument hinges on the time, 'after death'. Part of the ORIENTER in 1a-b is also included in the theme because of its features of prominence: (1) the rhetorical question 'do you not know . . . ?' (2) the vocative, (3) and the statement in 1a about their knowing the law. (In other words, 1a-b is more than an ordinary orienter.)

SECTION CONSTITUENT 7:7–12
(Expository Paragraph: Refutation of objection₁ to claim₁ of 7:1–25)

THEME: My reply to the objection that the law of Moses is evil because it causes us to sin is that the law is holy and good; what the law does is simply reveal that what we are doing is sinful.

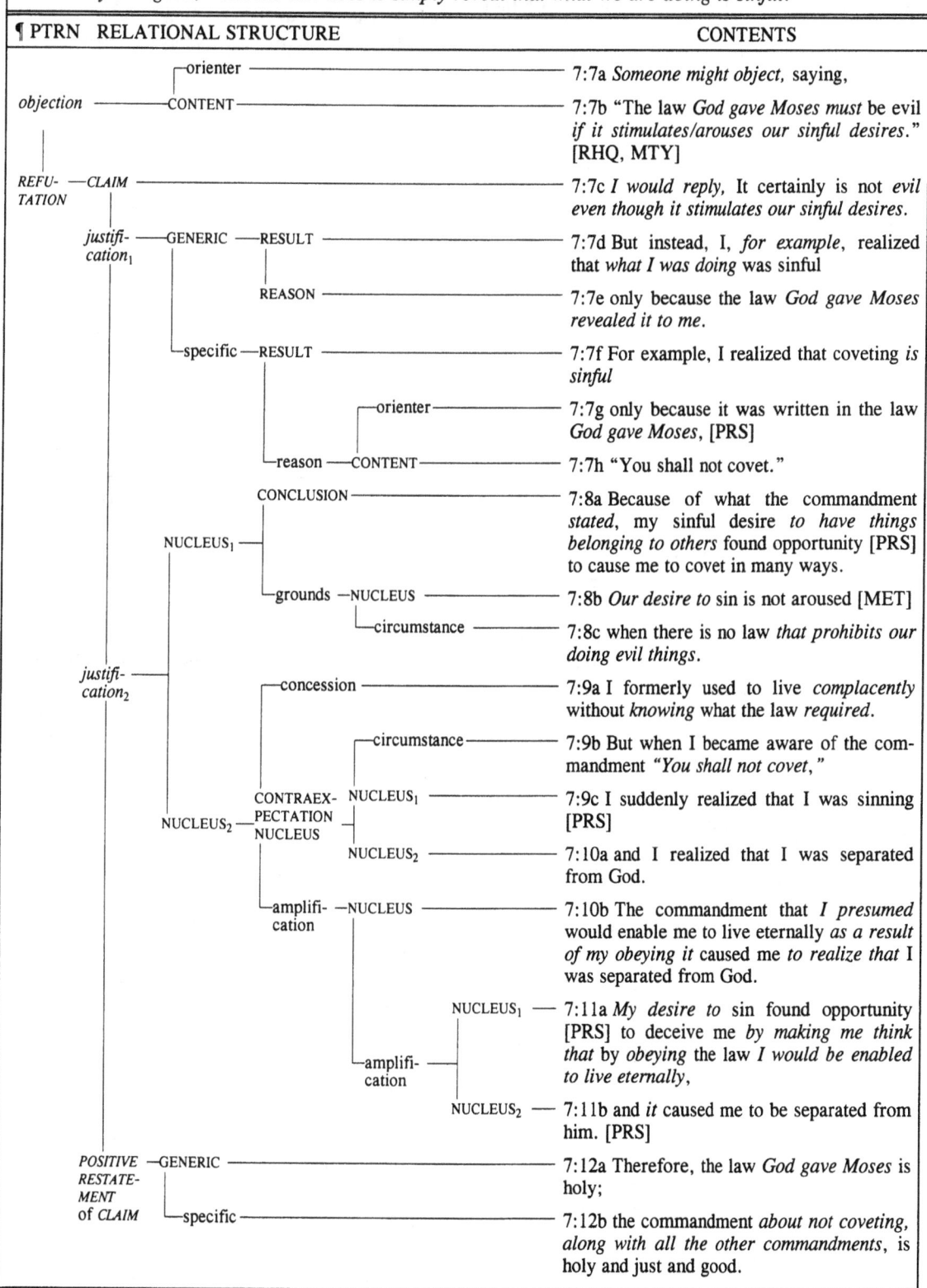

INTENT AND PARAGRAPH PATTERN

The finite verbs in the 7:7-12 paragraph are all indicative; thus its genre is expository. A further implication of the doctrine that justification is by faith, not by obedience of the law, is presented here. In 7a-b there is an *objection* and in 7c-12 a REFUTATION. Within the latter is another level of paragraph pattern: there is in 7:7c a CLAIM and in 7d-h a justification (we realize what we are doing is sinful because the law reveals that to us), though it is expressed in first person singular form; and this is followed by a second justification (8-11) using Paul's own experience in regard to coveting and then a restatement of the CLAIM in positive form (12) answering the original *objection*.

Justification₁ states the positive effects of the law, while justification₂ shows how the law incidentally arouses sinful passions, something that Paul must speak to in order to satisfy the objection and still maintain his earlier points in vv. 5-6.

NOTES

7:7a-b See the notes on 6:1 and 15 for the treatment of the rhetorical question here.

The law . . . *must be* evil *if it stimulates/ arouses our sinful desires* The clause ὁ νόμος ἁμαρτία 'is the law sin?' can be taken as either 'is the (Mosaic) law sinful?' or 'does the law cause/lead to sin?' Commentators are divided. Some have suggested that since Paul nowhere uses the noun 'sin' as a predicate adjective, he would have used the adjective ἁμαρτωλός if the adjectival meaning 'sinful' had been intended. However, Paul, in his v. 12 summary statement in reply to the query, does answer the question 'Is the law sinful?' On the other hand, 'sin' here can be taken as a metonymy: 'Is the law the cause of sin?' (see Bullinger, p. 565). It seems best to conclude that Paul in using ἁμαρτία meant *both* 'is it sinful?' and 'is it the cause of sin?'

7:7c-d It certainly is not *evil even though it stimulates our sinful desires*. But instead, I, *for example*, realized that *what I was doing* was sinful Here ἀλλά could be considered as introducing a contrast, in the sense of 'but nevertheless it is true that' (see Lenski). But since ἀλλά almost always introduces a contrast by substitution ('not . . . , but instead . . .'), we look for what 7d-h might contrast with; and we see that ἀλλά does introduce a contrast to 7b's 'is the law sin' as implied in 7c's 'certainly not'. "No, the law isn't the cause of sin, but it only shows us that what we are doing is actually sinful." To convey this contrast, the implied words 'cause us to sin' are supplied after 'certainly does not' and before 'But instead'.

The words ἁμαρτίαν ἔγνων 'I knew sin' do not mean 'I became a sinner' or even 'I became aware of sin' but rather 'I recognized sin for what it was' (so Cranfield; cf. Haldane, Hodge, Morris). In the Greek the word 'sin' is emphasized by forefronting.

Since many languages do not have an 'except' construction, the negative in οὐκ ᾔδειν εἰ μή 'not I knew except' is best rendered by omitting both the negative and the 'except' clause and rendering it positively with the word 'only' being placed in the clause to which it belongs semantically: 'I knew/realized (7d) . . . only (7e)'.

Starting with v. 7 and continuing through most of the rest of the chapter, Paul switches to the first person singular. Theologians have debated whether the intention is autobiographical or not. Some take it as a reference to non-Christian Jews, others to believers in general, and also debate whether the experiences mentioned are pre-Christian, worldly-Christian, or (regrettably) pan-Christian (i.e., those of all believers, including mature ones). The arguments as to whether Paul is referring to Jews or people before conversion or even immature Christians are largely theological and probably no more than wishful thinking. The evidence from the text itself with its repetition of 'I' and the present tense, is too strong to be rejected as anything but Paul's own experience. (For a superb discussion of the alternatives see Cranfield, pp. 344-47.)

The question of whether Paul is referring to himself alone or to believers in general is important to translators because of its possible effect on the translation. In the light of the context, in which Paul is discussing the relation of believers to the Mosaic law, and specifically in his giving a reply to a theoretical objection concerning believers in general, it is clear that he is using himself and his experiences as an example of what he knows is true of all of us. Paul is being honest and open in admitting his present struggle, but the implication is that it is the struggle of all of us. The translator would hardly be justified in changing all the 'I' references to 'we believers', but could make Paul's intention explicit either here at the start of the passage or at the end, and thus avoid the wrong meaning that what is described in vv. 7–25 is unique to Paul (see 24d in the 7:21–25b expansion display).

7:7e only because the law *God gave Moses revealed it to me* In this reference to Exod. 20:17 and Deut. 5:21, the phrase διὰ νόμου 'through law' needs some verb to make the proposition complete, hence 'revealed' in the display. TEV has "made me know" and LB "showed me." See 6:14b in regard to the words 'God gave Moses'.

7:7f For example Here γάρ introduces a specific example of 'knowing sin' from Paul's own experience.

I realized that The sense of the words 'I knew' in ἐπιθυμίαν ᾔδειν 'I knew coveting' is the same as in 'I knew sin' in 7d: 'I came to know that it was sinful'.

7:7g it was written in the law *God gave Moses* The personification of law in ὁ νόμος ἔλεγεν 'the law said' is rendered nonfiguratively.

7:7h You The Greek command is second person singular, but to avoid wrong meaning it may be necessary to render it as second person plural.

7:8 Here δέ introduces v. 8 as the beginning of justification$_2$. It is not to be taken in an adversative sense. It is omitted in many English translations.

7:8a Because of what the commandment *stated* The means phrase διὰ τῆς ἐντολῆς 'through the commandment' implies some verb: 'stated' is supplied. The phrase containing this proposition is placed first in 8a so that the word 'opportunity' might immediately precede the infinitive phrase which is its complement and specifies what the opportunity is. But this is not the Greek order, and the initial position does not imply emphasis.

my sinful desire *to have things belonging to others* **found opportunity** The sense of the word 'sin' in ἀφορμὴν λαβοῦσα ἡ ἁμαρτία 'sin taking opportunity' is 'the desire to sin', both here and in 8d, as it often is in chapters 6–7. The display retains the personification, but it could be rendered 'because I desired to sin I took the opportunity'. There are many kinds of sinful desire, of course, but the one in view here is coveting, as mentioned next.

to cause me to covet in many ways The word 'lust' in the clause κατειργάσατο ἐν ἐμοὶ πᾶσαν ἐπιθυμίαν 'produced in me every lust' is an event semantically, hence 'to covet'. Here πᾶς means 'every kind of, all sorts of' (BAGD, p. 631.1αβ). NCV has "want all kinds of things I should not want."

7:8b–c *Our desire to* **sin is not aroused when there is no law** *that prohibits our doing evil things* These propositions supply the justification for Paul's statement in 8a. At first glance it seems hard to see how this cluster relates to what immediately precedes it, but this is largely due to the double negative. When the negatives are removed, it becomes 'our desire to sin *is* aroused when there is a law that prohibits our doing evil things', which fits very well as the grounds for 8a.

The word νεκρά 'dead' at the end of v. 8 is used metaphorically; spelled out, it means 'our desire to sin is unable to be aroused as a dead person is unable to be aroused'. In the display the rendering is abbreviated because this metaphor has been used by Paul several times previously. An alternative would be 'it is as though it were dead'.

This 8b–c propositional cluster is a generic statement and does not refer to Paul alone. Thus it bears on the question of who is being described in this passage, Paul only or Christians in general (see the note on 7c–d).

The phrase χωρὶς νόμου 'without law' requires a modifying phrase such as 'that prohibits or commands certain things' in order for it to make sense.

7:9a Here δέ introduces a further point in the justification.

I formerly used to live It is the free pronoun ἐγώ 'I' that occurs here (and six more times in chap. 7). Normally this pronoun indicates emphasis, often by way of contrast with someone else, but such is not the case here. It is only the means by which Paul keeps pointing to his own life as illustrating the internal conflict he is describing. Therefore there is no special marking of it in the display.

BAGD (p. 695.1) give the meaning of ποτέ 'then' here as 'once/formerly'. Commentators disagree as to what time period the adverb refers to, but most feel that the reference is to Paul's childhood or youth. This could be made explicit if the ambiguous 'formerly' causes confusion.

complacently Commentators seem unanimous in agreeing that ἔζων 'was living' must mean more than existing/being alive. Murray says, "He is speaking of the unperturbed, self-complacent, self-righteous life which he once lived." Barnes, Hodge, and Lightfoot concur.

without *knowing* what the law *required* The phrase χωρὶς νόμου 'without law' semantically requires that some verb be supplied to make the proposition complete. It probably does not mean 'without knowing the law' because even as a child Paul was undoubtedly well instructed in the Scriptures. In this context it must mean 'without fully understanding' or, more specifically, 'without really knowing what the law required'. LB has "I did not understand what the law really demanded."

7:9b when I became aware of the commandment The phrase ἐλθούσης τῆς ἐντολῆς 'the commandment coming' is something of a personification in which 'arrival of the commandment' signifies Paul's becoming aware of it. Most commentators agree that the reference is to the tenth commandment, "You shall not covet," mentioned in v. 7. If Paul had meant God's law in general, he would have used the word νόμος 'law'.

7:9c suddenly realized that I was sinning In the expression ἁμαρτία ἀνέζησεν 'sin sprang to life', sin is personified. The display tries to capture the sense nonfiguratively, as does LB with "I realized that I had broken the law."

7:10a realized that I was separated from God The clause ἐγὼ ἀπέθανον 'I died' is figurative, the sense being the same as in 6:16 and 23. As nearly all commentators point out, however, it is not the event of separation from God that is being referred to, but Paul's realization of it. In this context the content of Paul's awareness is 'I was spiritually dead' or 'I was condemned' or even 'I was in a hopeless spiritual state'. The same holds true for 10b.

7:10b The commandment that *I presumed* would enable me to live eternally *as a result of my obeying it* caused me *to realize that* I was separated from God The phrase ἡ εἰς ζωήν 'which (was) unto life' modifies the word 'commandment' and expresses either purpose or result. However, in the light of 3:19-20 and Gal. 3:24, etc., it does not seem possible to take the phrase as expressing God's intention. Thus, both occurrences of εἰς in ἡ εἰς ζωήν, αὕτη εἰς θάνατον 'that which was unto life, this unto death' can be taken as a parallelism expressing result if a cognitive verb is supplied, hence 'I presumed' with the first phrase and 'I realized' with the second.

There is something that needs to be understood as an implied event, viz. obedience, relating the commandment to eternal life. It could be considered the means (i.e., 'by my obeying'), but it is probably better taken as the reason, as in the display.

7:11 The semantic content of v. 11 is relationally coherent if γάρ is taken as expressing amplification, not reason or grounds. The first participial phrase of this verse is identical to 8a (except for word order) and is rendered the same way.

7:11a *My desire to* sin found opportunity to deceive me The personification of ἁμαρτία 'sin' is rendered following Barnes, who says, "The meaning here seems to be that his corrupt and rebellious propensities, excited by the law, led him astray; caused him more and more to sin; practiced a species of deception on him by urging him on headlong, and without deliberation, into aggravated transgression." Its being first in the clause is no doubt a topicalization.

by making me think that* by *obeying* the law *I would be enabled to live eternally Deception implies some understanding of the content of the deception, and this is supplied in the display (see Haldane, Cranfield, Murray, Hodge).

7:11b *it* caused me to be separated from him Sin is personified in the expression δι' αὐτῆς ἀπέκτεινεν 'by it killed (me)'. The sense is almost identical to 'I died' in 10a. An attempt is made in the display to retain something of the transitive sense of 'killed'. A nonfigurative alternative is 'by it God revealed to me that I was spiritually dead'.

7:12a Therefore Here ὥστε 'therefore' introduces the positive restatement of the CLAIM answering the question in 7b. In some languages this might have to be rendered something like 'So my answer to the question of whether the law causes us to sin is'.

7:12b the commandment is holy and just and good Here again (cf. 8a) the singular form of ἐντολή 'commandment' is probably a reference to the tenth commandment, "You shall not covet" (so Murray, Lenski, Shedd, Hodge). However, as part of a main thesis giving Paul's reply to the question about the law in general, it probably also means 'this commandment and every other one' (so Dunn, Sanday and Headlam, Haldane,

Barnes). In any case, the translator should not imply that this commandment is good and the others are not.

Moore (p. 40) considers 'just and good' a near-synonymous doublet; however, there is enough difference in meaning that the words have not been so treated here.

BOUNDARIES AND COHERENCE

The initial boundary of the 7:7-12 paragraph is marked by the conjunction οὖν 'therefore' and two rhetorical questions. The start of the next paragraph is marked by another rhetorical question.

It is in vv. 7-12 that Paul shifts to using first person singular pronouns. Lexical coherence is also provided by five occurrences of ἐντολή 'commandment' and six of ἁμαρτία 'sin' in this short passage. Additional coherence in the 7-12 paragraph is seen in that the whole paragraph deals with the question of what the relationship is between the Mosaic law and our sinning.

PROMINENCE AND THEME

The theme of 7:7-12 is taken from both the *objection* and the REFUTATION. From the REFUTATION are included the *justification*, and the restatement of the CLAIM, the latter because it contains the real answer to the question posed in 7b and because it is introduced by ὥστε 'therefore', which indicates that it is a conclusion.

SECTION CONSTITUENT 7:13
(Expository Paragraph: Refutation of objection$_2$ to claim$_1$ of 7:1-25)

THEME: My reply to the objection that God's law, being good, causes people to become spiritually dead is no, but instead that it is our desire to commit sin that causes us to sin and become spiritually dead.

¶ PTRN RELATIONAL STRUCTURE	CONTENTS
objection — orienter	7:13a Therefore, *if someone were to object*
— CONTENT	7:13b that *the law God gave Moses*, which is good, resulted in my being separated from God, [RHQ]
REFUTATION — NEGATIVE	7:13c *I would reply*, "Certainly it did not *do that*."
POSITIVE MEANS — REASON — RESULT	7:13d But instead it is *my desire to commit* sin which caused me to *sin*
— means	7:13e by *being stimulated by* the *law*, which is good,
— result	7:13f with the result that I was separated from God,
— purpose$_1$	7:13g in order that it would be apparent that sinful desire (*or*, what I was doing) was truly sinful
— purpose$_2$	7:13h and in order that I could realize by *my disobeying* the commandment that sin is exceedingly detestable/sinful.

INTENT AND PARAGRAPH PATTERN

The 7:13 paragraph continues Paul's exposition of the implications of the doctrine of justification by faith. There are again an *objection* and a REFUTATION.

NOTES

7:13a The rhetorical question here is a hypothetical objection to Paul's teaching (see the notes on 6:1 and 6:15).

7:13b *the law God gave Moses* The referent for τὸ ἀγαθόν 'the good' is probably the law since the question is similar to the one in v. 7 and there 'the law' was specified. Moreover, 'the law' is explicitly identified in the new paragraph beginning in v. 14. A less probable referent is 'the commandment', which was just labeled as 'good' in 12b.

resulted in my being separated from God The word ἐγένετο means 'resulted in' (BAGD, p. 160.III1), and θάνατος denotes 'spiritual death' or, as it has been rendered consistently in these chapters, 'separation from God' (see the notes on 6:23 and 7:10a).

7:13d-f But instead Here ἀλλά indicates that instead of the law, it is rather my sinful desire which leads to my separation from God.

it is *my desire to commit* sin The word ἁμαρτία 'sin' is prominent in that it is nominalized and no verb occurs in the clause (the verb phrase is assumed to be repeated from 13b). This prominence is indicated in the display by a cleft construction. 'Sin' is rendered as it was in 8a.

which caused me to *sin* . . . with the result that I was separated from God The main verb phrase here is elided in the Greek; it is presumed to be 'resulted in death' from 13a. But if this were to be supplied, it would be redundant with κατεργαζομένη θάνατον 'producing death', so the idea of death is stated only once in the display.

The participial phrase κατεργαζομένη θάνατον 'producing death', when combined with the subject ἁμαρτία 'desire to sin', produces a semantic ellipsis as well. Our sinful desire causes spiritual death (i.e., separation from God) only as we give in to that desire and actually sin, hence the rendering 'caused me to sin . . . with the result that I was separated from God'.

by *being stimulated by* the *law*, which is good The phrase διὰ τοῦ ἀγαθοῦ 'through that which is good' expresses means and therefore requires some verb to complete it semantically: 'being stimulated by' is supplied as the most appropriate (see the note on 7:5c). Alternatively, the personification could be avoided with 'by making me want to disobey the law'. As in 13b, 'the good' is identified as 'the law' to avoid confusion.

7:13g in order that it would be apparent that sinful desire (*or*, what I was doing) was truly sinful The subject of the main clause, ἁμαρτία 'sin', is also the subject of this purpose clause (ἵνα φανῇ ἁμαρτία 'in order that it might appear sin'). But to say 'that sinful desire might appear as sinful desire' does not make much sense. The sense of the latter is 'that it truly is sin' or, as in the display, 'truly sinful'. The question then is, What was shown to be truly sinful, his sinful desire or the sinful deeds Paul was doing? It could be either or both; the display gives both alternatives.

7:13h and in order that I could realize by *my disobeying* the commandment that sin is exceedingly detestable/sinful The phrase καθ' ὑπερβολὴν ἁμαρτωλός means 'sinful beyond comparison' (BAGD, p. 407.II5bβ), but to say 'sin is very sinful' doesn't make much sense.

The word γένηται 'become' in this context means 'become to me' or 'become in my eyes'. It is rendered 'I could realize' in the display. Several commentators suggest 'be shown/demonstrated to be' or 'be shown up as'.

Some commentators (e.g., Murray, Stuart) have suggested that the phrase διὰ τῆς ἐντολῆς 'through the commandment' is a means proposition with the implied verb idea being 'abuse of', hence 'my disobeying'.

BOUNDARIES AND COHERENCE

The great majority of the commentators consulted make a paragraph division before v. 14. The evidence for doing so is: (1) the generic statement introducing v. 14 that uses the first person plural pronoun with the orienter verb (οἴδαμεν 'we know'), (2) the change from past tense to present tense, and (3) a new paragraph pattern. Lexical coherence within this unit is shown by three occurrences of ἁμαρτία 'sin' and one of the cognate adjective ἁμαρτωλός 'sinful'.

PROMINENCE AND THEME

The theme for 7:13 is simply a condensed version of the *objection* in 13a–b and the NEGATIVE and POSITIVE propositions of the *REFUTATION* in 13c–d.

SECTION CONSTITUENT 7:14–25
(Expository Paragraph: Claim₂ of 7:1–25)

THEME: The law is from God's Spirit, but you and I are influenced by our sinful nature. We often do not do the things we desire and do the things we detest, because of a desire to sin which permeates us and prevents us from doing good—unless Christ frees us from being controlled by these desires.

¶ PTRN RELATIONAL STRUCTURE	CONTENTS
CLAIM — NUCLEUS — NUCLEUS — CONTRAST	7:14a We know that the law *God gave Moses* is from *God's Spirit*;
	7:14b but as for me, I am *influenced by my* self-directed/sinful nature.
amplification	7:14c *It is as though* I have been forced to become a slave of *my desire to* sin. [MET]
justification₁ — SPECIFIC — generic	7:15a The things that I do I *often* do not understand. [HYP]
NUCLEUS₁	7:15b That is, *at times* it is what I want *to do* [HYP] that I do not practice,
NUCLEUS₂	7:15c and contrariwise *at times* it is what I detest *doing* [HYP] that I do.
justification₂	7:16–20 You and I do evil things not because we will it, but because of the desire to sin which permeates us. [*See the expansion on p. 168.*]
justification₃	7:21–25b What happens is that when you and I want to do good an evil desire prevents us. There is a force permeating us which opposes what we desire to do and puts us under the control of our sinful desires. [*See the expansion on p. 170.*]
SUMMARY CONCLUSION — CONTRAST	7:25c *So then, you and* I on the one hand *with our minds* want to obey God's law,
NUCLEUS	7:25d but on the other hand because of our self-directed/sinful human nature *you and* I *obey* the principle of being controlled by sinful desires.

INTENT AND PARAGRAPH PATTERN

It is not easy to decide on the paragraph pattern of 7:14–25, even though it is part of a long expository section. Several parts of it are expressive: (1) the first person singular pronoun is used; (2) the expressions in v. 24 are emotion charged; (3) conflicting emotions are expressed in vv. 21–22; and (4) following Paul's seeking of a solution in v. 24, the solution to his conflicts is pronounced with triumph in v. 25. It is an "expression of a strong and sudden emotion of gratitude" (Hodge). Thus the paragraph closes with a statement and question of great emotive force. But because 7:14–25 is part of a long expository section and its overall internal pattern is a CLAIM plus a series of *justifications*, it is considered an expository paragraph of the volitionality subtype.

NOTES

7:14a Here γάρ introduces a new CLAIM. It is omitted in the display and also in most English versions.

from God's Spirit The word πνευματικός 'spiritual' could be a reference to the human spirit, referring to matters that relate to our spirits and which require spiritual perception and obedience. Or it could be a reference to the Holy Spirit (i.e., as the author of the law). In the light of Paul's use of the same word in other epistles to mean 'originating from the Holy Spirit', the latter is undoubtedly correct. Most commentators support this view, as do BAGD (p. 679.2aβ).

7:14b *influenced by my* self-directed/sinful nature This is the only occurrence of σάρκινος 'fleshly' in Romans. Its sense is 'influenced/controlled by the self-directed sinful human nature'.

7:14c *It is as though* **I have been forced to become a slave of** *my desire to* **sin** Commentators agree that the phrase πεπραμένος ὑπὸ τὴν ἁμαρτίαν 'having been sold under sin' is a metaphor referring to slavery. The words 'it is as though' indicate that a comparison is intended. The idea of 'sold' is rendered as 'forced to become a slave'. The figure could also be considered a metonymy, with the cause (selling) standing for the effect (being made a slave). The metaphor could be spelled out more completely: 'controlled by desire to sin as a person who is sold as a slave is controlled by his master'. The preposition ὑπό 'under' signifies 'being controlled by'.

7:15a The things that I do, I *often* **do not understand** The object phrase 'the things that I do' is forefronted in the Greek, hence prominent; it is forefronted also in the display. The word 'often' is supplied (and 'at times' in 15b and c) because Paul's statement is hyperbolic; obviously he does understand many of the things he does. An alternative would be 'sometimes' or 'some of the things I do'.

7:15b Here γάρ does not have logical force but introduces what may be considered a specific or an amplification of 15a.

at times These words have been supplied to avoid the connotation that Paul never did what he wanted to or always did what he detested.

it is what I want *to do* **that I do not practice** The somewhat hyperbolic phrase ὃ θέλω 'what I wish' stands for 'what I wish to do', 'to do' being understood from ποιῶ 'I do' which follows. Though ὅ in this phrase is singular, the sense is generic: 'the things'. This phrase as well as ὃ μισῶ 'what I detest' in 15c is emphasized in the Greek by forefronting, hence the cleft construction in both 15b and 15c.

7:15c it is what I detest *doing* **that I do** The Greek is ὃ μισῶ 'what I detest', with 'to do' or 'doing' being understood for the same reason mentioned in the note on 15b. The other comments regarding ὃ θέλω 'what I wish' also apply to ὃ μισῶ.

EXPANSION OF *JUSTIFICATION*₂ IN THE 7:14–25 DISPLAY

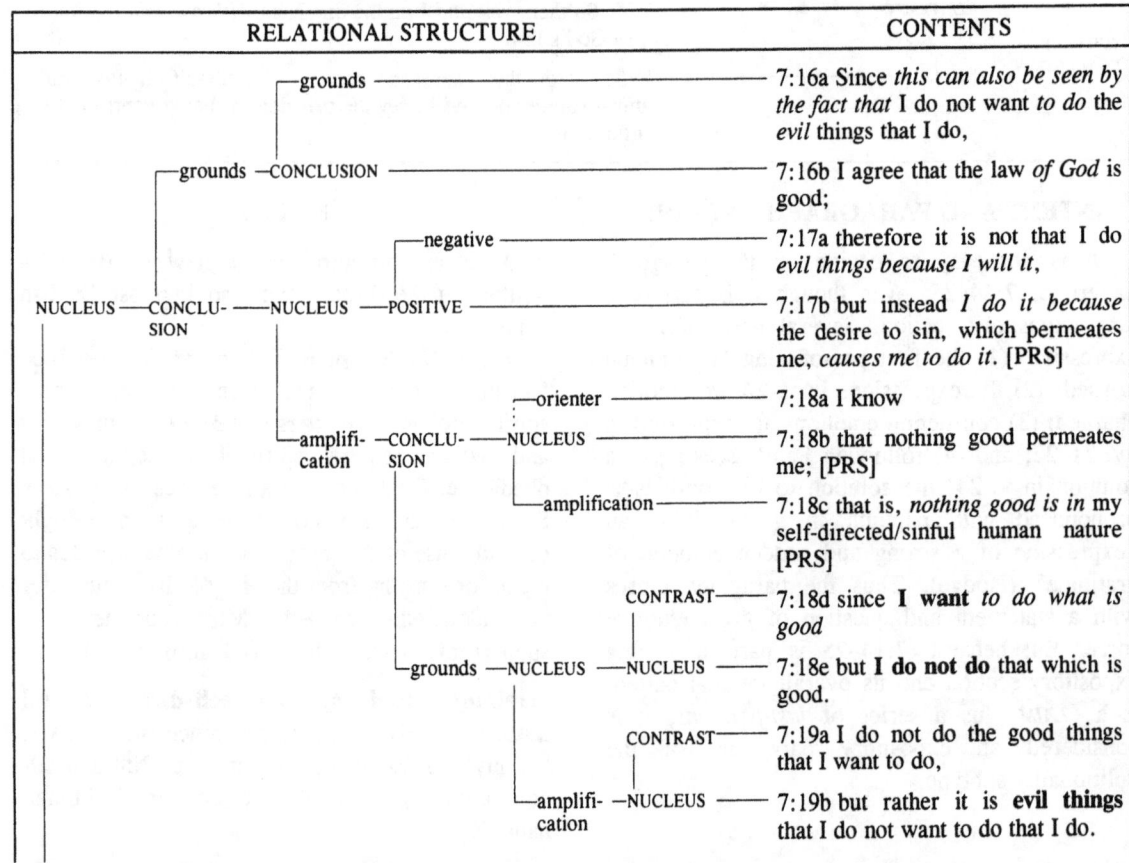

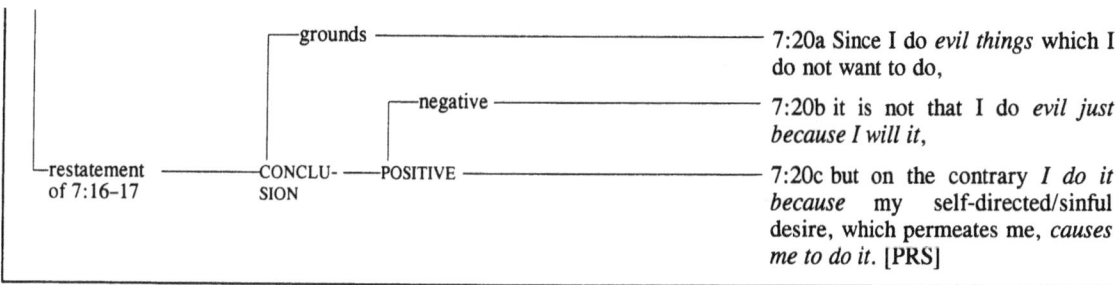

7:16a Since Here the introducer εἰ has a causal, not a conditional, sense, hence the grounds relationship.

7:17a therefore it is not that I do *evil things* Here δέ moves the argument along; it introduces the conclusion of the argument begun in 16a. The adverb νυνί 'now', as many commentators note, is not temporal but logical: 'the present situation is that' or 'as it is'. The logical force is brought out by the word 'therefore' in the display (TEV, RSV, JB, NASB, and CEV all have "so").

In the display, 'evil things' is supplied as the referent for αὐτό 'it'.

because I will it The clause ἐγὼ κατεργάζομαι αὐτό 'I do it' cannot be taken in a literal sense; for as Barnes declares, "It is really the man that sins when evil is committed." But it is linguistically unwarranted to try on theological grounds alone to maintain that 'I' refers to Paul's renewed nature. The better explanation (so Murray) is that Paul "identifies his ego, his person, with that determinate will which is in agreement with the law of God." Thus a reason clause is implied: by including 'because I will it' wrong meaning is avoided.

7:17b the desire to sin ... causes me to do it With no verb in the Greek here, it is assumed to be carried over from the previous clause, hence 'causes me to do it'. The subject of the verb is ἁμαρτία 'sinful desire', a personification that is kept in the display (cf. 7:8).

permeates me Sin is personified here (also in 18b) in that the ability to dwell in something is attributed to it: οἰκοῦσα ἐν ἐμοί 'indwelling in me' and οἰκεῖ ἐν ἐμοί 'dwells in me'. The display attempts to capture the sense nonfiguratively with 'permeates me'.

7:18c my self-directed/sinful human nature In the phrase ἐν τῇ σαρκί μου 'in my flesh', the word σάρξ signifies the sinful or self-directed human nature.

7:18d–e I want *to do what is good* **but I do not do** *that which is good* In the Greek the infinitive phrase θέλειν παράκειταί μοι 'to wish is present to me' (in 18d), 'wish' has no object. Therefore 'to do what is good' is supplied as the object, based on the following clause. Note that this phrase and the next one (in 18e), τὸ κατεργάζεσθαι ... οὔ 'to do (is) not', are mismatched ways of stating 'I want' and 'I don't do'. In the Greek, 'wanting' and 'doing' are emphasized by being substantive forms preposed to the stative verb παράκειμαι 'to be at hand', and an implied verb 'to do' for which θέλειν 'to wish' is, semantically speaking, the auxiliary. The emphasis thus signaled is indicated in the display by bold type.

Due to the lack in 18e of a Greek finite verb, some early manuscripts have supplied a verb, most notably εὑρίσκω 'I find'. But the best manuscripts have no verb, and there is no uniformity among the manuscripts that do have one, so clearly the GNT is correct. The fourth edition GNT assigns the shorter reading a B rating ("almost certain").

7:19a Here γάρ introduces not a grounds for what precedes it, but an amplification of 18d–e. It is also a restatement of v. 15.

7:19b The word κακόν 'evil' is emphasized by forefronting and by being followed by the demonstrative τοῦτο 'this'. The emphasis is indicated in the display by bold type and by forefronting, using a cleft construction.

7:20a Since Here εἰ has a causal sense as in 16a.

7:20b–c *just because I will it* See the notes on 17a and 17b.

7:20c *I do it because* **my self-directed/sinful desire, which permeates me,** *causes me to do it* There is no verb in the Greek in the last part of the verse, but 'does' can be supplied following the noun 'sin' on the basis of κατεργάζομαι 'does (it)' in 20b. (NIV, NCV, CEV supply this verb.) Though 'sin does it' is personified here, Paul does not by such a figure absolve himself of all responsibility. The display mitigates the personification with the words 'causes me to do it'.

EXPANSION OF *JUSTIFICATION*₃ IN THE 7:14–25 DISPLAY

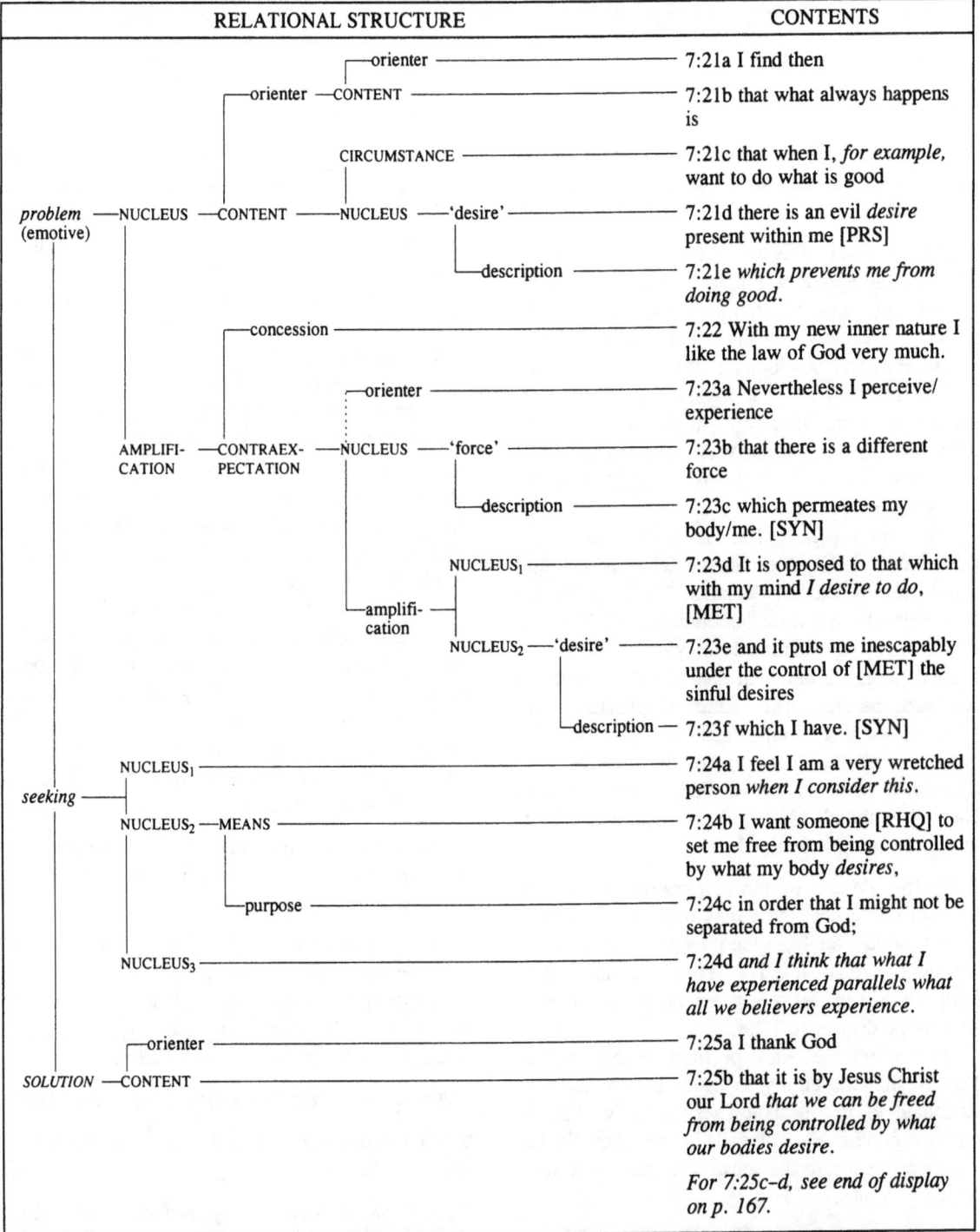

7:21b what always happens is The word νόμος here means 'rule' or 'principle', according to BAGD (p. 542.2). REB renders it "principle"; NCV and JB, "rule." However, 'principle' is difficult to express in many languages, and the English *rule* has a different primary sense than that intended by νόμος. Therefore it is rendered differently here—and quite simply. LB is similar:

"it seems to be a fact of life." Though some have suggested that the meaning is 'the law', since that is Paul's usual usage, that sense does not fit the context. On the other hand, 'as a general rule' fits very well (also in 3:27; 7:23, 25b; and 8:2). Furthermore, it is well documented that νόμος is used in the sense of 'general rule' in extrabiblical writings of the time. As Dunn notes, it is hard to know what other word Paul could have used to mean 'general rule'.

7:21c when I, *for example*, want to do what is good The dative construction τῷ θέλοντι ἐμοί 'to/for me the one wishing' represents a circumstantial relation, 'when I wish'. Nearly all the English versions give this sense.

Paul is using his experience as an illustrative example (see the note on 7:7d). It should not be suggested that his experience is unique. Thus the words 'for example' are supplied.

7:21d there is an evil *desire* present within me Evil is personified in the expression ἐμοὶ τὸ κακὸν παράκειται 'to me the evil is at hand'; in the display it is rendered nonfiguratively.

7:21e *which prevents me from doing good* This proposition is supplied because in Paul's argument in nearly every one of the preceding six verses he is stating not just that the evil desire is there, but that it prevents him from doing the good that he desires to do. CEV also supplies this: "something in me keeps me from doing what I know is right."

7:22 Here γάρ introduces a further amplification expounding in further detail the statement in v. 21.

With my new inner nature The phrase κατὰ τὸν ἔσω ἄνθρωπον 'according to the inner man' has been much discussed. Is Paul following a Hellenistic sense, referring to a higher aspect of an individual's nature in contrast to a base, more earthly aspect? In 2 Cor. 4:16 and Eph. 3:16 the same expression is used to refer to our new nature as transformed by Christ, so it is probably used in that sense here. Paul certainly does not mean people have a higher nature which, whether they are regenerate or not, would delight in God's law. It is accordingly rendered 'my new inner nature' here. It is almost synonymous with 'my mind' in 23d, which would tend to make the sense 'my conscious mind'.

7:23b force See the note on 21b for νόμος 'rule'. This is probably a play on the word νόμος, occurring here with a different meaning than in v. 21. BAGD suggest the meaning here is "principle of action" (p. 542.2). Bullinger says (p. 676) of Paul's meaning here, "He means that he sees *sin*: which, through the authority with which it rules his members, he calls by Catachresis, '*law*.'"

7:23c permeates my body/me The expression 'in my members' is taken as in 5b to mean 'in my body' or 'in me'.

7:23d It is opposed to that which with my mind *I desire to do* There is a military metaphor here, ἀντιστρατευόμενον 'which is warring against', in which the point of similarity with the topic is 'being opposed to'. Other acceptable nonfigurative renderings would be 'is in conflict with', 'resists', 'acts contrary to'.

The thing that is being warred against is τῷ νόμῳ τοῦ νοός μου 'the law/principle of my mind'. The genitive form 'of my mind' can be taken to signify 'which operates in my mind', 'mind' being almost synonymous with 'inner man' in v. 22. The desire to do good is the principle in his mind that evil desire is fighting against.

7:23e and it puts me inescapably under the control of The military metaphor continues with a participial phrase: αἰχμαλωτίζοντά με 'taking me captive' or 'making me a prisoner'. The point of similarity is 'to put someone unwillingly and inescapably under the control of another'. Spelled out completely, it means 'puts me inescapably under its control, as one captured in war is put unwillingly under the control of his captors'.

7:24a I feel I am a very wretched person *when I consider this* The exclamatory expression ταλαίπωρος ἐγὼ ἄνθρωπος 'wretched I man' has no verb. It expresses not so much Paul's state as his feelings about himself in the situation he has been describing.

7:24b I want someone to set me free The force of the rhetorical question 'who will set me free?' is somewhat difficult to determine. It could be taken as in the display; alternatively it could be taken as a negative statement such as 'I doubt if anyone can' or even 'I think no one can' (as is appropriate for similar questions in 8:31, 33, 34, 35). The display follows Hodge: "this is the expression, not of despair, but of earnest desire of help from without and above himself."

from being controlled by what my body desires The Greek is ἐκ τοῦ σώματος τοῦ θανάτου τούτου 'from the body of this death'. There is a question here of whether the final 'this' modifies only the word 'death' or the whole phrase. The argument from grammar is probably decisive: the genitive phrase τοῦ θανάτου modifies the word 'body', and "such phrases would never have a pronoun or some other modifier that makes them definite, for they would then cease to be adjectival" (BDF, p. 165).

As regards the interpretation of 'body', it has been variously interpreted. Some take σῶμα to refer to the physical body; others, to the sinful human nature; still others, to the principle of subjection to sinful desire. Hodge even suggests the burden or weight of being in such a bondage. In any case, it can hardly refer to Paul's physical body, for his cry in this passage is not to be released by death, but to be released from the struggle he experiences in this life against his sinful desires. On the other hand, if it meant 'sinful human nature', why would Paul not have used σάρξ? In the display, therefore, the word 'body' is retained, amplified with 'from being controlled by what my body desires'.

7:24c in order that I might not be separated from God The genitive 'of death' is taken by most commentators as 'which leads to' or 'which results in'. Since more than physical death is being referred to, 'death' is rendered as in vv. 10 and 13.

7:24d *and I think that what I have experienced parallels what all we believers experience* See the note on 7:7d. In this passage Paul is not merely reciting his own experience without relevance to anyone else. Rather, he is using his struggle with self-directed, sinful desire to illustrate what all believers experience. The proposition supplied here is to make Paul's meaning clear and avoid wrong meaning if it cannot be made clear by some other means.

7:25a I thank God See the note on 6:17a. The fourth edition GNT has χάρις τῷ θεῷ 'thanks to God' with a B rating ("almost certain"). There is some Western support for ἡ χάρις τοῦ θεοῦ 'the grace of God' and ἡ χάρις κυρίου 'the grace of (the) Lord', which evidently arose in order to supply a more direct answer to the question in 24b.

7:25b it is by Jesus Christ our Lord *that we can be freed from being controlled by what our bodies desire* The Greek phrase 'through Jesus Christ our Lord' lacks a subject and verb, giving rise to the Western variants in 25a. But most commentators recognize the phrase as an answer to Paul's rhetorical question in 24b. A simple 'Let us thank God through Christ our Lord' would not make sense in this context.

Commentators agree that the verb ῥύομαι 'set free' (repeated from 24b) needs to be supplied, but they disagree as to whether the tense should be present (or perfect) or future. The arguments are inconclusive and probably irrelevant. Paul knows that at least partial deliverance *is* possible (otherwise the triumphant exclamation and abrupt end to the discussion of the conflict make little sense), but he knows it will never be complete until death. The implied verb supplied here is intended to preserve the tense ambiguity. JBP retains the ambiguity with "I thank God there is a way out"; LB chooses the past tense; CEV opts for the future tense.

7:25c So then, *you and* **I** The function of the first words, ἄρα οὖν 'so then', in this final sentence of chapter 7 is to introduce the summary conclusion for the paragraph. Bruce (1963) states that here, "after his brief indication that the situation is not hopeless, Paul goes back to summarize the moral predicament of 7:14–24." Best, Hodge, and Shedd concur. Some have objected that logically this conclusion belongs before the triumphant statement of deliverance in v. 24, but 25c–d are related semantically not to v. 24, but to the chapter as a whole. And because this is a summary statement, it is appropriate to note that Paul intends the preceding discussion as a description of what all believers experience. Therefore the pronominal subject αὐτὸς ἐγώ 'I myself', which follows ἄρα οὖν, is here rendered as 'you and I'. An alternate rendering is simply 'I', with 24d moved to follow 25d.

There is a question whether αὐτός means 'I myself, without the aid of Christ' (in contrast to 'by Jesus Christ' in 25b) or simply 'I myself'. But since this is a summary conclusion for the whole chapter, it is best not to take it as a contrast with 25b.

7:25d because of our self-directed/sinful human nature The word σάρξ means 'sinful or self-directed human nature', but the dative (used to give a parallel to the dative τῷ νοΐ 'with the mind' in 25c) can hardly mean 'by the instrument of', hence the causal sense in the display.

***you and* I *obey* the principle of being controlled by our sinful desires** There is no verb in the last part of the verse. 'I serve' could be supplied from 25c, but in the light of vv. 4–6, it could be that the sense is 'you and I act as though we were compelled to obey'. In the display 'obey' is supplied rather than 'serve' because 'serve' implies a human recipient of the action. The object of the implied verb 'obey' is νόμῳ ἁμαρτίας 'the law of sin', that is, 'the principle of sinful desire' or 'the sinful nature'.

BOUNDARIES AND COHERENCE

Lexical coherence is provided by seven occurrences of νόμος 'law', four of ἁμαρτία 'sin', seven of θέλω 'to wish', and four of κατεργάζομαι 'to work'. The boundary with 8:1 has already been discussed (see p. 146).

PROMINENCE AND THEME

The theme of 7:14–25 is taken from the CONTRAST and NUCLEUS of the *CLAIM* in v. 14, plus condensations of the naturally prominent propositions of the three *justifications*. It also includes in abbreviated form the CONTENT (25b) of the *SOLUTION*, which is considered prominent because it is a solution that is led up to by *seeking* it (v. 24).

In the theme the pronouns have been changed from the first person singular to 'you and I' to avoid wrong meaning and confusion. (Paul is really making a generic claim, using his own experience as an example, as brought out in (implied) 24d; he is not simply answering a query about his own life.) The theme statement would not cohere with that of the previous paragraph if it did not say "you and I." An alternative to "you and I" would be to retain the pronominal references as first person singular and then either change the theme to "but I, for example, am influenced" or add an extra sentence at the end, "And what is true for me is true for all believers."

SUBDIVISION CONSTITUENT 8:1-39
(Expository Section: Claim₃ of 6:1-8:39)

THEME: God will not in any way condemn those who are united to Christ Jesus; we are compelled to live as God's Spirit directs, not as our sinful human nature directs. What we suffer now is not worth paying attention to as we consider the future splendor that God will reveal to us. The Spirit helps us as our spirits feel weak. And God works out all things in a way that produces good to us who love him. Therefore no one can prevail against us, and nothing can separate us from Christ's and God's loving us.

MACROSTRUCTURE	CONTENTS
justification₁ —JUSTIFICATION—	8:1-11 God will not in any way condemn those who are united to Christ Jesus, for God's Spirit has freed us from the inevitability of sinning and from spiritual death.
CLAIM—	8:12-13 We are compelled to live as the Spirit directs, not as our sinful human nature directs, because if you do the latter you will be eternally separated from God, but if you cease doing the latter you will live eternally.
justification₂	8:14-17 Since it is we who allow the Spirit of God to guide us who are God's children, we will also inherit eternal blessing from God.
justification₃	8:18-25 Since everything God has created is eagerly awaiting the time when he will reveal who are his true children, I consider that what we suffer now is not worth paying attention to.
justification₄	8:26-27 The Spirit helps us as our spirits feel weak; the Spirit prays for us and God understands what the Spirit intends.
justification₅	8:28-30 God works out all things in a way that produces good to us who love him. He does this because, having known that we would be saved and thus have the character of his Son, he chose us and declared us righteous, and he will surely give us future splendor.
CLAIM—	8:31-39 We must conclude from these things that no one can prevail against us, and absolutely no one and nothing can separate us from Christ's and God's loving us.

INTENT AND MACROSTRUCTURE

Although the final paragraph in the 8:1-39 section contains a succession of emotive rhetorical questions, still that paragraph is expository as are the other five paragraphs within the unit. Hence the whole section is considered expository, continuing Paul's exposition of the applications to daily life of the doctrine of justification by faith set forth in 3:21-26. The unit contains a CLAIM (31-39) preceded by a series of *justifications* that lead Paul to it, along with the emotive elements that signal the end of the higher-level unit, 6:1-8:39. The alternative would be to consider the section expressive, but the first five constituent paragraphs would then have to be classified as *situations* leading to Paul's REACTION in 31-39, and they are clearly not simply *situations*.

BOUNDARIES AND COHERENCE

The initial and final boundaries of the 8:1-39 section have already been discussed. All commentators recognize chapter 8 as one unit, giving it some such title as "A life characterized by the indwelling of God's Spirit" (Cranfield) or "The Spirit and New Life" (Michel). Indeed, πνεῦμα 'Spirit' occurs twenty times in the chapter (though not after v. 27) and only fourteen times in the rest of the epistle. It is quite possible to take the section's final paragraph (vv. 31-39) as the conclusion not just of the section but of the whole exposition of the implications of justification by faith (i.e., everything from 5:1 onwards). Cranfield says, "Verses 31-39 may justifiably be regarded as the conclusion not only to chapter 8 but also to the whole argument of the epistle so far." It depends on how much is covered by 'these things' in 8:31, τί οὖν ἐροῦμεν πρὸς ταῦτα; 'What therefore shall we say to these things?' But it is impossible to say for certain.

PROMINENCE AND THEME

The theme of 8:1-39 is drawn from the themes of the constituent paragraphs, but only from their CLAIMS, which are more naturally prominent than their corresponding *justifications*.

SECTION CONSTITUENT 8:1–11
(Expository Paragraph: Justification₁ for 8:31–39, justification for 8:12–13)

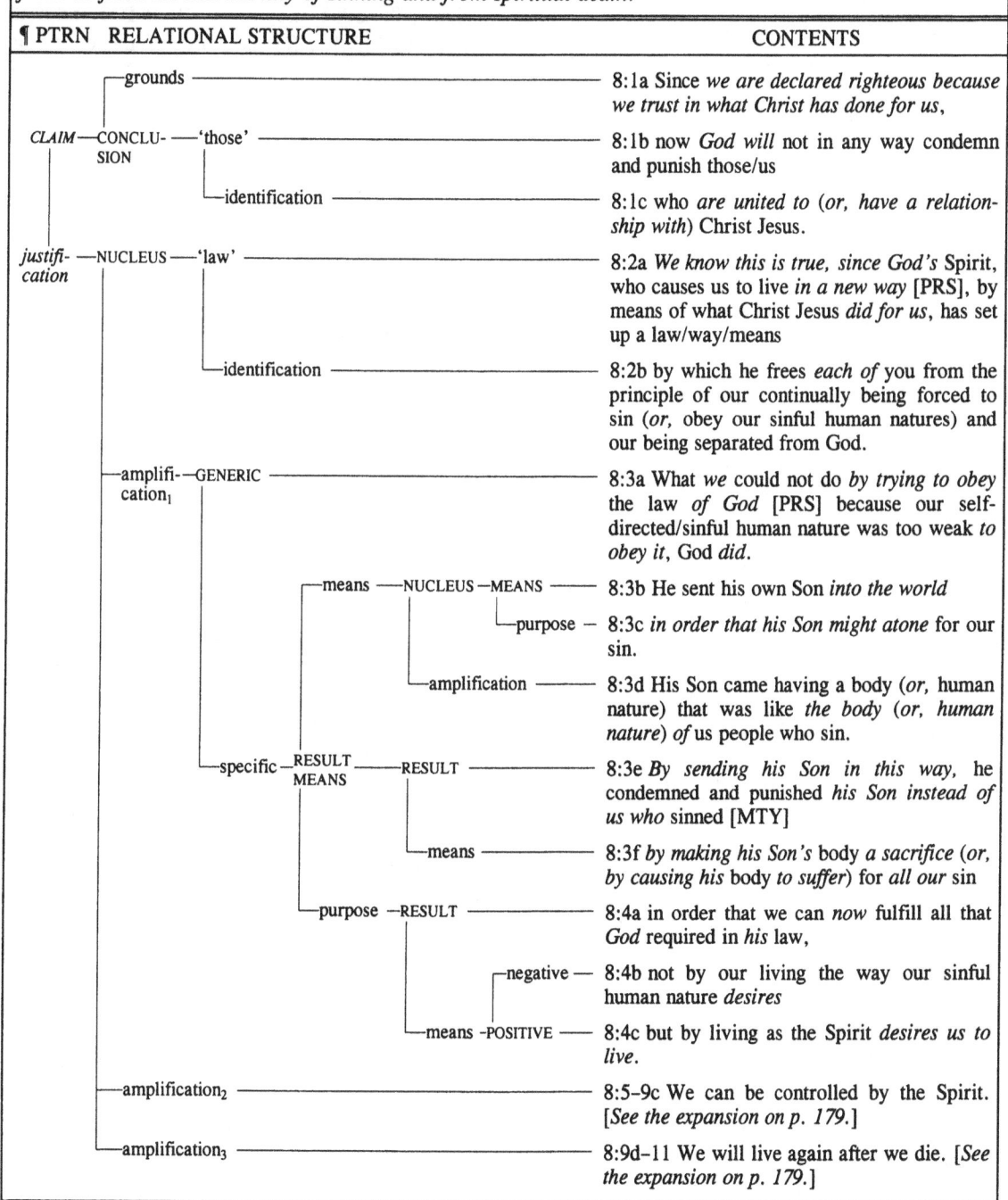

INTENT AND PARAGRAPH PATTERN

In the 8:1-11 paragraph Paul continues expounding the implications of justification by faith. It is clearly expository. All finite verbs are indicative except for the one in a subjunctive purpose clause introduced by ἵνα. The paragraph pattern is straightforward. It opens with a CLAIM in v. 1, followed by its *justification* in vv. 2–11.

NOTES

8:1a Since *we are declared righteous because we trust in what Christ has done for us* Here ἄρα 'therefore' marks what follows as being final in the succession of great implications of justification by faith set forth in 3:21-26. To make clear that this section is not just the conclusion of what immediately precedes it, some of what 'therefore' refers to is supplied.

8:1b now Commentators are somewhat divided as to whether the word νῦν 'now' has temporal or logical force. Most choose the temporal sense. Hodge gives the meaning as "under . . . the circumstances set forth in the previous part of the epistle," and this is surely correct. Dunn curiously hedges: "Paul most likely intended a pause between 7:25 and 8:1. . . . The linking words (ἄρα νῦν) should probably be read with this force." But there is little evidence to support such a conjecture; it is not mentioned by BAGD that the two words go together. There is no reason to depart from the primary sense of the word, which is temporal.

not in any way condemn and punish The meaning of οὐδὲν κατάκριμα 'no condemnation' is stronger than simply 'is not condemned'. As a number of commentators point out, 'condemnation' is not just passing a sentence of punishment, but the carrying out of the sentence, a metonymy in which cause stands for effect, hence 'and punish'.

those/us The goal of the event of condemnaion is expressed in the Greek by the masculine plural pronoun τοῖς 'to those'. But in some languages 'those' would imply exclusion of the writer, and the pronoun should be rendered 'those of us' or 'us'.

8:1c *united to* (*or, have a relationship with*) Christ Jesus For the phrase ἐν Χριστῷ Ἰησοῦ 'in Christ Jesus', see the notes on 6:11 and 6:23. The external evidence to support the first part of the KJV rendering ("who walk not after the flesh but after the spirit") is very weak. It was probably copied by mistake from v. 4 in some fairly early manuscript.

8:2a Here γάρ is taken as introducing the *justification* for the CLAIM made in 1b-c.

God's* Spirit, who causes us to live *in a new way The subject of the verb 'freed' is ὁ νόμος τοῦ πνεύματος τῆς ζωῆς 'the law of the spirit of life', a personification which Paul uses to balance the similar construction at the end of the sentence, τοῦ νόμου τῆς ἁμαρτίας καὶ τοῦ θανάτου 'the law of sin and death'. It is the Spirit who sets us free by causing us to respond to the 'law' he has established. These considerations enable us to decide between the views of various commentators on this phrase.

The word πνεῦμα 'spirit' occurs twenty-two times in this chapter. All but two of these occurrences are best taken as referring to God's Spirit. (The other two, in vv. 10 and 16, refer to the human spirit.) So the sense of the phrase is clearly not 'the law of the mind', nor 'the gospel', but 'the Spirit who is the author of life' (so Murray, Morris, Cranfield). The rendering in the display avoids the use of the verbal noun 'life'.

Paul uses the term νόμος 'law' in various ways. One meaning is the Mosaic law. But in 2a and 2b it means 'a principle' or 'way of operation' or 'what always happens', as also in its three immediately preceding occurrences (7:21, 23, and 25). There is nothing in the Mosaic law itself which points to life through Christ, and Paul has just gone to great lengths in chapter 7 to show that what the law did was reveal our spiritual death.

8:2b *each of* you There is a textual problem here. The fourth edition GNT has 'you(sg)', with a B rating ("almost certain"), as the object of the verb 'set free', in preference to 'me'. However, the problem is irrelevant; as Morris notes, "Paul clearly means the term to apply to any believer" (including himself). Assuming the 'you' reading to be correct, following Paul's use of the second singular pronoun elsewhere in the epistle, the display renders it as 'each of you'; in some languages it may be necessary to say 'you(pl) and me'.

from the principle of our continually being forced to sin The word ἁμαρτία refers to that from which we are set free. It could mean 'continual sinning' or, following Paul's use of the word in 7:25, 'continual obedience to our sinful nature'. Another alternative is 'the inevitability of sin'.

and our being separated from God The phrase τῆς ἁμαρτίας καὶ τοῦ θανάτου is, literally, 'of sin and of death', but semantically it seems best to recognize that death is the result of sin (so Barnes, Murray, Barrett), hence 'being separated from God' (see 7:10, 11). An alternative would be 'being spiritually dead'.

8:3a Here γάρ introduces an explanation of the method of our being set free, not a reason for it.

What *we* could not do *by trying to obey* the law *of God* The subject of the clause is τὸ ἀδύνατον τοῦ νόμου 'the inability of the law', a mismatched way of saying 'the law was unable'. This is a personification (it is 'we' who were unable). In the display it is rendered nonfiguratively, and an implicit verb, 'by trying to obey', is supplied. The law here refers either to the Mosaic law or God's law in general (see 7:25). Among the modern versions, only LB removes the personification: "We aren't saved from sin's grasp by knowing the commandments of God, because we can't and don't keep them."

because our self-directed/sinful nature was too weak *to obey it* The literal meaning of ἐν ᾧ ἠσθένει διὰ τῆς σαρκός is 'in which it was weak through the flesh'. It seems best here to take 'in which' in the causal sense, as suggested by BAGD (p. 261.IV6d) and other commentators. The weakness is that of the σάρξ, our sinful or self-directed human nature, as in chapter 7. The sphere of weakness is made specific in the display.

God *did* In the Greek, ὁ θεός 'God' is the subject of the verb κατέκρινεν 'condemned' (rendered in proposition 3e). The verb 'did' is supplied following 'God' to balance the verb in 'we could not do' in 3a. RSV, TEV, NIV, NEB, and JB likewise supply 'did'.

8:3b his own Son See the note on 1:3-4. Though 'son of God' is a dead metaphor in many cultures, it is not in others, and may have to be rendered some other way.

into the world This locative phrase is supplied because the case frame for the verb 'send' semantically requires a destination. NCV supplies "to earth."

8:3c *in order that his Son might atone* for our sin The words 'and for sin' require some event to be understood. BAGD (p. 644.1g) suggest that when the preposition περί 'concerning' is used with ἁμαρτία 'sin' it has the sense 'to take away, atone for'. Many commentators agree.

8:3d came having a body (*or,* human nature) that was like *the* body (*or,* human nature) *of* us people who sin The literal meaning of ἐν ὁμοιώματι σαρκὸς ἁμαρτίας καὶ περὶ ἁμαρτίας is 'in likeness of flesh of sin and concerning sin'. The noun ὁμοίωμα 'resemblance' is a mismatched way of expressing the event 'to resemble, to be like'. The word σάρξ here means 'body' or 'human nature'. Hence the first three words of the phrase mean 'having a body or human nature'. But σάρξ is modified by the genitive 'of sin', not to indicate that Christ's nature was sinful, but that ours is, and that the body or nature he assumed, though different from ours in that it was not sinful, resembled it. If Paul had meant 'he assumed sinful human nature', he would have said ἐν σαρκὶ ἁμαρτίας 'in a sinful nature'.

8:3e-f he condemned and punished *his Son instead of us who* sinned *by making his Son's* body *a sacrifice* (or, *by causing his* body *to suffer*) for *all our* sin There are two problems regarding κατέκρινεν τὴν ἁμαρτίαν ἐν τῇ σαρκί 'he condemned sin in the flesh'. First, what does the verb 'condemn' mean? Second, what is the sense of 'in the flesh'? It is clear that the latter phrase is not to be connected with 'sin'. In the context of discussing the whole purpose of the atonement (3d) Paul's meaning cannot be that 'God condemned sin in the flesh' (whatever that might mean), but not other types of sin. It seems best to follow the majority of commentators by taking ἐν in a means sense and taking 'flesh' to refer to the human body of Jesus (so Sanday and Headlam, Morris, Shedd, Hodge, Haldane, Robertson,).

The primary meaning of the word 'condemned' is the passing of sentence, a statement that punishment is deserved. Here it should be taken as a metonymy in which cause stands for effect (as with the cognate word κατάκριμα in 8:1b). The passing of sentence on an individual, expressed in Greek by cognates of the verb κρίνω 'to judge', is the cause of the effect which follows—namely, the punishment of the offenders. Thus the meaning is 'condemned and punished' (so Cranfield, Morris, Bruce 1985, Haldane, Murray, and others).

How, then, should the two concepts be put together? 'God condemned and punished sin in Christ's body' must mean that Christ was condemned and punished in his body for our sin. The means proposition being expressed by 'in (his) flesh' requires a verb to be complete: good alternatives are 'by afflicting his body', 'by causing his body to suffer', or 'by making his body a sacrifice'.

8:4a we can *now* fulfill all that *God* required in *his* law The phrase δικαίωμα τοῦ νόμου is taken as in 2:26 to mean 'the requirements of the law' (BAGD, p. 198.1), even though the word is cognate with several words (e.g., δίκαιος) in which the sense is 'righteous'. Extrabiblical use of δικαίωμα in the sense of 'commandment' supports taking it as 'requirement'. Moreover, righteous deeds are not in focus in the context.

Some commentators have suggested that the passive construction πληρωθῇ ἐν ἡμῖν 'may be fulfilled in us' points to the Holy Spirit as the agent of the fulfilling. This ignores the fact that both biblical and extrabiblical writers used ἐν in an agentive sense (see 3:24). Doing so here allows Paul to attach more easily to the pronoun 'us' the descriptive relative clause which follows. Furthermore, the relative clause clearly indicates that "we" are not just passive participants in the fulfilling: we fulfill the law's requirement by the way we live. Both LB and CEV make 'we' the agent of the clause.

8:4b–c not by our living the way our sinful nature *desires* but by living as the Spirit *desires us to live* The literal meaning of the relative clause τοῖς μὴ κατὰ σάρκα περιπατοῦσιν ἀλλὰ κατὰ πνεῦμα is 'to those who not according to flesh walk but according to (God's) Spirit'. The use of 'walk' is figurative, signifying 'the way one lives' or 'conducts his life' (see 6:4).

As in chapter 7, 'flesh' here means 'sinful human nature'. The preposition κατά 'according to' requires a verb to make a complete proposition, hence 'desires'. An alternative would be 'directs us'. NEB has "whose conduct, no longer under the control of our lower nature, is directed by the Spirit." JB and JBP have "dictates."

In view of the emphasis on the Holy Spirit in this chapter (see the note on 8:2a), it seems best to follow the majority of commentators and take πνεῦμα as referring to the Holy Spirit.

EXPANSION OF AMPLIFICATION₂ AND AMPLIFICATION₃ IN THE 8:1-11 DISPLAY

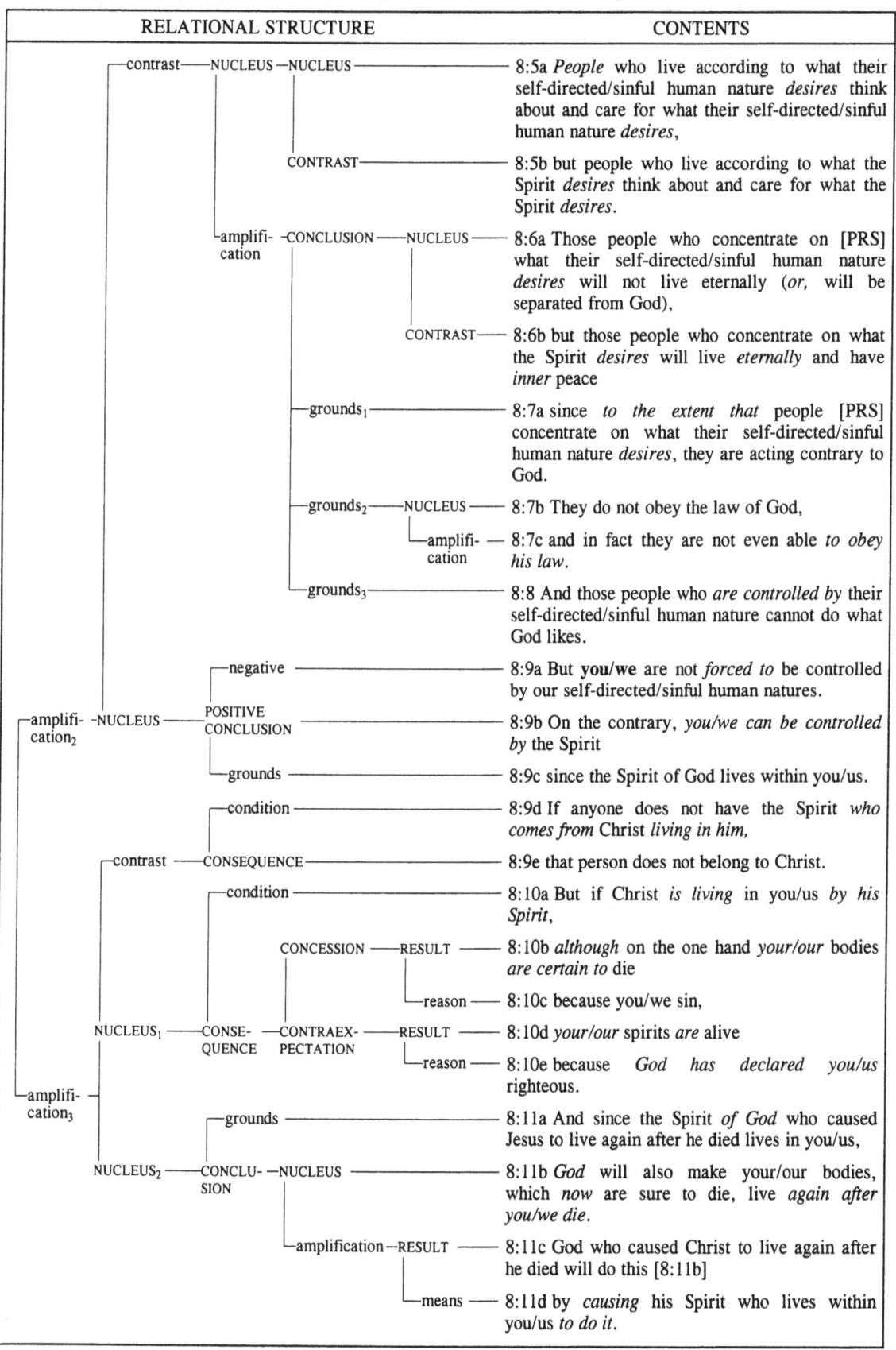

8:5a think about and care for what their self-directed/sinful nature *desires* The participle ὄντες 'being', which occurs in the relative clause here, substitutes for 'walk' from v. 4. The main verb is φρονοῦσιν 'they set their minds on, are intent on' (BAGD, p. 866.2).

8:5b what the Spirit *desires* The phrase τὰ τοῦ πνεύματος 'the things of the Spirit' could mean 'spiritual things'. However, in view of Paul's emphasis on the Holy Spirit in this chapter and the fact that 5a and 5b reflect a grammatical parallelism expressing conflict between two opposing forces, it is more natural to take 'the things of the flesh' and 'the things of the Spirit' the same way, as subjective genitives, with 'desires' being supplied as in 4b. NCV, TEV, and NIV follow this interpretation.

8:6a–b Those people who concentrate on what their self-directed/sinful human nature *desires* **will not live eternally (*or*, will be separated from God), but those people who concentrate on what the Spirit** *desires* **will live** *eternally* The Greek subjects are τὸ φρόνημα τῆς σαρκός 'the minding of the flesh' and τὸ φρόνημα πνεύματος 'the minding of (the) Spirit', in which the action stands for the individual performing the action. The sense of the word φρόνημα, which is found in the GNT only in vv. 6–7, is 'mind-set' (BAGD, p. 866). It is best taken as the nominalization of the concept expressed by the cognate verb in 5a, 'think about and care for'. The display has 'concentrate on'. A personification is involved: it is people who die, not their mind-set.

The predicate nominative in the first clause (6a), is θάνατος 'death', an event concept (there is no stative verb). Physical death is not in view here; Paul is referring to spiritual death. This seems rather surprising since Paul is not referring to unregenerate people here. The contrast with '(eternal) life' in 6b suggests for 6a the negative of life: 'not live eternally'. But since several commentators have suggested the notion 'be separated from God' (e.g., Hodge, Murray, Harrison), that is the alternative in the display.

and have *inner* **peace** The word εἰρήνη 'peace' can mean either peace with God (i.e., reconciliation as in 5:1) or inner tranquility of soul. In the context of life under the control of God's Spirit, the latter sense is preferable here.

8:7a *to the extent that* In the light of Paul's discussion in chapter 7 of the believer's continual struggle with self-directed or sinful human nature, it is probably incorrect to conclude that he is here describing believers whose whole mind-set is to follow their sinful desires as though they contrasted with others who never had such a problem. Hence 'to the extent that' is supplied.

people The personification in φρόνημα τῆς σαρκός 'the minding of the flesh' (see 6a) is rendered nonfiguratively by making 'people' the subject of the several verbs in 8:7a–c.

they are acting contrary to God The predicate of the clause is ἔχθρα εἰς θεόν 'enmity against God' (there is no verb). This event concept is rendered by 'acting contrary to God'. It could be represented somewhat more literally as 'acting hostilely toward'.

8:7c they are not even able *to obey his law* The Greek is elliptical. Only the negative-ability aspect of the preceding verb is expressed. In some languages it might be necessary to make a contrafactual sentence here: 'they would not be able to obey, even if they wanted to'.

8:8 And Some commentators and versions suggest various meanings for the conjunction δέ here, such as introducing a conclusion, but there seems no good reason to take v. 8 as other than an additional grounds for v. 6.

who *are controlled by* **their self-directed/ sinful human nature** The Greek here is ἐν σαρκὶ ὄντες 'in the flesh being', which is an alternate or abbreviated way of saying 'being under the control of the sinful human nature'. NIV, LB, REB, and Berkeley have 'control' here. An alternative would be 'obey' as in TEV and Weymouth.

8:9a you/we The subject of the clause is the emphatic ὑμεῖς 'you'. In some languages it may be necessary to translate it as 'we' (or 'you and I') to avoid implying that Paul does not include himself.

not *forced to* **be controlled by** As in v. 8, ἐν signifies 'under the control of'. But, in the light of his argument in chapter 7, Paul is hardly talking about his readers' having achieved sinless perfection (Dunn, p. 443). This somewhat hyperbolic statement is made clear with the words 'not forced to be controlled' in 9a, and 'you/we can be controlled' in 9b.

8:9c since The conjunction here is εἴπερ. As commentators note, it does not express doubt, but the factual grounds (as NRSV, CEV, TEV, and JB have it).

8:9d–e It is rather difficult to determine the relation of this propositional cluster to the whole argument. At first glance it seems something of a parenthetical comment following 9c. JB introduces it with "In fact" and JBP is similar with "indeed"; LB puts it in parentheses and introduces it with "And remember that. . . ." Barrett calls 9d–e "a fundamental definition," and Cranfield, though calling it parenthetical, says "it is clear that its purpose here is the positive one of asserting that every Christian is indwelt by the Spirit." A somewhat different approach could be taken by making 9d–e grounds for an implied conclusion of 9c (a repetition of 9a):

9c since the Spirit of God lives within you/us, *you can be controlled by the Spirit*
9d since, if anyone does not have the Spirit of Christ living in him,
9e that person does not belong to Christ.

But that would require an additional proposition, and 9d–e would not cohere well as grounds for the repeated statement in 9c. Furthermore, if d–e were to be taken as a grounds, one would certainly expect it to be introduced by γάρ, but better analysis shows it to relate more closely to what follows. In the display it is shown as a contrast expressing a negative condition-CONSEQUENCE cluster, balancing the positive condition-CONSEQUENCE cluster in 10a–e.

8:9d the Spirit *who comes from* Christ The phrase πνεῦμα Χριστοῦ 'Spirit of Christ' occurs only here and in 1 Pet. 1:11. (Similar phrases are 'Spirit of Jesus' in Acts 16:7 and 'Spirit of Jesus Christ' in Phil. 1:9.) It seems best to take the genitive 'of Christ' as expressing origin, hence 'who comes from Christ' (so Hodge, Barrett).

living in him The words 'living in' make clear what is meant by 'have the Spirit'—one does not possess the Spirit in the same way as, for example, a shirt.

8:10a To balance the conditional εἰ in 9d, εἰ here is taken as conditional. But Paul is not expressing doubt; he is stating that for the Romans (or anyone else) for whom 10a is valid, the rest of the verse is valid as well.

Christ *is living* in you/us *by his Spirit* The Greek is εἰ Χριστὸς ἐν ὑμῖν 'if Christ (is) in you'. These words do not mean that Christ and the Spirit are identical, but rather that, if the Spirit indwells someone, in some sense Christ dwells in him. Since the statement by itself is not literally true, the display attempts to clarify this by supplying 'by his Spirit'. Note that for some languages the pronoun 'you' may have to be changed to 'us' here and in v. 10.

8:10b *your/our* bodies The word 'body' in τὸ σῶμα νεκρόν 'the body (is) dead' is singular, but the sense is plural. In many translations an appropriate possessive pronoun will have to be supplied.

are certain to **die** Commentators are divided as to whether 'dead' means 'as good as dead' (i.e., 'certain to die') or 'to be reckoned as dead' because of our union with Christ. Some take it to be synonymous with σάρξ 'flesh' in the sense of being as useless as the sinful human nature. This last interpretation can be excluded on the grounds that since Paul uses σάρξ in the previous verse, he would not use an entirely different word here if the same sense were meant. Nor does the sense 'reckoned dead' fit well as a contrast to what follows about their spirits being alive: your bodies are (in some sense) dead but your spirits are alive. Therefore we take this as 'certain to die', as do most commentators. It could thus be considered a hyperbole. TEV renders it "going to die"; CEV ,"must die."

8:10d *your/our* spirits The word πνεῦμα 'spirit' is singular and without a possessive modifier; a few commentators therefore suggest it refers to the Holy Spirit. This fails to recognize that the unmodified singular 'spirit' balances the unmodified singular 'body' in 10b (not singular in sense). The display follows the great majority of commentators in giving it the sense of the human spirit, which makes more sense as a contrast with the body.

8:10e *God has declared you/us* righteous In order to match the grammatical form with the basic semantic category, διὰ δικαιοσύνην 'on account of righteousness' requires an event concept to accompany the attribute 'righteous'. What is supplied in the display is based on Paul's use of the word in earlier chapters of the epistle. TEV has "you have been put right with God"; JB and REB, "you have been justified."

8:11a since Here εἰ can clearly be given the factual causal sense.

who caused Jesus to live again after he died The word ἐγείραντος 'raised' here means 'caused to live again'. The phrase ἐκ νεκρῶν 'from the dead' is rendered in the display as 'after he died', death being an event concept.

8:11b God will also make your/our bodies, which now are sure to die, live *again after you/we die* The word ζῳοποιήσει means 'will cause to live (again)'. Paul does not mean that our *same* bodies will come to life again (see 1 Cor. 15), but that we will be alive again with bodies. This is hinted at by his use here of θνητὰ σώματα 'mortal bodies', the adjective 'mortal' meaning 'certain to die'. The clause 'after you/we die' is supplied to express the implicit intervening action.

8:11c Christ There is a great deal of variation among manuscripts here. Variants include 'Jesus', 'Christ Jesus', 'Jesus Christ', omission of 'from the dead', and even omission of 'who raised Christ from the dead'. The fourth edition GNT has 'Christ' and lists no variants. This reading seems best because there are logical explanations to account for all the other variants.

8:11d who lives within you/us The textual problem here regarding the grammatical form of the word that means 'living' does not affect the meaning.

BOUNDARIES AND COHERENCE

The 8:1-11 paragraph is relationally coherent in that it consists of a CLAIM (v. 1) and an extensive *justification* (vv. 2-11). Lexical coherence is provided by nine occurrences of σάρξ 'flesh', plus one of the verb φρονέω 'be intent on' and three of the cognate noun φρόνημα 'setting the mind on'.

The boundary between 8:1-11 and the following paragraph is marked, in 8:12, by ἄρα οὖν 'so then' and the vocative ἀδελφοί 'brothers'.

PROMINENCE AND THEME

The theme of 8:1-11 is drawn from the 1b-c CONCLUSION of the CLAIM and from the 2a-b NUCLEUS of the *justification*. In 2b, for the word νόμος 'law, rule, principle' the theme uses the alternative suggested in the notes, 'the inevitability of'.

SECTION CONSTITUENT 8:12-13
(Expository Paragraph: Claim based on 8:1-11)

THEME: We are compelled to live as the Spirit directs, not as our sinful human nature directs, because if you do the latter you will be eternally separated from God, but if you cease doing the latter you will live eternally.

¶ PTRN RELATIONAL STRUCTURE	CONTENTS
CLAIM — POSITIVE	8:12a So then, my fellow believers, we are compelled *to live as the Spirit directs us*.
— NEGATIVE	8:12b What we are not compelled to do is to live as our sinful human nature *guides us*,
justification — NUCLEUS — condition	8:13a since if you live the way the self-directed/sinful human nature directs you
— CONSEQUENCE	8:13b you will surely not live *eternally* (*or*, will surely be eternally separated from God).
— CONTRASTIVE NUCLEUS — condition	8:13c But if by *the power of* the Spirit you continue to cease doing the *sinful* things that our bodies *desire*, [MET]
— CONSEQUENCE	8:13d you will live *eternally*.

INTENT AND PARAGRAPH PATTERN

Like the previous paragraph, the 8:12-13 paragraph is expository, all the verbs being indicative. Although the concept of not living under the control of our sinful desire and our self-directed will is an important hortatory theme of Paul's (cf. 6:11-14), there is no imperative here, not even δεῖ 'must'. As to the paragraph pattern, it consists of a CLAIM and its *justification*, arranged in somewhat of a chiasm. This may be represented (with the material in vv. 12-13 simplified) as follows:

- A We are compelled to live as the Spirit directs (12a)
  - B We are not compelled to live as our self-directed will directs (12b)
  - B' If you live as the self-directed will directs, you will die (13a-b)
- A' If by the Spirit you cease obeying your sinful desires, you will live (13c-d)

NOTES

8:12a The conjunction cluster ἄρα οὖν appears to signal some type of "inference drawn from the preceding verses" (Murray), and it is more prescriptive than the preceding paragraph. Murray states, "The inference has hortatory implications, though not expressly in the language of exhortation." Lenski is similar: "The tone is hortative . . . , but the wording itself is didactic." Sanday and Headlam agree. The 8:12-13 paragraph is thus considered to be a CLAIM based on 8:1-11, but still a paragraph on its own. The alternative is to consider ἄρα οὖν having a resumptive function, introducing a new justification for the CLAIM in 8:31-39 following a long *justification* (vv. 2-11) for the CLAIM in 8:1.

we are compelled *to live as the Spirit directs us* The words ὀφειλέται ἐσμέν 'debtors we are' are followed by a negative construction stating what we are *not* obligated to do. Harrison (p. 92) says, "Only the negative side is stated; the positive side—that we are debtors to the Spirit—must be inferred." Morris, Lenski, Erdman, Alford, Hodge, and Shedd concur. The word 'debtor' is taken here as a dead metaphor.

8:12b What we are not compelled to do is to live as our self-directed/sinful human nature *guides us* In the phrase τῇ σαρκὶ τοῦ κατὰ σάρκα ζῆν 'to the flesh, according to flesh to live', everything is preposed to the verb, giving it emphasis; the display tries to convey this by preposing the 'what' clause.

For κατὰ σάρκα 'according to flesh' see the note on 8:4b. The word σάρξ occurs twice in this phrase, but since the word 'debtor' is considered a dead metaphor and rendered by a verb, it would be superfluous to translate 'flesh' twice.

8:13b you will surely not live *eternally (or,* will surely be eternally separated from God) The Greek is μέλλετε ἀποθνῄσκειν 'you(pl) are about to die'. The words 'about to' express the certainty of the event, hence 'surely going to' in the display. The word 'die' does not refer to physical death (see the note on 8:6a-b). NCV has "die spiritually"; JBP translates the sense quite well as "leads to certain spiritual death."

8:13c by *the power of* the Spirit In some languages πνεύματι 'by (the) Spirit' will need to be translated by a full clause (e.g., 'by the Spirit helping you') since it expresses means, which is a relationship between propositions. Some languages, however, will allow the wording expressed in the display (see LB).

continue to cease doing the *sinful* things that our bodies *desire* The metaphor θανατοῦτε 'you(pl) put to death' signifies 'to do away with as completely and decisively as by putting a person to death' (see 7:4). The present tense gives the idea of 'continue'. The word is rendered nonfiguratively by JB: "put an end to."

The object of this verb is τὰς πράξεις τοῦ σώματος 'the deeds of the body'. The deeds being referred to are sinful ones (NIV has "misdeeds"). The subjective genitive 'of the body' expresses the agent of an implicit verb such as 'desire'.

8:13d you will live *eternally* The verb ζήσεσθε 'you will live' is the antonym of 'die'. It refers to eternal life, not physical life. Among the versions only NCV seems to make this clear: "you will have true life."

BOUNDARIES AND COHERENCE

The main evidence for a boundary at v. 14 is (1) the chiastic structure in vv. 12-13; (2) the introduction of the concept of sonship in v. 14, a metaphor running throughout vv. 14-17; and (3) the fact that vv. 12-13 form a complete paragraph pattern with a CLAIM and its *justification*.

PROMINENCE AND THEME

The theme of 8:12-13 is drawn from all the elements in the chiastic structure (see "Intent and Paragraph Pattern"), since they all seem equally prominent and without all of them Paul's argument would not cohere.

SECTION CONSTITUENT 8:14–17
(Expository Paragraph: Justification$_2$ for 8:31–39)

THEME: *Since it is we who allow the Spirit of God to guide us who are God's children, we will also inherit eternal blessing from God.*

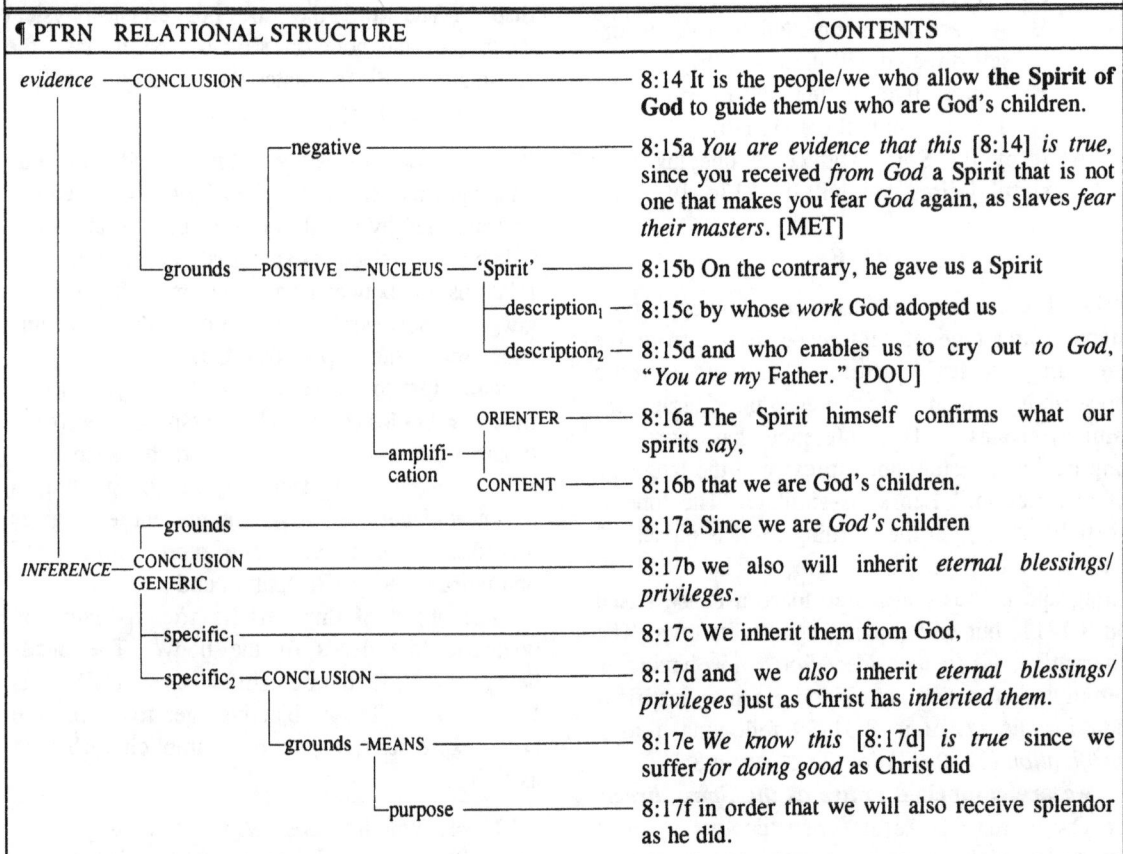

INTENT AND PARAGRAPH PATTERN

The 8:14–17 unit contains no imperatives or expressive elements and hence is another expository paragraph of the causality subtype. It consists of the *evidence* (vv. 14–16) and the INFERENCE (v. 17).

NOTES

8:14 It is the people/we who allow the Spirit of God to guide them/us who are God's children "The connection of thought between v 13 and v 14 is unclear to many commentators" (Dunn, p. 449). While v. 14 could be taken as the grounds for 13c-d, vv. 14–17 have a unity based on the concept of sonship which is totally absent in the preceding context. Furthermore, if v. 14 were the grounds of 13c-d, it would indeed be a tedious line of argument: v. 15 would be the grounds of v. 14, which would in turn be the grounds of 13c, which would in turn be the grounds (i.e., justification) of 12a-b. The display takes the view that 14–16 is an amplification of Paul's thought as represented in the implied 12a proposition.

The grammatically dependent clause that begins ὅσοι 'as many as' is forefronted and followed by the word οὗτοι 'these'; it is thereby topicalized. For this reason it is forefronted in the display. In this clause, the agent of the passive verb ἄγονται 'are led' precedes it (πνεύματι θεοῦ 'by the Spirit of God'). The prominence thus given to the agent is indicated in the display both by bold type and by making 'the Spirit of God' the subject of 'guide'. The 'as many as' is technically a third person plural concept, but Paul obviously intends to include himself. Of the two alternatives in the display, 'the people' or 'we', the second would be necessary in those languages where the writer/speaker would be excluded by the use of a third person plural.

The phrase υἱοὶ θεοῦ 'sons of God' is rendered as 'children of God' to make clear the intended generic sense of the expression. It is a dead metaphor, 'sons' not being used in its primary biological sense. CEV and NRSV adjust it similarly.

8:15a *You are evidence that this is true since* These words are supplied since v. 15 is the grounds of v. 14 (as signaled by γάρ) and since a link between 15a and v. 14 is needed to resolve the seeming conflict of the different pronouns in vv. 14 and 15 with the same referents.

you received *from God* **a Spirit that is not one that makes you fear** *God* **again, as slaves** *fear their masters* The Greek is οὐ ἐλάβετε πνεῦμα δουλείας 'you did not receive a spirit of slavery'. But they did receive the Spirit, so the negative is placed with the concept with which it belongs. Note that the Greek second person plural pronoun in no way implies 'you have received the Spirit but I have not'.

The phrase 'spirit of slavery' has been interpreted by many to refer to a state of mind that belongs to, is produced by, or is characteristic of slavery. However, in view of the fact that Paul refers to the Spirit of God so often in this chapter, it is best to assume he continues to do so here. Furthermore, the same word in the contrastive clause in 15b clearly refers to God's Spirit, and the parallelism in the contrast would be distorted if a different sense were taken in 15a. The analysis of the words that follow, πάλιν εἰς φόβον 'again unto fear' also makes it clear that the reference is to the Holy Spirit.

'Slavery again unto fear' is a metaphor: Just as slaves fear their masters, believers may be in a state of fear of punishment by God. But on the contrary, Paul says in what follows, by God's Spirit we have been adopted as sons of God, and sons need not live in fear of the one they can address in an intimate way. So whereas we might once have lived in fear of God, we do not need to live that way now.

8:15b-c he gave us a Spirit by whose *work* **God adopted us** The phrase πνεῦμα υἱοθεσίας 'Spirit of adoption' contrasts with and grammatically balances 'spirit of slavery'. The reference here is to God's Spirit as suggested by vv. 14 and 16. Though it is possible to make the Spirit the agent of adoption, the rendering here is based on what immediately follows; it is through the work of the Spirit via the new birth that we are made the adopted children of God the Father.

8:15d cry out *to God,* **"You are my Father"** The verb κράζω 'cry' denotes crying out in prayer by someone in need (BAGD, p. 448.2bα). The word ἀββά from the Aramaic is considered by many scholars (e.g., Morris, Dunn, Cranfield) to have been used by young children in addressing their father in an intimate way (cf. CEV, NCV). Since Jesus used the Aramaic and Greek terms in succession as he prayed in Gethsemane (Mark 14:36), just as they are used here, many suspect the words were taken up by the Greek-speaking Christians so that the Greek word πατήρ 'father' here is not to be seen as a translation for those unfamiliar with the Aramaic. The words are rather to be considered a repetition, perhaps indicating intensity (so Barnes, Sanday and Headlam, Dunn). In languages where both a familiar and a formal term for 'father' exist, there may be a possibility of using both of these instead of trying to introduce a meaningless Aramaic term. Among the few versions which have tried to translate by something more meaningful than 'Abba' the best is NCV with "Father, dear Father." As to whether the word 'Abba' is equivalent to the word *Daddy* in current English, see Barr's article. Käsemann says, "It is hard to believe... that with Abba Jesus was adopting the familiar term used in the family and especially by children."

8:16a The Spirit himself confirms what our spirits *say* The two references to 'spirit' here are to God's Spirit and the human spirit respectively. The word συμμαρτυρέω means 'to testify along with another (BAGD, p. 778).

8:17a Since Here εἰ is factual and means 'since' or 'because'.

8:17b will inherit *eternal blessings/privileges* The noun κληρονόμοι 'heirs' semantically entails an event and this is rendered by a verb, 'inherit'. This, in turn, requires an object to be supplied; and because of the future sense in the context ('being glorified with him' in 17f and 'the glory to be revealed to us' in 18c-d), 'eternal blessings or privileges' is supplied as the object of 'will inherit'. NCV is similar: "receive the blessings God has for us." TEV has "possess the blessings he keeps for his people"; NCV, "the blessings God has for us."

8:17c We inherit them from God The phrase κληρονόμοι θεοῦ 'heirs of God' means "to receive something as a possession from him" (BAGD, p. 435.2b).

8:17d we *also* inherit *eternal blessings/privileges just as* Christ has *inherited them* The phrase συγκληρονόμοι Χριστοῦ 'fellow heirs of Christ' is grammatically parallel with 'heirs of God' in 17c, but the sense of the construction is different. The Scriptures speak of Christ departing to inherit a kingdom (Luke 19:12). Therefore this phrase must mean 'to inherit as Christ has inherited'. Since some object is required, 'eternal blessings' is supplied as a good generic alternative (cf. 17b), but 'privileges' is given as an alternative: that which a son obtains in virtue of his position in the family. As that which is appropriate in respect to what Christ received from the Father, note that it is privileges rather than possessions.

8:17e *We know this is true* since The conjunction εἴπερ is not to be translated 'if' in the sense of introducing a condition which must be met before the consequence (17a–d) can be fulfilled. Rather, it states the grounds by which we are assured of the validity of the statements in 17a–d. Cranfield says the clause introduced by εἴπερ "is not to be understood as introducing a condition, but rather as stating a fact which confirms what has just been said."

In BAGD (p. 220.VI1) the potential meanings for εἴπερ in this verse are given as "if indeed, if all, since," showing the possibility of other than a conditional sense. Although Murray and Barnes support the conditional sense, Lenski, Barrett, Vine, and Haldane do not. Another suggestion is to make 17e–f an amplification of 17d. Newman and Nida state that εἴπερ "implies that Paul assumes that his statement represents the circumstances as they do in fact exist; that is, 'since we do in fact share Christ's suffering, we will share his glory'." This is an ingenious solution, but does not do justice to ἵνα 'in order to', which begins 17f. There is no doubt that theological bias influences the interpretation here, but the display captures the grounds relationship, and by supplying the words 'we know this is true' it coheres well relationally and should avoid theological objections.

we suffer *for doing good* The verb συμπάσχομεν 'we suffer with (him)' obviously cannot mean 'suffer at the same time as', but 'suffer similarly to'. The words 'for doing good' make clear that Paul is not talking about common infirmities but, as Morris states, "suffering that arises directly from our Christian profession in a world that rejects Christ."

8:17f receive splendor as he did The verb συνδοξασθῶμεν 'we may be glorified with (him)' refers to "the blessedness of the future state" (Hodge) as we share some of what Christ has received.

BOUNDARIES AND COHERENCE

Lexical coherence in the 8:14–17 paragraph is provided by words referring to close kinship relationships: υἱοί 'sons' in v. 14, υἱοθεσία 'adoption' in v. 15, ἀββά and πατήρ 'father' in v. 15, τέκνα 'children' in vv. 16 and 17, and κληρονόμοι 'heirs' twice in v. 17.

The boundary between 8:14–17 and the following paragraph is marked, in 8:18, by the first person singular orienter λογίζομαι 'I consider'. (The only other first person singular reference in the chapter is in v. 38, the beginning of the final sentence in the section.) In v. 18 γάρ is not given its logical sense; it marks a progression in Paul's thought to a new implication. The word συμπάσχομεν 'we suffer with (him)' at the end of the 8:14–17 paragraph provides the tail-head linkage to his discussion of suffering in the next paragraph.

PROMINENCE AND THEME

The theme of 8:14–17 is taken from the CONCLUSION propositions of the *evidence* and of the *INFERENCE*.

SECTION CONSTITUENT 8:18–25
(Expository Paragraph: Justification₃ for 8:31–39)

THEME: Since everything God has created is eagerly awaiting the time when he will reveal who are his true children, I consider that what we suffer now is not worth paying attention to.

¶ PTRN RELATIONAL STRUCTURE	CONTENTS
ORIENTER	8:18a I consider
CLAIM — CONCLUSION	8:18b that what we suffer during the present time is not worth *paying attention to*
grounds — 'splendor'	8:18c *since* the future splendor/glory *is so great*
identification	8:18d which *God* will reveal to us.
justification — NUCLEUS — 'time'	8:19a What the things that *God* has created are very eagerly awaiting is the time [PRS, DOU]
identification	8:19b when God will reveal who his true children are.
amplification₁ — RESULT	8:20a Those things that God created were caused *by him* to be unable to achieve *what God purposed*,
negative	8:20b not because they wanted to *be unable to do that*,
reason — POSITIVE — RESULT	8:20c but on the contrary *God* made them that way
reason — ORIENTER	8:20d because he wanted them to keep confidently expecting
CONTENT — MEANS	8:21a that the things that were created he will free from their sure decay [MET]
purpose	8:21b in order that *he can give them* the same glory that belongs to his children.
orienter	8:22a We know
NUCLEUS₁	8:22b that *it is as though* all *things* that were created *by God* still groan together
amplification₂ — NUCLEUS₂	8:22c *and long for that glory* [8:21b]
comparison	8:22d *just as a mother in labor* groans *and longs for her baby's birth.* [MET]
amplification₃	8:23 We also groan inwardly. [*See the expansion on p. 190.*]
amplification₄	8:24–25 But we continue to hope for the future glory. [*See the expansion on p. 190.*]

INTENT AND PARAGRAPH PATTERN

The 8:18-25 paragraph continues Paul's exposition of the implications of justification by faith. Its expository nature is clear: all finite verbs are indicative. Its structure is simple: a CLAIM in v. 18 and its *justification* (including several amplifications) in vv. 19-25.

NOTES

8:18b-c what we suffer during the present time is not worth *paying attention to since* the future splendor/glory *is so great* The Greek is οὐκ ἄξια τὰ παθήματα τοῦ νῦν καιροῦ πρὸς τὴν μέλλουσαν δόξαν 'not worthy the sufferings of the present time to the coming glory'. Most English translations supply the words 'to be compared to', which are not in the Greek. Actually that notion is inappropriate: in what way can two totally antithetical concepts such as suffering and glory be compared? In the display the idea is conveyed differently: the concepts of suffering and glory are joined by the words 'paying attention to'. This is in line with the citations of extrabiblical sources by BAGD (p. 78.1a) in which the sense of 'worthy' is 'worthy of consideration'. Another way of expressing the meaning might be 'I consider that the future splendor is so great that what we suffer is not worth paying attention to'.

8:19a What the things that *God* has created are very eagerly awaiting is The Greek is grammatically mismatched: ἡ ἀποκαραδοκία τῆς κτίσεως τὴν ἀποκάλυψιν τῶν υἱῶν τοῦ θεοῦ ἀπεκδέχεται 'the anxious waiting of the creation the revelation of the sons of God eagerly awaits'. This is an unusual construction involving repetition that emphasizes the eager anticipation. The noun ἀποκαραδοκία and the verb ἀπεκδέχεται are thus taken to be a doublet. If not taken in this way, the two concepts matched to their semantic categories would be something like 'are eagerly waiting while they eagerly await it', which is redundant. Since the function of the doublet is to emphasize the one concept, 'very' is supplied.

It is the creation that is doing the eager waiting, so 'the things which (God) has created' is made the subject of the clause in the display. Note that Paul uses personification here along with the doublet.

8:19b when God will reveal who his true children are In the phrase τὴν ἀποκάλυψιν τῶν υἱῶν τοῦ θεοῦ 'the revelation of the sons of God', the double genitive 'of the sons of God' is taken as an objective genitive; that is, what God (the implicit agent) reveals is the sons of God. But in what sense are the sons of God to be revealed? Several commentators assume that it is their splendor and glorious status which will be revealed, but Paul does not say 'the revelation of the glory of the sons of God'. (That concept does occur in the previous verse.) Rather, the meaning is 'reveal who his true children are' (so NCV and CEV). But Dunn suggests *both*, saying that with respect to "that final curtain call ... the audience's eagerness is to see who [the actors] are and what is this transformation they have undergone" (p. 470). If Paul meant both, the sense could be expressed by 'reveal that splendor of those who are his children'.

8:20a Those things that God created were caused *by him* to be unable to achieve *what God purposed* There are two problems with ματαιότητι ἡ κτίσις ὑπετάγη 'to futility the creation was subjected'. First of all, who is the implied agent of the verb 'subjected'? Some assume it is either Adam or Satan. But as Murray notes, "Neither Satan nor man could have subjected it in hope; only God could have subjected it with such a design." Therefore the implicit agent is God. Secondly, what does 'to futility' mean? The sense that fits best is, as Lenski gives it, "failure to reach the proper end," hence 'unable to achieve what God purposed'.

8:20b not because they wanted to *be unable to do that* The Greek expression οὐχ ἑκοῦσα 'not willing' is an elliptical way of expressing the negative of an event using only the aspect of the verb, which has to be understood from 20a. An alternative rendering is 'it was not because they wanted it that way'.

8:20c-d but on the contrary *God* made them that way because he wanted them to keep confidently expecting The Greek here is ἀλλὰ διὰ τὸν ὑποτάξαντα ἐφ' ἐλπίδι 'but because of the one subjecting (it) in hope'. The word 'hope' means 'confidently expecting', and ἐπί is taken as 'on the basis of' (BAGD, p. 287.III1bγ). The agent of the subjecting is God; the agent of the hope is the believer.

8:21a that The fourth edition GNT has the conjunction ὅτι 'that' introducing the content of v. 20's 'hope', giving it an A rating ("certain"), rather than διότι 'because', which probably arose in an early manuscript from an accidental repetition of the final syllable of the previous word. Cranfield argues for διότι,

> As far as transcriptional probability is concerned, there is not much to choose between διότι and the variant ὅτι (the former could be explained as due to dittography after the final δι of ἐλπίδι, the latter due to haplography). But ὅτι is the easier reading since it would be the obvious word to use to introduce a statement of the content of the hope. The more difficult διότι should probably be read. It is conceivable that it is used in the sense 'that', since the use of διότι in this sense is attested in Hellenistic Greek; but, as it is not used elsewhere in Paul (or indeed in the rest of the NT) in this sense, it seems preferable to understand it here to mean 'because' or 'for'—that is, as introducing a statement explaining why the creation is said to have been subjected ἐφ' ἐλπίδι. ..."

Cranfield's argument is rejected, however, because if διότι with a causal sense were to be chosen, it would not cohere relationally. On the other hand, the choice of ὅτι as introducing the content makes for excellent relational coherence. Hence the GNT reading is followed here.

the things that were created The form and ordering of the words καὶ αὐτὴ ἡ κτίσις 'even itself the creation' preceding the verb result in emphasis on the phrase. In the display the phrase is forefronted in order to convey this.

he will free from their sure decay In the metaphor τῆς δουλείας τῆς φθορᾶς 'the slavery of corruption', the point of similarity with the topic seems to be the inevitability or inescapability of decay. Spelled out, the metaphor would be 'the decay they will experience as inescapably as slaves must obey their masters'.

8:21b in order that *he can give them* the same glory that belongs to his children The Greek is εἰς τὴν ἐλευθερίαν τῆς δόξης τῶν τέκνων τοῦ θεοῦ 'unto the freedom of the glory of the children of God'. Many commentators suggest that the words 'freedom of glory' mean 'glorious freedom', but this ignores the fact that 'freedom' is a metaphor balancing 'slavery' in 21a. Paul's main foci are the decay and the glory (note 'glory' in vv. 17, 18, and the implicit 'glory' in 19, 23, and 24), not slavery and freedom (so Sanday and Headlam, Dunn, Alford, Murray, Morris, Barrett).

The phrase 'glory of the children of God' is taken, as commentators suggest, to mean 'the glory that belongs to God's children'. A verb must be supplied for which 'glory' is the object, hence 'he can give them'. Another possibility is 'they will share'.

8:22b-d *it is as though* all *things . . .* still groan together *and long for that glory just as a mother in labor* groans *and longs for her baby's birth* Commentators agree that the συν- prefix in συστενάζει 'groans together' and συνωδίνει 'travails together' means 'together with the other parts of creation', not 'with Christ' or 'with believers'. These verbs are in the present tense, followed by the phrase ἄχρι τοῦ νῦν 'until now'. Since a literal rendering, 'groans until now', would be awkward in English, the display captures the sense by using the present tense with the adverb 'still'; CEV does likewise. JB makes it very specific: "From the beginning till now."

The two verbs in the expression συστενάζει καὶ συνωδίνει 'groans and suffers agony together' are taken as a doublet, though Moore (p. 40) does not so consider them. He rejects them as a near-synonymous doublet, saying that the groaning is the result of the suffering agony together, but this would seem to be splitting hairs.

However, the creation is not literally groaning. What is referred to is sickness, erosion, and the many other evidences of the effects of man's sin in animal and plant life. It is for this reason that the words 'it is as though' are supplied in the display. Most commentators and versions take this as a live metaphor likening the condition of the creation to a woman suffering labor pains. The only question is why Paul refers to such agonizing here. The answer may be found in 24b-e. The groaning of a mother-to-be is at a time when she eagerly awaits the results (i.e., her baby's birth); here the idea of longing for results is the implied point of similarity. All of creation is groaning as it awaits better things to come. Therefore, since the point of similarity in the metaphor in this case involves not only the groaning but the eager awaiting (23d) that accompanies it, both concepts are included in the display in both the topic (22b-c) and the image (22d) of the metaphor.

EXPANSION OF AMPLIFICATION₃ AND AMPLIFICATION₄ IN THE 8:18–25 DISPLAY

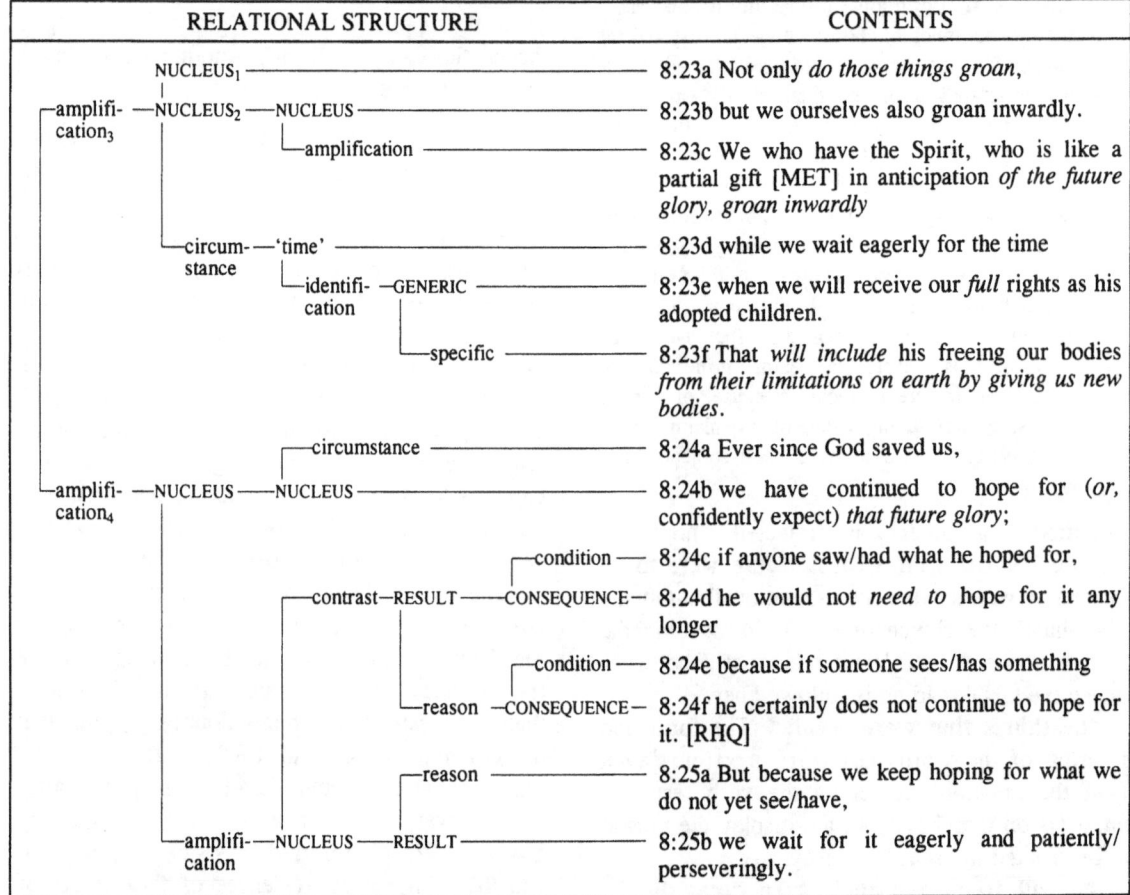

8:23c have the Spirit, who is like a partial gift in anticipation *of the future glory* Commentators disagree as to the meaning of the genitive 'of the Spirit' in τὴν ἀπαρχὴν τοῦ πνεύματος ἔχοντες 'the firstfruit of the Spirit having'. Is it 'the firstfruit which *is* the Spirit', or 'the firstfruit that the Spirit produces in our lives'? In the display it is taken as the former. In either case, 'firstfruit' is a metaphor (used by Paul in a figurative sense in several other passages) that refers to the first part of the harvest. It was the Jews' custom to bring the firstfruits to the temple as an offering to God, a sort of down payment or guarantee of more to come. The metaphor is rendered in the display 'like a partial gift in anticipation'. This in turn requires the expression of some content of what is anticipated: 'the future glory' is supplied from the preceding context. TEV renders it "the first of God's gifts"; NCV has "first part of God's promise."

Though grammatically the object of the participle 'having' is τὴν ἀπαρχήν, semantically the patient of the action is considered to be 'Spirit', with 'firstfruit' modifying 'Spirit'. The opposite route (i.e., making 'firstfruit' the object of the event and having 'of the Spirit' modify 'firstfruit') does not make sense semantically, as the great majority of commentators agree.

8:23d–e while we wait eagerly for the time when we will receive our *full* rights as his adopted children The Greek is υἱοθεσίαν ἀπεκδεχόμενοι 'adoption eagerly awaiting'. In v. 15, Paul says we have already been adopted as God's children; therefore, the event referred to here must be a further completion of what we already have. Another possible rendering besides the one in the display is 'fully enjoy the blessings of being his adopted children'.

A fair number of mainly Western manuscripts omit the word 'adoption'; it was probably deliberately omitted in some early text because it seemed unnecessary as well as contradictory to v. 15. It is now given an A rating ("certain") in the fourth edition GNT.

8:23f his freeing our bodies *from their limitations on earth by giving us new bodies* BAGD (p. 96.2a) suggest that 'redemption' in the phrase ἀπολύτρωσιν τοῦ σώματος ἡμῶν 'the redemption of our body' means the freeing of the body from earthly limitations at the resurrection when we receive new bodies. At least seven commentators consulted support this interpretation. This is made specific in the display; 'body' is made plural because of its generic sense referring to the bodies of all believers. LB, with "bodies that will never be sick again and will never die," is extremely free, but at least captures some of the sense.

8:24a-b Ever since God saved us, we have continued to hope for (*or,* confidently expect) *that future glory* Here γάρ is taken as introducing an amplification. It could be considered an amplification of the subject of the redemption of the body, because the contents of vv. 24–25 do not express a reason for everything in v. 23. But because v. 19 ends with the verb ἀπεκδέχομαι 'to eagerly expect' and the same verb occurs in v. 25, it is more accurately related back to v. 19.

The function signaled by the dative form ἐλπίδι in ἐλπίδι ἐσώθημεν 'in/by hope we are saved' is not clear. It could be taken as means (so Alford, Murray), but since the agent of salvation is 'God' and the agent of hope is 'we believers' yet the means relationship demands that the agents be the same, this interpretation is ruled out. It could be taken as expressing the circumstance of our salvation, 'it is while we were hoping', but this just does not fit the facts. God did not save us while we were hoping for any future glory. The better sense is 'characterized by hope' (the word having prominence by virtue of preceding the verb). This is the sense chosen by Vine, Denney, Sanday and Headlam, and Dunn. The sense of 'in hope' is chosen by Morris and also by Murray, who says it "refers to the fact that the salvation bestowed in the past, the salvation now in possession, is characterized by hope." This is the sense chosen here, with Murray's "characterized by" represented as 'Ever since God saved us (circumstance), we have continued to hope'. According to Harrison, the sense is anticipation (as in the display): "from the very moment of the reception of the gospel one must look forward to the final phase set forth in v. 23."

8:24c if anyone saw/had what he hoped for The Greek for 24c-d is ἐλπὶς βλεπομένη οὐκ ἔστιν ἐλπίς 'hope seen is not hope'. Hope is an event and is not visible. Here the word is a metonymy, standing for the goal of the event. The agent both of 'see' and 'hope', 'anyone', is supplied since in the Greek 'hope' is a noun, being used in a generic sense. In some languages some pronoun other than 'anyone' may be more suitable to express the agent.

8:24d he would not *need to* hope To connect the concept of hope with seeing in 24c the display supplies the reason why anyone who saw would not hope: there would be no need to. CEV and LB similarly supply "need to."

8:24f he certainly does not continue to hope for it The rhetorical question here, τί . . . ἐλπίζει 'why does he hope', is taken as an expression of an emphatic negative. Alternatively, it could be an expression of ridicule: 'it would be ridiculous for anyone to hope'.

There are two textual problems here. As to the first, whether there is an additional interrogative pronoun in the text or not, the sense would not be altered either way. The second is whether the text should have ὑπομένει 'waits for' instead of ἐλπίζει 'hopes for'. But since the verb ὑπομένω does not occur elsewhere in the NT with this sense, the conclusion is that it was probably wrongly copied by someone who saw the similar word ὑπομονῆς 'patience' in the next verse. Also, the manuscript evidence is stronger for the latter. Thus the compilers of the fourth edition GNT chose the reading 'hopes for', giving it a B rating, "almost certain."

8:25a because Here εἰ is factual, not conditional. It introduces the reason for 25b.

8:25b patiently/perseveringly Commentators disagree on the sense of ὑπομονή. It could mean either 'patience' (a resigned acceptance of the situation) or 'perseverance' (a continuing on with fortitude and determination). BAGD (p. 846.1) give both senses; Louw and Nida, only 'perseverance'. Both senses fit well.

BOUNDARIES AND COHERENCE

The 8:18–25 paragraph, which consists of a *CLAIM* and *justification*, including several amplifications, deals with the groaning and suffering experienced by all of creation. The Spirit is mentioned only once. The paragraph that follows deals with the way the Spirit helps us, which is a change in topic and thus the beginning of the next paragraph. This is signaled by the words ὡσαύτως δὲ καί 'likewise also'. Note how the amplifications relate to the *justification* in v. 19. Paul states in v. 19 that all of creation is eagerly waiting for what will happen when God reveals who his true children are. In the first amplification (vv. 20–21) Paul states that all that God created is intended by him to keep on constantly waiting for deliverance from decay; in the second (v. 22) he states that the creation is indeed longing for these things eagerly; in the third (v. 23) he states that we who have the Spirit are also eagerly waiting for our full rights as God's children; in the fourth (vv. 24–25) he states that we have to wait for the future glory eagerly and patiently because we do not yet see what we wait for.

Lexical coherence is exhibited by words in the semantic domain of suffering: παθήματα 'sufferings' (v. 18), φθορά 'decay' (v. 21), συστενάζω 'groan together' (v. 22), and στενάζω 'groan' (v. 23). Coherence is also shown by ἀπεκδέχεται 'is eagerly expecting' (in v. 19) and ἀπεκδεχόμεθα 'we are eagerly expecting' (in v. 25).

PROMINENCE AND THEME

The theme of 8:18–25 is taken from the naturally prominent propositions of both the CLAIM and *justification*. The 18a orienter (λογίζομαι 'I consider') is not deemed thematic and is therefore not included in the theme.

SECTION CONSTITUENT 8:26–27
(Expository Paragraph: Justification₄ for 8:31–39)

THEME: The Spirit helps us as our spirits feel weak; the Spirit prays for us and God understands what the Spirit intends.

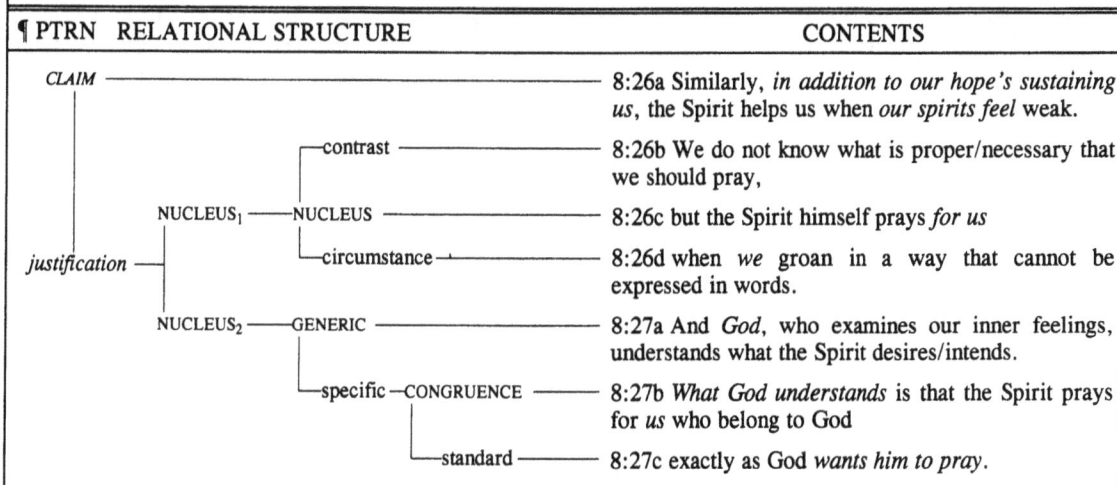

INTENT AND PARAGRAPH PATTERN

The 8:26–27 paragraph, which is a further *justification* for the 8:31–39 CLAIM, is deemed expository, since its finite verbs are indicative and it continues Paul's exposition on the implications of the Spirit-controlled life of a believer justified by faith. Although this could perhaps be considered a descriptive paragraph—descriptive of the Spirit in 26a and 26c-27—the description element is minimal. The presence of γάρ as an introducer of 26b would suggest such a pattern only if the declaration in 26b-27 preceded the 26a description. Here it fits well introducing the *justification*. Thus γάρ introduces, not a reason for the Spirit's helping us, but a *justification* of the CLAIM in 26a telling how he does it.

NOTES

8:26a Similarly, *in addition to our hope's sustaining us*, the Spirit helps us Concerning ὡσαύτως 'in the same way', the question is, In the same way as what? Based on what precedes, it seems best to take the sense as 'similarly to how our hope sustains us' (so Murray, Haldane, Hodge, Harrison). The other alternative would be to connect it with v. 23, stating another way in which the Spirit helps us. But if this were the sense, the phrase 'in our weakness' would surely occur before the verb to highlight this as an additional sphere of the Spirit's help. But it is 'the Spirit' that is forefronted, indicating that it is the Spirit (in contrast to something else just stated) who helps us in a similar manner.

***when our spirits feel* weak** The verb συναντιλαμβάνεται means 'comes to our assistance'. The phrase τῇ ἀσθενείᾳ ἡμῶν 'in our weakness' expresses circumstance and refers to weakness in our spirits, not primarily physical weakness. (Some later manuscripts have the plural, which KJV's "infirmities" is based on.)

8:26b what is proper/necessary that we should pray The Greek is τί προσευξώμεθα καθὸ δεῖ 'what we should pray as it is necessary'. There does not seem to be any good reason to depart from a fairly literal rendering.

8:26c prays *for us* The words 'for us' are clearly implied by the verb ὑπερεντυγχάνει 'supplicates on behalf of'. They are made explicit in the Textus Receptus.

8:26d when *we* groan The question regarding στεναγμοῖς ἀλαλήτοις 'with groanings unexpressed' is whether it is the Spirit who makes the groanings or the believer. Most commentators agree with Morris: "when we cannot find words in which to express our prayer and can do no better than make inarticulate sounds, the Spirit takes these sounds and makes them into effective intercession." That still does not clearly answer whether the Spirit prays for us (ὑπερεντυγχάνει) *when* we groan or *through* our groans. Since the answer could depend on one's theological orientation and the Greek seems ambiguous, the display, by postulating a circumstance relation here, preserves the ambiguity. REB renders it "through our inarticulate groans the Spirit himself is pleading for us."

cannot be expressed in words There is a question as to whether ἀλάλητος means 'unexpressed' or 'inexpressible'. The word does not occur elsewhere in the NT. As Hodge points out, the sense 'unutterable' is preferable because it is "more in accordance with the experience and language of men"; that is also the sense given in BAGD (p. 34).

8:27a The δέ introducing this proposition is not a clear signal of the semantic relationship with 26c; but since v. 27 seems to be a generic statement and not an expression of a logical relationship with 26c, it is taken as a coordinate NUCLEUS.

God, who examines our inner feelings The verb ἐραυνάω means "to examine or investigate" (BAGD, p. 306); the referent of 'the one who examines' is identified in the display as God. The word καρδία 'heart' signifies a person's inner feelings, as is usual in the NT.

what the Spirit desires/intends The phrase τὸ φρόνημα τοῦ πνεύματος 'the mind of the Spirit' is a metonymy, the mind standing for what a person does with his mind.

8:27b–c ***What God understands* is that the Spirit prays for *us* who belong to God exactly as God wants him to pray*** The introductory conjunction ὅτι can mean either 'because' or 'that'. Commentators are divided as to its meaning here. The arguments are not conclusive, but the better argument is that it would hardly be true that God would know the mind of the Spirit only for the reason given (his intercession). The rendering in the display therefore gives the sense 'that', rather than 'because', and takes ὅτι as introducing a fuller specification of what God 'understands' (27a).

The word ἁγίων 'saints' is rendered as 'us who belong to God'; it could be rendered 'believers' or 'Christians' (see the note on 1:7).

The phrase κατὰ θεόν 'according to God' requires some event word to complete the construction. Most English translations supply the noun 'will'. But in the display it is rendered 'as God wants him to pray'. The emphasis created by its preceding the verb is represented in the display by the word 'exactly'.

BOUNDARIES AND COHERENCE

The relational coherence of 8:26–27 derives from its being a CLAIM (26a) and its *justification* (26b–27). Lexical coherence is provided by three occurrences of 'Spirit' and words in the semantic domain of prayer: προσευξώμεθα 'we may pray', ὑπερεντυγχάνει 'supplicates for (us)', and ἐντυγχάνει 'supplicates'.

The boundary between this paragraph and the next is marked by the conjunction δέ and the orienter οἴδαμεν ὅτι 'we know that' leading to a change of subject matter, from the subject of the Spirit's help to God's working everything for good to those who love him.

PROMINENCE AND THEME

The theme of 8:26–27 is taken from the CLAIM in 26a and the two NUCLEI in the *justification*. Since the implicit information in 26a and the description of God in the 27a relative clause are not considered thematic or essential, they are not included in the theme.

SECTION CONSTITUENT 8:28–30
(Expository Paragraph: Justification₅ for 8:31–39)

THEME: God works out all things in a way that produces good to us who love him. He does this because, having known that we would be saved and thus have the character of his Son, he chose us and declared us righteous, and he will surely give us future splendor.

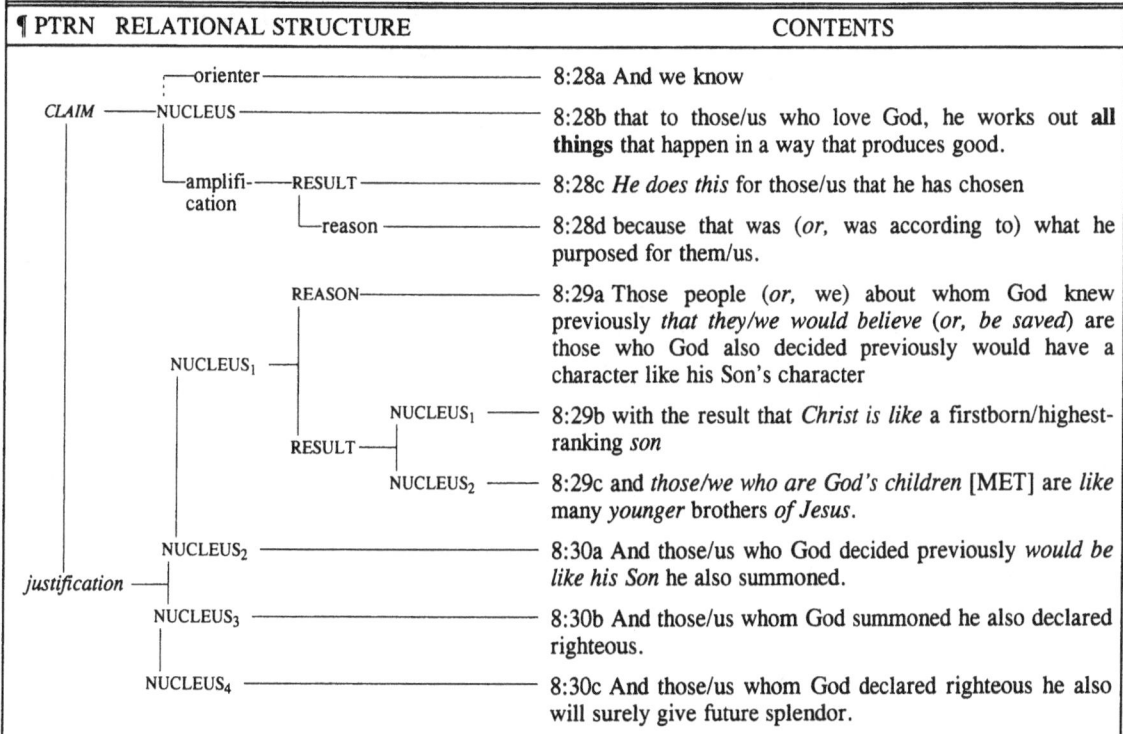

INTENT AND PARAGRAPH PATTERN

All the finite verbs in the 8:28–30 paragraph are indicative; hence this is another expository paragraph. Paul continues developing the topic of the life of a believer. Structurally, it consists of a CLAIM in v. 28 and a *justification* in vv. 29–30.

NOTES

8:28b to those/us who love God, he works out all things that happen Commentators are divided as to the subject of the clause πάντα συνεργεῖ 'all things works together'. In a number of good manuscripts ὁ θεός 'God' is the subject. But the fourth edition GNT omits ὁ θεός, giving the omission a B rating ("almost certain"). It is natural to suppose that these words were added in an early Alexandrian manuscript to avoid the "evolutionary optimism" idea of having 'all things' as the subject of 'work together for good'. That still leaves unanswered the question of whether the subject of the clause is 'all things' or an understood 'God' or 'the Spirit', which is the subject of four of the propositions in vv. 24–27. This last possibility is rather well ruled out by the fact that although 'the Spirit' is the subject of a subordinate clause in 27, 'God' is the subject of 27c, as well as the final participant mentioned in v. 27 and the agent in vv. 29–30, though not named. A change of subject would surely have been indicated. As to the first possibility, πάντα 'all things' could be either nominative or accusative (qualifying either as subject or object); and if nominative, it could indeed take the third person singular verb form that is here. However, semantically (i.e., in the world of experience) that solution faces the almost insuperable obstacle that, as Morris states, "mere 'things' do not work together (for good or ill)." Thus it seems best to take 'God', the implied subject of 27a, as the agent of 28b, as well as the subject of the main verbs of 29–30 (so TEV, NIV, JB, REB, CEV, and NCV).

As to the function of 'all things', since there are no examples of the verb συνεργέω 'work together' in a causative sense, it seems best to take it as an accusative of respect: 'with respect to all things'.

In the Greek, 'to those that love God' and 'all things' both have some prominence since they precede the verb. In the display the former is forefronted and 'all things' is in bold type to indicate emphasis.

in a way that produces good The phrase εἰς ἀγαθόν 'unto good' indicates result: 'that leads to, produces'.

8:28c chosen The word κλητοῖς 'called' is rendered in the display as 'chosen', since 'called' has the primary sense of 'summon vocally', which would be inappropriate.

8:28d because that was (*or,* was according to) what he purposed for them/us The preposition κατά in the phrase κατὰ πρόθεσιν 'according to purpose' merges the senses of 'in accordance with' and 'because of' (BAGD, p. 407.II5aδ). The display includes both senses as alternatives.

8:29–30 There is a climactic progression of the four main statements in these two verses. The vertical line from the second to third NUCLEUS, and from the third to fourth NUCLEUS, is drawn to the left of the previous one to show the progression. Depending on the given language, it may be possible to convey the progression in translation.

8:29a Those people (*or,* we) The Greek has the pronoun 'those', but in some languages it may be necessary to say 'we' or 'those of us' through v. 30.

God knew previously *that they/we would believe (or, be saved)* The verb προέγνω 'he foreknew' expresses cognition, and case role considerations require some content of 'knowing'. Commentators have suggested that our faith or our salvation is in view here. The verb is rendered 'knew previously' to avoid having to answer the question 'before what'; but in languages requiring the use of 'before' and an object to accompany it, one could render it by something such as 'before he created the world'.

are those who God also decided previously would have a character like his Son's character The verb προώρισεν is taken to mean 'decide upon beforehand' (BAGD, p. 709). The adjective συμμόρφους 'having the same form as' is semantically expressing an event which is the nucleus of the proposition 'they would be conformed'; this is the content of the event expressed by προώρισεν 'he decided upon beforehand'.

The phrase συμμόρφους τῆς εἰκόνος τοῦ υἱοῦ αὐτοῦ 'having the same form as the image of his son' does not refer to physical appearance. Most commentators suggest conformity of character.

8:29b–c with the result that *Christ is like* a firstborn/highest-ranking *son* and *those/we who are God's children* are *like* many *younger brothers of Jesus* The Greek is a metaphor: εἰς τὸ εἶναι αὐτὸν πρωτότοκον ἐν πολλοῖς ἀδελφοῖς 'unto him being the firstborn in many brothers'. The firstborn son in a family was the one with the highest privileges. Christ as the Son of God was in his relation to God as a firstborn son is to his father, and we who are God's children are like younger brothers in the family. The word 'like' is supplied in the display to show that a comparison is intended. CEV has "his son would be the first of many children," rendering 'sons' as 'children' in order to avoid sexist language, but such a rendering would not be well received in Muslim cultures where the idea of God's having children is highly objectionable.

8:30a summoned For the verb ἐκάλεσεν 'called' see the note on 28c. In some languages it may be necessary to express the purpose or location of the summoning. If so, something such as 'in order that they might be his people' or 'to himself' might be appropriate. Hodge says that God "effectually calls, *i.e.*, leads by the external invitation of the gospel, and by the efficacious operation of his grace, to the end to which they are destined."

8:30b, c declared righteous For ἐδικαίωσεν 'justified', see the note on 3:21.

8:30c will surely give future splendor The tense of the verb ἐδόξασεν 'he glorified' is aorist, suggesting that the action was completed; however, we know that glorification is still to take place in the future (cf. v. 18). Thus Morris says, "So certain is it that it can be spoken of as already accomplished." The display indicates this sense by 'surely', and the verb is translated in the display as 'will give future splendor' (cf. 18c). Another possible rendering is 'let us share the glory Christ has', which takes v. 17 into consideration.

BOUNDARIES AND COHERENCE

The 8:28–30 paragraph is relationally coherent in that it consists of a CLAIM (28) and a four-headed *justification* (29–30). Coherence within vv. 29–30 is maintained by a set of four clauses almost identical in structure: οὕς 'those whom' + third person singular aorist verb + καί 'also' + third person singular aorist verb, the first verb in the second through the fourth set repeating the second verb in the previous set.

The boundary with the following paragraph is clearly marked by the next unit's being a series of rhetorical questions.

PROMINENCE AND THEME

The theme of 8:28–30 is drawn from the naturally prominent parts of both the 28b CLAIM and the 29–30 *justification*. Though there is a progression towards a climax in the four NUCLEI of the *justification*, there do not seem to be any markers indicating the prominence of one over the other such that any of them could be omitted from the theme. There does not seem to be a simple way of wording the theme to indicate the progression towards a climax, but some attempt to do so was made.

A SEMANTIC AND STRUCTURAL ANALYSIS OF ROMANS

SECTION CONSTITUENT 8:31-39
(Expository Paragraph: Claim based on 8:1-30)

THEME: We must conclude from these things that no can prevail against us, and absolutely no one and nothing can separate us from Christ's and God's loving us.

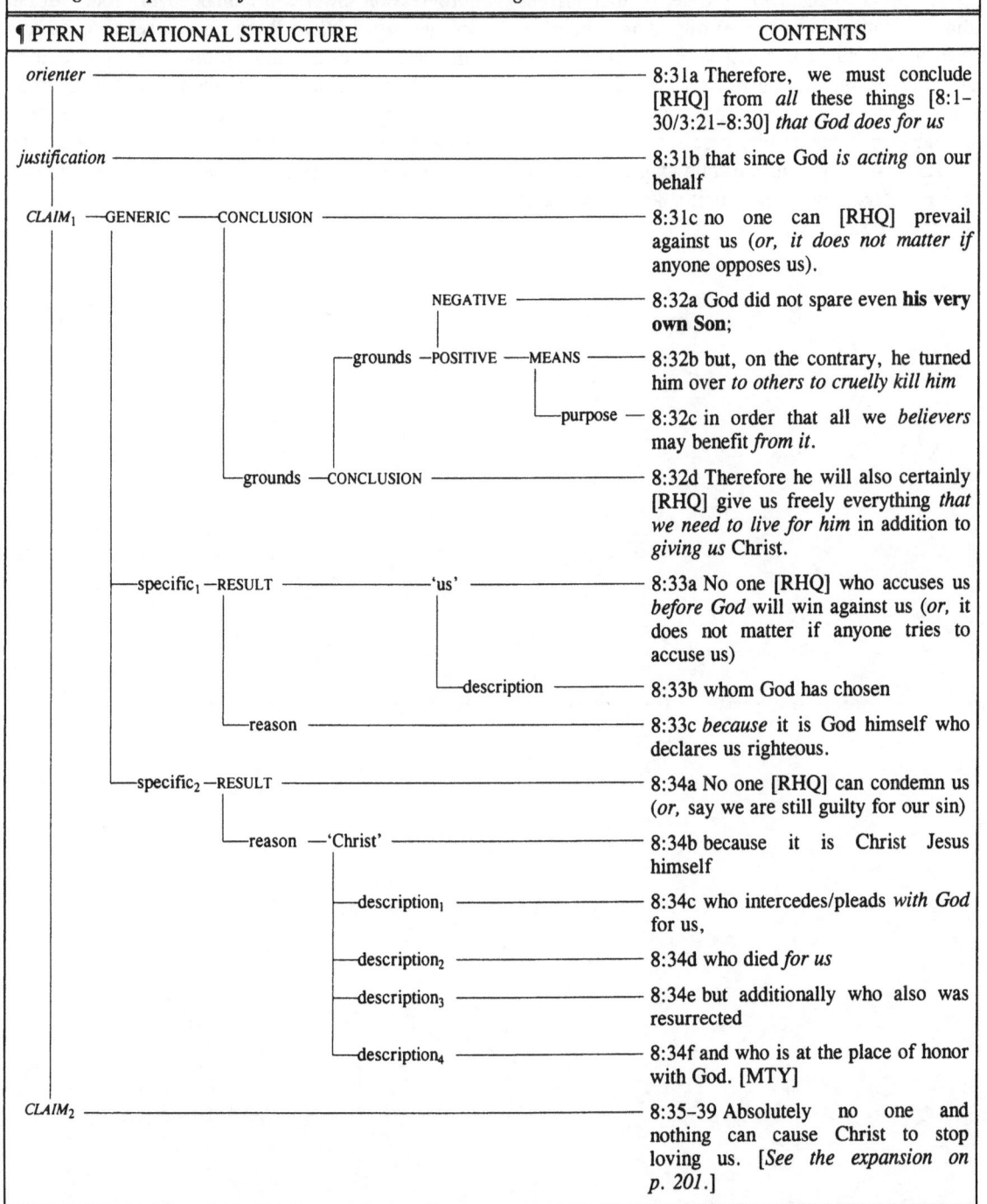

INTENT AND PARAGRAPH PATTERN

In the 8:31-39 paragraph the implications of justification by faith continue to be expounded. This paragraph is the climactic CLAIM Paul draws from the *justification* presented in 8:1-30 (see the 8:1-39 display). The density of rhetorical questions in 8:31-39 might lead us to consider this an expressive unit, but at the end of a long expository section without further evidence of any expressive paragraph pattern such as *situation-REACTION*, it seems much better to consider it expository with expressive overtones. Its paragraph pattern is a brief *justification* followed by two extensively developed CLAIMS, each with a series of specifics.

NOTES

8:31a Therefore, we must conclude from *all* these things *that God does for us* The rhetorical question τί οὖν ἐροῦμεν πρὸς ταῦτα; 'What therefore shall we say to these things?' is not introducing a hypothetical objection here, even though the identical construction in 3:5 does. It is instead inviting the readers to consider the implications of what has preceded. It probably refers to everything from the theme statement of 3:21-26 on, since this paragraph climactically completes the list of the inferences of 3:21-26. The display gives a nonquestion form and a generic specification of 'these things': 'that God does for us'. Another suitable declarative rendering is 'Consider what is implied from all these things'.

8:31b since God *is acting* on our behalf Here εἰ introduces a grounds, not a condition. JB seems to be alone among the versions in recognizing this in its rendering "with God on our side." The words εἰ ὁ θεὸς ὑπὲρ ἡμῶν 'if God on behalf of us' imply some verb. Most English translations supply the verb to be (e.g., "If God is for us"), but this does not do justice to 'on our behalf'; 'is acting' is closer to the sense. The word 'God' is probably somewhat emphasized in that 'God' is here contrasted with any and all others.

8:31c no one can prevail against us (*or, it does not matter if* anyone opposes us) This is a rhetorical question, the second in the series in vv. 31-35: τίς καθ' ἡμῶν; 'who against us?'. It might be taken as a question whose answer is 'no one'. But that would be untrue. Paul, for example, had many who opposed him. It should be noted that there is no verb in the original and that a verb needs to be supplied as in 31b. The real force of what is here semantically an emphatic negative statement may be conveyed by supplying a verb such as 'prevail against' (Morris). This is the first choice chosen for the display (NCV, for example, has "then no one can defeat us"). Or it may be conveyed as Cranfield suggests: 'we need fear no one'. A third alternative is the alternative in the display as supported by Hunter, Murray, Lenski, and Vine (see the note on 33a). How one interprets the rhetorical question has some bearing on the content and relationships signaled by the rhetorical questions in the subsequent verses. If one chooses the alternative 'no one can prevail against us' in 31c, he will probably choose 'no one' also in 33a, with the main propositions in 32d, 33a, and 34a fitting very well as specifics. If one chooses 'it does not matter' in 31c, he will choose it also for 33a.

8:32a God did not spare even his very own Son As in previous verses, Paul intends the reader to understand 'God the Father' as the agent of τοῦ ἰδίου υἱοῦ οὐκ ἐφείσατο 'his own Son did not spare'. The words 'his own Son' come before the verb; the resulting emphasis is indicated by bold type in the display.

8:32b he turned him over *to others to cruelly kill him* The verb in παρέδωκεν αὐτόν 'he delivered him' is identical with the one used to describe Judas's actions towards Jesus in John 18:5 and the actions of the religious rulers in Matt. 27:2, of the people of Jerusalem in Acts 3:13, and of Pilate in Matt. 27:26. The sense is 'to turn someone over to the custody of others'. Case roles require that a recipient of the action be stated, and perhaps the purpose of the turning over.

8:32c in order that all we *believers* may benefit *from it* The preposition ὑπέρ denotes 'for the benefit of'. The object of the preposition is 'us all', which refers to believers, the ones in focus in this passage. The phrase is emphasized by its position before the verb.

8:32d Therefore he will also certainly give us freely everything *that we need to live for him* The rhetorical question here begins with the words πῶς οὐχί 'how (will he) not?', the negative being a means of emphasis. Its meaning is 'it is impossible that he will not'. In making this into a positive expression, the emphasis is shown by 'certainly'. NCV changes the rhetorical question to a statement: "God will surely give us all things." JB is similar.

The hyperbolic τὰ πάντα 'all things' needs some qualification such as 'necessary for our salvation' (Sanday and Headlam, Morris, Cranfield, Erdman), 'necessary for eternal life and blessedness' (Shedd), or more generically 'that we need' (Lenski, Barnes). Since the first two suggestions would be redundant, the most appropriate one, in view of the focus of chapters

6-8, is 'that we need to live for him'. JBP renders it "everything else that we can need."

in addition to *giving us* Christ The words σὺν αὐτῷ 'with him' immediately following 'delivered him' refer to God's giving us Christ. In languages where a person cannot be the object of 'give', an alternative would be 'sending Christ to us'.

8:33-34 There is considerable disagreement among commentators as to the punctuation of vv. 33-34. As Morris notes, "it would be strange to have such a long series of questions without an answer anywhere." Therefore it seems best, following the majority of commentators and versions, to postulate two rhetorical questions (which represent emphatic negative statements) and two "answers" or reasons for them.

8:33a No one who accuses us *before God* will win against us (*or*, it does not matter if anyone tries to accuse us) The first of the two questions introduced by τίς 'who' is equivalent to an emphatic 'absolutely no one'. The words ἐγκαλέσει κατά mean 'bring a charge against, accuse'. However, it is not true that no one brings charges against believers (see the note on 31c). The sense is either "no one can successfully press charges [i.e., in God's sight]" (Harrison) or, like the alternative given in 31c, 'it does not matter if anyone tries to'. The first alternative seems better; it fits the triumphant conclusion in vv. 37-38 better also.

8:33b whom God has chosen The phrase ἐκλεκτῶν θεοῦ 'elect of God' is a mismatched way of stating 'those whom God has chosen'.

8:33c *because* it is God himself who declares us righteous There is no conjunction introducing this clause, but semantically it functions very nicely as the reason for 33a-b. Semantically the clause θεὸς ὁ δικαιῶν 'God (is) he who justifies' puts emphasis on 'God', which is conveyed in the display by 'it is God himself'. TEV and JBP have 'God himself'; NIV, NCV, RSV, and LB use a cleft construction to indicate the emphasis.

8:34a No one can condemn us Here the sense of the rhetorical question introduced by τίς 'who' may be said to be emphatic negative: 'certainly no one'. CEV and NCV retain the rhetorical question here, followed by emphatic negative replies. An alternative, the one suggested for 31c, is also valid here: 'It does not matter if anyone condemns us'.

8:34b it is Christ Jesus himself The grammatical construction here is identical to the one in 33c, creating emphasis on the agent. This emphasis is conveyed by a cleft construction (cf. TEV, LB). The best manuscript evidence supports the rendering in the display, but the word 'Jesus' is omitted in quite a few manuscripts. The fourth edition GNT has it, but with a C rating, indicating a fair degree of uncertainty.

8:34d who died *for us* The words 'for us' are supplied because it is Christ's death on our behalf that is in view here (see JB, JBP, LB).

8:34e but additionally The words μᾶλλον δέ 'but rather' introduce a statement that supplements the previous one. It is not a substitution for the previous one; neither is it a more important statement.

was resurrected The words ἐκ νεκρῶν 'from the dead' occur in many manuscripts but were obviously added for clarification. With or without these words, the sense is unaffected.

8:34f at the place of honor with God The connotation of the phrase ἐν δεξιᾷ τοῦ θεοῦ 'at the right (hand) of God' is more important than the denotation. LB's "at the place of highest honor next to God" is excellent.

EXPANSION OF *CLAIM₂* IN THE 8:31–39 DISPLAY

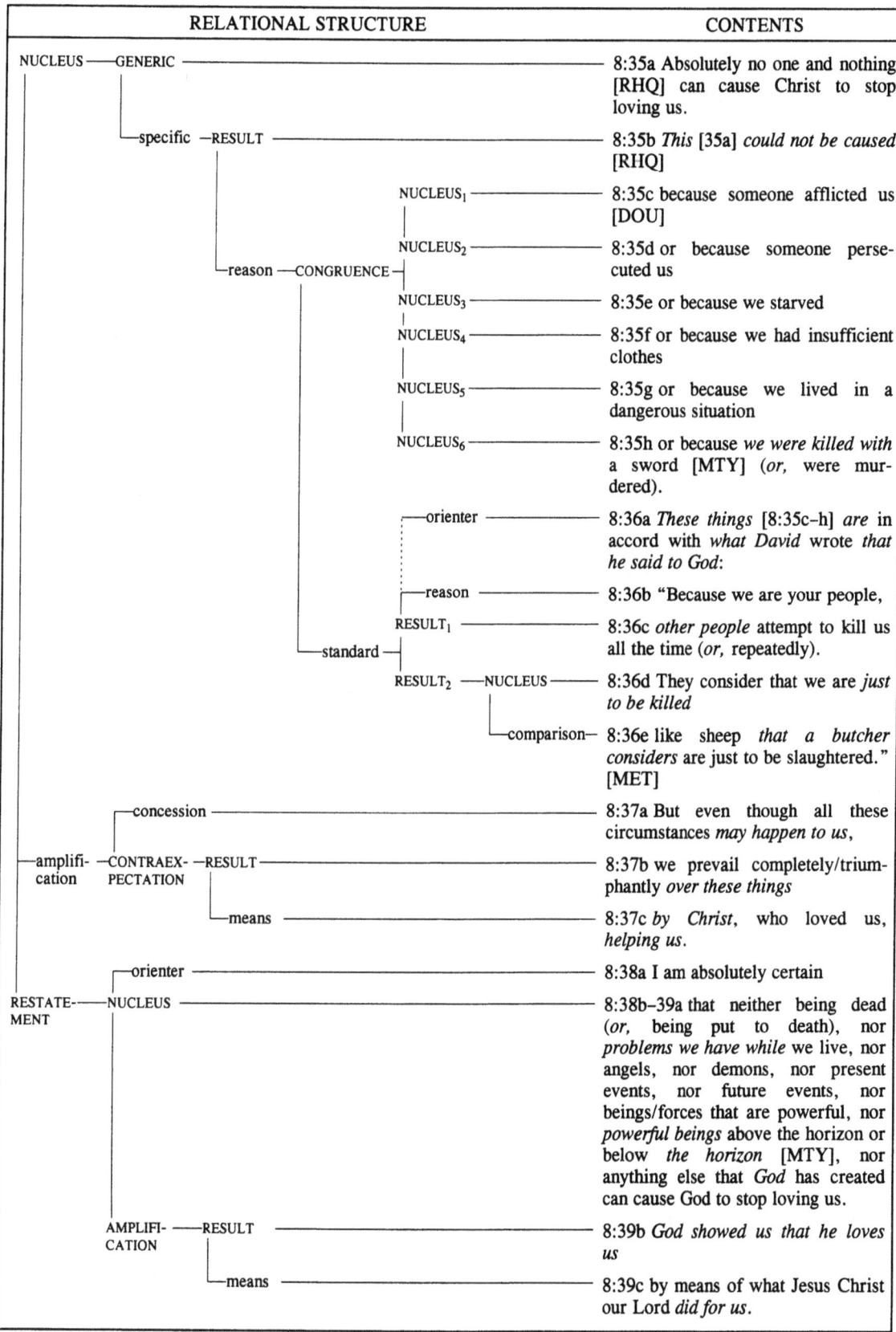

8:35a Absolutely no one and nothing can cause Christ to stop loving us Here the semantic force of the rhetorical question introduced by τίς 'who?' is an emphatic 'absolutely no one'. Things or events could be considered as agents, hence 'no one and nothing'.

The phrase τῆς ἀγάπης τοῦ Χριστοῦ 'the love of Christ' could refer to our love for Christ or his love for us. The display follows the great majority of commentators in taking the sense as Christ's love for us.

8:35c–h These propositions represent a series of seven nouns, all of which encode events. Each is an abbreviated rhetorical question with the verb phrase 'separate us from the love of Christ' being understood: 'Can trouble separate . . . ?', etc. Semantically, these rhetorical questions represent emphatic negative statements. In the display the statement, 'this could not be caused' (repeated from 35a), is supplied as 35b, and following that the seven events (in six propositions because two are considered a doublet expressing only one event) are rendered as reason propositions in which the indefinite agent 'someone' is supplied where possible (namely, in c and d, but for the rest a human agent is not necessarily implied). An alternative to rendering these as reason propositions would be to express them as individual ones: 'this could not be caused if someone afflicted us', etc. They could even be expressed as means propositions: 'this could not be caused by someone's afflicting us,' etc.

The noun γυμνότης can mean 'nakedness', but here it means simply 'lack of sufficient clothing' (BAGD, p. 168.2). Louw and Nida (49.23) suggest it was a state resulting from poverty.

8:35c someone afflicted us Moore (p. 40) considers the words θλῖψις 'affliction' and στενοχωρία 'distress' a doublet. They are so treated here. If the translator wishes to retain them both, the second might be rendered 'because something caused us distress'.

8:35h sword The word μάχαιρα 'sword' is a metonymy in which the instrument stands for the associated action of killing or murdering. It could also be taken as a specific event (killing with a sword) standing for the generic ('putting to death, murdering'). Several versions (e.g., TEV, CEV, LB) render 'sword' as 'death' here.

8:36a *These things are* in accord with *what David* wrote *that he said to God* The formula καθὼς γέγραπται 'as it was written' often, as here, introduces an OT passage (Psa. 44:22) that supports the argument. As Denney says, it implies that "such experiences as those named in verse 35 are in agreement with what Scripture holds out as the fortune of God's people." This sense is supplied in the display. The words 'David wrote' provide a frame of reference that identifies the source of the quotation. The words 'to God' identify the referent of 'your' in v. 36. A fuller explication would be 'these things which we experience are in accord with what is written in Scripture that David said to God'.

8:36b Because we are your people The words ἕνεκεν σοῦ 'for thy sake' occur before the verb and are thereby prominent. The prominence is shown in the display in the same way, with 36b preceding the proposition that contains the main verb.

8:36c *other people* attempt to kill us all the time (*or,* repeatedly) The words θανατούμεθα ὅλην τὴν ἡμέραν 'we are being killed all the day' are hyperbole: 'all the day' means 'constantly, repeatedly', and 'we are being put to death' must mean 'we face death' (so LB, NIV, CEV) or 'we are being threatened with death'.

8:36d–e They consider that we are *just to be killed* like sheep . . . just to be slaughtered Concerning the metaphor πρόβατα σφαγῆς 'sheep of slaughter', several commentators note that the reference is not to sacrifice but to slaughtering of animals that will be sold in a market (so Shedd). C. B. Williams has "sheep for the butcher's knife"; CEV, "sheep on their way to the butcher." Morris's idea of 'destined to be' is the basis for the rendering in the display, 'just to be'.

8:37a But even though all these circumstances *may happen to us* Commentators disagree as to what relation is indicated by ἀλλ' ἐν τούτοις πᾶσιν 'but in all these things'. The adversative ἀλλά plus the semantic content of the phrase which follows suggests concession, hence 'even though' in the display. (LB has "but despite all this.") The preposition ἐν suggests attendant circumstance, 'while we are in the middle of them'. Perhaps both are in view: 'although these things may happen, in the midst of them'.

8:37b we prevail completely/triumphantly The Greek is ὑπερνικῶμεν 'we overconquer'. Several commentators and versions suggest renderings such as 'achieve an overwhelming victory' or 'are gloriously victorious'.

8:37c by Christ, who loved us, *helping us* The preposition διά expresses means, and therefore some verb will be required in many languages. The display supplies a generic 'helping us'. Nearly all the commentators take 'him who loved us' as referring to Christ. The past tense of the participle probably points to the love of Christ expressed in his substitutionary death but with no implication that his love ceased then.

8:38a Here γάρ introduces a further statement about not being separated from the love of Christ (see 35a); thus it is taken as introducing a restatement of 35a. This restatement has prominence because of the orienter 'I am absolutely certain that'.

I am absolutely certain The verb πέπεισμαι 'I have been persuaded' is not to be taken in a transitive sense, but rather in the sense 'to be convinced, sure' (see 14:14, 15:14, and 2 Tim. 1:5, 12).

8:38b–39a In this series of nine nouns and a final noun phrase, each one is preceded by οὔτε 'nor'. Semantically, some of the nouns express events, which here are almost impossible to express without a nominalized clause. The list seems to be arranged with four lexical pairs of items and two single items.

being dead A few commentators suggest that θάνατος 'death' refers to the threats of death referred to in v. 36, but most think it is actual death itself, which would be the outcome of the threats.

problems we have while **we live** The word ζωή 'life' here is surprising; life is not ordinarily thought of as something that can separate us from Christ. Several commentators (e.g., Morris, Hodge, Dayton, Dunn, Cranfield) suggest the meaning given in the display. REB gives an excellent generic rendering of the two phrases: "nothing in death or life."

demons The word ἀρχαί 'rulers' may refer to earthly political rulers; but here since it is paired with and contrasted to ἄγγελοι 'angels', there is no doubt that it refers to evil angelic beings (cf. Rev. 12:7). Cranfield says that this pair means "no spiritual cosmic power, whether benevolent or malevolent." The NIV renders it "demons."

nor present events, nor future events The terms ἐνεστῶτα '(things) which are present' and μέλλοντα '(things) which are to come' are taken as referring to events and circumstances, not things (Cranfield, Hodge, Barnes, Haldane). The events would include the agents of those events.

beings/forces that are powerful The Textus Receptus puts οὔτε δυνάμεις 'nor powers' before οὔτε ἐνεστῶτα 'nor things to come' instead of at the end of the verse, but textual support for doing so is extremely weak. Evidently some copyist(s) wished to make the meaning clearer by collocating the words that seemed most alike semantically, or wished to make the reference to 'powers' clearer. The order in the display follows the fourth edition GNT, which gives this order an A rating (i.e., a high degree of certainty).

What Paul means by 'powers' is not clear. Some suggest other forces of evil, but this would seem to be covered by ἀρχαί. Others suggest the powerful physical forces of nature such as storms and earthquakes. Still others suggest miracles, or mighty works, since the term is often used with that sense in the NT. REB's "superhuman powers" is superb.

powerful beings **above the horizon or below** *the horizon* The terms ὕψωμα and βάθος, rendered as "height" and "depth" in the KJV, NIV, RSV, and JB, are technical astronomical terms. The former refers to the space above the horizon, and the latter to the space below the horizon. Here they are a metonymy in which the place stands for the beings that hold sway there (BAGD, p. 130.1).

nor anything else that *God* **has created** The final term in the list is τις κτίσις ἑτέρα 'any other creature'. It sums up all that might be necessary to make the list absolutely complete. In English 'creature' denotes an animal; the display renders it more generically.

8:39b–c *God showed us that he loves us* **by means of what Jesus Christ our Lord** *did for us* The phrase τῆς ἐν Χριστῷ Ἰησοῦ τῷ κυρίῳ ἡμῶν 'which (is) in Christ Jesus our Lord' modifies 'the love of God', love being semantically an event of which God is the agent. (Commentators give 'showed, manifested, displayed' as an implicit verb here, of which God is the subject.) Since ἐν is taken as introducing a means proposition, an event must be expressed: 'did for us' is supplied to complement the expressed agent. LB spells out the meaning very well with "the love of God demonstrated by our Lord Jesus Christ when he died for us." This propositional cluster, most specifically the

MEANS, is prominent since in the Greek text this construction is postponed to the very end of the final clause in the final paragraph of the 8:1-39 section.

BOUNDARIES AND COHERENCE

The 8:31-39 paragraph is one unit consisting of two separate *CLAIMS*: first, no one can prevail against us; second, nothing can separate us from Christ's loving us.

Coherence within this paragraph is provided by the series of rhetorical questions in 31-35 and then by the parallel clauses ἡμᾶς χωρίσει ἀπὸ τῆς ἀγάπης τοῦ Χριστοῦ 'will separate us from the love of Christ' in v. 35 and ἡμᾶς χωρίσαι ἀπὸ τῆς ἀγάπης τοῦ θεοῦ 'to separate us from the love of God' in v. 39.

The end of the unit (which is marked by the phrase 'in Christ Jesus our Lord') and the start of the next, in which Paul discusses the Jews, have already been commented on (see "Boundaries and Coherence" for 6:1-8:39).

PROMINENCE AND THEME

The theme of 8:31-39 is drawn from the two most naturally prominent propositions within each of the *CLAIMS*. These naturally prominent propositions have added prominence in that they are rhetorical questions with the function of lending emphasis. (Since it is difficult to indicate the added prominence in the theme statement, this is not done.) The theme also includes material from the introductory orienter, since its being a rhetorical question (τί οὖν ἐροῦμεν πρὸς ταῦτα; 'What shall we say to these things?') gives it marked prominence.

DIVISION CLUSTER CONSTITUENT 9:1–11:36
(Expository Subdivision Cluster: Application₃ of 3:21–26)

THEME: I grieve greatly because most of the Jews have rejected Jesus as their promised deliverer, but this does not prove that God has failed to give many descendants to Abraham as he promised. Nor can we conclude that God is unjust in choosing the ones he wants to or that it is not right for God to condemn people. The Jews did not succeed in fulfilling what the Mosaic law requires; they tried to find a way to be declared righteous by doing things in order that God would accept them. To you Jews I say that God has certainly not rejected all of us, and that God is saving many non-Jews to make the Jews jealous and thus seek to be saved. To you non-Jews I say that I hope my work among you will accomplish just that. But don't despise the Jews that God has rejected and become proud, because just as God did not spare the Jews he will not spare you if you fall away from him. And I want you to know that all the Jews will some day be saved.

MACROSTRUCTURE	CONTENTS
problem	9:1a–b Most of my fellow Israelites have rejected Christ.
Paul's reaction	9:1c–5 I tell you very sincerely that I grieve greatly about this, and I would be willing to be separated from Christ if that would help them believe in Christ.
wrong evaluation	9:6–29 This does not prove that God has failed in his promise to Abraham. Nor can we conclude that God is unjust in choosing the ones he wants to, or that it is not right for God to condemn people.
correct evaluation	9:30–10:21 The Jews did not succeed in fulfilling what the Mosaic law requires; they tried to find a way to be declared righteous by doing things in order that God would accept them. The Jews do not understand how to seek him correctly, which according to Scripture is that if anyone, Jew or non-Jew, confesses publicly that Jesus is Lord and believes inwardly that God raised him from the dead, he will be saved. People have been sent to preach about Christ to the Jews, but most Jews have not accepted the gospel. They certainly have heard it and should have understood it, because even the non-Jews, who were not searching for God, understood it.
SOLUTION	11:1–32 God has certainly not rejected all of us Jews, and God is saving many non-Jews to make the Jews jealous and thus seek to be saved. To you non-Jews I say that I hope my work among you will accomplish just that; but do not despise the Jews whom God has rejected and become proud, because just as God did not spare the Jews he will not spare you if you fall away from him. And I want you to know that all the Jews will some day be saved, as the Scriptures predict.
doxology	11:33–36 I marvel at how great God's wisdom and knowledge are, and his decisions and actions toward us.

INTENT AND MACROSTRUCTURE

In the 9:1–11:36 unit Paul presents a specific application for the Jews of justification by faith as presented in 3:21–26. Although four components (9:1c–5; 10:1–4; 11:13–16; 11:33–36) are expressive and one (11:17–24) hortatory, all the others are expository. Thus in spite of the highly emotive nature of some parts of 9:1–11:36 (witness the number of emotive rhetorical questions) and in spite of its being bracketed by emotive paragraphs, the unit is considered to be expository, of the volitionality subtype.

The unit centers around a problem arising from Paul's exposition of justification by faith in the previous chapters, namely the Jews' rejection of Christ; Paul's statement of the expected SOLUTION to the problem is given in the 11:25–32 paragraph. Erdman says, "The problem is Israel's rejection." Morris states it even more clearly, "Paul must face squarely the fact that, as a whole, Israel had rejected its Messiah." All the subparts of the three chapters relate directly to this problem. This problem, however, is nowhere stated overtly by Paul; and without it, as far as the macrostructure is concerned, it is difficult to show the relationships. It is for this reason that 9:1a–b is supplied as the most crucial implicature of the whole argument in these three chapters. With this in place, although it is still not easy to determine the high-level divisions and relationships, the subparts are seen as Paul's *reaction* to the problem (9:1c–5), Paul's answers to the anticipated *wrong evaluation* of the problem (9:6–

29), Paul's presentation of the *correct evaluation* of the problem (9:30-10:21), the *SOLUTION* to the problem (11:1-32), and finally a *doxology* (11:33-36).

As to Paul's intent in chapters 9-11 with regard to the explication of the doctrine of justification by faith which has preceded it, Paul knows that some among his intended audience will object, saying that if the good news that people are justified by faith in God's atonement is true, then why haven't most of the Jews been accepting it? The three central sections of chapters 9-11 answer this question.

BOUNDARIES AND COHERENCE

The coherence of the 9:1-11:36 subdivision cluster consists mainly of its having one topic: the implications of the doctrine of justification by faith in Christ for the Jews as a whole, inasmuch as the vast majority have rejected Christ. Within the unit there are five closely related constituents (the first one being an implied statement of the problem) plus a concluding doxology. After the problem of the Jews' rejection of Christ and Paul's reaction to it come lengthy discussions of the source of the problem and replies to anticipated objections, then the solution to the problem.

The main source of lexical coherence in 9:1-11:36 is ten occurrences of the word Ἰσραήλ 'Israel' and at least fifty other phrases and pronouns referring to Israel, including two occurrences of Ἰσραηλίτης 'Israelite' and two of Ἰουδαῖος 'Jew'.

The boundary between 9:1-11:36 and the one that follows it is marked by οὖν 'therefore' in 12:1 and the vocative ἀδελφοί 'brethren'. It is a major *APPEAL* that οὖν introduces, the orienter of which is παρακαλῶ ὑμᾶς 'I appeal to you', signaling a change to hortatory genre.

PROMINENCE AND THEME

The theme of 9:1-11:36 is taken from the themes of its constituents. The theme of the *problem* (1a-b) is included in its entirety. From the *reaction* (9:1c-5) condensations of the prominent propositions of its two *REACTIONS* are included. The theme of the *wrong evaluation* is included in its entirety. From the *correct evaluation* only the *CLAIM* is included, the other elements being of less natural prominence (e.g., the *REFUTATION* to the *objection* to the *CLAIM*, and *RESPONSES* to *queries* about the *CLAIM*). The theme of the *SOLUTION* is included because it is the most thematic element in the unit. The *doxology* is not included because it is not thematic.

SUBDIVISION CLUSTER CONSTITUENT 9:1a-b
(Expository Propositional Cluster: Problem in 9:1-11:36)

THEME: *Most of my fellow Israelites have rejected Christ.*	
MACROSTRUCTURE	CONTENTS
orienter	9:1a *Now I would like to discuss the fact*
CONTENT	9:1b *that most of my fellow Israelites have rejected Christ.*

It seems strange to call what is only implicit a unit on its own, but 9:1a-b is clearly the pivotal unit on which the whole of the next three chapters hinges. (See "Intent and Macrostructure" for 9:1-11:36 in regard to the need to supply 9:1a-b.)

Surprisingly, none of the major versions have a section heading at 9:1 that specifically refers to the Jews' rejection of Christ. Charles Williams's section heading here is the only one that does: "Paul's grief over God's rejecting Israel for their unbelief in Jesus. . . ."

SUBDIVISION CLUSTER CONSTITUENT 9:1c-5
(Expressive Paragraph: Paul's reaction to the problem of the Jews' rejection of Christ)

THEME: I tell you very sincerely that I grieve greatly about this, and I would be willing to be separated from Christ if that would help them believe in Christ.

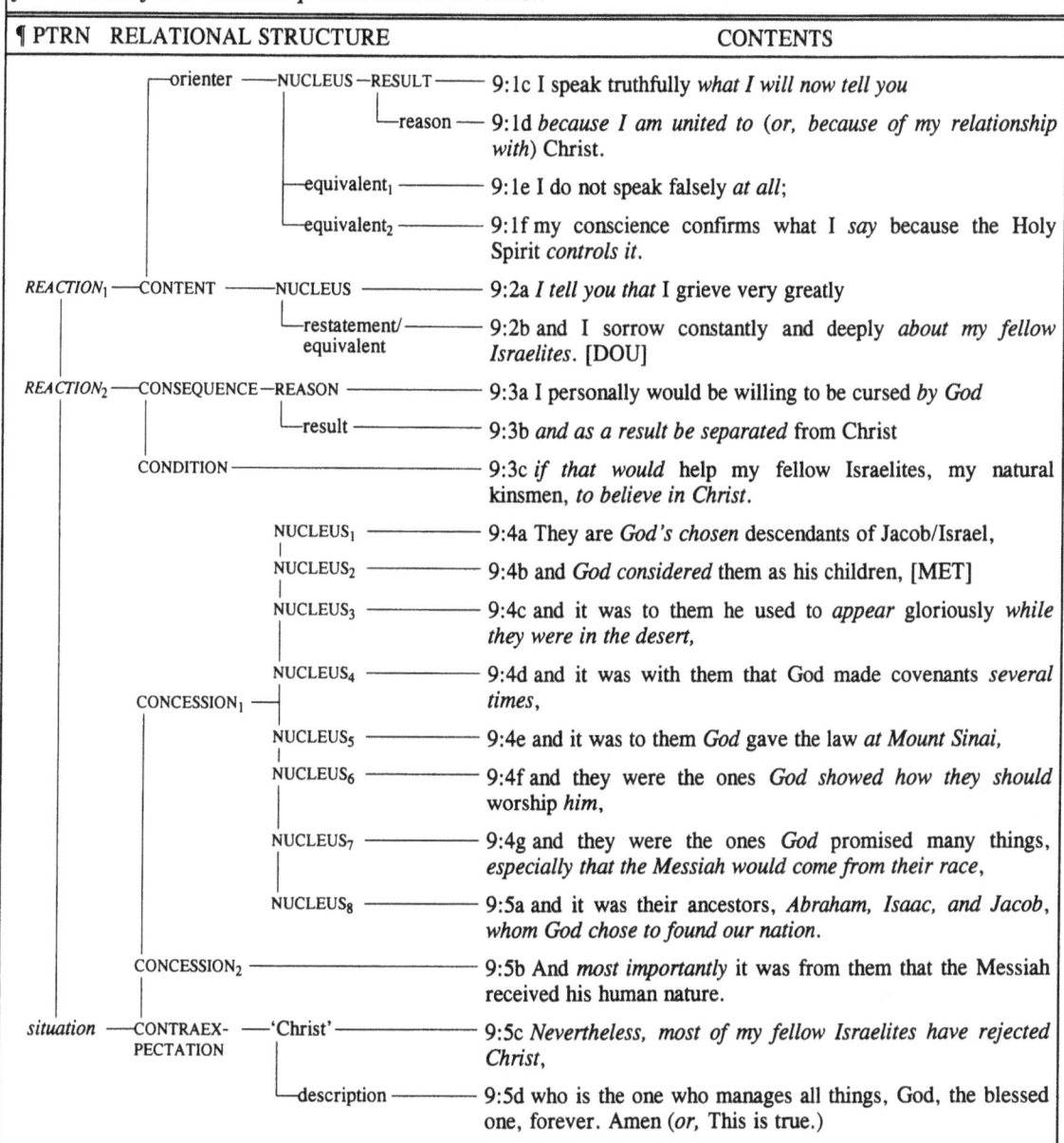

INTENT AND PARAGRAPH PATTERN

The 9:1c-5 paragraph is a series of expressions of Paul's feelings, making it an expressive paragraph. The relations consist of the statement of his REACTIONS to the *situation* that gave rise to these deep feelings.

NOTES

9:1c-f Verse 1 functions as an orienter to what follows in v. 2. It consists of a positive affirmation of the truthfulness of what Paul is about to state and a denial of the negative. As such, 1c and 1e could be considered a doublet; but since each statement is amplified in a different way, they are not combined into one proposition in the display.

9:1c I speak truthfully *what I will now tell you* Commentators agree that ὅτι 'that' in v. 2 introduces the content of what Paul is speaking truthfully about. (JB has "what I want to say now . . . is the truth.") Verse 1 is not meant as a generic statement that Paul always tells the truth, nor that he does not tell the truth in what he writes elsewhere.

9:1d *because I am united to* Christ The phrase ἐν Χριστῷ 'in Christ' borders between 'on the grounds of my union/relationship with Christ' and a circumstantial 'as I am united to Christ'. It frequently has this sense in Paul's writings.

9:1f my conscience confirms what I *say* because the Holy Spirit *controls* it The Greek here is συμμαρτυρούσης μοι τῆς συνειδήσεώς μου ἐν πνεύματι ἁγίῳ 'witnessing with the conscience of me in (the) Holy Spirit'. The genitive absolute suggests a loose connection with what precedes. The display therefore proposes a second equivalent relationship with 1c.

The phrase 'in the Holy Spirit' is taken as expressing the control or guidance of the Spirit, with ἐν signifying reason. Both NCV and TEV have "ruled by the Holy Spirit."

9:2a *I tell you that* I grieve very greatly The form of λύπη μοί ἐστιν μεγάλη 'grief to me is great' puts emphasis on the adjective, hence '*very* greatly'.

9:2b and I sorrow constantly and deeply Cranfield states, "It is doubtful whether any clear distinction between λύπη ['grief'] and ὀδύνη ['pain'] can really be sustained." Moore (p. 40) calls them a synonymous doublet. In the display both terms are retained as events ('grieve' in 2a and 'sorrow' in 2b) only because putting all the qualifying adverbs with one verb would sound unnatural in English.

The idiom τῇ καρδίᾳ μου 'in my heart' is rendered nonfiguratively as 'deeply'.

about my fellow Israelites Paul does not state the reason for his sorrow (see Morris, Denney, Barnes). It is crucial that the reason be understood here, because all that follows is a further explanation of it. The reason, as commentators supply it, is the Jews' lack of faith in or rejection of Christ as the Messiah (see the comments under the 9:1a-b display).

In the entire 9:1-11:36 subdivision cluster, Paul usually uses 'Israel' when he refers to his fellow Jews. For this reason the word 'Israelites' is used in the displays most of the time, even though nowadays English words built on the name *Israel* refer to citizens of the modern nation of Israel, whereas *Jews* refers to people around the world who claim descent from Abraham. The translator will have to determine what term will be understood by and acceptable to the receptor audience.

9:3a I personally would be willing to be cursed *by God* Here γάρ introduces not the reason for the sorrow, but a different expression of his reaction to the sorrow.

The verb ηὐχόμην 'I could wish' expresses what Harrison calls "an impossible wish," one that is impossible of fulfillment. In some languages it may be necessary to include the words 'if it were possible' to make clear the contrafactual nature of the verb.

9:3b *and as a result be separated* from Christ The Greek is ἀπὸ τοῦ Χριστοῦ 'from Christ'. There is no verb. Most English translations supply 'separated' or 'cut off'. Commentators suggest that this implicit action is either the result of being cursed or a specification of the nature of the curse. In the display it is taken as the former (cf. BAGD, p. 54.2a).

9:3c *if that would* help The preposition ὑπέρ means 'for the benefit of' (cf. 8:32). The complete propositionalization would include a purpose clause: 'in order to help my fellow Israelites if that were possible'. NCV has "if that would help them"; CEV, "for the good of my own Jewish people."

my fellow Israelites, my natural kinsmen The word ἀδελφοί 'brothers' is usually used by Paul to refer to fellow believers, but here it means Paul's fellow countrymen or, more precisely, those of Jewish ancestry. Some languages may have an appropriate term (e.g., in Tok Pisin, *wanblut* 'one related by blood'), but 'Israelites' might still have to be supplied to make the referent clear. The phrase τῶν συγγενῶν μου κατὰ σάρκα 'my kinsmen according to flesh' is in apposition to 'brothers' and defines it more specifically. The term technically means those to whom one is related; 'according to flesh' clarifies that it refers to others of the same race, but not those with whom he had a spiritual bond.

to believe in Christ These words are supplied to define the nature of the help referred to.

9:4a-5b These propositions represent a series of relative clauses all describing 'brothers' (i.e., Jews) in 3c. Each is represented in the display by an independent clause connected to the preceding one by 'and'. They, and the constituent elements within them, enumerate the great list of privileges and blessings that belonged to the Jews. The question is, Why does Paul give this list and how does it contribute to his argument? The answer seems to lie in the fact that the Jews rejected Christ in spite of these privileges. Therefore this whole cluster is labeled concessive (see the note on 5c).

9:4a They are *God's chosen* descendants of Jacob/Israel Commentators say that the word Ἰσραηλῖται 'Israelites' points to the Jews as being the chosen people of God (Cranfield, Morris, Dunn). This is true, but if that is all Paul meant, he probably would have said so more directly. Thus in the display the denotation 'descendants of Israel/Jacob' is considered to be at least as important (cf. Hodge, Murray) as the connotation "God's chosen people" (TEV).

9:4b and *God considered* them as his children The Greek here is ὧν ἡ υἱοθεσία 'whose (was) the adoption'. The word 'adoption' is the first of six unmodified nouns that follow the understood verb 'was'. Paul uses them for effect. This one, 'adoption', and several others involve event concepts and are rendered in the display by clauses. God's adopting the Jews is a way of saying that he considered them his children. It is a metaphor: God gave the Jews special privileges just as an adopted child receives the same rights that are conferred on natural-born sons.

9:4c it was to them he used to *appear* gloriously *while they were in the desert* Most commentators agree that the word δόξα 'glory' here refers to the Shekinah glory of God, the radiance symbolizing the presence of God while the Israelites were in the wilderness. LB is quite specific with "led you along with a bright cloud of glory"; REB is much less specific with "theirs is the glory of the divine presence." But the Israelites did not literally possess this radiance; saying it was theirs is equivalent to saying that it was to them that God manifested himself in this way. Since Paul would expect his readers to know the location where this happened, it is supplied here. While the Shekinah glory of God appeared at the dedication of Solomon's temple (2 Chron. 7:1-3), the focus here is on what happened in the desert.

9:4d it was with them that God made covenants *several times* The phrase 'theirs (were) ... the covenants' means that it was with them that God made covenants. There is fairly strong manuscript support for the singular form here, but GNT's choice for the plural form is preferred (it is given a B rating of "almost certain" in the fourth edition). One can understand how some copyist would object to the plural, thinking of the one great covenant at Mount Sinai, and change the plural to the singular to agree with the other singular words in the series.

9:4e it was to them *God* gave the law *at Mount Sinai* The words 'at Mount Sinai' are supplied here, not because the place is so important, but to identify the law as that which God gave through Moses. NCV has "the law of Moses."

9:4f they were the ones *God showed how they should* worship *him* The word λατρεία 'worship' denotes all the rituals involved in the worship of God, not only in the temple but probably also in the tabernacle, perhaps in synagogues as well. REB specifies "the temple worship." NCV's rendering, "the right way of worship," is closer to what is in the display.

9:4g they were the ones *God* promised many things, *especially that the Messiah would come from their race* Nearly all commentators state that the plural αἱ ἐπαγγελίαι 'the promises' refers to all the promises God gave to Israel in the OT, but especially the promise of a coming Messiah.

9:5a and it was their ancestors, *Abraham, Isaac, and Jacob,* whom God chose to found our nation There is a new relative clause here, ὧν οἱ πατέρες 'whose (were) the fathers', referring to the ancestors of the Jews. In Jewish minds this means Abraham, Isaac, and Jacob, as commentators suggest. CEV renders the clause as "they have those famous ancestors," but such a translation will not be very meaningful to people who do not automatically know who the famous ancestors were. But the clause also implies some sort of event connecting the patriarchs with their Jewish descendants, such as the founding of the nation. Perhaps the sense would be carried equally well by 'it is they who are the descendants of Abraham, Isaac, and Jacob'.

9:5b And *most importantly* it was from them that the Messiah received his human nature Paul's description of the privileges of the Jews moves to a climax with καὶ ἐξ ὧν ὁ Χριστὸς τὸ κατὰ σάρκα 'and from whom (is) the Messiah according to flesh'. That it is climactic is indicated in the display by 'most importantly'.

The introducer καί indicates that 'them' refers to the 'brothers' and 'fellow kinsmen' in v. 3, not the 'ancestors' in 5a. The word Χριστός 'Messiah' is to be taken as a title, not a name (cf. Morris). The phrase 'according to flesh' means "as to his human nature" (Hodge) or "as far as physical descent is concerned" (Moule). It is implied that Christ, like all the Jews, was descended from Jacob (i.e., Israel).

9:5c Nevertheless, most of my fellow Israelites have rejected Christ This proposition (most of which is repeated from implied 1b) is supplied to clarify the concessive force of the preceding list of privileges enjoyed by the Jews. It also supplies the contextually implied *situation* to which Paul is stating his REACTION in vv. 1-3. Paul's grief (v. 2) is heightened by the fact that the Jews rejected Christ in spite of all these blessings. LB summarizes the content of vv. 4-5 well, indicating the concessive relationship, and gives the essence of 5c with "God has given you so much, but still you will not listen to him."

9:5d the one who manages all things, God, the blessed one, forever. Amen. As Morris notes, the meaning here "is one of the most hotly disputed questions of the New Testament." Both Cranfield and Sanday and Headlam devote more than five pages to it. There is no problem with ὁ ἐπὶ πάντων 'who is over all': the preposition ἐπί means 'in control of' (BAGD, p. 286.II bα). But it is the words θεὸς εὐλογητός 'God blessed' that are problematic. It is largely a matter of punctuation. Does the description of ὁ Χριστός 'the Messiah' end with σάρκα (or with πάντων), or does it continue until 'Amen' at the end of the verse? The possibilities are:

(a) 'May God who is over all be blessed forever', or 'He who is over all is God, blessed forever'.

(b) '. . . Christ, who is over all. May God be blessed forever!'

(c) '. . . Christ, who is God over all, blessed forever'.

Interpretation c is chosen here for the following reasons, several of which summarize Metzger's (pp. 459-62) discussion: (1) It allows the sentence to flow naturally, while either *a* or *b* makes an extremely abrupt semantic change, for which there is no explanation at all. (2) The presence of the participle ὤν 'being' would be superfluous if the 'who' began a doxology, but is natural if it is part of a relative clause modifying ὁ Χριστός. (3) Elsewhere in the NT, doxologies begin either with a relative pronoun whose unambiguous antecedent is in the immediately preceding context or else with the conjunction δέ. (4) If this were a doxology that lacked an introductory conjunction or pronoun, the verbal adjective εὐλογητός 'blessed' would precede 'God', not follow it. But here it does follow it. (5) The main reason for rejecting interpretation c is that nowhere else in the NT is Christ unambiguously referred to as God. (Phil. 2:6, "he did not count equality with God a thing to be grasped," is close.) However, there is no reason to assume that Paul could not refer to him as God here. As a climax of his description of the advantages and privileges of the Jews, that from their race came the Messiah, who is the blessed second member of the Trinity, it is, in fact, very appropriate. (This is the interpretation followed by NIV, JB, NCV, and NRSV.)

BOUNDARIES AND COHERENCE

The 9:1c-5 paragraph is relationally coherent in that it consists of Paul's emotional REACTIONS (1c-3) to the *situation* that called it forth (vv. 4-5). Lexical coherence is provided through a whole series of terms expressing Paul's feelings, followed by a series of terms describing the Jews and the advantages they have (3c-5b).

The clearest mark of a boundary between this paragraph and the next is the fact that the list of advantages the Jews have builds up to a ringing description of the Messiah (in 5d) followed by 'Amen'.

PROMINENCE AND THEME

The theme of 9:1c-5 is primarily drawn from the v. 1 orienter and the prominent propositions of the REACTIONS. The CONTRAEXPECTATION in the *situation* is also included because 'I grieve greatly' is semantically incomplete without a statement of the cause of the grief and because Paul elaborates so much in this paragraph on the cause of the grief.

Ordinarily a speech orienter would not be included in a theme statement, but here the complex orienter in v. 1 is so extensive that it is very prominent. Therefore v. 1 is condensed and the words "I tell you very sincerely that" are made part of the theme.

SUBDIVISION CLUSTER CONSTITUENT 9:6–29
(Expository Section: Wrong evaluation of the Jews' rejection of Christ)

THEME: This does not prove that God has failed in his promise to Abraham. Nor can we conclude that God is unjust in choosing the ones he wants to, or that it is not right for God to condemn people.

MACROSTRUCTURE	CONTENTS
CLAIM₁	9:6–13 This does not prove that God has failed to do for Abraham what he promised, because, as Scripture illustrates, it is not all who are naturally descended from Jacob or Abraham whom God considers his children, but it is those who were born as a result of what God promised whom he considers his children.
CLAIM₂	9:14–18 As Scripture indicates, God's choosing people depends not on their wishes or efforts. But God helps whomever he wants to and he makes stubborn whomever he wants to. We cannot conclude that God is unjust in choosing the ones he wants to.
CLAIM₃	9:19–29 My reply to anyone's objection to this doctrine is that God has a right to carry out his purposes; he tolerated the people who caused him to be angry, in order that he might disclose how gloriously he acts toward those on whom he intends to have mercy.

INTENT AND MACROSTRUCTURE

The three paragraphs in the 9:6–29 unit are expository, the first (6–13) containing a CLAIM and its *justification*, the second (14–18) an *objection* and Paul's REFUTATION, the third (19–29) another *objection* and REFUTATION.

BOUNDARIES AND COHERENCE

Coherence in 9:6–29 is seen in the three occurrences of Ἰσραήλ 'Israel' (in v. 6 and v. 27) and in the names of prominent people in Israel's history: Abraham, Isaac, Sarah, Rebecca, Jacob, Esau, Moses, Hosea, and Isaiah.

The start of the next unit is marked at 9:30 by the rhetorical question τί οὖν ἐροῦμεν; 'what then shall we say?'. The words δικαιοσύνη 'righteousness' (nine times) and πίστις 'faith' (five times), and πιστεύω 'believe' (eight times) occur in 9:30–10:21, but not in 9:6–29.

PROMINENCE AND THEME

The theme of 9:6–29 is drawn from the themes of its three constituent paragraphs. The *justification* in 6–13 is omitted as being less prominent than the CLAIM. The *objections* in 14–18 and 19–29 are omitted as being less thematic than the REFUTATIONS.

SECTION CONSTITUENT 9:6-13
(Expository Paragraph: Claim₁ of 9:6-29)

> **THEME:** *This does not prove that God has failed to do for Abraham what he promised, because, as Scripture illustrates, it is not all who are naturally descended from Jacob or Abraham whom God considers his children, but it is those who were born as a result of what God promised whom he considers his children.*

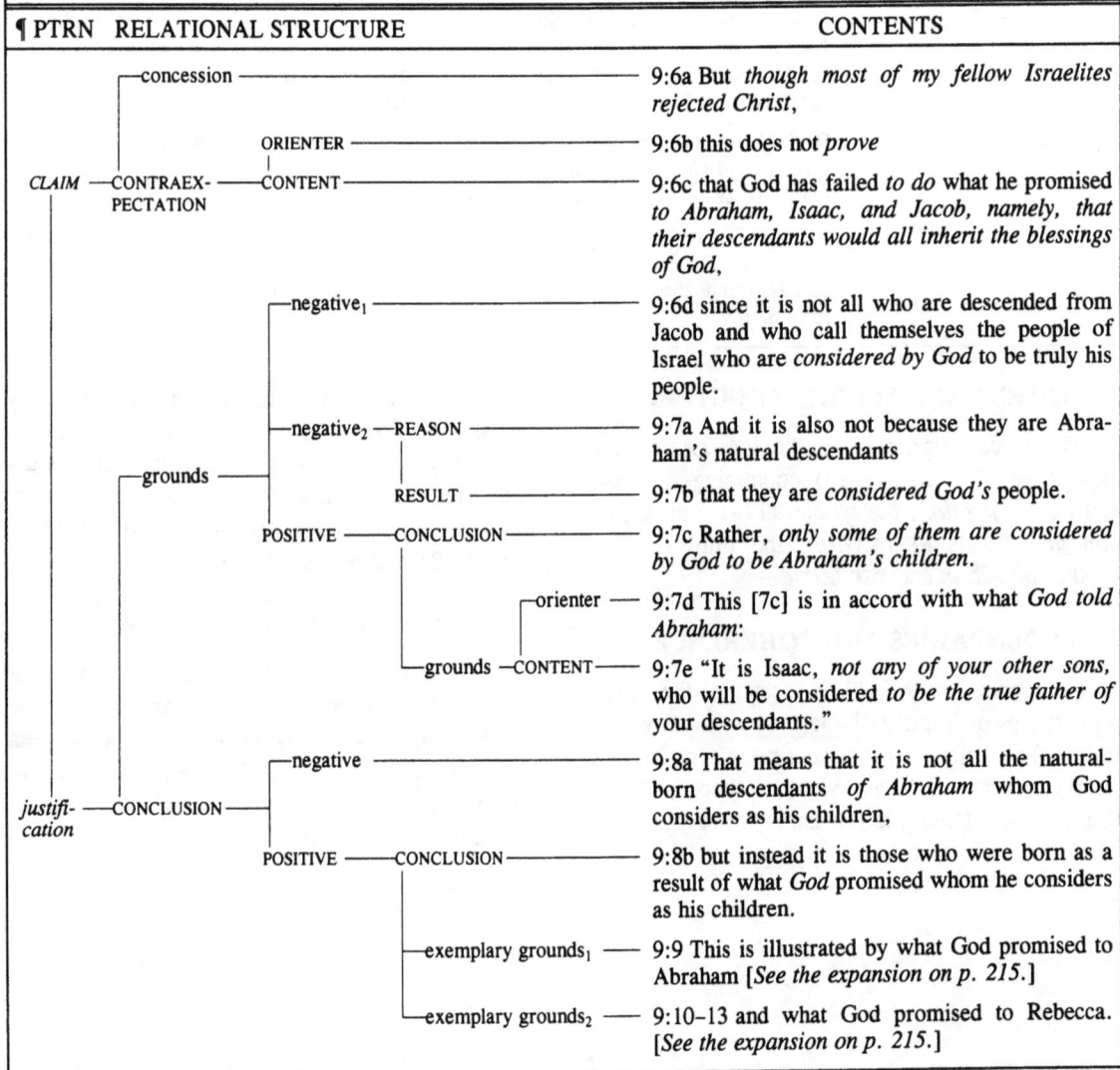

INTENT AND PARAGRAPH PATTERN

In 9:6-13, Paul begins his long discussion on the present spiritual state of the Jews and God's future plans for them. It is clear that this is an expository paragraph, consisting of a CLAIM about the Jews in 6b-c and its *justification* in 6d-13.

NOTES

9:6a-c But *though most of my fellow Israelites rejected Christ,* **this does not** *prove* **that God has failed** *to do* **what he promised** *to Abraham, Isaac, and Jacob, namely, that their descendants would all inherit the blessings of God* The Greek is οὐχ οἷον δὲ ὅτι ἐκπέπτωκεν ὁ λόγος τοῦ θεοῦ 'but not as though the word of God had failed'. Here Paul clearly is introducing a contrast or contraexpectation. What it is contrasted to is the Jews' rejection of Jesus as the Messiah (see 1a-b). Therefore, this idea is supplied in 6a, the relation being concessive.

Commentators and some versions (TEV, LB, JB, CEV, NCV) render λόγος as 'promise'. To say 'the promise has not failed' is something of a personification, a short way of saying 'God has not failed to do what he promised'. Since case role considerations require that the recipients of the promise be specified, Abraham might be considered the recipient in the light of the following context (vv. 7-8). But since Isaac is mentioned in v. 10 (and probably is in view in 7a), and since the promise to Abraham was repeated to Isaac (Gen. 26:4) and to Jacob (28:14), all three may be in view here, as suggested in the display. Another alternative is 'the patriarchs' (cf. v. 5).

Case considerations (as well as the following context) require that the promise Paul was referring to be understood. The display supplies 'that their descendants would all inherit the blessings of God' as the content of the promise. Although the following context discusses who the true descendants of Abraham, Jacob, and Isaac are, the Jews remembered God's promise in Gen. 17:7, "I will establish an everlasting covenant . . . between me and you and your descendants . . . to be your God and the God of your descendants"; and they wrongly concluded that this promise guaranteed redemption to all Abraham's descendants. (Paul specifically deals with this wrong belief in the following context.)

The connection between 'the promise has not failed' and what precedes is somewhat nebulous. A complete clause to go with the introductory negative οὐχ at the beginning of the verse would make the connection clearer, hence 'this does not prove that'. Another possibility would be 'one should not infer that'.

9:6d it is not all who are descended from Jacob and who call themselves the people of Israel who are *considered by God* **to be truly his people** The Greek is οὐ πάντες οἱ ἐξ Ἰσραήλ, οὗτοι Ἰσραήλ 'not all who (are) out of Israel, these (are) Israel'. The first 'Israel' refers either to Jacob (his new name being Israel) or to the people of Israel. Or it could be a play on the word, referring to both, since the word 'Israel' indeed refers to both the individual and the nation or race. The latter is very likely here, since the reference to Israel occurs before the reference to Abraham, Jacob's grandfather. In some languages the conceptual idea denoted by the first occurrence of the word 'Israel' may have to be rendered with different terms, to capture the play on words; for example, 'although there are many descendants of Jacob who call themselves the people of Israel'.

In the OT, the people of Israel were viewed as the people of God. But from God's point of view, Paul says, this is not necessarily so. The display thus renders the second 'Israel' as 'truly God's people' (as in CEV, NCV, NEB, and TEV). The play on words is probably untranslatable.

9:7a-b And it is also not because they are Abraham's natural descendants that they are *considered God's* **people** The grammatical construction here is parallel to the one in 6d-e, and therefore the display includes the word 'considered' to connect πάντες 'all' and τέκνα 'children'. In some languages the grammar may require 'God', the implicit agent of 'consider', to be made specific, or it may be necessary in order to avoid ambiguity.

9:7c Rather, *only some of them are considered by God to be Abraham's children* Except for the word 'rather' (which represents the conjunction ἀλλά), this proposition is only implied. It is contextually crucial as the main implicature of the argument. LB tries to make some of this clear by adding at the end of the verse "though Abraham had other children too."

9:7d *God told Abraham* Since 7d is a direct quotation from the OT and Paul clearly expects his readers to realize this, the display identifies the speaker and addressee of the quoted words (as does NCV).

9:7e "It is Isaac, *not any of your other sons,* **who will be considered** *to be the true father of your descendants."* Paul is quoting Gen. 21:12 here. The words ἐν Ἰσαάκ 'in Isaac' occur before the verb and are thereby in focus. The force of this focus can be expressed as 'only in Isaac' (so Morris, Alford, LB, CEV) or, more specifically, 'in Isaac and not in any other son', or perhaps 'in Isaac and not in Ishmael' (see Cranfield, Hodge). Although at the time God gave this promise to Abraham his only other child was Ishmael, he later had several other sons (Gen. 25:2), so either alternative is appropriate. Morris makes this comment: "Paul can cite Genesis 21:12 to show that it is only the descendants through Isaac that constitute the seed (here used of the true successors of Abraham)."

It may have to be made specific that these words were written in Scripture.

The clause ἐν Ἰσαάκ κληθήσεταί σοι σπέρμα 'in Isaac will be called your seed' is a literal translation of the Hebrew, and it is difficult to know from the Greek the exact senses of the preposition and the verb. The display has 'who will be considered to be the true father of'. An alternative is 'from whom your descendants will be considered to come'. English versions use "counted as" (TEV), "come" (NIV), "be carried on" (JB), "traced" (NEB).

9:8a That means Most commentators take the words τοῦτ᾽ ἔστιν 'that is' as introducing an explanation of the preceding verse. This would give 7c, nearly all of which is an implied proposition, as the NUCLEUS of the *justification*. What seems a better alternative is to consider τοῦτ᾽ ἔστιν as introducing a general principle deduced from v. 7 (cf. Sanday and Headlam, Whedon, Cranfield). RSV, LB, TEV, NCV, JBP all render it as "This means" or "That means," which can be taken as introducing a conclusion which is drawn from what precedes it.

the natural-born descendants *of Abraham* The phrase τῆς σαρκός 'of the flesh' means "natural children" (NIV) or "children born in the natural way" (TEV).

9:8b instead it is those who were born as a result of what *God* promised whom he considers as his children There is little difference between the two main interpretations of τὰ τέκνα τῆς ἐπαγγελίας 'the children of the promise'. Some suggest 'children to whom the promise was given' in the sense of 'those who receive or inherit it'; others suggest 'those who are born because of, as a result of, or according to the promise' (cf. *BAGD*, p. 280.2a). The display follows the latter. One could say that the genitive implies an understood verb. In this context, and in the light of chapter 4, 'believe' would seem the best verb to supply (so LB). But the event of believing is not in focus.

ROMANS 9:6–13

EXPANSION OF THE EXEMPLARY GROUNDS IN THE 9:6–13 DISPLAY

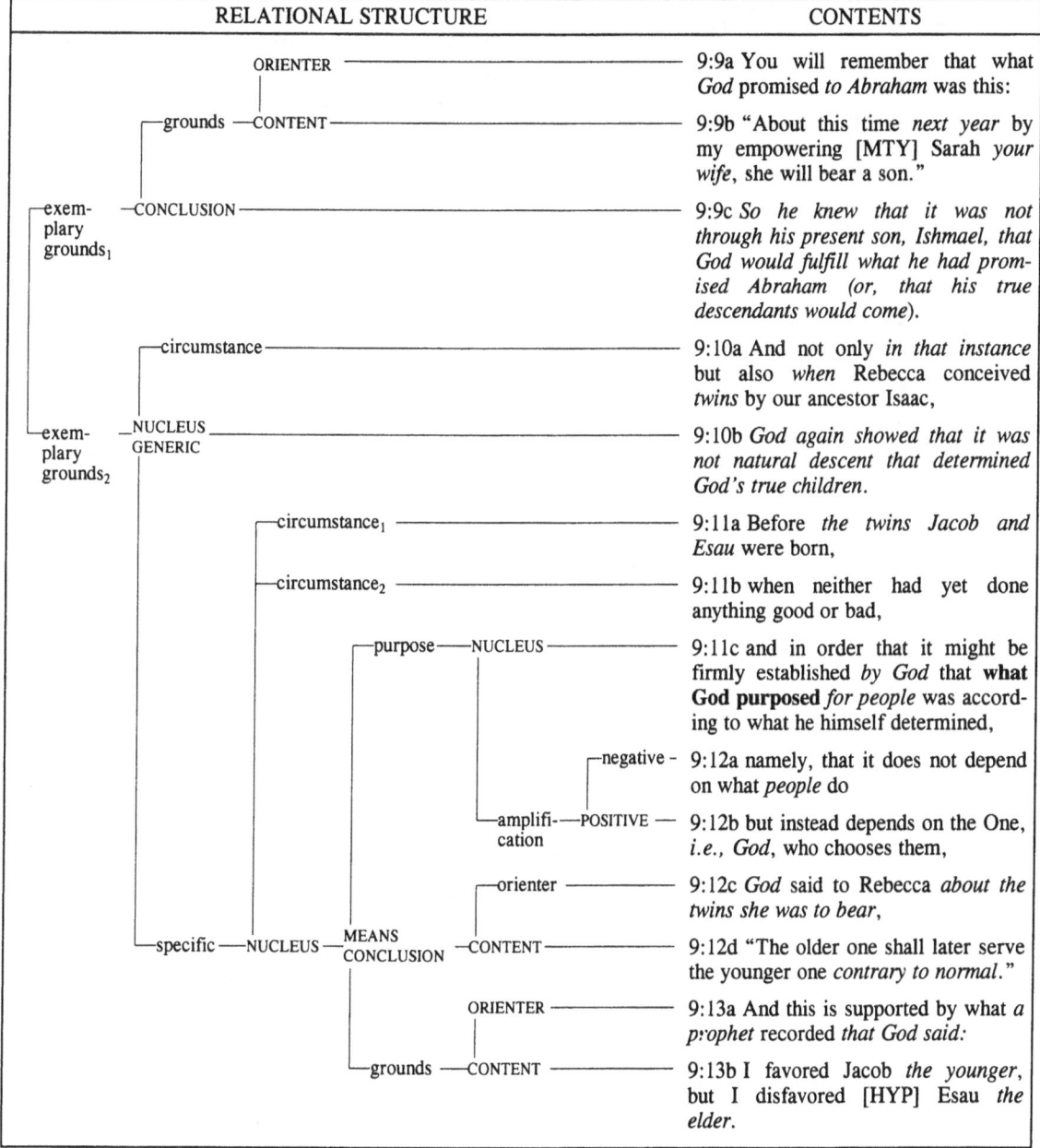

9:9a You will remember that Here γάρ is introducing, not a reason, but an additional bit of Scripture as an exemplary grounds of the 8c statement.

what God promised to Abraham was this The phrase ἐπαγγελίας ὁ λόγος οὗτος 'of promise this word' refers to the words that God promised; 'promise' is forefronted and is thereby emphasized. It is likewise forefronted in the display. The recipient of the promise, 'Abraham', is supplied to complete the case roles.

9:9b About this time next year by my empowering Sarah your wife, she will bear a son The Greek κατὰ τὸν καιρὸν τοῦτον 'according to this time' is a rather free translation from the Hebrew (Gen. 18:10 or 14). It could mean either 'at the proper time' or 'the time I have determined' or, more specifically, 'at this time next year'. Some have suggested 'at the time required between conception and birth'. But to do justice to the word 'this', the best choice is 'at this time next year'. It is so rendered by CEV; LB has simply "next year." (The exact time is not in focus here;

Paul was only reminding readers of the promise of a son.) But there is still a problem of when the empowering/enabling was to take place: right away or in the following year. CEV makes a fairly clear choice: "At this time next year I will return, and you will already have a son." Morris says regarding the possible ambiguity of the phrase 'the appointed time', "In Genesis it means 'this time next year' (Gen. 18:10, 14), but Paul's abbreviated quotation could be understood as 'the time between conception and birth'."

The verb ἐλεύσομαι 'I will come' must have some semantic connection with the words 'Sarah will have a son'. Hodge says, "God is said to come, wherever he specially manifests his presence or power"; the birth of his son was obviously the miraculous consequence of God's coming. The verb is therefore taken as a metonymy and rendered 'by my empowering Sarah'. In support of this is the fact that the fulfillment of this prophecy in Genesis 21 does not mention any reappearance of the angel. The words 'your wife' are supplied to indicate the relationship between Abraham and Sarah that Paul expected his audience to know.

9:9c *So he knew that it was not through his present son, Ishmael, that God would fulfill what he had promised Abraham (or, that his true descendants would come)* This implicit proposition is the conclusion that Abraham drew and which Paul expects his readers to know. It also supplies the purpose of Paul's quoting what God told Abraham (so Morris).

9:10a not only . . . but also The expression οὐ μόνον δέ, ἀλλὰ καί 'and not only, but also' is an elliptical expression, whose missing words in every other instance in the NT are clear from the context, but not so clear here. What *is* clear is that Paul is saying, in effect, "there is not just that example, but another one, to prove my point." The point is stated in 10b.

when Rebecca conceived twins In some languages an object for 'conceive' (κοίτην ἔχουσα, literally 'having intercourse') will be required; in this case 'twins' may be supplied (as in LB, CEV, JBP, and JB).

by our ancestor Isaac The preposition ἐξ 'out of' is rendered here as 'by', but in some languages an appropriate euphemistic clause may be necessary, for example, 'after sleeping with'. Several versions have 'Rebecca's twins had the same father, our ancestor Isaac', but saying the twins had the same father doesn't seem very profound.

9:10b *God again showed that it was not natural descent that determined God's true children* The display follows Hodge, who says, "The choice of God does not depend on natural descent." Murray has a longer alternative: "not by natural descent did the descendants of Abraham become partakers of God's covenant grace and promises."

9:11a Before *the twins Jacob and Esau* were born In the Greek no subject is given for the first two participles. Supplying 'the twins Jacob and Esau' helps the reader to connect the discussion here with the quotation in v. 13, where both names are given.

9:11c–12d The display follows the Greek order rather closely, but it may be somewhat confusing to follow this in translation. An alternative would be to transpose 9:12c–d to precede 11c–12b. Then 11c could begin with a new sentence, 'He said this in order that . . .'.

9:11c in order that it might be firmly established *by God* **that** <u>what God purposed</u> *for* **people** **was according to what he himself determined** The Greek is ἵνα ἡ κατ' ἐκλογὴν πρόθεσις τοῦ θεοῦ μένῃ 'in order that the according to selection purpose of God might remain'. What Paul means by 'remain' is that it would be recognized or firmly established. What was to be established was not God's purpose but the principle related to it (specified in 12a–b). The phrase κατ' ἐκλογήν 'according to election' can be made into a full clause: 'according to what he determined/selected/chose'. Note that the context demands that emphasis be given to 'God' as the agent of 'determined'. The phrase 'he himself' in the display attempts to bring this out (TEV has "God's own purpose"). Everything in the Greek clause precedes the verb and is thereby prominent, and the fact that κατ' ἐκλογήν occurs within the subject phrase gives it special emphasis. This is difficult to bring out in translation, but the display attempts to do so with bold type and the forefronting of 'what God purposed'.

9:12a–b namely, that it does not depend on what *people* **do but instead depends on the One,** *i.e., God,* **who chooses them** These two propositions can be viewed as appositional, not parenthetical, to the word 'purpose' ('what God purposed') in 11c. They specify the content of the principle referred to in 11c.

The negative part of the principle is οὐκ ἐξ ἔργων 'not from works', which is an abbreviated way of saying 'it does not depend on what people do', 'it' being a pronominal ellipsis for 'God's selection of people'.

The positive part of the principle is ἀλλ' ἐκ τοῦ καλοῦντος 'but instead from the one who calls'. A verb is again needed to make a full clause, so 'depends on' is supplied (cf. JB). (TEV and REB have "based on.") The one who 'calls' or 'chooses' is God.

9:12c-d *God* **said to Rebecca** *about the twins she was to bear*, **"The older one shall later serve the younger one** *contrary to normal*.**"** In 12c the pronominal referents are specified as in NCV and CEV, and the words 'about the twins she was to bear' are supplied so that it will be clear who 'the elder' and 'the younger' mentioned in 12d are.

Verse 13, which contains a quotation from Malachi, mentions Jacob and Esau by name. Even though the context in Malachi is about the descendants of Jacob and Esau, Malachi does name the two individuals. And in Gen. 25:23, where the quotation cited in Rom. 9:13 first was spoken, the two individuals are also in view as well as the two peoples to be descended from them.

As for the quotation here in 12d, the emphasis is clearly on God's choice of individuals, not on races or nations: "the older shall serve the younger." Some commentators object that Esau never really served Jacob, but Jacob did dominate Esau as a master dominates a slave who serves him.

The words 'contrary to normal' are supplied in the display to make specific what was culturally understood and essential information to Paul's argument. Without it Paul's point would not be clear. Since according to custom Esau would have been over Jacob, Jacob's being over Esau was only because of God's determination and choice.

9:13a this is supported by what *a prophet recorded* **that** *God said* The words καθὼς γέγραπται 'just as it is written' introduce the 13b quotation from Mal. 1:2-3. Usually these and similar words convey the notion that the evidential grounds to support a theological point are about to be given (cf. 1:17, 3:10, 4:17). Here, however, 12d is also a quotation from Scripture.

To satisfy the case frame the agent of 'written/recorded' is specified: 'a prophet'. In order to identify the referent for 'I' in 13b, 'that God said' is supplied here in 13a.

9:13b I favored Jacob *the younger*, **but I disfavored Esau** *the elder* The word ἐμίσησα 'hated' is a hyperbole and means "to love less, to regard and treat with less favour" (Hodge). The words 'the younger' and 'the elder' are supplied to make clear that the reference here is to the same two individuals alluded to in 12b.

BOUNDARIES AND COHERENCE

Relational coherence in the 9:6-13 paragraph is provided by its consisting of one CLAIM and *justification*. Lexical coherence is provided by references to Abraham and his wife, his son, his son's wife, and his two grandsons, and also by lexemes referring to descendants: σπέρμα 'seed' (three times) and τέκνα 'children' (three times). And while the next unit refers to various individuals (Moses and Pharaoh), it contains no reference to Abraham's descendants per se. The start of the next unit is marked by the rhetorical question τί οὖν ἐροῦμεν 'what then shall we say?'

PROMINENCE AND THEME

The theme of 9:6-13 is drawn from elements of both the CLAIM and the *justification*. The ORIENTER in 9:6b and CONTENT in 9:6c are essential parts of the CLAIM; the word 'this' in 6b refers to the implied statement in 9:1b that most of the Jews have rejected Christ. The most prominent element in the *justification* is the v. 8 CONCLUSION.

SECTION CONSTITUENT 9:14–18
(Expository Paragraph: Claim₂ of 9:6–29)

> **THEME:** *As Scripture indicates, God's choosing people depends not on their wishes or efforts. But God helps whomever he wants to and he makes stubborn whomever he wants to. We cannot conclude that God is unjust in choosing the ones he wants to.*

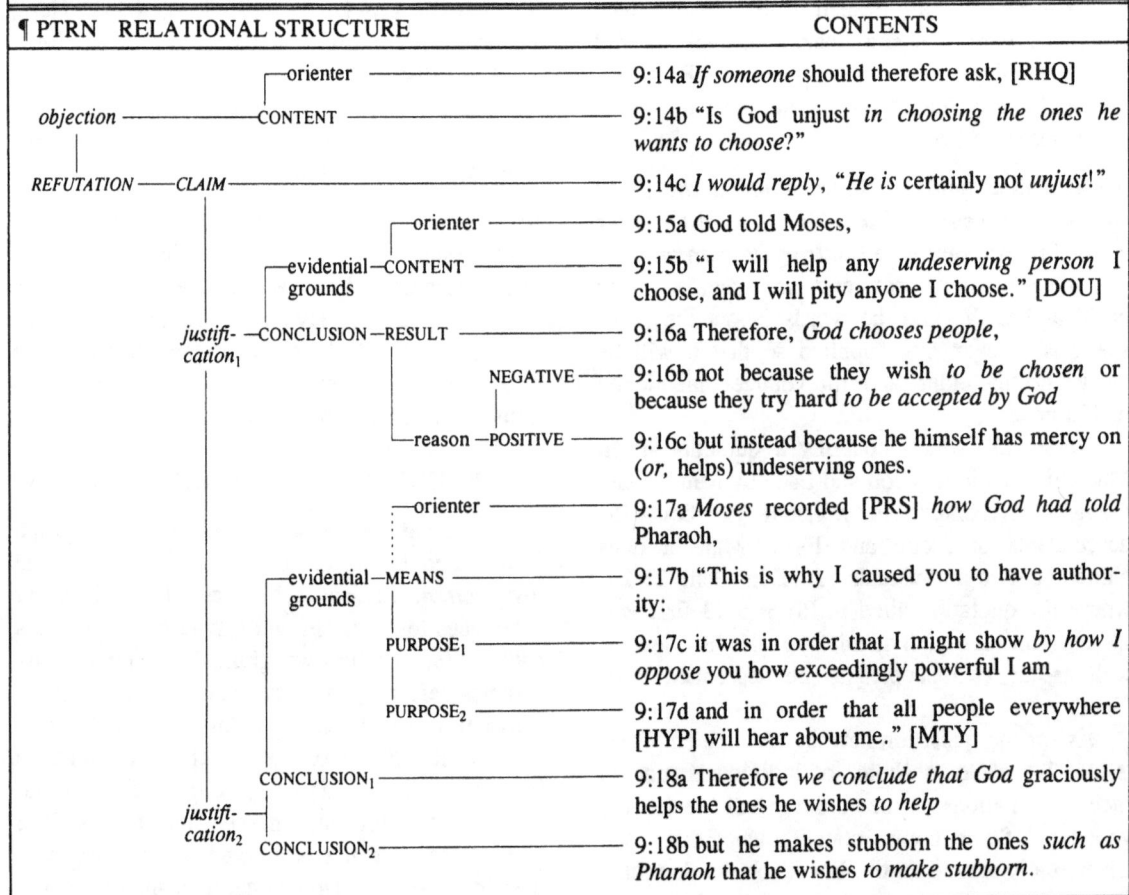

INTENT AND PARAGRAPH PATTERN

The questions at the beginning of 9:14–18 indicate that Paul is about to answer an objection, either hypothetical or actual, to his statements about the Jews. This is therefore an expository paragraph. There are two levels of paragraph pattern: an *objection* (14a-b) and a REFUTATION (14c-18); and within the REFUTATION, a brief CLAIM (14c) followed by two *justifications* supporting it.

NOTES

9:14a *If someone* should therefore ask Verse 14 begins in the same way as 6:1, with τί οὖν ἐροῦμεν 'what therefore shall we say' followed by a yes/no question and then Paul's answer μὴ γένοιτο 'may it not be so'. It is therefore treated in the same way as a question, real or hypothetical, which Paul raises and then answers (see the note on 6:1).

The οὖν 'therefore' is not really relating this paragraph on a higher level as a conclusion to the preceding one. Rather, it relates the *justification* (or some element of it) in the preceding paragraph to the *objection* in this paragraph.

9:14b "Is God unjust *in choosing the ones he wants to choose?*" The italicized words here indicate the object of possible injustice that is in focus in this context. It is implied that the one asking this question would be a Jew.

9:15a Here γάρ introduces the *justification* to support the emphatic negative reply in 14c. Something like 'when Moses pleaded for all of Jacob's descendants' may be required in the text or in a footnote for readers who need to be informed of the situational background of this quotation from Exod. 33:19.

9:15b "I will help any *undeserving person* I choose, and I will pity anyone I choose." The words 'any undeserving person' define more precisely the semantic content of the verb ἐλεήσω 'I will have mercy on'. The two clauses here are a doublet, but since this comes from a poetic passage, both are left in the display. Moore (p. 40) classifies it as a near-synonymous doublet. Most commentators agree that it is very difficult to see any difference in meaning between the two verbs. The doublet lends emphasis, as though God were saying, "If you didn't hear me the first time, I'll say it again." The sense could be represented as well by something like 'I will take pity on precisely anyone I choose'.

9:16a *God chooses people* In the Greek there is neither subject nor main verb in this verse. But the implicit subject is akin to the implicit referent in 14b, namely 'God's election' (Bullinger, Hodge) or possibly 'God's mercy' (from 15b). NCV makes the subject clear: "God will choose the one he decides to show mercy to."

not because they wish *to be chosen* Of the three genitive phrases here, the first two are negative and the third (the most prominent, introduced by ἀλλά 'but instead') is positive. They are taken as having a causal force. Most commentators and versions suggest 'it does not depend on' instead of 'it is not because of' (so RSV, TEV, NIV, NEB), but that, of course, is equally causal. LB has 'not because'.

9:17a Here γάρ is introducing, not a reason, but a second evidential grounds from Scripture to support the argument.

***Moses* recorded *how God had told* Pharaoh** The Greek is λέγει ἡ γραφὴ τῷ Φαραώ 'the Scripture says to Pharaoh', a personification. The agent of the writing of the Scripture cited here (Exod. 9:16) was Moses and the speaker of the message to Pharaoh was God. CEV handles it well: "In the Scriptures the Lord says to Pharaoh." In many languages it may be better to translate 'Pharaoh' as 'King of Egypt' as in NCV; LB has both.

9:17b This is why I caused you to have authority The function of the cataphoric expression εἰς αὐτὸ τοῦτο 'unto this very thing' is to place prominence on the purpose clauses that follow. The words ἐξήγειρά σε 'I raised you up' are not to be taken in their primary sense here. Although in the LXX this verb clearly has the sense of 'preserved', Paul has something more general in mind here. The sense is "caused him to appear on the stage of history" (Cranfield), which is difficult to express nonfiguratively. Alternatively, 'established' or 'gave authority to' or 'allowed you to rule' might convey the sense.

9:17c in order that I might show *by how I oppose* you how exceedingly powerful I am The Greek here is ὅπως ἐνδείξωμαι ἐν σοὶ τὴν δύναμίν μου 'so as I will show in you my power'. Power is basically an attribute, hence 'show how exceedingly powerful I am'; for some languages it may have to be expressed as 'act very powerfully'. The reference is to God's displaying his power through the miracles that preceded the Exodus. The words 'in you' are a little more difficult. God's power was not demonstrated in anything he did *in* or *for* Pharaoh. NEB has "in my dealings with you" and LB "against." The words in the display convey the same idea. An alternative would be 'when I oppose you'.

9:17d and in order that all people everywhere will hear about me The Greek is καὶ ὅπως διαγγελῇ τὸ ὄνομά μου ἐν πάσῃ τῇ γῇ 'and so that might be announced everywhere my name in all the earth'. The word 'name' is a metonymy standing for the person or the power exercised by the person or the person's fame or reputation. Any of these is appropriate here, except that power has already been mentioned in 17c. REB has "spread my fame."

The hyperbolic 'in all the earth' is here rendered 'everywhere'. Though still hyperbolic, it is more translatable than 'in all the earth'.

In the display the reciprocal of 'proclaiming', namely 'hearing about me', is used because the focus is not so much on proclaiming (or who will do it) as on people's hearing about God's mighty power.

9:18a Therefore *we conclude that* The words ἄρα οὖν 'so therefore' introduce the conclusion Paul expects his readers to draw from the passage about Pharaoh.

9:18b but he makes stubborn the ones *such as Pharaoh* that he wishes *to make stubborn* The idiomatic expression 'hardens' is rendered "makes stubborn" by REB, TEV, CEV, and NCV. LB has "causes to refuse to listen." The reference to Pharaoh is supplied to clarify Paul's point in mentioning Pharaoh in v. 17.

BOUNDARIES AND COHERENCE

The relational coherence of 9:14–18 is shown by its consisting of the hypothetical *objection* Paul expected the Jews among the epistle's readers to raise, and then Paul's REFUTATION of it. This, along with lower-level CLAIM and its two *justifications*, gives the paragraph its relational coherence. Lexical coherence is provided by references to Moses and Pharaoh as well as three occurrences of the verb ἐλεέω 'to have mercy on'.

The start of a new paragraph is signaled in v. 19 by another question expressing another hypothetical objection to Paul's presentation of the problem of the Jews' rejection of Christ.

PROMINENCE AND THEME

The theme of 9:14–18 is drawn from the 14c CLAIM and the three CONCLUSIONS in the two *justifications*. A slightly longer theme would bring out the fact that Paul was answering an objection ('My reply to a query as to whether God is unjust . . . is no, because . . .'). This alternative is not chosen because Paul does not specify here that he is answering an objection (though he does in v. 19). The words 'as Scripture indicates' are included in the theme because the fact that he can cite Scripture to prove his point is always an essential part of Paul's argument.

SECTION CONSTITUENT 9:19–29
(Expository Paragraph: Claim₃ of 9:6–29)

THEME: My reply to anyone's objection to this doctrine is that God has a right to carry out his purposes; he tolerated the people who caused him to be angry, in order that he might disclose how gloriously he acts toward those on whom he intends to have mercy.

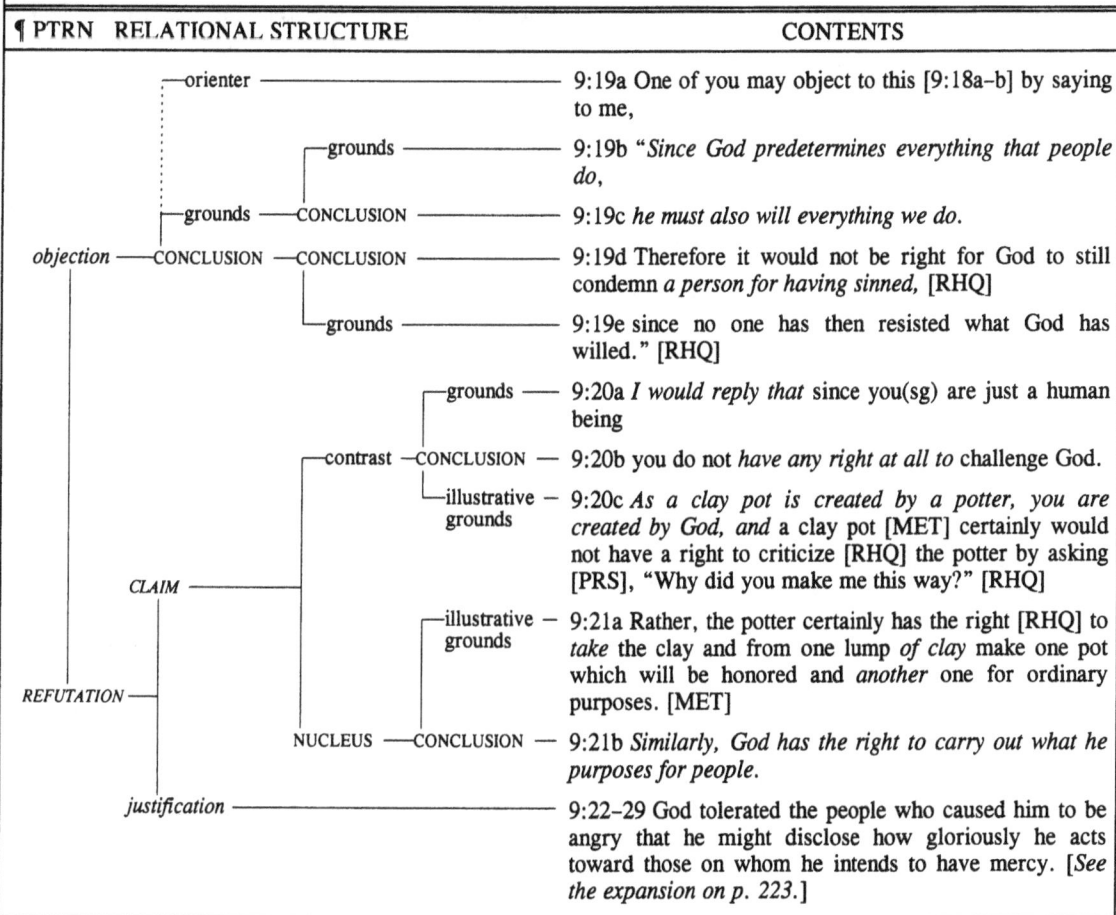

INTENT AND PARAGRAPH PATTERN

In 9:19–29 Paul continues to raise and answer possible objections. The verbs are in the indicative mood; thus this is an expository paragraph. The manner of argumentation also makes it clear that it is expository (Paul is answering a hypothetical objection). There are two levels of paragraph pattern: On the higher level there are an *objection* and REFUTATION; on the lower level, within the REFUTATION, a CLAIM and a *justification*.

NOTES

9:19a One of you may object to this by saying to me The words ἐρεῖς μοι 'you(sg) will say to me' are rendered in the display as 'one of you(pl)' because Paul is addressing the Roman church as a whole, not an individual; and 'will say' is expressed as 'may say' because Paul does not necessarily know that someone will raise the objection—he is simply stating that he has a reply ready in case someone does. In Greek the use of the second person singular and future tense is characteristic of a certain type of argument. We should not expect that the same forms used for this type of argument would necessarily carry over into other languages. CEV has "Someone may ask." The οὖν is represented by 'object to this' (i.e., object to what was said in 18a-b) because the possible objection in v. 19 arises out of what Paul has just said.

9:19b *Since God predetermines everything that people do* This is the expression of τί ἔτι 'why still?' in 19d, which by itself implies some grounds of objection. Another option is to consider the grounds to be 'since God is the one who chooses or rejects people', which also repeats the main point of Paul's argument in the previous two paragraphs. But the words supplied here are more generic and fit the following context better (the objection stated in v. 19 is more closely related to what follows).

9:19c *he must also will everything we do* This too is an integral and crucial step in the logic of the objection. Whedon comments,

> The Jew's question . . . is this: Since . . . God, as you say, has it all his own way, why does he hold us Jews responsible? . . . it is to a false Calvinistic view of the matter that the Jew objects. He understands that Paul is a predestinarian in his putting of the case, and against that putting his query is perfectly just. And Paul will reply, not by denying the validity of the objection to the fatalistic view, but by denying that the fatalistic view is the one he puts.

9:19d it would not be right for God to still condemn a person for *having sinned* The words τί ἔτι μέμφεται 'why does he still find fault?' are considered a rhetorical question expressing a negative evaluation. In the display it is rendered as a statement, but in many languages a literal translation may convey the sense well, or perhaps some other rhetorical question may be suitable, for example, 'how can God still . . . ?' The verb μέμφομαι means to blame someone for a wrong that has been committed; in this context it means to condemn a person for his sin. NCV supplies "for our sins"; JBP has "for what they do."

9:19e no one has resisted what God has willed This is another rhetorical question: τῷ γὰρ βουλήματι αὐτοῦ τίς ἀνθέστηκεν; 'for his purpose who has resisted?' If taken literally, the answer would be 'no one' or, more emphatically, 'absolutely no one!' The noun βούλημα expresses an event concept: 'to intend, to purpose, to will'. The forefronting of the words 'his purpose' give them prominence, which might be expressed in English by rephrasing, for example, 'what God has willed is something that no one has resisted'.

The display uses a perfect tense 'has resisted' for the verb because the Greek also uses a perfect tense. Surprisingly, nearly all the versions take the sense as 'can resist'. (LB is an exception with "Haven't they done what he made them do?") Commentators do not discuss it. Probably Paul intends both: 'No one has ever resisted and no one ever will'.

9:20a–b *I would reply that* **since you(sg) are just a human being you do not** *have any right at all to* **challenge God** This is a reply or counter remark to the objection raised in v. 19 by means of a rhetorical question: μενοῦν γε σὺ τίς εἶ ὁ ἀνταποκρινόμενος τῷ θεῷ; 'on the contrary, who are you, the one replying against God?' The words μενοῦν γε indicate a contrast and a degree of emphasis on what follows. The contrast is shown in the display by the words 'I would reply'; the emphasis, by 'just' and 'any right at all'. An alternative for the latter would be 'have absolutely no right'. The NCV rendering is close to the one here: "You are only human. And human beings have no right to question God."

The words ὦ ἄνθρωπε 'O man' do not mean that Paul thought a potential objector would be male, nor are they just rhetorical; but, as Dunn says, "an antithesis between man and God is intended." RSV and JBP have "a man"; JB is better with "a human being."

9:20c *As a clay pot is created by a potter, you are created by God, and* **a clay pot certainly would not have a right to criticize the potter by asking** The metaphor μὴ ἐρεῖ τὸ πλάσμα τῷ πλάσαντι 'the thing molded will not say to the molder' refers to a potter who molds clay to form pots. Its topic is: having been created by God, human beings have no right to criticize God. Both the image and topic are spelled out in the display. In Greek this is a rhetorical question with the force of an emphatic negative statement.

Since clay pots cannot talk, in some languages it may need to be rendered 'If clay pots could talk, they would not have a right to criticize the potter by asking. . . .' To mitigate the personification, the display has 'certainly would not have a right to' rather than simply 'will not'.

The rhetorical question in 20c, 'Why did you make me thus?' is retained as such in the display since a 'why' question is almost universally used to convey criticism. This function is expressed in the display with the words 'to criticize by asking'.

9:21a the potter certainly has the right to *take* **the clay and from one lump** *of clay* **make one pot which will be honored and** *another* **one for ordinary purposes** The rhetorical question here has the force of an emphatic positive statement and is rendered as such in the display. The phrase ἐξουσίαν . . . τοῦ πηλοῦ 'the authority of the clay' is rendered 'the right to take the clay' since some sort of event relationship is being signaled.

The two parallel but contrastive prepositional phrases at the end of v. 21, εἰς τιμήν 'unto honor' and εἰς ἀτιμίαν 'unto dishonor', are rhetorically forceful in Greek, but the intended sense of the second one is probably not so strong as 'dishonor' suggests. The sense of the first phrase is 'in order that people will honor it', but the sense of the second is not 'in order that people will dishonor/disparage it'. (No potter would make a pot for that purpose.) Instead the sense of the second phrase may be taken as "for ordinary use" (TEV), "for common use" (NIV, NEB). However, it may be that Paul makes this extreme statement on purpose to highlight the fact that the creator has the authority to do whatever he may wish with something he has made.

9:21b *Similarly God has the right to carry out what he purposes for people* The unexpressed but implicit topic of the metaphor is supplied here.

EXPANSION OF THE *JUSTIFICATION* IN THE 9:19–29 DISPLAY

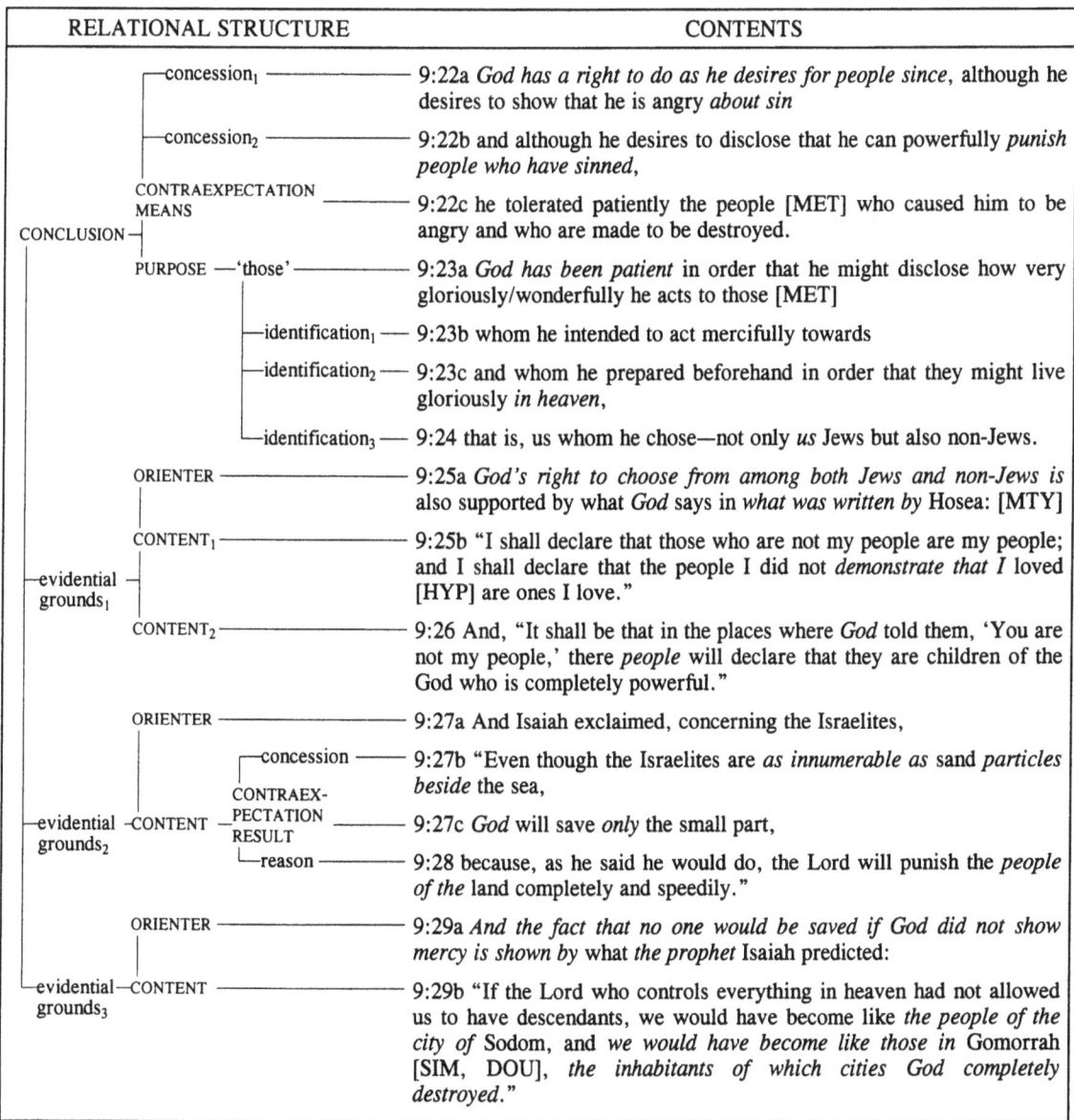

9:22–24 Commentators have wrestled at great length with this passage. John Knox (1978) says, "Only a few passages in Paul are more obscure than this one (i.e. vv. 22–23), and no certainty is possible as to how it ought to be translated." The first problem is grammatical in that vv. 22–24

form a subordinate clause beginning with εἰ 'if', making it an unfinished sentence. Commentators suggest 'what will you say?' or 'what reply will you make?' as an 'understood' main clause. Either of these would be appropriate, but they would still be rhetorical questions. In the display, therefore, the first part of 22a is included to carry the sense of what the commentators propose, but as a negative statement, not a rhetorical question. Interestingly enough, even without a main clause, the compilers of the GNT have concluded the sentence at the end of v. 23 with the Greek equivalent of a question mark. Many versions have a question somewhere in these three verses. (JB, CEV, TEV, and Beck are among those who render 22-24 as a statement.) However, since there is no textual evidence for considering the passage to be a question, 22a has no RHQ label, and in the display the more straightforward alternative of an emphatic negative statement is given: 'not one of you can challenge God'. This in effect places the implied apodosis at the beginning of the sentence, rather than at the end, as the commentators would suggest.

9:22a *God has a right to do as he desires for people* This clause simply repeats the content of 21b to enable a new sentence to begin with v. 22, relating the CLAIM in vv. 20-21 to the *justification* which follows.

since, **although he desires to show that he is angry** *about sin* The participle θέλων 'wishing' has been taken by commentators as expressing either cause or concession. If it is causal, the idea would be that God tolerated sin patiently because he desired to show his anger (with sin). This has a lot of support from commentators, but does not make sense. The opposite would be the case: if God wanted to show anger concerning sin, he would *not* have tolerated it patiently. If it is concessive, the idea would be that God tolerated sin patiently even though he desired to show his anger (with sin). This makes for excellent relational coherence, and is the choice in the display.

The words 'about sin' are supplied to define the sphere of God's anger (cf. JBP, "his wrath against sin"). God is not angry for no reason.

9:22b although he desires to disclose that he can powerfully *punish people who have sinned* The main verb from 22a is repeated here since this is the second part of the compound object of θέλων 'wishing': γνωρίσαι τὸ δυνατὸν αὐτοῦ 'to make known his power'. This is the only occurrence of δυνατόν in the NT in which it is equivalent to δύναμις 'power' (so BAGD, p. 209.2d). The question now is, What did God wish to disclose about his power? The grammatical parallelism of the two infinitive phrases ('to show his anger' in 22a and 'to make known his power' in 22b) indicates their close relationship, so the answer to the question is that God is not only angry about sin, but that he has the power to do something about it (so Morris), namely punish it. With the mismatch between the meaning and the grammar removed, 'to make known his power' becomes 'to disclose that he can powerfully punish people who have sinned'.

9:22c he tolerated patiently the people who caused him to be angry The phrase ἤνεγκεν ἐν πολλῇ μακροθυμίᾳ 'he endured in much forbearance' is a mismatched way of saying 'he tolerated very patiently'. The object of the verb is σκεύη ὀργῆς 'pots of anger', a continuation of the v. 21 metaphor. Since it is a live metaphor, it could be spelled out in the display as 'the people who cause God to be angry just as ill-formed pots cause the potter to be angry'. However, the metaphor, which is quite extended (see 20c-21b), here consists of only one word (as also in 23a). Therefore, it is rendered here simply by the topic of the metaphor, 'people'. CEV, NCV, LB, and TEV similarly remove the figurative language.

Some event relationship between 'pots' (i.e., people) and 'anger' (God is angry)' is required. If 'anger' is taken literally, then the sense is 'the people who caused God to be angry (because they have sinned)'. But if 'anger' is a metonymy standing for the result of God's anger, namely the punishment which results, then the sense of the phrase is 'the people who deserve to be punished (because they have sinned)'. The first of these two interpretations is chosen here because the punishment is mentioned in the following phrase and because both God's anger with sin and his power to punish it have already been mentioned in v. 22.

and who are made to be destroyed The final phrase in v. 22 is κατηρτισμένα εἰς ἀπώλειαν 'having been made/created unto destruction'. It is clear from the parallel phrase in v. 23, σκεύη ἐλέους ἃ προητοίμασεν εἰς δόξαν 'pots of mercy which he prepared beforehand unto glory', that a contrast is intended between the two phrases. The objection to taking the v. 22 phrase at face value is theological: the implication is that God has determined beforehand not only who will be saved but who will be eternally lost. (There are other passages that point to the former, e.g., Rom. 8:29, Acts 13:48, and Eph. 1:4, but none which mention the latter.) Either Paul indeed intended to say this, or else there is a second exegetical alternative for which textual clues need to be found.

In favor of the first alternative, it can be argued that (1) this seems to be the clear sense of the words, considering the contrastive parallelism; (2) there are other doctrines presented in only one passage but generally accepted as true; and (3) if predestination to eternal life is valid, the other must be true logically, simply by default.

In favor of the second alternative are the following points: (1) The verb in 22c is καταρτίζω, which in no way connotes 'beforehand' (contrast προκαταρτίζω 'arrange for beforehand' in 2 Cor. 9:5). The verb in 23c, on the other hand, does have προ- 'beforehand'. (2) The verb in 22c is a passive participle in the perfect tense, suggesting a possible ambiguity as to agent and time, while the verb in 23c is an active verb in the aorist tense, in which God is clearly the agent.

It is therefore likely that by using the verb καταρτίζω in v. 22 Paul is pointing to the people's having been made for and deserving of destruction, but not to the agent (whether God, or themselves, or even Satan). *What* has brought them to that state or *when* they are brought to it is not explicit. The display therefore renders the phrase as 'who are made to be destroyed' without suggesting an agent.

9:23a This verse is taken as supplying the purpose of v. 22. In the best Greek manuscripts it starts with καί 'and', and the fourth edition GNT includes καί with an A rating ("certain"). In some manuscripts καί is omitted, probably having been omitted by some scribe who took v. 23 as supplying the *only* purpose of v. 22 and therefore saw no function for καί.

God has been patient These words echo the idea of God's patience that is in 22c in order to provide a main clause for the ἵνα purpose clause to relate to in a new sentence.

in order that he might disclose how very gloriously/wonderfully he acts In the phrase τὸν πλοῦτον τῆς δόξης αὐτοῦ 'the riches of his glory', the word 'riches' is, semantically, a modifier of 'glory'. The word 'glory' is taken by most commentators as summarizing the attributes of God: 'how very glorious God is'. But several others suggest a slightly different alternative that seems more suitable to the context: 'how very gloriously God acts'. What God desires to reveal to the 'vessels of mercy' is "the glory of his boundless mercy" (Cranfield). This is the interpretation followed in the display. CEV is somewhere between with "showing how glorious he is when he has pity."

9:23b whom he intended to act mercifully towards The phrase σκεύη ἐλέους 'pots of mercy' parallels and contrasts with 'pots of anger' in 22c. But the semantic relationship between 'pots' and 'mercy' is not causative as it is between 'pots' and 'anger'. Rather, the sense here is 'those towards whom he intended/desired to act mercifully'.

9:23c in order that they might live gloriously *in heaven* The phrase εἰς δόξαν 'unto glory' is taken as expressing purpose, and 'glory' as referring to the state of believers in heaven. This word is also in 2:10 and 5:2, and the corresponding verb is in 8:17 and 8:30. For languages in which 'gloriously' is not easily translated, 'in heaven' may be a suitable substitute.

9:24 us whom he chose Here ἐκάλεσεν 'he called' is rendered as 'he chose' since the primary meaning of 'called' is not in view.

not only *us* Jews but also non-Jews The pronoun 'us' is supplied along with the word 'Jews' to make it clear that Paul himself was a Jew. For languages in which an inclusive-exclusive distinction exists, it is difficult to know which pronoun would be better here, because some of Paul's audience were Jews and many were not. The decision should be based on the reaction of the receptor-language speakers.

9:25a *God's right to choose from among both Jews and non-Jews is* also supported by what *God* says in *what was written by* Hosea Verses 25-26 present evidential grounds from the OT to support the argument that God chooses Gentiles as well as Jews to be among his own people, as stated in v. 24. Since there is no subject or verb to complete the statement introduced by ὡς in the orienter to the quotations, these are repeated from v. 24 and supplied in the display.

The phrase ἐν τῷ Ὡσηέ 'in Hosea' is a metonymy in which the writer stands for his writings. In some translations it will be necessary to say something like 'in the paper that Hosea (or, the prophet Hosea) wrote'.

9:25b I shall declare In this quotation (Hos. 2:23), the verb καλέσω 'I will call' is used in a somewhat extended sense to mean 'consider/declare that they are'. BAGD (p. 399.1aβ) give 'designate as' as the sense here.

are my people When God speaks of 'my people', the readers were normally intended to understand that the reference was to the Jews.

I shall declare that the people I did not *demonstrate that I* loved are ones I love The phrase τὴν οὐκ ἠγαπημένην 'the (people) not loved' refers to the non-Jews. But since it is not literally true that God did not love the Gentiles, the display softens this hyperbole with the supplied words 'demonstrate that'.

9:26 And This quotation (Hos. 1:10) is from a passage that precedes the one quoted in 25b. The LXX (from which this verse is quoted) has καί 'and' to begin the verse. The question here is, Is καί part of the quotation itself or does it introduce another Scripture quotation? Since the latter is actually the case, the display makes this specific. The NIV seems to be the only English version that takes the καί introducing this quotation as introducing a quotation separate from the previous one, although some versions (e.g., RSV, NCV) attempt to indicate it by beginning this verse with a new set of quotation marks.

in the places Here Hosea was referring to one specific place or area, namely the northern kingdom of Israel. Paul in citing it uses a singular form as in the LXX: ἐν τῷ τόπῳ 'in the place'. But Paul's intention is to refer to wherever Gentiles become God's people, hence the plural in the display. Alternatively, it could be translated as 'each place', retaining the singular.

***God* told them** The Greek is ἐρρέθη αὐτοῖς 'it was said to them', the agent being God and the referent of 'them' being the non-Jews. This can be made specific in a translation.

they are children of the God who is completely powerful The word 'sons' in υἱοὶ θεοῦ ζῶντος 'sons of the living God' (a dead metaphor) is rendered as the gender-neutral 'children'. The term 'living God' occurs some fifteen times in the OT, and fifteen in the NT. Although the term was originally used to contrast God with dead idols, in its NT usage it almost always has the connotation of 'all powerful', which is essential to the argument.

9:27a And Here δέ introduces a new grounds, another evidential grounds for Paul's statement in 22c–24. Paul now turns from the inclusion of the Gentiles to the fact that many Jews will be excluded.

concerning the Israelites Here the preposition ὑπέρ means 'concerning' (see BAGD, p. 839.1f).

9:27b Israelites Though the Hebrew term that is translated by the Greek as υἱῶν Ἰσραήλ 'sons of Israel' was originally used to mean 'the descendants of Israel/Jacob' in a literal sense, it soon came to mean the people of Israel as a nation, or the Jews. (It is so used 120 times in Exodus alone.) CEV has "the people of Israel"; LB, simply "the Jews."

are *as innumerable as* sand *particles beside* the sea The phrase 'sand of the sea' is taken to mean the sand which is along the shore of the sea. The point of similarity is innumerability. As in the display, this is made specific by REB, CEV, NCV, TEV, and JB.

9:27c *God* will save *only* the small part The word ὑπόλειμμα used to translate a Hebrew term in Isa. 10:22 means 'small left-over part, residue'. Most modern English translations supply the emphatic 'only' to modify 'remnant' due to the emphatic position in Greek of the phrase before the verb.

9:28 because, as he said he would do, the Lord will punish the *people of the* land This verse involves several problems. First of all, as a rendering of Isa. 10:23 it is very free. Second, the meaning that Paul gives to it is quite different from Isaiah's meaning (which is obscure to begin with). Moreover, it is difficult to understand the sense Paul intended by the two participles and one noun that he used. Finally, there is a textual uncertainty.

Regarding the last problem, it should be noted that support for the additional words in the Textus Receptus (ἐν δικαιοσύνῃ, ὅτι λόγον συντετμημένον 'in rigteousness, because [his] sentence [will be] shortened') is weak. These words appear in the LXX in Isa. 10:22–23; but since Paul so freely departs from the LXX in v. 27, it is not likely that he would have slavishly copied these words that are so hard to fit in grammatically. It is more likely that some scribe inserted them from the LXX to make up for Paul's apparent deficiency.

The noun λόγος in its primary sense means 'word', but as the object of the verb ποιήσει 'he will do', the phrase must mean 'the word that he said, he will do', and in this context 'he will carry out his threat'. The implication is 'carry out the threat to punish them (for their sin)'. The display thus renders it 'as he said he would . . . he will punish'. The manner clause is forefronted because it represents the word λόγον, which receives prominence by being the first word in the clause.

completely and speedily The first of the two participles here is συντελῶν. Literally, it means 'accomplishing', which by itself would add no meaning to that of the main verb ποιήσει 'he will do', being synonymous with it. But in combination with the next participle, it probably conveys the sense of 'with finality, decisively'. The second participle συντέμνων 'shortening, cutting off' is from a verb used nowhere else in the NT. This could refer to a shortening of his threat by only partially fulfilling it, but this is clearly opposed to the sense of the passage. It could refer to the cutting off of the number of the remnant, but this is likewise contrary to the context. The sense must be a shortening of the time required to complete the action; thus the two participles are rendered "with speed and finality" in the NIV and "will be summary and final" in the NEB. In the display the sense is the same but adverbs are used.

9:29a *And the fact that no one would be saved if God did not show mercy is shown by* **what** *the prophet* **Isaiah predicted** Verse 29 supports Paul's argument as an evidential grounds from Scripture, but again the main point that he supports is left unstated, the main point being that it is only by God's mercy that even a small number will be saved. (This is somewhat different from the main point in 27c, which was that only a small number would be saved.)

The word προείρηκεν could mean 'predicted', 'said long ago', or 'said previously'. A number of commentators prefer the last of these ('in a passage in Isaiah prior to the one I just quoted'). But "this would be a trivial literary observation" (Lenski) and is rejected for that reason as being unworthy of Paul. Similarly, 'said long ago' would be trivial and inappropriate considering that *all* the quotations of chapter 9 were written long ago. Therefore the first interpretation, which is the one given by BAGD (p. 704.1) and used in NRSV, is chosen for the display.

9:29b the Lord who controls everything in heaven The expression κύριος Σαβαώθ 'Lord of hosts' is a translation of a common OT phrase (occurring in some form sixty-two times in Isaiah alone). The word 'hosts' can refer to the sun, moon, and stars, or to the angels conceived of as constituting the army of heaven. The role relation signaled by the genitive is 'who rules/controls', hence 'the Lord who controls everything in heaven'. The 1988 edition of NCV has "Lord of heaven's armies," but the 1991 edition has "Lord All Powerful," as do NIV and CEV. Many translators may prefer to translate by using something equivalent to 'all powerful Lord', which would be taking the words to be figurative, a type of metonymy in which the grounds ('controls everything in heaven') stands for the conclusion ('he is all powerful').

descendants The word σπέρμα means 'descendants', as in v. 8.

we would have become like *the people of the city of* **Sodom, and . . .** *those in* **Gomorrah,** *the inhabitants of which cities God completely destroyed* The comparisons stated by ὡς Σόδομα . . . ὡς Γόμορρα 'like Sodom . . . like Gomorrah' are between groups of people, not between people and a city. The clauses form a doublet from a poetic passage in Isa. 1:9. Both are retained in the display, but one needs to make sure that readers do not get the impression that the fate of one was different from the fate of the other. The passage may have to be translated as 'become like the people in the cities of Sodom and Gomorrah' in some languages. The point of similarity is that they were both completely destroyed with no survivors. These words are supplied in the display to convey what Paul expected his readers to know.

BOUNDARIES AND COHERENCE

The relational coherence of the 9:19-29 paragraph is seen in its consisting of a hypothetical *objection* and Paul's REFUTATION of it and also by an extended metaphor involving pottery (vv. 20-24). The last five verses of the paragraph consist of a series of OT references supporting Paul's CLAIM. The boundary at 9:30 has already been discussed (see p. 211).

PROMINENCE AND THEME

The theme of 9:19-29 is drawn from the central elements of both the *objection* (19b-e) and the REFUTATION (20-29); in view of the two operative paragraph pattern levels, the theme draws from the naturally prominent propositions of both the CLAIM and *justification* in the REFUTATION. The rhetorical question in vv. 22-24 gives these verses a certain amount of prominence. The anantapodoton construction (a conditional clause without a statement of consequence) that begins with εἰ δὲ θέλων ὁ θεός 'but if God, wishing' is also a rhetorical device that creates prominence.

SUBDIVISION CLUSTER CONSTITUENT 9:30–10:21
(Expository Section: Correct evaluation of the Jews' rejection of Christ)

THEME: The Jews did not succeed in fulfilling what the Mosaic law requires; they tried to find a way to be declared righteous by doing things in order that God would accept them. The Jews do not understand how to seek him correctly, which according to Scripture is that if anyone, Jew or non-Jew, confesses publicly that Jesus is Lord and believes inwardly that God raised him from the dead, he will be saved. People have been sent to preach about Christ to the Jews, but most Jews have not accepted the gospel. They certainly have heard it and should have understood it, because even the non-Jews, who were not searching for God, understood it.

MACROSTRUCTURE	CONTENTS
CLAIM	9:30–33 The non-Jews found the way by which God could declare them righteous. The Jews did not succeed in fulfilling what the Mosaic law requires; they tried to find a way to be declared righteous by doing things in order that God would accept them.
Paul's feeling about the source of the problem	10:1–4 My deep desire and earnest prayer is that God would save the Jews, who do not understand how to seek him correctly.
justification for CLAIM	10:5–13 The message of Scripture is that if anyone confesses publicly that Jesus is Lord and believes inwardly that God raised him from the dead, he will be saved, because God treats Jews and non-Jews alike.
REFUTATION of objection to CLAIM	10:14–17 My reply to the objection that the Jews cannot ask Christ to save them if God does not send someone to preach to them is that God has sent people to preach about Christ to them, but most of the Jews have not accepted the gospel. People are indeed believing in Christ and people are indeed hearing the message.
RESPONSES to queries about CLAIM	10:18–21 In reply to a query of whether the Jews have heard or understood about Christ, I would say that, as is supported by Scripture, they have heard it and should have understood it, because even the non-Jews, who were not searching for God, understood it.

INTENT AND MACROSTRUCTURE

There are five paragraphs in 9:30–10:21. The first (30–33) is expository, containing two contrastive CLAIMS and the *justification* for the second one. The second (10:1–4) is expressive of Paul's feelings about the 9:30–33 CLAIM. The third (10:5–13) is expository, stating the *justification* supporting the CLAIM. The fourth and fifth are likewise expository, 10:14–17 refuting an anticipated objection and 10:18–21 responding to two hypothetical queries related to the 9:30–33 CLAIM. Since most of these paragraphs are expository, and since the first one is the CLAIM to which the others are related, the whole unit is considered expository.

BOUNDARIES AND COHERENCE

Though the 9:30–10:21 section is primarily focused on the Jews and their failure to heed the gospel, coherence as a unit is seen in references to the contrast between the responses of the Jews (Ἰσραήλ 'Israel') and of the Gentiles at the beginning of the section in 9:30–31 and at its very end in 10:20–21. The start of the next section is marked at 11:1 by οὖν 'therefore', the orienter λέγω 'I say', and a question that expresses a new anticipated query.

PROMINENCE AND THEME

The theme of 9:30–10:21 is drawn from the theme statements of all its constituent paragraphs. Since the first paragraph is the most prominent, expressing the CLAIM to which the other paragraphs relate, its theme is included in toto. The emotive part of the theme for the second paragraph is not included because it is less thematic (and in any case difficult to fit into the theme). The *justification* portion of the third paragraph is omitted as being less thematic. From the last two paragraphs the *objection* and the *queries* are likewise omitted from the 9:30–10:21 theme as being less thematic portions.

SECTION CONSTITUENT 9:30–33
(Expository Paragraph: Claim of 9:30–10:21)

THEME: *The non-Jews found the way by which God could declare them righteous. The Jews did not succeed in fulfilling what the Mosaic law requires; they tried to find a way to be declared righteous by doing things in order that God would accept them.*

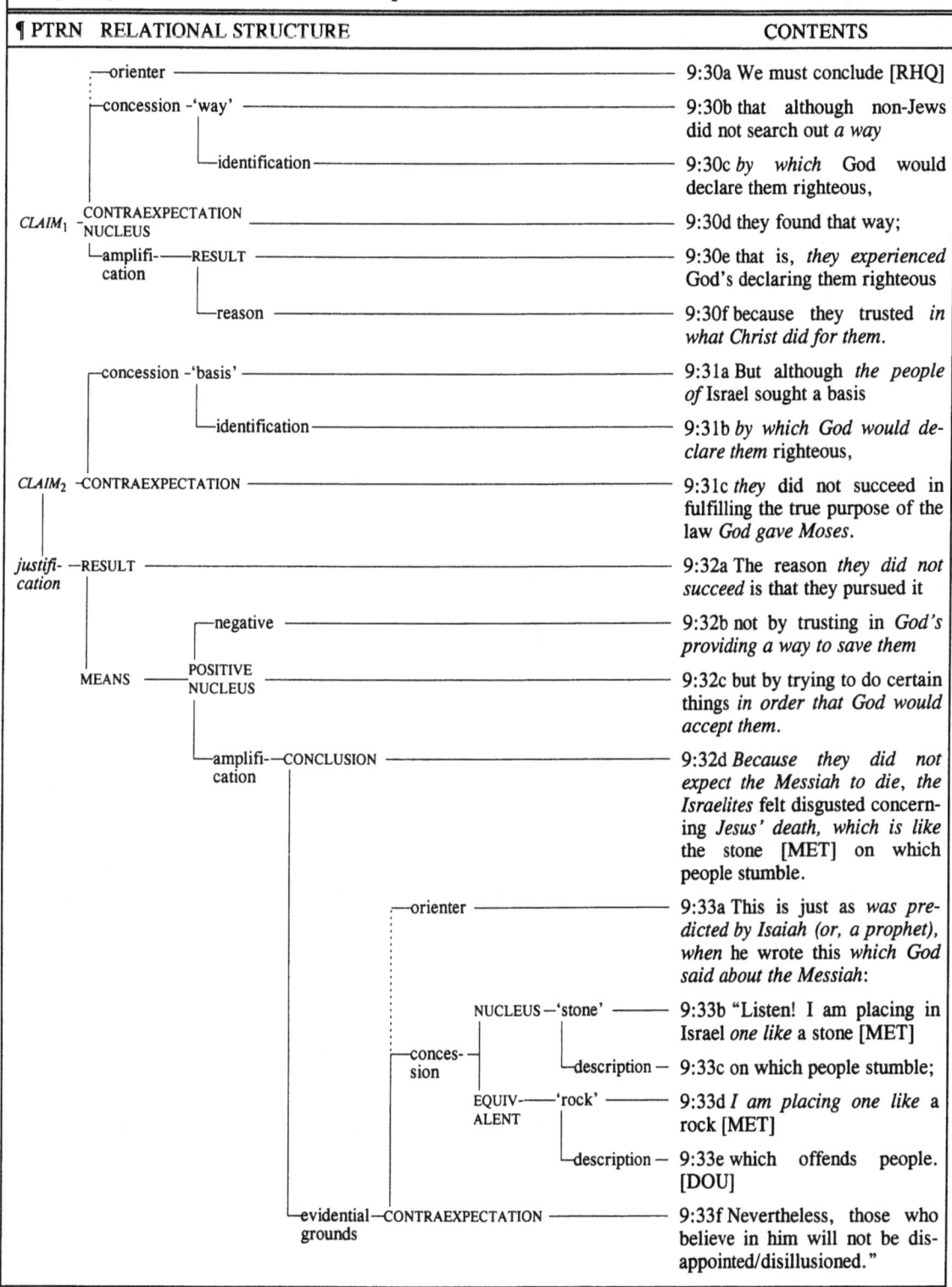

INTENT AND PARAGRAPH PATTERN

Since there do not seem to be elements of causality or solutionality between them, the three main parts of the 9:30-33 paragraph are considered to be CLAIMS (v. 30 and v. 31) referring to the contrast between Jews and Gentiles and a *justification* of the second CLAIM (vv. 32-33).

NOTES

9:30a We must conclude Verse 30 begins with τί οὖν ἐροῦμεν 'what therefore shall we say?' as do Rom. 4:1, 6:1, 7:7, 8:31, and 9:14. In some of these other occurrences an anticipated objection follows the question. But here there is only the question. Therefore it is taken as introducing a new part of the argument: a conclusion to be drawn from the preceding paragraphs. JB also removes the rhetorical question with "From this it follows that. . . ."

9:30b-c although non-Jews did not search out *a way by which* God would declare them righteous The phrase 'search out' is admittedly a bit metaphoric; in some languages it may be necessary to say 'try to find/seek'. The participial phrase τὰ μὴ διώκοντα δικαιοσύνην 'the ones not pursuing righteousness' is taken as in a concessive relationship with 30d. The alternative is to take it as descriptive of 'non-Jews'. There is little difference in the sense either way. Since 'righteousness' expresses both an event and an attribute concept semantically, it is expressed here as 'a way by which God could declare them righteous' (cf. NCV, CEV). For other ways of translating 'righteousness' see the note on 3:21.

9:30d-f they found that way; that is, *they experienced* God's declaring them righteous because they trusted *in what Christ did for them* The Greek here is κατέλαβεν δικαιοσύνην, δικαιοσύνην δὲ τὴν ἐκ πίστεως 'they attained righteousness, a righteousness which (is) from faith'. Since the two occurrences of 'righteousness' follow each other, and the second further develops the first, the second is taken as an amplification of the first, and in the display the first occurrence of 'righteousness' is rendered as 'that way' to avoid stating 'the way by which God could declare them righteous' three times in the same verse.

The problem of stating 'a way by which God could declare them righteous' as the object of the verb 'found' is handled by using the verb 'experienced' in the 30e amplification.

The noun πίστις 'faith' represents an event which may be expressed as 'trust' or 'believe'. This then requires a cognitive content as the goal, supplied here as 'in what Christ did for them'. An alternative would be 'believing that Christ died for their sin'. A shorter form, 'in Christ', would be possible in many languages.

9:31a-b although Grammatically, 31a parallels 30b, and the participle is again taken as expressing a concessive relationship.

a basis *by which God would declare them righteous* Commentators interpret the phrase νόμον δικαιοσύνης 'law of righteousness' in several ways. One suggestion is that 'law' is redundant and that the phrase simply means 'righteousness', but Paul is not known for using extra words to no purpose. A second suggestion, supported by several commentators and versions, is 'a righteousness which is based on (obeying) the law'. This fits with what Paul said in chapter 3, but if this is what Paul meant he certainly would have used a different grammatical construction (e.g., δικαιοσύνην διὰ/ἐκ νόμου 'righteous through/from law'). The third alternative is to take it as in 3:27b to mean 'basis/means' or 'principle/rule' (see the note on 3:27b). This is supported by a number of commentators. In certain languages, the actual means, 'by obeying God's laws', may have to be supplied to convey what Paul expected his readers to know.

9:31c *they* did not succeed in fulfilling the true purpose of the law *God gave Moses* The problem in εἰς νόμον οὐκ ἔφθασεν 'unto a law they did not attain' is whether 'law' here again means 'basis/means', giving the sense 'they did not attain such a law', or whether there is something of a play on the word 'law' so that here it means the law of Moses, giving the sense "they did not succeed in fulfilling that law" (NRSV). If the first alternative had been what Paul meant, he would have said τοιοῦτον νόμον 'such a law'. The second alternative seems closer to the sense and is therefore chosen for the display (cf. also JB, LB).

9:32a The reason *they did not succeed* is Dunn suggests that διὰ τί 'Why?' at this point expresses the shock that the Jewish reader would feel after reading the preceding statement. This 'Why?' prepares the reader to consider the defense Paul is about to make. In the display an attempt is made to convey this intention without a rhetorical question.

9:32a-c they pursued it not by trusting in *God's providing a way to save them* but by trying to do The phrases οὐκ ἐκ πίστεως 'not of/from faith' and ὡς ἐξ ἔργων 'as of/from works' contain no verb. Nearly all commentators and versions agree that the verb ἐδίωξα 'they pursued' from 31a is to be assumed.

The phrase 'of/from faith' in 32b occurs also in 30f, but it is not rendered exactly the same in both places. Means is the appropriate relationship in 32b, whereas reason fits in 30f. CEV's "instead of having faith in God" is inadequate: the Jews did believe in God, but not in what Christ had done.

9:32c by trying to do certain things *in order that God would accept them* The word ὡς 'as' ('as of works') indicates that this method was one that could not be successful—the Jews were mistaken to think it could be. An alternative to what is given in the display is 'thinking that by doing certain things'. Good alternatives to the phrase 'by works' would be 'by doing good deeds' (cf. JB) or 'by obeying the laws of Moses'. LB has both: "by keeping the law and being good." The way 'works' is rendered in the display makes the purpose of works specific, because this purpose, which Paul expected his Jewish readers to know, is a crucial part of his argument.

The Textus Receptus has νόμου 'of law' following ἔργων 'works'. It is evidently a scribal addition prompted by Paul's use of the longer expression in 3:20 and 28 and several times in Galatians. The shorter text has much stronger manuscript support and is given a B rating ("almost certain") in the fourth edition GNT.

9:32d *Because they did not expect the Messiah to die, the Israelites* felt disgusted concerning *Jesus' death, which is like* the stone on which people stumble The Greek is προσέκοψαν τῷ λίθῳ τοῦ προσκόμματος 'they stumbled at the stone of stumbling'. (This metaphor is more fully developed in v. 33.) The word play involved in the verb προσκόπτω 'stumble' and the noun πρόσκομμα 'stumbling' (which may be impossible to reproduce in translation) involves the word's two senses, the literal one and the extended sense 'feel repugnance for' (BAGD, p. 716). The literal sense of 'stumble' is in view when collocated with 'stone', but the Jews did not literally stumble—they felt repugnance at or were offended by the thing the stone stands for metaphorically. What offended them was Jesus' death on the cross, and this is made specific in the display (cf. Thomson, Sanday and Headlam). The specific reason the Jews felt repugnance is also made specific, because it is cultural information Paul expected his audience to know but which would not be understood in most cultures today. An alternative might be 'because they didn't think that any death was needed for their spiritual benefit'. The rendering in the display of the genitive phrase 'stone of stumbling' resolves the mismatch between the grammatical and semantic categories: 'stone on which people stumble'. In some languages it might be necessary to state the point of similarity between repugnance at Jesus' death and stumbling over a stone: rejection of the implications of Jesus' death is something that hinders spiritual progress just as falling over a stone hinders physical progress.

9:33a This is just as *was predicted by Isaiah (or, a prophet), when* he wrote this The phrase καθὼς γέγραπται 'as it is written' is often used to introduce an OT quotation that supports an argument, as it does here. But here the sense is 'which is just as was predicted by what was written' (cf. Hodge, Sanday and Headlam; also Norlie). The display supplies this; and as the agent of the predicting, 'Isaiah' or the generic 'prophet' is also supplied. Since Isaiah was mentioned in the text as the source of the quotation in v. 29, it is justified to supply his name here. (The source is Isa. 8:14 and 28:16.)

which God said about the Messiah The words 'which God said' are supplied so that it will be clear who 'I' in 33b refers to. The words 'about the Messiah' are supplied to clarify what Paul's Jewish audience already understood. That the 28:16 passage referred to the Messiah was generally understood in Jewish circles (cf. Dunn, Cranfield).

9:33b Listen! In its primary sense, the word ἰδού means 'behold!', but semantically it is just an attention-getter calling attention to the importance of what follows.

I am placing in Israel *one like* a stone The word 'Zion' in the phrase ἐν Σιών 'in Zion' is the name for the hill upon which Jerusalem was built. But it came to stand for Jerusalem itself and then for the nation of Israel. It is this last sense that Paul has in mind here, since he is speaking of the relation of Christ to the Jews as a whole. No matter which term is used in translation, it should be a meaningful term to the receptor-language audience. Even 'the land dominated by Mount Zion' is a good possibility.

The significance of the metaphor that begins τίθημι ἐν Σιὼν λίθον 'I am placing in Zion a stone' is made clear in 33f: that the stone refers to an individual. Therefore, in keeping with 33f, the display supplies 'one' (= a person) as the metaphor's topic. The word 'like' is used to show that this is a comparison.

9:33c on which people stumble See the note on 32d. LB tries to make the topic of the metaphor clear with "many will stumble over him (Jesus)," but it is anachronistic to put the name of Jesus in an OT quotation. Such specification needs to be done outside the quotation (see the second note on 33a).

9:33d-e a rock which offends people The metaphor continues with πέτραν σκανδάλου 'rock of offense'. The sense of 'offense' here is 'one who causes opposition' (BAGD, p. 753.3).

Moore (p. 41) considers 'stone that will make men stumble' (33b-c) and 'rock that will make them fall' (33d-e) to be a figurative doublet, which they undoubtedly are. But since this comes from a poetic OT passage, both are retained in the display.

9:33f those who believe in him The phrase ὁ πιστεύων ἐπ' αὐτῷ 'he who believes in him' is plural in the display (as in several modern versions) because of the generic sense; in some languages a singular rendering would be taken as referring to some one individual. The word 'believe' (or 'trust') may require a full clause to supply its content, such as 'in what he has done for them'.

In the Textus Receptus the word πᾶς 'all' appears, added to 'those who' evidently to make the claim more vivid and to correspond with the same quotation in 10:11. But πᾶς does not appear in the better manuscripts, that is, the much older ones from across a much wider geographical area. The text followed in the display is given an A rating ("certain") in the fourth edition GNT.

BOUNDARIES AND COHERENCE

Relational coherence in the 9:30-33 paragraph is shown by its consisting of two contrasting CLAIMS (one regarding the non-Jews and one regarding the Jews) and a *justification* for the second CLAIM. One bit of lexical coherence in this paragraph is seen in four occurrences of δικαιοσύνη 'righteousness'.

The boundary with the following paragraph is marked by a vocative, ἀδελφοί 'brethren', in 10:1 and an emotive expression about the Jews.

PROMINENCE AND THEME

The theme of 9:30-33 is drawn from the naturally prominent elements of the two CLAIMS and the RESULT and MEANS propositions of the *justification*, which are needed to express a complete thought. From within the first CLAIM, parts of 30b-c are included along with the CONTRAEXPECTATION in 30d for the purpose of identifying the pronoun 'they' and the demonstrative 'that way'.

SECTION CONSTITUENT 10:1-4 (Expressive Paragraph: Paul's feeling about the source of the problem of 9:1-11:36)

THEME: My deep desire and earnest prayer is that God would save the Jews, who do not understand how to seek him correctly.

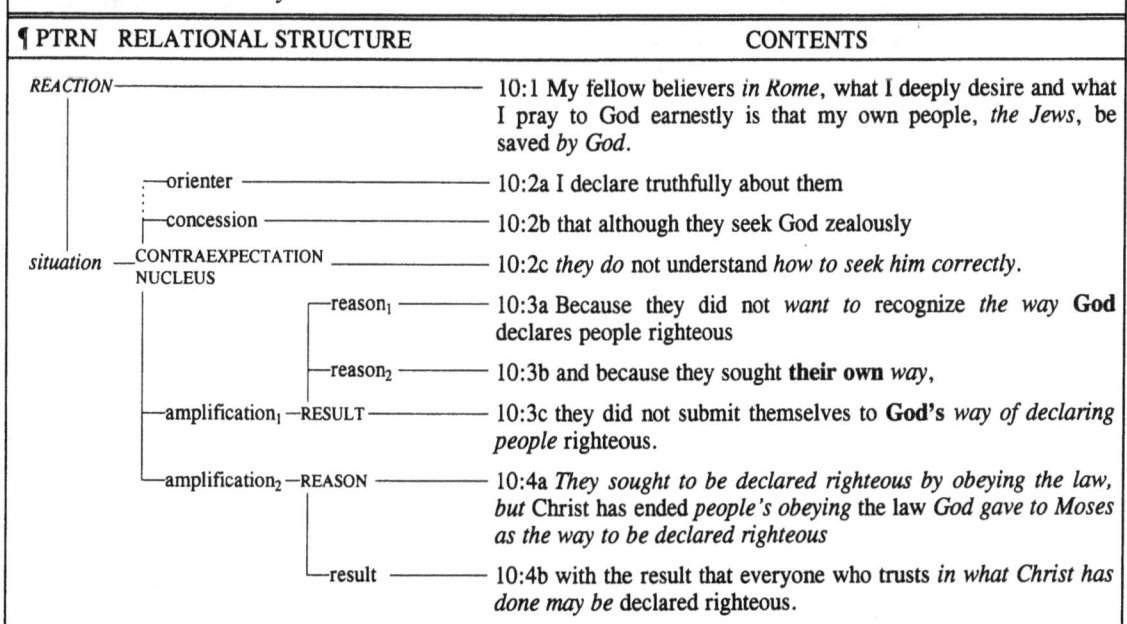

INTENT AND PARAGRAPH PATTERN

The 10:1-4 paragraph continues the topic of God's apparent rejection of the Jews. The first sentence expresses Paul's hope or desire and is considered his REACTION to the problem of the Jews' rejection of Christ, thus putting the paragraph into the expressive genre. Verses 2-4, introduced by γάρ, express the *situation* that gave rise to Paul's feelings.

NOTES

10:1 My fellow believers *in Rome* The word ἀδελφοί 'brothers' is here rendered 'fellow believers' as usual. The words 'in Rome' are supplied, not for semantic necessity, but to remind the receptor-language readers that Paul's addressees were in Rome.

what I deeply desire and what I pray to God earnestly is that my own people, *the Jews*, be saved *by God* In the best Greek manuscripts there is no verb in this verse. In some manuscripts the verb 'to be' has been inserted to take care of the grammatical ellipsis. But the main semantic events are conveyed by εὐδοκία 'desire' and δέησις 'prayer', both of which are nouns, apparently a device to heighten the expression of Paul's emotion. In the display this is represented by 'what I desire and what I pray is that'. The figurative expression τῆς ἐμῆς καρδίας 'of my heart' is rendered by 'deeply', a nonfigurative equivalent (cf. 9:2b).

The phrase εἰς σωτηρίαν 'unto salvation' technically presents the goal or purpose of Paul's prayer, but at the same time it is the content of his prayer. In the display it is represented as 'be saved *by God*'. The focus is not on the agent at all; use of an agent should be avoided if possible (e.g., the passive 'that they will be saved' would be better).

The display identifies 'them' as 'my own people, the Jews', repeated from 9:3. The words 'of Israel', which convey almost the same sense, are found in a great many Western texts, and hence in the KJV. To identify 'them', the majority of versions supply some phrase such as 'the people of Israel', 'the Jews', or 'my own people'.

10:2a I declare truthfully about them Here γάρ introduces not so much a logical reason or grounds for the statement in v. 1, but the situation which lies behind Paul's emotional expression.

The word μαρτυρῶ 'I witness' is expressed in the display as 'I declare truthfully'.

10:2b they seek God zealously The words ζῆλον θεοῦ ἔχουσιν 'a zeal of God they have' are a mismatched way of saying 'they seek God zealously/energetically'.

10:2c they do not understand how to seek him correctly The phrase οὐ κατ' ἐπίγνωσιν 'not according to knowledge' must mean 'not according to proper knowledge of how to seek him'. In keeping with this, typical renderings are "they do not know the right way" (NCV), "correct views" (Barnes), "accurate apprehension" (Alford), "proper understanding" (Stuart).

10:3a–b Here γάρ introduces an amplification of 2c, not a reason for it.

Because they did not *want to* recognize *the way* God declares people righteous and because they sought their own *way* The two present participles here, ἀγνοοῦντες 'not knowing' and ζητοῦντες 'seeking', precede the main verb and are taken as expressing reasons. As many commentators point out, the verb ἀγνοέω here means "to fail to recognize" (Dodd) or "misunderstand" (Michel). REB renders it "ignored." BAGD (p. 11.2) suggest "disregard" (so also NIV), hence the rendering in the display.

What they disregarded was τὴν τοῦ θεοῦ δικαιοσύνην 'the of God righteousness'. The genitive 'of God' is taken to mean 'the way God declares people righteous' (cf. 3:21, 9:31). It is in an emphatic position, and this emphasis is conveyed by bold type here.

The words τὴν ἰδίαν 'their own' occur before the verb and are thereby emphatic, hence the bold type in the display. The supplied word 'way' is repeated from 3a.

10:3c they did not submit themselves to God's way of declaring people righteous The words 'righteousness of God' are rendered as in 3a. In the Greek they occur before the verb and are thereby emphasized (by way of contrast). This emphasis on 'God's' in contrast to 'their own' is shown by bold type in the display.

10:4 Commentators are divided as to how this verse relates to what precedes it. Some (Murray, Cranfield) take it as giving the reason for v. 3, but it does not cohere relationally as the reason for v. 3: Christ's ending obedience to the law was not the *reason* the Jews did not submit to this way of being declared righteous. Denney and also Sanday and Headlam take v. 4 as the reason for 2c, which is close to how it is interpreted in the display. Morris says it gives the reason for what was implied in v. 3, that "they were wrong in the way they looked for righteousness." The verse coheres very well as an amplification of 2c, if one understands the whole verse to be saying 'they sought to be declared righteous by obeying the law, but Christ has ended the law . . .'.

10:4a Christ has ended *people's obeying* the law *God gave to Moses as the way to be declared righteous* There are several possible interpretations for the phrase τέλος νόμου 'end of the law' used to describe Christ. A few commentators support 'object/aim of the law', in the sense that Christ "brings about that which the law was designed to accomplish" (Stuart). This might be true, but does not fit the context. Another interpretation is that Christ meets all the requirements of the law, which likewise might be true, but again does not fit the context. The context is about the Jews' failure to seek a proper way of being declared righteous, not what Christ did to fulfill the law. The vast majority of commentators and versions support the interpretation that Christ terminated the law. The question then is, In what way is the law ended? In this context the answer, as Morris states, is that it is "an end to the law of Moses considered as a way of attaining righteousness." Since the rendering in the display is somewhat awkward grammatically, a better alternative might be 'has made unnecessary our obeying the law in order to be declared righteous' or 'has said we can cease trying to be declared righteous by obeying the law'. JBP has "Christ means the end of the struggle for righteousness by the Law," which carries the sense quite well. Most commentators who say anything about the preposition εἰς take it as signifying result, which is probably the intended meaning of "so that" in NIV, TEV, and NCV.

10:4b who trusts *in what Christ has done* The phrase δικαιοσύνην παντὶ τῷ πιστεύοντι 'righteousness unto every (one) who believes' is a mismatched way of saying 'everyone who believes is declared righteous'. As elsewhere, the display supplies 'in what he has done' as the implicit cognitive content of 'believe/trust'.

BOUNDARIES AND COHERENCE

The 10:1–4 paragraph is relationally coherent in that it consists of Paul's REACTION (v. 1) to the *situation* (vv. 2–4) regarding the Jews. Lexical coherence is provided by occurrences of δικαιοσύνη 'righteousness', which occurs at least twice in v. 3 and once in v. 4. (The third occurrence in v. 3 is found in brackets in the fourth edition GNT, meaning it is of dubious textual validity; but it is in any case clearly implied.)

The boundary between the 10:1-4 paragraph and the following one is marked by γάρ in 10:5, which introduces not a reason for any statement in 10:1-4, but a return to Paul's general argument regarding the source of the problem of the Jews' rejection of Christ from a human perspective.

PROMINENCE AND THEME

The theme of 10:1-4 is drawn from the statement in v. 1 of Paul's *REACTION* to the problem of the Jews (their rejection of the gospel) and from the naturally prominent CONTRAEXPECTATION/NUCLEUS proposition in 2c that describes the *situation* at the heart of the problem.

SECTION CONSTITUENT 10:5-13
(Expository Paragraph: Justification for the claim in 9:30-33)

THEME: The message of Scripture is that if anyone confesses publicly that Jesus is Lord and believes inwardly that God raised him from the dead, he will be saved, because God treats Jews and non-Jews alike.

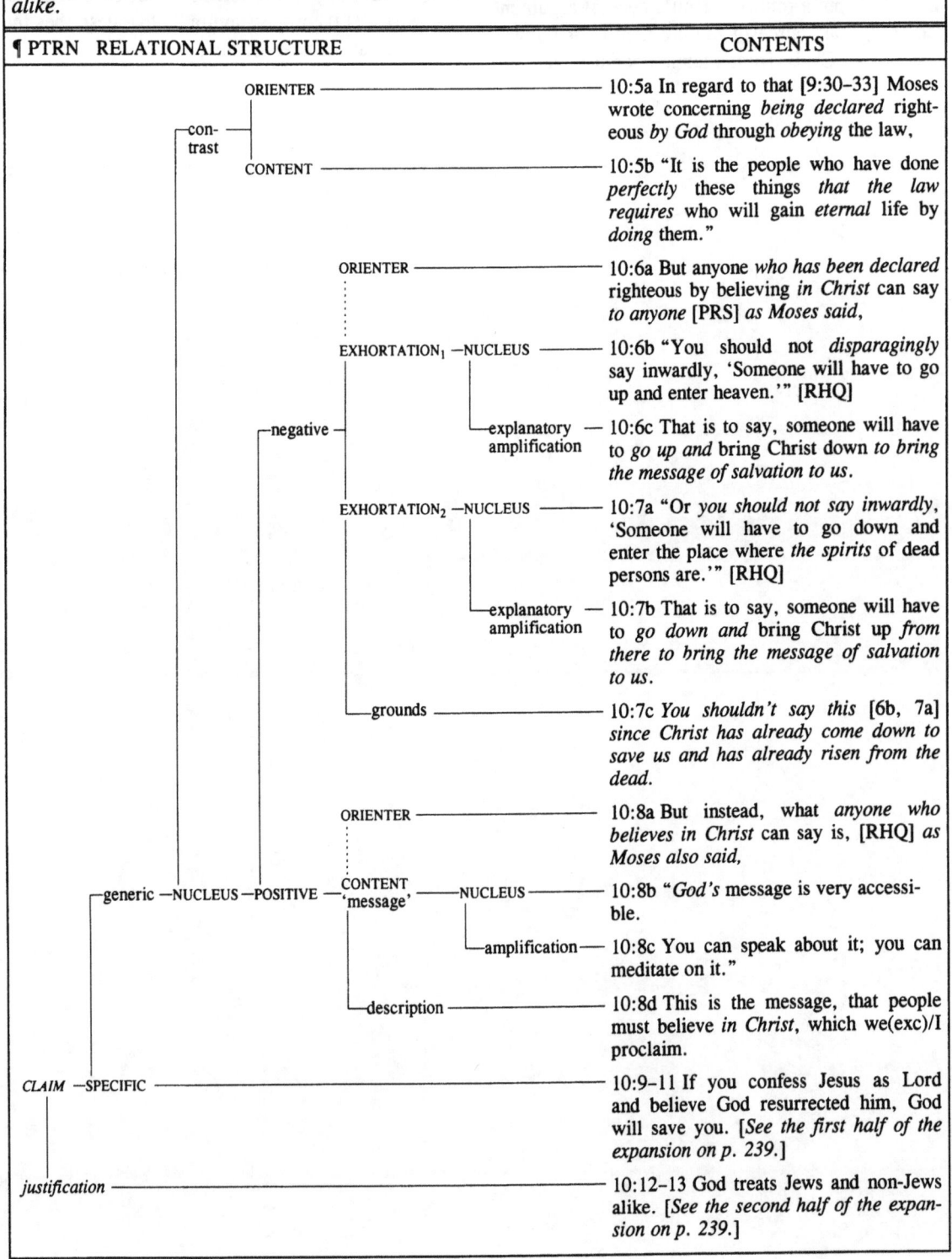

INTENT AND PARAGRAPH PATTERN

There are a number of Scripture quotations in the 10:5-13 paragraph leading up to the SPECIFIC statement of the CLAIM in v. 9 about whom God will save. Thus this is an expository paragraph. The CLAIM is supported by a factual *justification* in vv. 12-13.

NOTES

10:5 Granted that γάρ 'for' introduces what follows as evidence for what precedes, should the 10:5-13 paragraph be taken as relating to 9:30-33 or to 10:1-4? Cranfield supports the latter interpretation, saying that it is in some way "explanatory of v. 4." But 10:5-13 does not provide an explanation for the *situation-REACTION* of vv. 1-4. Furthermore, the two types of righteousness (by obedience of law vs. by faith) are clearly contrasted in both 9:30-33 and 10:5-13, but not in 10:1-4. All this suggests that 10:5-13 relates back to 9:30-33, not to 10:1-4. It is recognized, however, that 10:4 is in a real sense a crucial transition to what follows, what Cranfield calls "one of the fundamental theses of Pauline theology as a whole." In v. 5 γάρ builds on that transition. All the versions make a paragraph break here; TEV, JB, and NCV have section headings.

10:5a In regard to that [9:30-33] Since this paragraph relates to 9:30-33, it may be useful in some languages to summarize 9:30-33 by saying something like 'In regard to the Jews not succeeding in fulfilling what the Mosaic law requires. . . .'

concerning *being declared* righteous *by God* through *obeying* the law GNT's fourth edition has τὴν δικαιοσύνην τὴν ἐκ τοῦ νόμου '(concerning) the righteousness from the law'. Here 'righteousness' is rendered as 'being declared righteous by God' (but see the note on 3:21). The words 'from the law' may be rendered 'by/through the law', supplying the implicit verb 'obeying' as in TEV and CEV. JB has "keep the law"; NCV, "follow the law."

10:5b It is the people who have done *perfectly* these things *that the law requires* The Greek is ὁ ποιήσας αὐτὰ ἄνθρωπος 'the having done these things man'. Since 'the man' is used in a generic and not a definite singular sense, it is plural in the display: 'the people'. The word 'completely' or 'perfectly' is implied as a modifier of the verb 'have done' (supported by Paul's statement in 3:20 that no one can be declared righteous by works). JBP renders it similarly ("perfectly obeys"), as does LB ("could be perfectly good . . . and never sin once"). This sense is probably implied by the fact that the clause 'who has done these things' is in the emphatic position preceding the noun 'man' which it modifies.

The pronoun 'these (things)', which is the object of the verb 'has done', probably needs to be specified to avoid ambiguity or zero meaning. The display supplies 'that the law requires'. TEV has "what the law commands"; Beck, "demanded by the law"; and Hodge, "the things prescribed in the law."

There are two significant textual problems in this verse. First, in quite a few Greek manuscripts the conjunction ὅτι occurs before the words τὴν δικαιοσύνην in 5a. But the evidence for its position here before ὁ ποιήσας is strong: a copyist would have been much more likely to move it from its position later in the sentence to a position earlier in the sentence than vice versa. Some copyists evidently thought it was much more natural to have ὅτι 'that' immediately follow the words 'Moses wrote', considering 'the righteousness of the law' to be part of what Moses wrote. The only difference in meaning would be that everything following γράφει 'he writes' would be part of the quotation (but this would make it difficult to fit 'the righteousness from the law' into the rest of the clause). The second textual problem is whether the pronoun αὐτά belongs in the text. It was probably omitted deliberately by some copyist because of the lack of an antecedent for it or because it was not part of the original OT passage. (Its omission is not even mentioned in the fourth edition GNT.)

who will gain *eternal* life by *doing* them The final words in the quotation as found in the best Greek manuscripts and GNT are ζήσεται ἐν αὐτοῖς 'will live in them'. It is probable that Paul gives to these words a different sense from that in Lev. 18:5. The context here in Romans concerns whether a person is justified or not, not his manner of life. Following BAGD (p. 336.2bβ) the display has 'have eternal life'. NEB has "gain life by it"; NCV, "have life forever."

The phrase 'in them' is an abbreviated means expression, with the verb 'doing' being implicit. Although there is a fair amount of manuscript evidence to support a singular pronoun instead of 'them' in this final phrase (with manuscript variations on contiguous words), the singular form was probably a change made from the plural by an early copyist who, having a manuscript without the word αὐτά (see the previous note), saw no plural antecedent nearby and so took it to refer to 'law' earlier in the verse.

10:6a anyone *who has been declared* righteous by believing *in Christ* can say *to anyone as Moses said* The Greek is ἡ ἐκ πίστεως δικαιοσύνη οὕτως λέγει 'the by faith righteousness thus says'. This personification is rendered here by making the agent generic: 'anyone who'. CEV has "people who" as the subject. An alternative is to completely recast the clause with something like NCV's "This is what the Scripture says about being made right through faith." The words 'in Christ' are supplied as the cognitive content of 'believe'; but in some languages something like 'trusting in what Christ has done' may be preferred (or required). Since no specific Christian is in view who actually uttered the words that follow, 'he says' is rendered as 'can say'; 'to anyone' is supplied as a generic antecedent for 'you' in 6b. The words 'as Moses said' show that what follows is an OT quotation (Deut. 30:12-14). As Dunn states, "The text is too close to that of the Deuteronomy passage to be accidental."

10:6b You should not *disparagingly* say inwardly The idiomatic phrase ἐν τῇ καρδίᾳ σου 'in your heart' is rendered as 'inwardly'. The word 'disparagingly' is included to carry some of the impact of the rhetorical question, here rendered as a positive statement (so also LB). Lenski has "the man who has this question in his heart would be left helpless and hopeless," but it would be more correct to say that Paul conceives of an objector asking the questions that follow with a very critical attitude toward what Paul has said thus far.

10:6b, 7a Someone will have to go up and enter heaven. . . . Someone will have to go down The questions in 6b and 7a that begin with τίς 'Who?' are taken as rhetorical questions that express the emotion of doubt or unbelief (Bruce 1963, Shedd, Murray, Whedon) or hopelessness (Lenski). In the display, they are changed to statements, the emotion being conveyed by the word 'disparagingly' in the introduction to the quotation. In many languages, rhetorical questions would be appropriate, with either 'Who?' or 'Will someone have to?'

10:6c someone will have to *go up and* bring Christ down *to bring the message of salvation to us* These words represent Paul's comment; they are not part of the quotation. The same is true of 7b. The words 'go up and' are supplied to make 6c correspond with 6b and because they represent an implicit intervening action.

The italicized words at the end of 6c are supplied as the contextually implicit purpose of the action. Alternatives are 'to teach us God's truth' and 'to explain God's way of salvation to us'. LB has the generic "to help you." The point Paul makes in v. 8 is that the message of salvation was already with them (Hodge, Murray, Barrett). The translator should make it clear that 6c is Paul's explanation, not part of Deut. 30. (It is almost impossible to show this in the display.)

10:7a the place where *the spirits* of dead persons are The word ἄβυσσος 'abyss' means "the abode of the dead" (BAGD, p. 2.2). The words 'the spirits of' are included in the display to avoid wrong meaning concerning the nature of such people.

10:7b See the note on 6c.

10:7c This proposition is supplied because it is implicit as the reason why neither the 6b nor 7a statement of doubt is appropriate (Cranfield, Sanday and Headlam, Hodge, Harrison).

10:8a But instead, what *anyone who believes in Christ* can say is As in 6a, λέγει 'it says' is rendered as 'he can say', 'he' referring to anyone justified by faith. CEV renders the sense very well: "All who are acceptable because of their faith simply say."

In the Greek, τί 'What?' begins a rhetorical question that is translated as a statement by TEV, JB, and JBP. Its force is to focus attention on what follows as a positive statement contrasting with the negative ones in 6b and 7a. As in the display, TEV attempts to convey this with "What it says is this."

as Moses also said As in 6a, the display makes clear that Paul is citing these words from Scripture (Deut. 30:14).

10:8b *God's* message is very accessible The word ῥῆμα is rendered here as 'God's message' (so TEV). BAGD (p. 735.1) suggest 'gospel', as do Hodge, Barrett, Harrison, and Denney. The words ἐγγύς σου 'near you' are somewhat figurative; in this context they mean 'very accessible'. LB has "within easy reach of us."

10:8c You can speak about it; you can meditate on it The phrases 'in your mouth' and 'in your heart' are metonymies in which the place stands for the event associated with it. They mean, respectively, 'you are able to talk about them' (Lenski, Barnes) and 'you can think about them' (cf. Stuart, Barnes).

It is recognized that there is some kind of connection between the words στόμα 'mouth' and καρδία 'heart' when they occur together as they do here three times in vv. 8–10 (and also in Matt. 12:34, 15:18, and Luke 6:45). The connection is blurred by rendering the figures nonfiguratively. In translating, it may be possible to use appropriate body parts and retain some of the imagery simply by adding something like 'with your mouth/lips', 'within your hearts/minds/livers'. LB has "it is as near as our own hearts and mouths." Moore (p. 41) considers the figures here to be a doublet, but that is not the interpretation taken here. Rather the words 'near you' in 8b are taken as generic, and the phrases 'on your lips' and 'in your heart' in 8c are taken as figurative amplifications (metonymies, the body parts standing for the events associated with each).

10:8d This is the message, that people must believe *in Christ* The phrase ῥῆμα τῆς πίστεως 'word of faith' has been taken by some commentators as 'message concerning faith' and by others as 'message that is to be believed'. As Hodge and Dunn indicate, there is little difference in the sense either way and Paul may have intended both. The display tries to preserve some of the ambiguity.

which we(exc)/I proclaim Most commentators assume that Paul and the other apostles are in view as the subject of κηρύσσομεν 'we preach'. But it may well be that it is the editorial 'we', referring to Paul alone (see Alford). Lenski offers a third possibility: that it means all Christians, in which case it would be 'we(inc)'.

EXPANSION OF THE *CLAIM'S SPECIFIC* AND ITS *JUSTIFICATION* IN THE 10:5-13 DISPLAY

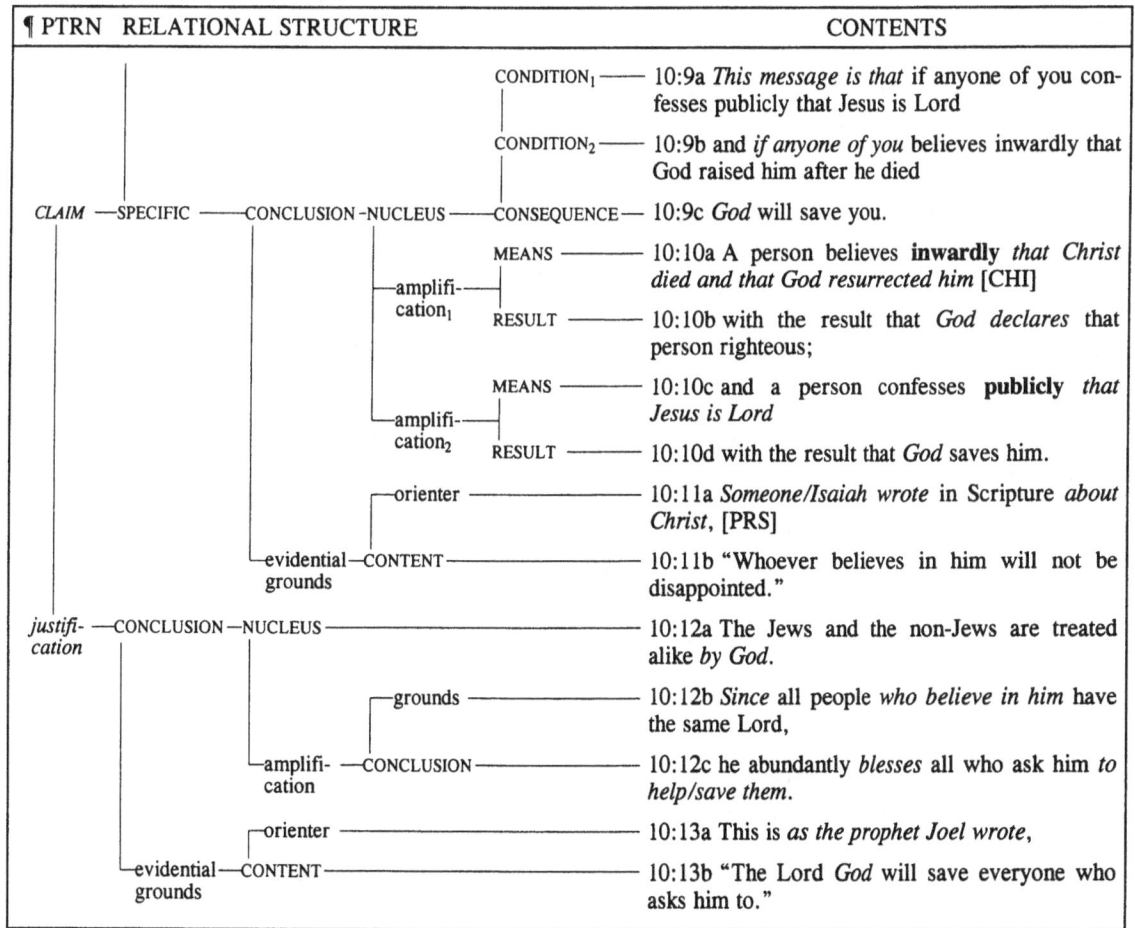

10:9a *This message is that* **if any one of you confess publicly that Jesus is Lord** The word ὅτι introducing this verse could mean either 'that' or 'because'. The former, which signals the content of what Paul and others preach, is chosen here because semantically v. 9 does not cohere well as the reason for 8b-c, and also because 9a and 9b are obviously related to the phrases 'in your mouth' and 'in your heart' in 8c. Note that Paul follows the order of the phrases in the quotation, though chronologically we expect belief 'in your heart' to precede confession 'with your mouth'.

As some commentators suggest, 8d is a somewhat parenthetical comment regarding 'the message of faith'. So to maintain the connection with 8b-d, v. 9 is made to begin a new sentence with the words 'This message is that' supplied.

The subject of the verb 'confess' is a second person singular pronoun, but the sense is generic, 'anyone'. Paul is not here addressing some particular individual.

The words ἐν τῷ στόματί σου 'in thy mouth' are an idiom meaning 'publicly' (also in 10c). They could be taken as a metonymy meaning 'by what he says', but this would be redundant and inappropriate unless this were a poetic passage, which it is not. The rendering in the display follows Shedd, Barnes, Hodge, Dunn, and others.

The words κύριον Ἰησοῦν 'Lord Jesus' have the sense '(that) Jesus is Lord', an expression of the supreme lordship of Christ in view of his deity and not so much of his lordship over the person making the confession.

10:9b inwardly The Greek is ἐν τῇ καρδίᾳ σου 'in thy heart'. See 6b.

10:10a-d Here γάρ introduces an amplification of the public confession and inward belief mentioned in v. 9, not a reason for it. Of the versions examined, three (CEV, NCV, and JB) seem to indicate this by using asyndeton here. In this verse the two events are discussed in the proper chronological sequence. The structure of the two verses is thus a chiasmus.

10:10a believes inwardly *that Christ died and that God resurrected him* In the Greek there is no cognitive content for the object of the impersonal passive verb 'believe'. Paul is talking about faith in general, but of course he means faith in what Christ has done. The display supplies the cognitive content from the context: 'that Christ died but God resurrected him'. Appropriate alternatives are 'the message about Christ' or 'the gospel'. In a language that does not require an object of the verb to be expressed, it would be best to leave the cognitive content unspecified.

10:10a, c inwardly . . . publicly The phrase 'in (your) heart' is rendered 'inwardly' in the display, and the phrase 'with the mouth' is rendered 'publicly'. The emphasis these phrases receive by virtue of an initial position in their respective clauses is shown by bold type.

10:10b-d with the result that *God declares* **the person righteous; and . . . with the result that** *God* **saves him** The prepositional phrases εἰς δικαιοσύνην 'unto righteousness' and εἰς σωτηρίαν 'unto salvation' indicate result; they are expressed as clauses in the display. But, as pointed out by both Morris and Bullinger, it is not that the one action leads to the one result and the other action to the other result; they both lead to both results.

10:11a *Someone/Isaiah wrote* **in Scripture** *about Christ* Here γάρ introduces Scripture, Isa. 28:16, quoted as evidential grounds for the statements in vv. 9-10. The words λέγει ἡ γραφή 'the Scripture says' are rendered 'someone/Isaiah wrote in Scripture', removing the personification (cf. 4:3 and 9:17). The words 'about Christ' are supplied to serve as the antecedent for 'him' in the quotation that follows.

10:11b Whoever believes in him will not be disappointed The verb καταισχυνθήσεται means 'will be disappointed' (BAGD, p. 411). In some languages a statement of the reason for or reference of the disappointment may be needed. Lenski suggests "as far as righteousness (justification) and salvation are concerned when he faces God and his judgment."

10:12a-b Several commentators say that here Paul "gives the reason for the 'whosoever' of verse 11" (Murray; see also Hodge, Newman and Nida). Several commentators do not discuss relationships, including Dunn, who points out that "this is the positive equivalent of 3:22" (also Barrett). But it would be most unusual to have these two verses hinge on only the word πᾶς 'everyone' in v. 11 and not on the whole verse. The interpretation given here is that γάρ introduces the *justification* for the main CLAIM in vv. 9-10. By doing so, this allows the v. 12 NUCLEUS statement to appear in the theme for the paragraph. Without this, it is very difficult to see how 10:5–13 fits into the argument Paul is making in chapters 9 to 11. That is, making vv. 10–12 an amplification of 'whoever' in 11b would reduce its prominence and there would be no mention of Jews and Gentiles in the theme for this paragraph. Yet these two groups *are* the central participants of Paul's exposition in these three chapters.

10:12a The Jews and the non-Jews are treated alike *by God* Here γαρ is introducing all of v. 12 as the *justification* for the CLAIM stated in v. 9. The word Ἕλλην 'Greek' refers to Gentiles here, as it most frequently does in the NT (BAGD, p. 252.2a). The statement 'there is no difference between Jews and Gentiles' obviously needs qualification. Barnes suggests "in regard to justification before God"; Murray suggests "in respect of sin and condemnation, on the one hand, and opportunity of salvation, on the other"; Hodge suggests "in relation to the law or to God." Instead of choosing one of these, a different approach is taken for the display, with the positive statement 'are treated alike by God'.

10:12b This proposition supplies the grounds for 12c, not a reason why God treats them equally (12a). The γάρ here is introducing 12b–c as an amplification of 12a.

all people *who believe in him* **have the same Lord** The phrase ὁ αὐτὸς κύριος πάντων 'the same Lord of all' is an elliptical way of saying 'the same (Lord is) Lord of all'. The 'all' needs qualification, and in the light of 11b the words 'who believe in him' are supplied. An alternative to the wording in the display is 'there is only one person/Lord who is Lord of all *who believe in him*'.

10:12c he abundantly *blesses* **all** The Greek is πλουτῶν εἰς πάντας τοὺς ἐπικαλουμένους αὐτόν 'is rich unto all who call on him'. Here the verb πλουτέω, which is usually rendered in English by 'is rich', is an attribute modifying an implied verb. It is not to be taken in its literal sense, but means 'gives generously' (BAGD, p. 674.2). But since giving is not in focus in this passage, the display renders it as 'abundantly blesses'. TEV has "richly blesses"; NCV, "give many blessings to."

who ask him *to help/save them* The verb 'call on' means 'to appeal to someone for aid' (BAGD, p. 294.2b).

10:13a This is *as the prophet Joel wrote* Here γάρ again introduces a Scripture passage as evidential grounds to support the previous statement. The passage is assumed to be so well known to his readers that Paul gives no introduction to it such as 'it is written'. But since it may not be so well known by receptor-language readers, the display supplies 'It is as the prophet Joel wrote'. A good alternative is 'as a prophet wrote in Scripture' (cf. TEV's "as the Scripture says").

10:13b "The Lord *God* **will save everyone who asks him to"** Here 'the name of' is omitted from the Joel 2:32 quotation because "To call on the name of the Lord is the same as to call on the Lord himself" (Barnes).

BOUNDARIES AND COHERENCE

The 10:5–13 paragraph is relationally coherent in that it consists of a CLAIM (vv. 5–11) and the *justification* for it (vv. 12–13). Coherence is also provided by a series of five Scripture quotations given as evidential grounds for Paul's CLAIM. There is a certain amount of lexical coherence in the recurring words στόμα 'mouth' and καρδία 'heart' in vv. 8–10 (arranged chiastically).

The boundary with 10:14–17 is marked by the fact that that paragraph contains a series of four uninterrupted rhetorical questions.

PROMINENCE AND THEME

The theme of 10:5–13 is mainly drawn from the naturally prominent elements of the CLAIM and its *justification*, namely 9a–c and 12a. The initial words of the theme ("The message of Scripture is that") are added because everything leading up to v. 9 centers around the accessibility of the message, and one can hardly talk about 'the message' without defining it.

SECTION CONSTITUENT 10:14-17
(Expository Paragraph: Refutation of objection to the claim in 9:30-10:21)

THEME: My reply to the objection that the Jews cannot ask Christ to save them if God does not send someone to preach to them is that God has sent people to preach about Christ to them, but most of the Jews have not accepted the gospel. People are indeed believing in Christ and people are indeed hearing the message.

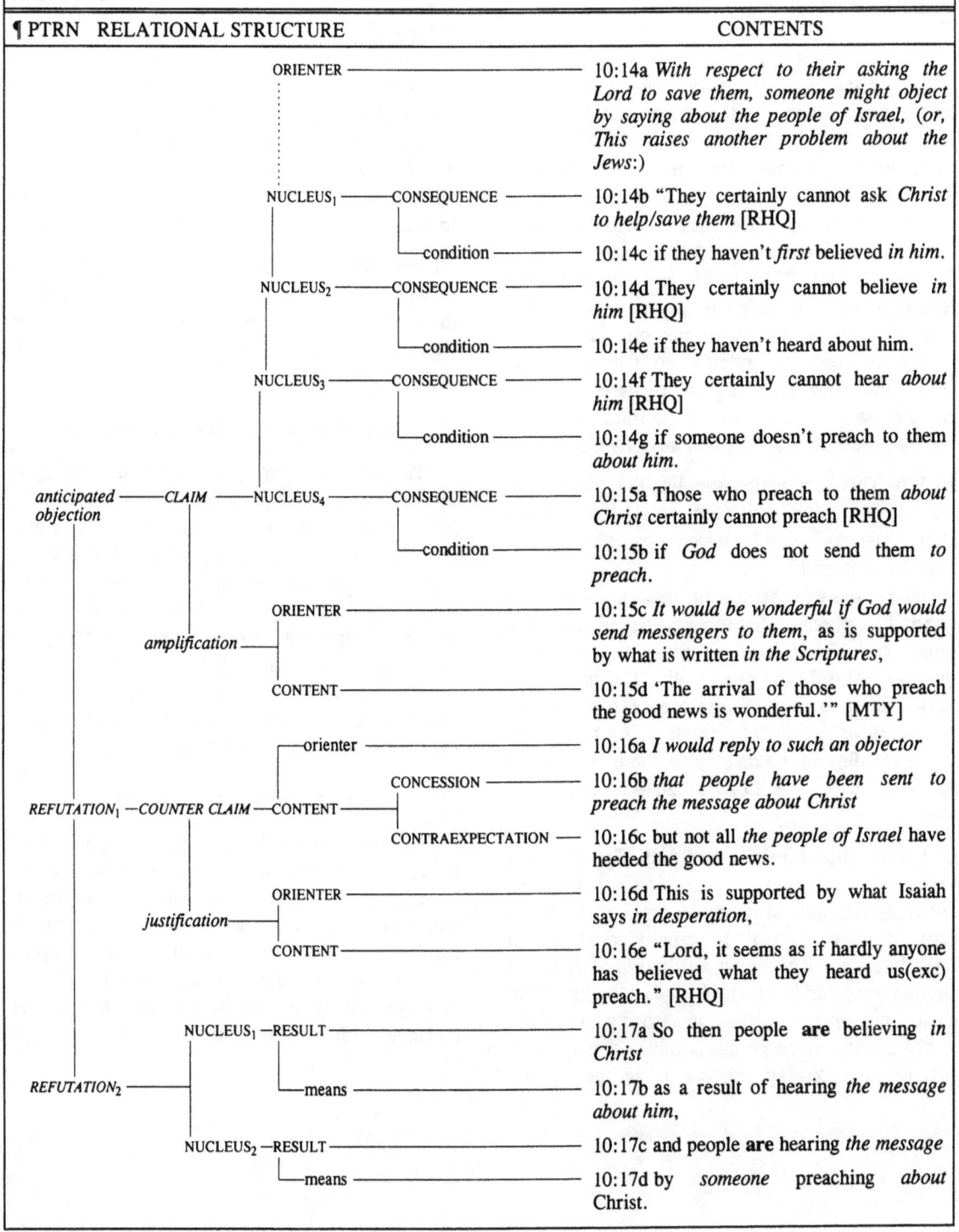

INTENT AND PARAGRAPH PATTERN

On the highest level of paragraph pattern relations in 10:14–17, Paul presents another *anticipated objection* to his argument and then two REFUTATIONs of it. The *objection* is, in essence, that you can't expect the Jews to believe if the gospel isn't preached to them. Paul's first REFUTATION is, "Well, that might be so, but the fact is that they *have* had the gospel preached to them, and even so most of the Jews haven't heeded the message." The second REFUTATION in essence throws back the content of 14b–15b at the potential accusers as a general principle that is valid.

On the lower level, the *objection* consists of a multiheaded CLAIM, and the first REFUTATION contains what can be considered a COUNTER-CLAIM and its *justification*.

NOTES

10:14–15 Verses 14–15 are often taken in a generic sense to support the concept of missions, as though Paul were here arguing for the Great Commission. There are a couple of very deep questions regarding these verses. First, to whom does the third person plural subject of the verbs refer—Jews, Gentiles, or both? Cranfield notes,

> The third person plural verbs of the first three questions are sometimes understood as indefinite ('How then shall men call . . .'); but in view of the argument of the section 9.30–10.21 as a whole, it is more natural to assume that the subject of these verbs is the same as that of the third person plural verbs in 9.32; 10.2, 3— namely, the Jews.

Dunn finds the question irrelevant: "Paul leaves the subject ambiguous, so that a decision between 'the Jews' (as Cranfield) and the πάντες of v 12 . . . is unnecessary." Hodge takes vv. 14–15 as a discussion on how the Gentiles should be saved. Morris leans more towards Cranfield's view, saying, "Throughout these chapters he is discussing the plight of his own nation, and they will be prominently in mind, whatever other application we may fairly discern." Since the context of chapters 8–11 supports this view, the words 'about the people of Israel' and 'about the Jews' are supplied in 14a.

As to Paul's use of the questions in vv. 14 and 15, they introduce a set of objections to his argument thus far. As he has done several times previously, Paul asks a question and then supplies the answer. For similar renderings of such questions, see 6:15, 7:7, and 7:13. But are these Paul's words or the words of an anticipated challenger? No commentary consulted discusses the problem. One could say that Paul elsewhere does not have any objector quoting Scripture (as is assumed for 15d). But Satan quotes Scripture in his challenge to Jesus in Matt. 4:6 and Luke 4:10. An investigation of all the questions in Romans, especially those that introduce anticipated challenges, would show that there is no uniformly clear signal of these challenges. Many of the questions begin with τί οὖν; 'what therefore?' or τί οὖν ἐροῦμεν; 'what then shall we say?' but one (7:13) simply is a yes/no question, and several others have 'you will say to me' or 'I say therefore' followed by a question. One (3:3) has τί γάρ plus a question. Furthermore, 9:30 has τί ἐροῦμεν and it is not an anticipated challenge. So the evidence is not clearly conclusive. For that reason two alternative versions of 14a are given in the display. The first (the preferred one) assumes that vv. 14–15 present an anticipated challenge by some of the Jewish audience. So we see that calling vv. 14–15 the *basis* of a "Great Commission" APPEAL is quite far from Paul's intent.

The 14b–15b series of objections is an ordered progression of condition-consequence statements that climax in 15a–b (see the discussion of these verses in BDF, sec. 493.3). This progression is indicated by the staggered set of NUCLEUS labels in the display. The series concludes with a Scripture an objector might cite to justify his claim.

The questions here can be considered either real (posed by a hypothetical objector) or rhetorical (equivalent to emphatic negative statements). Either way, it is probably possible in most languages to translate them literally as *How* questions.

As presented here, the *anticipated objection* consists of a CLAIM composed of several related NUCLEI. Semantically, one would expect a *justification* also. Actually all the conditional propositions in 10:14c–15b function as *justifications*. It is as though the writer were saying in his objection, "They certainly cannot ask Christ to help/save them [14b], since they haven't first believed in him [14c]," etc.

10:14b They certainly cannot ask *Christ to help/save them* Verse 14 begins a rare instance in which οὖν, which usually means 'therefore', means 'but' (BAGD, p. 593.4); it is so rendered by NCV, RSV, TEV, JB, AND LB. The word 'Christ' is supplied here to serve as the referent of the pronoun 'him' in 14c (it could be supplied in 14a: 'I would say about the Jews' believing in Christ'). For the words 'to help/save them', see the note on 12a. CEV has "ask the Lord to save them."

10:14c if they haven't *first* believed *in him* The Greek relative clause here is rendered in the display as a conditional clause, as also in 14e, 14g, and 15b, the sense being the same.

The word 'first' is supplied to make the chronological order of the events clear. The words 'in him' are supplied as the minimal cognitive content of 'believe' (also in 14d).

10:14e if they haven't heard about him Commentators doubt that ἀκούω followed by the genitive means 'hear about' someone; but as Barrett says, "Christ must be heard either in his own person, or in the person of his preachers." (Barrett's view is supported by Sanday and Headlam.) The relative pronoun is therefore taken as a metonymy, meaning 'message about'. Paul knows no one would argue it was necessary to hear Christ's actual voice. As Morris says, "The point is that Christ is present in the preachers; to hear them is to hear him." TEV supplies "the message," but "the message about him" would be clearer.

10:14g preach to them *about him* The words 'about him' are supplied as the minimal cognitive content of 'to preach'. Again TEV supplies "the message," but "the message about Christ" would be better.

10:15a preach to them *about Christ* See the note on 14g.

10:15b if *God* does not send them Commentators agree that the implied agent of 'send' is 'God'.

10:15c *It would be wonderful if God would send messengers to them* There is a big question as to just what the quotation in 15d is supporting. Most take it as supporting the idea that God has sent them; this would require them to understand the questions in vv. 14–15 as "They would not have been able to call on him [contrafactual condition] if they had not believed in him [contrafactual consequence]...." But no commentator hints that that is the real sense of the questions.

Commentators do not seem to realize that beginning in v. 14 Paul is raising another anticipated objection by the Jewish believers among the audience (see "Intent and Paragraph Pattern" and note on 10:14–15). Comments such as "Paul implies that the commissioned members have been sent" (Sanday and Headlam) are typical. However, once the *anticipated objection-REFUTATION* pattern is recognized it is clear that 'as it is written' is supporting the objection. The thrust is, 'it would be wonderful if the gospel were preached to the Jews', not 'it is wonderful that it *has* been preached to them'.

It could be maintained that there is no *anticipated objection* here. In that case, the two verses could be rewritten as shown in the following abbreviated display:

```
axiom ─────────────── 10:14–15b ...
 │
CLAIM₁ ─────────────── 10:15c God has sent preachers to them
 │
justification ─────────── 10:15d which is in accord with what is written in the Scriptures ...
         ┌─concession──── 10:16a People have been sent to preach the message about Christ to them,
CLAIM₂ ──┴─CONTRAEXPECTATION── 10:16b but not all the people of Israel have heeded the good news
```

But then it is difficult to see how 15c would follow logically from 14–15b. Moreover, the quotation in v. 15 would seem much less necessary as bolstering Paul's argument than as bolstering the argument of potential critics among the Jewish believers at Rome.

written *in the Scriptures* The words 'in the Scriptures' are supplied to show where it is written (cf. 3:4, 3:10, 8:36, 9:33). Quite a few versions render this as a personification: "the Scriptures say."

10:15d 'The arrival of those who preach the good news is wonderful' Paul here quotes from Isa. 52:7. The Greek 'feet' is a metonymy in which the body part, feet, stands for the action associated with it, namely movement—more specifically, arrival at a destination (cf. TEV's "how wonderful is the coming"). JB captures some of the flavor of the figure with "the footsteps of those who bring good news is a welcome sound."

The words τῶν εὐαγγελιζομένων εἰρήνην rendered in the KJV as "who preach the gospel of peace" are considered to be an insertion by some later scribe who wanted to make the quotation conform more closely to Isa. 52:7 as found in the LXX. The shorter version, which is followed here, is given an A rating ("certain") in the fourth edition GNT.

10:16a–b *I would reply to such an objector that people have been sent to preach the message about Christ* These propositions are supplied because they are essential parts of Paul's argument. For one thing, 16a–b, which introduces Paul's reply to the foregoing objection, is the necessary counterpart to 14a. Also, the strong adversative ἀλλά 'but/nevertheless' that introduces 16c requires some contrastive proposition to relate to; 16a–b supplies this (16c would not cohere relationally as a contrast to 14–15 without 16a–b being understood).

10:16c but not all *the people of Israel* **have heeded the good news** The subject pronoun 'they' refers to 'the Jews'. While the statement is applicable to all people, Paul's focus in the section starting with 9:1 is on the failure of most of the Jews to respond to God's way of salvation.

The word ὑπακούω 'to obey, embrace in full surrender' (BAGD, p. 837.1) is rendered 'heeded' in the display. TEV has "accepted"; JBP, NEB, and NIV have "responded to." Both are good alternatives.

10:16d Here γάρ introduces a Scripture, Isa. 53:1, in support of the contention in 16c. (It is not the reason for it.)

10:16e "Lord, it seems as if hardly anyone has believed what they heard us(exc) preach" The rhetorical question introduced by 'Who?' expresses an emotive component of frustration and disappointment. This is represented in the display by 'it seems as if hardly anyone', and also by 'in desperation' in 16d. CEV captures the sense with a different rhetorical question: "Lord, has anyone believed?"

The event in τῇ ἀκοῇ ἡμῶν 'our preaching' is represented by the verb 'preach' in the display. As to the referent of 'our', it could, in the original context of Isaiah, mean "that which he and other prophets heard from God" (Denney). As far as it expresses Paul's own thoughts and experience, it would probably refer to himself and the other apostles. In either case it is exclusive. LB seems alone in suggesting an editorial first person plural.

10:17 Commentaries are not clear as to how this verse relates to what precedes and follows. Morris calls it a summarizing conclusion, and nearly all the versions (NIV and CEV being exceptions) make a paragraph break after v. 17, not before. Cranfield agrees, but notes that "hearing [in v. 17] becomes the hinge, so that it leads naturally into v. 18." His view is supported by Newman and Nida, Sanday and Headlam, and Morris. But in Paul's arguments here, ἄρα 'therefore'—far from introducing something parenthetical (so Denney, Sanday and Headlam)— is taken as Paul's throwing back at his objectors what actually is happening: some Jews (and others) *are* believing in Christ and people *are* hearing the message about him. Unfortunately there is no verb in the verse, and translators supply a present tense verb, most often 'comes'. (Beck, however, comes close to the interpretation in the display with "So when we tell people, they believe.") Those who supply a present tense verb do so assuming a timeless aspect is in view, whereas in the display a present progressive aspect is used on the verbs in 17a and 17c (with the word 'are' in bold) to make Paul's real meaning clear.

10:17a people are **believing** *in Christ* The noun πίστις 'faith' is here spelled out semantically.

10:17b–c hearing *the message* In this context ἀκοή 'report' must mean 'hearing' or, more precisely, hearing what has been preached about Christ' (cf. 16e, where the sense of ἀκοή is different, the focus there being on the preaching).

10:17d *someone* **preaching** *about* **Christ** The phrase διὰ ῥήματος Χριστοῦ 'through the preaching of Christ' is taken as expressing means, though it could be attendant circumstance: 'when someone preaches about Christ'. The genitive phrase 'of Christ' could mean 'which has Christ as its source', but it is much more natural to take it as meaning 'about Christ', especially if Paul has Isaiah 53 in mind—there the Messianic servant is suffering, not proclaiming.

The Textus Receptus follows manuscripts which have ῥῆμα θεοῦ 'word of God' instead of ῥῆμα Χριστοῦ 'word of Christ'. The change was evidently made because that form was more familiar, occurring five times elsewhere in the

NT, whereas this form, which is in the best manuscripts, occurs only here. The display follows the fourth edition GNT, which gives it an A rating ("certain").

BOUNDARIES AND COHERENCE

Coherence derives from the four rhetorical questions in vv. 14–15, each of which begins with πῶς 'how?' Each question consists, semantically, of a CONSEQUENCE and a condition, with the main clause in each succeeding question repeating the verb of the condition of the preceding question. The REFUTATION in v. 17 contains three verbs that are semantically the same as verbs used in the questions in vv. 14–15.

The boundary with the next paragraph (10:18–21) is marked by a new hypothetical question in v. 18. This question follows upon Paul's REFUTATION in v. 17 which expresses his very different point of view concerning the 10:14–15 *objection* answered in v. 16.

PROMINENCE AND THEME

The theme of 10:14–17 is drawn from parts of both the *objection* and the REFUTATIONS. Though the *objection*'s CLAIM consists of four NUCLEI each of which leads in logical progression to the next, the central two NUCLEI are omitted from the theme, the first and last parts being the crucial ones in the argument. (The central two are simply logical links in the chain.) This multiheaded CLAIM is supported by Scripture, but the fact that Paul is willing to admit it has some scriptural justification is not considered thematic. The CLAIM within the *objection* is, in fact, essentially refuted—it is the REFUTATIONS that are thematic. In the first REFUTATION, the CONCESSION and CONTRAEXPECTATION elements of the CLAIM (16b-c) are thematic because the argument is incomplete without them. And although v. 17 seems to be mostly a restatement, here Paul is really throwing back at the anticipated objectors their own *objection* as part of his REFUTATION, which makes the two NUCLEI of the second REFUTATION necessary parts of the theme as well.

SECTION CONSTITUENT 10:18–21
(Expository Paragraph: Responses to queries about the claim in 9:30–33)

THEME: In reply to a query of whether the Jews have heard or understood about Christ, I would say that, as is supported by Scripture, they have heard it and should have understood it, because even the non-Jews, who were not searching for God, understood it.

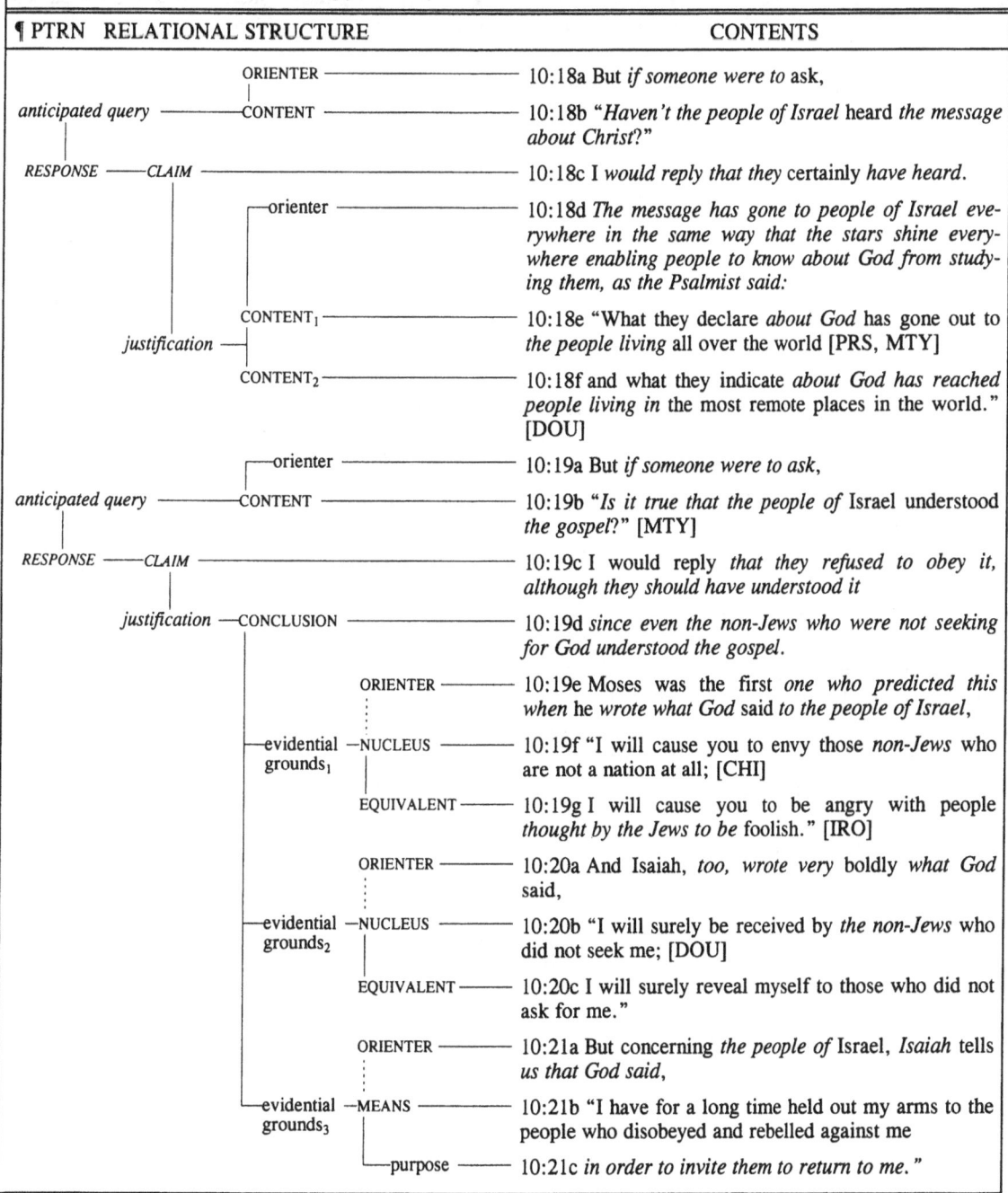

INTENT AND PARAGRAPH PATTERN

The 10:18–21 expository paragraph consists of two closely related *anticipated queries* and a RESPONSE to each one. Within the first RESPONSE is a CLAIM with its *justification* by way of a Scripture quotation, as is common in Paul's writing. The second RESPONSE is likewise made up of a CLAIM (19c) and its *justification* (19d–21), though 19c and the introduction to the justification (19d) are both implicit, as shown by the italicizing. They are supplied just prior to the Scripture quotation (see the note on 19d).

NOTES

10:18a-b *But if someone were to ask, "Haven't the people of Israel heard the message about Christ?"* Paul here introduces another question with λέγω 'I say', but for the display it is assumed he is expressing a theoretical question arising from what he has just said in vv. 16-17. Almost none of the commentators discuss just what this question represents. Vine says that the question here is the first of "two possible excuses which might be advanced on behalf of Jewish unbelief." Sanday and Headlam also seem to put these words into the mouth of someone replying to Paul. Morris specifically states, "Paul proceeds to an objection that might be raised." But the double negative question in 18b (μὴ οὐκ ἤκουσαν 'is it not that they have not heard?'), which anticipates an affirmative reply, makes the question acceptable as an anticipated query, but rules it out as an anticipated objection.

If one chooses not to accept the interpretation followed here, one alternative would be to retain the 18b double negative but change the question form: 'It is not true that the Jews have not heard'. Then 18c would become 'On the contrary/indeed, they certainly have heard'; and the *anticipated query-RESPONSE* labels would be omitted from the paragraph pattern column of the display. But this wording would be awkward. Another possibility takes 18b as a question Paul is asking himself. The question's literal sense is 'You don't mean to say that they did not hear?' (so Denney), giving the sense of 18b that is in the display or, in even more idiomatic English, 'They have heard, haven't they?' According to BDF (427.2), "In questions with μή the verb itself can already be negated ..., producing μή ... οὐ with an affirmative answer implied: R[om.] 10:18 μὴ οὐκ ἤκουσαν; 'have they not heard?' (Answer: 'Indeed they have'). ..." Regarding the words μενοῦν γε that introduce 18c, BAGD (p. 503) say they are "particles used esp. in answers, to emphasize or correct ... *Indeed* Ro 10:18." In other words, although the particle has some nuance of an adversative in all contexts, it is not enough to translate it as 'on the contrary' in all contexts, and probably not here. A similar case is Paul's question in 1 Cor. 11:22, μὴ οἰκίας οὐκ ἔχετε 'don't you have houses?' with an emphatic positive reply implied.

The subject pronoun 'they' is here identified as 'the people of Israel' (cf. LB's "the Jews" and CEV's "the people of Israel"). As the object of the verb 'heard', 'the message about Christ' is supplied (cf. TEV's "the message").

10:18c *they certainly have heard* Paul's answer begins with the particle μενοῦνγε (see note immediately above). The display conveys the sense with 'certainly'. TEV and NIV have "Of course they did." There is no verb in the Greek, but 'they have heard' is implied, and that—or an abbreviated form of it—is supplied in all modern versions.

10:18d *The message has gone to the people of Israel everywhere in the same way that the stars shine everywhere enabling people to know about God from studying them, as the Psalmist said* In 18e-f Paul quotes Psalm 19:4. He does not state that he is quoting Scripture; but since he quotes the verse exactly, it is reasonable to suppose he assumed his audience knew that. Therefore the display supplies the words 'as the Psalmist said'.

In giving this quotation Paul makes an implied comparison between the fact that people everywhere can know about God from studying the stars and the fact that Jews everywhere can know the gospel because its message, too, has gone all over the world. The implied comparison is supplied in 18d.

10:18e *What they declare* In the quotation the subject of the first clause is ὁ φθόγγος αὐτῶν 'their voice'. This is a personification—stars don't talk. In the original context the Psalmist was speaking about the witness of the heavenly bodies to God's glory. The display uses the word 'declare' even though it is still somewhat personified. NCV has "their message."

all over the world The words πᾶσαν τὴν γῆν 'all the earth' are a metonymy in which the earth stands for the people of the earth. A good alternative to the rendering 'all over the world' is 'everywhere'.

10:18f *and what they indicate* about God has reached people living in *the most remote places in the world* This is the second part of a doublet, a restatement of 18e; but since it has its source in a poetic passage, it is retained in the display. It is rendered generically: 'what they indicate about God'.

The figurative phrase 'to the ends of the earth' is rendered in the display by 'to the most remote places of the world'. This is hyperbolic, equivalent to 'everywhere'.

10:19a–b But *if someone were to ask, "Is it true that the people of* Israel understood *the gospel?"* The word λέγω 'I say' is handled as in v. 18. Paul here gives another query that someone might make, but makes it sound as though he himself were raising it.

'Israel' is a metonymy standing for the people of Israel.

Since the word ἔγνω 'understood' is a verb of cognition, the question arises, What should be understood as the content? Many commentators suggest 'that he would reject the Jews and accept the Gentiles'. Murray, for example, says that "the answer is indicated in the quotations that follow" (cf. LB). The problem is that the content cannot be supplied from something which is yet to come. The reader needs to know the implicit cognitive content from what has preceded, not from what follows. Furthermore, the parallelism between 'didn't they know?' and ἀγνοοῦντες 'not knowing' in 10:3 cannot be ignored. The content given in 10:3 was 'how God declares people righteous'. Therefore, the generic word 'gospel' is supplied here as the implicit cognitive content of 'understood', as is supported by many commentators.

10:19c–d I would reply *that they refused to obey it although they should have understood it since even the non-Jews who were not seeking for God understood the gospel* The Scripture quotation (Deut. 32:21) in 19f–g is given by Paul as an answer to the 19b *query*. But how does the quotation support a yes-or-no answer to the question? What Paul is clearly implying is that they should have understood, so if they did not it must be their own fault (Hodge, Barnes, Nygren, Denney, Dayton). In the display this connection between the quotation and the question is supplied. The first part of 19c is included because the quotation in v. 21 refers to the Jews' disobedience, not their lack of understanding.

10:19e Moses was the first *one who predicted this when* he *wrote what God said to the people of Israel* A few commentators join the word πρῶτος 'first' to the previous clause to give the sense 'didn't Israel know first?' But the parallelism in the questions in 18b and 19b, which both end in verbs, would be destroyed if 'first' went with 19b. Furthermore, it should be noted that Paul does give a second scriptural support in vv. 20–21, this time from Isaiah; thus Moses was the first to make this prediction and then Isaiah. And, finally, 'didn't Israel know first?' does not cohere relationally with the preceding context. Therefore 'Moses was the first one' is the interpretation chosen here. Most commentators support this.

The words 'wrote what God said' are supplied to provide a referent for 'I' in the quotation that follows, and 'to the people of Israel' is supplied to make the referent of 'you' in the quotation clear.

10:19f–g "I will cause you to envy those *non-Jews* who are not a nation at all; I will cause you to be angry with people *thought by the Jews to be* foolish" There is a chiastic structure in the Greek, which may not be translatable:

A I will provoke you to jealousy
  B by *ones who are* not a nation;
  B' by a foolish nation
A' I will anger you

The question here is, What is the cause of the jealousy and anger, and how does it relate to the context? In the words of Murray, it is that "another nation which had not enjoyed God's covenant favour as Israel had would become recipient of the favour which Israel had despised." If this is not clear to the receptor-language audience, the word 'this' in 19e may have to be spelled out: 'that Gentiles would accept the gospel (or, God's way of salvation)'.

non-Jews Both Moses and Paul were referring to Gentiles as those the Jews would become jealous of. This is made clear in the display. LB has "the foolish heathen nations."

not a nation at all The word 'nation' here is not used in its primary sense. Paul, quoting Deut. 32:21, is using it in a pejorative sense: 'who are a non-people, who are a bunch of nobodies in God's sight.'

foolish The word ἀσύνετος 'foolish' is used with irony; it means that the Gentiles were considered by the Jews to be foolish (Bruce 1985, Erdman, Sanday and Headlam).

The background of the communication situation here is that the Jews thought they alone would be accepted by God, but such information is not really in focus here.

10:20a Isaiah, *too, wrote very* boldly *what God* said The words 'wrote what God said' are supplied for the same reason as in 19e. CEV has "Isaiah was fearless enough to tell that the Lord had said. . . ." The word 'too' is supplied in view of 19e: 'Moses was the first'.

There is a question as to whether ἀποτολμᾷ 'is quite bold' means that Isaiah was very bold in saying this or 'more bold than Moses'. Either way, it probably implies that Isaiah's statement would be more likely to arouse the ire of the Jews than Moses' statement would, for it was risky to say openly that God might turn away from favoring the Jews.

10:20b–c The two parts of the doublet are retained because of the poetic nature of the OT passage cited (Isa. 65:1).

I will surely be received by *the non-Jews* who did not seek me The word εὑρέθην 'I have been found' is rendered 'received' here, since in English 'find' usually implies that what was found was previously lost. It is aorist passive, and the sense is probably more precisely 'I have let myself be found'. In the display it is taken as a prophetic past, hence the definite future tense here and in 20c (cf. Beck's "I will let those who don't look for Me find Me" and LB's "would be found"). The third person plural pronoun is identified as 'the non-Jews'.

I will surely reveal myself to those who did not ask for me The verb phrase ἐμφανὴς ἐγενόμην 'I became manifest' is a somewhat mismatched way of saying 'I revealed myself to' (cf. JB, NIV, REB).

10:21a concerning *the people of* Israel, *Isaiah tells us that God said* Some commentators and versions take the phrase πρὸς τὸν Ἰσραήλ 'toward Israel' as meaning 'to Israel'. But there is no second person pronoun in the quotation, as there would be if God were speaking *to* Israel. Therefore the display follows the great majority of commentators in rendering it 'concerning Israel'. The word 'Israel' again stands for 'the people of Israel'.

The verb λέγει 'he says' could mean 'God says', but more probably it is 'Isaiah says'; in either case it needs to be made clear, as in the display, that God is the referent of 'I' in the quotation and that this is an additional quotation from Isaiah. CEV specifies it ("And Isaiah said") but changes the pronoun 'I' in the quotation to 'the Lord', which translators are not encouraged to do.

10:21b–c "I have for a long time held out my arms to the people who disobeyed and rebelled against me *in order to invite them to return to me*" In this quotation from Isa. 65:2 the verb phrase ἐξεπέτασα τὰς χεῖράς μου 'I stretched out my arms' expresses a symbolic action whose purpose is 'to invite them to return to me'. This is specified to avoid a zero or wrong meaning. NCV renders it nonfiguratively: "I stood ready to accept." Moore (p. 41) considers ἀπειθοῦντα 'disobedient' and ἀντιλέγοντα 'contrary' a near-synonymous doublet, but they are different enough to warrant their both being included here.

BOUNDARIES AND COHERENCE

The 10:18–21 paragraph is relationally coherent in that it consists of two hypothetical *queries* and Paul's RESPONSE to each. Coherence is also shown by each RESPONSE's consisting of a CLAIM and one or more OT quotations providing their *justification*. The start of the next section is marked at 11:1 by οὖν 'therefore' and the orienter λέγω 'I say', which introduces the next hypothetical question.

PROMINENCE AND THEME

The 10:18–21 theme makes it clear that Paul is responding to two hypothetical *queries*; but the two *queries*, since they are very similar, are compressed into one compound predicate. The theme also contains the CLAIM of the 18c RESPONSE and the CLAIM of the 19c RESPONSE as well as the generic CONCLUSION in 19d of the *justification* within the second RESPONSE. The fact that Paul supports each of the CLAIMS by Scripture is represented by the words "as is supported by Scripture."

SUBDIVISION CLUSTER CONSTITUENT 11:1–32
(Expository Section: Solution to the problem of 9:1–11:36)

THEME: God has certainly not rejected all of us Jews, and God is saving many non-Jews to make the Jews jealous and thus seek to be saved. To you non-Jews I say that I hope my work among you will accomplish just that; but do not despise the Jews whom God has rejected and do not become proud, because just as God did not spare the Jews he will not spare you if you fall away from him. And I want you to know that all the Jews will some day be saved, as the Scriptures predict.

MACROSTRUCTURE	CONTENTS
query$_1$ about God's rejection of the Jews, and Paul's *RESPONSE*	11:1–6 My reply to a query whether God has rejected the Jews is that he has certainly not rejected all of us. I am evidence of that. Just as in the past, there is at the present time a small group of us Jews who have become believers.
general statement about the problem of God's rejection of the Jews	11:7–10 The people of Israel as a whole did not find the way of being declared righteous, which is confirmed by the scriptures, though those whom God had chosen did find it.
query$_2$ about God's rejection of the Jews, and Paul's *RESPONSE*	11:11–12 My reply to a query whether the result of the Jews' unbelief is a permanent falling away from God is no, but that God is saving many non-Jews to make the Jews envious and thus seek to be saved.
statement to non-Jews of Paul's *REACTION* to the problem of God's rejection of the Jews	11:13–16 I highly esteem the work God has given me to do among you non-Jews. I hope that my making my fellow Jews jealous will result in some of them being saved.
APPEALS to non-Jews	11:17–24 You non-Jews must not despise the Jews whom God has rejected, and you must not become proud, but instead beware. God will not spare you if you fall away from him, and he will act kindly toward the Jews and be reunited to them if they trust in Christ.
SOLUTION to the problem of God's rejection of the Jews	11:25–32 I want you to know that all the people of Israel will some day be saved, as the Scriptures predict. God still loves them because of their ancestors. It is God's purpose to act mercifully towards them as well as toward all Gentiles.

INTENT AND MACROSTRUCTURE

The 11:1–32 unit, which consists of six paragraphs, is difficult to classify as to intent. The first, second, and third paragraphs (1–6, 7–10, 11–12) are expository. The fourth (13–16) is expressive. The fifth (17–24) is hortatory, and the final paragraph (25–32) is expository. The whole unit is classified as expository, of the solutionality subtype, since most of the paragraphs are expository, and since it is part of the expository division cluster 1:16–11:36, and since the final paragraph, an expository one, expresses the expected resolution to the problem of the Jews' rejection of Christ stated in the first paragraph (9:1–5) of the 9:1–11:36 subdivision cluster of which it is a part. (A *SOLUTION* is by definition more thematic than the *problem* relating to it.) An alternative is to consider 11:1–32 as hortatory, with the *APPEALS* paragraph (17–24) being the focus and the first, second, and final paragraphs expressing *bases* for the *APPEALS*. But while the γάρ introducing the final paragraph would support this, such an analysis would do violence to the topic that the 9:1–11:36 subdivision cluster clearly expresses: the problem of the Jews' rejection of Christ and God's solution.

What is Paul's main intent in chapters 9, 10, and 11? Is it to express the question that would arise in the minds of his Jewish audience about the implications of the doctrine of justification by faith as far as the relation of God to his chosen people, the Jews, and God's answer to that question? Or is his main intent to warn the non-Jews in his audience not to despise the Jews? Supporting the first view is the doxology in 11:33–36. Verses 33–36 do not fit well as the outcome of vv. 1–32 if the 1–32 theme is "do not despise the Jews." Rather, it is vv. 25–32, God's climactic solution to the problem of the Jews, which calls forth this paean of praise. According to this view, the 17–24 *APPEALS*, then, are somewhat parenthetical. Thus it is assumed for this analysis that the unit is expository, but with the *APPEALS* in 17–

24 and the *SOLUTION* in 25-32 being equally prominent.

BOUNDARIES AND COHERENCE

Coherence within the 11:1-32 unit is maintained by references to Ἰσραήλ 'Israel' (four times, plus many pronominal and other references), Ἰσραηλίτης 'Israelite' (once), and ἔθνη 'Gentiles' (five times). The boundary between this unit and the next (11:33-36) is marked in v. 33 with the exclamatory interjection Ὦ 'O', which introduces two verbless statements listing God's attributes.

PROMINENCE AND THEME

The theme of 11:1-32 is drawn from the themes of all its constituent paragraphs. The *query* parts of the themes of the first and third paragraphs are omitted; they are less thematic than the *RESPONSES*. From the first paragraph only the *INFERENCE* is included (the *CLAIM* is a repetition and largely supportive). The NUCLEUS propositions of the *REACTION* (fourth paragraph) are included as naturally prominent. Similarly the NUCLEUS proposition of the *INFERENCE* of the final paragraph is included as is the TOPIC ORIENTER, which points to its prominence within the whole 9:1-11:36 subdivision cluster. The *evidence* for the *INFERENCE* in this final paragraph is represented by the words "as the Scriptures predict."

SECTION CONSTITUENT 11:1–6 (Expository Paragraph: Query₁ about God's rejection of the Jews, and Paul's response)

THEME: My reply to a query whether God has rejected the Jews is that he has certainly not rejected all of us. I am evidence of that. Just as in the past, there is at the present time a small group of us Jews who have become believers.

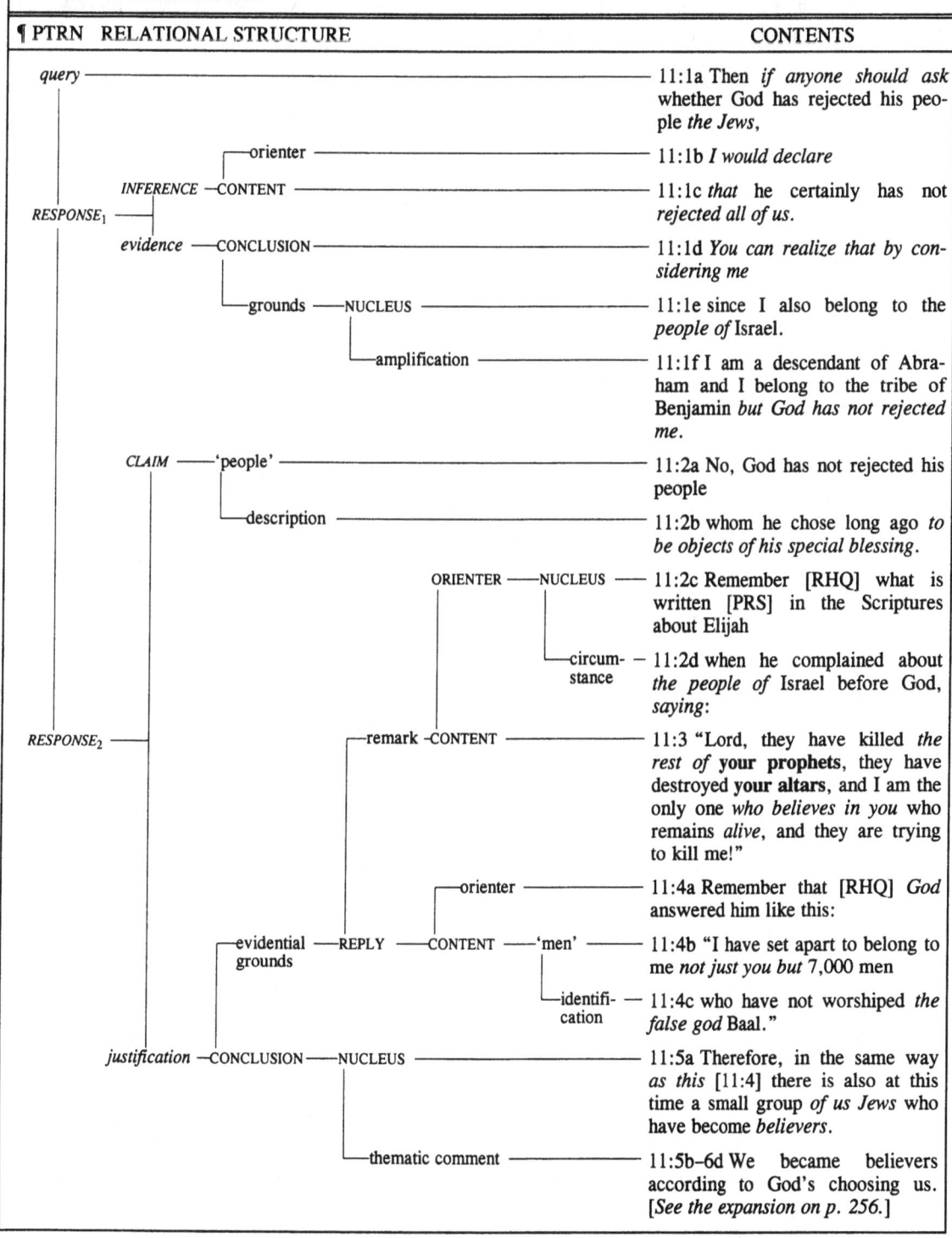

INTENT AND PARAGRAPH PATTERN

There are two levels of paragraph pattern relations in 11:1-6: On the higher level is an expository pattern with a *query* in 1a and two RESPONSES in the rest of the paragraph (1b-f and vv. 2-6); then in each of the RESPONSES is a statement about a present or past situation with evidence to validate it. These lower-level subunits are also expository, the first being INFERENCE-*evidence*, the second being CLAIM-*justification*.

NOTES

11:1a-b Then *if anyone should ask* **whether God has rejected his people** *the Jews, I would declare* Paul's first word in this verse is λέγω 'I say', an abbreviated way of raising a query that he thinks some of his Jewish audience might raise. Then he goes on to answer it. The words 'the Jews' are supplied to make clear who is meant by τὸν λαὸν αὐτοῦ 'his people'.

11:1c he certainly has not *rejected all of us* Paul's reply to the query is μὴ γένοιτο 'absolutely not'. This is made into a full sentence here by repeating the verb 'rejected' from 1a. The phrase 'all of us' is supplied to make it clear that Paul himself was an Israelite. If it is so translated, the decision on whether the pronoun 'us' in this context should be rendered by the inclusive or the exclusive form should be made in consultation with RL speakers, keeping in mind that some, though not all, of Paul's readers are Jews and that he may have been speaking more directly to the Jews at this point.

11:1d *You can realize that by considering me* This supplied proposition provides the connection between 1c and 1e-f. Alternatives would be 'I am proof that he has not rejected us all' or 'I am evidence of that'. Some commentators have suggested that 1e-f is the reason that Paul so vehemently rejects the idea in 1a. (To him as a Jew the idea in 1a would be almost blasphemous.) This would be far more plausible if Paul had simply said, 'For I myself am an Israelite'. But since he lists three statements regarding his Jewishness, this interpretation seems far less likely than the one chosen for the display, which is held by the great majority of commentators.

11:1f I am a descendant of Abraham and I belong to the tribe of Benjamin *but God has not rejected me* The words 'but God has not rejected me' supply the implicit statement of contraexpectation to accompany the three concessive statements of 1e-f. It is a crucial implicature of the argument.

11:2a-b his people whom he chose long ago *to be objects of his special blessing* In the relative clause ὃν προέγνω 'whom he foreknew' the meaning of 'foreknew' in this context is 'chose beforehand' (so Dunn, TEV, Beck, Norlie, JB, LB), as in the display. Hodge says that the verb can mean 'to approve' or 'select'; NEB has "acknowledged as his own."

However, commentators are divided as to the meaning of the whole phrase—mostly on theological grounds. One camp says it is a statement about the people of Israel as a whole, the other that it refers to 'spiritual Israel' (i.e., those among the Jews who were the elect). Both interpretations require some semantic content to be supplied as the object of the cognitive verb 'know'. Interpretation 1 would require something like 'that they would be objects of his special blessings' (so Morris). Interpretation 2 would require something like 'that they would believe in Christ' or 'that they would be saved' (cf. 8:29). But there are serious difficulties in regard to interpretation 2. For one thing, the phrase 'his people' that occurs here occurs also in v. 1 where it clearly means all the people in Israel. The other difficulty, as Morris notes, is that Paul refers to 'the people he foreknew' and not 'those out of (ἐκ) his people whom he foreknew'. (Note that if interpretation 2 *were* to be followed, proposition 2b would be labeled identification, not description, as it is here. Note also that although the label here is description, 2b could be taken as grounds, in which case it would be rendered 'since he chose them' or 'as seen by the fact that he chose them'.)

11:2c Remember The words οὐκ οἴδατε 'do you not know?' (found also in 6:3, 6:16, 7:1) are taken as introducing a rhetorical question whose function is to ask the readers to keep something in mind, whether or not they realized it before.

what is written in the Scriptures The words λέγει ἡ γραφή 'says the Scripture' are a personification as in 10:11a. It is rendered nonfiguratively here. CEV also eliminates the figure: "Don't you remember reading in the Scriptures . . . ?"

11:2d when he complained about *the people of Israel* The verb ἐντυγχάνω here means "to appeal to someone against a third person"

11:3 Lord, they have killed *the rest of* **your prophets** In this quotation from 1 Kings 19:10 and 14 'they' refers to the Israelites who acted under the orders of the evil king and queen. The phrase 'your prophets' is given emphasis by its position before the verb and is therefore in bold type in the display. (The same is true of 'your altars' in the next clause.) The words 'the rest of' are supplied to make clear that Elijah is also a prophet.

they have destroyed your altars The verb κατέσκαψαν means literally 'to raze to the ground'.

I am the only one *who believes in you* **who remains** *alive* In the clause καγὼ ὑπελείφθην μόνος 'and I alone am left', 'I alone' needs to be qualified in order to be properly understood. NCV has "the only prophet left"; LB supplies "in all the land who still loved God." Vine, Hodge, and Dodd all suggest "who is faithful"; Morris and Lenski, "who is a worshipper." The display supplies 'who believes in you', but 'who faithfully worships/serves you' is a good alternative that fits both the OT and NT contexts.

11:4a Remember that *God* **answered him like this** The Greek is τί λέγει αὐτῷ ὁ χρηματισμός 'What says to him the divine answer?' This rhetorical question has the same function as the one in 2c and again is rendered as 'Remember'. The 'divine answer says' is a personification using a word which occurs nowhere else in the NT; it is rendered nonfiguratively as 'God answered'. Paul here quotes 1 Kings 19:18 as God's answer to Elijah.

11:4b I have set apart to belong to me *not just you but* **7,000 men** The word ἐμαυτῷ 'to myself' is rendered here as 'to belong to me ' (see Hodge). Others suggest 'to serve me'. Another alternative would be 'There are still 7,000 men who belong to me' (cf. CEV's "I still have").

The words 'not just you but' are supplied to make God's reply fit Elijah's complaint. What Elijah said was, 'I am the only one'. God replied, '7,000 besides you' (see LB).

11:4c who have not worshiped *the false god* **Baal** The function of the verb phrase οἵτινες οὐκ ἔκαμψαν γόνυ 'who have not bowed knees' is more important than the form by which it is conveyed; it is therefore rendered as 'have not worshiped' (so TEV, CEV). The words 'the false god' are supplied as implicit cultural information essential to understanding the meaning. TEV also includes these words.

11:5a in the same way *as this* The word οὕτως means 'similarly, in the same way'. In the display the phrase 'as this' is supplied to complete the comparison. An alternative would be 'as in the past'.

a small group *of us Jews* The word λεῖμμα 'remnant' is probably figurative, referring to a small left-over amount. (A similar word occurs in 9:27.) It is rendered in the display as 'a small group', with 'of us Jews' supplied to specify what group Paul was referring to. It also makes clear that he was one of them (see the note on 1c concerning inclusive/exclusive).

who have become *believers* The words κατ' ἐκλογὴν χάριτος γέγονεν mean 'according to choice of grace become' or, more freely, 'who have become according to being chosen by grace'. Since 'become' requires a complement, 'believers' is supplied. 'God's people' would also be appropriate.

EXPANSION OF THE THEMATIC COMMENT IN THE 11:1-6 DISPLAY

RELATIONAL STRUCTURE	CONTENTS
NUCLEUS—RESULT	11:5b *God* has chosen us *to become believers* (*or*, *his people*)
—reason	11:5c only because *he* acts graciously (*or*, is gracious).
—amplification—grounds	11:6a Since *it is* because he acts graciously *toward people that he chooses them*,
CONCLUSION—CONCLUSION	11:6b *it is* not because they have done good things *that he has chosen them*.
—condition	11:6c If *God chose people because they did good things*,
—grounds—CONSEQUENCE	11:6d then it wouldn't be because he was acting graciously.

11:5b-c *God* **has chosen us . . . only because** *he* **is gracious (*or*, acts graciously)** The words 'election' and 'grace', which refer to events, are rendered here as verbs and the appropriate agent ('God'/'he') supplied. In some languages it will be more natural to say 'because he is gracious'.

11:6a Since *it is* **because he acts graciously** *toward people that he chooses them* Here εἰ means 'if, as is actually the case'. That is, it is introducing the factual grounds, not an uncertain condition. Since there is no explicit result clause for the reason clause ('it is because he acts graciously') to relate to, 'that he chooses them' is supplied. TEV has "His choice"; NCV, "God chose them."

11:6b *it is* **not because they have done good things** *that he has chosen them* The prepositional phrase ἐξ ἔργων 'from works' is rendered here as in 4:2. The same phrase in 9:32 is rendered 'because of doing certain things in order that God would accept them', which is appropriate here as well. CEV has "not because of anything they have done"; LB, "not by their being good enough."

11:6c-d *If God chose people because they did good things*, **then it wouldn't be because he was acting graciously** The Greek is ἐπεὶ ἡ χάρις οὐκέτι γίνεται χάρις 'for (otherwise) grace no longer would be grace'. A contrafactual apodosis (conclusion) implies a contrafactual protasis (condition), so one is supplied. The rendering of the self-contradictory 'grace would no longer be grace' is more straightforward here. An alternative is 'then the statement that God acts graciously towards us would no longer really be true'.

There are several textual variants at the end of this verse. The KJV, following the Textus Receptus, has a long extra sentence, "But if it be of works, then is it no more grace; otherwise work is no more work." Quite apart from the difficulty of trying to make sense of the final clause, it is clear that some scribe added the words to amplify the text; but as Morris notes, "It is impossible to understand why they would have been deleted if they had been in the original." The shorter text is given an A rating ("certain") in the fourth edition GNT.

BOUNDARIES AND COHERENCE

The main feature of coherence in the 11:1-6 paragraph is two occurrences of the phrase 'his people'. The start of the next paragraph at 11:7 is marked by the rhetorical question τί οὖν 'What therefore?' All the modern versions have a paragraph break here.

PROMINENCE AND THEME

The theme of 11:1-6 is drawn from a condensation of the *query* and the prominent propositions of the first *RESPONSE*, namely 1c and 1d. From the second *RESPONSE* the *CLAIM* in 2a is not included because it is simply a repetition of 1c; however, the prominent part of its *justification* (5a) is included.

SECTION CONSTITUENT 11:7–10 (Expository Paragraph: General statement about the problem of God's rejection of the Jews)

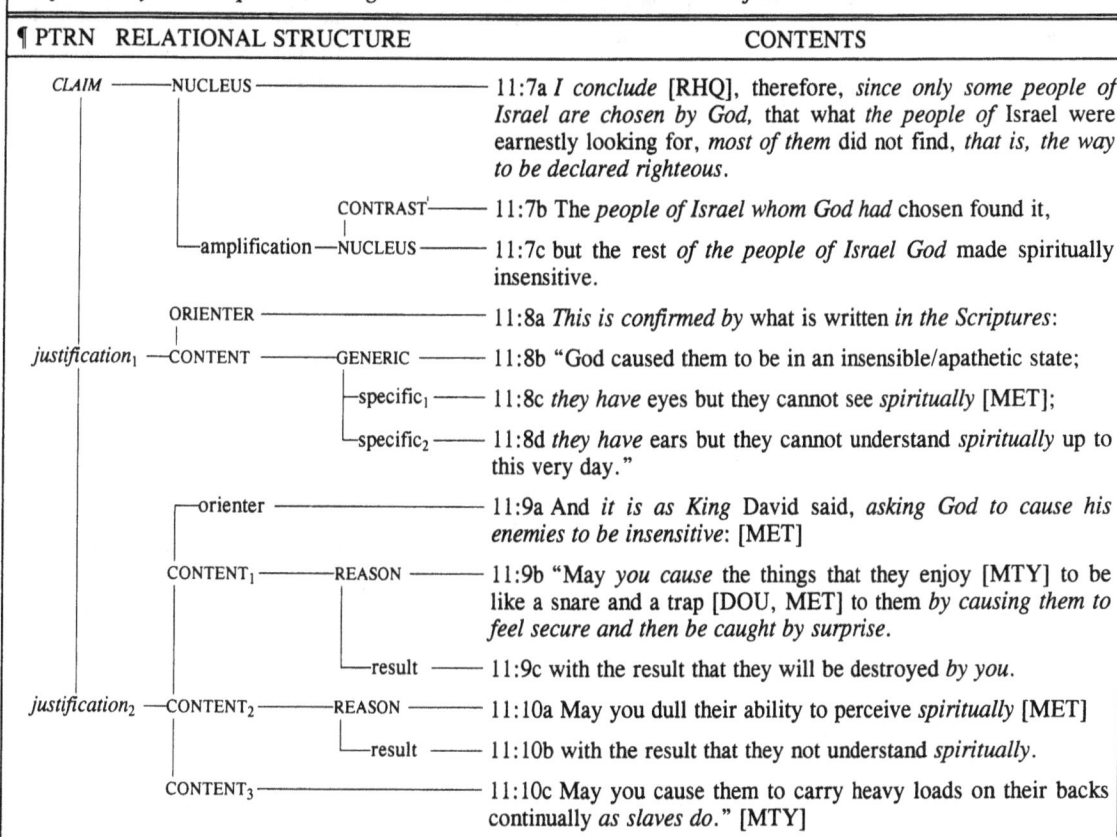

INTENT AND PARAGRAPH PATTERN

The lack of imperatives (except in the plea to God in the final quote) or expressive elements in 11:7–10 indicates that it continues as another in a long sequence of expository paragraphs. It consists of a CLAIM (v. 7) and two *justifications* (v. 8 and vv. 9–10).

NOTES

11:7a *I conclude*, therefore, *since only some people of Israel are chosen by God* The rhetorical question τί οὖν; 'What therefore?' is considered to be calling attention to a conclusion (as in 6:16), but here it is one Paul himself is about to make, not a possible one by others. Thus 'I conclude' is supplied, as well as 'since only some people of Israel are chosen by God', which summarizes the referent of 'therefore' (the gist of the previous paragraph).

what *the people of* Israel were earnestly looking for, *most of them* The word 'Israel' stands for the people of Israel, as it usually does, but here the words 'most of them' are supplied (cf. JB, JBP) because, obviously, it does not refer to all of them, as just indicated by the mention of the faithful remnant of believers among the Jews. CEV renders the word 'Israel' with a positive phrase: "only a chosen few of the people of Israel."

The prefix on the verb ἐπιζητεῖ 'seeks, strives for' intensifies it, hence 'earnestly' (so NIV).

that is, the way to be declared righteous The object of the verb 'seeks' is not in the text, but it is assumed to be carried over from 9:31 and 10:3. As commentators suggest, it is best taken as 'the way to be declared righteous'.

11:7b The *people of Israel whom God had chosen found it* The phrase ἡ ἐκλογή 'the elect' usually refers to the Gentiles, but in this context, especially with 'the rest' in 7c clearly referring to unbelieving Jews, it must be taken here as referring primarily to 'the remnant' of v. 5. NCV has "the ones God chose."

11:7c the rest *of the people of Israel* The Greek is οἱ λοιποί 'the rest'; the phrase 'of the people of Israel' is supplied to make it clear who are referred to.

God **made spiritually insensitive** In the extant Greek literature the verb πωρόω 'harden' is used only in the figurative sense of being made spiritually insensitive to the truth (BAGD, p. 732). Several translations have "made callous," but that too is figurative. Louw and Nida give the meaning "have a closed mind" (2:21c), which is itself an idiom. The use of the passive is considered to be euphemistic, God being the implied agent. (The supporting quotation in v. 8 explicitly states that God is the agent.)

11:8a *This is confirmed by* **what is written** *in the Scriptures* The phrase καθὼς γέγραπται 'just as it is written' introduces a Scripture passage that confirms what has just been said. An alternative here might be 'This happened just as'. The display makes explicit where it was written. In some languages, the agent of the writing may have to be made explicit; in such a case, 'which two of the prophets have written' could be supplied, since what follows appears to come partly from Deut. 29:4 and partly from Isa. 29:10.

11:8b God caused them to be in an insensible/ apathetic state The Greek is ἔδωκεν αὐτοῖς ὁ θεὸς πνεῦμα κατανύξεως 'God gave them a spirit of stupor'. The word 'spirit' ought not be taken to refer to some supernatural being, but to a state (Morris, Sanday and Headlam) or pervading tendency (Murray). Barnes says, "The 'spirit' of slumber is not different from slumber itself." TEV has "God made them dull of heart and mind"; REB has "God has dulled their senses."

11:8c-d *they have* **eyes but they cannot see** *spiritually*; *they have* **ears but they cannot understand** *spiritually* The phrases ὀφθαλμοὺς τοῦ μὴ βλέπειν 'eyes of not seeing' and ὦτα τοῦ μὴ ἀκούειν 'ears of not hearing' are rather unusual constructions. As Morris notes, the genitive article followed by an infinitive usually denotes purpose or sometimes result, "but neither suits this passage very well." In some versions the genitives in these phrases are taken as attributive, the first one being rendered as "unseeing" (JB) or "blind" (NEB). The two parts of each phrase are considered to be in a concession-CONTRAEXPECTATION relation and hence are joined with 'but'.

The words 'seeing' and 'hearing' both refer to spiritual, not physical, perception. In many languages there may be no problem using the words 'seeing' and 'hearing' in a metaphorical sense. But for languages where 'seeing' cannot be taken as anything but physical seeing, the display supplies 'spiritually'. In some languages it may be necessary to spell it out in more detail with something like 'Because they have minds that cannot understand any of God's truth, they are like people who have eyes but cannot see anything, and like people who have ears but cannot hear anything.'

11:9a And *it is as King* **David said** The Scripture Paul is about to quote from Psa. 69:22-23 is introduced only by καὶ Δαυὶδ λέγει 'and David says'. But since this quotation is added evidential grounds to support the statement in 7c about the Jews being spiritually insensitive, the words 'it is as' are supplied. In some languages, 'God's making the Jews spiritually insensitive is as' may have to be supplied. LB introduces the quotation with "King David spoke of the same thing when he said."

asking God to cause his enemies to be insensitive This propositional cluster supplies an antecedent that identifies the pronoun 'they' in the quotation that follows (it was the enemies of the Jews, not the Jews themselves, that the Psalmist speaks of). It also provides the point of similarity between those described in the quotation and the Jews themselves.

11:9b May *you cause* **the things that they enjoy** The Greek is γενηθήτω ἡ τράπεζα αὐτῶν 'let their table become'. The word 'table' is a spatial metonymy standing for the things on the table, specifically the things spread on the table that people delight in. CEV has "their meals"; LB has "their good food and other blessings." Since the prayer is directed to God, the words 'you cause' are supplied to show that God is the implied agent.

to be like a snare and a trap to them *by causing them to feel secure and then be caught by surprise* Four phrases with the same grammatical form occur in succession in 9b-c: εἰς παγίδα καὶ εἰς θήραν καὶ εἰς σκάνδαλον καὶ εἰς ἀνταπόδομα 'for a snare and for a trap and for a stumbling block and for a recompense'. The first two are taken as a doublet: they refer to objects with the same function. Both are retained in the display because of the poetic nature of the OT passage from which they come. According to Morris, the third of the three words, σκάνδαλον, "properly means the bait stick of a trap, the stick which triggers off the trapping mechanism when a bird or animal makes contact." Thus it is a synecdoche, the part standing for the whole trap. Since its meaning is the same as that of the preceding word, it is not included in the display. An alternative is to consider that 'stumbling block' refers to the event of falling away (from God) (cf. TEV, "May they fall"), but this lacks support from commentators.

The first three of the four terms are metaphors. Commentators disagree on how much weight should be given to the three respective items versus their combined connotation. A number of commentators (e.g., Erdman, Murray, Sanday and Headlam) suggest that the uniting idea is things that give a false sense of security. In the case of the Jews of Paul's day, it was their delight in the law and rituals and consequent feeling of spiritual security that Paul is referring to. The display supplies as the point of similarity two separate clauses to try to convey the notion of a false sense of security. LB conveys the same sense with "trap them into thinking all is well between themselves and God." Though the expression 'caught by surprise' is an English idiom, there does not seem to be a better way to express it.

11:9c with the result that they will be destroyed by you The fourth phrase, καὶ εἰς ἀνταπόδομα αὐτοῖς 'and for a recompense to them', is rendered as a full clause, a separate proposition, because it expresses an event. Lenski and Sanday and Headlam take it to refer to destruction or death; Morris, on the other hand, thinks it means only trouble (JB has "let that be their punishment"). Here in view of the notion of recompense it is rendered 'will be destroyed' in line with the former interpretation. The agent of 'recompense' is clearly God.

Even though the εἰς phrase here is grammatically parallel to the three phrases that precede it, it is taken as expressing a result proposition because semantically it is the outcome of the others. The first three are figurative; and, as Lenski says, "The fourth term, 'recompense', is the literal interpretation which states the point of the figure, namely due retribution."

11:10a May you dull their ability to perceive *spiritually* The Greek is σκοτισθήτωσαν οἱ ὀφθαλμοὶ αὐτῶν 'let be darkened their eyes'. It is a metaphor in which 'eyes' stands for spiritual perception and 'darkened' means being made dull, being obscured.

11:10b with the result that they not understand *spiritually* The Greek is τοῦ μὴ βλέπειν 'of not seeing', in which 'seeing' refers to spiritual understanding (see the note on 8c regarding 'eyes of not seeing'). Here the result relationship is very appropriate. In many versions (e.g., NIV, TEV, NEB, RSV, LB) the two clauses are joined with "so that," which could be taken as expressing either purpose or result.

11:10c May you cause them to carry heavy loads on their backs continually *as slaves do* In τὸν νῶτον αὐτῶν διὰ παντὸς σύγκαμψον 'their back continually bending' the word 'bending' is probably a metonymy, the effect standing for the cause: bearing heavy loads. But is it also metaphorical, at least in Paul's understanding ('carry loads as slaves do for their masters')? Most commentators suggest that the allusion is to the burdens imposed on slaves, hence 'as slaves do'. In the display no attempt is made to define exactly what slavery Paul may be referring to.

BOUNDARIES AND COHERENCE

The 11:7-10 paragraph is relationally coherent in that it consists of a CLAIM and two *justifications* for it. The quotations and the figures they contain also provide coherence.

The boundary with the next unit is signaled in v. 11 by the same marker that is in v. 1: οὖν 'therefore' plus the orienter λέγω 'I say'. It introduces yet another hypothetical question.

PROMINENCE AND THEME

The theme of 11:7-10 is drawn from the CLAIM (v. 7) and its two *justifications*. Since the *justifications* consist of Scripture supporting the CLAIM, the theme includes the fact of the confirmation by Scripture. The parts of the actual quotations are not included since the appeal to Scripture was more important in making the point than the quotations themselves.

SECTION CONSTITUENT 11:11–12 (Expository Paragraph: Query₂ about God's rejection of the Jews, and Paul's response)

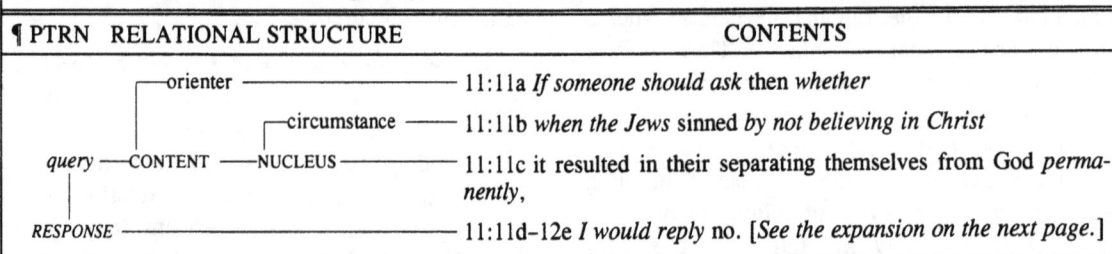

INTENT AND PARAGRAPH PATTERN

It is difficult to decide whether 11:11–12 is a *query-RESPONSE* unit or an *objection-REFUTATION*. It seems to be more a hypothetical reply "someone" would make to what Paul said in 9:30–32 (about the Jews falling away), followed by Paul's rejection of such a view. Therefore in 11:11–12, as in the previous paragraph, the paragraph pattern is considered as consisting of a *query* and RESPONSE, which relation marks the paragraph as being expository.

NOTES

11:11a *If someone should ask* Paul is about to pose a question which he suspects some of his audience might raise, and then he answers it. It is handled here as similar questions were previously (cf. 10:18, 19; 11:1).

11:11b *when the Jews* **sinned** *by not believing in Christ* The pronominal subject is here specified as 'the Jews' (so NCV). CEV has "the people of Israel."

The verb ἔπταισαν 'they stumbled' in its figurative use means "to make a mistake, go astray, sin" (BAGD, p. 727.1). But what sin is Paul referring to? Murray says that "what is in view is . . . their rejection of Christ as Saviour." Since this fits the context and failure to understand this could easily give a wrong or zero meaning, it is included in the display.

11:11c it resulted in their separating themselves from God *permanently* The conjunction ἵνα usually denotes purpose, but that would not be relationally coherent here. According to Morris, "if that is the meaning here it ought to be the purpose of the subject of the verb ἔπταισαν, i.e., of the Jews. But obviously it was not their purpose that they would fall." Most commentators agree that result or outcome is meant, and it is so rendered in the display.

The word 'permanently' is supplied as required by the context. Obviously the Jews have 'fallen away', but Paul is leading up to the subject of their eventual reinclusion in v. 12. Thus, as commentators note, permanency is implied; the figure is of stumbling, in which a person usually, but not always, gets up again. NIV has "beyond recovery"; JB and LB, "forever"; CEV, "never to get up again."

EXPANSION OF *RESPONSE* IN THE 11:11-12 DISPLAY

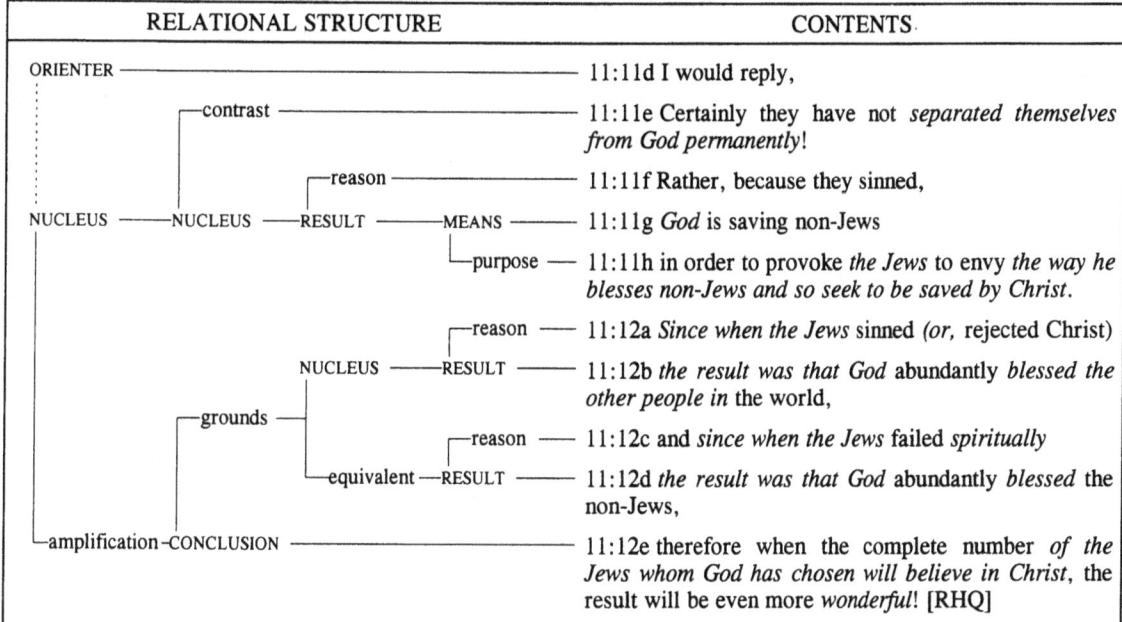

11:11f because they sinned The dative expression τῷ αὐτῶν παραπτώματι 'by their trespass' could be taken as means, but since means almost always introduces a proposition with the same agent as that of the preceding action, it is best to consider it a reason (following Cranfield, TEV, NIV, and NEB).

11:11g God is saving non-Jews The construction ἡ σωτηρία τοῖς ἔθνεσιν 'salvation to the Gentiles' has no verb. Most English versions supply 'has come', which is fine for a literal translation. An alternative is to render the event expressed by 'salvation' as a verb with 'God' the agent. The term 'non-Jews' is not intended to imply that all Gentiles are being saved. If necessary, the word 'many' could be supplied to avoid wrong meaning.

11:11h in order to provoke *the Jews* to envy *the way he blesses non-Jews and so seek to be saved by Christ* In the display 'them' is identified as 'the Jews'. The verb παραζηλῶσαι 'provoke to jealousy' semantically requires that the object of the jealousy/envy be understood: 'the way he blesses non-Jews'. But more is in view than the Jews' being provoked to envy; what is implied is the ultimate purpose, that it will result in their seeking salvation through Christ (so Hodge, Cranfield, Morris). LB has "begin to want God's salvation for themselves."

11:12a *Since when the Jews* sinned (*or,* rejected Christ) As in 11:6a, εἰ is factual, not conditional. The noun παράπτωμα is rendered as in 11f by the verb 'sinned'; but the reader needs to know what sin is in view. Therefore 'rejected Christ' is supplied as an alternative (so Murray). Cranfield suggests 'unbelief'.

11:12b *the result was that God* abundantly *blessed the other people in* the world The Greek is simply πλοῦτος κόσμου 'riches of the world', with no verb. Some verb such as 'brought' (TEV) or 'meant' (NIV, NEB, RSV) is usually supplied. In the display 'the result was' is supplied following C. B. Williams (also in 12d for the identical construction).

As in 2:4 and 9:23, 'riches' is semantically an attribute modifying an unexpressed event. Here 'blessed' is supplied as the event (also in 12d). TEV has "rich blessings"; Morris, "an abundance of blessings"; CEV, "the rest of the world's people were helped so much."

The word κόσμος 'world' is a spatial metonymy standing for the people of the world. But here it obviously also means 'other people in the world' and is more or less equivalent to 'non-Jews'.

11:12c and *since when the Jews* failed *spiritually* The phrase τὸ ἥττημα αὐτῶν means 'their defeat' (BAGD, p. 349). As Cranfield points out, the sense 'diminution' often given by commentators is not a proper sense of the word. (There is no reason why the word must be taken as an antonym of πλήρωμα 'fulness' in 12e.) Spiritual defeat fits the context quite well. The idiom 'lost out spiritually' carries the sense very well. If one cannot express this concept naturally, it may be necessary to say simply 'rejected Christ'. LB has "turned down [God's offer of salvation]."

The paired expressions 'the Jews sinned . . . riches for the world' (12a-b) and 'their failure . . . riches for the Gentiles' (12c-d) are considered by Moore (p. 41) a near-synonymous doublet. In the display the second is labeled an equivalent of the first.

11:12e therefore when the complete number *of the Jews whom God has chosen will believe in Christ***, the result will be even more** *wonderful* The Greek is terse: πόσῳ μᾶλλον τὸ πλήρωμα αὐτῶν 'by how much more their fulness'. It is difficult to know exactly what Paul meant by this. The word πόσῳ 'how much?' has an exclamatory sense, as in many other passages, calling the reader to consider how much greater something is than something else. Hence the display has 'even more'.

Since 12e is clearly the conclusion to which the grounds in 12a-d relate, the question is, What will it result in, and for whom? To answer the first part of the question, 'blessing', which was used in b and d, could be appropriate here also (cf. TEV, LB). But since the text is not explicit, the word 'wonderful' is supplied modified by 'even more'. An alternative would be to nominalize the word 'bless' and render it as 'an even greater blessing', following TEV. The answer to the second part of the question is not clear. Morris says, "[Their] salvation will mean no diminution of the blessing that had come to the Gentiles, but rather an enrichment." The display makes no attempt to solve the problem. (Neither of the alternatives just given states for whom it will be more wonderful or more greatly blessed, and it is not likely that Paul's expression was intended to specify this.) In the display it has deliberately been left ambiguous as to whether the result will be more wonderful to the Jews or to everyone. LB, JB, and NCV specify "to/for the world"; Dunn, "to humankind."

The word 'fullness' has been variously interpreted. Some suggest 'fulfillment' (see BAGD, p. 672.4) and then supply 'of all that God demands' as the implicit object, even though the same word with seemingly the same sense in v. 25 is given the meaning 'the full number'. Other ideas are complete conversion, complete restoration, perfection. Lenski suggests fullness of salvation. But the rest of the chapter supports the sense of 'the full number'. The question then is, the full number of what? Most commentators support the sense given in the display, as it fits the context best. JB has "the conversion of them all"; LB, "the Jews, too, come to Christ." NCV has "enough Jews became the kind of people God wants," which is not very satisfactory.

BOUNDARIES AND COHERENCE

Lexical coherence in the 11:11-12 paragraph is provided by two occurrences of ἔθνη 'Gentiles', two of παράπτωμα 'trespass', and two of πλοῦτος 'riches'. The boundary between this paragraph and the next is clearly marked, at v. 13, by the orienter ὑμῖν δὲ λέγω 'but (now) I say'. But the clearest indication of a paragraph break at v. 13 is that at that point Paul makes it specific that he is switching from addressing the Jews to addressing the Gentiles in his audience. Furthermore, his whole thrust switches from God's rejection of the Jews to their eventual reinstatement as God's people.

PROMINENCE AND THEME

The theme of 11:11-12 is drawn from a condensation of the *query* in v. 11 and the two main propositions of the NUCLEUS of the RESPONSE. None of the amplification is included because it would be repetitious of what is stated in vv. 25-32, which is a more prominent paragraph.

SECTION CONSTITUENT 11:13–16 (Expressive Paragraph: Statement to non-Jews of Paul's reaction to the problem of God's rejection of the Jews)

THEME: I highly esteem the work God has called me to do as an apostle among you non-Jews. I hope that my making my fellow Jews jealous will result in some of them being saved.

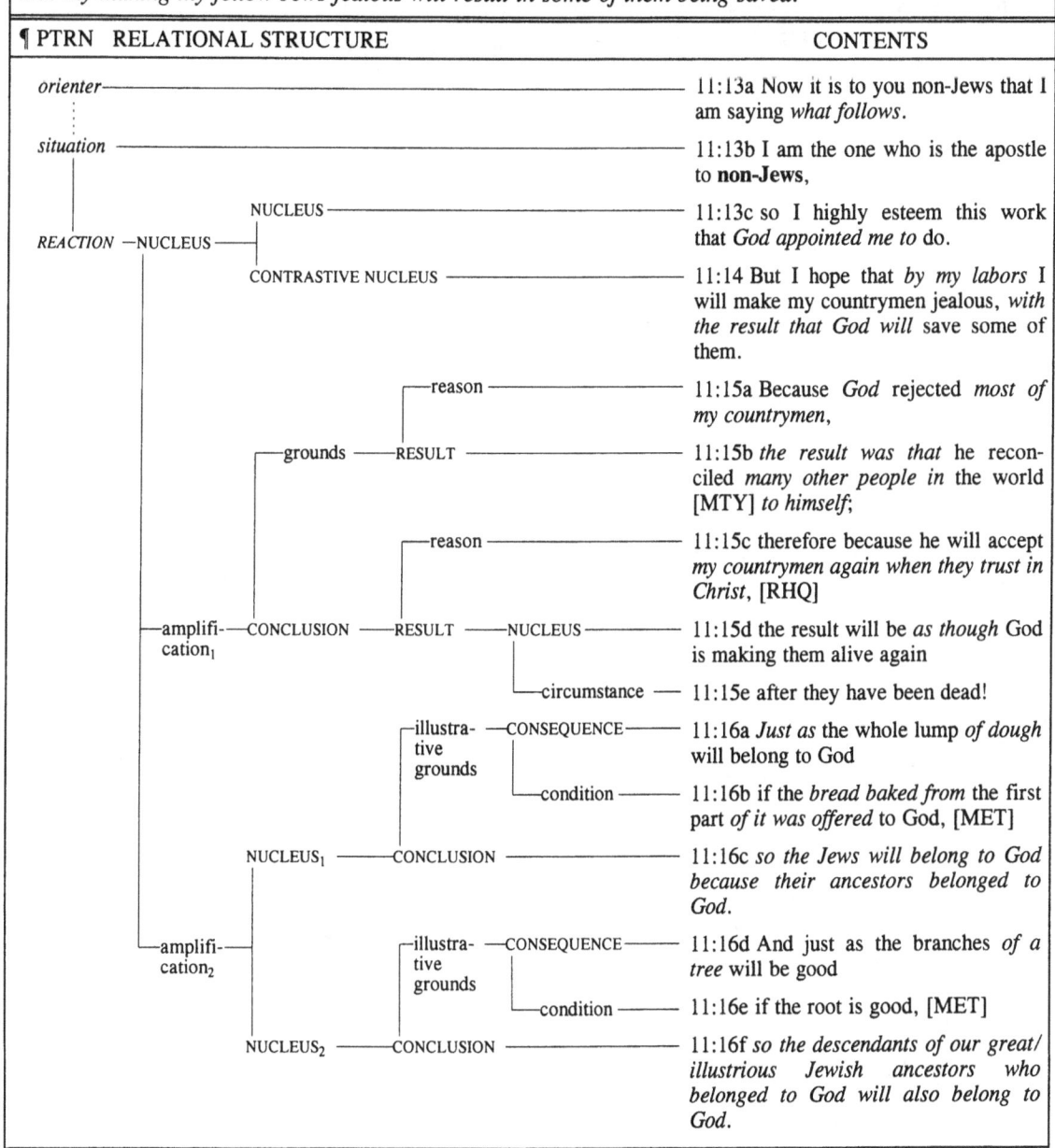

INTENT AND PARAGRAPH PATTERN

The 11:13–16 paragraph is considered expressive. In v. 13 (τὴν διακονίαν μου δοξάζω 'I highly esteem this work that I do'), Paul is expressing his feelings and in vv. 14–16 he expresses a hope which relates directly to and contributes to his feelings. The paragraph consists of a short statement of the *situation* (13b) and an extended statement of his REACTION to it (13c–16).

NOTES

11:13a Now it is to you non-Jews that I am saying *what follows* The pronoun ὑμῖν 'to you' occurs before the verb, a marker of either topicalization or prominence. It is therefore forefronted in the display. (JBP has "Now a word to you who are gentiles.") Paul here changes the focus of his discussion about the Jews from a long series of questions he thinks the Jews among his audience might ask to the attitude the Gentiles should have to all this.

11:13b I am the one who is the apostle to <u>non-Jews</u> The word combination ἐφ' ὅσον means 'inasmuch as, since' (not "as long as" as in the TEV). BAGD (p. 289.III3) have "insofar as." It introduces a clause expressing what on a lower level would probably be labeled a grounds or reason relation; therefore ἐφ' ὅσον might also be rendered as 'on the basis of'.

Following ἐφ' ὅσον is the particle μέν and then the conjunction οὖν 'therefore'. According to Cranfield, the sequence μέν οὖν gives the sense 'contrary to what you may think', but this does not fit the communication situation very well. BAGD (p. 503.2b) suggest that μέν always indicates contrast, and that here "the contrast is actually expressed, but not in adversative form . . . (the contrast follows in vs. 14)." Therefore in the display v. 14 begins with 'But'. Since "a genitive preceding the word it modifies (instead of following, which is normal word order) is emphatic" (Greenlee, p. 68), the emphasis is on 'Gentiles' (in the phrase ἐθνῶν ἀπόστολος 'of Gentiles apostle'); hence 'non-Jews' is in bold type.

11:13c so I highly esteem this work that *God appointed me to* do The phrase τὴν διακονίαν μου 'my ministry' is rendered as 'this work that God appointed me to do' to make clear what work Paul was referring to: it was his work as an apostle to the Gentiles.

The verb δοξάζω 'I glorify' is translated in some versions as "take pride in" (TEV, CEV). Cranfield, Hodge, and Sanday and Headlam suggest 'do it with all my ability to make it successful', but this explains the motive of the action more than the action itself. The sense in the display (quite different from TEV's "take pride in") follows Bruce 1985, Barnes, and Dunn.

11:14 But I hope that *by my labors* I will make my countrymen jealous, *with the result that God will* save some of them The Greek here begins with εἴ πως 'if perhaps' (cf. 1:10), which is a rather unusual construction. Though εἰ usually expresses expectation (BDF, p. 191), in conjunction with πώς it expresses hope more than expectation. NIV begins this verse with "in the hope that," and CEV and NCV both begin a new sentence here beginning with "I hope." The verb in the first clause, παραζηλώσω μου τὴν σάρκα 'I may provoke to jealousy my flesh', is rendered 'make jealous'. It is somewhat difficult to know exactly what Paul intends by using the phrase 'my flesh' to refer to his fellow countrymen. It seems to signify his racial, ethnic, religious, and linguistic (rather than political) oneness with them (cf. τῶν συγγενῶν μου κατὰ σάρκα 'my kinsmen according to flesh' in 9:3).

The subject of the verb σώσω 'I will save' is the first person singular subject pronoun. This is very unusual, because God is the one who saves, and the verb is almost always used in the passive with 'God' as the implied agent or in the active with 'God' as the expressed agent. Semantically, it seems best to include both agents as in the display: 'by <u>my</u> labors' and '<u>God</u> will save'. NCV solves the problem neatly with "it can help some of them to be saved."

11:15a–b Because *God* rejected *most of my countrymen, the result was that* he reconciled many other people *in* the world *to himself* Here γάρ introduces an amplification of what Paul has just said, not a reason why God will save them. It is true that the subject matter of 15d seems to build on 12e, but since v. 13 clearly marks a new paragraph directed to a different audience, 15a is seen as relating to 14b.

The 15a–b construction is the same one as in 12a–b, c–d, and e (the causal εἰ is the introducer, without a stative verb between the subject and predicate). Therefore 'the result was that' is again supplied.

The word ἀποβολή (found only twice in the NT) here means 'rejection' (BAGD, p. 89.1); 'God' is its implied agent, as TEV, LB, and NCV make clear. CEV's "When Israel rejected God" is totally unwarranted.

The pronoun αὐτῶν 'of them' refers to the Jews; in the display it is rendered 'most of my countrymen' to avoid an overstatement.

In the phrase καταλλαγὴ κόσμου 'reconciling of (the) world', the word 'world' is a metonymy meaning the people of the world. But it means 'many of the people in the world' or 'others in the world', not all of them.

The words 'to himself' are supplied to remove the ambiguity as to who is being reconciled to whom.

11:15c–d because he will accept *my countrymen again when they trust in Christ*, the result will be *as though* God is making them alive again The construction here is like that in 12e and is similarly expressed: 'the result will be'.

The only difference is that here in 15c–d the agent, 'God', is the same in the two propositions.

Proposition 15c is, in Greek, simply ἡ πρόσλημψις 'the acceptance'. The agent of the event is clearly 'God'; 'my countrymen' is supplied, carried over from 14a (and 15a), as the implicit object. (NCV has "the Jews.") The words 'when they trust in Christ' are to make clear what Paul is implying in his argument.

Just as the a fortiori argument in v. 12 ended with a clause introduced by 'how much' with exclamatory force, so here the climax of the a fortiori argument ends with a clause introduced by τίς 'what?' In the display the rhetorical question is changed to a statement ending with an exclamation point (in 15e). The Greek construction is τίς εἰ μή, literally 'what if not?' There is a difference in interpretation among the commentators here. Several say 'life from the dead' refers to the Gentiles. Their argument goes like this: First note that 15a clearly refers to the Jews and 15b to the Gentiles with a reason-RESULT relation between them. Then note the grounds-CONCLUSION relation between 15a–b and 15c–d plus the fact that 15c refers to the Jews (shown by the context). Therefore by analogy 15d must refer to the Gentiles, since there is a reason-RESULT relationship between 15c and 15d just as there is between 15a and 15b. This view is rejected, however, because vv. 15–16 are clearly an amplification of 14, which deals with Paul's hope for the salvation of the *Jews*, not the Gentiles.

11:15e after they have been dead! The result, Paul says, will be ζωὴ ἐκ νεκρῶν 'life from the dead'. There are two problems here. First, is Paul speaking figuratively of a massive conversion of a great number of people, or is he speaking of a literal bodily resurrection coinciding with the return of Christ, which according to this view is to follow Israel's conversion? The figurative interpretation is preferable, because if the literal one were to be adopted, 15e would seem an abrupt, unusual intrusion with no contextual support. Moreover, Paul elsewhere always speaks of the resurrection as ἀνάστασις νεκρῶν 'resurrection from the dead', not 'life from the dead'. The words 'will be as though' in 15d are intended to indicate the figurative sense.

The second problem is the matter of who is being referred to as receiving 'life from the dead'. Several commentators say it is the Gentiles, because of the 15a and 15b analogy contrasting the Jews and Gentiles in a reason-RESULT relationship. But as already noted, it is clear that vv. 15–16 are an amplification of 14a, which deals with Paul's hope for the salvation of the Jews, not the Gentiles. And ἡ πρόσλημψις 'the reception' (in 15c), in contrast to ἡ ἀποβολή 'the rejection' in 15a, clearly refers to the Jews, and Paul would probably expect his readers to supply the same referent unless he explicitly indicated otherwise. Furthermore, in the analogy to follow in v. 16 the referent of the 'whole lump' and 'branches' is clearly the Jews.

11:16 The two illustrations in v. 16 are in the form of proverb-like statements introduced by εἰ, which may be taken as the conditional 'if', in the sense of 'given X, Y holds too'.

11:16a–b *Just as the* whole lump *of dough* will belong to God if the *bread baked from* the first part *of it was offered* to God There is considerable assumed cultural information in the metaphorical εἰ ἡ ἀπαρχὴ ἁγία, καὶ τὸ φύραμα 'if the firstfruit (is) holy, also the lump'. According to nearly all commentators, the reference is to dough offered to the Lord as a sacrifice (described in Numbers 15). The rendering here is 'bread baked from' because it was the bread, not the dough, that was to be offered to the Lord (Num. 15:17–21). TEV and NCV both have "first piece of bread."

The word ἁγία 'holy' means 'separated or consecrated unto God'; and since the main point Paul is making has to do with Jews belonging to God (by faith in Christ), the display translates it as 'belongs to God'.

11:16c *so the Jews will belong to God because their ancestors belonged to God* The topic of the 16a–b metaphor is supplied in 16c. A few commentators say the reference is to the first Jewish Christians. Hodge says, "Since the first converts to the gospel were Jews, it is evident that the nation, as such, is not cast off by God; as a portion of them is holy (or have been accepted by God), so may the residue be." While it is impossible to exclude this as Paul's meaning here, even the commentators who hold this view agree that the metaphor in 16d–e is referring to the godly Jewish patriarchs. Since there is an obvious parallelism in both parts of v. 16, it would seem unnatural to make it refer to two entirely different groups so distant in time. Furthermore, the analogy would not be clear: The "rest of the dough" is inextricably of the same stock as the first portion offered, but future Jewish converts will not be of exactly the same ancestral stock as the first converts. The other interpretation, which is followed in the display and by the vast majority of commentators, is that the references in both a–b and d–e are to the same group, namely the Jewish patriarchs; and certainly all Jews consider themselves of the same stock as the patriarchs. LB, the only version to give a nonmetaphorical rendering, makes the topic clear: "Since Abraham and the prophets are God's people, their children will be too."

11:16d the branches *of a tree* The implied words 'of a tree' are supplied here. In many languages it will be necessary to include them.

11:16f *so the descendants of our great/illustrious Jewish ancestors who belonged to God will also belong to God* As in 16c, the topic of the metaphor is spelled out. The word 'great' or 'illustrious' is included to convey the implied connotation of 'patriarchs', not because of any signal from the word 'root'.

BOUNDARIES AND COHERENCE

The relational coherence of the 11:13–16 paragraph derives from its unity as an expressive unit. It consists of Paul's feelings about his *situation* as the apostle to the Gentiles and his REACTION to it, including his hopes about how his ministry will affect the Jews. (Both 'I highly esteem this work' in 13c and 'I hope that' in 14 are expressive.)

The boundary between the 11:13–16 paragraph and the next one is marked by a new sentence at v. 17, beginning with δέ and the start of an extended metaphor on the grafting of olive trees. There is a tail-head linkage at the end of v. 16 in which are introduced the words ῥίζα 'root' and κλάδοι 'branches', which form an integral part of the next paragraph.

PROMINENCE AND THEME

The 11:13–16 theme is drawn from the *situation* in 13b and the NUCLEI of the REACTION.

SECTION CONSTITUENT 11:17-24
(Hortatory Paragraph: Appeals to non-Jews)

THEME: You non-Jews must not despise the Jews whom God has rejected, and you must not become proud, but instead beware. God will not spare you if you fall away from him, and he will act kindly toward the Jews and be reunited to them if they trust in Christ.

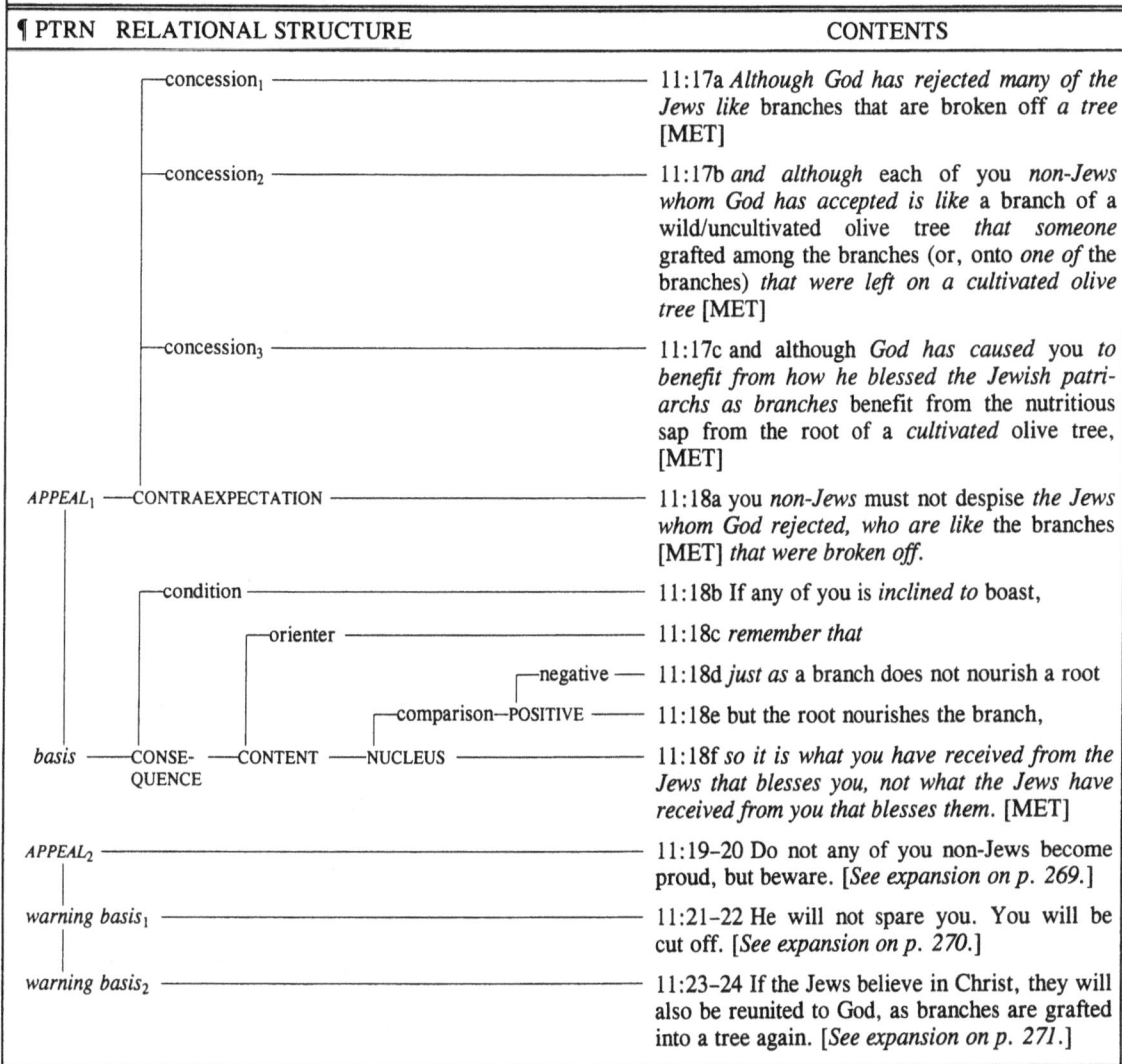

INTENT AND PARAGRAPH PATTERN

Verses 11:17-24 form a complex paragraph, with different levels of patterns operating. It probably could be divided into two units; however, there is a clear unity in that it is addressed to the non-Jews on the subject of God's rejection of most of the Jews. The negative imperative expressions μὴ κατακαυχῶ 'do not despise' in 18a and μὴ ὑψηλὰ φρόνει 'do not become proud' in 20f and the positive imperative φοβοῦ 'beware' in 20g show that the paragraph is mainly hortatory. The imperative in 18a is an *APPEAL* supported by the incentive in 18b-f for not despising the Jews. Similarly the imperatives in 20f-g constitute an *APPEAL* supported by the *warning bases* in vv. 21-24. On the lower level within 19-20 is a hypothetical *anticipated challenge* by Paul's non-Jewish readers (19a-c) to which v. 20 is his *RESPONSE*.

NOTES

11:17a *Although God has rejected many of the Jews like* Here εἰ is not introducing an uncertain condition. The sense is 'if it is true, and it is'. (The construction parallels the one in vv. 15-16.) The clause *could* be considered a grounds. (NCV and TEV ignore εἰ and begin v. 18 with "so," indicating a grounds-CONCLUSION relationship.) But even though a causal relationship might seem to be indicated by εἰ, semantically 'God has rejected many Jews' (17a) does not cohere as a grounds of 'you non-Jews must not despise them' (18a). Therefore, 17a is taken as in a concession relationship, which fits the context well.

The branches metaphor introduced in v. 16 continues in 11:17-24. Its topic is spelled out here in 17a (cf. LB's "some of these branches from Abraham's tree, some of the Jews, have been broken off").

11:17b each of you *non-Jews whom God has accepted is like* The Greek pronoun 'you' in σὺ ἀγριέλαιος 'you(sg) a wild olive' is singular for effect; but since Paul is not addressing one individual, the sense is captured here with 'each of you'. The topical referent is made clear with the words 'you non-Jews'. CEV has "You Gentiles are like. . . ."

a branch of a wild/uncultivated olive tree *that someone* grafted among the branches (or, onto *one of* the branches) *that were left on a cultivated olive tree* The word ἀγριέλαιος 'wild olive tree' here refers to a branch or shoot of such a tree. Since 'wild' in some languages refers only to animals, 'uncultivated' is given as an alternate.

The words ἐν αὐτοῖς 'among them' are rendered in the display by 'among the branches that were left on a cultivated olive tree' in order to specify the pronoun and complete the metaphor. Cranfield says that ἐν αὐτοῖς means "among the remaining branches of the cultivated olive tree, the Jewish Christians. The meaning is imprecisely expressed: αὐτοῖς must be understood to refer to those of the κλάδοι [branches] which are not denoted by the preceding τινες τῶν κλάδων [some of the branches]." A few commentators suggest that ἐν αὐτοῖς means 'instead of them' because 'them' should refer to its nearest antecedent, the 'broken branches' of 17a. But Paul does not say that believing Gentiles have completely replaced believing Jews, but rather that they have been joined to them.

11:17c and although *God has caused* you *to benefit from how he blessed the Jewish patriarchs as branches* benefit from the nutritious sap from the root of a *cultivated* olive tree The Greek is καὶ συγκοινωνὸς τῆς ῥίζης τῆς πιότητος τῆς ἐλαίας ἐγένου 'a partaker of the root of the fatness of the olive tree you(sg) became'. The topic of this metaphor is supplied in the 17c proposition. Commentators agree that 'the root' refers to the Jewish patriarchs.

The noun 'partaker' is rendered as a verb, 'benefit from', which is the point of similarity between the metaphor's image and topic. An alternative would be 'share some of'.

Though 'root of fatness' is not textually certain (it has a B "almost certain" rating in the fourth edition GNT), it is the variant that seems the best one. The other longer variants seem to be attempts to improve on the original somewhat strange construction. The genitive 'of fatness' could be taken as appositional, giving the sense 'the root, that is, its fatness'; but this is strained. Or it could be considered attributive, which, as many suggest, would then mean "the rich sap which flows from the root" (Sanday and Headlam). Rich sap is sap that is full of nutrients, hence 'nutritious' (cf. NIV). LB is alone among the versions in supplying the topic of the metaphor: "So now you, too, receive the blessing God has promised Abraham and his children."

11:18a you *non-Jews* must not despise *the Jews whom God rejected, who are like* the branches *that were broken off* The Greek is μὴ κατακαυχῶ τῶν κλάδων 'do not exult over the branches', in which the second person singular continues. In the display the referent is made clear with the plural 'you non-Jews'. For 'not exult over' TEV has "must not despise"; Goodspeed, "must not look down upon"; NJB, "not consider yourself superior to." The point of similarity between the topic and branches image, 'rejected', is supplied. The topic, 'the Jews whom God rejected', is also supplied. TEV has "those who were broken off."

11:18b If any of you is *inclined to* boast The literal meaning of εἰ κατακαυχᾶσαι is 'if you(sg) boast'. But the sense is "if thou art disposed to do it" (Hodge), not 'if you actually do it'. JBP has "If you feel inclined that way."

11:18c remember that These words are not in the text but are essential to the sense of what follows. NRSV, NEB, JB, and LB have them; other versions have something comparable.

11:18f This proposition supplies the topic of the metaphor. Hodge has "the Jews were the channel of blessings to the Gentiles, and not the reverse."

EXPANSION OF *APPEAL₂* IN THE 11:17-24 DISPLAY

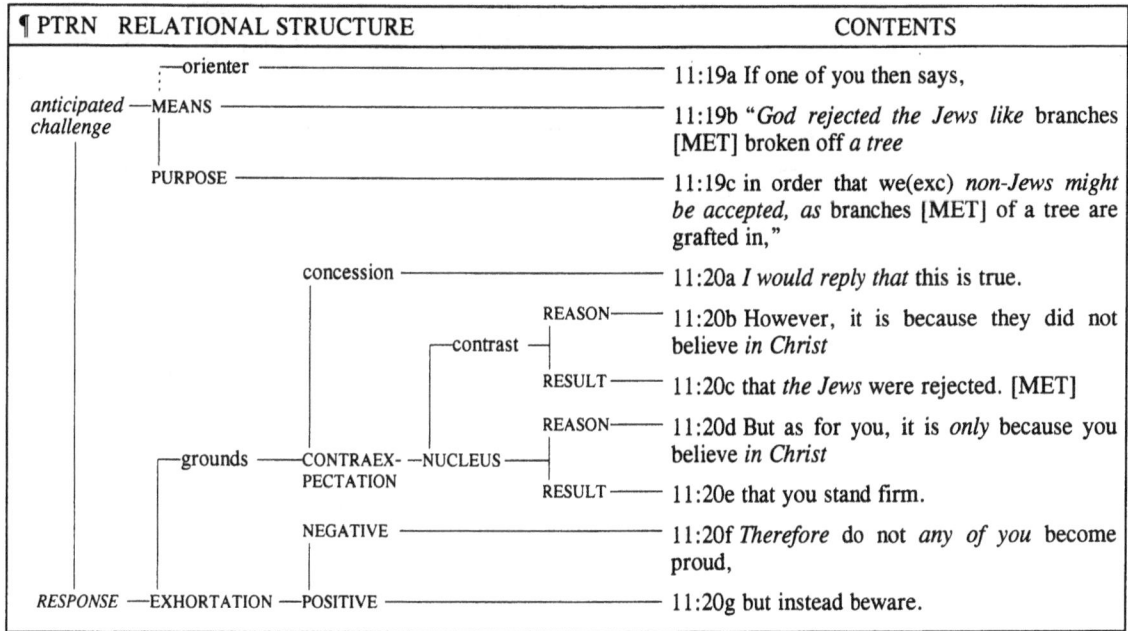

11:19a If one of you then says The Greek is ἐρεῖς οὖν 'you(sg) will say therefore'. The conjunction οὖν does not indicate a grounds-CONCLUSION relation between the parts of the paragraph pattern. Rather, it introduces an *anticipated challenge* arising from the immediately preceding context. In the display, the word 'then' indicates the connection. As in 17a and 18a, the second person singular pronoun is rendered by 'any of you'. To translate this 'if any of you would boast, saying' would also capture the force. LB puts it well: "those branches were broken off to make room for me so I must be pretty good."

11:19b *God rejected the Jews like* **branches broken off** *a tree* The topic of the branches metaphor is represented as in 18a.

11:19c in order that we(exc) *non-Jews might be accepted, as* **branches of a tree are grafted in** The metaphorical 'grafted' is spelled out in the display by 'accepted'. Paul uses the first person singular here but with the generic sense, so it is rendered 'we(exc) non-Jews' to make the referent clear.

11:20a *I would reply that* The change of speakers is made specific. (In 19a the speaker was 'you'.)

11:20b it is because they did not believe The phrase τῇ ἀπιστίᾳ 'by unbelief', rendered here as 'because they did not believe', is forefronted in the Greek. That prominence is represented in the display by a cleft construction.

11:20c that *the Jews* **were rejected** The Greek is ἐξεκλάσθησαν 'were broken off', a continuation of the metaphor. Since the metaphor was fully spelled out previously, only the topic is given here.

11:20d But as for you, it is *only* **because you believe** The pronoun σύ 'you(sg)' is forefronted, probably as a feature of topicalization, but it also conveys some emphasis by way of contrast with the Jews in 20c. This contrast/emphasis is rendered in the display by 'as for you', and a cleft construction and the word 'only' are used to convey the contrast/emphasis of τῇ πίστει 'by belief', which is also forefronted (cf. LB, JB, RSV, JBP, NCV).

11:20e you stand firm The verb ἕστηκας 'you(sg) stand' is in the perfect tense and has the sense of 'stand firm' as in several other places (note esp. Rom. 5:2; 1 Cor. 10:12, 15:1; and 2 Cor. 1:24). The English rendering here is still somewhat figurative.

11:20f *Therefore* **do not** *any of you* **become proud** Although there is no conjunction here, 20b-e is clearly the grounds for the EXHORTATION that begins here. Accordingly the proposition begins with 'Therefore'. (RSV and

CEV have "So.") The second person singular of the imperative is again represented as 'any of you'.

11:20g beware The verb φοβοῦ 'be afraid' has the sense of reverential awe here. It is clearly a warning. NEB has "be on your guard"; JB, "be careful."

EXPANSION OF *WARNING BASIS*₁ IN THE 11:17-24 DISPLAY

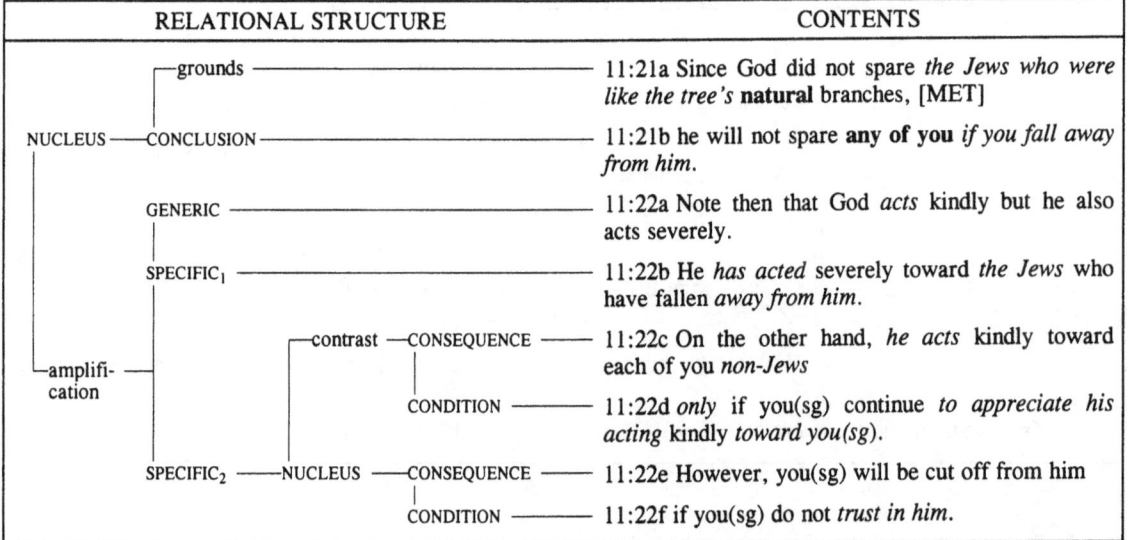

11:21a *the Jews who were like the tree's natural branches* The Greek is τῶν κατὰ φύσιν κλάδων, literally 'the according to nature branches' or, more idiomatically, 'the natural branches'. The prominence given to 'natural' by its position extends to the topic of the metaphor (the Jews), and this prominence is indicated by bold type in the display.

11:21b he will not spare any of you *if you fall away from him* Since 'he will not spare you' is not intended to be understood unconditionally, the implied words 'if you fall away from him' are supplied (see Barrett, Denney, Cranfield, Dunn). NCV has "if you don't believe." The pronoun 'you(sg)' is forefronted for emphasis, as indicated by bold type in the display.

There is a textual problem here that is not easily resolved. In some very old and excellent manuscripts this clause begins with μή πως 'lest'. While it is quite possible that μή πως was inserted by some scribe to tone down the force of the warning, Metzger (p. 465) suggests that "copyists may have taken offense at its presence here because of its apparent unrelatedness" and thus omitted it. (The expression does occur elsewhere in Paul's writings, nine other times.) Although this internal evidence is inconclusive, the better external evidence of the manuscripts supports omitting the words, as in the display.

Including μή πως requires the addition of several words, something like 'I fear that'. But with or without these words, it does not cohere well relationally with the first part of the verse. Normally the shorter text is to be preferred, and including the italicized conditional clause is more or less equivalent to toning down the warning, as would be indicated by μή πως.

11:22a Note then that God *acts* kindly but he also *acts* severely To resolve the mismatch between the grammatical and semantic categories in χρηστότητα καὶ ἀποτομίαν θεοῦ '(the) kindness and severity of God' the attributive quality of the nouns is represented by adverbs and the verb 'acts' is supplied to accompany the expressed agent, 'God'. The mismatches in 22b and c are handled similarly.

11:22b *the Jews* who have fallen *away from him* The phrase τοὺς πεσόντας 'those who have fallen' is clarified by supplying 'the Jews' and 'away from him'. Note that in English 'fallen away' is a dead metaphor. NCV has "if you stop following him."

11:22c each of you *non-Jews* The pronoun 'you(sg)' is again rendered as 'each of you non-Jews'.

11:22d *only* **if you(sg) continue** *to appreciate his acting* **kindly** *toward you(sg)* The Greek is ἐὰν ἐπιμένῃς τῇ χρηστότητι 'if you(sg) remain in the kindness'. The argument seems to demand an implicature: "continue to be indebted to it, and to it alone, for your religious position" (Denney). The sense of exclusiveness is represented by 'only' in the display. JB has "only for as long as"; NEB, "if only."

Since 'remain/continue' is an aspect of an action, 'continue in his kindness' must mean 'continue to ⎯ his acting kindly toward you', with some verb filling the blank. Denney suggests "be indebted to"; Murray suggests "enjoy"; Morris suggests "lean on"; Newman and Nida suggest "merit" (but this is definitely un-Pauline). An alternative to the display rendering is 'accept'. Some languages may require an even more verb-oriented translation such as 'if you continue *to trust* in *him who* is acting kindly *toward you*'.

11:22e–f you(sg) will be cut off from him *if you(sg) do not* The conjunction ἐπεί here means 'otherwise' (as in 6c); it is an elliptical way of stating a consequence with an implied condition. This is made specific in the display.

The verb ἐκκοπήσῃ 'will be cut off', which continues the metaphor, is retained in the display although it is somewhat figurative.

EXPANSION OF *WARNING BASIS₂* IN THE 11:17–24 DISPLAY

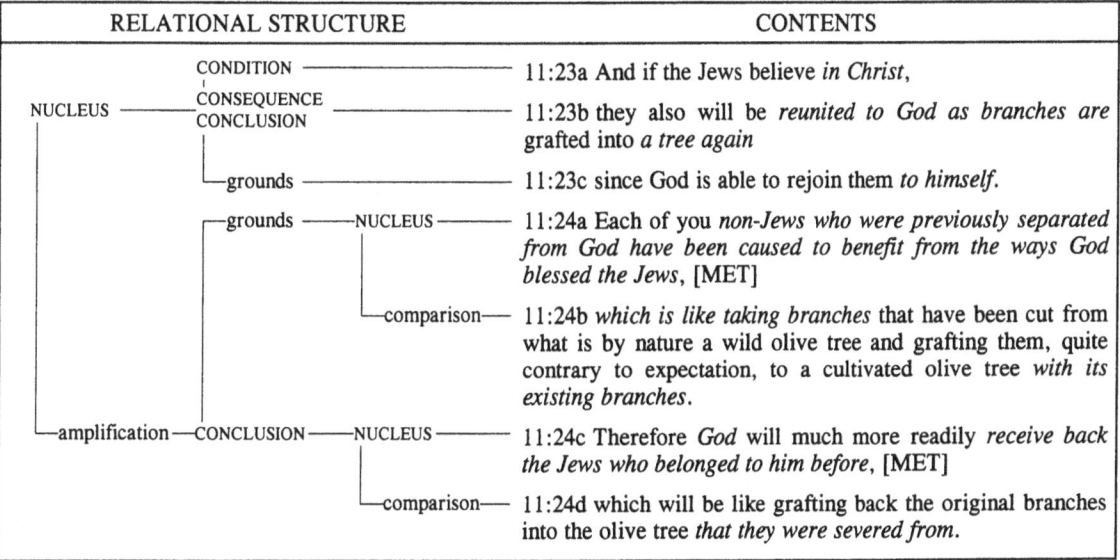

11:23a And if the Jews believe *in Christ* The pronoun κἀκεῖνοι 'and they also' is identified as 'the Jews' (so TEV, NCV, JB, LB). For some languages the equivalent of 'who have not trusted in Christ' may have to be included.

The clause ἐὰν μὴ ἐπιμένωσιν τῇ ἀπιστίᾳ 'if they do not remain in unbelief' contains a double negative, an impossible construction in many languages. The display therefore gives a positive. CEV is similar: "start having faith."

11:23b–c will be *reunited to God as branches are* **grafted into** *a tree again* **since God is able to rejoin them** *to himself* The grafting metaphor continues with ἐγκεντρισθήσονται 'they will be grafted in', the topic of which is 'reunited to God'. It, with the rest of the image of the figure, is included in the display, the figure being completely spelled out in 23b, but dropped in 23c to avoid repetition.

11:24 This verse is an amplification of v. 23, not a reason why God has the power to graft them in again.

11:24a–b Each of you *non-Jews* Here εἰ is a factual 'if': it expresses grounds, not condition. Paul is still using the singular σύ 'you' for effect; the display makes clear just whom he is addressing. TEV has "you Gentiles."

who were previously separated from God have been caused to benefit from the ways God blessed the Jews, which is like taking branches **that have been cut from what is by nature a wild olive tree and grafting them, quite contrary to expectation, to a cultivated olive tree** *with its existing branches* The Greek is ἐκ τῆς κατὰ φύσιν ἐξεκόπης ἀγριελαίου καὶ παρὰ φύσιν ἐνεκεντρίσθης εἰς καλλιέλαιον 'out of according to nature you were cut off (from) a wild olive (tree) and against nature you were grafted into a cultivated olive (tree)'. The metaphor is completely spelled out in the display: The topic of 'cut off' in 24b is specified in 24a by the relative clause 'who were previously separated from God' (an alternative would be 'were not previously united to God'); and the topic of 'grafting to a cultivated olive tree' in 24b is specified in 24a by 'caused to benefit from the ways God blessed the Jews'. An alternative would be 'begin to enjoy the privileges the Jews had previously'.

The word 'nature' in the phrases κατὰ φύσιν and παρὰ φύσιν is a play on words. The first phrase means 'naturally' and the second 'contrary to what would be expected'. In many languages it would not be possible to use the same word in both phrases. The phrase 'with its existing branches' is included in order to avoid the wrong meaning that the grafting was done on a bare trunk, and also to carry some of the sense of the phrase τῇ ἰδίᾳ ἐλαίᾳ 'the(ir) own olive-tree' at the end of v. 24.

11:24c-d Therefore *God* **will much more readily** *receive back the Jews who belonged to him before*, **which will be like grafting back the original branches into the olive tree** *that they were severed from* The Greek is πόσῳ μᾶλλον οὗτοι οἱ κατὰ φύσιν ἐγκεντρισθήσονται τῇ ἰδίᾳ ἐλαίᾳ 'by how much rather these according to nature will be grafted into (their) own olive tree'. The metaphor is spelled out in the display, the topic of 'grafted back' being 'received back' and the topic of 'those according to nature' being 'the Jews who belonged to him before'. Because this could cause some problems in understanding, it might have to be translated as 'considered to belong to him before' or 'called his people before'. The topic of 'their own' is spelled out as 'who belonged to him before'. The words 'that they were severed from' are supplied because they are implied by 'grafted back'.

The last part of the verse begins with the question word 'by how much?' and may be rendered either as a rhetorical question (as in JBP, NIV, LB, C. B. Williams) or as a statement (as in TEV, JB, RSV, CEV, NCV, REB). But in either case its force should be that of an emphatic statement, the same as in v. 12 and v. 15. (NEB uses an exclamation point.)

BOUNDARIES AND COHERENCE

In the 11:17-24 paragraph there is a return to hortatory discourse. The coherence in this paragraph is seen in the use of the second person singular pronoun to address readers plus the references to olive grafting: κλάδοι 'branches' (in 16, 17, 18, 19, 21); ἐλαία 'olive tree' (in 17, 24); ἀγριέλαιος 'wild olive tree' (in 17, 24); καλλιέλαιος 'cultivated olive tree' (in 24); ἐγκεντρίζω 'graft' in 17, 19, twice in 23, twice in 24); and ῥίζα 'root' (in 16, 17, 18). The relational coherence of 11:17-24 is seen in its being composed of two APPEALS and, within the second APPEAL, an *anticipated challenge* (19) and Paul's RESPONSE (20). The second APPEAL is supported by two *bases* in 21-24.

The boundary with the next paragraph is marked by a vocative in v. 25 (ἀδελφοί 'brothers'), a return to the second person plural pronoun, and the orienter οὐ γὰρ θέλω ὑμᾶς ἀγνοεῖν 'for I do not wish you to be ignorant'.

PROMINENCE AND THEME

The theme of 11:17-24 is drawn from the central elements of both APPEALS and both *bases* for the second APPEAL, namely 18a (minus the figurative elements), the NEGATIVE and POSITIVE propositions of the RESPONSE within the second APPEAL, the NUCLEUS of the first *warning basis* (21b), and the CONDITION and CONSEQUENCE propositions of the second *warning basis* (23a-b). Two prominence devices in this paragraph mark it as a thematic lead-in to the epistle's hortatory section: the metaphors and the dialogue nature of the paragraph with its second person singular pronouns. Following Longacre (pp. 25-31), 11:17-24 is considered to be a pre-peak leading to the peak in chapter 12 (the start of the hortatory section). Specifically, the 11:17-24 paragraph leads to the central hortatory section dealing with the problems between the Jewish and Gentile believers discussed in 14:1-15:13.

SECTION CONSTITUENT 11:25-32
(Expository Paragraph: Solution to the problem of God's rejection of the Jews)

THEME: *I want you to know that all the people of Israel will some day be saved, as the Scriptures predict. God still loves them because of their ancestors. It is God's purpose to act mercifully towards them as well as toward all Gentiles.*

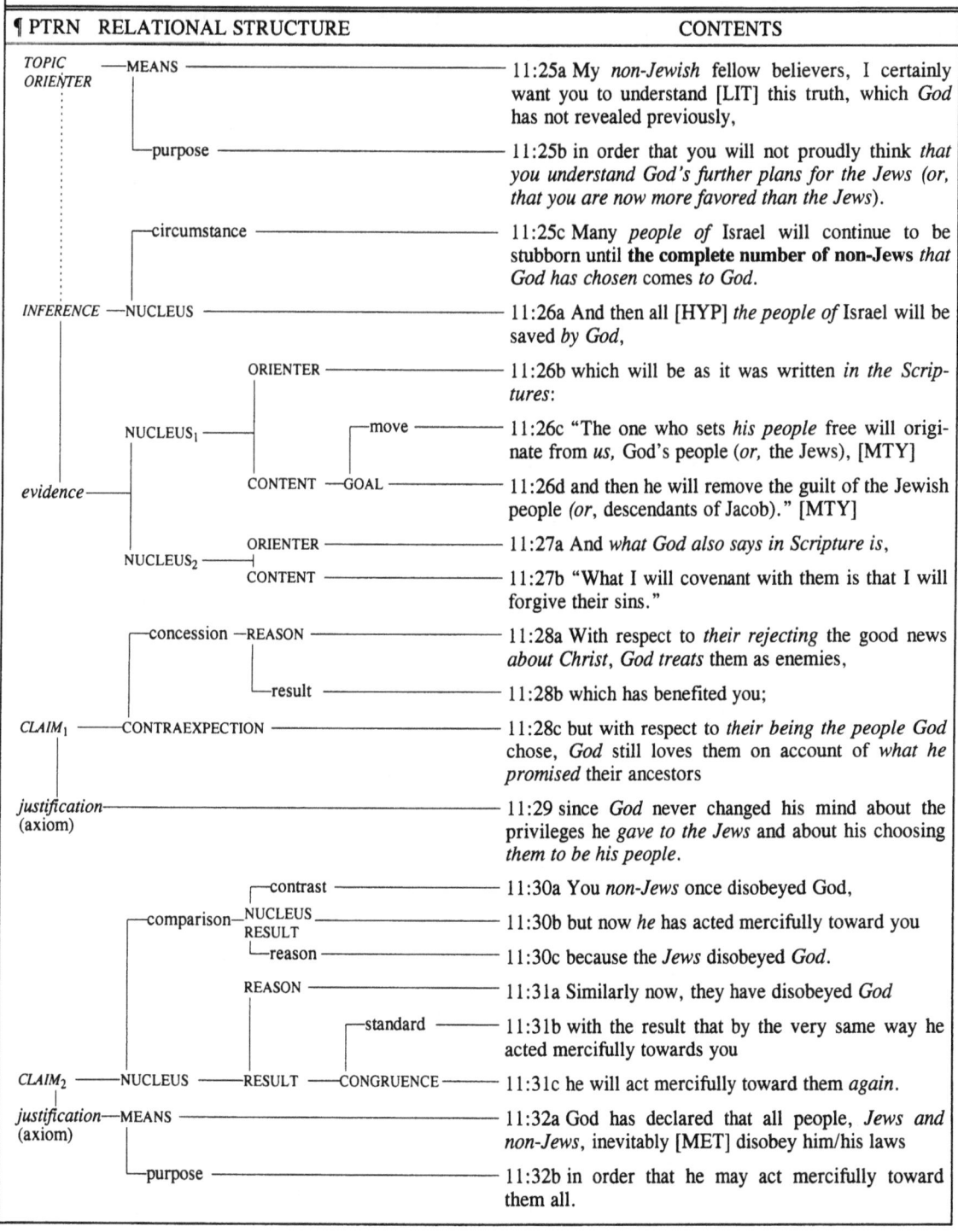

INTENT AND PARAGRAPH PATTERN

In the 11:25–32 paragraph Paul makes a number of statements about the Jews and Gentiles. Since there are no expressive or hortatory elements, it is considered expository. It consists of a number of closely related subunits. The first one (vv. 25–27), with its main proposition being a statement about what will happen, comprises an ORIENTER, an INFERENCE, and its *evidence*. This is followed by two CLAIMS, each with its *justification*. However, vv. 30–32 are really more than CLAIM-*justification*: they function as a summary, not just of this paragraph but of all of 9:1–11:29. Of v. 32 Sanday and Headlam say, "St. Paul now generalizes from these instances the character of God's plan, and concludes his argument with a maxim which solves the riddle of the Divine action."

NOTES

11:25a My *non-Jewish* fellow believers, I certainly want you to understand The word ἀδελφοί 'brothers' is rendered 'fellow believers' as usual, but 'non-Jewish' is supplied to make clear that it is this particular group Paul refers to when he says 'you'. The double negative οὐ θέλω ὑμᾶς ἀγνοεῖν 'I do not wish you to be ignorant' is a litotes (as in 1:13), a literary device that emphasizes the positive 'I want you to know' (cf. TEV, LB).

this truth, which *God* has not revealed previously This is the sense of the Greek word μυστήριον 'mystery'.

11:25b that you will not proudly think *that you understand God's further plans for the Jews* (*or, that you are now more favored than the Jews*) The clause ἵνα μὴ ἦτε παρ' ἑαυτοῖς φρόνιμοι means 'lest you be wise in your own estimation' (BAGD, p. 866) and thus "proudly imagine" (Hodge). But what were the Gentile believers in danger of proudly thinking themselves wise about? Commentators suggest two possibilities, both of which are equally valid (Denney). Both are given in the display.

11:25c will continue to be stubborn until the complete number of non-Jews that God has chosen comes to God The word πώρωσις means 'obstinacy' (BAGD, p. 732) and is rendered here by 'be stubborn'.

The phrase πλήρωμα τῶν ἐθνῶν 'fullness of the Gentiles' precedes the verb and is thereby prominent; this is indicated by bold type. 'Fullness' is rendered as it was in 12e.

The verb εἰσέλθῃ 'comes in' implies coming in to something, and case roles require that some location be understood. Commentators make several suggestions, all of which are somewhat figurative: 'into God's blessings', 'into life', or 'into God's kingdom'. This last might seem the best in view of the repeated use of εἰσέρχομαι in the phrase 'enter the kingdom' in the Gospels or where 'kingdom' is mentioned in the near context. Paul, however, never speaks of entering God's kingdom elsewhere. Moreover, that phrase is figurative: it means 'entering God's presence'. Thus the display has simply 'comes to God', as TEV and NCV do. But in some languages it may not be possible to say 'comes to God'. An alternative in such cases is 'trusts in God'.

11:26a And then all *the people of* Israel The phrase πᾶς Ἰσραήλ 'all Israel' here has been variously interpreted as meaning (1) 'all those who are spiritually God's people, all believers'; (2) 'all the elect Jews' (Lenski); or (3) 'all the people of Israel' (i.e., Israel as a nation or the vast number of those who claim Jewish descent). Interpretation 1 treats the phrase as a metaphor; however, the word 'Israel' in the preceding verse clearly does mean 'the Jews', and to consider it to mean 'all believers' here is hardly valid. Interpretation 2 treats the phrase as a synecdoche (the whole standing for the part); it has the same problem as interpretation 1, plus the fact that 'all the elect Jews' could be a very small number, thus making a very insignificant claim. Interpretation 3 is therefore chosen for the display even though it is hyperbolic: 'all' is not to be understood as all without exception.

11:26b which will be as it was written *in the Scriptures* The words καθὼς γέγραπται again introduce evidential grounds from Scripture, the sense being 'which is supported by what is written'. (REB has "in accordance with Scripture.") As previously, the words 'in the Scriptures' are supplied in the display to provide the location of where it was written, since Paul expected his audience to know this.

11:26c The one who sets *his people* free The event in ὁ ῥυόμενος 'the Deliverer' is here rendered 'sets his people free' instead of 'delivers' because the primary sense of 'delivers' in English is different and because case roles require a patient of the action to be understood. In some translations it will have to be made explicit what it is the people are set free from: Paul would have expected his audience to understand it as 'from (the guilt of) their sins'. This may come out the same as the expression used for 'Messiah'; in fact, this seems to be how this term in this passage was understood, not only by Paul but by later Jewish rabbis.

will originate from us, God's people (*or,* **the Jews**) In the phrase ἐκ Σιών 'out of Zion' the word 'Zion' is considered a metonymy signifying the people with which the place was associated (as in 9:33; see BAGD, p. 752.2b). An alternative is "from Jerusalem," as NCV and NLT have it. The pronoun 'us' is supplied because both Paul and Isaiah, the writer of the original passage, were Jews.

11:26d and then he will remove the guilt of the Jewish people (*or, descendants of* **Jacob**) The Greek is ἀποστρέψει ἀσεβείας ἀπὸ Ἰακώβ 'he will remove ungodliness from Jacob'. There is a problem as to whether 'ungodliness' means ungodly living or the guilt of ungodliness. In the context of the conversion of Jews and especially in the light of v. 27, the latter sense is taken for the display (see Morris).

'Jacob' is used figuratively: the name stands for Jacob's descendants. As with the name 'Israel', it had come to signify all the Jewish people. Both 'the Jewish people' and 'descendants of Jacob' are given here as alternatives. LB has "the Jews"; TEV, CEV, "descendants of Jacob."

11:27a-b And *what God also says in Scripture is,* **"What I will covenant with them is that I will forgive their sins."** 'God says' is supplied here to make the referent of the first person singular pronoun in the quotation clear. Note the quotation does not come from one source: the first part is from Isa. 59:20-21 (as in the latter part of v. 26), and the second part from Isa. 27:9 or Jer. 31:33-34.

A literal rendering of the quotation is 'this is my covenant with them, when I take away their sins', with no indication of what the covenant will be. Since Paul is citing it to show that God will forgive the sins of the people of Israel, the display, following Hodge and Cranfield, takes ὅταν 'when' as introducing the content of the covenant. LB does the same.

The word αὕτη 'this' at the beginning of the verse functions cataphorically and thereby puts prominence on the material to follow. This prominence is represented in the display with the rendering 'what I will covenant ... is that'.

The word ἀφέλωμαι 'I take away' is rendered here as 'forgive'; an alternative would be 'I will take away (the guilt of) their sins'.

11:28a With respect to *their rejecting* **the good news** *about Christ,* **God treats them as enemies** The Greek is κατὰ τὸ εὐαγγέλιον ἐχθροί 'with respect to the gospel (they are) enemies'. But in what respect regarding the gospel are they enemies? Barrett suggests "so far as the immediate results of the preaching of the gospel," but this does not cohere well. In view of the context, 'their rejecting the gospel' is more appropriate (so Denney, Dayton, Morris; also TEV). The NCV has "the Jews refuse to accept the Good News, so . . ."

Saying that they are enemies is somewhat overstated; they are not literally enemies, but as Hodge and Sanday and Headlam suggest, God treats them as such. The word εὐαγγέλιον is again rendered 'good news about Christ' (see the note on 1:16a).

11:28b which has benefited you In the phrase δι' ὑμᾶς the accusative following διά gives the sense 'for your sake'. This is made a little clearer in the display by a full clause. LB and JBP do the same (see also Barnes, Barrett).

11:28c with respect to *their being the people God* **chose,** *God* **still loves them** The noun 'election' in κατὰ τὴν ἐκλογήν 'with respect to the election' refers to an event, which is rendered in the display by 'their being the people God chose'. JB, CEV, and NCV render it similarly. The adjective ἀγαπητοί 'beloved', also an event, is rendered by 'God still loves them'.

on account of *what he promised* **their ancestors** As Cranfield, Morris, Alford, and Murray point out, the phrase διὰ τοὺς πατέρας 'on account of the fathers' means not 'on account of their ancestors' merits', but 'on account of the covenant he made with them'. NCV has "because of the promises he made to," and LB is very similar. The word 'fathers' refers to Abraham, Isaac, and Jacob, and this may have to be specified for some languages.

11:29 since *God* **never changed his mind about the privileges he** *gave to the Jews* **and about his choosing** *them to be his people* The Greek is ἀμεταμέλητα γὰρ τὰ χαρίσματα καὶ ἡ κλῆσις τοῦ θεοῦ 'for irrevocable (are) the gifts and the calling of God'. Since the adjective 'irrevocable' and the noun 'calling' represent events, they are rendered as clauses in the display. This construction that uses nouns and an adjective without a verb has a cryptic or epigrammatic quality, as though Paul were making a generic statement. But as Hodge says, "it is evident that the calling and election which he here has in view, are such as pertain to the Jews as a nation, and not such as contemplate the salvation of individuals." Thus the implied words 'he gave to the Jews' are supplied. The alternative would be to render it as a generic statement and then make the application specific: for example, 'since God never changes his mind about giving things to people or choosing them to be his people, that is true with respect to his giving privileges to the Jews and choosing them'.

The word 'gifts' that Paul uses here is the same one used of the gifts or enabling of the Spirit in chapters 12-14 of 1 Corinthians. This word can also refer to natural abilities, but neither of these is in focus here. "He is speaking rather of the gifts he has listed in [Rom.] 9:4-5" (Morris; see also Murray); and since the things listed in that passage are more privileges than spiritual gifts, 'privileges' is the word used here.

The word 'election' is rendered here as 'choosing them to be the people of God' (see the note on 28c). TEV renders the verse very nicely with "God does not change his mind about whom he chooses and blesses."

11:30-31 Dunn (vol. 2, p. 687) says, "This is the most contrived or carefully constructed formulation which Paul ever produced in such a tight epigrammatic form, with so many balancing elements . . . set within a chiastic structure." It is probably impossible to reproduce the form in translation. The following attempt to reproduce it in English uses bolding to represent pronouns in topicalized position and italics to represent the temporal words in emphatic position (the main verbs are in capital letters):

> Just as *once* **you** DISOBEYED God
> > but *now* **you** HAVE BEEN SHOWN MERCY
> > > because of their DISOBEDIENCE,
> > similarly *now* **these** HAVE DISOBEYED
> > > so that through his showing mercy to you
> > > > *now* **they** MIGHT BE SHOWN MERCY.

The four central elements here (lines 2-5) could be seen to have a chiastic structure involving the verbs 'show mercy' and 'obey', but in fact they do not (see the note on 31b). In the display the referents indicated by the pronouns in these two verses are made specific to avoid ambiguity (as in TEV).

11:30a You *non-Jews* once disobeyed God The fact that the pronoun is referring to the non-Jews is made specific in the display (also in TEV, NLT, and CEV).

11:30b but now *he* has acted mercifully toward you The Greek is νῦν δὲ ἠλεήθητε 'but now you have been pitied'. This can be represented in English by 'but now you have been shown mercy'; but due to case frame considerations (plus the fact that Paul may simply be avoiding stating the agent), it is rendered with an active form in the display.

11:30c because the *Jews* disobeyed *God* In the phrase τῇ τούτων ἀπειθείᾳ 'by their disobedience' the noun 'disobedience' represents an event; hence it is rendered as a verb with the participants in the action being supplied.

11:31b by the very same way he acted mercifully towards you The Greek is τῷ ὑμετέρῳ ἐλέει 'by your mercy' or, more freely, 'by the mercy shown to you'. (The emphasis shown by its being forefronted is conveyed by 'the very same way'.) A number of versions translate it as 'because of your mercy', but this is not supported in the commentaries. If Paul had meant a causal relationship, he surely would have used διά. Several commentators suggest 'by the same mercy you received'. This is good, but resolving the mismatch here is problematic: filling out the comparison gives 'by God's acting mercifully towards (them just as he acted mercifully towards you)'. This would make the final clause (31c) completely redundant. Moule suggests that the phrase has a temporal sense, "at the time when pity is shown to you"; and Beck follows this interpretation, which makes good sense semantically but is hard to justify grammatically. Another problem in the interpretation of this phrase is whether it actually goes with the final ἵνα purpose clause or whether it goes with the preceding clauses. Some have suggested that since it precedes ἵνα, it cannot be taken as subordinate to the ἵνα clause. Dunn argues that there is a chiastic structure in 30-31 and that this forces it to relate to the preceding verb. But Dunn is wrong: since the first and last verbs in 30-31 are different, they cannot form part of a chiasm. As Morris and Hodge say, it is much better to assume that this phrase is forefronted for the purpose of emphasis; in this case it would occur before ἵνα, *seeming* to give a chiastic structure for the four elements in 30-31, but this is only accidental. Thus the interpretation chosen for the display fits best in spite of its being somewhat redundant when the mismatch is resolved.

The evidence for including 'now', which is in some texts, is divided. The manuscript evidence tends to support its omission. But internal evidence suggests that Paul could well have included it to balance the other temporal words in 30-31; then, since it refers to an event not yet underway, some copyist may have felt it inappropriate and omitted it. It is included in the fourth edition GNT with a C rating ("difficulty in deciding").

11:32 Here γάρ introduces a *justification* of the v. 31 CLAIM about God's acting mercifully towards all the Jews. Or it could be taken as a conclusion to the whole topic.

11:32a God has declared that all people, *Jews and non-Jews*, inevitably disobey him/his laws The Greek is συνέκλεισεν ὁ θεὸς τοὺς πάντας εἰς ἀπείθειαν 'God shut up all in disobedience', in which the verb συγκλείω means 'to confine, imprison', a metaphor signifying "put them under compulsion to be disobedient or given them over to disobedience" (BAGD, p. 774.2). Commentators are divided as to what Paul means here. Shedd lists three interpretations: "1. God declares and proves all men to be sinners. 2. He permits them to sin. 3. He judicially withdraws restraints, and gives them over to sin." Shedd, Barnes, Vine, Hodge, and Sanday and Headlam support the idea that this statement represents the divine purpose of God. There is a scarcity of arguments supporting the various views. Morris supports the first of Shedd's possible interpretations and the second of BAGD's definitions: "Paul is not saying that God predetermined that all should sin, but rather that he has so ordered things that all people, Jew and Gentile alike, being disobedient, show themselves to be sinners." This interpretation is followed in the display, and the sense of the metaphor is retained by the word 'inevitably'. (An alternative closer to the metaphor is 'inescapably'.)

The word 'all' presents certain problems. First, some manuscripts have τὰ πάντα 'all things', probably as a result of some copyist's recollection of Gal. 3:22, where συνέκλεισεν ἡ γραφὴ τὰ πάντα 'Scripture has shut up all things' occurs. But the reading τοὺς πάντας is given an A rating ("certain") in the fourth edition GNT.

Another problem is the referent: Some have postulated that the phrase refers to 'all the elect'; but in this context, and in view of Paul's deliberate use of 'all' early in the epistle (1:7, 8, 16) to refer to both the Jews and non-Jews, it is clear that Paul means both of these groups here. This information is supplied in the display.

BOUNDARIES AND COHERENCE

Lexical coherence within the 11:25-32 paragraph is provided by the phrases πλήρωμα τῶν ἐθνῶν 'fullness of the Gentiles' (v. 25) and πᾶς Ἰσραήλ 'all Israel' (v. 26) being balanced with τοὺς πάντας 'the all' in v. 32. The start of a new paragraph at v. 33 is clearly marked with the interjection Ὦ 'O', which introduces a very emotive description of God in an expressive paragraph (a doxology) that closes off the epistle's entire expository part.

PROMINENCE AND THEME

The first part of the 11:25-32 theme is drawn from the 26a INFERENCE, as well as the 25a TOPIC ORIENTER (the latter being considered thematic because of the litotes). The next part is drawn from 26b, which is the ORIENTER of the *evidence* supporting the 26a INFERENCE. (The quotation itself is not considered as thematic as the fact that Paul can support his INFERENCE with Scripture.) The next part of the theme is taken from the CLAIM in 28c. The final part of the theme is derived from the CLAIM in 31c plus a portion of the *justification* in 32a-b. The latter is considered thematic because of the two occurrences of πάντας 'all', which is a motif throughout the book.

SUBDIVISION CLUSTER CONSTITUENT 11:33-36
(Expressive Paragraph: Doxology concluding 11:1-32)

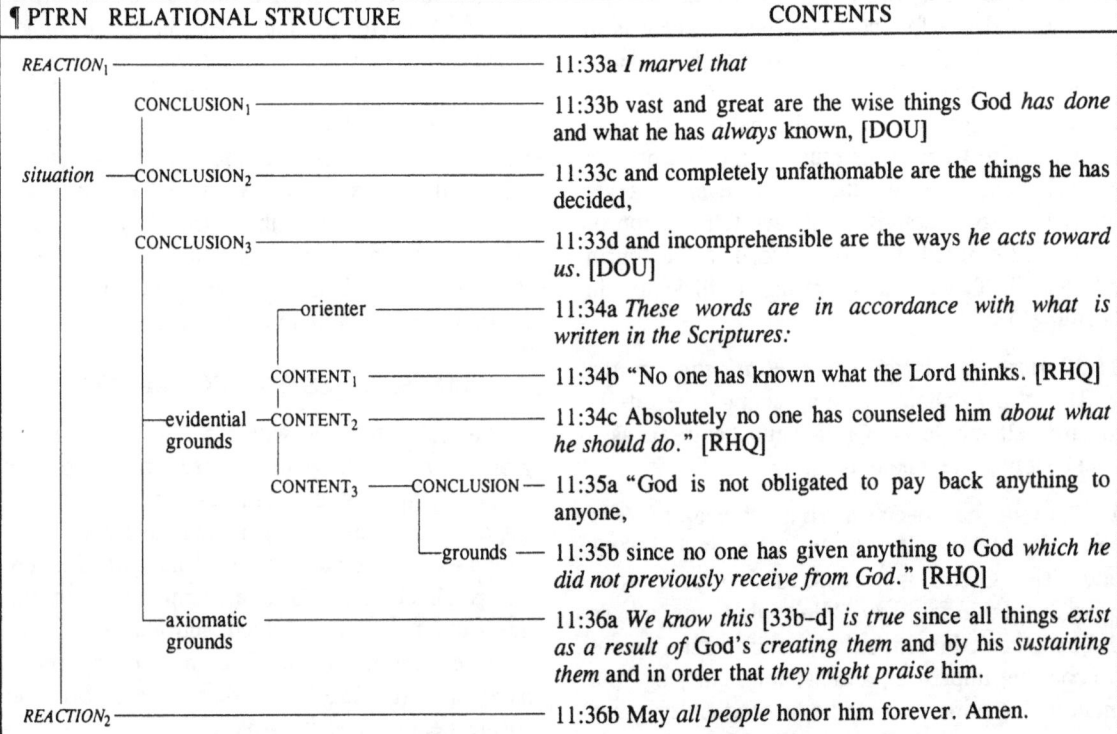

INTENT AND PARAGRAPH PATTERN

The 11:33-36 paragraph is a doxology concluding the 11:1-32 unit but also concludes the subdivision (9:1-11:32) and could also be said to conclude the first part of the epistle (cf. Murray). There are no verbs in vv. 33 and 36, and the intervening verses are quotations from Scripture. This is clearly an expressive paragraph: the 33a proposition with the introductory ˚Ω (rendered 'I marvel') and the wish in 36b are considered REACTIONS and what is between them the *situation* that calls it forth.

NOTES

11:33a *I marvel* Verse 33 is a verbless exclamatory construction introduced by ˚Ω 'O', an interjection expressing emotion (BAGD, p. 895.3a), the same one used previously in 2:1, 2:3, and 9:20, though in direct address in those references. In the display it is rendered 'I marvel' and given a *REACTION* label. JBP brings out the emotive impact with "I stand amazed at." The exclamatory sense is also conveyed by translating βάθος πλούτου 'depth of riches' in 33b with two strong adjectives, 'vast and great'.

11:33b *vast and great are the wise things God has done* and what he has *always* known The Greek is βάθος πλούτου καὶ σοφίας καὶ γνώσεως θεοῦ 'depth of the riches and of the wisdom and of the knowledge of God'. Even though 'riches', 'wisdom', and 'knowledge' are nouns connected by 'and', semantically 'riches' is an attribute modifying 'wisdom and knowledge'. (And it does not mean God's tangible wealth!) Many versions and commentators support this interpretation. Technically, 'wisdom' too can be said to represent an attribute, 'knowledge' being the cognitive event it modifies. However, in an emotive passage like this, it is likely that the meaning of the two terms is nearly identical. Moore (p. 41) classifies them as near-synonymous, but both are retained in the display since this is a poetic paragraph. It should be noted that in this context Paul is not just extolling these attributes of God in general, but in connection with what God has done to bring Jews and non-

Jews to himself. In the display 'wisdom' is therefore represented by 'wise things God has done' and 'knowledge' by 'what he has always known'.

11:33c-d completely unfathomable are the things he has decided and incomprehensible are the ways *he acts towards us* Though the word ὡς 'how' is exclamatory here, the construction is rendered as a statement, with the word 'completely' conveying something of the exclamatory impact. The word ἀνεξεραύνητα means 'unfathomable, unsearchable, not subject to full investigation'; and the word ἀνεξιχνίαστοι means 'incomprehensible, not subject to being fully understood'. Since there is so little difference between the two, they may be taken as a synonymous doublet, as Moore (p. 41) says. But in the display both words are kept because of the poetic nature of the passage. Commentators agree that κρίματα means 'decisions'. The figurative phrase αἱ ὁδοὶ αὐτοῦ 'his ways' at the end of v. 33 is rendered to fit the context.

11:34 Here γάρ introduces two Scripture passages that support the statements Paul has just made about God's nature; γάρ is not part of the original text in Isaiah. The quotations are evidential grounds.

11:34a *These words are in accordance with what is written in the Scriptures* This proposition is supplied to make it clear that Paul is citing Scripture. TEV and NCV similarly specify this.

11:34b-35 The fact that Paul cites two entirely different passages is indicated by the quotation marks. The first quotation is from Isa. 40:13; the second appears to be a free translation of Job 41:11. Both are rhetorical questions beginning with τίς 'who?' and are equivalent to emphatic negative statements beginning 'absolutely no one'. An alternative is CEV's "Has anyone known . . . ?" which is a different type of rhetorical question.

11:34c no one has counseled him *about what he should do* The words σύμβουλος αὐτοῦ ἐγένετο 'his counselor became' are rendered 'counseled him'. To make clear what God might need counseling about, the words 'about what he should do' are supplied.

11:35a-b "God is not obligated to pay back anything to anyone, since no one has given anything to God *which he did not previously receive from God"* The Greek is τίς προέδωκεν αὐτῷ, καὶ ἀνταποδοθήσεται αὐτῷ; 'who previously gave to him and it will be repaid to him?'. This is an instance of a construction (which may be peculiar to Indo-European languages) in which an initial question word relates to the first of the two clauses that follow—clauses connected by some conjunction but whose particular relationship to each other is not clearly signaled by that conjunction. The conjunction καί 'and' in 35b conveys a cause-effect relationship: 'What individual will God pay back *because* that individual has previously given him something?' The intention of the rhetorical question is to express that obviously there is no such individual. In the display, this relationship, as well as the participants, is made clear. The implied words 'obligated to' are supplied because, as Morris says, "we cannot place God under obligation."

The words 'which he did not previously receive from God' are included to make Paul's (and the OT writers') argument clear: people can give things to God but that doesn't put God under obligation because they came from God anyway (cf. 1 Chron. 29:14). In some languages the double negative in 35b will have to be changed to something like 'everything people have given to God they had previously received from him'.

11:36a *We know this is true* Here ὅτι introduces the grounds for the previous statements, but it is not clear whether 36b supports 35a-b or 34a-b or 33b-d. To help clarify the relationship 'We know this [33b-d] is true' is supplied.

since all things *exist as a result of* **God's** *creating them* **and by his** *sustaining them* **and in order that** *they might praise* **him** The Greek is ἐξ αὐτοῦ καὶ δι' αὐτοῦ καὶ εἰς αὐτὸν τὰ πάντα 'from him and through him and unto him (are) all things'. This is very cryptic, and commentators disagree as to its referent. Some have presumed it to be a reference to the Trinity, but this seems strained. (As Morris and Hodge point out, there is no statement elsewhere in Scripture of things being '*unto* the Spirit'.) The words 'from him' point to God as the creator or source of everything, hence 'as a result of God's creating them'. The words 'through him' point to God as the one who "preserves, directs, and controls them" (Stuart; cf. Hodge, Denney). The words 'unto him' suggest 'for his glory' (so Denney, Stuart, Haldane, Murray, LB), hence 'that they might praise him'.

In languages where one cannot have a purpose clause relating to a stative clause, it may be necessary to translate as 'he created all things in order that'.

11:36b May *all people* honor him forever The phrase αὐτῷ ἡ δόξα 'unto him the glory' is rendered as a complete clause though there is no verb in the Greek; the implicit subject is 'all people'.

Amen An alternative to 'Amen' is 'May it be so'; but if such an expression is used only in dialogue (as is usual where the Hebrew equivalent occurs in the OT), the translator may need to find some expression that is suitable in monologue.

BOUNDARIES AND COHERENCE

The 11:33-36 paragraph is relationally coherent in that it consists of Paul's emotive REACTION (33a) to a *situation* (33b-36a, listing the virtues of God) and another emotive REACTION (36b) arising from this same *situation*.

The initial and final boundaries of the doxology in 11:33-36 have already been discussed. It should also be added that 11:36 concludes with ἀμήν 'Amen', the normal signal of the end of a doxology.

PROMINENCE AND THEME

The theme of 11:33-36 is drawn from the 33a REACTION and the three 33b-d CONCLUSION statements of the *situation*. Since Paul is not making an appeal or claim here, the fact that he quotes Scripture is not considered thematic enough to include in the theme; neither is the final doxology in 36b.

SUBPART CONSTITUENT 12:1-15:13
(Hortatory Division Cluster: Appeals of the epistle)

THEME: (See the thematic outline in the Introduction.)	
MACROSTRUCTURE	CONTENTS
GENERIC APPEAL	12:1-2 I appeal to you that, because of all the ways God has acted mercifully towards you, you present yourselves to God by making yourselves like living sacrifices, which is the appropriate way to serve him. Do not let anything non-Christian determine how you act, but instead let God change your way of thinking.
SPECIFIC APPEAL₁	12:3-13:14 Think about yourselves sensibly, by considering the abilities God has given you; love others sincerely in the ways you act towards them and instead of avenging yourselves let God avenge you. Be subject to the civil authorities. Let your only continual obligation be to love one another.
SPECIFIC APPEAL₂	14:1-15:13 Accept those who doubt whether they are permitted to do certain things. Specifically, anyone who thinks it is all right to eat all kinds of food must not despise those who don't, and those who don't think so must not condemn those who do, because God has accepted them.

INTENT AND MACROSTRUCTURE

All three constituents of the 12:1-15:13 unit are hortatory; thus the unit as a whole is hortatory. It consists of an introductory GENERIC APPEAL (12:1-2) followed by two SPECIFIC APPEALS (12:3-13:14 and 14:1-15:13).

BOUNDARIES AND COHERENCE

The second of the two major constituents of the 1:16-15:13 CORE of the epistle, 12:1-15:13 is characterized by a set of APPEALS on several topics, some expressed by imperatives, some by independent subjunctive clauses, some by expressions such as παρακαλῶ 'I appeal' and ὀφείλομεν 'we ought to', and some by an implicit verb 'to be'. The end of the unit is marked in 15:13 by a benediction, and the start of the 15:14-33 unit is marked in 15:14 by a vocative and the absence of a further APPEAL until 16:17.

PROMINENCE AND THEME

The theme of 12:1-15:13 is drawn from the themes of its three constituent paragraphs. Only the *basis* and ORIENTER in the first paragraph are omitted.

DIVISION CLUSTER CONSTITUENT 12:1-2
(Hortatory Paragraph: Generic appeal of 12:1-15:13)

THEME: I appeal to you that, because of all the ways God has acted mercifully towards you, you present yourselves to God by making yourselves like living sacrifices, which is the appropriate way to serve him. Do not let anything non-Christian determine how you act, but instead let God change your way of thinking.

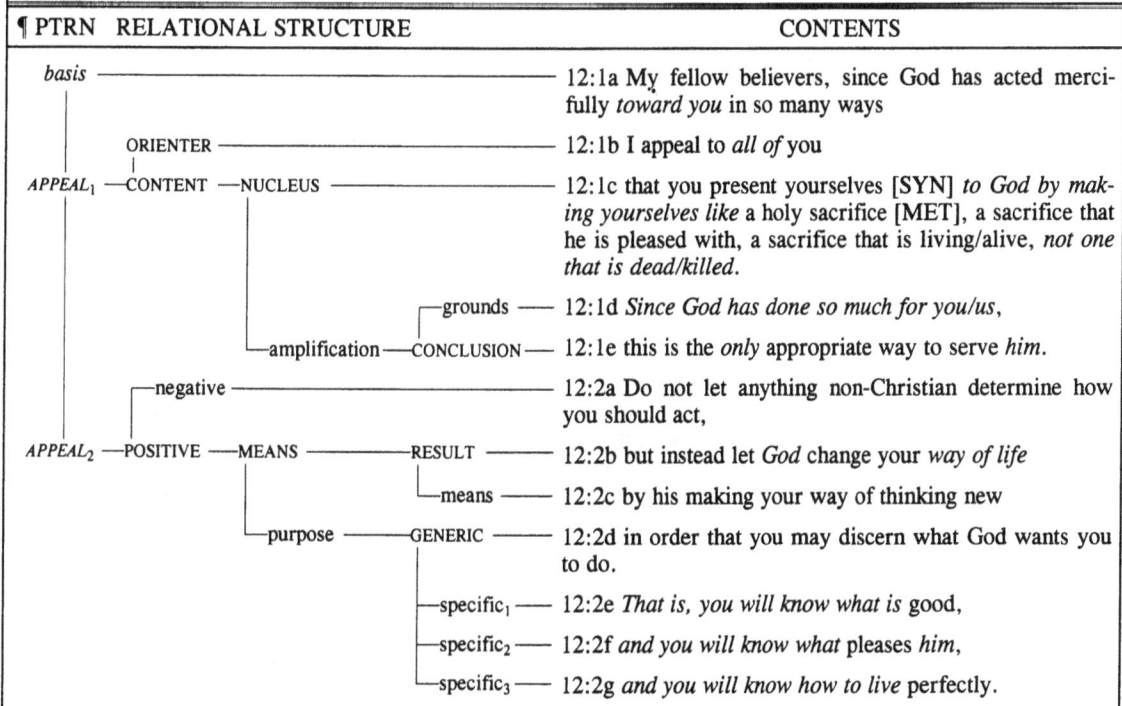

INTENT AND PARAGRAPH PATTERN

With two imperatives in 12:2, the negative μὴ συσχηματίζεσθε 'do not be conformed' and the positive μεταμορφοῦσθε 'be transformed', 12:1-2 is clearly a hortatory paragraph. The infinitive παραστῆσαι 'to present' in 1c, though not an imperative, functions as one, since it follows the verb phrase Παρακαλῶ ὑμᾶς 'I beseech you', a communicative verb introducing the first *APPEAL*. The phrase διὰ τῶν οἰκτιρμῶν τοῦ θεοῦ 'on account of the mercies of God' is considered a *basis* since it supplies the motivation for the two *APPEALS*, but in another sense the whole 1:16-11:36 division cluster is the *basis* for these *APPEALS*.

NOTES

12:1a since God has acted mercifully *toward you* in so many ways The phrase διὰ τῶν οἰκτιρμῶν τοῦ θεοῦ 'on account of the compassions of God' expresses the *basis* of the *APPEAL* (see Barnes, Cranfield, Morris; also TEV, NCV).

The noun 'compassions/mercies' is rendered 'act mercifully' since semantically it expresses an attribute of the event 'to act'. The force of the plural is conveyed by 'so many ways'. But what are these 'many ways'? It could be the things mentioned in the previous chapter (so Sanday and Headlam), but more probably it refers back to everything Paul has presented since 3:21-31.

12:1b I appeal to *all of* you Though 'all of' is not in the Greek, this is the sense here where Paul is beginning his exhortations to them all. Aune (p. 295) states it very well:

> Paul has brought the reader through the problems confronted by outsiders in the Christian gospel, whether Gentiles or Jews (Rom. 1:18-4:25), and he has further presented with great clarity his view of the nature of the Christian life as a life lived from the perspective of the Spirit rather than the flesh. He now appeals to the readers (12:1-2), no matter what their status, to devote themselves fully to God.

12:1c present yourselves *to God* The word σώματα 'bodies' is taken as a synecdoche in which the part stands for the whole person (supported by Barrett, Cranfield, Erdman, Lenski, Dunn, Hodge, Michel; cf. NEB, NIV, TEV, NCV, NRSV). The verb is probably metaphorical: 'as people offer the bodies of animals as sacrifices, so you should offer yourselves'. The phrase 'to God' is supplied to satisfy the case frame and remove ambiguity.

by making yourselves like a holy sacrifice The metaphor is rendered as a simile in the display. The phrase τὰ σώματα ὑμῶν θυσίαν 'your bodies a sacrifice' is a double accusative in Greek. Commentators do not discuss how the 'sacrifice' relates to 'bodies' (i.e., 'to present your bodies') semantically, but in the display it is treated as a means proposition with 'making' supplied. Alternatively it could be considered a specific of 'present yourselves'.

The sense of ἁγίαν 'holy' here is 'one that belongs completely to God'.

living/alive, *not one that is dead/killed* Commentators agree that ζῶσαν 'living' is used "in the sense that once an animal is sacrificed it is dead, but the Christian's sacrifice of himself is a continuously living action" (Best). Thus the italicized words are clearly implied.

12:1d Since God has done so much for you/us This is supplied to spell out the grounds of λογικός 'appropriate' in 1e. It echoes 1a.

12:1e this is the *only* appropriate way to serve him The phrase τὴν λογικὴν λατρείαν ὑμῶν could be glossed as 'the rational service of yours' or 'the rational worship of yours'. In its use in the LXX the word λατρεία nearly always refers to services of worship. As Paul turns to address aspects of believers' everyday functioning, he uses animal sacrifice as a metaphor: 'People used to worship God through offering him animal sacrifices, but I declare that now the rational way for us to worship or serve God is by offering ourselves to him continually'. Morris is right in saying that Paul probably has the components of both worship and service in mind.

Similarly, λογικός can mean either 'rational' or 'spiritual', and either meaning would be appropriate here. However, in the light of all that has preceded this verse, 'rational' or 'appropriate' seems best. CEV has "That's the most sensible way to serve God."

12:2a Do not let anything non-Christian determine how you should act The Greek is μὴ συσχηματίζεσθε τῷ αἰῶνι τούτῳ 'do not be conformed to this age'. Some versions take the verb as being in the middle mode, giving the sense of 'conform yourselves', but according to BAGD (p. 795) the verb is passive, giving the sense of 'be conformed to, be guided by'. The present tense of the imperative could be rendered even more clearly: 'Stop letting anything. . . .' Dunn suggests that the passive is conveying the notion that there is "a power or force which molds character and conduct and which 'this age' exercises; Paul in effect recognizes the power of social groups, cultural norms, institutions, and traditions to mold patterns of individual behavior." In the display, the sense of the verb is conveyed actively ('determine how you should act'), but an adequate term for the agent is hard to suggest.

JBP's classic rendering "Don't let the world around you squeeze you into its own mould" does not shed much light on the meaning of the word αἰών 'age'. Hodge suggests that αἰών means "the wicked," equivalent to κόσμος, "the mass of mankind, considered in opposition to the people of God." But it probably refers to anything which leaves God out of consideration as well as to individuals who are specifically opposed to God. Bullinger notes that the term is a metonymy, a temporal expression standing for what occurs during the period of the αἰών. Louw and Nida give as the meaning of αἰών "the system of practices and standards associated with secular society, that is, without reference to any demands or requirements of God." BAGD (p. 27.2a) suggest that it refers to "everything non-Christian"; this is what is used in the display.

12:2b but instead let *God* change your *way of life* Commentators have argued at length as to whether μὴ συσχηματίζεσθε 'be not conformed' in 2a and μεταμορφοῦσθε 'be transformed' in 2b are synonymous. Strictly speaking, the positive of 'do not be conformed' would be 'be different, be willing to stand out'. But Paul's word 'be transformed' goes beyond this. As Morris notes, "Paul is looking for a transformation at the deepest level that is infinitely more significant than the conformity to the world's pattern that is distinctive of so many lives." The implied agent of the transforming is God (so CEV, TEV) or perhaps, as Harrison more specifically suggests, the Spirit of God. The present imperative here points to a continual action, not a one-time action.

There is a question of whether the relation of 2c to 2b should be one of means or specific. In either case, taking it literally might suggest that the only thing that is to be changed is a person's thinking. Therefore 'way of life' is supplied to make clear that the change affects every aspect of life.

12:2c by his making your way of thinking new The phrase τῇ ἀνακαινώσει τοῦ νοός 'by the renewing of (your) mind' does not mean that the believer gets a new brain, but that his manner of thinking should be new. The Textus Receptus includes ὑμῶν 'your(pl)' after 'mind'; in any case 'your' is required semantically.

12:2d in order that The construction εἰς τό plus the infinitive is taken as expressing purpose. Morris says (p. 82, fn.) that this construction is used forty-three times by Paul compared to eighteen times by all the other NT writers combined, adding "Paul almost always uses it to express purpose." The only other alternative here would be to take it as result, but the result would only be anticipated, not an accomplished result, which in effect would express purpose anyway.

discern The verb here is δοκιμάζειν 'to examine and then approve'. NIV has "test and approve," But as noted by BAGD (p. 202.2b), it also means 'to discover' (JB has "discover" and NEB "discern"). Denney says the verb means to "discern in their experience." Erdman says it means to "find out by practical personal experience"; Dunn translates it as "ascertain." To try to capture both of these senses, the display uses 'discern' in 2d and then slightly modifies it by supplying 'you will know' in each of the next three propositions. REB translates it in exactly the same way.

what God wants you to do The noun phrase τὸ θέλημα τοῦ θεοῦ 'the will of God' is rendered in the display as a full clause.

12:2e–g *what is* good, ... *what* pleases *him*, ... *how to live* perfectly The Greek is τὸ ἀγαθὸν καὶ εὐάρεστον καὶ τέλειον 'the good and well pleasing and perfect'. These words are considered to be specific descriptions of 'the will of God'. In the display each is made into a full stative clause following the supplied verb 'you will know', which is a modified repetition of δοκιμάζειν 'discern' in 2d.

BOUNDARIES AND COHERENCE

Verses 12:1–2 are a brief paragraph recognized by many commentators as a set of generic APPEALS relating the 1:16–11:36 *basis* to the SPECIFIC APPEALS in 12:3–13:10. Cranfield says, "These two verses serve as an introduction to the rest of the main division 12:1–15:13, the theme of which they set forth."

The 12:1–2 paragraph consists of two generic APPEALS preceded by a *basis*. The boundary with the next unit is marked in 12:3 by the introductory γάρ and another performative introducing a SPECIFIC APPEAL about the appropriate use of spiritual gifts.

PROMINENCE AND THEME

The theme of 12:1–2 is drawn from the *basis* and the two APPEALS. The 1a *basis* refers to the entire expository first part of the book, and therefore it has prominence, which requires that it be included in the theme. The theme's final part is drawn from the 2a negative and the 2b POSITIVE APPEALS.

DIVISION CLUSTER CONSTITUENT 12:3-13:14
(Hortatory Subdivision Cluster: Specific appeal₁ of 12:1-15:13)

THEME: Think about yourselves sensibly, by considering the abilities God has given you; love others sincerely in the ways you act towards them and instead of avenging yourselves let God avenge you. Be subject to the civil authorities. Let your only continual obligation be to love one another.

MACROSTRUCTURE	CONTENTS
SPECIFIC APPEAL₁	12:3-8 Do not think about yourselves more highly than you should. Instead, think about yourselves sensibly, considering your abilities that have been given to you by God because you trust in Christ. Let us do diligently and cheerfully the things God has given us ability to do.
SPECIFIC APPEAL₂	12:9-21 Love others sincerely in the ways you act towards them. Instead of avenging yourselves, allow God to avenge you; and instead of being overcome by evil done to you, overcome these things by doing good deeds to those who do evil to you.
SPECIFIC APPEAL₃	13:1-7 Every believer must be subject to civil authorities, because anyone who opposes them opposes what God has established and will bring on himself punishment from the authorities as God considers fitting. Do what is good and then they will commend you. Give to all the authorities what you are obligated to give them.
SPECIFIC APPEAL₄	13:8-10 Do not leave any debt unpaid. Your only continual obligation is to love one another, since doing so fulfills all that God's law requires.
GENERIC APPEAL	13:11-14 Because it is time for us to be fully active, we must quit doing wicked deeds, we must do those things which will help us resist that which is evil, we must live properly, and we must be like Christ.

INTENT AND MACROSTRUCTURE

The 12:3-13:14 unit is hortatory, of the causality subtype, since all its constituents are hortatory. The unit comprises four SPECIFIC APPEALS followed by a GENERIC APPEAL.

BOUNDARIES AND COHERENCE

The APPEALS in 12:3-13:14, while not generic as those in 12:1-2, are still quite general, most without a *basis*. They are all brief except for the one in 13:1-7. The negative ones are immediately followed by a contrastive positive one, and it is not clear whether they are aimed to correct any problem Paul knows to exist. Even 13:1-7 probably does not address a problem but is aimed more at trying to avoid one. Morris says, "Sometimes it is argued that the Jews in Rome may well have been restive . . . ; Paul may have wanted to dissuade Christian Jews in the capital from taking part in revolutionary movements." (But with two *may have*'s this is hardly definitive.)

The end of the 12:3-13:14 unit is marked by a GENERIC APPEAL (13:11-14). The next unit, beginning at 14:1, contains a lengthy APPEAL regarding a specific problem in the Roman congregation. That it starts a new unit is clear from the forefronting of τὸν δὲ ἀσθενοῦντα τῇ πίστει 'now the one being weak in faith', which topicalizes the subject now to be addressed.

PROMINENCE AND THEME

The theme of 12:3-13:14 is drawn from the themes of its constituents, except for the final one, 13:11-14, which is not included because it is generic and has little or no reference to the other constituents' content. Moreover, it is highly figurative, hence nonthematic. It simply serves as a closure to this set of varied SPECIFIC APPEALS before the epistle's most prominent SPECIFIC APPEAL (14:1-15:13). The negative portion of the first paragraph is not included in the theme because a negative exhortation is almost always less thematic than a contrastive positive one connected to it. From the theme of the second constituent (12:9-21) the last portion is omitted because it is largely repetitive. From the theme of the third constituent only the first clause is included because the rest of it is either repetitive or only implied. From the fourth constituent, the first APPEAL, which is negative, and its *basis* are omitted, being less thematic.

SUBDIVISION CLUSTER CONSTITUENT 12:3–8
(Hortatory Paragraph: Specific appeal$_1$ of 12:3–13:14)

THEME: Do not think about yourselves more highly than you should. Instead, think about yourselves sensibly, considering your abilities that have been given to you by God because you trust in Christ. Let us do diligently and cheerfully the things God has given us ability to do.

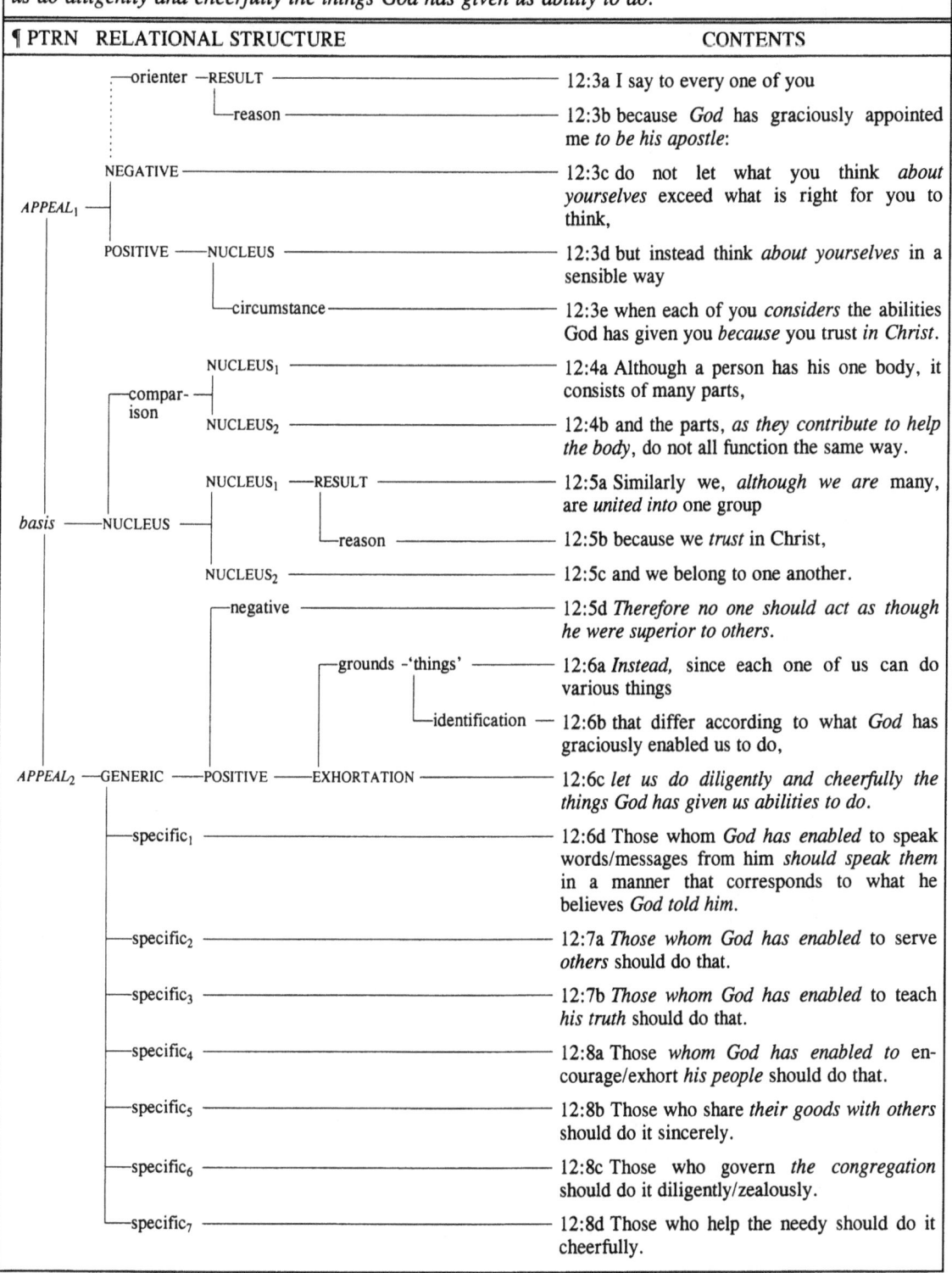

INTENT AND PARAGRAPH PATTERN

The 12:3-8 paragraph is made up of two APPEALS and a *basis*, making this a hortatory paragraph. The events expressed in 3a-d are in the form of a performative orienter plus two infinitives (μὴ ὑπερφρονεῖν 'not to think too highly' and φρονεῖν 'to think'); such a construction encodes exhortations. Verses 4-5 are introduced by γάρ; semantically, these verses are considered the *basis* for the more generic APPEAL in v. 3 but also for the specific ones in vv. 6-8. The reason the two APPEALS are considered to form one paragraph is that the first one is more generic and includes both negative and positive exhortations, and the second is more specific and expresses only positive exhortations that relate to the topic. Moreover, the *basis* applies to both of the APPEALS.

NOTES

12:3a The conjunction γάρ that introduces v. 3 does not give the reason for vv. 1-2, as is apparent from the fact that v. 3 contains further APPEALS, not statements. Rather, it introduces the first of a set of specific ways in which the APPEALS of 12:1-2 are to be carried out. The verb λέγω 'I say' here functions as a speech orienter giving prominence to 12:3c-e, the content of what Paul says.

12:3b because *God* **has graciously appointed me to be his apostle** The Greek is διὰ τῆς χάριτος τῆς δοθείσης μοι 'through the grace that was given to me'. Since χάρις 'grace', as noted previously (cf. 1:5 and 3:24), expresses an attribute modifying an implied event, it is expressed here in a straightforward manner as a verbal clause, exactly as it was in 1:5. Nearly all commentators support this interpretation.

12:3c do not let what you think *about yourselves* **exceed what is right for you to think** The Greek is μὴ ὑπερφρονεῖν παρ' ὃ δεῖ φρονεῖν 'not to think too highly beyond what it is proper to think'. The words 'about yourselves' (here and in 3d) are implied and taken for granted by versions and commentators. The verb 'exceed' is used in the display because it probably conveys the meaning of the Greek better than the words 'more highly than' found in most English versions, and it may solve the problem for languages that lack a comparative degree construction ('more than').

12:3d in a sensible way The Greek is εἰς τὸ σωφρονεῖν, literally 'unto being sober minded', meaning 'be reasonable, sensible, serious' (BAGD, p. 802.2). As in the previous verse, εἰς τό plus the infinitive expresses purpose or perhaps result, but most versions translate it with an adverbial sense. Moule (p. 70) suggests the sense "to adopt an outlook which tends to sobriety." NEB seems to capture a result sense with "think your way to a sober estimate"; CEV has "Use good sense."

12:3e when each of you *considers* **the abilities God has given you** The Greek is ἑκάστῳ ὡς ὁ θεὸς ἐμέρισεν μέτρον πίστεως 'to each as God has apportioned a measure of faith'. Some commentators maintain that 'measure' refers to "a standard (by which to measure, estimate, himself)" (Cranfield). But as Dunn notes, following the verb μερίζω the phrase 'measure of faith' is "more naturally taken as an apportioning of *different* measures." In view of what follows, the sense seems to parallel 1 Cor. 12:7-10: 'to each is given a manifestation of the Spirit' followed by a list of Spirit-given gifts or abilities. Since in vv. 6-8 there is a list of χαρίσματα 'gifts', the display expresses the clause as 'when each of you considers the abilities God has given you'.

because **you trust** *in Christ* Hodge says of the word πίστεως 'of faith',

> Faith may be taken in its usual sense, and the meaning of the clause be, 'Let every one think of himself according to the degree of faith or confidence in God which has been imparted to him. . . .' Or *faith* may be taken for what is believed, or for knowledge of divine truth. . . . Or it may be taken for *that which is confided* to any, and be equivalent to *gift*. The sense then is, 'Let every one think of himself according to the nature or character of the gifts which he has received.' This is perhaps the most generally received interpretation, although it is arrived at in different ways; many considering the word *faith* here as used metonymically for its effects, viz., for the various . . . *graces*, ordinary and extraordinary, of which it is the cause. This general sense is well suited to the context, as the following verses, containing a specification of the gifts . . . , appear to be an amplification of this clause.

The problem with the first of the interpretations that Hodge mentions is that nowhere else does the concept of degrees of faith seem to be supported by apostolic teaching, nor does saving faith seem to be in focus here. The second interpretation, faith as a body of truth, does not fit the context at all. The third interpretation is the one chosen for the display, but the primary sense of πίστις is also retained by the rendering 'abilities God has given because you trust in Christ'.

12:4-8 At first glance it seems that v. 4 has figurative parts which are stated nonfiguratively in vv. 6-8, but it is v. 5 that is the nonfigurative representation of 4a-b.

12:4a Here γάρ introduces the *basis* for the 3d-e APPEAL.

Although a person has his one body, it consists of many parts The Greek is ἐν ἑνὶ σώματι πολλὰ μέλη ἔχομεν 'in one body many members we have'. Since in many languages both the body and body parts are obligatorily possessed, the display has 'a person has his one body'; and since 'we have members' expresses a part-whole relationship, not a possessive one, this is expressed in the display as 'consists of'.

12:4b and the parts, *as they contribute to help the body*, **do not all function the same way** The Greek is τὰ μέλη πάντα οὐ τὴν αὐτὴν ἔχει πρᾶξιν 'the members do not all have the same function'. Paul is not just saying that we all have different abilities but that each ability is needed to help the body of Christ. In some languages this part of the simile will have to be made specific. For languages in which there is no word for 'function' it may be possible to translate this as 'they do not all have the same work'.

12:5a Similarly we, *although we are* **many, are united into one group** The Greek is οὕτως οἱ πολλοὶ ἓν σῶμά ἐσμεν 'thus the many, one body we are'. The words 'the many' seem to represent the comment of a stative topic-comment proposition of a concessive nature. The two parts of 5a thus express a concession-CONTRAEXPECTATION couplet (see RSV, TEV, JBP, REB, NCV).

In some languages 'we' may have to be specified as 'we believers'.

The words 'are united' are supplied to express the relationship between 'we' and 'one body'; alternatives would be 'compose' or 'form'. Since 'body' is figurative, and many languages will not allow such a figurative sense for the word 'body', it is rendered 'group' here.

12:5b *because we trust* **in Christ** The words ἐν Χριστῷ could be rendered 'because we are united to Christ' (cf. TEV's "in union with Christ," REB's "we who are united with Christ") or 'on the basis of our relationship with Christ' (see the note on 6:11f).

12:5c and we belong to one another The Greek is τὸ δὲ καθ' εἷς ἀλλήλων μέλη 'and each one members of one another'. There is no verb in the Greek; 'we are' is understood from 5a. In the display this is rendered as 'belong to', but this is somewhat figurative, as is TEV's "is joined to." Also in view here, probably, are the senses of 'serves' and 'is dependent on' (LB has "each needs all the others").

12:5d *Therefore no one should act as though he were superior to others* This is the negative part of the implied conclusion corresponding to 3c, the point of the one-body many-members illustration. An alternative is 'Therefore no one should act as though his abilities were superior to those of others', which would tie the first and second APPEALS together a bit more closely. Hodge says, "Nothing can present in a clearer light . . . the sinfulness of divisions and envyings among the members of Christ's body, than the apostle's comparison."

12:6a since each one of us can do various things The participial phrase ἔχοντες χαρίσματα 'having gifts' presents two problems for the translator. First, 'gifts' in its primary sense denotes tangible objects, whereas here the sense is special abilities for Christian service. Secondly, 'abilities' is a noun but it means 'being able to do something', an event concept. The rendering in the display is an attempt to solve these problems. LB has "God has given each of us the ability to do certain things well."

12:6b that differ according to what *God* **has graciously enabled us to do** In the phrase κατὰ τὴν χάριν τὴν δοθεῖσαν ἡμῖν διάφορα 'according to the grace given to us differing', the noun 'grace' expresses an attribute modifying an event. The event of giving is expressed as 'enabled us to do', and the implied agent of 'enabled' needs to be expressed. The display fills out the case frame by supplying 'God' as the implied agent.

12:6c *let us do* Commentators agree that this is a classic case of Paul's constructing a sentence without a finite verb. It is a mitigated exhortation, hence 'let us do' in the display (or 'we should' or 'we ought to'). Note that in the TEV and RSV the generic verb "use" is supplied here. One could say it is the specific verbs in vv. 7-8 that are being referred to; but by supplying verbs only in

vv. 7-8, one cannot express the grounds relationship being communicated by the participle ἔχοντες 'having' in 6a. For example, 'since we have gifts (6a) ... let us/him prophesy (6d)' does not cohere relationally. The NIV rendering, which makes the participle into a finite verb ("We have different gifts"), is not satisfactory because it ignores the grounds relation between 6a and the exhortations that follow.

diligently and cheerfully These adverbs, which are taken from the specific propositions 8c and 8d, are supplied here because the imperative 'let us do the things' seems semantically incomplete by itself.

12:6d Those whom *God has enabled* to speak words/messages from him The Greek is elliptical: εἴτε προφητείαν 'if prophecy'. Therefore in the display 'God has enabled' is repeated from 6b. The noun 'prophecy', which represents an event, is spelled out as 'speak words/messages from him'. The word 'prophecy' in the NT does not usually mean a prediction of the future but rather, in the words of Morris, "passing on direct words from God." REB calls it "the gift of inspired utterance."

in a manner that corresponds to what he believes *God told him* Commentators are divided as to the meaning of the noun πίστις in the phrase κατὰ τὴν ἀναλογίαν τῆς πίστεως 'according to the proportion of faith'. Some hold that πίστις refers to the event of believing with the implied content of the believing being 'that God has revealed it to him'. Others hold that it refers to faith in the sense of the body of revealed truth. The display follows the former interpretation. If the latter is followed, this would be rendered '*should speak* the truth which is in accord with what God has already revealed'.

The difficulty with the second view is that it does not fit the context: Paul is talking about exercising a prophetic gift, which by its nature involves an ability to discern what God wishes to convey through that individual to a specific audience. Obviously one should not have to think whether his prophetic utterance is in accord with scriptural teaching. Critics of the first interpretation note that the phrase 'proportion of faith' seems to be almost identical with 'measure of faith' in v. 3, which supposedly opens the door for an individual to introduce any doctrine he cares to, claiming that it is what God told him. But as commentators note, the answer to that is found in other passages warning of the need to beware of false prophets, to evaluate their prophecies (1 Cor. 14:29), to exercise the gift of discernment, and to test the spirits (1 John 4:1-6). Among the versions, only LB seems to try to clarify what Paul means, but its rendering, "as often as your faith is strong enough to receive a message from God," is quite different from the one given here.

12:7-8 The sets of Greek phrases in these two verses have no finite verbs; instead each set has two nouns or a participial phrase plus a noun. In every case the nouns and participles represent events; and in the display the first noun/participle in each pair is represented by a verb, and the second, simply to avoid redundancy, by the pro-verb 'do'.

12:7a *Those whom God has enabled* to serve *others* should do that The Greek is εἴτε διακονίαν, ἐν τῇ διακονίᾳ 'whether in service, in serving'. Commentators are divided as to whether διακονία is used generically, referring to all types of service, or specifically of a certain service such as administration (cf. JB, REB), or whether it refers to the office of a deacon. Against this last interpretation is the fact that Paul uses the word διακονία 'service', which basically refers to an event, not διάκονος or a relative pronoun followed by a participle, either of which would refer to the individual performing the action. Against both the second and third interpretations is the fact that Paul uses this term quite frequently to refer to his ministry as a whole or to individual acts of ministry. Therefore the more neutral first interpretation is chosen here (so also Dunn, Harrison, Morris, and others).

Although the instructions in vv. 7 and 8 delineate how believers should act within the life of the church, the display supplies only 'others' in 7a to complete the case frame. If the referent of 'others' is unclear, 'among the congregation' could be added.

12:7b to teach *his truth* The object of 'teach' is supplied as 'his truth' to satisfy the case frame and avoid ambiguity or wrong meaning as to what kind of teaching is meant.

12:8a Those *whom God has enabled to* encourage/exhort In the GNT ὁ παρακαλῶν 'he who encourages' is singular; but since the sense is generic, the display has 'those who'. An alternative would be 'anyone who'.

The verb could mean 'to encourage', 'to exhort', or 'to console'. Sometimes the sense is clear from the context, but not here. The sense of 'console' is a specific kind of encouragement and would not be the sense here unless the context indicated something for which consolation was needed. As to the other two senses, BAGD (p. 617.2) are undecided, nor is there any clear help from commentators, so in the display both alternatives are included.

his people Both 'encourage' and 'exhort' semantically require a patient to be expressed. The words 'his people' are supplied because in this context Paul is discussing ways of ministering within groups of believers.

12:8b Those who share *their goods with others* should do it sincerely The words 'their goods with others' are supplied as the object and recipient following the verb 'share' in order to satisfy the case frames. 'Their goods' is meant to include funds. Paul is probably referring primarily to sharing among other members of the Christian community.

The expression ἐν ἁπλότητι could mean 'with liberality' or 'with singleness'. Most versions render the word by "generously" or "freely," though the latter is somewhat ambiguous. Louw and Nida (57.106) give the meaning here as "generously." BAGD (p. 86.2) support the meaning 'with generosity' here and also in 2 Cor. 8:2, 9, but note that this meaning is disputed by some. Cranfield, Dunn, and Morris all support the sense of 'with sincerity'. And even if the word did come to mean 'with generosity', it would still carry the sense of 'with sincerity'. Therefore it is rendered here as 'sincerely', in the sense of 'without ulterior motives' or, to put it positively, 'with pure motives'.

12:8c Those who govern *the congregation* should do it diligently/zealously The verb προΐστημι means 'to govern'. Since Paul is discussing the life of the church, the object is supplied to complete the case frame and avoid wrong meaning about the kind of governing. The phrase ἐν σπουδῇ means 'in diligence'. When the mismatch between the grammatical and semantic categories is resolved, we have 'diligently/zealously', with the sense of 'putting one's whole being into it'.

12:8d Those who help the needy should do it cheerfully The verb ἐλεέω means 'to help someone out of pity' (BAGD, p. 249). This is rendered here 'help the needy', meaning those who are in need. Since the noun ἱλαρότης 'cheerfulness' represents an attribute, ἐν ἱλαρότητι is rendered as 'cheerfully'.

BOUNDARIES AND COHERENCE

Relational coherence in the 12:3-8 paragraph is evidenced by its consisting of one generic APPEAL in v. 3 regarding believers' abilities plus a series of specific APPEALS in vv. 6-8 about exercising those abilities and gifts as one group of believers. Lexical coherence is also maintained by use of first person plural pronouns, in contrast to the following paragraph. The paragraph ends with a long section consisting of verbless phrases. The beginning of the next paragraph is marked by a new sentence with the topicalized word 'love' as the subject, which is maintained throughout the paragraph.

PROMINENCE AND THEME

The theme of 12:3-8 is taken mostly from the positive and negative parts of the APPEAL in 3c-d and the implied generic APPEAL in 6c. The orienter is not included in the theme because its function is to mark the 3c-d CONTENT as prominent; it is not prominent itself. The 3e circumstance is included because of the extensive development in vv. 4-8 of the same subject mentioned in 3e: abilities.

SUBDIVISION CLUSTER CONSTITUENT 12:9–21
(Hortatory Section: Specific appeal₂ of 12:3–13:14)

THEME: Love others sincerely in the ways you act towards them. Instead of avenging yourselves, allow God to avenge you; and instead of being overcome by evil done to you, overcome these things by doing good deeds to those who do evil to you.

MACROSTRUCTURE	CONTENTS
SPECIFIC APPEAL₁	12:9–18 Love others sincerely in the various ways you act toward them.
SPECIFIC APPEAL₂	12:19–21 Instead of avenging yourselves, allow God to avenge you; and instead of being overcome by evil done to you, overcome these things by doing good deeds to those who do evil to you, since this is what the Scriptures command.

INTENT AND MACROSTRUCTURE

The 12:9–21 unit is composed of two hortatory paragraphs. Neither is subordinate to the other. Both are *SPECIFIC APPEALS*.

BOUNDARIES AND COHERENCE

The coherence of the 12:9–21 section is seen in its consisting of a long set of *SPECIFIC APPEALS* dealing with Christian attitudes and actions that demonstrate love. There is something of a sandwich structure to mark the boundaries, with references to 'the evil' and 'the good' in the opening and closing verses of the unit. The boundary with the next unit at 13:1 is clearly marked by a change of topic to subjection to civil authority.

PROMINENCE AND THEME

The theme of the 12:9–21 unit consists of the combined themes of its constituents except for the omission of the *scriptural basis* (the final clause), which is less thematic than the *APPEALS*.

SECTION CONSTITUENT 12:9–18
(Hortatory Paragraph: Specific appeal₁ of 12:9–21)

THEME: Love others sincerely in the various ways you act toward them.

¶ PTRN	RELATIONAL STRUCTURE	CONTENTS
GENERIC APPEALS	GENERIC	12:9a *The way you are to love people* is to love them sincerely;
	specific₁	12:9b abhor what is evil;
	specific₂	12:9c continue to eagerly do what is good *in God's sight*;
	specific₃	12:10a love one another as members of the same family do;
	specific₄	12:10b and be in the lead about honoring one another.
SPECIFIC APPEALS Set A	NUCLEUS₁	12:11a Do not be lazy, *but rather* be zealous *to serve God*;
	NUCLEUS₂	12:11b remain fervent spiritually;
	NUCLEUS₃	12:11c serve the Lord;
	NUCLEUS₄ — RESULT	12:12a rejoice
	reason	12:12b because you are confidently awaiting *what God will do for you.*
	circumstance	12:12c When you suffer,
	NUCLEUS₅ — NUCLEUS	12:12d be patient.
	NUCLEUS₆	12:12e Pray perseveringly.
	condition	12:13a If any of God's people lacks anything,
	NUCLEUS₇ — CONSEQUENCE	12:13b share with them *what you have*.
	NUCLEUS₈	12:13c Readily take care of travelers who need a place to stay.
SPECIFIC APPEALS Set B	NUCLEUS₁ — NUCLEUS	12:14a *Ask God to* be kind to those who persecute you.
	amplification	12:14b *Ask him to* be kind; do not *ask God to* curse them.
	condition	12:15a If someone is joyful,
	NUCLEUS₂ — CONSEQUENCE	12:15b you rejoice also.
	condition	12:15c If someone is sad,
	NUCLEUS₃ — CONSEQUENCE	12:15d you be sad also.
	NUCLEUS₄ — GENERIC	12:16a Seek for others what you seek for yourselves (*or*, Live harmoniously with each other).
	negative	12:16b Do not be too ambitious *to do things that will make you famous/proud*,
	specific — POSITIVE	12:16c but instead be content with humble *tasks*.
	NUCLEUS₅	12:16d Do not consider yourselves wise.
	NUCLEUS₆	12:17a Do not do evil *deeds* to anyone *who has done* evil to you.
	NUCLEUS₇	12:17b Act in a way that all people will recognize as good.
	NUCLEUS₈	12:18 Live peacefully with other people whenever it is possible, to the extent that you *can control it*.

INTENT AND PARAGRAPH PATTERN

The three imperatives in the 12:9–18 paragraph mark it as hortatory: εὐλογεῖτε 'bless' occurs twice in v. 14, and γίνεσθε 'become' once in 16d. In the main APPEAL of the paragraph, the one expressed in the first clause, the imperative verb 'to be' is understood, though not expressed. Since this first clause contains the GENERIC APPEAL under which all the other exhortations in the paragraph are subsumed (many of them expressed by participles, not finite verbs), and since there are no supporting *bases*, except possibly 12b, the paragraph does not fit the usual patterns. In a sense the *bases* for these APPEALS are in the preceding chapters.

NOTES

12:9a *The way you are to love people* **is to love them sincerely** In the clause ἡ ἀγάπη ἀνυπόκριτος '(may) love (be) sincere', the noun 'love' expresses an event concept. Rendering it as a verb and completing the case roles causes a problem, however: 'love people sincerely' puts the focus on the event, whereas Paul is focusing on the attribute modifying the event: 'sincerely is how you should love others'. A good alternative would be 'be sincere in the way you love (people)' (cf. CEV).

12:9b-18 Many commentators suggest that the series of participles following the implied copulative imperative in 9a are a Hebraistic pattern and that Paul often uses participles following an imperative to give an imperative sense. While that is true, in this instance it seems better to follow Dunn, who suggests that while they do have an imperative sense, they act more as specific ways of making love sincere. It is recognized, however, that some of the exhortations in vv. 9b-18 do not fit well as specifics of 'love'. It is also recognized that this long list of short appeals forms somewhat of a miscellaneous list. But there is *some* grouping within this list. Cranfield notes,

> it is a mistake to look too anxiously for precise connections of thought or for a logical sequence in these verses. . . . In vv. 9-13 Paul has been concerned mainly at any rate with the relations of Christians with their fellow Christians. In vv. 14-21 he is at any rate mainly concerned with the relation of Christians with those outside the Church.

The question is what to do with these groupings. And there is a further question of whether such groupings would even affect the translation. In the display some grouping has been done strictly on the basis of grammatical forms. For example, the participles that characterize 9b-13 are largely replaced by imperatives and infinitives in vv. 14-18.

12:9b **abhor what is evil** The word ἀποστυγέω means 'to abhor, hate', but in conjunction with κολλάω 'cling closely to' in 9c it carries the additional connotation of 'turn away from'.

12:9c **contine to eagerly do what is good** *in God's sight* The verb κολλάω means 'cling closely to', which is metaphorical. BAGD (p. 441.2c) suggest 'be devoted to' as a nonmetaphorical rendering.

The words rendered here as 'what is good' contrast with 'evil' in 9c. They refer to that which is morally good, hence 'in God's sight'.

The expression 'in God's sight' is admittedly somewhat idiomatic in English; it could be translated as 'what God considers good,' using a full clause.

12:10a **love one another as members of the same family do** The Greek is τῇ φιλαδελφίᾳ εἰς ἀλλήλους φιλόστοργοι 'in brotherly love loving each other dearly'. Brotherly love refers to love among siblings in the same family, hence 'as members of the same family do'. Paul is referring to the fact that spiritually all believers are members of God's family. NCV has "Love each other like brothers and sisters." CEV is similar.

12:10b **be in the lead about honoring one another** The Greek is τῇ τιμῇ ἀλλήλους προηγούμενοι 'in honor each other preceding', which lends itself to two interpretations: either "be eager to show respect for one another" (TEV) or "as far as honor is concerned, let each esteem the other more highly than himself" (BAGD, p. 706). Louw and Nida are undecided as to whether it means "to excel, do exceedingly" (78.35) or "do with eagerness" (68.70). In its literal sense the verb προηγέομαι, which occurs nowhere else in the NT, means to go ahead of someone to show him the way. It is used in a somewhat figurative sense here. One of the difficulties with the BAGD view is that it gives a transitive sense to an intransitive verb. On the other hand, the sense of 'show respect for' is not attested elsewhere. (BDF [p. 150] suggests that the verb is one which becomes transitive "by a preposition in composition.") It is the BAGD view that is chosen for the display, using the words 'be in the lead', the sense 'each of you' being understood. This retains the literal sense of the verb in a somewhat idiomatic way.

12:11a Do not be lazy, *but rather* be zealous *to serve God* The Greek is τῇ σπουδῇ μὴ ὀκνηροί 'in zeal not lazy'. Robertson (p. 1172) says that this adjective in the midst of participles that themselves carry an imperative sense also carries an imperative sense. That would give 'do not be lazy in zeal'. But since laziness and zeal are antonyms, they are both treated in the display as imperatives and are connected by 'but rather'. Since zeal can be for any cause, virtuous or not, the rather generic phrase 'to serve God' is supplied to define the sphere of the zeal. The context (11c) supports this.

12:11b remain fervent spiritually The verb ζέω in the phrase τῷ πνεύματι ζέοντες 'in spirit burning' means 'to boil' and is used figuratively here. But it is difficult to know whether the sense is "be aglow with the Spirit" (RSV), referring to the Spirit of God, or "in ardour of spirit" (NEB), referring to the human spirit. As Morris says, "Great names can be cited to support either view, and it is difficult to see a convincing reason for excluding either." In the display, 'in spirit' is treated as attributive and is rendered 'spiritually'. This perhaps preserves the ambiguity in that 'spiritually' refers to that which relates to the human spirit but is accomplished by the means of God's Spirit.

12:12a-b rejoice because you are confidently awaiting *what God will do for you* The Greek is τῇ ἐλπίδι χαίροντες 'in hope rejoicing'. Again the participle carries an imperative sense. 'Hope' is made into a verb phrase, 'confidently awaiting'. Case roles then require some goal to be supplied such as the generic 'what God will do for you'. LB supplies "all God is planning for you." As to the propositional relationship being expressed by the dative phrase 'in hope', it could be reason, as was chosen for the display, or it could be circumstantial: 'while you are waiting'.

12:12c-d When you suffer The noun phrase τῇ θλίψει 'in affliction' is represented by a full clause expressing a circumstantial relationship.

be patient The participle ὑπομένοντες 'enduring' connotes the activity of remaining steadfast; this is not just passive resignation.

12:12e Pray perseveringly The phrase προσευχῇ προσκαρτεροῦντες 'in prayer being devoted' involves somewhat of a mismatch: the noun 'prayer' is actually the event and thus is rendered in the display as a verb. Semantically speaking, the participle 'being devoted' modifies the event and states how the action is to be performed, namely perseveringly. An alternative rendering is 'be constantly devoted to praying'. REB's "persist in prayer" is excellent.

12:13a-b If any of God's people lacks anything, share with them *what you have* As in 8:27, οἱ ἅγιοι is rendered 'God's people'. The noun χρείαις 'needs' is rendered as a conditional clause with the verb 'lack'. Alternatively, it could be expressed as a relative clause: 'who lack or need anything'. To fill out the case roles, 'share' must have some object, 'what you have/possess', for example.

12:13c Readily take care of travelers who need a place to stay The Greek is τὴν φιλοξενίαν διώκοντες 'hospitality pursuing', which suggests active pursuit, "not merely bestowing it, perhaps grudgingly . . . when necessity makes it unavoidable" (Murray), hence 'readily' in the display. The phrase 'take care of' is intended to cover the provision of both meals and lodging. JBP captures it well with "never grudging a meal or a bed to those who need them." Several versions have "welcome strangers into your home" (CEV), but this is not really what Paul is telling the believers to do: he is not commanding them to take in homeless people off the streets.

12:14a *Ask God to* be kind to those who persecute you The Greek has a full imperative clause, εὐλογεῖτε τοὺς διώκοντας 'bless those (who are) persecuting'. In some Greek manuscripts the object pronoun 'you' does not occur (though it is included in the GNT), but either way it needs to be understood. Since the verb εὐλογέω means "to call down God's gracious power" (BAGD, p. 322.2a) for someone's benefit, the words 'ask God to' are implied (see TEV, CEV, LB, Murray, Cranfield, Morris).

12:14b do not *ask God to* curse them God is the actual agent of the cursing, as well as the blessing, as is made clear in the display. The verb καταράομαι can mean "to call on God to withhold his favor" as well as to ask him "to act as a power for ill" (Dunn).

12:15a-b If someone is joyful, you rejoice also In the Greek, v. 15 has two infinitive phrases with an imperative sense: 'to rejoice', 'to be sad'. This grammatical construction is rare in the NT but common in extrabiblical literature. Both participles in the infinitive phrases are rendered in the display as conditional clauses, but a circumstantial relation (i.e., 'whenever someone is joyful') would capture the sense equally well.

In the phrase μετὰ χαιρόντων 'with (those who are) rejoicing', the preposition 'with' can mean 'when you are in the presence of'. Hence the main clause is rendered 'you rejoice also'.

12:15c–d If . . . sad, you be sad The verb κλαίω means 'to weep', but the sense here is more generic, "an expression of any feeling of sadness, care, or anxiety" (BAGD, p. 433.1).

12:16a Seek for others what you seek for yourselves (*or*, Live harmoniously with each other) Again, there is a participle with an imperative sense (likewise in 16b and c). The Greek is τὸ αὐτὸ εἰς ἀλλήλους φρονοῦντες, literally 'thinking the same thing toward each other'. This has been given a diversity of meanings. Some suggest 'be agreed in your opinions and views', but as Dunn notes, "he is certainly not calling for a rote uniformity of thought." Other versions and commentaries support this by giving 'live in harmony with each other', a somewhat extended sense. But in the context of the two preceding verses and those which follow, it is better to give a more literal rendering, as BAGD do (p. 866.2): 'be intent on the same thing toward each other'. The first alternative rendering of 16a closely follows Barnes's "what you regard or seek for yourself, seek also for your brethren. . . ." (Morris, JB, NEB, and TEV are similar.) The second alternative follows most of the commentators, also NIV, REB, JBP, and RSV. If the second alternative is chosen, the 16b–c cluster would be another NUCLEUS.

12:16b Do not be too ambitious *to do things that will make you famous/proud* The Greek is μὴ τὰ ὑψηλὰ φρονοῦντες 'not the high things minding/thinking'. This is clearly figurative, but there is uncertainty as to whether the phrase means 'do not be ambitious' or 'do not be conceited'. Most commentators choose the former; most versions, the latter. Although the word ὑψηλός has the figurative sense of 'exalted, proud, haughty', it follows the verb φρονέω. Choosing 'do not be ambitious' allows the same basic sense to be given to the same verb in 16a and 16b. Thus this sense would seem the better choice. BAGD (p. 850.2) similarly renders the phrase as "strive after things that are (too) high, be too ambitious."

Another difficulty is that 'ambitious' in itself is quite neutral; God does not disapprove of someone being ambitious for accomplishing things that are pleasing to God. Therefore 'to do things that will make you famous/proud' has been supplied to avoid wrong meaning. LB has "Don't try to get into the good graces of important people."

12:16c be content with humble *tasks* The sense of the participial phrase τοῖς ταπεινοῖς συναπαγόμενοι 'to the humble (people/things) condescending' depends on whatever is chosen for 16b, since the phrases in 16b and c are clearly in a negative-positive relationship with each other (ἀλλά here has the sense 'but instead'). A few commentators, in support of this interpretation, point out that in all other occurrences of ταπεινός it refers to things, not people. Some (e.g., Barrett, Dunn, Murray) suggest that the ambiguity of the adjective may be deliberate, including condescension to both humble tasks *and* humble people.

12:16d Do not consider yourselves wise The Greek is a clause with a finite verb: μὴ γίνεσθε φρόνιμοι παρ' ἑαυτοῖς 'do not become wise with yourselves'. The phrase 'with yourselves' has the same sense of the idiomatic 'in your own eyes': "do not think of yourselves as wise" (TEV), "don't be conceited" (NIV).

12:17a Do not do evil *deeds* to anyone *who has done* evil to you The Greek is μηδενὶ κακὸν ἀντὶ κακοῦ ἀποδιδόντες 'to no one evil for evil recompensing'. This is somewhat elliptical, with the verbal idea in the second part assumed. In some languages there may be an idiomatic expression that conveys this thought.

12:17b Act in a way that all people will recognize as good The participle προνοούμενοι means 'taking into consideration, having regard for' (BAGD, p. 708.2), but the sense here is not just consider, but act accordingly. TEV has "try to do what all men consider to be good." While this is better than 'consider what is good', Paul is not telling them to make their lives conform to what nonbelievers might approve of. As Morris says, the sense is, rather, that "their lives will be lived on such a high plane that even the heathen will recognize the fact." JBP is close to the meaning with "See that your public behaviour is above criticism." The display expresses it positively, but in some languages the negative might be better: 'act in a way that no one will consider bad'.

The phrase ἐνώπιον πάντων ἀνθρώπων 'before all men' is idiomatic. In the display it is expressed nonidiomatically, but it could be expressed by the idiom 'in the eyes of all'.

12:18 whenever it is possible The expression εἰ δυνατόν 'if (it is) possible' occurs a number of times in the NT. This does not mean 'if you can' here, focusing on 'you', but rather "if others will allow it" (Alford).

to the extent that you *can control it* The Greek is τὸ ἐξ ὑμῶν, literally 'that (which is) from you'. This is an unusual use of an accusative neuter article in an adverbial sense; the meaning is quite well expressed by Moule: "as far as it is in your power."

BOUNDARIES AND COHERENCE

The 12:9-18 paragraph is relationally coherent in that it consists of a *GENERIC APPEAL* followed by a long set of short *SPECIFIC APPEALS*, most of which have to do with how believers are to express their love for one another.

The boundary with the 12:19-21 paragraph is marked by a vocative in 12:19 plus a switch from the subject of loving actions to the specific topic of revenge. Although NIV, TEV, and REB make a paragraph division at v. 17 and not at v. 19, most portions of vv. 17-18 do not deal with vengeance whereas all of vv. 19-21 does. Clearly vv. 19-21 have *bases* as well as *APPEALS*; on the other hand, vv. 17-18 are in a paragraph with no *bases*. Furthermore, at the beginning of v. 19 there is a change from the scattered, brief, mostly unrelated commands of vv. 11-18 to a more fully developed exhortation with a series of closely related supporting propositions.

PROMINENCE AND THEME

The theme of 12:9-18 is taken from the *GENERIC APPEAL* in 9a. Then since there is such a long list of specific exhortations in the rest of the paragraph, these are summarized by the words "in the various ways you act towards them" in the last part of the theme.

SECTION CONSTITUENT 12:19-21
(Hortatory Paragraph: Specific appeal₂ of 12:9-21)

THEME: *Instead of avenging yourselves, allow God to avenge you; and instead of being overcome by evil done to you, overcome these things by doing good deeds to those who do evil to you, since this is what the Scriptures command.*

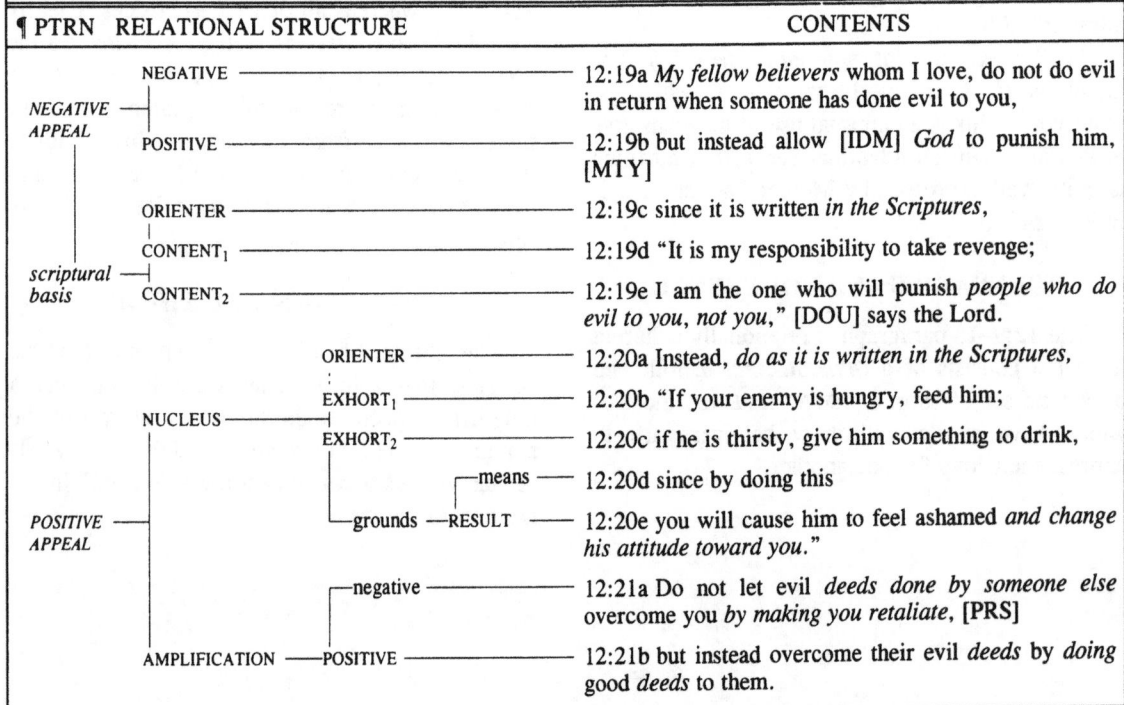

INTENT AND PARAGRAPH PATTERN

That 12:19-21 is a hortatory paragraph is signaled by the imperatives δότε 'give' in 19b, νικῶ 'be conquered' in 21a, νίκα 'conquer' in 21b, and ψώμιζε 'feed' and πότιζε 'give drink' in the quote (20b-c). These imperatives are expressions of APPEALS. The first APPEAL (19a-b) is supported by a *basis* (19c-e). The EXHORTATIONS in the NUCLEUS (20b-c) of the POSITIVE APPEAL are supported by the grounds in 20d-e.

NOTES

12:19a *My fellow believers* **whom I love** The vocative ἀγαπητοί 'beloved' expresses an event that is descriptive of an unexpressed noun or pronoun, for which 'my fellow believers' is supplied. An alternative to 'my fellow believers' is 'you'. (In English, however, 'you, whom I love, do not do evil in return' could be construed as being in the indicative mood.)

do not do evil in return when someone has done evil to you The Greek participial phrase ἑαυτοὺς ἐκδικοῦντες 'avenging yourselves' is fully spelled out in the display. Some languages, however, will have a simple expression for 'retaliate'.

12:19b allow *God* **to punish him** The Greek is δότε τόπον τῇ ὀργῇ 'give place to wrath'. Some suggest that this means that a believer is to let his opponent give opportunity to express his wrath; others suggest that it means to step aside, to get out of the way of his wrath. But in fact the expression is an idiom with its roots in intertestamental literature according to Dunn. It means 'let someone else take your place in performing it', which meaning is supported by the context. It is also supported by the fact that 'wrath' preceded by the article 'the', when 'wrath' has not been mentioned in the preceding context, points to that wrath the readers are assumed to know, namely God's wrath. As elsewhere in the NT (e.g., Rom. 2:5, 8 and 5:9) 'wrath' is somewhat of a metonymy, the cause standing for the effect. NCV expresses both with "wait for God to punish them with his anger."

12:19c since it is written *in the Scriptures* The verb γέγραπται 'it is written' requires specification to complete case roles and avoid wrong meaning, hence 'in the Scriptures'. For languages that must specify the agent, some generic specification of the writer ('someone', 'a prophet', or 'they') might be used. Several versions use a personification, "the Scripture says," to express this. The source of the quotation is Deut. 32:35.

12:19d It is my responsibility to take revenge The pronoun in ἐμοὶ ἐκδίκησις 'to me (is) vengeance' is prominent by its position. This emphasis is conveyed in the display by the word order (cf. NIV's "it is mine to avenge" and CEV's "I am the one to take revenge"). The noun rendered here as 'take revenge' has the same root as the participle in 19a and the same meaning. It is recognized that the English word *revenge* is an abstract noun, but there seems to be no good verb for 'take revenge' in English as there probably is in most languages.

12:19e I am the one who will punish . . . , *not you* The emphasis expressed by the free pronoun ἐγώ 'I' in Greek is for the purpose of contrast. This is brought out in the display by the word order and by the words 'not you'.

The expressions in 19d-e are a synonymous doublet (Moore, p. 41), but both are retained here since this is an OT poetic passage.

12:20a The conjunction ἀλλά that introduces the second APPEAL signals a contrast with the 19a negative proposition regarding retaliation. But it is difficult to show this in the relational structure labels of the display: the labels NEGATIVE APPEAL for 19a and POSITIVE APPEAL for 20-21 are an attempt to convey this.

12:20a–c The quotation here acts as an APPEAL itself, and this function is made specific in 20a. (The same device is used in 1 Cor. 5:13.) NCV captures the idea with "But you should do this: 'If your enemy. . . .'"

it is written in the Scriptures As in TEV, CEV, and JBP, these words are supplied to indicate what Paul expected his readers to know, that the rest of the verse is a quotation from the OT (Prov. 25:21-22).

12:20d–e since In the display 20d-e are labeled as the grounds of 20b-c. In effect, 20d-e are the *basis* for the 20b-c APPEALS; however, this is difficult to show due to constraints on making relational structure diagrams.

12:20e you will cause him to feel ashamed *and change his attitude toward you* There is a fair amount of disagreement by commentators on the origin and meaning of the saying 'heap coals of fire on his head'. The great majority say it refers to the pain of remorse felt by someone whose antagonism is repaid by deeds of kindness. LB makes this meaning explicit, following up its literal rendering with "In other words, he will feel ashamed of himself for what he has done to you." Some have suggested that such deeds of kindness have the effect of increasing the offender's guilt and punishment, but that would be contrary to the spirit of the context. Some recent commentators (Käsemann, Cranfield, Dunn, Morris) have suggested that the saying comes from an Egyptian custom in which coals of fire were offered as a symbol of a genuine change in attitude. Supposedly, in this ritual someone would, as a symbol of repentance, "purge his offense by carrying on his head a dish containing burning charcoal on a bed of ashes" (Cranfield). But even if such a custom existed, there is little chance that Paul would have known of it. It seems best to follow the interpretation accepted by most commentators and assume that it must have been a dead metaphor even to Paul. Therefore no attempt is made to retain it in the display. To include the image and spell out its meaning would distort the focus of the passage.

12:21a Do not let evil *deeds done by someone else* overcome you *by making you retaliate* In the clause μὴ νικῶ ὑπὸ τοῦ κακοῦ 'do not be conquered by evil' the word 'evil' stands for evil things done to you by someone else.

Note that in this context of Paul's exhortation to resist the urge to exact revenge, the means by which evil can overcome the believer is clearly implied and needs to be understood (see Cranfield, Denney, Murray, Erdman, Harrison, Hodge, Morris); hence the words 'by making you retaliate' are supplied.

It is recognized that the rendering here, with 'evil deeds' as the subject of the verb 'overcome', is a personification as in Greek, but it is difficult in English to express the thought without it. Possibly one could say 'Do not do evil deeds in return to anyone who does evil deeds to you', but this completely misses the impact of 'overcome'.

12:21b overcome their evil *deeds* by *doing* good *deeds* to them As in 21a, 'evil' refers to evil deeds done to you by someone else; 'good' refers to good deeds which you do in return. The word νίκα, literally 'conquer', is somewhat metaphorical: Paul uses it here because it is the same verb as in 21a. The sense Paul probably intended is 'shame him and thus make him your friend and less likely to continue treating you in an evil way'.

BOUNDARIES AND COHERENCE

The 12:19-21 unit consists of two *APPEALS*, the second of which (looked at semantically) repeats much of the first one. Between the two *APPEALS* is a *basis*. This sandwich structure is what marks the three verses as a unit and shows their relational coherence.

The boundary between the 12:19-21 unit and the next, 13:1-7, is marked by a change to a new topic: what the believers' attitude should be toward civil authorities.

PROMINENCE AND THEME

The theme of 12:19-21 is drawn from the naturally prominent propositions of the *APPEALS* and of the *basis,* all greatly condensed. The 19a vocative and the description of the believers are omitted as nonthematic, and the clauses are reduced by using the word "avenge." The CONTENT of the *scriptural basis* in 19c-e is summarized by "since this is what the scriptures command." The quotation in 20b-e includes an exhortation, but since it is more specific than its generic counterpart 21b, the latter is included in the theme instead of 20b-c.

ROMANS 13:1–7

SUBDIVISION CLUSTER CONSTITUENT 13:1–7
(Hortatory Paragraph: Specific appeal₃ of 12:3–13:14)

THEME: *Every believer must be subject to civil authorities, because anyone who opposes them opposes what God has established and will bring on himself punishment from the authorities as God considers fitting. Do what is good and then they will commend you. Give to all the authorities what you are obligated to give them.*

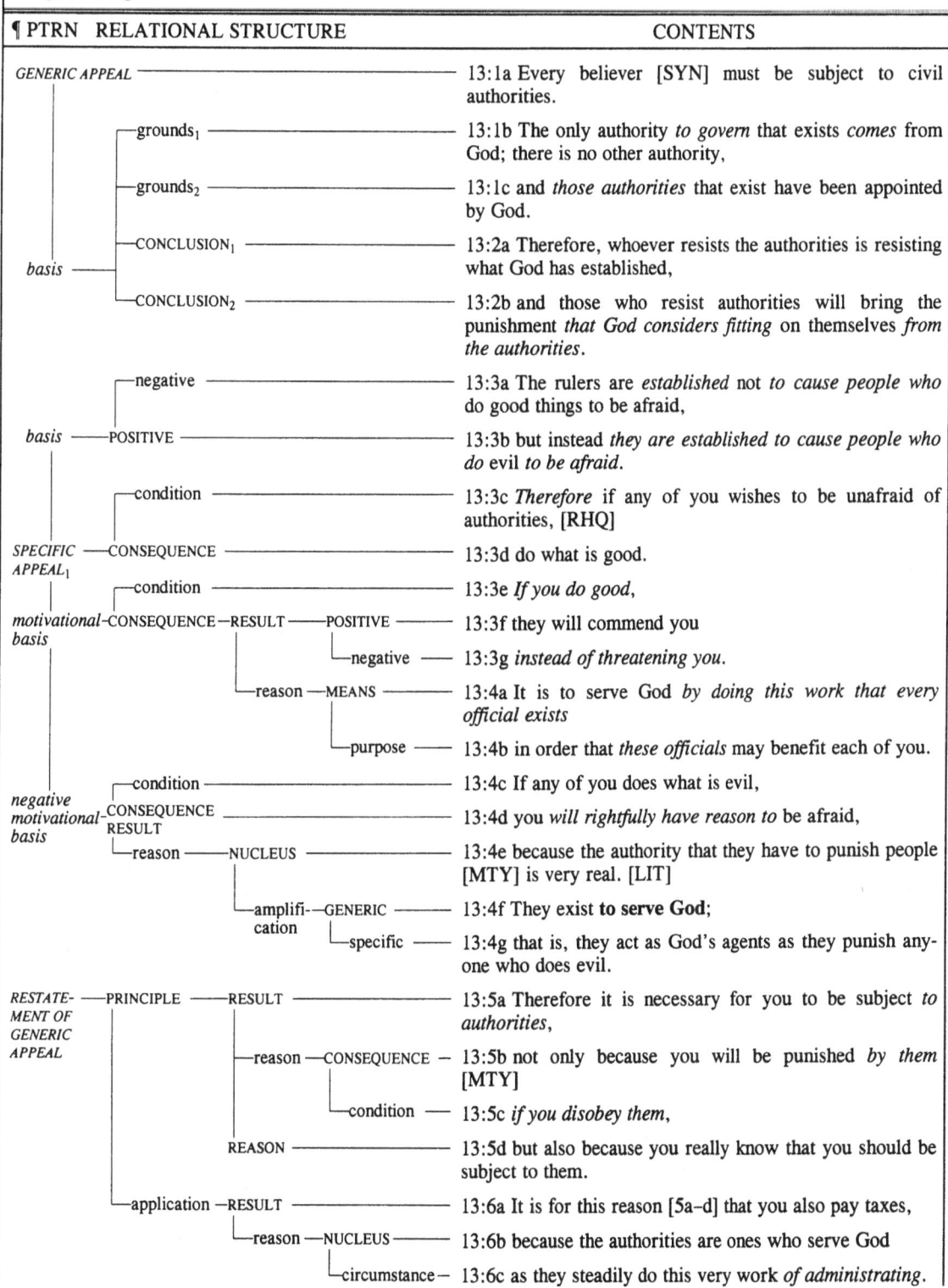

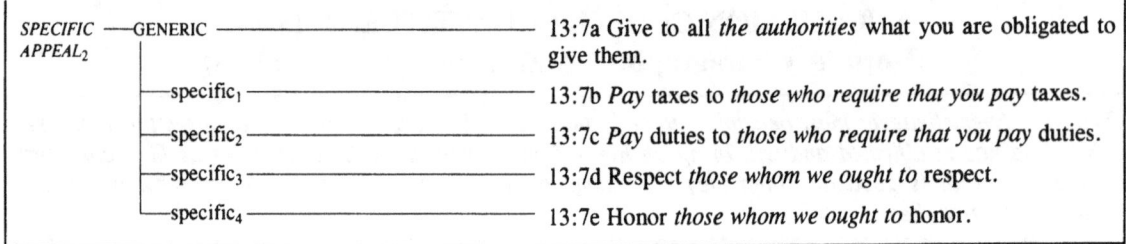

INTENT AND PARAGRAPH PATTERN

There are a number of indicators to show that 13:1-7 is a hortatory paragraph: the third person singular imperative ὑποτασσέσθω 'let him be subject' in 1a; the imperative ποίει 'do' in 3; the ἀνάγκη 'it is necessary' in 5a; and the imperative ἀπόδοτε 'render/give' in 7a.

The 1b-2b material introduced by γάρ gives grounds for the exhortation in 1a in the form of a warning; it therefore functions as a *basis* for the preceding APPEAL. It is difficult to know how to label 3d ('do good') with respect to 1a, but the best option seems to be to take it as a SPECIFIC APPEAL and 1a a GENERIC APPEAL, with v. 7 clearly a second SPECIFIC APPEAL. The first SPECIFIC APPEAL is supported by a general *basis* (3a-b) and two *motivational bases*, one positive (3e-4b) and one negative (4c-g). It is also difficult to decide whether to take 5a as a mitigated appeal or not. But Dunn says, "The use of ἀνάγκη here is striking, since its philosophical use in reference to divine or immanent necessity—the way things are (laws of nature) and have to be (fate, destiny)—would be well known." In view of this concept of 'necessity', vv. 5-6 are considered a mitigated APPEAL, specifically a restatement of the APPEAL in 1a.

NOTES

13:1a Every believer Paul is addressing believers here and prescribing their behavior, so 'believer' is made specific in the display. The Greek is πᾶσα ψυχή 'every soul', in which 'soul' is a synecdoche standing for the whole person. (Some manuscripts have πάσαις ἐξουσίαις ὑπερεχούσαις ὑποτάσσεσθε 'to all authorities governing be subject', perhaps in an effort to avoid the figure of speech and use a less formal style.) NCV's "All of you" is a good alternative.

civil authorities The phrase ἐξουσίαις ὑπερεχούσαις means 'to those that are in superior authority', officials at any level, not necessarily 'supreme authorities' (so Barrett). It is civil authorities that Paul has in mind, not religious, and certainly not angelic powers.

13:1b The only authority *to govern* that exists *comes* from God; there is no other authority The Greek is οὐ ἔστιν ἐξουσία εἰ μὴ ὑπὸ θεοῦ 'there is no authority except from God'. But, as noted previously in the note on 7:7, many languages do not have an 'except' construction, and in such a case the exception has to be stated as 'the only thing that exists' with the words 'there is no other' added.

The words 'to govern' make the kind of authority Paul refers to specific. (NCV has "power to rule.") The verb 'comes' is supplied because it is more natural in English than the verb 'to be' (similarly in REB); the sense is 'originates'.

13:1c *those authorities* that exist have been appointed by God The Greek is simply αἱ οὖσαι 'the existing (ones)'; 'the authorities' is supplied from 1a. The predicate 'have been ordained by God' may have to be expressed more fully in some languages, for example as 'are ones who have been ordained' or 'are ruling because they have been appointed'.

13:2a whoever resists the authorities The Greek has the singular article ὁ 'he who' but used in the generic sense of 'anyone who'. The word ἐξουσία 'authority' is also singular with the generic sense of 'any authority'. It is made plural in the display to capture the generic sense (cf. RSV). The verb ἀντιτάσσω here has the sense of 'set oneself against, oppose, resist' (BAGD, p. 67.3).

is resisting what God has established The object of the verb ἀνθέστηκεν 'has opposed' is τῇ τοῦ θεοῦ διαταγῇ 'the of God ordinance'. Since the noun 'ordinance' represents an event, it is made a full clause in the display.

13:2b This proposition is considered a second conclusion following from the grounds stated in v. 1 (so Hodge). It is possible to consider 2b as the result of 2a, but no commentators mention that possibility.

will bring the punishment *that God considers fitting* **on themselves** *from the authorities* There is no indication of the source of punishment; the Greek is simply κρίμα λήμψονται 'judgment will receive'. Most commentators state that Paul probably means that the punishment will be carried out by the authorities but that "it carries the sanction of God and its propriety is certified" (Murray). To avoid ambiguity both of these elements are supplied here.

It is recognized that 'punishment' is a verbal noun. Alternatives to avoid this would be 'those who resist authorities will be punished by the authorities as a result' or possibly 'those who resist authorities will be punished by them because they have resisted them'.

13:3a-b The 3a-b cluster sets up the principle or axiom on which the APPEAL in 3c-d is based. The initial γάρ here in 3a is either marking support for the primary APPEAL in 1a (the interpretation followed here) or an amplification of the general topic. There is little difference in sense. But on the level of v. 3 itself, the most direct support given by 3a-b is to 3c-d.

13:3a are *established* **not** *to cause people who* **do good things to be afraid** The Greek is οὐκ εἰσὶν φόβος τῷ ἀγαθῷ ἔργῳ 'are not a fear to the good work'. The word 'fear', which represents a state, is rendered in the display by 'to be afraid', and a causative relationship is supplied. Alternatively, 'those who do good' can be made the subject of 'do not need to fear' as in LB and NCV. But this distorts Paul's focus somewhat.

The verb 'to be' connects 'rulers' with 'fear', which is a mismatch between the grammatical and semantic categories. To resolve the mismatch, the verb 'are established' is supplied. In some languages and cultures 'appointed' would be possible. Other alternatives would be 'they exist' or 'they are there'. In the display the negative is put with the clause it refers to, not with the verb expressing existence. The phrase 'good work' is figurative, the effect standing for people who produce it.

13:3b but instead *they are established to cause people who do* **evil** *to be afraid* The Greek is elliptical: ἀλλὰ τῷ κακῷ 'but to evil'. Most of this proposition is repeated from 3a.

13:3c Therefore Since 3a-b functions as the *basis* for the APPEAL beginning in 3c, the display supplies 'therefore' to make the relationship specific. LB has "So" here.

if any of you wishes The Greek is a rhetorical question: θέλεις 'Do you(sg) wish . . . ?' Semantically, it expresses a conditional relationship (so Morris, Barrett) with the imperative clause that follows. It also relates 3a-b as the *basis* for the APPEAL in 3c-d. Paul uses the second person singular pronoun here for effect, but he is not addressing any one individual, and so the sense is represented by 'if any of you'.

13:3e *If you do good* This clause begins with καί, which often occurs after an imperative to signal the result that will follow. In this case the result functions as a motivational basis.

13:3f they will commend you The word ἔπαινον here means 'praise', but with a sense closer to 'approval' or 'commendation', since it is commendation from authorities that is in view.

13:3g *instead of threatening you* This proposition is implied as a contextual implicature of Paul's argument. If it is needed in translation, it may be necessary to reverse the order of 13:3f-g and render as 'they will not threaten you; instead they will commend you'.

13:4a It is to serve God *by doing this work that every official exists* The word θεοῦ 'of God' is first in the clause, indicating prominence (as also in 4f). The word order in the display similarly shows this emphasis. The words 'by doing this work' are supplied to express the implied means. Of course, many public servants are unaware that they are serving God; Paul is expressing the goal of their work from the divine perspective, not the human. This sense could perhaps be conveyed by 'God considers that they are serving him'.

The Greek uses the singular διάκονός ἐστιν 'a minister he is' in a generic sense, which is represented in the display by 'every official'.

13:4b that *these officials* **may benefit each of you** The Greek is σοὶ εἰς τὸ ἀγαθόν 'to you(sg) for the good'. The singular sense of the pronoun is again represented by 'each of you'. The phrase 'unto the good' is represented more naturally by a verb, hence the generic verb 'benefit', as in JB. LB and CEV have "to help you"; NIV, "to do you good."

13:4d you *will rightfully have reason to* **be afraid** The Greek is the imperative φοβοῦ 'be afraid', but such a state cannot be commanded in a literal sense. JB has the same sense as in the display: "you may well have fear." REB has "you will have cause to fear them"; JBP, "you have reason to be alarmed."

13:4e the authority that they have to punish people is very real Two figures of speech are involved in οὐ εἰκῇ τὴν μάχαιραν φορεῖ 'not in vain the sword he bears'. First, 'sword' is a metonymy, the instrument standing for the power to punish which is associated with it. NCV has "the ruler has the power to punish." Second, 'not in vain' is a litotes: the denial of the negative emphasizes the positive, hence 'very real'. Prominence is given to this phrase by virtue of its appearing first in the clause.

13:4g that is, they act as God's agents as they punish anyone who does evil Literally, this is 'for of God a servant he is, an avenger for wrath to him that evil does'. The word ἔκδικος 'avenger' is in apposition to διάκονος 'servant': being avengers is the way authorities serve God. Thus this proposition serves semantically as a specific of 4f.

The noun ὀργή 'wrath' is a metonymy in which the cause stands for the effect, as in 2:5, 2:8, 4:15, and 5:9, and is rendered 'punish'. As many versions and commentators bring out, the expresser of the wrath is God. The indirect object phrase τῷ τὸ κακὸν πράσσοντι 'to the one practicing evil' is singular but with a generic sense, hence 'anyone who does evil'.

13:5a to authorities This elided phrase is restated from 1a.

13:5b you will be punished by them The Greek is τὴν ὀργήν 'wrath', repeated from 4g. Since 'wrath' stands for the resultant punishment, it could be expressed by 'God will punish', but here it is rendered with the passive and the agent supplied: 'by them' (cf. the rendering of κρίμα in 2b). The sense is "the wrath of God manifested in the punishment inflicted by civil authorities" (Morris). NCV renders it as "because you might be punished."

13:5c if you disobey them This proposition is supplied as the understood condition for 5b to take place.

13:5d because you really know that you should be subject to them The Greek is simply διὰ τὴν συνείδησιν 'on account of conscience', but the 'because' relation requires a full proposition with some verb supplied. Since some languages will not have a word for 'conscience', the display avoids it, as do NCV and CEV. CEV has "because you know it is the right thing to do," using a verbal construction.

13:6a you also pay Although it is quite possible to take τελεῖτε as meaning 'you must pay', and a few commentators choose that interpretation, the vast majority of commentators and versions choose the indicative 'you pay'. It would be very difficult to have an imperative introduced by γάρ, which is seen here as introducing an application of the principle about being in subjection to authorities.

taxes The word φόρος technically refers to tribute paid by a people to a government that had conquered it, but here Paul probably means it to include any taxes.

13:6b the authorities are ones who serve God The phrase λειτουργοὶ θεοῦ 'ministers of God' is here rendered by a verb and its object to resolve the mismatch and clarify the case roles.

13:6c as they steadily do this very work of administrating As Dunn notes, the words εἰς αὐτὸ τοῦτο 'for this very thing' should not, theoretically, be the object of the verb because this verb takes a word in the dative case as object. But it is almost impossible to translate it otherwise and make any sense. Commentators are divided as to whether 'this very thing' refers to serving God or their work of administration or collecting taxes. The first part of the verse does not refer to what the administrators are doing (collecting taxes) but to what the people are doing (paying them). Thus it most likely refers to something previously attributed by Paul to the administrators, namely their administrating. The present participle προσκαρτεροῦντες 'being busily engaged in' is taken as expressing a simultaneously occurring event: God considers the one (6b) to be taking place at the same time as the other (6c).

13:7a what you are obligated to give them The word ὀφειλή 'debt' can mean 'what you owe them', but such a rendering in English implies unpaid outstanding obligations. 'What they require you to pay' is implied. JB has "what he has a right to ask."

13:7b Pay taxes to those who require that you pay taxes The Greek is τῷ τὸν φόρον τὸν φόρον 'to the one the tax, the tax', which is extremely elliptical: both the main verb and the verb linking 'the one who' and its object 'the tax' are elided. The same ellipsis occurs also in 7c, 7d, and 7e. The generic sense of 'the one who' in each of these is indicated by supplying the plural 'those who'.

13:7c *Pay* duties Grammatically, this construction parallels the one in 7b. Commentators are somewhat unclear as to the exact sense of the word τέλος, but most suggest it had come to refer primarily to indirect taxes, mostly duties of various kinds. In many languages it may be impossible to provide different terms for 'taxes' in 7b and 'duties' in 7c, in which case it may be necessary to say 'various kinds of taxes'. Moore (p. 41) calls 'taxes to whom taxes are due' (7b) and 'revenue to whom revenue is due' (7c) a near-synonymous doublet.

13:7d *ought to* respect The word φόβος usually means 'fear', but here it means 'respect'. The obligatory sense of ὀφειλή 'debt' in 7a is maintained by 'ought to'. Moore calls 7d and 7e a near-synonymous doublet, and, in fact, in some languages it will not be possible to distinguish 'respect' and 'honor'.

BOUNDARIES AND COHERENCE

The unity of the 13:1-7 paragraph, which consists of both hortatory and expository elements, derives from its overall subject matter: the relation of believers to authorities. Lexical coherence consists of references to authorities: ἐξουσία 'authority' in vv. 1, 2, and 3, ἄρχοντες 'rulers' in v. 3, and other pronominal or implied references to authorities in all the other verses.

Verse 8 is considered the beginning of a new paragraph because it deals with loving others, not with obedience to authorities.

PROMINENCE AND THEME

The first sentence of the 13:1-7 theme is drawn from the GENERIC APPEAL (1a) and the two CONCLUSIONS (2a-b) in its supporting *basis*. The theme's second sentence is from the first SPECIFIC APPEAL (3d) and also from 3e-f, the condition and CONSEQUENCE propositions of its motivational *basis*. The theme's third sentence is from the GENERIC exhortation of the second SPECIFIC APPEAL (7a). The 5a RESTATEMENT OF GENERIC APPEAL is not included in the theme because it would be redundant.

SUBDIVISION CLUSTER CONSTITUENT 13:8-10
(Hortatory Paragraph: Specific appeal₄ of 12:3-13:14)

THEME: Do not leave any debt unpaid. Your only continual obligation is to love one another, since doing so fulfills all that God's law requires.

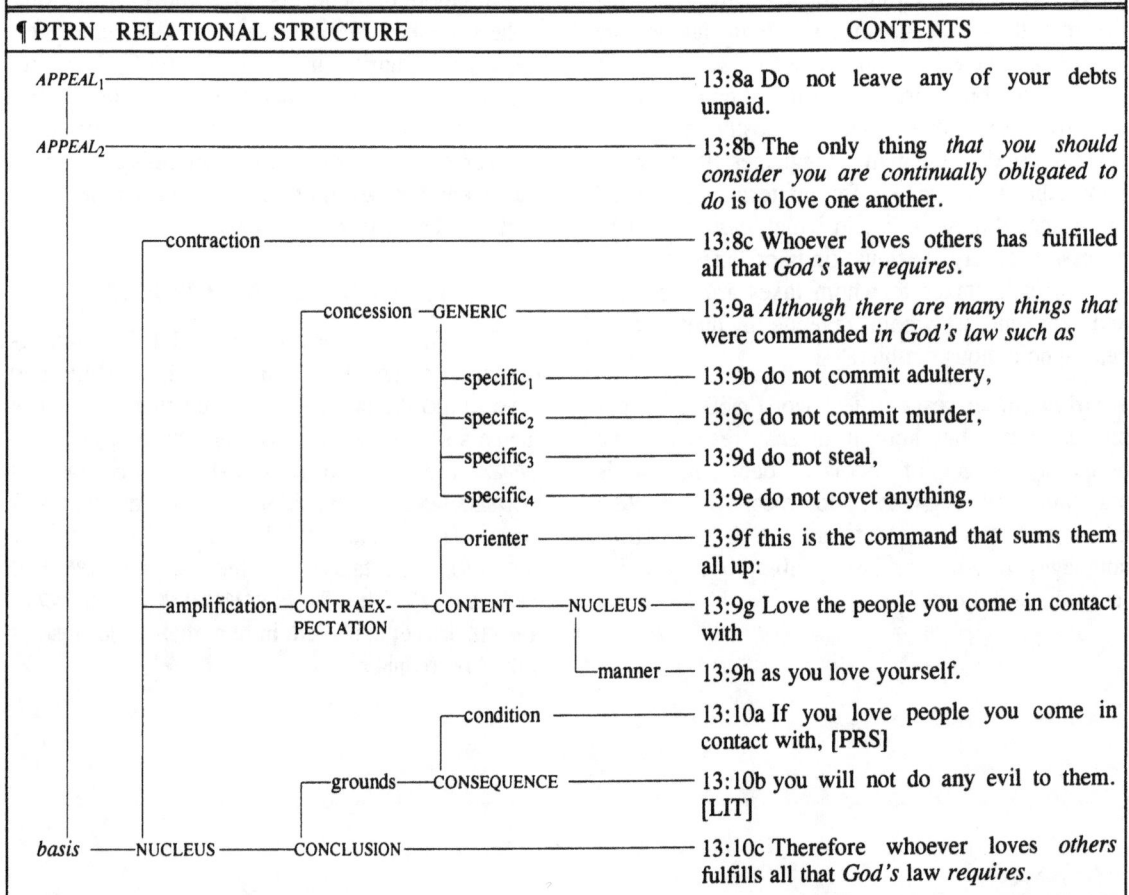

INTENT AND PARAGRAPH PATTERN

The 13:8-10 paragraph, in view of the imperative ὀφείλετε 'owe' in 8a, is seen as hortatory. The same verb is implied in 8b and so is supplied in the display, hence the APPEAL label for each of these propositions. Since 8c-10 states an incentive for the APPEALS, it is the *basis* for them.

NOTES

13:8a Do not leave any of your debts unpaid The Greek is μηδενὶ μηδὲν ὀφείλετε 'to no one nothing owe'. Commentators agree that this does not mean that a Christian is not to go into debt for anything since both OT and NT allow borrowing. The sense is captured well by the NIV: "let no debt remain outstanding." REB and LB are similar. Implied, of course, is the temporal phrase 'beyond the time when payment is due'. To make the meaning clear, in some languages it may be necessary to add 'which you should have paid previously'. JBP's "Keep out of debt altogether" is unjustified.

13:8b The only thing *that you should consider you are continually obligated to do* is to love one another The Greek clause here is connected with 8a by εἰ μή, which normally means 'except'. If that were the meaning here, it would be saying that loving others is an unpaid debt, which doesn't make much sense.

Note that there is a play on words between ὀφείλετε 'you are obligated' in its overt occurrence in 8a and its implied presence here in the εἰ μή 'except' clause. This word play cannot be translated easily. In the display, two different verb phrases are used, 'leave unpaid' and 'obligated to do', thus losing the play on words.

As Murray states it, Paul is here reminding his readers that loving others (i.e., fellow Christians) "is a perpetual obligation."

The words 'you should consider' are supplied to avoid wrong meaning: Paul does not mean it is a literal obligation but that it should be considered as such.

The word ὀφείλετε 'you are obligated' rendered 'do not leave unpaid' in 8a is carried over here since there is no verb in the 'except' clause in the Greek. The supplied words 'you are continually obligated' fill in the ellipsis.

13:8c Commentators are divided as to how this part of v. 8 (and what follows) relates to the first part of the verse. Cranfield summarizes the two options well:

> Verse 8b may be understood as stating a reason for loving one another: to do so is to fulfil the law.... [Alternatively,] Verse 8b may be understood as explaining why the debt of love cannot be fully discharged, because if there were people who were in the fullest sense loving their neighbors, they would have done what we have seen impossible for fallen men—they would have perfectly fulfilled the law.

The problem with the second interpretation is that it does not exhibit relational coherence: 8b says 'love one another', and then 8c-10 would say why it is impossible to completely do so—it would be ridiculous as an explication of γάρ. Note that 8c is essentially restated in 10c, but 10c is supported by the material in 10a-b. Since v. 10 coheres so well as the *basis* for 8b, it is the first interpretation that is essentially followed here.

Whoever loves others The subject and object in the clause ὁ ἀγαπῶν τὸν ἕτερον 'he who loves the other' are represented by 'whoever' and the plural 'others' since they are used in a generic sense. Cranfield, like a number of other commentators, says in regard to τὸν ἕτερον 'the other' that it "means not just 'another' (KJV) or 'his fellow man' (NIV, TEV) or 'someone other than himself' (Barrett), but 'the other', that is, the one who at a particular moment confronts him...." The sense is thus more likely 'others that he has contact with'.

God's **law** *requires* The display specifies that it is God's law that is referred to. Commentators (e.g., Barrett, Murray, Denney) suggest that the word 'requires' is needed to complete the sense of 'fulfill the law'. LB has "fulfilling all his requirements"; CEV, "done all that the Law demands."

13:9a *Although there are many things which were commanded in God's law such as* A full proposition with a concessive relationship to 9f-h is given here for smoothness and clarity. In the Greek, the clause καὶ εἴ τις ἑτέρα ἐντολή 'and if (there is) any other command' follows the specific commands (9b-e in the display). But if this were to be translated literally, following the Greek order, it would convey the sense that Paul did not know that there were other commandments besides the ones mentioned. In reality he mentions only a few representative ones with the full knowledge that there are many others. Thus in the display a generic statement is placed before the specific examples with 'such as' supplied (cf. JB's "and so on"). The source of the commandments is also supplied: 'in God's law'. CEV conveys the sense well: "In the Law there are many commandments, such as . . . ."

13:9b-e In citing these commandments from Exod. 20:13-15, 17, and Deut. 5:17-19, 21, Paul uses the second person singular imperative. For some languages the second person plural may be necessary.

Some may wonder why Paul cites these four, and no more, of the Ten Commandments. The answer seems to be that these have to do with human interrelationships. A few Greek manuscripts have here a fifth commandment, 'you shall not bear false witness', probably because in the Exod. 20 and Deut. 5 passages this commandment lies between 'do not steal' and 'do not covet'. Other manuscripts omit one or another of the four or rearrange the order, but the supportive evidence for doing so is very weak.

13:9f this is the command The Greek is ἐν τῷ λόγῳ τούτῳ ἀνακεφαλαιοῦται, ἐν τῷ 'in this word is summed up, in the (command)'. Because the first part (τῷ λόγῳ τούτῳ 'in this word') is given emphasis by its form and by being first in the clause, 'this' is forefronted here to retain this emphasis. (Note that the article τῷ points to the sense of 'the well-known command'.) Although λόγος means 'command', it is omitted in what would have been its second occurrence so that 'command' would not be used twice in 9f; but it is the understood word that is elided in the phrase ἐν τῷ 'in the (command)'.

13:9g the people you come in contact with This is taken as the intended sense of the word πλησίον 'neighbor' in the NT references that cite Lev. 19:18. See the second note on 8c.

13:10 The chiastic structure in v. 10 occurs at the end of the section on the believer's obligations to others, and perhaps serves to emphasize the importance of love:

  A love
    B to its neighbor no evil works; so
    B' fulfillment of law *is*
  A' love

13:10a-b If you love . . . , you will not do any evil to them In ἡ ἀγάπη κακὸν οὐκ ἐργάζεται 'love evil does not work', the event 'love' is nominalized. In the display 'love' is made a full proposition with the subject 'you'. But since the subject is not in focus, the translator should use whatever form expresses this sense generically when the agent and the patient are not in focus.

13:10c whoever loves *others* See the note on 8c. This is virtually a restatement of 8c, except that here, as in 10a, the Greek word 'love' is nominalized. (In 8c it is a verbal form in a participial phrase.) This mismatch is resolved in the display, though no English version of those examined resolves it.

BOUNDARIES AND COHERENCE

The 13:8-10 paragraph has a tail-head linkage with the preceding paragraph: In 13:7 the word ὀφειλή 'debt' is used in a literal sense; in 13:8 ὀφείλατε 'owe' is used in a figurative sense. The former is simply a lead-in to the topic of loving others, which is introduced immediately after the word 'owe' by an εἰ μή 'except' clause. The paragraph is a sandwich structure that has a number of chiastic elements within it, marking the paragraph as a coherent unit:

(v. 8)	
ὁ ἀγαπῶν τὸν ἕτερον	the one loving another
νόμον	law
πεπλήρωκεν	has fulfilled
(v. 9) τὸ γὰρ . . .	(four specific commands)
(v. 10)	
πλήρωμα	fulfillment
νόμου	of law
ἡ ἀγάπη	love

PROMINENCE AND THEME

The theme of 13:8-10 is drawn from the 8a and 8b *APPEALS* and the 10c NUCLEUS of the *basis*. In the interest of conciseness, repetition is avoided and the gerund of the pro-verb 'do' is used in the final part of the theme.

SUBDIVISION CLUSTER CONSTITUENT 13:11–14
(Hortatory Paragraph: Generic appeal of 12:3–13:14)

THEME: Because it is time for us to be fully active, we must quit doing wicked deeds, we must do those things which will help us resist that which is evil, we must live properly, and we must be like Christ.

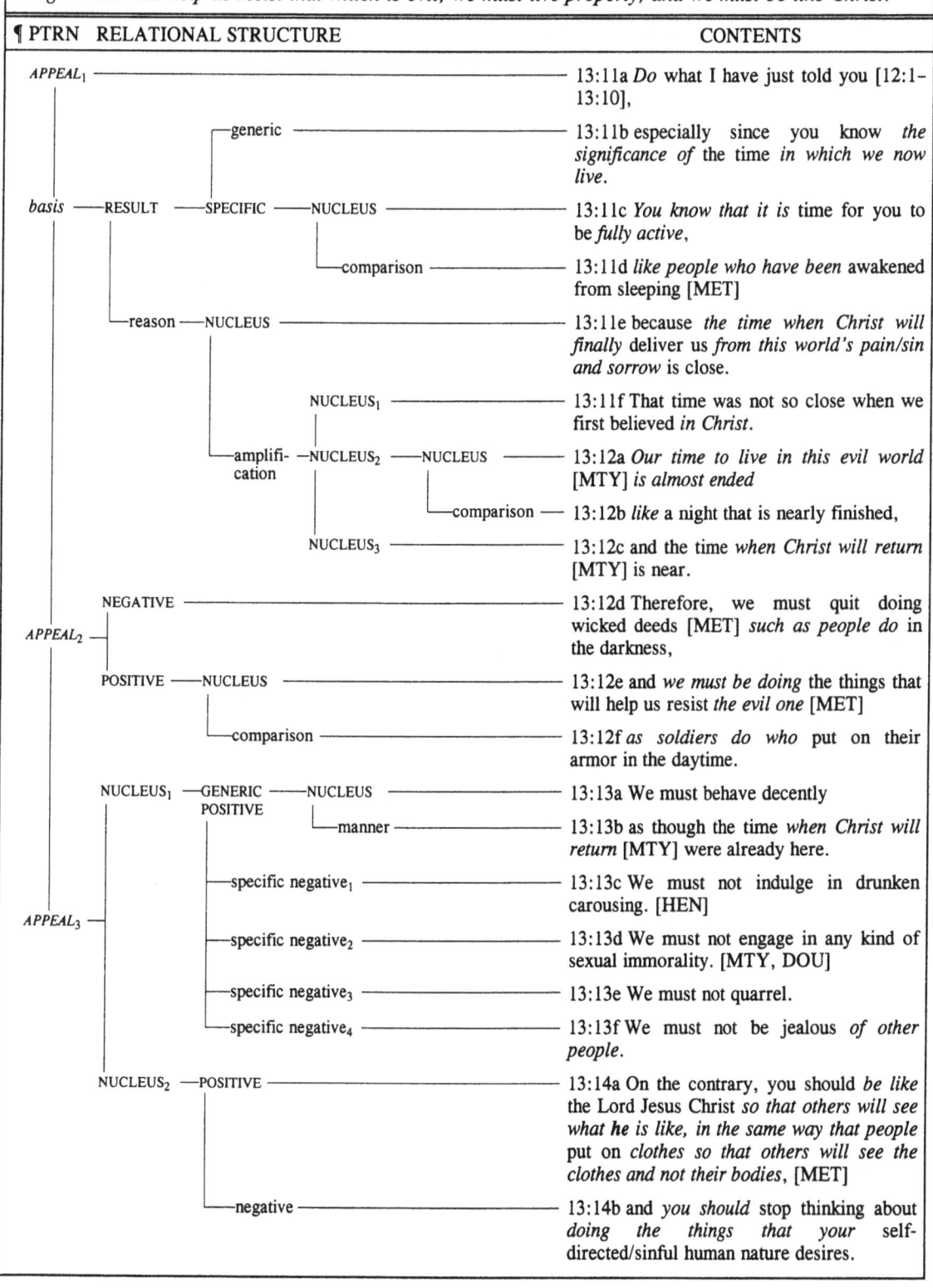

INTENT AND PARAGRAPH PATTERN

The 13:11-14 paragraph is hortatory, as is evident from three first person plural subjunctives (ἀποθώμεθα 'let us put off' in 12d, ἐνδυσώμεθα 'let us put on' in 12f, and περιπατήσωμεν 'let us walk' in 13a) and one imperative (ἐνδύσασθε 'put on' in 14a). The propositions containing these forms are all labeled as APPEALS. Since the APPEAL in 12d begins with οὖν 'therefore' and since the material in 11b-12c provides a motivation for that, 11b-12c is considered the *basis* for the second APPEAL and also for the third APPEAL. Note that every proposition in 12d-14b except for 12f and 13b is an APPEAL.

Hodge says of this paragraph, "From this verse [v. 11] to the end of the chapter, Paul exhorts his readers to discharge the duties already enjoined, and urges on them to live a holy and exemplary life." The problem is that some parts are truly generic (the *basis* in 11b-12c is generic), while some parts are specific. Nevertheless, the 13:11-14 paragraph is labeled a GENERIC APPEAL in the display heading for want of a better term.

NOTES

13:11a-b Do what I have just told you, especially since you know Commentators disagree as to the meaning of καὶ τοῦτο εἰδότες 'and this knowing'. The vast majority say an ellipsis occurs here, and that the verb 'do' needs to be supplied (cf. TEV, NCV, NIV). Some have suggested 'besides this' as in the RSV and JB. Cranfield considers 'and this' an idiom used "to introduce an additional circumstance heightening the force of what has been said." In other words, the readers are to strive all the more earnestly to do what Paul has been urging them to do in chapters 12 and 13 because they know the significance of the law. Dunn's discussion (p. 785) is quite good:

> The καὶ τοῦτο is awkward to translate. The nearest parallels suggest that the phrase is resumptive or recapitulative, gathering up what has already been said; cf. particularly 1 Cor 6:6, 8 and Eph 2:8.... To regard it as an ellipse with verb omitted... is less satisfactory, since choice of a particular verb ("do this" [... NIV]) rather weakens the breadth of the reference back. ... But καὶ τοῦτο could also be understood as adding a further thought—"besides this" (RSV, NJB), "in addition"....

Hodge says of the pronoun that it "is frequently used to mark the importance of the connection between two circumstances for the case in hand ... and is, therefore, often equivalent to the phrases, *and indeed, the more,* &c. So in this case, 'We must discharge our various duties, *and that* knowing,' &c., i.e., 'the rather, because we know,' &c." Beck renders it well: "Do this especially since." If knowing is the reason for what precedes, there seems no purpose at all for the words 'and this'. In the other few occurrences of καὶ τοῦτο it is the object of some verb in the immediate context, but here it is the object of the implied pro-verb 'do'. Quite a few commentators note that τοῦτο is often used to mark the importance of the connection between two thoughts, hence 'especially' in the display.

There is a question of how much preceding material the word τοῦτο 'this' in v. 11 refers to. It could refer to the material in the previous paragraph about loving one another, or to everything from 12:3 to 13:10, forming a sort of closure to set all this material off from the extensive discussion of 'the weak' beginning in 14:1. In view of its generic nature and the length of the unit that follows, the second alternative seems the better one.

Regarding the reference of τοῦτο 'this' to everything since the beginning of chapter 12, Cranfield has this to say:

> Paul has already referred to the eschatological context of Christian obedience in 12:2 (μὴ συσχηματίζεσθε τῷ αἰῶνι τούτῳ, ἀλλὰ μεταμορφοῦσθε τῇ ἀνακαινώσει τοῦ νοός) ['do not be conformed to this world but be transformed by the renewal of the mind']. Throughout chapters 12 and 13 it is assumed. Now at the end of the more general part of his ethical exhortation Paul takes up again the reference of 12:2, and makes explicit the eschatological motivation of Christian obedience.

the significance of **the time** *in which we now live* The Greek is simply τὸν καιρόν 'the time', which obviously does not mean the time of day. The display follows Hodge. The same sense is captured fairly well by NEB's "remember how critical the moment is," but CEV's "you know what sort of times we live in" is somewhat better.

13:11c-d *it is* **time for you to be** *fully active like people who have been* **awakened from sleeping** The expression ὥρα ἤδη ὑμᾶς ἐξ ὕπνου ἐγερθῆναι 'now *(is)* the hour for you to be raised out of sleep' is a metaphor. Although some commentators take the point of similarity to be alertness, the great majority follow BAGD (p. 215.2a), who say it is waking from 'thoughtless indolence'. Dunn says that

> ὥρα + infinitive is a familiar construction in Greek to indicate the right time to do something.... The ἤδη naturally increases the sense of urgency: the hour has already struck.

There is no main verb in the Greek; 'it is' is supplied. TEV, NIV, and JB supply "has come."

There is considerable manuscript support for the pronoun 'us' instead of 'you', but it seems likely that 'you' is correct, since a scribe would have been more inclined to change 'you' to 'us' to conform to 'our' in the next clause than to change 'us' to 'you', for which there would be no reason. In the fourth edition GNT 'you' is given a B rating ("almost certain"). In some languages it would be necessary to say 'us' in any case to avoid the implication that Paul did not consider that what he was suggesting applied to himself. (The omission of the pronoun in KJV is very poorly supported.)

13:11e–f *the time when Christ will finally deliver us from this world's pain/sin and sorrow* Proposition 13:11e represents ἡμῶν ἡ σωτηρία 'our salvation'. A subject of the salvation event must be supplied to complete the case frame. Since Paul elsewhere says that we await a Savior from heaven (Phil. 3:20), 'Christ' is supplied as the agent here. (The subject is not in focus, however.)

The words 'the time when' are supplied because in some languages one cannot say an action is near. TEV has "the moment when." To avoid ambiguity it may be necessary in some translations to specify 'when Christ returns'. LB's "the coming of the Lord is near" is unwarranted as a rendering of "our salvation."

Usually salvation is referred to in Scripture as a past accomplishment, but occasionally as a present operation, and sometimes (as here) a future event. To avoid the wrong meaning that salvation from the guilt of sin is still a future event, things Paul may have had in mind are supplied: 'pain/sin and sorrow'. An alternative would be Hodge's more generic "from this present evil world."

is close. That time was not so close when we first believed *in Christ* The comparative ἐγγύτερον ... ἢ ὅτε ἐπιστεύσαμεν 'nearer ... than when we believed' is spelled out with two clauses because many languages do not have a comparative degree construction and must use two clauses.

The word 'first' does not occur in the Greek, but nearly all versions include it. The meaning is not that there are a number of believings, this being the first, but rather "when we were converted" (JB).

13:12a–b *Our time to live in this evil world is almost ended like* **a night that is nearly finished** The Greek is ἡ νὺξ προέκοψεν 'the night is well advanced', a continuation of the metaphor of waking from sleep begun in 11c–d. It is not clear whether the word 'night' in this clause is simply referring to our life span on earth or whether it has strong evil connotations, such as 'this present evil age'. Commentators suggest the latter is probable. Both ideas are given in the display, but without trying to spell out exactly in what way night represents the evil world.

13:12c the time *when Christ will return* **is near** Paul does not specify what day he was referring to in ἡ ἡμέρα ἤγγικεν 'the day has come near', except for the oblique reference in 11e to the time when Christ will complete our salvation. This expression is a metonymy, the day standing for the events of that day. Several commentators support the rendering in the display. LB has "the day of his return will soon be here." Translators should use whatever generic expression refers to this time.

13:12d we must quit doing wicked deeds *such as people do* **in the darkness** The words ἀποθώμεθα τὰ ἔργα τοῦ σκότους 'let us cast off the works of darkness' involve two metaphors. As to the first, the word 'cast off' refers to removal of clothes. Since it is used frequently by NT writers, it might be considered a dead metaphor (see the note on 12e–f); but, combined with ἐνδυσώμεθα 'let us put on' in 12f it is, to some extent, at least, a live metaphor here. Rendering 'cast off' and 'put on' nonfiguratively is for the benefit of those translators who anticipate constraints in the receptor language. The figure is rendered nicely by CEV: "we must stop behaving as people do in the dark." (A number of Western manuscripts have ἀποβαλώμεθα instead of ἀποθώμεθα, but the meaning is the same.)

The second metaphor involves 'darkness', the topic of which, according to some commentators, is wicked deeds, as shown in the display. But it may be that this is a dead figure with the sense 'wicked deeds'.

13:12e-f and *we must be doing* **the things that will help us resist** *the evil one as soldiers do who put on their armor in the daytime* There are a number of textual variants of the conjunction that introduces 12e-f. But whichever one is correct, 12d and 12e are connected and contrasted by a negative-positive relationship.

The clothing metaphor (see the note on 12d) continues here with ἐνδυσώμεθα τὰ ὅπλα τοῦ φωτός 'let us put on the weapons of light'. Since believers do not literally put on armor, the topic of the figure is given as 'those things which help us resist'. The problem then, since case frames require an object, is to know who it is we are resisting. Suggestions such as Hodge's "sin and evil" are still figurative. The best solutions seem to be "spiritual foes" (Barnes) or "the evil one."

Commentators disagree as to whether or not 'putting off' (in 12d) refers to a soldier's removing his sleeping garments when he awakes and 'putting on' (in 12f) to his donning weapons when he awakes. The best historical evidence indicates that Roman soldiers did not have night clothing; they simply removed their outer clothing to sleep. Therefore, 'put off', since it is considered a dead metaphor, is rendered 'quit' in the display and the phrase 'who put aside their sleeping garments' is not added in 12f, as it would be if this were a live metaphor being spelled out.

Commentators are not clear on the meaning of the genitive 'of light' (in the expression 'weapons/armor of light') which contrasts with 'of darkness' in 12d. Suggestions are (1) 'used in the daytime', (2) 'of God', (3) 'belonging to the children of light' (i.e., to believers), or (4) "for fighting in the light" (TEV), whatever that might mean. The meaning is difficult to determine because Paul does not say 'deeds of light' but 'weapons of light'. The first alternative is chosen for the display because 'putting on weapons' seems to require an expression of time to be complete, both to explain the cultural background and as a contrast to 'in the darkness' in 12d.

13:13a We must behave decently The verb περιπατήσωμεν 'let us walk' is a dead metaphor referring to conduct. The rendering here follows the NIV. The word εὐσχημόνως means 'decently' and refers literally to one who is properly dressed.

13:13b as though the time *when Christ will return* **were already here** The expression ὡς ἐν ἡμέρᾳ 'as in day' is capable of several interpretations: (1) 'as people do in the daytime', the literal meaning; (2) 'as we will do in the time following Christ's return', which is the meaning of 'day' if it is taken as a metonymy; (3) 'as though that time following Christ's return were already here'; or (4) 'as is suitable for believers who are living according to Christ's revelation', which is the meaning of 'day' if it is taken as a metaphor. Quite a few versions choose the first interpretation, but against the first (also the fourth) interpretation is the fact that 'day' would be taken in a different sense from the same word in the previous verse. As to the second and third interpretations, there is not much difference between them, but the third fits better with Paul's 'as though' expressions of the Christian life in Romans. See, for example, the SSA renderings for 5:21; 6:3, 4, 6, 8, 22; and 11:15.

13:13c drunken carousing There are two terms here: κώμοις καὶ μέθαις 'revelings and drunkenness'. Moore (p. 41) does not consider this pair a near-synonymous doublet. Barrett says it is likely that the one is reinforcing the other. Hence, they properly constitute a hendiadys and one is given a modifying status in the display. JB and REB have "drunken orgies."

13:13d any kind of sexual immorality The term κοίτη in its primary sense means 'bed', but by metonymy comes to mean sexual intercourse and then more specifically immoral sexual relations. The word here is 'beds', plural like the other nouns of this verse, giving the sense of 'various kinds of'.

The conjoined noun following κοίτη is ἀσέλγεια 'licentiousness'. It is very difficult to see any contrasting component of meaning between the two words; they clearly form a doublet (so Moore, p. 41). The one possibly reinforces the other; thus Dunn has "debauched sexual excess."

13:13e quarrel The word ἔρις means "strife, discord, contention" (BAGD, p. 309). Since it denotes an action, it is represented by a verb here. The same is true for all the words rendered as verbs in 13c-f.

13:14a you should *be like* **the Lord Jesus Christ** *so that others will see what* he *is like, in the same way that people* **put on** *clothes so that others will see the clothes and not their bodies* This is another metaphor regarding clothing. Most commentators do not do justice to the figure, but those that do (Barnes, and esp. Harrison and Hodge) give the sense indicated here. Among the English versions, only CEV tries to retain some of both the metaphorical image and the topic: "Let the Lord Jesus Christ be as near to you as the clothes you wear." Although it is recognized that 'and not their bodies' is not in focus, it does seem to be implied. To complete the comparison, the words 'and not what you are like' should be included. The display hints at this by bolding 'he', referring to Christ. Commentators do not discuss the change from 'we' in vv. 12-13 to the second person plural in v. 14, even though the same verb, 'put on', is used in both v. 12 and v. 14. Though vv. 12-14 all contain *APPEALS*, those with 'we' are mitigated or softened.

13:14b *you should* **stop thinking about** *doing the things that your* **self-directed/sinful human nature desires** The Greek is τῆς σαρκὸς πρόνοιαν μὴ ποιεῖσθε εἰς ἐπιθυμίας, which means, literally, 'of the flesh forethought do not take for (its) desire'. The object of the verb is 'forethought', prominent by virtue of its occurring before the verb. The word 'flesh', rendered as "sinful nature" by the NIV, has the same meaning here as in chapter 7.

BOUNDARIES AND COHERENCE

The coherence of the 13:11-14 paragraph derives from the metaphors relating to time and light: καιρός 'time' (v. 11), ἡμέρα 'day' (vv. 12, 13), νύξ 'night' (v. 12), φῶς 'light' (v. 12), σκότος 'darkness' (v. 12), ὕπνος 'sleep' (v. 11), and ὥρα 'hour' (v. 11). Words in the semantic domain of changing clothes also lend coherence: ἀποτίθημι 'take off' (v. 12) and ἐνδύω 'put on' (vv. 12 and 14).

PROMINENCE AND THEME

The theme of 13:11-14 is drawn, first, from the most prominent proposition (11c) of the *basis*, which precedes the 12d *APPEAL*, giving it marked prominence. That not only justifies its being included in the theme but also its coming first in the theme. An alternative wording would be to make the first part of the theme an independent clause, "It is time for us to be fully active," followed by a new sentence beginning "Therefore."

The 11a *APPEAL* is not included in the theme because it is an extremely generic statement and not developed further; moreover, there is no overt verb expressing an *APPEAL* in 11a. (The 11b-12c material is really the *basis* more for the second and third *APPEALS* than for the first.) Note that 11d is not included in the theme, either, since it involves the image of a metaphor, and an image has less thematic prominence than a topic.

The 12d-e *APPEAL* is included in the theme in an abbreviated form, but the comparative clauses that state the metaphor's image are not because they do not have natural prominence. Also included in the theme is the POSITIVE NUCLEUS of 13a because it is more prominent than the specific negative appeals of 13c-f. The first part of the 14a *APPEAL* is included in the theme, but the embedded purpose clause and the 14b negative clause are omitted because these have less prominence.

DIVISION CLUSTER CONSTITUENT 14:1–15:13
(Hortatory Subdivision: Specific appeal₂ of 12:1–15:13)

THEME: Accept those who doubt whether they are permitted to do certain things. Specifically, anyone who thinks it is all right to eat all kinds of food must not despise those who don't, and those who don't think so must not condemn those who do, because God has accepted them.

MACROSTRUCTURE	CONTENTS
APPEAL — GENERIC APPEAL	14:1-4 Accept those who doubt whether they are permitted to do certain things. Anyone who thinks it is all right to eat all kinds of food must not despise those who don't, and those who don't think so must not condemn those who do, because God has accepted them.
specific appeal₁	14:5-9 Each person should be fully convinced about observing special days, thinking and deciding for himself. For doing such actions is not intrinsically wrong.
specific appeal₂	14:10-12 You should neither condemn nor despise your fellow believers who believe differently about religious regulations, because it is God who will say whether he approves of what we have done.
specific appeal₃	14:13-18 Instead of condemning each other, decide not to do anything that might lead your fellow believer to sin by following your example and which would then cause others to speak evil of you.
specific appeal₄	14:19-23 Try to do what will help fellow believers to be at peace with each other and grow spiritually. Do not destroy what God has done in others' lives as a result of your eating certain things. Keep between yourself and God what you believe about eating such things, and don't try to force your views on others, because if those who are not certain if they should eat such things do eat them, they will be condemned by God and their own consciences.
specific appeal₅	15:1-4 We should endure being irritated by the practices of those who are uncertain whether God will condemn them for doing certain things which the Mosaic law forbade, and do things which please our fellow Christians, since Christ has set us an example.
specific prayer regarding APPEAL	15:5-6 May God enable you all to live harmoniously with each other.
RESTATEMENT of APPEAL	15:7-12 Accept each other as Christ accepted you, remembering that what Christ has done was both to help the Jews and cause non-Jews to praise God.
generic prayer concluding 14:1-15:12	15:13 May God make you completely joyful and peaceful in order that you may have abundant hope.

INTENT AND MACROSTRUCTURE

All the constituent paragraphs of the 14:1-15:13 unit are hortatory except for two: 15:5-6, an expressive paragraph that is Paul's prayer regarding the topic of the preceding paragraphs; and 15:13, the final generic prayer. Since these are less thematic than the unit's APPEALS, the whole unit is considered hortatory. The macrostructure consists of a GENERIC APPEAL about how the Jewish and non-Jewish members of Paul's audience are to regard each other, followed by five *specific appeals,* then a *specific prayer* regarding the subject, a RESTATEMENT of the GENERIC APPEAL, and a final *generic prayer* to conclude the unit.

BOUNDARIES AND COHERENCE

The initial boundary of 14:1-15:13 is marked by the forefronted phrase τὸν ἀσθενοῦντα τῇ πίστει 'the one who is weak in faith' and the imperative προσλαμβάνεσθε 'accept'. This forefronted phrase provides the new topic, which continues throughout the unit. The end of the unit is marked by a benediction in 15:13. The start of the following unit is marked by a return to use of the first person singular pronoun and a vocative in 15:14.

The clearest indication of the unity of 14:1-15:13 is that the same imperative that is in 14:1 is repeated in 15:7 (διὸ προσλαμβάνεσθε ἀλλήλους 'therefore accept one another'), which is the start of the last hortatory paragraph in the unit.

Lexical coherence in 14:1-15:13 is seen in the occurrences of the verb ἀσθενέω 'be weak' in

14:1-2 and its cognate ἀσθένημα 'weakness' in 15:1, plus many references to eating and drinking throughout chapter 14. Another feature of coherence is the semantic concept 'one another', which in this context amounts to 'both the Jewish and non-Jewish believers among you'; the concept is represented by covert references to both groups in vv. 1-6, ἕκαστος 'each person' in 14:5 and 15:2, οὐδεὶς ἡμῶν 'none of us' twice in v. 7 and again in v. 12, and ἀλλήλους 'each other' in 14:13, 19, and 15:5, 7.

PROMINENCE AND THEME

The first paragraph in the 14:1-15:13 unit is the most thematic since it contains the *GENERIC APPEAL* addressed to both the Jews and Gentiles among the Roman believers not to despise or condemn the other group because of views about disputable matters. The *specific appeals* in the other paragraphs are less thematic. Therefore the 14:1-4 theme, with the addition of "specifically," is taken as the theme for the whole unit.

SUBDIVISION CONSTITUENT 14:1–4
(Hortatory Paragraph: Generic appeal of 14:1–15:13)

THEME: Accept those who doubt whether they are permitted to do certain things. Anyone who thinks it is all right to eat all kinds of food must not despise those who don't, and those who don't think so must not condemn those who do, because God has accepted them.

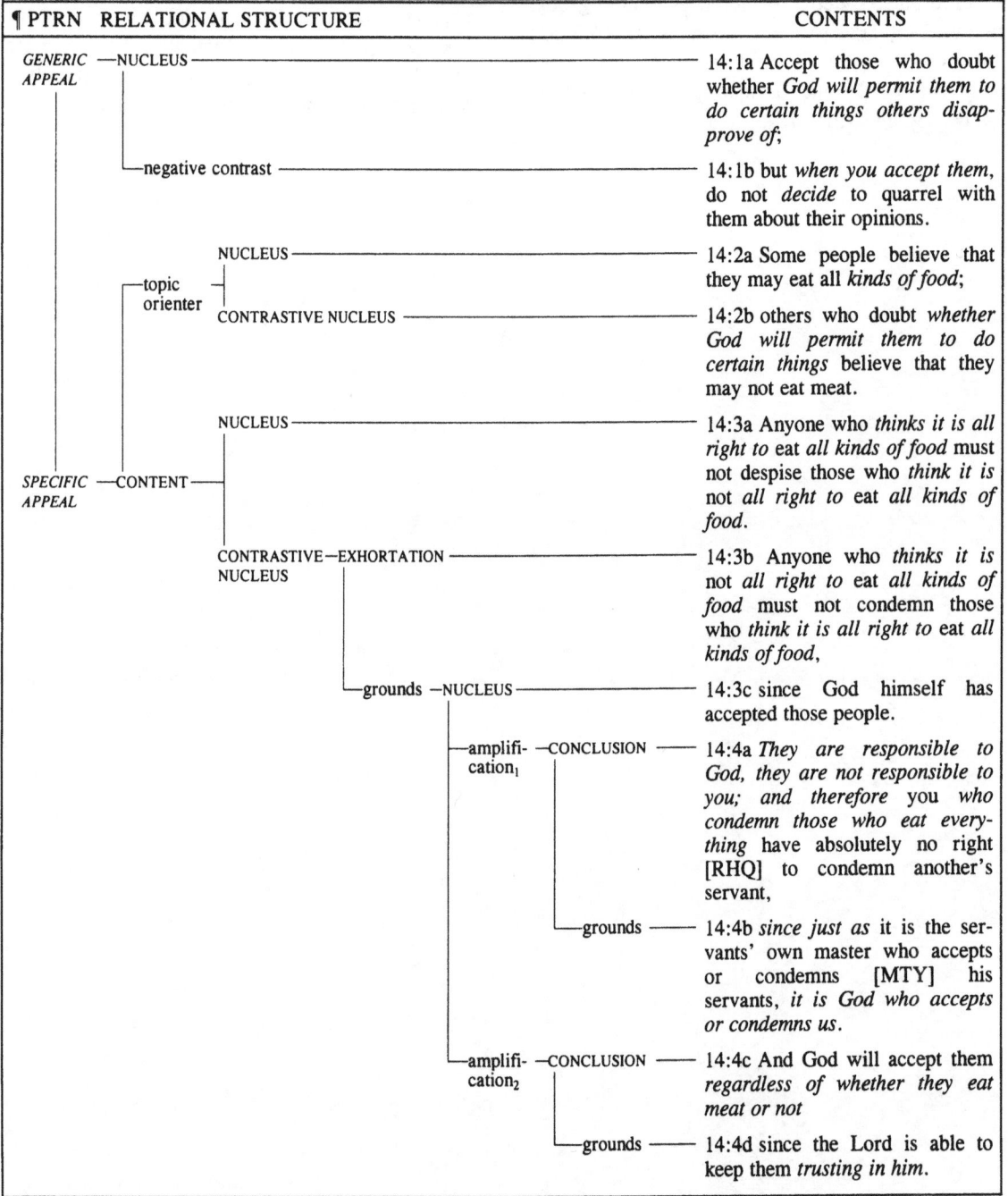

INTENT AND PARAGRAPH PATTERN

The first fully inflected verb in 14:1–4 is προσλαμβάνεσθε 'welcome', an imperative, so the paragraph is clearly hortatory. The first APPEAL (v. 1) is generic, and is followed in v. 3 by two negative third person imperatives: μὴ ἐξουθενείτω 'let him not despise' and μὴ κρινέτω 'let him not judge'. These are APPEALS also. (If the alternate interpretation of the pronominal referent mentioned in the note on 3c were to be followed, 3c–4d could be considered the *basis* for both APPEALS.)

NOTES

14:1a Accept those who doubt whether *God will permit them to do certain things others disapprove of* The sense of the verb προσλαμβάνομαι 'accept' is given by BAGD as "receive or accept in one's society, in(to) one's home or circle of acquaintances" (p. 717.2b). The generic sense of the singular article τόν 'the (one)' is conveyed by the plural 'those' in the display.

Most commentators agree that the expression τὸν ἀσθενοῦντα τῇ πίστει 'him being weak in the faith' does not refer to people who are uncertain whether they truly believe in Christ, but rather to those who are uncertain as to the implications and applications of that faith with respect to observing certain rules and regulations, especially regarding diet. The phrase 'weak in faith' is represented here by 'doubt'; it could also be expressed as 'not fully assured that'. Semantically, 'doubt' then requires a statement of the content of the doubt, hence 'whether God permits them to do certain things'. Since this is ambiguous (it is not referring to the things listed in the Ten Commandments), the display makes it clear with 'which others disapprove of'. There are a number of other ways the thought could be expressed: for example, 'those whose faith in Christ is not strong enough to cause them to know that God will not condemn them for doing certain things' or 'those who don't realize that because they believe in Christ it is irrelevant whether they do certain things'. But these are no shorter than the rendering in the display.

Since there are several groups of people being referred to in this verse, in some cases it may be necessary to identify the participants. Something like the following might be appropriate: 'You non-Jewish believers must accept those who doubt whether God will permit them to do certain things which some of your fellow Jews disapprove of'.

14:1b but *when you accept them*, **do not** *decide* **to quarrel with them about their opinions** The Greek is μὴ εἰς διακρίσεις διαλογισμῶν 'not unto quarrels of opinions', in which the verb is elided. Semantically the negative goes with 'unto quarrels', not with 'accept'. The nouns διάκρισις and διαλογισμός have various meanings in the NT, leading to various interpretations. The event expressed by the first noun could be 'criticizing' or 'passing judgment on', but the sense in the display (following BAGD, p. 185.2) fits the context very well. The second noun can mean 'thought', 'opinion', 'doubt', or 'dispute'. Some commentators and versions prefer 'dispute': NIV has "disputable matters"; NEB, "doubtful points." But here again the context supports the sense in the display, which is that of the majority of commentators and versions and also of BAGD (p. 186.1).

There is a problem on how to interpret μὴ εἰς 'not unto' here. Some versions (e.g., TEV, LB) simply start a new negative exhortation, but this does not seem to do justice to the force of εἰς. Several versions represent 'not unto' as 'without': NIV has "without passing judgment." The specific question is, Does the quarreling function as the purpose of the acceptance (as in JBP's "but not with the idea of arguing . . .") or the outcome of it? The latter seems to fit better: Paul is saying once the acceptance has taken place, don't let such criticism or passing of judgment follow.

14:2a–b The two Greek clauses represented by these propositions are simply introducing or describing the two sets of participants or groups of people within Paul's audience that he will be referring to in an abbreviated manner in subsequent verses.

14:2a Some people The pronoun ὅς 'one', here rendered 'some people', is singular (as also in 2b), but the sense is generic. It probably refers to the majority of Paul's readers.

all *kinds of food* The Greek is πάντα 'all things', but that is not to be taken literally. The display follows REB and NCV.

14:2b who doubt *whether God will permit them to do certain things* The Greek is simply ὁ ἀσθενῶν 'the weak', with the same sense as in 1a.

not eat meat The word λάχανα 'herbs/vegetables' occurs before the verb, which makes it emphatic; hence nearly all versions have "only vegetables." A literal translation would indicate that they would not eat fruit or grains, which was certainly not the case. What the word λάχανα conveys is that they were vegetarians: 'avoiding meat' (see JBP here).

Readers of a translation may question why someone would eat "only vegetables." This was a matter of Jewish scruples, and those with a different cultural background might suppose a totally different and wrong reason. Therefore it might be necessary to indicate, perhaps by a footnote, the reason why some of these Christians might think they had to eat only vegetables. Two typical explanations offered in commentaries are: (1) they wanted to avoid eating meat they thought God disapproved of; (2) specifically, they wanted to avoid eating meat that had been offered to idols. The latter is the interpretation the LB rendering follows.

14:3a-b Anyone who *thinks it is all right to eat all kinds of food* The phrase ὁ ἐσθίων 'he who eats' refers not to those who eat any food, but rather to those who think that such is permissible. LB has "those who think it is all right to eat . . ."; NCV, "The one who knows he can eat any kind of food." Since 'eat' has a transitive sense, the display repeats 'all kinds of food' from 2a as the object of the verb.

must not despise . . . must not condemn The verb κρίνω in 3b is glossed by BAGD (p. 452.6b) for contexts such as this one as 'pass an unfavorable judgment on, criticize, find fault with, condemn'. Rendered 'condemn' in the display, it should not be taken as synonymous with 'despise' in 3a. Cranfield says,

> The choice of the verbs ἐξουθενεῖν ['to despise'] and κρίνειν ['to condemn'] is significant; for in the situation which Paul envisages, in which the eaters (i.e., those who eat all things) are the great majority, the non-eaters (i.e., those who abstain from meat) a small minority, the eaters would be liable to despise the non-eaters as not worth taking seriously, while the non-eaters would be prone to adopt a censorious attitude to the eaters.

14:3c since God himself has accepted them The Greek is ὁ θεὸς γὰρ αὐτὸν προσελάβετο 'because God him accepted'. Commentators are divided concerning the referent of 'him', but the best evidence supports the notion that it refers to the one who thinks it is all right to eat anything. If Paul had wanted it to refer to both the strong and the weak believers, he could and would have made that clear. More importantly, as Dunn states, those who think it refers to both "have missed the importance of the distinction between the two preceding verbs and clauses in v 3, and so fail to appreciate that Paul's exhortation here (v 3c) is a rebuke particularly to the condemnatory attitude of the weak (vv 3b, 4): the one with the much tighter understanding of what is acceptable conduct for God's people would think that God has *not* accepted the other. . . ."

The prominence of the word 'God' as a result of its being first in the clause is expressed by 'himself'. Paul's point is that since God has accepted such people, fellow Christians are not justified in doing otherwise.

Though γάρ here introduces what is labeled as grounds for 3b, it is in effect the *basis* for the immediately preceding APPEAL (3b).

14:4a-b In Greek there is no conjunction to introduce the 4b clause here. For this reason it could be assumed there is a contrast relationship between 14a and 14b. But a better case can be made for positing a CONCLUSION-grounds relationship: 'you have no right to condemn another man's servant, since it is God (not you) who accepts or condemns us.'

14:4a *They are responsible to God, they are not responsible to you; and therefore* you *who condemn those who eat everything* have absolutely no right to condemn another's servant The Greek is σὺ τίς εἶ ὁ κρίνων ἀλλότριον οἰκέτην 'who are you(sg) the one condemning another's servant?' This is a rhetorical question with the force of an emphatic negative statement, hence 'absolutely no right'.

Paul is making a comparison here using the figure of slavery. The italicized words preceding 'therefore' supply the implied grounds for the nonfigurative part of the metaphor (cf. LB, "They are God's servants, not yours"). Spelled out, the figure would be 'because you and they are both God's servants, you have no right to condemn a fellow believer, just as a servant does not have the right to condemn someone who is another person's servant'.

The identification of 'you' is made clear in the display to avoid ambiguity. In some languages this identification will have to be made in the first clause, not the second. In the display it is made in the second clause to maintain the parallelism of the illustrative clause in 4b. The force of the singular pronoun in the original could be expressed by 'none of you'.

14:4b *since just as* it is the servants' own master who accepts or condemns his servants, *it is God who accepts or condemns us* The words τῷ ἰδίῳ κυρίῳ στήκει ἢ πίπτει 'to his own master he stands or falls' continue the slavery metaphor. The verbs 'stands' and 'falls' are metonymies in which the effect or result stands for the cause. To stand before one's master is the result of being vindicated by him; to fall before him is the result of being condemned by him. The metonymies are rendered nonfiguratively here. The metaphor concerning slavery is spelled out in the display, but in some translations it may be possible to abbreviate it in some such way as 'it is the servants' master who accepts or condemns them'. In such cases it may be necessary to say 'God our master' in 4c. LB is not far off the mark with "let him tell them whether they are right or wrong."

The words 'stand' and 'fall' are probably dead metaphors, as in English. But they are probably not dead metaphors in many languages and therefore will not lend themselves to literal translation.

The words 'it is the servants' own master' are forefronted in the Greek and thereby emphasized. The cleft construction in the display conveys this emphasis.

14:4c And God will accept them *regardless of whether they eat meat or not* The Greek is σταθήσεται δέ 'and/but he will stand'. As in 4b the verb is rendered nonfiguratively. The words in italics are clearly implied: Paul is not making an unqualified statement that God will accept everyone. In the context he is talking about the vegetarians and the nonvegetarians.

14:4d since the Lord is able to keep them *trusting in him* There is probably a play on the word 'stand' in δυνατεῖ γὰρ ὁ κύριος στῆσαι αὐτόν 'for is able the Lord to cause him to stand'—it can hardly have the same sense here as it did in 4c. If it did, it would be completely redundant. Hodge suggests that the meaning here is 'the Lord is able to save them', but the initial salvation of either group is not what was in question. Rather it was their continuing to live in a way that would be acceptable to God. It is difficult to give the sense without being too specific. Perhaps the sense would be captured by 'sustain them', except that it is not physical sustaining but spiritual that is in view. Barnes suggests "keep him from error, and from condemnation."

Some manuscripts have 'God' instead of 'Lord' here (cf. KJV). Support for this is very weak; a copyist was evidently trying to make the subject agree with the subject 'God' in 3c.

BOUNDARIES AND COHERENCE

Lexical coherence in the 14:1-4 paragraph is seen in the six occurrences of the verb ἐσθίω 'eat' and also in two occurrences of the verb κρίνω 'to judge' and one of the related noun διάκρισις 'quarrel'. (While there are also two occurrences of κρίνω in v. 5, they have a totally different meaning in v. 5 from the occurrences in 3b and 4a.)

The next paragraph, beginning at 14:5, involves a different example of the problem Paul is discussing: regarding certain days as special. The main evidence of a boundary at 14:5 is the fact that the topic changes from vegetables to special days.

PROMINENCE AND THEME

The three imperatives in 14:1-4 all express *APPEALS*. The first one, the *GENERIC APPEAL* in 1a, is included in the theme because it is naturally prominent: The weak in faith are referred to in one way or another, directly or indirectly, many times between 14:1 and 15:7 and therefore should be mentioned in the theme. The other two imperatives make up the *SPECIFIC APPEAL* (3a-b) and are included in the theme because of the frequent mention in this paragraph of both the ones 'weak in faith' and those 'strong in faith'. The specific problem about eating certain foods is also included in the theme because of its frequent mention throughout 14:1-15:13 and because it is needed for identification of the topic Paul is discussing. The 3c grounds proposition introduced by γάρ is included in the theme because in effect it serves as the *basis* for the 3b *APPEAL*.

SUBDIVISION CONSTITUENT 14:5-9
(Hortatory Paragraph: Specific appeal₁ of 14:1-15:13)

THEME: Each person should be fully convinced about observing special days, thinking and deciding for himself. For doing such actions is not intrinsically wrong.

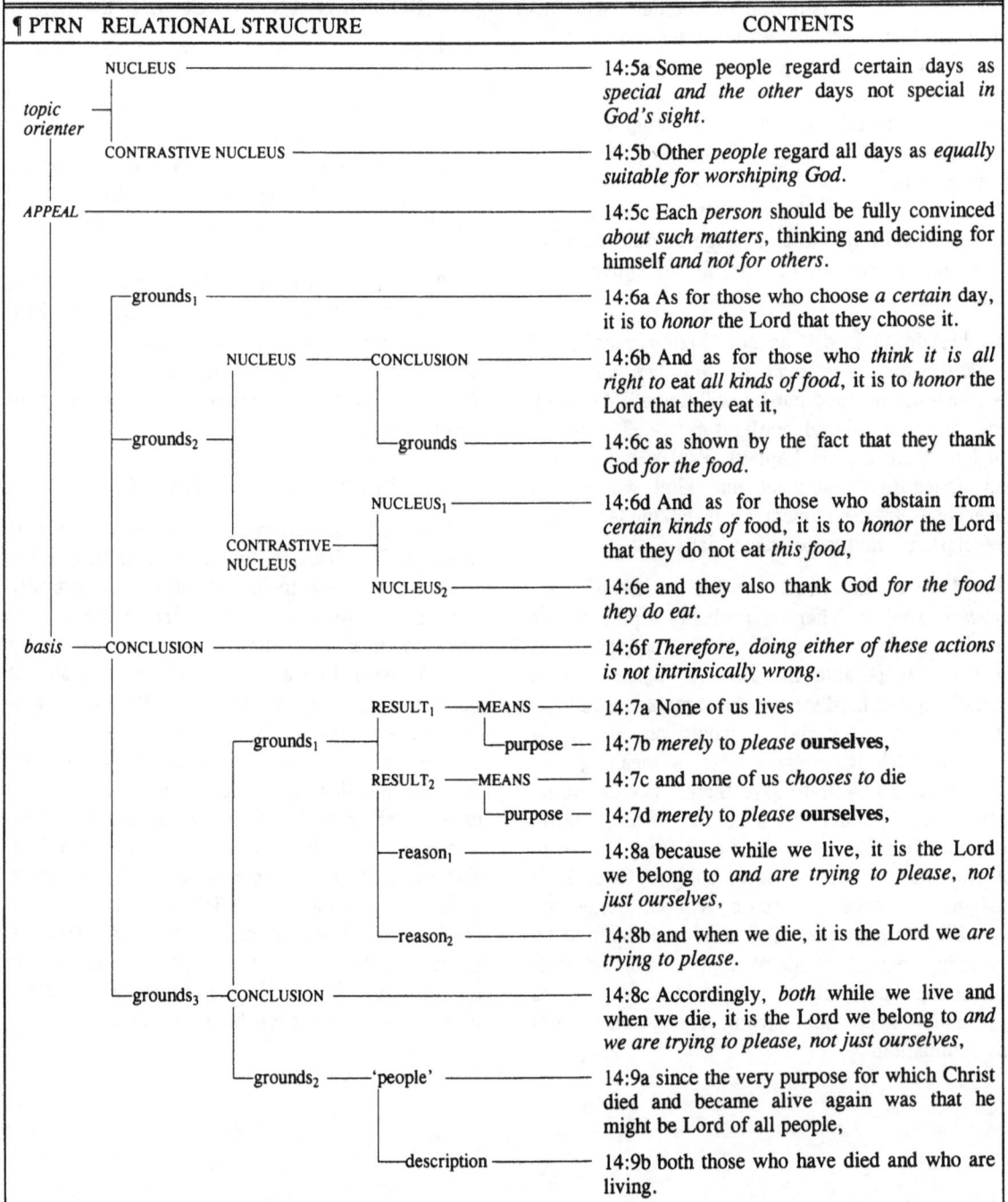

INTENT AND PARAGRAPH PATTERN

The 14:5-9 paragraph is hortatory as shown by the third person imperative πληροφορείσθω 'let him be fully persuaded' in 5c. This APPEAL is followed by the vv. 6-9 basis for the action proposed in 5c. The introductory γάρ in 7a is taken as introducing the vv. 7-9 grounds for the 6f CONCLUSION. The γάρ in 8a is taken as introducing the two reasons supporting the two RESULTS in 7a-d.

NOTES

14:5a-b As in 14:2a-b, the clauses here are simply introductory, descriptive of the two groups to whom Paul will make his appeal in v. 6.

14:5a Some people regard certain days as *special and the other* days not special *in God's sight* The GNT has ὃς γὰρ κρίνει ἡμέραν παρ' ἡμέραν 'for one judges a day more than a day'. This is idiomatic, the sense being 'considers one day more important than another' or, more specifically, "one day more sacred than another" (NIV, CEV, TEV), hence 'special in God's sight'. To avoid the comparative degree construction it is rendered as two clauses in the display.

As to what day or days Paul was referring to (the Sabbath, the special Jewish days of feasting or fasting, or both), commentators are divided. There are no strong reasons for rejecting any of the possibilities. Harrison's remark, however, deserves note: "if the day of worship is in view, it is strange that any believer could be said to consider 'every day alike'." The display therefore retains the ambiguity and renders the singular as a generic plural: 'days'.

Although there is very strong manuscript evidence for the omission of γάρ at the start of this verse, it is very likely that an early copyist did not understand the noncausal use of the conjunction and therefore deleted it. In the context the relationship of 5a-b with what immediately precedes is clearly not causal. Rather, 5a-b provide an additional specific example of the people being referred to in v. 1.

14:5b Other *people* regard all days as *equally suitable for worshiping God* The Greek is ὃς δὲ κρίνει πᾶσαν ἡμέραν 'one judges all days', with the words 'to be the same' or 'as equal' implied. This idea is expressed in all versions; even the KJV has "alike" (in italics). The words 'suitable for worship' are also implied. LB has "days to worship God"; JB, "equally holy." (Paul is not talking about government holidays.)

14:5c fully convinced *about such matters*, thinking and deciding for himself The Greek is ἐν τῷ ἰδίῳ νοΐ πληροφορείσθω 'in his own mind let him be fully convinced'. The words 'about such matters' are implied. LB has "on questions of this kind."

The phrase ἐν τῷ ἰδίῳ νοΐ 'in his own mind' refers to mental activity, and is rendered here so as to include thinking and then deciding.

and not for others This is the implied contrast that is the crucial implicature of Paul's argument.

14:6a As for those who choose *a certain* day, it is to *honor* the Lord that they choose it The Greek is ὁ φρονῶν τὴν ἡμέραν κυρίῳ φρονεῖ 'he who sets his mind on the day, to the Lord he sets his mind on (it)'. The singular pronoun 'he' has the generic sense, hence the plural 'those'.

In this context the verb, whose ordinary sense is 'to be intent on', means 'is intent on observing' in the sense of choosing that day for special religious observance, hence 'choose' in the display. Alternatives are 'think highly of' (TEV), 'prefer', 'select', and 'espouse'. The word 'keep' in English carries the sense of 'observe as being special', as in the expression 'keeping the Sabbath', but this is very idiomatic. The sense is 'to select from those already available as options'. In some languages it may be helpful to translate as 'decide (to worship on)'.

Many English versions supply 'to honor' to complete the phrase 'to the Lord'; an alternative would be 'to please'. The word κυρίῳ 'to the Lord' occurs before the verb, emphasizing it (the same is true in 6b and 6d); this emphasis is conveyed by a cleft construction in the display.

The Textus Receptus has an additional clause here, ὁ μὴ φρονῶν τὴν ἡμέραν κυρίῳ οὐ φρονεῖ 'he who does not set his mind on the day, to the Lord does not set his mind on it'. Support for it is very weak, and it no doubt was added by someone to provide a contrastive negative clause to go along with the corresponding negative clause about eating at the end of the verse. The variant is not even mentioned in the fourth edition GNT.

14:6b those who *think it is all right to* eat *all kinds of food* See the note on 3a.

14:6c *for the food* These words are implied (cf. TEV, LB, NCV).

14:6d abstain from *certain kinds of* food The Greek is μὴ ἐσθίων, literally 'not eating', but in the context this does not refer to fasting, as JBP renders it. Paul is still speaking of vegetarians. LB is closer (though too restrictive) with "the person who won't touch such meat," that is, meat offered to idols. NCV is much better with "refuses to eat some foods." See the note on 2b.

14:6e and they also thank God *for the food they do eat* It should be noted that καί is used here, not γάρ. Thus, what follows is not a reason for his abstaining, but simply a statement that he also gives thanks (cf. JB, NEB, LB). As for the content of the thanking, Dunn states correctly that "he gives thanks not for his abstaining, but for what he does eat (vegetables)." JBP's rendering, "for the benefits of fasting," is unwarranted.

14:6f *Therefore, doing either of these actions is not intrinsically wrong* This is the implied conclusion that Paul expects his readers to reach on the basis of his two supporting arguments in 6a, 6b-e. It is an essential step in the logic of his argument.

14:7-8 Some commentators take these two verses as an amplification of v. 6, but structurally they fit much better as the grounds for the implied 6f CONCLUSION, which is the most central proposition of vv. 6-9.

14:7a-b **None of us lives** *merely* **to** *please* **ourselves** The forefronting of the reflexive pronoun in ἑαυτῷ ζῇ 'to himself lives' is for emphasis. In the display this is conveyed by bold type and by 'merely' (a number of versions have 'only' or 'alone'). The generic singular 'himself' is rendered 'ourselves, both in 7b and 7d.

The dative 'to himself' (used in the generic sense of 'oneself' or 'ourselves' in 7b and 7d) contrasts with the dative 'to the Lord' in v. 6; therefore, the verb 'to please', suggested as an alternative in 6a, is supplied here as being the most appropriate verb to complete the proposition. Note that the same type of phrase occurs in v. 8 (τῷ κυρίῳ 'to the Lord') as here in this verse (ἑαυτῷ 'to himself'); for this reason 'to please' is used in each of the propositions where one of these phrases occurs. Cranfield says regarding this that "all Christians live 'to the Lord', that is, they live with the object of pleasing Christ."

Taken literally, 7a-b would seem to be a universal statement applying to all believers. Although the thrust of Paul's argument in this chapter is to correct the situation wherein the Roman church were not showing due respect for members with differing opinions, here Paul is making a general statement of universal validity to all believers (and perhaps all people in general). It functions within the *basis* as the grounds for the general statement of 8c. (The CEV rendering of the verb as 'must', as though v. 7 were a mitigated exhortation, does not seem justified.)

14:7c-d *chooses* **to die** *merely* **to** *please* **ourselves** It is somewhat difficult to determine exactly what Paul means by ἑαυτῷ ἀποθνῄσκει 'to himself dies', because the manner or time of our death is usually not something a person decides for himself. However, this, according to Morris, is exactly what the first-century Stoics sought to do; therefore 'should choose to' is an alternative to 'chooses to' in the display. Hodge comments that "death as well as life must be left in the hands of God, to be directed by his will and for his glory."

merely This word is implied. TEV, REB, and NIV supply "alone" or "only." To please oneself, but not oneself alone, is in keeping with the teaching of Jesus to "love your neighbor as yourself." He did not say to love your neighbor and not yourself.

14:8a-b **while we live, ... and when we die** By his use of the conditional conjunction ἐάν 'if' Paul is not saying that there is anything uncertain about whether people will die. It is expressing a circumstantial relation. Barnes has "as long as we live"; JBP, "when we die."

it is the Lord we *are trying to please* The phrase 'to the Lord', which occurs both in 8a and 8b, is emphatic in each occurrence since it precedes the verb. This emphasis is represented in the display by forefronting, using a cleft construction.

14:8c it is the Lord we belong to *and we are trying to please, not just ourselves* At the end of v. 8 the Greek is τοῦ κυρίου ἐσμέν 'of the Lord we are'. The forefronting of the genitive phrase gives it emphasis; this is shown in the display by the cleft construction 'it is the Lord'. The genitive indicates possession, but in the context possession is not the main thing in focus. As Hodge says, it is the "right of possession, and the consequent duty of devotion and obedience" (cf. also Murray, "the conscious service of the Lord ... must govern the sense of 'unto the Lord' in verse 8").

14:9a-b the very purpose for which Christ died ... was that The cataphoric expression εἰς τοῦτο 'unto this' gives strong emphasis to the subjunctive clause which follows. This emphasis is conveyed in the display by a cleft construction and the word 'very'. An alternative would be to reverse the order, putting 'It was in order that' at the beginning of the clause.

and became alive again The GNT has ἔζησεν 'lived', the sense of which is "rose to life" (TEV) or "returned to life" (NIV). There are a number of manuscript variants, probably due to the awkwardness of 'he lived' and the fact that the resurrection of Christ is usually indicated by ἀνέστη 'he rose'. In some manuscripts ἀνέστη occurs, replacing 'he lived'; in others it occurs along with 'he lived' but in varying sequence in different manuscripts. The fourth edition GNT reading, ἀπέθανεν καὶ ἔζησεν 'he died and he lived', is supported by the best and oldest manuscripts and is given an A rating ("certain").

that he might be Lord of all people, both those who have died and those who are living In καὶ νεκρῶν καὶ ζώντων κυριεύσῃ 'both of the dead and of the living he might be Lord', the genitive phrases are emphasized by occurring before the verb. This emphasis is conveyed in the display by the word 'all'. The aorist verb is taken to express an ingressive sense: 'become Lord' (so Morris).

BOUNDARIES AND COHERENCE

Coherence in the 14:5-9 paragraph consists in its being a set of contrasts between those who regard certain days as special and those who don't, between those who eat all foods and those who don't, and between living and dying.

It is very difficult to decide paragraph boundaries and relationships in vv. 5-12. There are several options besides the one given in the display:

1. Make v. 5 a paragraph by itself dealing with days (in contrast to vv. 2-4, which deal with food). With this interpretation vv. 6-9 would then be two *bases* for the APPEAL in v. 10. In support of this interpretation is the fact that v. 6 deals with both days and food.
2. Make a paragraph break at v. 7 (as in CEV and NEB). With this interpretation, v. 6 would be the *basis* for the APPEAL in 5c, and vv. 7-8 the *basis* for v. 10.
3. Make a paragraph break at v. 9 (as in NCV).
4. Make a paragraph break at v. 10. This is done by LB, JBP, and RSV (perhaps because of a switch to the second person singular pronouns there).

In this analysis the next paragraph is begun at v. 10. The introductory οὖν in the second half of v. 8 is seen as introducing the 8c CONCLUSION to the 7a-8b grounds. Then 7a-9 fit well as the grounds for the 6f implied CONCLUSION, and 7a-8b as the grounds for the 8c CONCLUSION.

PROMINENCE AND THEME

Since 14:5-9 is a hortatory paragraph, the first part of the theme is drawn from the APPEAL in 5c: ἕκαστος πληροφορείσθω 'let each be fully convinced'. The second part of the theme is drawn from the prominent part of the 6-9 *basis*, namely the CONCLUSION proposition in 6f. It is slightly modified to "such actions" instead of "either of these actions." (If vv. 7-9 were taken as an amplification of 5-6, the theme would consist of only 5c; but this alternative is rejected since we do, in fact, expect APPEALS to be supported by *bases,* and since 6-9 coheres quite well as a *basis*.)

SUBDIVISION CONSTITUENT 14:10–12
(Hortatory Paragraph: Specific appeal₂ of 14:1–15:13)

THEME: You should neither condemn nor despise your fellow believers who believe differently about religious regulations, because it is God who will say whether he approves of what we have done.

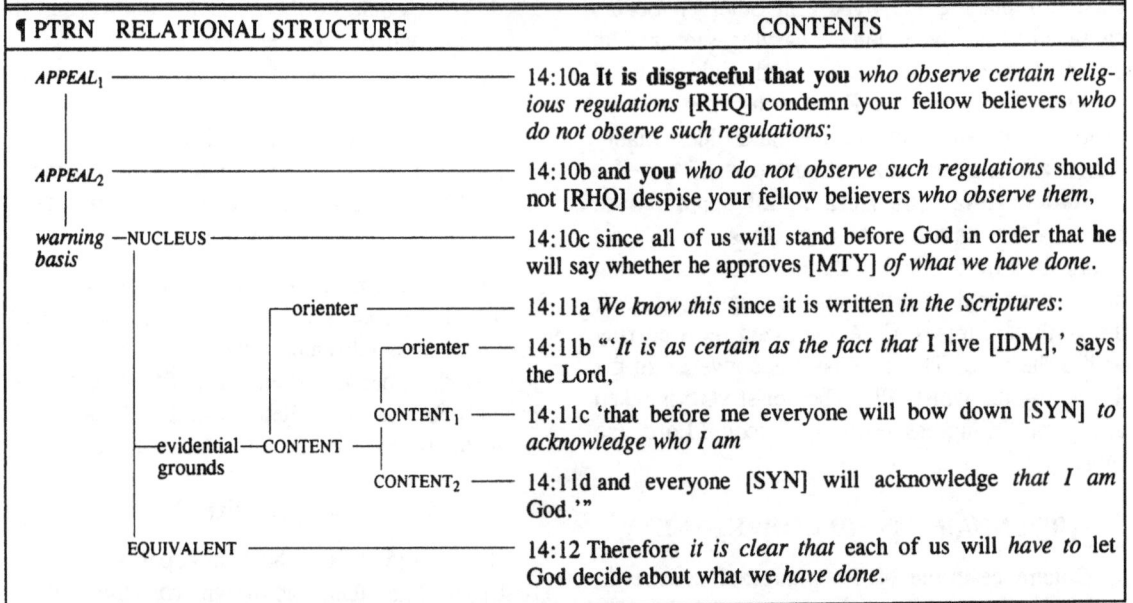

INTENT AND PARAGRAPH PATTERN

The 14:10–12 paragraph is considered hortatory because the two rhetorical questions (τί κρίνεις; 'why do you judge?' and τί ἐξουθενεῖς; 'why do you despise?') are, semantically, expressions of negative commands. The material in 10c–12 presents what may be considered warnings and is therefore classified as *a warning basis* supporting the two APPEALS.

NOTES

14:10a–b <u>it is disgraceful that you</u> *who observe certain religious regulations* **condemn your fellow believers** *who do not observe such regulations*; **and you** *who do not observe such regulations* **should not despise your fellow believers** *who observe them* The Greek consists of two rhetorical questions: σὺ δὲ τί κρίνεις τὸν ἀδελφόν σου; ἢ καὶ σὺ τί ἐξουθενεῖς τὸν ἀδελφόν σου; 'and you(sg), why do you condemn your brother? Or also you(sg), why do you despise your brother?' These "reproachful questions" (Cranfield) express negative evaluations, either negative prohibitions or 'it is disgraceful that you are doing this'. The δέ here marks a switch in subject, from 'we' (v. 9) to σύ 'you (sg)', the Greek pronouns being singular for rhetorical effect. This might be conveyed in English by 'anyone of you who'. The pronouns are also emphatic. The recurrence of the singular pronoun σύ 'you' along with ἢ καί 'or also' is evidence that each question is directed to a different group: the display indicates by relative clauses exactly who is being addressed and who the object of criticism is in each case. These supplied relative clauses are as generic as possible—they cover both eating or abstaining from meat and observing or not observing Jewish holidays.

14:10c God The KJV has 'Christ' here based on many of the early Church Fathers and later manuscripts, but the best manuscripts support 'God'. (The fourth edition GNT has 'God', with a B "almost certain" rating.) The change was undoubtedly made by some copyist with 2 Cor. 5:10 in mind.

in order that <u>he</u> will say whether he approves *of what we have done* The word 'tribunal' in τῷ βήματι τοῦ θεοῦ 'the tribunal of God' refers to the platform on which a judge was seated. A metonymy in which the place stands for the events that occur there, it is here rendered nonfiguratively. But the purpose of the judgment is spelled out to avoid the wrong meaning that this judgment is about a person's eternal destiny. The point is that it is God who is to do the judging, not us; to help mark this contrast 'he' is in bold type in the display.

14:11a *We know this* since Here γάρ introduces not the reason we will stand before God but the evidential grounds supporting that claim.

in the Scriptures The implied location is specified. REB has "we read in Scripture."

14:11b *It is as certain as the fact that* I live The Greek is ζῶ ἐγώ 'live I', and nearly all versions render it 'as I live'. But 'I live' is a frequent idiomatic phrase in the OT, meaning "as surely as I live" (NIV, NCV).

14:11c–d before me everyone will bow down *to acknowledge who I am* and everyone will acknowledge *that I am* God The Greek is ἐμοὶ κάμψει πᾶν γόνυ, καὶ πᾶσα γλῶσσα ἐξομολογήσεται τῷ θεῷ 'to me will bend every knee, and every tongue will confess to God' (a poetic passage quoted from Isa. 45:23 in the LXX). It is a chiastic structure:

  A To me
    B will bend
      C every knee;
      C' every tongue
    B' will confess
  A' to God.

Here 'knee' is a synecdoche, the body part standing for the whole person (CEV, NCV, and TEV have "everyone"). Bowing is a symbolic action; its purpose is supplied in the display. The word 'tongue' is also a synecdoche: 'every tongue' means 'every person'.

Commentators and versions disagree as to the meaning of the verb ἐξομολογέω 'confess'. It can mean 'to promise', 'to confess (sins)', 'to praise', or 'to acknowledge'. The only other occurrences of this word in the Pauline epistles are in Phil. 2:11, where it clearly means 'to acknowledge', and in Rom. 15:9, where it could mean either 'to praise' or 'to acknowledge'. 'Acknowledge' fits the context much better here than 'praise'. (Though the word is used extrabiblically to mean 'praise' with the person praised in the dative, the dative here is seen as simply fulfilling the need for poetic balance in the chiasmus.) Semantically, 'acknowledge' requires a full proposition as its content. The display follows the NCV and TEV in supplying 'that I am' before 'God'.

14:12 *it is clear that* The words in 11b–d are from Isa. 45:23. They are not the reason but the evidential grounds by which we know that the v. 11 claim is true. Therefore, for the same reason that 'we know this' was included in 11a, 'it is clear that' is included here.

let God decide about what we *have done* This is an attempt to state more clearly just what is meant by περὶ ἑαυτοῦ λόγον δώσει τῷ θεῷ, literally 'will give a word concerning himself to God'. NCV's "answer to God for what he has done" is somewhat idiomatic but captures the sense fairly well. As Hodge notes, "we are to render our account to him, we should await his decision." The sense is therefore not so much our reporting to him but our awaiting his verdict on our actions.

In some manuscripts the words 'to God' are at the end of this verse, and in others they are absent. It is possible that they were originally absent and were later supplied by a copyist as the implied indirect object of the verb, although one would have expected 'to him' and not 'to God'. Conversely, it is possible that they appeared in the original and were later omitted accidentally by a copyist. The sense is not affected either way, since 'to God' is required, semantically, to complete the thought.

BOUNDARIES AND COHERENCE

The boundary between the 14:10–12 paragraph and the next one is marked by οὖν 'therefore' in v. 13. The new APPEAL in v. 13 is expressed by verbs with plural pronominal subjects, being addressed to all the believers at Rome. This contrasts with the v. 10 APPEALS which use singular pronouns and are addressed to two different groups in conflict among the believers. Also, there is a change of topic at v. 13, the most prominent proposition in v. 13 being an APPEAL to stop spiritual injury. In v. 10 the APPEALS are to stop judging and despising one another.

PROMINENCE AND THEME

The theme of 14:10–12 is drawn from the two APPEALS, condensed to avoid repetition, and from the 10c NUCLEUS of the *basis*, also condensed. The words 'stand before' in 10c are omitted as not being thematic; but because of the repetition in v. 12 of the idea that God is the one who will ultimately approve or disapprove of what we have done, these words are included as thematic, with 'God' emphasized by the cleft construction.

SUBDIVISION CONSTITUENT 14:13-18
(Hortatory Paragraph: Specific appeal₃ of 14:1-15:13)

THEME: Instead of condemning each other, decide not to do anything that might lead your fellow believer to sin by following your example and which would then cause others to speak evil of you.

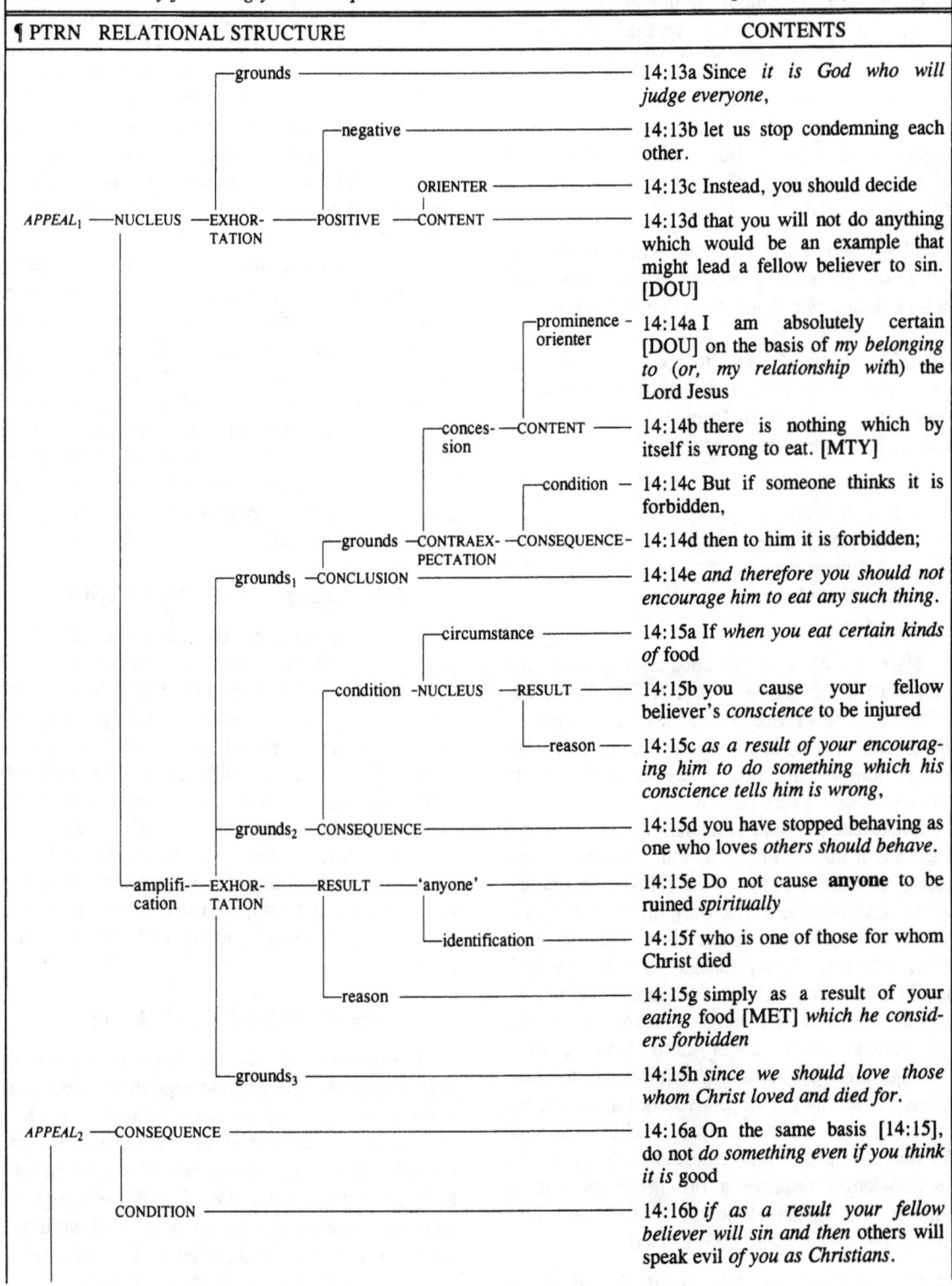

INTENT AND PARAGRAPH PATTERN

The 14:13-18 paragraph contains a number of imperatives; thus it is hortatory. The first APPEAL is a double-headed one (i.e., the negative μηκέτι κρίνωμεν 'let us no longer judge' in 13b followed by the positive κρίνατε 'judge' in 13c). Although vv. 14-15 might be expected to provide the *basis*, these verses do not in fact express a *basis*, nor are they introduced by γάρ as would be expected if that were the case. Rather, they express an amplification of v. 13. It is true that v. 15 would cohere as a *basis* for v. 13, but here 15h gives the grounds for 15e, not v. 13. The second APPEAL is in 16a-b, followed by the *basis* for that APPEAL in 17-18, which is introduced by γάρ (Cranfield and Hodge agree).

NOTES

14:13a Since *it is God who will judge everyone* Verse 13 begins with οὖν 'therefore', marking it as the logical conclusion of the preceding verses. The italicized words here are supplied to summarize vv. 10-12.

14:13b let us stop condemning The word μηκέτι 'no longer' combined with the present subjunctive of 'condemn/judge' implies that they have been doing this and they should stop. In some languages it may be necessary to change 'let us' to 'you(pl) should' in order to avoid implying that Paul had been doing this also.

14:13d you will not do anything which would be an example that might lead a fellow believer to sin In the phrase τὸ μὴ τιθέναι πρόσκομμα τῷ ἀδελφῷ ἢ σκάνδαλον 'not to put an obstacle to a brother or a temptation', there are two dead figures of speech (cf. 9:32-33). Moore (p. 41) calls them a figurative doublet. They are taken as such here, the two terms having the sense "every kind of occasion for stumbling" (Stuart). The display follows Bruce (1985), who says that the terms refer to "the setting of an example which might lead another into sin." In some languages a clause such as 'if he knew about it' might be needed at the end of the verse. LB suggests the setting of an example: "by letting him see you doing something he thinks is wrong."

It is somewhat strange that Paul changes abruptly from 'we' to 'you' in the middle of this verse. Morris notes that in the first part of the verse Paul "means that this is not a preemptory command given by someone who adopts a superior position. What he is saying is something to which he must give heed as well as they." In other words, the exhortation in 13b is somewhat mitigated.

14:14a I am absolutely certain The words οἶδα καὶ πέπεισμαι 'I know and am persuaded' are, according to Moore (p. 41), a borderline case of near-synonymy. They are here taken as a doublet for the sake of emphasis (cf. TEV, "know for certain"; NIV, "am fully convinced"; LB, "am perfectly sure").

on the basis of *my belonging to (or, my relationship with)* **the Lord Jesus** The prepositional phrase ἐν κυρίῳ Ἰησοῦ 'in the Lord Jesus' is taken as expressing the grounds or basis of Paul's certainty. Commentators are divided as to whether it means 'on the basis of my union with Christ' or 'on the basis of what Christ revealed to me'. If Paul had meant the latter he most certainly could have expressed it differently to avoid misunderstanding by his audience. Most commentators choose the first of these interpretations.

14:14b there is nothing which by itself is wrong to eat The Greek is οὐδὲν κοινὸν δι' ἑαυτοῦ 'nothing (is) common through itself'. In the context (cf. v. 17) Paul is talking specifically about food or drink, and the display makes this clear. The word κοινός means 'ceremonially impure' (BAGD, p. 438.2), but the point is not whether some food is 'unclean' or 'unholy' as most versions translate it, but whether it renders the consumer unacceptable to God. It can be considered a metonymy, the cause standing for the effect. An alternative based on Best, also Sanday and Headlam, would be 'forbidden *by God to eat or drink*'. NCV renders this as "no food that is wrong to eat," as in the display. It may be necessary in some cases to say 'which God considers wrong to eat'. CEV renders it positively: "God considers all foods fit to eat." Note that 'forbidden' is used in 14c.

14:14c But if someone thinks it is forbidden Most commentators agree that the force of εἰ μή here is 'but'. In τῷ λογιζομένῳ τι κοινὸν εἶναι 'to the (person) reckoning anything to be common', the dative phrase is a mismatched and abbreviated way of expressing a conditional clause.

14:14d to him The forefronting of ἐκείνῳ 'to that (person)' may be to give it emphasis. In the display, 'to him' is similarly forefronted.

14:14e *and therefore you should not encourage him to eat any such thing* These words supply the main conclusion Paul expects his readers to make. LB has "he shouldn't do it because for him it is wrong"; Hodge, "therefore, [they] should not be induced to act contrary to their consciences."

14:15a Almost none of the English versions represent the γάρ here. C. B. Williams and NASB are exceptions. The KJV rendering is evidently based on some manuscripts that have δέ instead of γάρ, probably because the copyists rightly failed to see how v. 15 was related as the reason of v. 14.

Some commentators (e.g., Cranfield, Morris) state that v. 15 assigns a reason for v. 13, not v. 14. Hodge thinks that "[v. 15] does not assign a reason for the principle asserted in v. 14, but does introduce a limitation to the practical application of that principle." However, relationally 15a–d coheres much better as supplying an additional grounds for the 15e exhortation. Therefore the display, following most English versions, does not represent γάρ, taking it instead as introducing this additional grounds.

***when you eat certain kinds of* food** The phrase διὰ βρῶμα 'on account of food' is an abbreviated expression. In the display it is given as a full clause. TEV has "because of something you eat"; LB, "by what you eat."

14:15b you cause your fellow believer's *conscience* to be injured The literal meaning of the passive form of the verb λυπέω is 'to be sad, to grieve'; but here, as commentators note, the verb means much more than to be annoyed or displeased or have hurt feelings. BAGD suggest 'to be injured, damaged' as a possible meaning here (p. 481.2b; see also RSV, Shedd, and Sanday and Headlam). The damage, of course, is to the soul or conscience.

14:15c *as a result of your encouraging him to do something which his conscience tells him is wrong* This proposition makes specific what can be considered either the means or the reason of the wounding of the conscience (see comments by Barrett, Cranfield, Morris, Sanday and Headlam, Murray), but reason coheres better semantically.

14:15d you have stopped behaving as one who loves *others should behave* The Greek is οὐκέτι κατὰ ἀγάπην περιπατεῖς 'no longer according to love are you(sg) walking'. Here the word 'walk' signifies a person's conduct or behavior (as also in 6:4, 8:4, 13:13). The phrase 'according to love' is rendered by an appropriate full clause to avoid the use of an abstract noun.

14:15e–g This propositional cluster, which has as its NUCLEUS 'Do not cause anyone to be ruined spiritually', is an indirect way of saying 'Do not eat food if that will cause anyone to be ruined spiritually'. (JB is similar.) In many languages it will have to be so translated. Paul's way of stating it highlights the result.

14:15e This exhortation is in effect the conclusion which follows the two grounds stated in 14:14c–15d. In some languages it may be appropriate to begin the proposition with the equivalent of 'therefore'.

Do not cause <u>anyone</u> to be ruined *spiritually* The sense of the verb ἀπόλλυε 'destroy' is eternal spiritual destruction, not physical. NCV has "hurt your brother's faith." Its object, ἐκεῖνον 'that one', is emphatic both lexically and positionally and hence is in bold type in the display. Since it does not refer to one specific individual, it is rendered 'anyone'.

14:15g simply as a result of your *eating* food which he considers forbidden The dative phrase τῷ βρώματί σου 'by your food' occurs before the verb, an emphatic position; this emphasis is conveyed in the display by 'simply'. The phrase is made into a full clause by supplying the word 'eat' as in most modern English versions, since 'food' here stands for the eating of food, specifically those foods which many Jewish believers considered defiling. Contextual information identifying the kind of food meant is also supplied.

14:15h *since we should love those whom Christ loved and died for* This proposition is a necessary part of the syllogism in Paul's argument, which, stated in a positive way is, If Christ loved them and died for them, should we not love them also?

14:16a-b On the same basis With the word οὖν, usually glossed 'therefore', Paul is referring back to the 15a-d grounds for the 15e exhortation (cf. Stuart). Just as believers were to avoid doing things that might induce fellow believers to sin, for the same reason they were to avoid doing things that would give believers a bad name among unbelievers.

do not *do something even if you think it is good if as a result your fellow believer will sin and then* **others will speak evil** *of you as Christians* The Greek is μὴ βλασφημείσθω ὑμῶν τὸ ἀγαθόν 'do not let be blasphemed (what is) good of yours'. A fair bit of information is omitted here; only the outcome is mentioned, not the steps that lead up to it. LB is alone in trying to do justice to the intervening steps: "Don't do anything that will cause criticism against yourself even though you know that what you do is right." An alternative might be "Don't do something that would encourage a fellow believer to sin with the result that others would speak ill of you."

A textual problem here is whether the pronoun is ὑμῶν 'yours' or ἡμῶν 'ours'. But 'yours' is supported by the better manuscripts and makes better sense with the imperative.

Another question is the meaning of 'good'. The answer to that depends on whether Paul is addressing this exhortation to the weak believers (those who were worried about eating certain things) or to the strong (those who felt such things were inconsequential) or to both. (Cranfield's two-page discussion is helpful here.) The context strongly favors what is in the display, namely that Paul is addressing the strong. In this case, 'the good' is taken as referring to the freedom they have in Christ (i.e., something they think is all right). This is the view of most commentators. An alternative is to take 'the good' as referring to the gospel (following Hodge, Hendriksen, Cranfield, and Morris), in which case the only change would be that the end of the verse would read 'speak evil *of the gospel*'. There is really not much difference in sense.

Still another problem is who the implied agent of the blaspheming is. Is it the "weak" Christians, outsiders, or both? That is difficult to say, but if the interpretation here is correct, it would be most natural to take the agent as unbelievers. In the display 'others' is supplied, since the agent is not in focus.

14:17a Letting God rule us This rendering is an attempt to spell out what Paul meant by the metaphor ἡ βασιλεία τοῦ θεοῦ 'the kingdom of God'.

is not *a matter of whether or not we obey regulations about* **eating or drinking** *something* The Greek is βρῶσις καὶ πόσις, literally 'eating and drinking'. JBP, with "is not a matter of whether you get what you like to eat and drink," comes close to the meaning; but Dunn is closer yet, saying that Paul was making a "denial that the kingdom should be understood . . . in terms of rules governing eating and drinking."

14:17b living righteously Some take δικαιοσύνη 'righteousness' here in the sense in which Paul used it in the early chapters of the epistle: the state of being declared righteous by God. Cranfield says this is the correct view since righteousness, peace, and joy "are combined as a definition of the kingdom of God" more naturally than considering them as moral qualities or human feelings. But to take this view is to ignore the strong component of God's absolute control of lives implied in the term 'kingdom of God'. Paul in this passage is talking not about justification, but about the conduct of one believer towards another. NCV renders it "living right with God." Morris says, "It seems likely that Paul is not differentiating sharply between these two views, and that he is using the expression in a way that suggests both." Denney agrees. If the other interpretation is preferred, it could be expressed as 'being declared righteous by God' or 'knowing that God has declared our guilt for having sinned to be ended'.

being peaceful with others Some commentators suggest that the word εἰρήνη 'peace' refers to peace with God as in 5:1. However, it is the conduct of one believer towards another that is in focus here (v. 19 says 'pursue those things that make for peace'). Therefore the ethical sense is chosen for the display: acting peacefully towards others.

being joyful by *the power of* **the Holy Spirit** Since χαρά 'joy' has to do with living the Christian life, its inclusion here is further evidence that the preceding words, 'righteousness and peace', refer to Christian conduct as well, not to entry into a right relationship with God.

There is a question concerning the final phrase ἐν πνεύματι ἁγίῳ 'in the Holy Spirit'. Is it linked only with χαρά 'joy', or also with 'living righteously' and 'being peaceful'? Most commentators assume the former, but a few (Hodge, Morris, and possibly Barrett) hold that there is no good reason to suppose that it is not related to all three. The display does not attempt to resolve the apparent ambiguity, however. The preposition 'in' is taken as indicating source. LB renders it "from"; REB, "inspired by"; and JB, "brought by."

14:18 Anyone who serves Christ *by acting* **in such ways** In the phrase ὁ ἐν τούτῳ δουλεύων τῷ Χριστῷ 'he who in this serves Christ', the singular 'he' is used in the generic sense and is rendered 'anyone' in the display.

The main problem here is the sense of 'in this'. Some, noting the singular form of the demonstrative pronoun, take it as a reference to the Holy Spirit in v. 17, but to refer to the Spirit like this would be extremely unusual. The majority of commentators take it as a generic singular referring to the three concepts in v. 17, the singular being used because Paul perceives the three as inseparable. This is the interpretation on which the rendering in the display is based (as also in LB and JBP).

pleases God and will be respected by others The adjectives εὐάρεστος 'well pleasing' and δόκιμος 'approved' express events; hence they are represented in the display by verbs.

BOUNDARIES AND COHERENCE

Lexical coherence in the 14:13-18 paragraph is provided by three references to Christ (vv. 14, 15, 18). He is not mentioned in the immediately preceding or following paragraphs.

The boundary between the 14:13-18 paragraph and the next one is signaled by οὖν 'therefore' in v. 19, introducing a new set of APPEALS. The APPEAL in v. 19 is positive, while the 13-18 APPEALS are negative. Though οὖν 'therefore' occurs in v. 16, the APPEAL in v. 16 is considered to be something of an amplification of the v. 13 APPEAL: both 13d and 16a-b express the concept 'do not do something that might lead to a fellow believer's sinning'. Hence, in v. 16 οὖν does not mark a paragraph boundary.

PROMINENCE AND THEME

There are several hortatory expressions in 14:13-18. The first is the first person plural subjunctive μηκέτι κρίνωμεν 'let us no longer judge' in 13b. This is included in the theme because, although it is negative, it refers to the problem Paul is addressing in 14:1-15:13 and it uses the verb κρίνω, which is prominent by virtue of its frequent use in 14:13-18. The 13c ORIENTER and the CONTENT in 13d that it introduces are also included in the theme, being prominent. The negative imperative μὴ ἀπόλλυε 'do not destroy' in 15e is not included in the theme because it is only an amplification of the 13c-d APPEAL. The rest of the theme is drawn, in an abbreviated form, from the 16a-b APPEAL. The portions of 16a-b that are repetitions of material in 13c-d are not included in the theme. The material from the *basis* in vv. 17-18 is not included because it is a generic positive statement not considered to be vital support of the two negative APPEALS.

SUBDIVISION CONSTITUENT 14:19–23
(Hortatory Paragraph: Specific appeal₄ of 14:1–15:13)

THEME: Try to do what will help fellow believers to be at peace with each other and grow spiritually. Do not destroy what God has done in others' lives as a result of your eating certain things. Keep between yourself and God what you believe about eating such things, and don't try to force your views on others, because if those who are not certain if they should eat such things do eat them, they will be condemned by God and their own consciences.

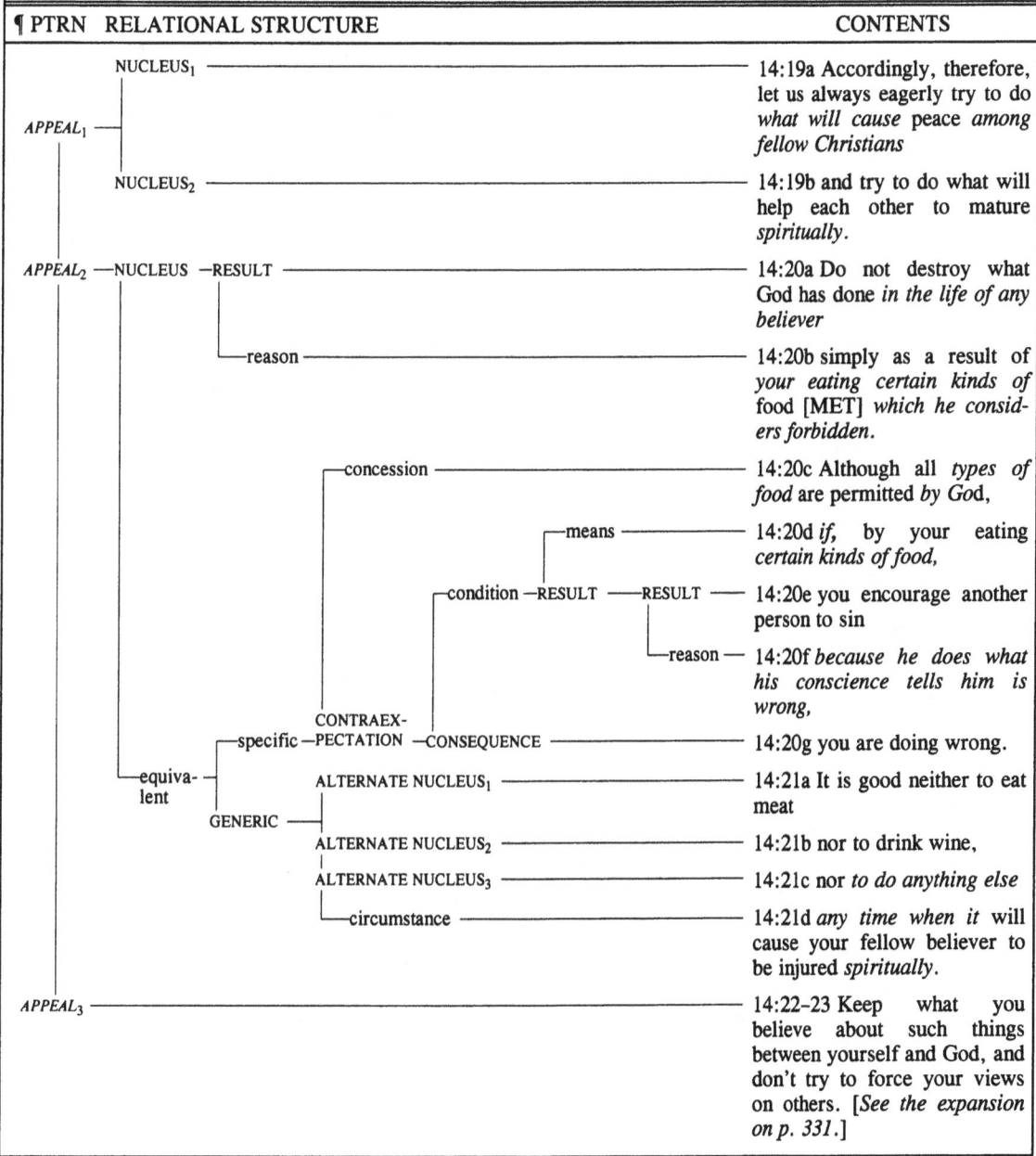

INTENT AND PARAGRAPH PATTERN

The hortatory nature of the 14:19–23 paragraph is signaled by the first person plural subjunctive διώκωμεν 'let us pursue' in 19a, the negative imperative μὴ κατάλυε 'do not undo' in 20a, and the imperative ἔχε 'keep' in 22a. These three words are closely related, two generic and one specific. The first *APPEAL*, in v. 19, is generic and has no *basis* supporting it. The second *APPEAL*, a negative and more specific one, in 20a is similarly without a *basis* supporting it.

(The 20c–21d material is an equivalent restatement of the 20a APPEAL, not its *basis*.) The third APPEAL in 22a is supported by a *basis* in 22b–23.

NOTES

14:19a let us always eagerly try to do *what will cause* peace *among fellow Christians* The GNT has διώκωμεν 'let us pursue'. Actually the better manuscripts support the indicative διώκομεν 'we pursue', as though Paul were describing the ideal. But since the context strongly favors this being an exhortation, and since "in ancient mss ω and ο are often confused" (Morris), the display follows the GNT. The continuative sense of the present subjunctive is conveyed by 'always' in the display.

All commentators and versions take 'things' in τὰ τῆς εἰρήνης 'the things of peace' as producing or causing peace. TEV has "bring"; JB, "leads to"; JBP, RSV, NEB, "make for." Note that the word 'peace' is more an attribute than a thing according to semantic theory. In some languages it may be necessary to render it in some such way as 'cause fellow Christians to act peacefully towards each other'.

The phrase 'among fellow Christians' is supplied to avoid wrong meaning (Paul is not talking about peace among nations) and to make specific just what sphere of peacemaking is in view. LB makes this clear with "aim for harmony in the church."

14:19b what will help each other to mature *spiritually* In the phrase τὰ τῆς οἰκοδομῆς τῆς εἰς ἀλλήλους 'the things of building up unto one another', the noun οἰκοδομή 'construction' is used figuratively. However, Paul uses it so often that it is taken as a dead metaphor and is rendered nonfiguratively in the display. CEV has "help each other have a strong faith."

14:20a–b As in 15e–g this is an indirect way of saying, "Don't eat . . . and as a result destroy." An alternative might be, "It would be a terrible thing if, as a result of your eating . . . you would destroy."

14:20a Do not destroy what God has done *in the life of any believer* The Greek is μὴ κατάλυε τὸ ἔργον τοῦ θεοῦ 'do not destroy the work of God'. Here the second person singular imperative is used for effect, as also in vv. 10 and 15. Commentators differ somewhat on the meaning of 'work of God', but they all agree that 'of God' is a subjective genitive: 'the work that God has done'. The majority refer it to what God has done in the lives of the weak believers, those with scruples about certain foods. It certainly includes such people, and the second half of the verse strongly supports this. But it could be taken more generically, which some commentators support, hence the generic identification of 'work' in the display.

14:20b simply as a result of *your eating certain kinds of* food *which he considers forbidden* The Greek is ἕνεκεν βρώματος 'for the sake of food'. Here, as in 15g, 'food' stands for the eating of food (so NCV), specifically those foods which many Jewish believers considered defiling. The phrase is forefronted in Greek (as in RSV and TEV). The emphasis it thus receives is conveyed in the display by 'simply'.

14:20c all *types of* food are permitted *by God* The Greek is πάντα μὲν καθαρά 'all things indeed (are) clean'. In the context, the reference 'all' clearly is to 'all food' (so TEV, CEV, NCV, NIV, JBP). The word 'clean', as Barnes states, means "lawful to be eaten." TEV has "may be eaten." JBP gives a wrong sense with "in itself, harmless."

14:20d–g *if,* by your eating *certain kinds of food*, you encourage another person to sin . . . you are doing wrong The Greek is very elliptical: κακὸν τῷ ἀνθρώπῳ τῷ διὰ προσκόμματος ἐσθίοντι '(it is) evil to the man who through stumbling eats'. In the display the object of 'eating' is supplied, and it is also made clear that not every food is in view. NCV has "eat food"; JBP and CEV, "what you eat."

There is a problem as to whether 'the man' refers to the weak believer (the one who is caused to be ruined spiritually when he eats such food) or the strong believer (the one who causes the weak believer to stumble by what he does). It depends somewhat on the meaning here of διά. BAGD (p. 180. AIII1c) take it as expressing attendant circumstance: "with offense (to the scruples of another)." But Barrett claims this still does not solve the problem of the identity of the 'man who eats':

> v. 21 suggests that he is the strong Christian, who by his eating causes offence and lays a stumblingblock before his weaker brother, who may be tempted to do that of which his conscience disapproves (v. 23). It is not, however, impossible that the eater is the weak Christian who eats because he has been tripped up

and made to stumble by the strong man's action, and thus suffers injury because he is acting against conscience.

But in either case the stumbling is the fault of the strong Christian. Moreover, as supported by the majority of commentators, the focus of this whole passage (cf. vv. 15, 19, 21) is on not injuring a brother. Therefore this interpretation is chosen for the display.

The word πρόσκομμα 'stumbling' is rendered as it was in v. 13, since the sense is the same. An alternative would be 'cause to be injured spiritually'.

14:20f *because he does what his conscience tells him is wrong* The implied connection between the "strong" individual's eating and the "weak" individual's stumbling/sinning is supplied here with precisely the information in Barrett's comment in the preceding note.

14:21a–c It is good neither to eat meat nor to drink wine nor *to do anything else* There is a question here as to whether 'meat' should be identified as 'certain kinds of meat' (i.e., the kinds which the Jews thought unacceptable). That could be done, but here Paul seems to be making a broad generic statement. This is borne out by his adding 'nor drink wine' with no indication of how this might have caused offense and, following that, the even broader elliptical expression μηδὲ ἐν ᾧ 'nor by which', taken by all versions (and supported by commentators) to mean 'or do anything else by which'. Therefore 'meat' is left unqualified in the display.

14:21d *any time when it* Morris notes that the aorist tense of the infinitives here is pointing to specific times, not to habitual abstention.

to be injured *spiritually* The verb προσκόπτω 'to take offense at' is cognate with πρόσκομμα in 20d. It clearly means more than 'being offended at'. In its literal sense it can mean 'to stumble'. Most English versions capture the sense with figurative expressions such as "fall," "downfall" (NEB), or "fall away" (JB), since Paul is using the verb in a figurative sense. The display follows Bruce's (1965) nonfigurative rendering: "which may hinder your brother in his spiritual life."

There are many textual variants here. The Textus Receptus has 'or be led into sin or be made weak'. However, there is no good reason why a copyist would have deliberately omitted these if they were in the original. Therefore, it seems best to follow the fourth edition GNT's shorter reading (it has a B "almost certain" rating), based on the assumption that the other variants were made by copyists familiar with these words or their cognates in Paul's discussion of the same topic in 1 Cor. 8:11-13.

EXPANSION OF *APPEAL₃* IN THE 14:19–23 DISPLAY

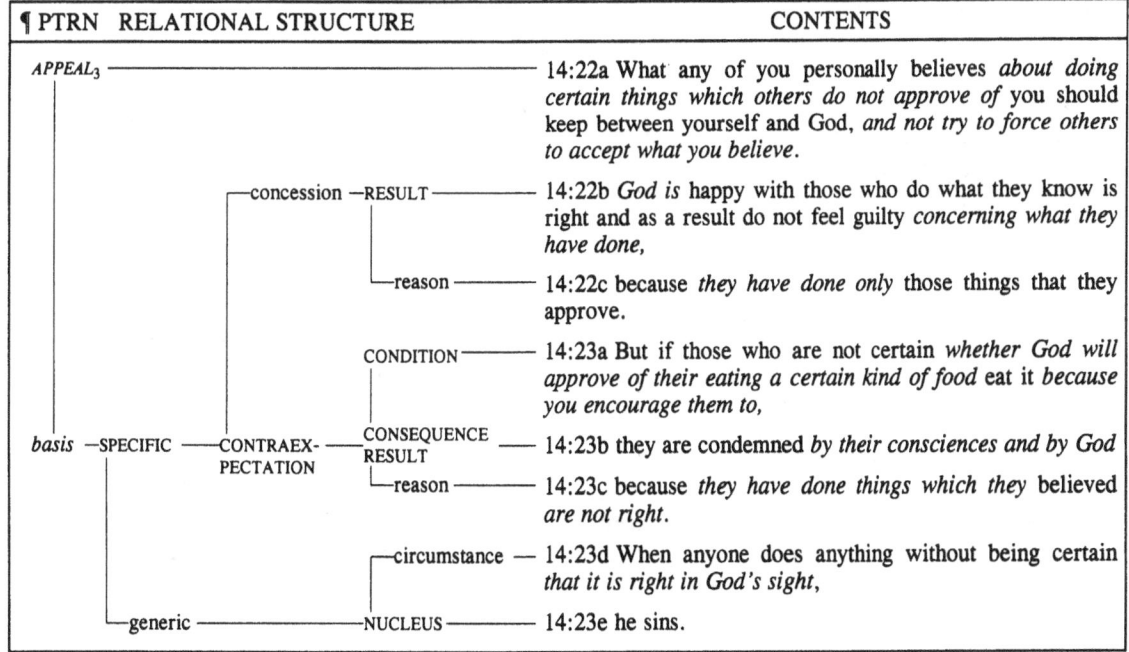

14:22-23 What Paul seems to be saying here is, "Don't you realize that you are causing these weaker brothers to sin? So keep between yourself and God your beliefs about doing things that they don't approve of, and don't try to force them to accept what you believe."

14:22a What any of you personally believes *about doing certain things which others do not approve of* Most commentators agree that the word 'faith' in the phrase σὺ πίστιν ἣν ἔχεις 'the faith which you(sg) have' is not referring to saving faith. Rather, it is used here in the same sense as in 14:1a. (There it was rendered, in its negative sense, as 'doubt whether God will permit them to do certain things which others disapprove of'.) Morris defines it as "the faith that enables anyone who has it to follow without hesitation or scruple a course of action which his weaker brother cannot follow." The display abbreviates this somewhat; an even more generic rendering would be 'what you believe about matters like this'. NIV, NCV, and CEV supply "about these things"; TEV has "about this matter." An alternative would be 'about eating and drinking certain kinds of food', which would fit the immediate context.

There is a textual problem here. The relative pronoun ἣν 'which' is supported by a number of excellent manuscripts, but it is omitted in the vast majority of Latin manuscripts and other early versions. (This omission prompted the rendering as a rhetorical question in KJV.) If 'which' were omitted, the semantic sense of the clause would be conditional: 'If you have personal convictions on such matters'. But it seems better, following the GNT, to assume that 'which' was in the original and then accidentally omitted due to the suffix -ιν on the preceding word.

The Greek emphatic pronoun 'you' is singular, continuing the use of second person pronouns in many places in this chapter for emphasis and personal application. The sense is conveyed by 'any of you personally'. JBP has "your personal convictions."

you should keep between yourself and God The words κατὰ σεαυτὸν ἔχε ἐνώπιον τοῦ θεοῦ 'by yourself have before God' are somewhat idiomatic, as is the rendering in the display.

and not try to force others to accept what you believe This implied contrast is an essential implicature of Paul's argument in this whole section; it is an integral part of carrying out the APPEAL in 19a.

14:22b *God is* happy with those who do what they know is right and as a result do not feel guilty *concerning what they have done* The subject of the clause μακάριος ὁ μὴ κρίνων ἑαυτόν 'blessed (is) the one who is not judging himself' is singular, but with a generic sense, hence the plural in the display.

In the NT, when a person is described as μακάριος 'blessed', it means he is in a state of God's approval and favor. This could be rendered 'God is happy with', but it does not mean the individual himself is necessarily happy with the situation (cf. Matt. 5:10–11).

The verb κρίνω here means 'condemn' (BAGD, p. 452.6b). In the display it is made clear that by 'condemn himself' Paul means that a person's conscience does the condemning (NEB has "with a clear conscience"); in other words, it makes him feel guilty. NCV has "if he can do what he thinks is right without feeling guilty," which is close to the rendering in the display.

14:22c because *they have done only* those things that they approve The Greek is ἐν ᾧ δοκιμάζει 'in what he approves'. To make a full proposition some verb is necessary, hence 'do', as in TEV and LB. JBP is more specific ("allow yourself to eat"), but since Paul is making a generic statement here, a generic verb is better, along with the plural 'they'. Harrison suggests that the 'blessed' one is fortunate "because he is free from doubt and because no one who might be scandalized is looking on."

14:23a those who are not certain *whether God will approve of their eating a certain kind of food* The generic sense of ὁ διακρινόμενος 'he who doubts' is conveyed by the plural in the display. Case frame considerations require an object to be supplied for 'doubt'. TEV has "about what he eats"; LB, "believes that something he wants to do is wrong." NCV is more full with "eats something without being sure that it is right." To make the thrust of Paul's argument clear here it may be necessary to include something like this at the end, because it is a crucial implicature of the argument (see the note on 14:22–23).

14:23b they are condemned *by their consciences and by God* The Greek is the perfect passive κατακέκριται 'he is (or stands) condemned'. A number of commentators suggest that the implied agent is God; others, that it is both God and his own conscience. The use of the passive may well be a deliberate attempt to suggest both. Both are supplied in the display, but when translating in a language that has a passive, it would be good to preserve the ambiguity by omitting the agent.

14:23c because *they have done things which they believed* **are not right** The Greek is ὅτι οὐκ ἐκ πίστεως 'because not out of faith'. Some verb phrase needs to be supplied, and the display supplies 'they have done things' (cf. RSV's "because he does not act from").

The noun 'faith', when translated by a verb, requires a content of the cognitive event, hence 'are not right'. LB has "he thinks it is wrong." Harrison renders it "he lacks confidence that the step is in line with the will of God." NCV is very clear with "because he did not believe that it was right."

14:23d–e When anyone does anything without being certain *that it is right in God's sight*, **he sins** The Greek is πᾶν ὃ οὐκ ἐκ πίστεως ἁμαρτία ἐστίν 'everything which is not out of faith is sin'. In the display the content of the faith is supplied somewhat idiomatically. An alternative is 'whether God will approve it or not'.

In the Greek, the agent of 'faith' is unstated; but when 'faith' is changed to a verb form, an agent must be expressed. It should be rendered by whatever pronoun or other form is natural for generic statements, hence 'anyone' here.

BOUNDARIES AND COHERENCE

Lexical coherence in 14:19–23 is provided by references to food: βρῶμα 'food' in v. 19; the verbs ἐσθίω 'eat' in vv. 20, 21, and 23; and πίνω 'drink' in v. 21.

It is possible to posit a paragraph boundary at 14:22, as in NIV and JB; but this is not done in any other versions examined, nor do any commentators consider a boundary to be here. The reasons for seeing 14:19–23 as one paragraph are: (1) v. 22 continues the same genre, hortatory; (2) there is no conjunction at v. 22; and (3) v. 22 continues the second person singular pronoun.

The boundary between 14:19–23 and the next paragraph is marked at 15:1 by a change from the second person singular imperative in v. 22 to the indicative ὀφείλομεν 'we ought' with the free first person plural form of the pronoun. These, along with the conjunction δέ, mark a progression to a new turn of thought.

PROMINENCE AND THEME

The theme of 14:19–23 is drawn from the APPEALS in 19a–b, 20a–b and 22a, and from the naturally prominent CONDITION and CONSEQUENCE propositions of 23a–b of the *basis* that supports 22a. The vv. 20c–21 exhortations are not included because a summary of them ('do not do anything to injure a fellow believer spiritually') would be no more than a negatively phrased repetition of 19b ('do things which will help each other to mature spiritually').

SUBDIVISION CONSTITUENT 15:1-4
(Hortatory Paragraph: Specific appeal₅ of 14:1-15:13)

THEME: We should endure being irritated by the practices of those who are uncertain whether God will condemn them for doing certain things which the Mosaic law forbade, and do things which please our fellow Christians, since Christ has set us an example.

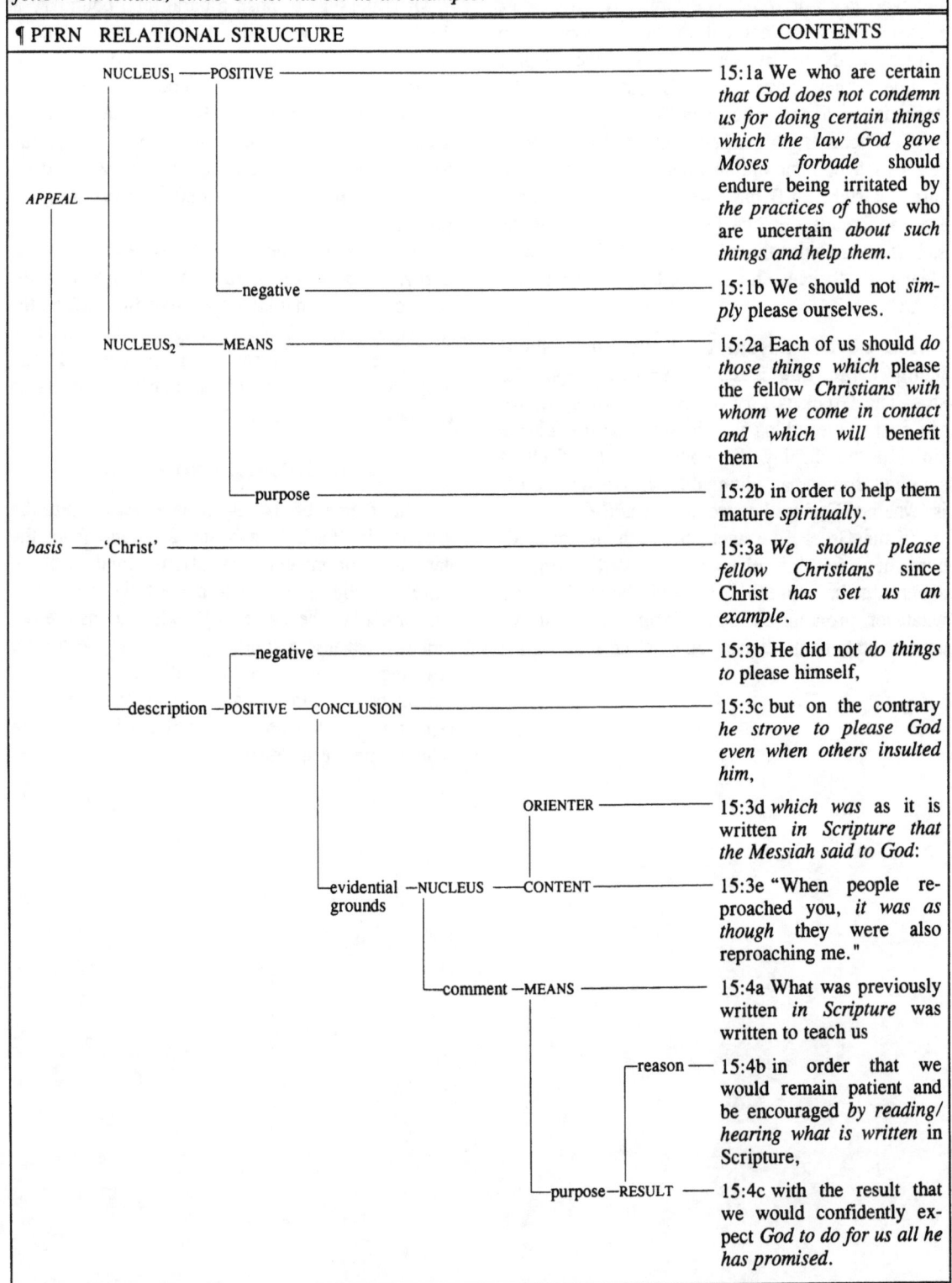

INTENT AND PARAGRAPH PATTERN

That 15:1-4 is a hortatory paragraph is evident from the first verb, ὀφείλομεν 'we ought to', which expresses a somewhat mitigated APPEAL. The third person imperative ἀρεσκέτω 'let him please' in 2a also expresses an exhortation. Verses 3-4 are seen as supplying the *basis* for the two APPEALS, although they are more directly a *basis* for 2a than for v. 1.

NOTES

15:1a We who are certain *that God does not condemn us for doing certain things which the law God gave Moses forbade* The word 'able' in the phrase ἡμεῖς οἱ δυνατοί 'we who are able', contrasts with 'weak' in 14:1. But it should not be rendered as 'strong' or 'strong Christians'; this would not convey Paul's meaning. Regardless of how the word is rendered, it is difficult to convey the sense without using several clauses. LB has "believe that it makes no difference to the Lord whether we do these things." (LB is the only one among the English versions that attempts to make this meaning clear.) Hodge says the sense is "strong in reference to . . . faith in the Christian doctrine of the lawfulness of all kinds of food, and the abrogation of the Mosaic law." Hodge's statement is good except for the fact that in chapter 15 Paul makes no further reference to food and eating; his subsequent comments are more generic. In the display, the words 'are able' are rendered as 'are certain' and the content of the certainty is supplied. The literal 'able' might be retained if a qualifying phrase is added: 'able to do certain things which the law of Moses forbade without feeling condemned'.

should endure being irritated by *the practices of* **those who are uncertain** *about such things and help them* The Greek is ὀφείλομεν τὰ ἀσθενήματα τῶν ἀδυνάτων βαστάζειν 'we ought to bear the weaknesses of those not able'. Here 'weaknesses' is taken by many as meaning 'scruples', but 'should endure' implies some source of irritation. The verb βαστάζω 'to bear', Morris notes, implies toleration of the weaknesses. The primary sense of the word is 'carry'; 'and help them' is implied. TEV has "help the weak" (so also Morris, Newman and Nida). The immediately following context supports this rendering; more than 'put up with' is involved. Murray says the word here "is not to be understood in the sense of 'bear with' frequent in our common speech but in the sense of 'bear up' or 'carry'. . . . The strong are to help the weak."

15:1b We should not *simply* **please ourselves** As Morris notes, "This does not mean that we are never to do anything that we want to do, but that we are never to do what pleases us regardless of its effects on others." Thus 'simply', 'merely', or 'only' must be supplied in order to avoid wrong meaning. JBP has "not just go our own sweet way"; LB, "we cannot just go ahead and do them to please ourselves"; NCV, "not only ourselves"; REB, "not just please ourselves."

15:2a the fellow *Christians with whom we come in contact* For πλησίον 'neighbor' see the note on 13:9g. In this context Paul is referring to fellow believers specifically. The plural is used in the display because Paul is using the word in a generic sense, not just referring to one specific individual.

and which will **benefit them** The Greek is εἰς τὸ ἀγαθόν 'unto the good'. Most English translations use the phrase 'for his good', but this is an idiom. Semantically an event is in view, hence 'benefit'.

15:2b in order to help them mature *spiritually* The phrase πρὸς οἰκοδομήν 'for upbuilding' is a dead metaphor. It is rendered here as in 14:19b. Cranfield comments "the pleasing of the neighbour which is here commanded is such a pleasing as has regard to his true good, to his salvation, a pleasing which is directed toward his edification."

15:3a *since* **Christ** *has set us an example* This verse is introduced by γάρ as the reason we are not to please ourselves, but a major logical step is omitted. The fact that Christ did not do things to please himself (3b) does not relationally cohere as the *basis* for the APPEAL that we should please our neighbors (2a); what coheres as the *basis* for the APPEAL is that by Christ's not doing things to please himself, he set us an example. Murray says, "Here is an appeal to the supreme example in order to reinforce the obligation enjoined in the two preceding verses." Denney is similar: "The duty of not pleasing ourselves is enforced by the example of Christ." CEV and NIV allude to the missing step in the logic here with "even Christ did not . . ."

15:3b He did not *do things to* **please himself** The Greek, οὐχ ἑαυτῷ ἤρεσεν 'did not himself please', is by itself ambiguous in English. It could be taken to mean 'he was not pleased with his own behavior' or 'the purpose of his behavior was not to please himself.' The latter is what Paul means, and thus 'do things' is implied.

15:3c but on the contrary *he strove to please God* The Greek here is simply ἀλλά 'but instead' followed by the 3d introduction to the Scripture quotation. However, a clause contrasting with 'he pleased himself' is implied; and since the following quotation gives the supreme example of Christ's espousing his Father's cause, not his own, 'he strove to please God' is taken as the implied clause that completes the contrast.

even when others insulted him This implied clause is supplied as the circumstantial setting of the events concerning which the Psalmist prophetically spoke.

15:3d *which was* **as it is written** *in Scripture* The expression καθὼς γέγραπται 'as it is written' is used here, as it was previously, to relate an event that is the fulfillment of a Scripture to its prediction (cf. 9:33). REB condenses the material covered in propositions 3c–d with "to him apply the words of Scripture."

that the Messiah said to God Cranfield notes that "Christ is addressing God" here. Hence the identification of the pronouns 'I' and 'you' in the quotation is made outside the quotation (cf. 8:36 and 9:33). The term 'Messiah' is used in the display instead of 'Christ', which would be anachronistic.

15:3e "When people reproached you, *it was as though* **they were also reproaching me."** The words οἱ ὀνειδισμοὶ τῶν ὀνειδιζόντων σε ἐπέπεσαν ἐπ' ἐμέ 'the reproaches of those who reproached you fell on me' can be taken in various ways. The first part could mean 'the reproaches that were intended for you' or 'the reproaches that were, in your estimation, directed toward you'. The second part could mean 'actually fell on me' or 'I considered that they fell on me'. But neither in the case of the Psalmist (Psa. 69:9) nor of Christ did the reproachers consider that they were reproaching God; the sense chosen for the display fits the situation better. It is very difficult to express the sense without using a verbal noun such as 'reproaches'. An alternative might be 'When people were, in your estimation, reproaching you, they actually reproached me'. NCV's "when people insult you, it hurts me" comes closest among the versions to making the meaning clear without figurative language.

15:4 Verse 4 is labeled comment because it does not give a reason for any previous statement, but only a justification of Paul's use of Scriptures here and elsewhere in his epistle. Thus γάρ here is taken as introducing a parenthetical comment, a rare use of it. If Paul had said '*this* Scripture was previously written . . .', it would be the grounds of 15:3d–e, but that is not the case. There seems to be no good explanation why this statement is given here rather than following any of the many other Scripture quotations by Paul in this letter or in any of his other letters. Cranfield comments that Paul "justifies the use for the purpose of exhortation of the christologically understood OT passages just quoted," but immediately goes on to say, "All Scripture has its relevance and applicability to us." The great majority of commentators would support a grounds relationship for v. 4 to 3d. Best, on the other hand, says, "Paul digresses," and Barnes says, "This is a *general* observation which struck the mind of the apostle, from the particular case which he has just specified. . . . It should be read as a parenthesis." These views support the interpretation followed in the display. Moreover, at least eleven modern translations do not signal a grounds relationship here.

15:4a *in Scripture* This phrase is supplied to specify the place where it was written. TEV, REB, LB, and CEV do likewise.

15:4b remain patient and be encouraged The compound noun phrase διὰ τῆς ὑπομονῆς καὶ διὰ τῆς παρακλήσεως 'through patience and through encouragement' represents two events, which in the display are conveyed by verb expressions. Several commentators suggest that the sense of the first of these nouns is 'fortitude, perseverance, steadfastness' rather than 'patience'. But since 4b is taken as the reason leading to the result of confident expectation in 4c, the sense of patience coheres better. The second word can mean 'encouragement, comfort, or exhortation', but 'encouragement' fits the context best in English and is used in nearly all English versions.

by reading/hearing what is written **in Scripture** Commentators agree that the genitive τῶν γραφῶν 'of the Scriptures' indicates source; thus either the hearing or reading (an event) of the Scriptures is implied. But commentators are undecided as to whether it modifies 'encouragement' only, or both 'steadfastness' and 'encouragement'. Grammatically, the repetition of the preposition διά (in the best manuscripts) makes it almost certain that it refers only to 'encouragement'.

15:4c confidently expect *God to do for us all he has promised* The abstract noun 'hope' in τὴν ἐλπίδα ἔχωμεν 'we might have hope' is translated here as 'confidently expect', as before. Case frame considerations require the cognitive content of 'hope' to be supplied. What is supplied here is generic, but 'promised' does carry the idea of implicit reference to Scripture, which is the focus of the verse.

BOUNDARIES AND COHERENCE

The coherence of the 15:1-4 paragraph is seen in its consisting of one APPEAL and its *basis*.

Lexical coherence is seen in three occurrences of ἀρέσκειν 'to please (in vv. 1, 2, 3).

The beginning of the next paragraph is marked in 15:5 by a change from the indicative 'ought to' and imperative 'let each one please' to the third person optative of the main verb in the 15:5-6 prayer.

PROMINENCE AND THEME

The theme of 15:1-4 is drawn from the two NUCLEI of the APPEAL in vv. 1-2 and from 3a, the most naturally prominent proposition of the *basis*. To keep it shorter the long relative clause in 1a that identifies 'we' has been omitted from the theme.

SUBDIVISION CONSTITUENT 15:5-6
(Expressive Paragraph: Specific prayer regarding 14:1-15:4)

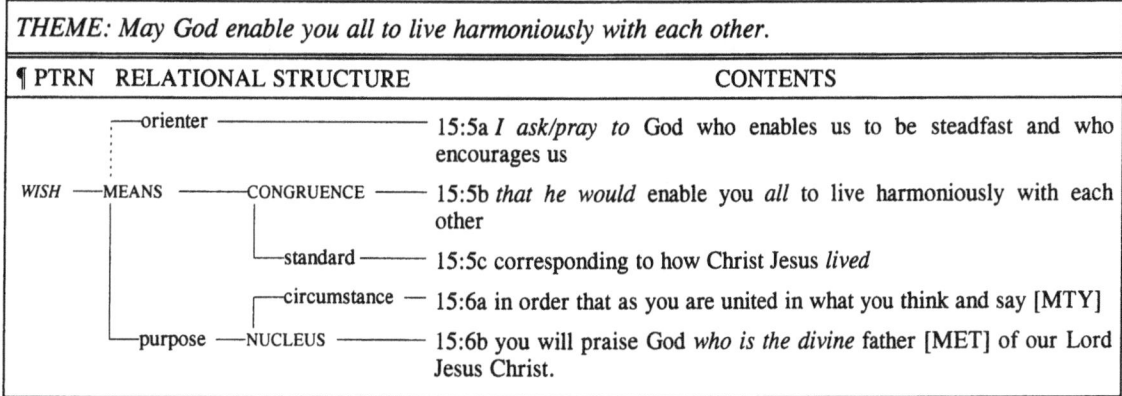

INTENT AND PARAGRAPH PATTERN

The 15:5-6 paragraph is an expression of Paul's WISH or desire; in effect, it is a prayer. The main verb in the paragraph is δῴη 'give', a third person optative form. The meaning of ὁ θεὸς δῴη ὑμῖν is 'may God give you', the subject of the verb being 'God'. The paragraph is thus considered to be of the expressive genre, of the causality type. It might be said that there is an implied *situation* here, 'because of my concern for your spiritual growth'.

NOTES

15:5a *I ask/pray to* The third person singular optative δῴη (5b) is represented in all English versions by 'may'. But since many languages do not have such a form, and since many commentators say it is equivalent to a prayer, the optative is represented by 'I ask/pray' in the display. Cranfield says that "it is surely more closely akin to prayer than to exhortation." Both CEV and NCV have "I pray that."

God who enables us to be steadfast and who encourages us The genitives in ὁ θεὸς τῆς ὑπομονῆς καὶ τῆς παρακλήσεως 'God of patience and of encouragement' are genitives of source. These abstract nouns are rendered here as verbs.

15:5b enable you *all* to live harmoniously with each other The Greek is δῴη ὑμῖν τὸ αὐτὸ φρονεῖν ἐν ἀλλήλοις 'give to you the same thinking among each other', which means "be in agreement, live in harmony" (BAGD, p. 866.1). The word 'all' is supplied because it is clearly the sense of this prayer, following as it does upon an extended hortatory section addressed to the whole Roman church and dealing with the main problem that Paul gives attention to in this epistle. JB has "help you all to be tolerant with each other"; CEV has "live at peace with each other."

15:5c corresponding to how Christ Jesus *lived* The phrase κατὰ Χριστὸν Ἰησοῦν 'according to Christ Jesus' can mean either 'according to the will of Christ' or 'according to the example of Christ'. In view of the example of Christ in v.3, the latter is almost certainly the meaning. This is supported by the majority of commentators. JB and TEV have "following the example of"; REB, "after the manner of."

15:6a as you are united in what you think and say The word ὁμοθυμαδόν means "with one mind or purpose" (BAGD, p. 566). The phrase ἐν ἑνὶ στόματι 'with one mouth' is a metonymy that means being unified in what they utter with their mouths.

15:6b praise The verb δοξάζω can mean 'to honor', but here where it is immediately preceded by 'with one mouth' it is better taken as 'praise', as most English versions render it.

God *who is the divine* father The Greek is τὸν θεὸν καὶ πατέρα 'the God and father', but a literal translation could give the idea that Paul was talking about two persons.

In some languages it may be necessary to make some sort of adjustment to make clear that 'father' is a metaphor here. The word 'divine' is included because the primary sense of πατήρ is 'human father'. In some languages it is not possible to use the ordinary word for 'father' without qualification. This problem is similar to that involving 'Son of God' (see the note on 1:3a).

BOUNDARIES AND COHERENCE

The 15:5-6 paragraph consists of Paul's prayer that his readers live harmoniously. The boundary with the next paragraph is marked by διό 'therefore' in 15:7 and an imperative expressing another APPEAL with exactly the same verb form (προσλαμβάνεσθε 'accept') that introduced the 14:1-15:13 subdivision at 14:1.

PROMINENCE AND THEME

The theme of 15:5-6 is drawn from the prominent MEANS proposition (5b). 'May' is used rather than 'I pray that' because it is shorter and also is in keeping with the Greek.

SUBDIVISION CONSTITUENT 15:7–12
(Hortatory Paragraph: Restatement of 14:1–15:4)

THEME: Accept each other as Christ has accepted you, remembering that what Christ has done was both to help the Jews and cause non-Jews to praise God.

¶ PTRN RELATIONAL STRUCTURE	CONTENTS
APPEAL — MEANS	15:7a Therefore, *I say to all of you at Rome*, accept each other
└─purpose — NUCLEUS	15:7b in order that *people* will praise God
└─circumstance	15:7c *as they see you thus behaving like Christ*.
motivational basis	15:7d *Accept each other* just as Christ accepted you/us.
basis NUCLEUS₁ — MEANS	15:8a I want *you to remember* that what Christ has done was to help *us* Jews [MTY]
└─purpose — GENERIC	15:8b in order to show that God is faithful.
└─specific	15:8c *That is*, he caused to come true what he promised to *our Jewish* patriarchs *about sending the Messiah*.
NUCLEUS₂ — CONCLUSION — RESULT	15:9a And *what he has done was also in order to* cause the non-Jews to praise God
└─reason	15:9b because he acted mercifully *to them*.
ORIENTER	15:9c *What he has done for the non-Jews* fulfills what was written *in the Scriptures that David said to God*:
evidential grounds₁ — CONTENT	15:9d "So I will praise you *when I am* among the non-Jews and I will sing to you." [MTY]
┌─orienter	15:10a And it is written in another *Scripture passage*,
evidential grounds₂ — CONTENT	15:10b "Rejoice, non-Jews, with God's people *the Jews*."
┌─orienter	15:11a *And it is written in* another *Scripture passage*,
evidential grounds₃ — CONTENT	15:11b "Praise the Lord, all *you* non-Jews, and may everyone praise him." [DOU]
┌─orienter	15:12a And Isaiah wrote *in the Scriptures*,
evidential grounds₄ — CONTENT₁	15:12b "There shall be a descendant [MET] of Jesse who will begin to rule the non-Jews.
└─CONTENT₂	15:12c They will confidently expect him *to fulfill what he has promised*."

INTENT AND PARAGRAPH PATTERN

The imperative προσλαμβάνεσθε 'accept' in the first clause in the 15:7–12 paragraph, to which all the other clauses are subordinate relationally, is a clear indication that this is a hortatory paragraph. This verb expresses the *APPEAL*. It is supported by two *bases*, one motivational (15:7d) and the other evidential (15:8–12).

NOTES

15:7 There is a division among commentators as to whether the phrase εἰς δόξαν τοῦ θεοῦ 'for the glory of God' relates to 'Christ has accepted you' or to 'accept each other'. The majority support the former view, which is spelled out in the diagram on the next page. But in this context that does not seem to make sense: 'Christ has accepted you that he might glorify God'. The second interpretation is the one chosen for the main display; it coheres very well once 7c is understood as given here. (It is the interpretation given by Cranfield, TEV, LB, NJB, and NIV.)

```
APPEAL ─────────────── 15:7a . . . accept each other
   │
 basis ───── MEANS ──── 15:7b since Christ has accepted you/us
             └─purpose ─ 15:7c in order that he/we might glorify God
```

15:7a Therefore In this context the conjunction διό 'therefore' probably means 'on the basis of all the evidence mentioned in this section'. The use of 'accept' in 7a, the same verb used in 14:1a to introduce the whole subdivision, supports the analysis that the 15:7-12 paragraph is a summary of 14:1-15:6.

I say to all of you at Rome This paragraph concludes Paul's discussion of "the weak" and "the strong"; as his final appeal, it "is surely addressed to the whole community" (Morris). Thus this is an appropriate speech act orienter expressing what Paul is doing at this point.

accept See the note on 14:1.

15:7b in order that *people* **will praise God** Since the verb δοξάζω in 6b was rendered 'praise', the cognate noun δόξα here is also rendered 'praise'.

15:7c *as they see you thus behaving like Christ* This proposition is needed to complete the logic of the argument; otherwise the reason for others' praising God is not apparent. The relation could be one of circumstance or reason.

15:7d you/us KJV has 'us', but it is based on weak manuscript evidence; 'you', on the other hand, has an A rating in the fourth edition GNT, indicating "certain" in their opinion. It could be that some copyist changed 'you' to 'us' accidentally, or even deliberately, thinking Paul should have included himself. In view of all the second person plural pronominal forms in the context, 'you' is indeed more likely than 'us'. But in a language where 'you' here would imply that Paul was not accepted by Christ, it will be necessary to render this as 'us' in any case.

15:8-12 Cranfield considers 15:8-12 to be related to 7a:

> "We get a more straightforward and natural connexion of thought . . . if we take vv. 8-12 as intended as additional support for the command of v. 7 . . . than we get if we regard vv. 8-12 as intended simply as support for, or explanation of, the subordinate clause of v. 7."

15:8a I want *you to remember* **that** The Greek has the speech act verb λέγω 'I say' with the relator γάρ. The function of this orienter is to put prominence on what follows, hence 'I want you to remember that' (as also in LB and REB). Good alternatives are 'note that', 'keep in mind that', 'don't forget that'. The material that follows is not the reason for what precedes; it introduces the second *basis* for the APPEAL in v. 7. This *basis* has two main statements: v. 8 discusses Christ's acceptance of believing Jews; vv. 9-11, his acceptance of believing Gentiles.

what Christ has done was to help The Greek is Χριστὸν διάκονον γεγενῆσθαι 'Christ a servant became'. The sense of διάκονος here is 'helper' (BAGD, p. 184.1b), hence 'to help' in the display. The verb 'became' needs to be expressed by a verb with more semantic content. JB uses 'came', which is good; but in the context of what Christ accomplished and continues to accomplish by his life and death and present ministry at the Father's side, 'what Christ has done' is more to the point. The English perfect tense points not only to past acts but his continuing ministry.

us **Jews** The word περιτομῆς 'of the circumcision' is a metonymy used previously to refer to the Jews—nearly all modern English versions render it 'the Jews'. In the display, 'us' is supplied to indicate that Paul was a Jew. It is not easy to determine whether 'us' is inclusive or exclusive. If Paul is addressing the Gentiles in his audience, an exclusive 'us' would be appropriate. But if he is here addressing both Jews and non-Jews, the decision between exclusive and inclusive is difficult. Though not all of Paul's audience were Jews, some were; hence the decision for the display is on the side of its being inclusive.

15:8b to show that God is faithful The phrase ὑπὲρ ἀληθείας θεοῦ 'on behalf of the truth of God' is difficult. Several commentators (Denney, Hodge, Barrett) suggest the sense that is in the display (see also TEV): God is reliable, he has been faithful to perform what he has promised. This fits very well as the generic statement of which 8c is the specification. A good alternative would be 'God faithfully fulfills what he has promised'.

15:8c caused to come true what he promised to our Jewish patriarchs The Greek is εἰς τὸ βεβαιῶσαι τὰς ἐπαγγελίας τῶν πατέρων 'unto the confirming of the promises of the fathers'. According to BAGD (p. 138.1), the verb 'confirm' here means 'prove the promises reliable, fulfill them'. Causing them to come true is what he means by confirming them (cf. TEV). JB has "carry out the promises"; NEB has "making good his promises."

Most modern versions render 'fathers' as 'patriarchs' here, meaning Abraham, Isaac, and Jacob (see the note on 11:28). The words 'our Jewish' are supplied to identify them and to specify that they were Paul's ancestors too.

about sending the Messiah In the context of Christ's ministry to the Jews, the specific promises in view are those related to the coming of the Messiah (so Barnes). The promises about giving them the land of Canaan or bringing them back from slavery in Egypt are not in view.

15:9a And . . . in order to The conjunction δέ indicates a change of referent: here the change is from the Jews to the Gentiles. The fact that Paul fails to repeat the purposive construction εἰς τό has led a few commentators to suggest that this clause depends on λέγω in 8a. Cranfield, for instance, insists that vv. 9-12 are "support, not just for v. 9a but for Paul's solemn declaration (vv. 8-9a) as a whole." Dunn agrees. But in each of the four Scripture references that follow in 9c-12, the Gentiles are referred to, and in only one (10b) are the Jews referred to, and that only secondarily. The great majority of commentators recognize the ellipsis and relate what follows as a second purpose of Christ's ministry.

praise God The Greek is δοξάσαι 'to glorify'. See the note on 6b.

15:9b because he acted mercifully to them The rendering in the display resolves the mismatch in ὑπὲρ ἐλέους 'on behalf of mercy'. The words 'to them' are supplied to make it clear who the recipients of God's mercy were.

15:9c What he has done for the non-Jews The main clause of 9a is repeated here as a means of starting a new sentence.

fulfills The word 'fulfills' expresses the function of καθώς 'according as', the introducer of an OT quotation that predicted what Paul has just alluded to.

what was written in the Scriptures that David said to God The speaker of the words from Psa. 18:49 is specified here in order to provide a referent for the first person pronoun in the quotation. (LB supplies "the Psalmist.") The inscription to Psalm 18 cites David as author. Sanday and Headlam say, "In the original, David, as the author of the Psalm, is celebrating a victory over surrounding nations." However, due to the messianic application of the quotation, they suggest that the speaker could be Christ: "Christ is presented as declaring that among the Gentiles . . . He will praise God." Denney would agree with this, declaring, "Christ is assumed to be the speaker"; he takes the sense that David wrote what the Messiah said to God. But both of these implicitly ignore the original communication situation: there is nothing in Psalm 18 about the Messiah; this is David's song of praise to God after his victory over Saul and other enemies. But in any case, the name of the speaker, David, is irrelevant here since it is not in focus.

The location (i.e., 'in the Scriptures') is specified in the display; likewise, for vv. 10-12.

The phrase 'to God' is supplied to provide a referent for the second person pronoun in the quotation.

15:9d I will praise you when I am among the non-Jews The verb ἐξομολογέω usually means 'to confess', but BAGD (p. 277.2c) say it means 'praise' here. It is so rendered in most modern English versions.

Several commentators suggest that ἐν ἔθνεσιν 'among Gentiles' means that David is surrounded by Gentiles who are also praising God; but Dunn says "it is significant that the verse does not necessarily envisage the Gentiles themselves joining in the praise." No such instance is recorded in 1 Samuel, and in the display therefore it is not suggested that the Gentiles were praising God.

I will sing to you In the clause τῷ ὀνόματί σου ψαλῶ 'to your name I will sing', 'name' is a metonymy. It is rendered nonfiguratively in the display.

15:10a it is written in another Scripture passage The Greek is πάλιν λέγει 'again it/he says'. Here where it is used in a series of quotations, πάλιν means 'elsewhere' (JB and LB have "in another place"). Since Paul is referring to another passage of Scripture (Deut. 32:43), the display uses 'it is written' instead of 'it says'. The passive is used in order to retain the ambiguity of the subject of 'says', which could be either

'Scripture', 'God', or 'Moses'. CEV has "the Scriptures also say."

15:10b with God's people, *the Jews* The words 'the Jews' are supplied in the display to make clear who, according to the OT, God's people are. LB also makes this specific.

15:11a The quotation is from Psa. 117:1. See the note on 10a.

15:11b Praise the Lord, all *you* **non-Jews, and may everyone praise him** Moore (p. 41) considers these two clauses a near-synonymous doublet involving rhetorical parallelism. Both are retained in the display because this is a poetic passage.

15:12a In some languages it may be necessary to add the words 'about the Messiah' at the end of 12a to make it clear that the descendant of Jesse is the Messiah, not David.

15:12b There shall be a descendant of Jesse In this quotation from Isa. 11:10 the word 'root' in the clause ἔσται ἡ ῥίζα τοῦ Ἰεσσαί 'there will be the root of Jesse' is a dead metaphor. It is used throughout Scripture to refer to someone's descendants. The display follows TEV and Weymouth; an alternative is NCV's "from Jesse's family." It could be well argued that CEV's "someone from David's family" is justified: Rev. 5:5 refers to Christ as ἡ ῥίζα Δαυίδ 'the root of David'. Those familiar with the OT would know that Jesse was the father of King David. Another alternative is 'a descendant of Jesse's son, King David'.

who will begin to rule the non-Jews In Greek this is a participial phrase beginning with καί 'and'. Since the phrase seems to be a description of the individual mentioned in 12b, it is represented here by a relative clause. Most English versions omit 'and'. The participle, ἀνιστάμενος 'rising up', is used in the extended sense of 'to appear, to come upon the scene'. It refers to the rule of a king, and here means 'to come to power' (cf. Acts 7:18). Since 'rising up' is used in conjunction with ἄρχειν 'to rule', it is represented simply as 'begin' in the display. (According to BAGD, p. 70.2d, ἀνίστημι is sometimes used "to indicate the beginning of an action.") The phrase 'begin to' is not intended to imply that the action will begin and not be completed. In languages where that would be implied, these words can be eliminated. What is meant is simply that an action that had not occurred before will now begin—and continue.

15:12c confidently expect See the note on 4c concerning 'hope'.

BOUNDARIES AND COHERENCE

The 15:7-12 paragraph is relationally coherent in that it consists of an APPEAL plus its supporting *bases*. The coherence in the second *basis* is seen in the set of four OT quotations regarding the non-Jews.

The paragraph's closing boundary is marked by the return in v. 13 to the third person optative. This optative verb is the main verb in what may be considered another prayer by Paul to conclude the unit; the genre shifts in v. 13 from hortatory to expressive.

PROMINENCE AND THEME

The theme of 15:7-12 is basically drawn from the APPEAL in 7a and the two *bases*. The material from the two NUCLEI in the second *basis* (vv. 8-12) has been condensed to eliminate repetitiveness.

SUBDIVISION CONSTITUENT 15:13
(Expressive Paragraph: Generic prayer concluding 14:1–15:13)

THEME: May God make you completely joyful and peaceful in order that you may have abundant hope.

¶ PTRN RELATIONAL STRUCTURE	CONTENTS
WISH — MEANS — orienter	15:13a *I pray/ask*
— NUCLEUS	15:13b that the God who causes you to be confidently expecting *him to do what he has promised* will cause you to be completely joyful and peaceful
— circumstance	15:13c as you trust in God
— purpose	15:13d in order that by the power of the Holy Spirit you will more and more confidently expect *to receive what God has promised you.*

INTENT AND PARAGRAPH PATTERN

The 15:13 paragraph is similar to 15:5-6 in that it expresses a *WISH* or prayer by Paul. The main verb, πληρώσαι 'may he fill', is a third person optative with 'God' as the subject.

NOTES

15:13a *I pray/ask* NCV, LB, and CEV have "I pray that." See the note on 5a.

15:13b causes you to be confidently expecting The phrase θεὸς τῆς ἐλπίδος 'God of hope' could mean 'the God who is the object of our hope', but since the goal of hope in v. 12 is the descendant of Jesse, the phrase almost certainly is a subjective genitive and means 'God, the one who is the source of hope', as most commentators hold.

will cause you to be completely joyful In πληρῶσαι ὑμᾶς πάσης χαρᾶς 'fill you of all joy' the verb 'fill' is figurative and indicates (as in 1:29) that some quality fully or completely applies to individuals.

peaceful While εἰρήνη 'peace' sometimes refers to peace with God, this is not the subject being dealt with in this passage; nor does 'full of peace with God' make much sense. The alternative is inner peace, which collocates well with 'joy'. But some commentators suggest that in view of the larger context dealing with harmonious relations between believers at Rome, 'peace' here probably includes "concord among yourselves" (Hodge). The rendering here as 'peaceful' is intended to embrace both inner peace and concord.

15:13c as you trust in God The construction ἐν + τῷ + an infinitive (which is quite rare, used only four times by Paul) could be taken as expressing reason. But Morris (p. 156, fn. 25) says, "It is mostly temporal, and means 'while' (cf. BDF 404)." Thus in the display the phrase ἐν τῷ πιστεύειν 'in believing' is taken as a concomitant circumstance. NIV has "as you trust in him."

15:13d by the power of the Holy Spirit In languages where 'power' cannot be expressed as an abstract term, it could be rendered as 'by the Holy Spirit powerfully (helping you)'.

you will more and more confidently expect In εἰς τὸ περισσεύειν ὑμᾶς ἐν τῇ ἐλπίδι 'unto your abounding in hope', the word 'abounding' is a means of intensifying the event of hope. It expresses Paul's desire that their confident expectation of what God will do for them will continue to increase. For the noun 'hope', see the note on 4c.

BOUNDARIES AND COHERENCE

The 15:13 paragraph expresses a *WISH* by Paul for his readers. This is a different genre than seen in the hortatory unit which precedes it and the expository unit which follows it. It is therefore considered a separate unit.

PROMINENCE AND THEME

The theme of 15:13 is a condensation of the 13b NUCLEUS of the MEANS and the 13d purpose clause. The latter is included because 'hope', being mentioned twice in the one verse, is prominent and therefore thematic.

PART CLUSTER CONSTITUENT 15:14–33
(Hortatory Subpart: Epilogue of epistle)

THEME: Because of the work of proclaiming the gospel among the non-Jews in places where they have not heard about Christ, I have often been hindered from visiting you, but I hope to see you and be helped by you for my next journey. But now I am about to go to Jerusalem, and I urge you to pray that God will protect me from the unbelieving Jews in Judea and that the believers there will accept the money I take to them.

MACROSTRUCTURE	CONTENTS
introduction	15:14–16 I have written frankly to you in this letter because of what God has graciously commissioned me to do among the non-Jews.
description	15:17–21 I am proud of my work for God, which I have now completed in this region by proclaiming the gospel in places where they have not heard about Christ.
basis — DECLARATION	15:22–29 Because of this work, I have often been hindered from visiting you, but I hope to see you as I journey through your area and I hope that you will give me what I need for my next journey. But now I am about to go to Jerusalem to take funds to God's people there. So later I shall visit you in Rome and I know that Christ will bless us there.
APPEAL	15:30–33 I urge you to pray fervently that God will protect me from the unbelieving Jews in Judea and that God's people there will accept the money I take to them and that I may be refreshed by visiting you. May God be with you all.

INTENT AND MACROSTRUCTURE

Here near the end of his letter Paul has a number of things that he wants to say, each of a different genre. For this reason, it is difficult to identify the structure or genre of the 15:14–33 unit. Even its constituent paragraphs defy neat classification. Paul does lead up to an APPEAL in 30–33 (an APPEAL of a very personal nature, quite different from the other APPEALS in the epistle), which some might say is the most significant one in the epistle. Based on this, the 15:14–33 unit is considered hortatory. It consists of four paragraphs: an introductory expository paragraph (14–16); an expressive paragraph (17–21) that functions as a *description* supporting 22–29; then a DECLARATION (22–29), which functions as the *basis* for the fourth and final paragraph, the 30–33 APPEAL.

BOUNDARIES AND COHERENCE

The 15:14–33 unit deals with matters concerning Paul and the church at Rome. The main topic is his proposed visit, and the coherence consists in a succession of I-you references: 'I am convinced about you' (v. 15); 'I have written you frankly' (v. 15); 'I have been hindered from visiting you' (v. 22); 'I hope to see you' and 'I hope to be helped by you' (v. 24); 'I will visit you' (vv. 28–29); and 'I urge you to pray for me' (v. 30). The close of the 15:14–33 unit is signaled by the brief prayer in v. 33 and the closing 'Amen'. The next unit, chapter 16, is clearly distinct, consisting of a succession of references to specific individuals.

PROMINENCE AND THEME

The theme for 15:14–33 consists of the themes of its two most prominent constituents, in accordance with the principle that in a hortatory unit the theme is drawn from both the *basis* and the APPEAL. It also includes the portion of the theme of the 17–21 *description* needed to identify Paul's "work," but omits certain parts of the theme for 22–29 as being less thematic.

SUBPART CONSTITUENT 15:14–16
(Expository Paragraph: Introduction to 15:17–33)

THEME: I have written frankly to you in this letter because of what God has graciously commissioned me to do among the non-Jews.

¶ PTRN	RELATIONAL STRUCTURE	CONTENTS
CLAIM	concession — CONCLUSION — ORIENTER	15:14a My fellow believers, I myself am *thoroughly* convinced about you
	CONTENT	15:14b that you yourselves *have acted* in a completely good way *toward others*
	grounds₁	15:14c since you have known completely *all that God wants you to know* [HYP]
	grounds₂	15:14d and since you are able to instruct each other.
	CONTRAEXPECTATION MEANS	15:15a Yet I have written to you quite frankly *in this letter* about some things
	purpose	15:15b in order to remind you *about these things*
justification	MEANS	15:15c since God has graciously *commissioned* me
	PURPOSE — GENERIC	15:16a in order that I work for Jesus Christ among the non-Jews;
	specific — MEANS	15:16b that is, *he has commissioned me* to act like a priest as I *proclaim* the good news from God *to them*
	purpose — RESULT	15:16c in order that the non-Jews *who believe in Christ* may become accepted *by God* like an offering [MET]
	reason	15:16d as a result of their having been dedicated *to God* by the Holy Spirit.

INTENT AND PARAGRAPH PATTERN

The 15:14–16 paragraph is made up of two independent clauses, each with verbs in the indicative expressing Paul's declarations about his relations with his readers at Rome. It is thus a rapport-building unit. At the same time, due to Paul's claim to authority, it is an expository paragraph. In 15–16 Paul is expressing a CLAIM and introducing his *justification* for it: he is saying, "I have the right to write you frankly on these things since . . ."

In an apostolic letter the author often includes both rapport-building and authority-claiming elements. These are balanced in the 15:14–16 paragraph—v. 14 builds rapport and vv. 15–16 state authority—even though Paul's claim to authority is more naturally prominent.

NOTES

15:14a I myself am *thoroughly* convinced about you In the construction πέπεισμαι, καὶ αὐτὸς ἐγώ 'I am persuaded, even I myself' the subject pronoun is emphasized. But more than just emphasis seems to be involved. According to Dunn, Paul uses these words to convey "a deep personal conviction and feeling for his unknown readers." Cranfield agrees. Hodge, however, suggests that it means "I of myself, without the testimony of others. Paul . . . did not need to be informed by others." It could mean that Paul had heard nothing from others about their spiritual maturity, but this is unlikely in view of clear indications that Paul knew a lot about the church there. It could mean that Paul's evaluation of them was higher than might be expected from those reports. The display follows this sense by supplying 'thoroughly. JB renders it as "It is not because I have any doubts about you, my brethren; on the contrary, I am quite certain that you are full of good intentions, perfectly well instructed and able to advise each other."

15:14b you yourselves *have acted* in a completely good way *toward others* The Greek is καὶ αὐτοὶ μεστοί ἐστε ἀγαθωσύνης 'also (your)selves you are full of goodness'. It has the same emphatic pronoun as in 14a (αὐτός). According to Dunn, "their healthy condition . . . is something they have come to without the help of outsiders (or apostles?) like him." To carry this implied aspect of Paul's argument here, it may be necessary in some translations to include the words 'without others helping you'. 'Goodness' here does not refer to moral excellence by itself, but "a disposition to do good, to show a kindly activity toward others" (Vine), which has been the focus of Paul's concern in chapters 14–15. Most commentators agree with this interpretation.

15:14c since you have known completely *all that God wants you to know* The phrase πεπληρωμένοι πάσης τῆς γνώσεως 'filled with all knowledge' does not mean they knew everything there was to know. Instead, it must refer to "our Christian knowledge in its entirety" (Sanday and Headlam). But they cannot have known all Christian truth either. Lenski qualifies it as "all necessary knowledge so that they could proceed safely and securely." Knox renders it as "knowing all you need to know." It is clearly hyperbolic, though in the display the hyperbole is somewhat downplayed in the interest of clarity.

15:15a I have written to you quite frankly The literal meaning of the adverb τολμηρότερον is 'more boldly', but the sense of the comparative degree here is not 'more boldly than before' or 'more boldly than others' but 'quite boldly'. The word does not indicate lack of fear or timidity, however; rather the meaning is "quite frankly." JBP has "with a greater frankness"; C. B. Williams, "rather freely."

The Textus Receptus follows manuscripts that add the word ἀδελφοί 'brethren' after 'you'. There is much stronger manuscript support for its omission; there would be no reason to omit it if it had been in the original.

in this letter The tense of the verb ἔγραψα 'I have written' is the epistolary aorist (so Robertson), indicating what has just been written, not a previous epistle. The display makes this specific to avoid ambiguity, as does TEV. Aune (p. 295) says that Paul "is referring to the paraenetic [i.e., hortatory] section (12:1– 15:13) which he has just concluded," and this is probably correct.

about some things A few commentators suggest that the phrase ἀπὸ μέρους 'in part' should be taken with the verb phrase to qualify the boldness, giving the sense of 'in some measure boldly' or 'rather boldly'. But this seems to stretch the syntax too much, and it does not fit the communication situation. Most commentators take the sense as "on some points" (BAGD, p. 506.1c), which fits the letter well.

15:15b in order to remind you *about these things* The phrase ὡς ἐπαναμιμνῄσκων ὑμᾶς 'as reminding you' expresses purpose (cf. JB's "to refresh your memories"; see also JBP, NEB). The words 'about these things' are required to satisfy the case frame.

15:15c since God has graciously *commissioned* me The Greek is διὰ τὴν χάριν τὴν δοθεῖσάν μοι ὑπὸ τοῦ θεοῦ 'by the grace given me by God'. Since 'grace' in this phrase is best taken as representing an attribute of an event, it is rendered as an adverb here. What Paul is referring to, probably, is the 'grace of apostleship' mentioned in 1:5. A possible alternative is 'what God has graciously enabled me to do'.

It is not entirely clear whether this proposition supports 15a or 15b. The former is assumed for the display, the analysis here being that this paragraph presents not only a CLAIM but the *justification* for it.

15:16a in order that I work for Christ Jesus This verse is introduced by εἰς τό, which could signal either purpose or result, but most English versions and a number of commentators take it as elucidating the 'grace' or work as an apostle that Paul has referred to in 15c. It could be considered the content of what God had commissioned Paul to do.

In the clause εἶναί με λειτουργὸν Χριστοῦ Ἰησοῦ 'that I might be a minister of Christ Jesus', λειτουργός can mean 'servant'. BAGD (p. 471.2), however, prefer a religious rendering: "in our literature always with religious connotations . . . of priests." It could be specified as 'do religious work' but that would be redundant with 16b.

among the non-Jews If 'servant of Jesus Christ' is rendered 'work for Jesus Christ', then in the phrase εἰς τὰ ἔθνη 'unto the non-Jews' an English preposition other than 'unto' must be used. Best has "among the non-Jewish nations." In some languages it may be necessary to say 'among you non-Jews' (so LB).

15:16b to act like a priest The present participle ἱερουργοῦντα, which means "perform holy service, act like a priest" (BAGD, p. 373), expresses either manner or simultaneous action. CEV has "do the work of a priest."

proclaim **the good news from God** *to them* The phrase τὸ εὐαγγέλιον τοῦ θεοῦ 'the gospel of God' is the object of the participle ἱερουργοῦντα. Rendering the participle as 'acting like a priest' requires a verb to be supplied to connect 'acting like a priest' and 'gospel'. The display follows NIV in supplying 'proclaim'. TEV and NEB have "preaching"; LB and JB have "bringing"; NCV has "teaching." The genitive 'of God' is taken as indicating source (so TEV and JB).

15:16c in order that the non-Jews *who believe in Christ* **may become accepted** *by God* **like an offering** In ἵνα γένηται ἡ προσφορὰ τῶν ἐθνῶν εὐπρόσδεκτος 'in order that may become the offering of the Gentiles acceptable', the Gentiles are compared metaphorically to a προσφορά, "that which is brought, gift" (BAGD, p. 720.2). A few commentators take the genitive 'of the Gentiles' as meaning an offering made by the Gentiles, but Paul is speaking here of his apostolic ministry of bringing Gentiles to Christ—he is not speaking about Gentiles bringing something to God. The great majority of commentators take 'of the Gentiles' as appositional, defining the offering. This sense is followed in the display. If the metaphor were fully spelled out, it would be something like 'may become accepted by God as sacrifices are accepted by God'.

The words 'who believe in Christ' are supplied because Paul does not mean all the Gentiles, only "the Gentiles who were converted to Christianity" (Barnes). See also BAGD (p. 720.2), Murray, Bruce (1963), and Morris.

15:16d as a result of their having been dedicated *to God* Following the description of the Gentiles as being like a sacrifice, the sense of ἡγιασμένη 'having been sanctified' here is 'set apart, dedicated to God', in the way that sacrifices were.

by the Holy Spirit The preposition in the phrase ἐν πνεύματι ἁγίῳ 'in the Holy Spirit' could mean 'in union with' (so Lenski); Paul elsewhere often uses it in this sense as, for example, in ἐν Χριστῷ 'in Christ' in the next verse. However, ἐν never occurs with 'Spirit' in this sense. Nearly all versions and commentators therefore take the sense as 'by'.

BOUNDARIES AND COHERENCE

The 15:14–16 paragraph serves as an *introduction* of the 15:14–33 subpart on Paul's relations with the church at Rome. It is intended to further establish rapport with them in anticipation of a future visit to them and his request for their prayers on his behalf. It includes Paul's commendations of them and a claim to authority in view of his commission by God as a minister to the Gentiles.

The boundary with the next paragraph is marked in v. 17 by οὖν 'therefore', which expresses the transition to the new topic of Paul's recent ministry in places where people had not heard about Christ.

PROMINENCE AND THEME

The theme of 15:14–16 is drawn from the most prominent propositions in the two central elements in the paragraph, the CLAIM in 15a and the MEANS and PURPOSE propositions of the *justification* in 15c and 16a.

SUBPART CONSTITUENT 15:17–21
(Expressive Paragraph: Description related to 15:22–29)

THEME: I am proud of my work for God which I have now completed in this region by proclaiming the gospel in places where they have not heard about Christ.

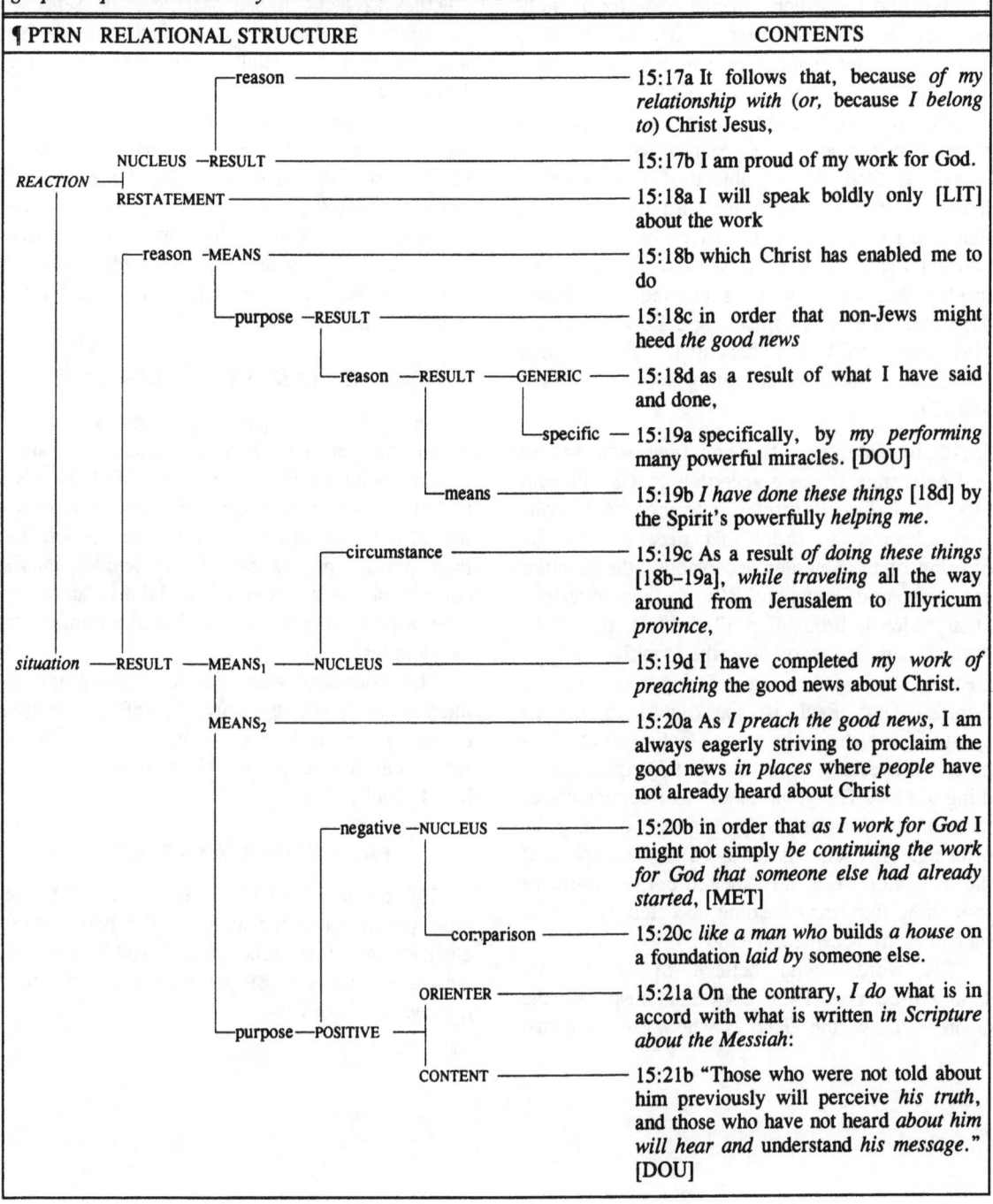

INTENT AND PARAGRAPH PATTERN

The main independent clause in the 15:17-21 paragraph contains the words ἔχω καύχησιν 'I have boasting' (represented in 17b by 'I am proud'). It expresses Paul's emotive REACTION to the *situation* described in vv. 18b-21. Thus this is an expressive paragraph.

NOTES

15:17a It follows that The word οὖν 'then' marks the beginning of the new paragraph, but there is a question whether it is related to what precedes it as the EFFECT following the *cause* or whether it simply marks a transition to a new point. There is clearly not a logical relationship between 14-16 and 17-21 as whole units. The display rendering uses the somewhat idiomatic 'It follows that' (similar to NRSV, TEV, NEB's 'then'), but it is to be understood that this is not meant in its primary sense of temporal progression.

because *of my relationship with* (*or*, **because** *I belong to*) **Christ Jesus** Here the preposition ἐν 'in', followed by Χριστῷ 'Christ', has its usual sense of 'in union with'. See the note on 6:11f.

15:17b I am proud of my work for God The Greek is ἔχω τὴν καύχησιν τὰ πρὸς τὸν θεόν 'I have the boasting the things with God'. There is a mismatch here in that the noun 'boasting' represents an event. Also, the last part of the expression is very unusual grammatically. The accusative τά could be taken as an adverbial accusative or an accusative of respect. In any case, the sense of the whole phrase is 'with respect to what concerns God'. Most English versions have "for God" (e.g., NCV, "I am proud of what I have done for God"). The neuter pronoun τά, which is generic, is rendered by most English versions as 'service' or 'work'. The work Paul specifically has in mind is that of preaching to non-Jews.

The Greek word 'boasting' does not have the negative connotation of its English equivalent. It may be necessary in some languages to say something like 'I am happy about' or 'I feel good about': Paul is talking about his own feelings, not about expressing them to others in a boastful way.

15:18a Here γάρ introduces a restatement of 17b, not the reason for it.

I will speak boldly only about the work The double negative οὐ τολμήσω τι λαλεῖν ὧν οὐ 'I will not dare to speak anything which is not', which is a litotes, has the effect of emphasizing 'only'. In the display this is rendered as a positive as in several recent versions.

15:18b Christ has enabled me to do The clause κατειργάσατο Χριστὸς δι' ἐμοῦ 'Christ worked through me' is expressed more straightforwardly in the display. Though the tense is aorist, Paul is referring to all his ministry to the Gentiles, not just one event.

15:18c in order that non-Jews might heed *the good news* The phrase εἰς ὑπακοὴν ἐθνῶν 'unto obedience of non-Jews' is the equivalent of a purpose clause and is so rendered in the display. The genitive form ἐθνῶν is a subjective genitive; it expresses the agent of 'obedience', the non-Jews.

Case considerations require an object of 'heed' to be supplied. TEV and NIV supply 'God', but most commentators supply 'gospel', which seems more appropriate in this context concerning the ministry of Paul. In some languages 'good news about/from Christ' may need to be specified.

15:18d as a result of what I have said and done The nouns of the phrase λόγῳ καὶ ἔργῳ 'by word and deed' are rendered as a compound verbal construction (as in NIV).

15:19a specifically, by *my performing* **many powerful miracles** The phrase ἐν δυνάμει σημείων καὶ τεράτων 'by the power of signs and wonders' is taken as an explication of 'deed' and perhaps of both 'word and deed' in 18c. As a means clause, it requires a verb, hence 'my performing'. LB has "miracles done through me." But as Dunn notes, the phrase 'signs and wonders' recalls its OT equivalent, which was "a traditional way of referring to the miracles of the Exodus." Thus it is a fixed expression—a doublet—with no difference in meaning between the two terms. Moore (p. 41) likewise considers this a near-synonymous doublet.

15:19b *I have done these things* **by the Spirit's powerfully helping me** The Greek is ἐν δυνάμει πνεύματος 'in the power of the Spirit'. Some suggest that this expresses the means of 19a. But if this were the case, Paul would have used a relative pronoun to introduce it to make this clear. Others suggest that it refers to gifts of the Spirit, but Paul would surely have used the word χαρίσματα in this case. It could be coordinate with 19a; but if it were, the connector καί would most likely have been used. Thus Cranfield's view seems best: two distinct relationships are signaled by the two successive ἐν δυνάμει phrases, and this one relates to λόγῳ καὶ ἔργῳ 'by word and work' in 18d (so Cranfield, Dunn, Vine, Morris). In languages where 'power' can be expressed as a noun, it could be rendered by a phrase, 'by the power of the Spirit', instead of a full clause.

The KJV has 'the Spirit of God', but whether θεοῦ 'of God' was in the original text is open to question. Many excellent manuscripts have 'of God', and many others have ἁγίου 'holy'. One excellent manuscript and one church father have neither, strongly suggesting that the text with neither was the original form. Since the oldest extant manuscript (p⁴⁶) contains 'of God', the fourth edition GNT chooses it, but with a C rating ("difficulty in deciding"). There is no plausible explanation to account for a change from ἁγίου to θεοῦ, from θεοῦ to ἁγίου, or from either one to its omission if either had been in the original. On the other hand, if the original text had had neither one, it is easy to see why some scribes might supply the one and some the other to complete the reference. Hence, the display does not follow the GNT here (nor does TEV or NIV). Having said that, however, it is admitted that the sense is the same, with or without a qualifier to 'Spirit'.

15:19c As a result The word ὥστε introduces the result of Paul's determination to win the Gentiles just mentioned in 18a–19b.

while traveling The mention of two locations, one the place of origin and the other the final destination, semantically requires a verb such as 'traveled' to connect them (cf. TEV).

all the way around . . . to Illyricum *province* There is some uncertainty regarding the words κύκλῳ μέχρι 'around unto': the first word means 'in a circle' or 'round about', and the second means 'up to, as far as'. Some commentators suggest that 'around' refers to Jerusalem and a circle around it. But to use the word 'circle' to refer to Jerusalem, or even as its vicinity, would be very strange; and even if Paul had intended this, he probably would have used a different grammatical construction (so Sanday and Headlam, Cranfield). It is much more likely that 'around' refers to "the broad arc which can be drawn roughly from Jerusalem through Syrian Antioch, through Asia Minor, 'right up to Illyricum' " (Dunn). Most commentators agree. But there is no record of Paul's having gone into the province of Illyricum (nor, for that matter, does it seem right for Paul to claim that his ministry started in Jerusalem). Perhaps he meant that his ministry extended from the vicinity or boundary of one to the vicinity of the other.

The word 'province' is supplied as geographical information that would have been known by Paul's audience. The province of Illyricum was located on the Adriatic Sea in the approximate vicinity of what is now northern Albania.

15:19d I have completed A number of possible senses are suggested for πεπληρωκέναι 'to have fulfilled': (1) thoroughly preached, (2) caused it to be thoroughly effective in the lives of its hearers, (3) completed all the preaching needed before the return of Christ, or (4) completed laying the foundation of the churches in this area. The first three of these are very unlikely as claims by Paul. In the context of what immediately follows, the fourth interpretation is clearly the best; that is, the sense of 'completed' is much more in focus than the concept of 'thoroughly'. This interpretation has the most support from commentators (see JBP, NEB, Best, and C. B. Williams).

my work of preaching All four of these interpretations of 'to have fulfilled' require the verb 'preach' or its equivalent to be supplied. To go along with interpretation 4, 'my work of preaching' is supplied to avoid the meaning that Paul considered no more preaching by others was needed in this area. NCV makes it quite clear: "And so I have finished that part of my work."

the good news about Christ For τὸ εὐαγγέλιον τοῦ Χριστοῦ 'the gospel of Christ', see the note on 1:9.

15:20a As *I preach the good news,* **I am always eagerly striving** Many English versions start a new sentence here even though φιλοτιμούμενον 'eagerly striving' is a present participle, which suggests that it relates to the preceding clause. It is taken as expressing an action simultaneous with the action in 19d; that is, it is an action that accompanied the completion of Paul's work of preaching in these areas. The introductory δέ 'but' is taken as introducing a contrast with 19d, the subject pronoun 'I' being assumed to be repeated from the verb in 19d. Thus, Paul feels, he has been able to complete his work of preaching in these areas, but the work God specifically assigned to him was to preach in unreached areas. The word οὕτως 'thus' is taken as a pro-form representing 19c–d, summarized in the display by 'As I preach the good news'.

in places where people have not already heard about Christ The Greek is οὐχ ὅπου ὠνομάσθη Χριστός 'not where was named Christ'. The phrase 'in places' is supplied here simply to provide an antecedent noun for the relative 'where' (cf. TEV, NEB). The verb 'named' means 'known' (BAGD, p. 574.3). In the display, the reason for Christ's name not being known is substituted for 'named', namely that people had not heard about him (cf. TEV, LB, JB). It could thus be considered a metonymy, the effect standing for the cause.

15:20b–c in order that *as I work for God* I might not simply *be continuing the work for God that someone else had already started*, *like a man who* builds *a house* on a foundation *laid by someone else* The clause ἵνα μὴ ἐπ' ἀλλότριον θεμέλιον οἰκοδομῶ 'lest on another's foundation I build' is a live metaphor; its meaning is fully spelled out in the display. Building on a foundation is the image; continuing the work someone else has started is the topic. CEV changes the metaphor to a simile: "I am like a builder." The words 'for God' specify what type of work is meant.

15:21a *I do* The words 'I do' are to summarize 20a. In some cases it might be expressed as 'my way of working' or 'what I have done'.

is in accord with what is written See the note on 15:9c. Among the English versions only LB is clear here: "I have been following the plan spoken of in the Scriptures."

in Scripture The location Paul's readers understood by 'it is written' is supplied.

about the Messiah This phrase supplies the referent of 'him' in the quotation from Isa. 52:15 which follows.

15:21b will perceive *his truth*, ... *will hear and understand his message* The Greek is ὄψονται καὶ ... συνήσουσιν 'will see and understand', but case considerations require some object to be supplied for each of these verbs. The words supplied here are made as generic as possible: 'his truth' and 'his message'.

The verb 'see' is figurative here; it refers to mental perception, not perception with the eyes. The verb 'hear' is supplied to fit the context, in which Paul talks about people hearing about Christ from his preaching. It is the implicit intervening action: hearing precedes understanding.

These two lines from Isa. 52:15 are considered by Moore (p. 42) to be a figurative doublet involving rhetorical parallelism. Both are retained since this is a poetic passage.

BOUNDARIES AND COHERENCE

The 15:17–21 paragraph further describes Paul's work among the Gentiles. It is at the same time an explanation of why he has not come to see them. Lexical coherence is provided by a number of first person pronouns and references by Paul to his work: κατειργάσατο Χριστὸς δι' ἐμοῦ 'Christ worked out through me', ἔργῳ 'work', φιλοτιμούμενον 'eagerly striving', and οἰκοδομῶ 'I would build'.

The boundary with the following paragraph is marked by διό 'therefore' in v. 22, which introduces a new topic, Paul's intended visit to Rome.

PROMINENCE AND THEME

The 15:17–21 theme is drawn from the 17b RESULT proposition stating Paul's REACTION and from 19d, the first MEANS proposition in the RESULT part of the *situation*. The locative construction in the second MEANS (20a) is also included because Paul develops this idea in vv. 20–21 and defends it with a Scripture quotation; furthermore, it is necessary to understand this aspect of the *situation* in order for Paul's argument in v. 22 about being hindered from visiting Rome to make sense.

SUBPART CONSTITUENT 15:22-29
(Descriptive Paragraph: Declaration based on 15:17-21 and basis for 15:30-33)

THEME: Because of this work, I have often been hindered from visiting you, but I hope to see you as I journey through your area and I hope that you will give me what I need for my next journey. But now I am about to go to Jerusalem to take funds to God's people there. So later I shall visit you in Rome and I know that Christ will bless us there.

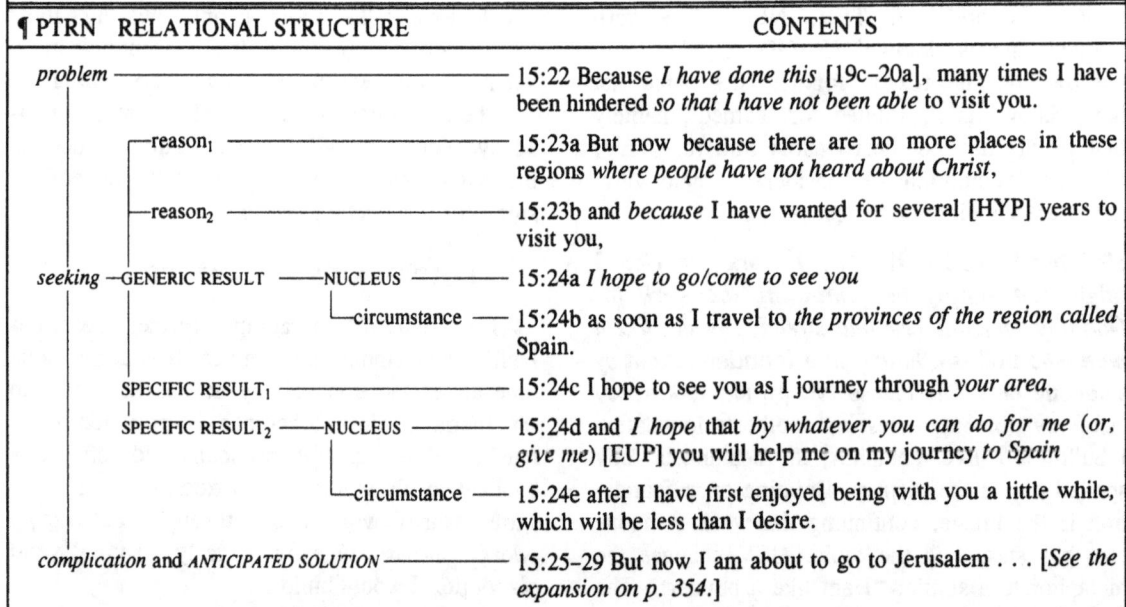

INTENT AND PARAGRAPH PATTERN

The 15:22-29 paragraph is considered to be of the solutionality type because the first fully inflected verb, ἐνεκοπτόμην 'I was hindered', in v. 22, states a *problem*: Paul has not, as he had hoped, been able to visit Rome before this time. The paragraph is considered to be descriptive rather than narrative since its sequencing is future. The use of 'desire/longing' (23b) and 'I hope' (24c) also indicates its emotive nature. Verses 23-24 have to do with seeking a solution to the problem. The ANTICIPATED SOLUTION is that he will see them on his way to Spain. The fact that first he plans to go to Jerusalem (with its uncertainties) is a *complication*.

NOTES

15:22 Because *I have done this* This rendering is an attempt to convey some of the semantic content of the initial διό 'wherefore'. More specifically, it is 'because I have attempted to preach about Christ in places where they had not heard about him'.

many times Although a few have suggested that the phrase τὰ πολλά 'the many' means 'in many ways' or 'for the most part', the best evidence from lexicons and commentaries is that it is somewhat idiomatic and means 'often, frequently, regularly'.

I have been hindered *so that I have not been able* to visit you The Greek is ἐνεκοπτόμην τοῦ ἐλθεῖν πρὸς ὑμᾶς 'I was hindered of coming to you'. Idiomatic English would be 'hindered from coming', but from the point of view of semantic theory the sense is 'hindered with the result that I could not come'.

15:23a because there are no more places in these regions *where people have not heard about Christ* The Greek is μηκέτι τόπον ἔχων ἐν τοῖς κλίμασι τούτοις 'no longer having place in these regions'. The meaning of τόπος is problematic. BAGD (p. 822.1c) give the basic meaning as "place, position, region," but in this passage "opportunity (to do the work of an apostle)" (p. 823.2c). Quite a few versions and commentators choose this sense. Some other versions render it as "no further work," which partially conveys the sense, though it is clearly not the meaning of the Greek word. What Paul means is clear from the context; it's not that there was no room for him there or no opportunities to preach.

(CEV's "there is nothing left for me to do in this part of the world" is definitely misleading.) Rather, as Hodge says, he means "having no longer a place in these parts where Christ is not known." The italicized words in the display convey this and are needed to avoid wrong meaning. An alternative would be the more generic "now that I have finished my work in these regions," as TEV has it.

15:23b for several years There is a textual problem here as to whether the word for 'several' is ἱκανῶν or πολλῶν, but both have the same sense. These Greek words literally mean 'many', which is a hyperbole. In English 'several' is more correct.

15:24a *I hope to go/come to see you* This clause is not explicit in the Greek, but all English versions supply either this or something very similar. It is made specific by 24c.

15:24b as soon as The words ὡς ἄν introduce an event which it is anticipated will immediately precede the one just referred to: the start of Paul's travel to Spain will immediately precede his going to Rome. BAGD give 'when, as soon as' for ὡς ἄν here (p. 898.IV1ca). To avoid confusion as to the sequence of events, it may be necessary in some languages to render the clause as 'when I travel' or 'while I am traveling'.

the provinces of the region called **Spain** Some term of geographic classification is needed; 'provinces' is supplied since by the time of Paul Spain consisted of three provinces. The words 'the region called' are included because otherwise the modern reader would probably conclude that Spain was a country, whereas Spain was not classified as a country in those days as it is now.

15:24c as I journey through *your area* The present participle διαπορευόμενος 'journeying through' expresses simultaneous action. Case considerations require specification of a location to complete 'through'.

15:24d *I hope* that *by whatever you can do for me (or, give me) you will help me on my journey* The verb προπέμπω means "help on one's journey with food, money, by arranging for companions, means of travel, etc." (BAGD, p. 709.2). What Paul meant by this euphemistic expression is made clear in 24d, and without this being supplied the meaning may not be clear to the reader. The translator should carefully consider both the cultural attitude toward solicitation of financial support and the receptor audience's understanding of Paul's intention before translating the verse. REB makes it clear by including the words "with your support."

15:24e after When used with the subjunctive, the conjunction ἐάν ordinarily means 'if'. Here it seems clearly to have the sense 'after', although grammars and lexicons provide no support for this.

I have first enjoyed being with you a little while, which will be less than I desire The expression ἐὰν ὑμῶν πρῶτον ἀπὸ μέρους ἐμπλησθῶ is difficult. Literally, it seems to mean 'if of you first in part I may be filled'. The verb ἐμπί(μ)πλημι means 'to enjoy someone's company' in this context (BAGD, p. 256.3). The difficulty is in regard to the sense of 'in part'. Some commentators and most versions take it as meaning 'a little while'; a few other versions and most commentators take it as meaning 'partially'. But, in fact, it means both here: the basic meaning is 'partial satisfaction', but the implied reason for the partial satisfaction is that Paul is not going to be able to stay as long as he would like. As Murray says, "he is again courteously reminding his readers that he will not be able to enjoy the full measure of satisfaction because his visit will only be a passing one." The partial satisfaction is thus 'less than I desire'.

EXPANSION OF vv. 25-29 IN THE 15:22-29 DISPLAY

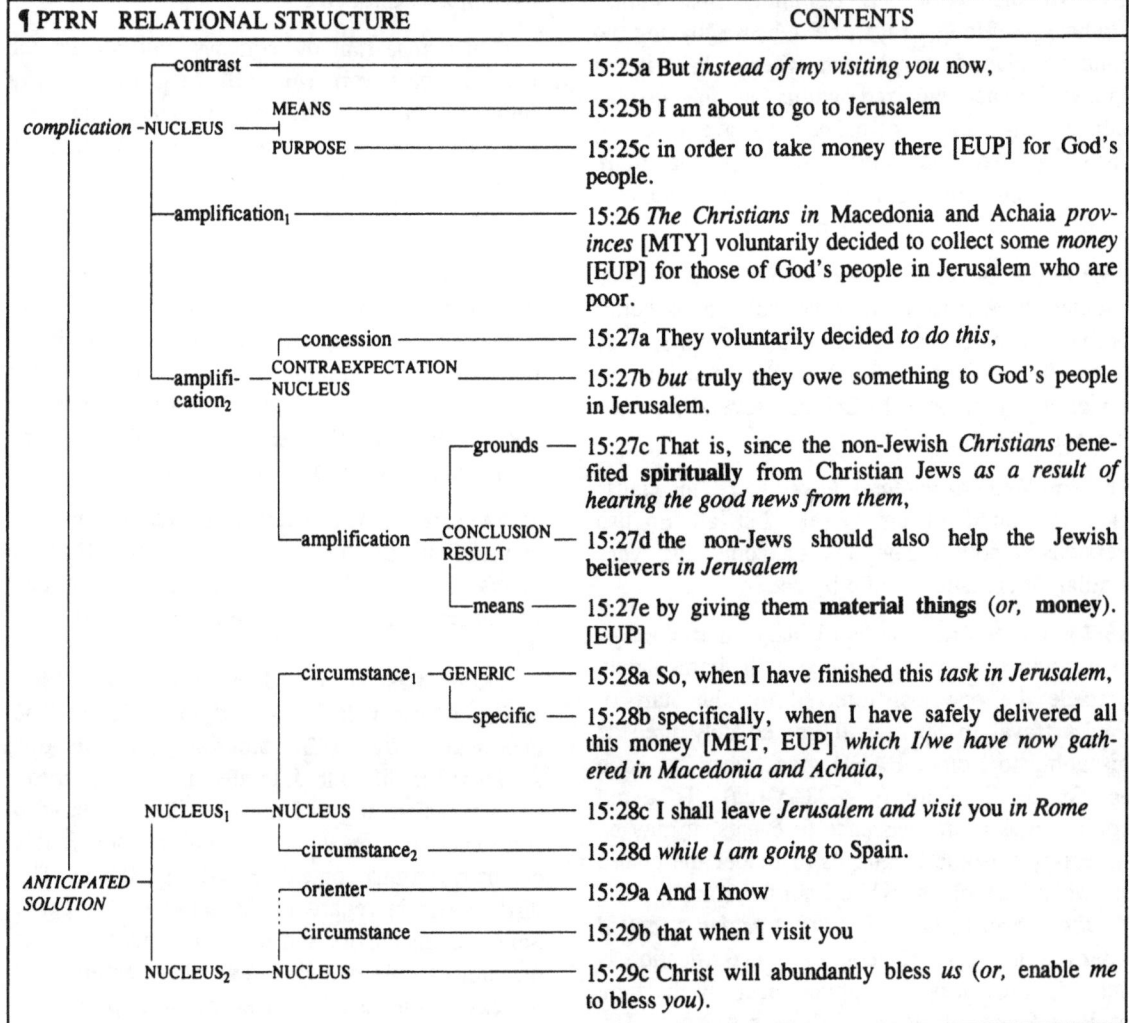

15:25a But Here δέ introduces a contrast; the v. 25 statement about going to Jerusalem contrasts with the v. 24 mention of going to Spain (so Shedd, Cranfield, Sanday and Headlam).

instead of my visiting you **now** The implicit words about Paul's not immediately visiting them explain the contrast between v. 24 and v. 25 and makes the sequence of events clearer. Shedd has "But now I am (not going to Spain but) going to Jerusalem." LB has "But before I come," which is a good alternative to the rendering in the display.

15:25b I am about to go The present tense of πορεύομαι 'I am going' indicates the imminence of the action.

15:25c to take money there The participle διακονῶν 'ministering' is a typical Pauline euphemism; it refers to collecting and distributing a financial offering. "The participle is usually taken as expressing purpose" (Dunn). JB spells out the euphemism with "I must take a present of money to."

God's people This is the usual rendering of οἱ ἅγιοι 'the saints'. JBP's "the poor Christians" is excellent, but the fact of their being poor is specified in v. 26.

15:26 *The Christians in* **Macedonia and Achaia** *provinces* The place names here are metonymies, the place standing for the people who live there, more specifically the believers there. This is spelled out in the display. TEV and JBP have "the churches in"; NCV, "the believers in"; and CEV, "the Lord's followers in." The geographical term 'provinces' is supplied to provide information Paul's readers would know.

voluntarily decided The verb εὐδόκησαν could mean either 'they determined to' or 'they were delighted to'. Both senses fit the context; but as several commentators point out, the main thought seems to be that the Christians' decision to take a collection was voluntary. The sense would also be captured by 'quite readily'. TEV has "freely decided."

to collect some *money* The Greek is κοινωνίαν τινὰ ποιήσασθαι 'to make some (proof of) fellowship', which is somewhat euphemistic. All the versions render it noneuphemistically with terms such as "offering," "contribution," or "money."

for those of God's people . . . who are poor The phrase εἰς τοὺς πτωχοὺς τῶν ἁγίων 'for the poor of the saints' makes it clear that not all the believers in Jerusalem were poor.

15:27a They voluntarily decided *to do this* This is the same verb as in 26a and is here rendered the same; thus γάρ is taken as introducing an amplification of the subject of the contribution, not a reason for it. The pronoun 'they' refers to the believers in the two provinces. The words 'to do this' are supplied as the generic content completing the verb 'decided'; 'this' refers to collecting and sending an offering.

15:27b *but* **truly** Many commentators point out that καί is emphatic here; in many versions it is translated 'and indeed'. The sense of the proposition shows that it is a CONTRAEXPECTATION rather than additive, hence 'but' in the display. TEV's "But, as a matter of fact" is excellent.

they owe something to God's people in Jerusalem This rendering resolves the mismatch in ὀφειλέται εἰσὶν αὐτῶν 'debtors they are of them'. The referent of the indirect object pronoun 'of them' is specified for clarity's sake. (The referent of the subject pronoun 'they' is the believers in Macedonia and Achaia.)

15:27c That is, since Propositions 27c-e do not give the reason for the obligation stated in 27b, but an amplification of it. The grounds for 27d are given in c, introduced by εἰ, literally 'if'.

the non-Jewish *Christians* **benefited spiritually from Christian Jews** The Greek is τοῖς πνευματικοῖς αὐτῶν ἐκοινώνησαν τὰ ἔθνη 'in their spiritual things shared the Gentiles'. In the display the referent of 'their' is specified, and the fact that both groups being referred to are believers is also made clear. The verb 'shared' in this context means to receive a portion of what someone else already has. Since it refers to spiritual things here, not physical, it is rendered 'benefited spiritually'. An alternative is to use the reciprocal of 'benefited from' as in the NRSV: "the Jewish Christians shared their spiritual treasures with the Gentiles." In the Greek the phrase 'in spiritual things' occurs before the verb and is thereby prominent, hence the bold type in the display.

as a result of hearing the good news from them These supplied words specify in what way the Gentiles shared in what the Jewish believers had. Morris says that "there is no doubting that Paul means the gospel above everything else," and other commentators agree. LB has "Because the news about Christ came to these Gentiles from the church in Jerusalem."

15:27d-e the non-Jews should also help the Jewish believers *in Jerusalem* **by giving them material things** (*or,* **money**) The Greek is ὀφείλουσιν καὶ ἐν τοῖς σαρκικοῖς λειτουργῆσαι αὐτοῖς 'they ought also in the fleshly things to minister to them'. The conjunction καί here can be taken as 'also' or 'in a similar way'. Both referents of the third person plural pronouns are specified. The euphemistic 'minister' is made clear with 'giving'. The word σαρκικός means "belonging to the order of earthly things, material" (BAGD, p. 742.1); REB has "contribute to their material needs." In languages that have no idiomatic expression for 'material things' such as 'the things of the body', the word 'money' may do, since that was exactly what was involved here. CEV has "sharing their money with."

The phrase 'material things' occurs before the verb in Greek and is thereby prominent, hence the bold type in the display.

15:28a this *task in Jerusalem* The words in italics specify the referent of the demonstrative pronoun τοῦτο 'this'.

15:28b when I have safely delivered all this money *which I/we have gathered in Macedonia and Achaia* The words καὶ σφραγισάμενος αὐτοῖς τὸν καρπὸν τοῦτον 'and having sealed to them this fruit' are euphemistic as well as metaphorical. The image is 'fruit', signifying the financial gift. To seal something is, generally, to guarantee it. But as Morris says, "the meaning of 'sealing' in this context remains doubtful." According to the various commentators, it could mean (1) 'to guarantee that they have received it', or (2) 'guarantee that the full amount is there', or (3) 'guarantee that it has all been done properly', or even (4) 'to seal the end of his work in Asia Minor'. This last badly strains the sense of 'guarantee' and is the least likely. Of the other three, it is very hard to say exactly which if any Paul had in mind. The display follows Hodge, JBP, REB, and a number of lesser-known English versions in suggesting that the figure is something of an idiom drawn from commerce and refers to safe delivery.

15:28c–d I shall leave *Jerusalem and visit* you *in Rome while I am going* to Spain A fair amount of semantic material is condensed in ἀπελεύσομαι δι' ὑμῶν εἰς Σπανίαν 'I will go away through you unto Spain'. The verb 'go away' refers to leaving Jerusalem, and 'through you' means visiting at Rome on the way to Spain. See the note on 24b concerning Spain.

15:29c Christ will abundantly bless *us* (*or*, enable *me* to bless *you*) The Greek is πληρώματι εὐλογίας Χριστοῦ 'in the fulness of the blessing of Christ'. Semantically, 'fulness' modifies the event expressed by the noun 'blessing'. Commentators are agreed that the genitive 'of Christ' indicates source, hence 'the blessing which Christ produces'. But there is a real question as to the relation between Paul's coming and the blessing. It could mean 'Christ will enable me to bless you' (so LB), or 'Christ will enable us to bless each other', or 'Christ will bless us all', or 'Christ will bless me'. The latter is the least likely, and there is perhaps not much difference between the second and third options. In the display the equally valid first and third alternatives are both given. A translation that preserves the ambiguity is preferable, for example, 'bringing an abundant blessing from Christ'.

In the manuscripts followed by the Textus Receptus are two additional words, translated by the KJV as "of the blessing of the gospel of Christ." Based on the principle that the shorter text is more likely to be the original, and since there is no apparent reason why the words would have been omitted if they had been in the original, the GNT adopts the shorter text. In fact, it has an A rating ("certain") in the fourth edition. This is the basis for the rendering in the display.

BOUNDARIES AND COHERENCE

In the 15:22–29 paragraph Paul states his plans to visit Rome soon, but to visit Jerusalem first. Again it is full of first person singular pronominal references. The words ἐλθεῖν πρὸς ὑμᾶς 'to come to you' in v. 22 and ἐρχόμενος πρὸς ὑμᾶς 'coming to you' in v. 29 form a rhetorical bracket around the unit. The references to his proposed visit provide further coherence. There are references to going to see them in vv. 22, 23, 24, and twice in v. 29.

The beginning of the next paragraph is marked in v. 30 by a vocative and an *APPEAL* introduced with παρακαλῶ ὑμᾶς 'I beseech you'. Thus in v. 30 there is a switch to the hortatory mode.

PROMINENCE AND THEME

The 15:22–29 theme is drawn from the v. 22 *problem* and the two SPECIFIC statements in 24c–d, the thematic MEANS and PURPOSE propositions of the 25b–c *complication*, and the two NUCLEI of the *ANTICIPATED SOLUTION* in vv. 28–29.

SUBPART CONSTITUENT 15:30–33
(Hortatory Paragraph: Appeal of 15:14–33)

THEME: I urge you to pray fervently that God will protect me from the unbelieving Jews in Judea and that God's people there will accept the money I take to them and that I may be refreshed by visiting you. May God be with you all.

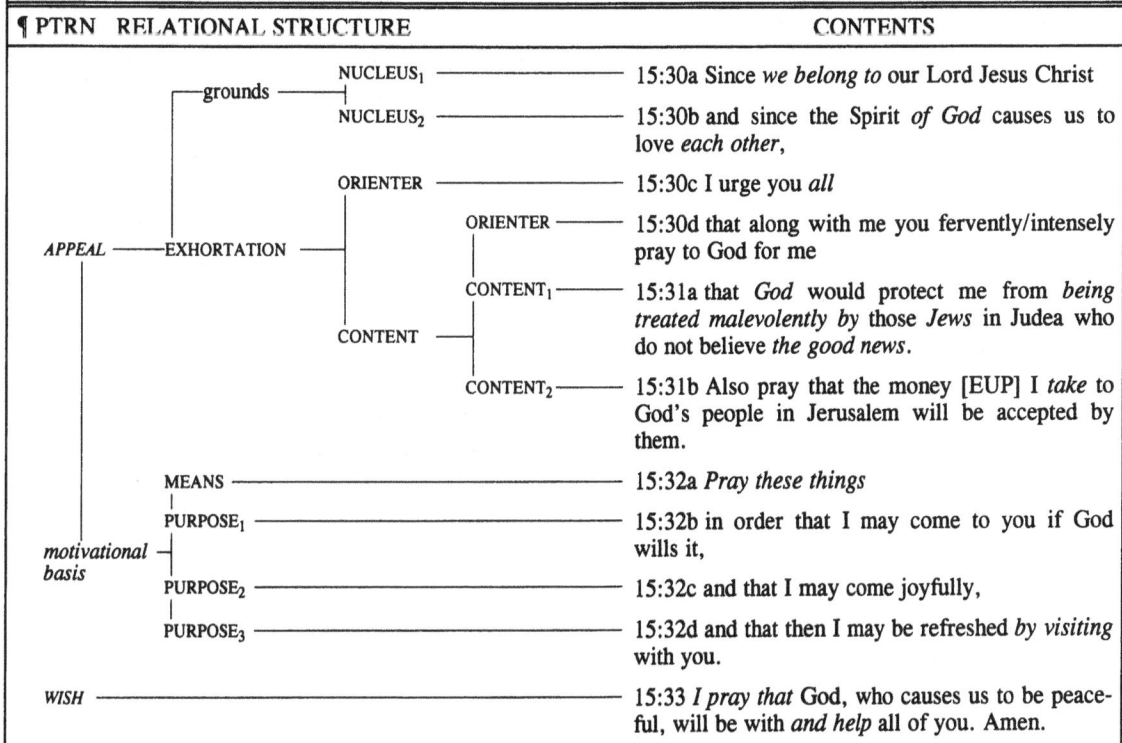

INTENT AND PARAGRAPH PATTERN

The 15:30–33 paragraph begins with παρακαλῶ ὑμᾶς 'I urge you' followed by the infinitive phrase expressing the content of Paul's APPEAL. Thus this is a hortatory paragraph. The APPEAL is supported by a *motivational basis* in v. 32, expressing what Paul hopes will be the outcome of the readers' prayers. The paragraph ends with a WISH or prayer for God's blessing on the Roman believers.

Theoretically, since the v. 33 WISH is expressive, it is a different genre from vv. 30–32 and therefore should be a paragraph on its own. However, it is included in the 30–33 paragraph for two reasons, the first being simply because of its brevity. The second is that one can well argue that there is a close relationship between Paul's request for prayer in vv. 30–32 and his own prayer in v. 33. The former can be seen as the *situation* that calls for his prayer as a REACTION, or v. 33 could be taken as another *motivational basis* for the v. 31 APPEAL. (Hodge says, "As he begged them to pray for him, so he prays for them.")

NOTES

15:30a Since *we belong to* our Lord Jesus Christ The preposition διά followed by a genitive form usually means 'by means of'; but when the genitive is a person's name, it does not cohere semantically to take it in an instrumental sense. A number of commentators suggest the generic sense 'out of concern/regard for', hence 'for the sake of' (as in JBP, LB; NCV has "because of"). The other possible interpretation is 'by the authority of' (CEV has "by the power of"), but that hardly seems an appropriate grounds of asking them to pray for him. Newman and Nida say that perhaps the most satisfactory rendering is "because of our faith in"; Barnes suggests "out of love and regard to"; Dunn thinks that it points to Paul's belief that the coming trip was at Christ's direction and also to the fact of their common experience of Christ's lordship. A good alternative might be 'because of all that the Lord Jesus Christ means to you(pl) and me'.

15:30b since the Spirit *of God* causes us to love *each other* The prepositional phrase διὰ τῆς ἀγάπης τοῦ πνεύματος 'through the love of the Spirit' is grammatically coordinate with the preceding prepositional phrase (30a), but it does not necessarily have the same semantic function, even though both are introduced by διά. The one here in 30b could refer either to the love which the Spirit has for all believers or the love which the Spirit engenders among believers for one another. The latter suits the context—Paul is appealing to their mutual love as a basis for their prayers for him. (This interpretation is supported by nearly all commentators.)

The words 'of God' are supplied following 'the Spirit' to avoid any ambiguity.

15:30d along with me you fervently/intensely pray 'With me' in συναγωνίσασθαί μοι ἐν ταῖς προσευχαῖς 'strive/agonize with me in prayers' means that Paul is already praying intensely and he asks them to join in this prayer struggle. The words 'agonize in prayers' are a figure from wrestling that emphasizes the intensity with which they are asked to pray. Semantically, 'agonize' modifies the event of praying. TEV has "praying fervently." (The Col. 4:12 note on 'agonizing' in John Callow's SSA of Colossians is helpful.)

15:31a that *God* would protect me from *being treated malevolently by* The Greek is ἵνα ῥυσθῶ ἀπό 'that I may be delivered from'. As Morris notes, "Paul is asking that he not fall into the hands of his opponents, not that he may be rescued after they have taken him." This 'deliver from' implies some event of which his enemies in Judea are the agents, an event which 'fall into the hands of' expresses in an idiomatic way. The display supplies 'being treated malevolently by', which is generic enough to cover all contingencies.

those *Jews* in Judea who do not believe *the good news* The phrase τῶν ἀπειθούντων ἐν τῇ Ἰουδαίᾳ 'the disobeying ones in Judea' does not specify the group Paul was referring to, but commentators state unanimously that he was referring to Jews (e.g., Morris, Denney, Cranfield, Dunn). This is supplied in the display to avoid wrong meaning. The primary sense of the verb is 'disobey', but versions all support BAGD (p. 82.3) in saying the meaning here is 'unbelievers'. When this word is changed to a verb, case considerations require that an object be supplied, hence 'the gospel' or, alternatively, 'in Christ'.

15:31b the money I *take* to . . . Jerusalem The expression ἡ διακονία μου ἡ εἰς Ἰερουσαλήμ 'my ministry unto Jerusalem' is euphemistic; Paul is referring to taking funds there. JB has "the aid I carry to Jerusalem." JBP is similar. LB has "the money I am bringing them." Jerusalem could be taken as a metonymy here, standing for the believers in Jerusalem.

Some manuscripts have the more specific δωροφορία 'gift', which occurs nowhere else in the NT, while others have διακονία. It may be that to clarify the euphemism expressed by διακονία some copyist replaced it with δωροφορία, but the manuscript evidence for δωροφορία is not strong. The fourth edition of the GNT has διακονία with an A rating ("certain").

God's people The Greek is τοῖς ἁγίοις 'the saints', meaning the believers who live in Jerusalem, as made clear in the display.

will be accepted by them The wording here is εὐπρόσδεκτος τοῖς ἁγίοις γένηται 'may be acceptable to the saints'. It is difficult to know why Paul thought the gift might not be accepted. The most cogent possible reason is that the Jewish believers might have been unhappy with the concept of freedom from the Mosaic law that Paul preached among the Gentiles and thus were not on very good terms with him. They may also have felt unhappy about accepting help from Gentiles. But this information is not considered essential to the understanding of the text and is not included in the display.

15:32b if God wills it The Greek is διὰ θελήματος θεοῦ 'through the will of God'. The noun 'will' is rendered as a verb because it expresses a cognitive event. This requires an appropriate relation to be given between this proposition and the preceding one, and it is a conditional relation that coheres best. However, in translating it needs to be made clear that what Paul is somewhat uncertain about is not his being joyful but his coming to them.

15:32d and that then I may be refreshed *by visiting* with you The Greek is συναναπαύσωμαι ὑμῖν 'I may find rest with you'. English versions are unanimous in translating this as a clause joined to 32c by 'and'. In the display 'and' makes it clear that there are in 32b-d three distinct goals to be accomplished by the Roman believers' prayers. But since 'and' does not unambiguously signal a temporal relationship and in 32b the Greek has an aorist participle, ἐλθών 'coming', which expresses a temporal relationship, 'then' is used here in addition to 'and' to signal this temporality.

Commentators are unanimous in saying that it was not physical rest that Paul had in mind, but refreshment of spirit by their fellowship together. The phrase 'with you' means 'in your presence' or 'among you', but the wording in the display makes it clear that Paul's hope was to be refreshed *by* them, not independently of them. CEV renders this as "and have a pleasant and refreshing visit."

There are many textual variants in the latter part of this verse. Some of them have 'will of Jesus Christ' or 'will of Christ Jesus', but Paul never uses such expressions elsewhere. In one variant the words 'find rest with you' are omitted, but this appears to have been an accidental omission. Other variants seem to have been the result of a desire to simplify the syntax or provide a more specific word for 'be refreshed'. The GNT gives an A rating ("certain") to συναναπαύσωμαι ὑμῖν, and there is no good reason to reject it.

15:33 *I pray that* This verse in effect expresses a hope or prayer by Paul (cf. 15:13). As in the display here, CEV has "I pray that."

God, who causes us to be peaceful In the phrase ὁ θεὸς τῆς εἰρήνης 'the God of peace', the genitive is taken as expressing source. TEV has "God, our source of peace." In the display the article before 'God' is omitted and the genitive rendered as a relative clause of description, not of identification. Retaining the article would give the sense that there were other gods, ones who do not cause us to be peaceful.

The sense of 'peace' is the same as in 15:13 (see the note there).

be with *and help* all of you In the Scriptures, when God is spoken of as being with someone, the sense is that he is with the individual to aid him (e.g., 1 Sam. 17:37). Paul is not suggesting that God is not always present.

Amen A few manuscripts omit this word. Although it is true that it could have been added by some copyists as appropriate after Paul's benedictory prayer, it also could have been omitted by copyists who thought it was not appropriate to have this word both here and at the end of the epistle. However, its inclusion in the fourth edition GNT is with an A rating ("certain").

BOUNDARIES AND COHERENCE

The 15:30–33 paragraph is relationally coherent in that it contains the APPEAL to pray, a *motivational basis*, and a concluding WISH. Coherence is also provided by the words that have to do with prayer (ἐν ταῖς προσευχαῖς 'in the prayers') as well as the contents and purposes of the prayers. The close of the unit is clearly marked in v. 33 with a benediction and the closing 'amen'. This closing benediction and 'amen' are a transition between the 15:14–33 subpart and the personal APPEALS that begin in 16:1.

PROMINENCE AND THEME

The theme of 15:30–33 includes the 30c generic ORIENTER 'I urge you' and the 30d specific ORIENTER 'pray fervently', although the former could be eliminated and the theme shortened by omitting "I urge you to." The theme also includes the 31a and 31b CONTENTS of the prayer and the third PURPOSE in the *motivational basis* (32d). (The PURPOSE in 32b is probably implied by the one in 32d and therefore need not be explicitly stated in the theme, and the PURPOSE in 32c is considered less thematic.) A condensation of the WISH in v. 33 is also included.

EPISTLE CONSTITUENT 16:1-27
(Hortatory Part: Closing of the epistle)

THEME: Finally, receive and help Phoebe. Greet many individuals among the believers there. Note those who cause quarrels among you and those who cause people to turn away from God, and avoid them. Several of the people here send their greetings. Let us forever praise that One who alone is God and is truly wise.

MACROSTRUCTURE	CONTENTS
SPECIFIC APPEAL	16:1-2 I am introducing and commending Phoebe to you, and I ask that you receive her as a fellow believer and give her whatever she needs.
GREETINGS	16:3-16 Greet many individuals among the believers there. All the congregations in this area greet you.
GENERIC APPEAL	16:17-20 Note those who are causing quarrels among you and those who cause people to turn away from God. Avoid them, since they only want to satisfy their own desires and deceive those who do not suspect their motives. If you avoid such people, God will soon crush Satan under your feet.
declaration of greetings	16:21-23 Several of those who are with me send their greetings.
doxology	16:25-27 Let us forever praise that One who alone is God, who alone is truly wise.

INTENT AND MACROSTRUCTURE

The 16:1-27 unit consists of five paragraphs, the first three of which are hortatory and the last two expressive. These last two are less prominent by virtue of their being expressive. Furthermore, the status of 16:25-27 as Pauline is very much in doubt, a good reason for not letting it influence the classification of the whole unit. Because of the hortatory nature of the first three paragraphs the whole unit is therefore classified as hortatory.

The unit consists of a SPECIFIC APPEAL (1-2) concerning Phoebe, the bearer of the letter; a set of GREETINGS (3-16) to greet a long list of individuals; a GENERIC APPEAL (17-20) to avoid those who cause quarrels among them; a *declaration of greetings* (21-23) being sent by Paul's companions; and a final *doxology* (25-27).

BOUNDARIES AND COHERENCE

In spite of the diversity of its contents, 16:1-27 is considered a unit because all of its constituents are appropriate to the closing of an epistle. Most deal with individuals—a commendation of and request for assistance for Phoebe (1-2), Paul's greetings to named individuals at Rome (3-16), and greetings from named companions of Paul's that he relays to the Roman congregation (21-23). Right before vv. 21-23 there is a closing GENERIC APPEAL dealing with the central theme of the book (17-20). Then finally there is a *doxology* as a benediction (25-27).

PROMINENCE AND THEME

The theme of 16:1-27 is taken from the themes of all the constituent paragraphs. The less prominent parts of each are omitted (i.e., the description of Phoebe and the *bases* of the GENERIC APPEAL). One could argue that the GENERIC APPEAL is the most thematic and that the theme for 16:1-27 should consist of its theme alone, but obviously the request to receive and assist Phoebe as the bearer of the letter is extremely important for the whole epistle, and the fact that Paul greets so many individuals among the recipients seems to be extremely important to Paul's whole purpose (see pp 15-19 in the introduction).

PART CONSTITUENT 16:1-2
(Hortatory Paragraph: Specific appeal of 16:1-27)

THEME: I am introducing and commending Phoebe to you, and I ask that you receive her as a fellow believer and give her whatever she needs.

¶ PTRN	RELATIONAL STRUCTURE	CONTENTS
basis	NUCLEUS	16:1a I am introducing and commending to you our fellow believer Phoebe,
	—description	16:1b who is a deacon in the congregation at Cenchrea *city*.
APPEAL₁	EXHORTATION	16:2a *I ask that* you receive her as *one who belongs to* the Lord,
	—grounds	16:2b since those who are God's people ought to receive *their fellow believers that way*,
APPEAL₂	EXHORTATION	16:2c and that you assist her *by giving her* [EUP] whatever she needs
	—grounds	16:2d since she has helped many *people*, including me.

INTENT AND PARAGRAPH PATTERN

On the surface, the 16:1-2 paragraph consists of a main clause with an indicative verb followed by a set of two purpose clauses. It contains no imperative. But since the paragraph is at the beginning of a long series of low-level APPEALS in which Paul requests that his greetings be passed on to various individuals, and since Paul's purpose in the commendation is that they receive Phoebe appropriately, it is taken as two mitigated APPEALS (v. 2) preceded by their *basis* (v. 1).

NOTES

16:1 This verse is labeled as the *basis* for the v. 2 APPEALS. Paul here introduces and commends Phoebe as the basis for his request that they accept and assist her.

16:1a I am introducing and commending to you The expression συνίστημι ὑμῖν can mean either 'I recommend to you' or 'I introduce to you'. Those are two very different senses in English: either one can be done without the other being done. But clearly Paul is doing both here; therefore both are in the display. Commentators strongly suggest that Phoebe was to be the bearer of the letter; and since she was evidently unknown to the Romans, Paul introduces her and then authenticates his letter as coming from him, at the same time authenticating her as its legitimate bearer, so that she will be well looked after. In some languages it may be necessary to include 'who is taking this letter to you' to make the situational meaning clear. JBP has "I want this letter to introduce to you."

fellow believer Phoebe The feminine ἀδελφή 'sister' is rendered 'fellow believer' in the display just as ἀδελφός 'brother' was in earlier passages. The fact that this believer is a woman is made clear in subsequent propositions by feminine pronouns. In languages without gender-specific pronouns, this fact may have to be expressed by other means.

16:1b a deacon There is much discussion by commentators as to whether διάκονος here means 'deaconess' in the sense of a woman holding a recognized office in the congregation (JB, JBP, RSV) or 'servant' (NIV) or something in between. CEV has "leader"; NEB, "who holds office." It cannot mean simply 'who serves' (TEV) because Paul uses a noun with the present participle οὖσαν 'being', pointing to an official position, not just a habitual activity. It does not mean 'deaconess' in the sense of referring specifically to a woman since this is not a gender-specific noun. Such a Greek word for 'deaconess' did not come into use until much later. Thus, since the word can be used to refer to either a man or a woman (BAGD, p. 184.2b), we conclude that Phoebe was an officially appointed deacon in the church, as NRSV has it.

in the congregation The phrase τῆς ἐκκλησίας 'of the church' is genitive, but the relationship signaled is location, not possession, hence 'in' in the display. The word 'church' is avoided because in English that word most commonly refers to a building.

16:2a *I ask that* Morris deplores the NIV rendering with its insertion of "I ask," but he ignores the fact that nearly all the modern translations begin the verse with a new sentence and an imperative verb, which is in effect the same thing.

The verse starts with ἵνα, which could be taken in its most common sense as expressing purpose. This would fit the context very well, but would mean that "I commend Phoebe to you" was the main theme of the paragraph, whereas it is clear from what follows that the paragraph's main function is to request that they receive and treat her well—an APPEAL. Another way to take ἵνα is as introducing the content of an appeal, which it often does—in this case the words 'I request' would be considered to be implied. The NIV and NCV rendering is based on this, and it is the interpretation followed in the display.

as *one who belongs to* the Lord The Greek has only ἐν κυρίῳ 'in the Lord'. An alternative rendering is 'receive her because of her relationship to the Lord'. Most commentators who attempt to explicate the phrase say that it means "as a fellow Christian" (Bruce 1963). LB has "giving her a warm Christian welcome"; CEV, "who has faith in the Lord."

16:2b since those who are God's people ought to receive *their fellow believers that way* The expression ἀξίως τῶν ἁγίων 'worthily of the saints' is capable of two meanings: 'as the saints ought to be received' or 'as saints ought to receive fellow believers'. As part of an exhortation as to what Paul wants the believers at Rome to do, the latter meaning is far more plausible and is supported by the great majority of commentators (also REB).

16:2c and that you assist her *by giving her whatever she needs* The verb παρίστημι means literally 'to stand by' but here in a somewhat euphemistic way clearly means "come to the aid of, help" (BAGD, p. 628.2αγ). The phrase ἐν ᾧ ἂν ὑμῶν χρῄζῃ πράγματι 'in whatever thing of you she may need' is taken as expressing means. Making it a full clause requires a verb to be supplied; the display follows many English versions in using 'give'. Since the subject of the verb 'stand by' is second person plural, the words 'of you' are redundant, but could be rendered by 'whatever she needs to receive from you' if desired. The word πρᾶγμα is taken by all versions in a generic sense of 'task, thing, matter', but some commentators note that the term can refer specifically to a lawsuit or dispute (as in 1 Cor. 6:1). However, all the other occurrences of the word in the NT have the generic sense, and the specific sense does not seem required here.

16:2d she has helped many *people*, including me There is some disagreement among commentators as to the meaning of the noun in the clause αὐτὴ προστάτις πολλῶν ἐγενήθη καὶ ἐμοῦ αὐτοῦ 'she herself a protectress of many became and of me myself'. The masculine form of the word was well known in the sense of a "wealthy or influential person as patron (and so protector) of Hellenistic religious societies" (Dunn). But Morris and Cranfield say that a woman could not hold a position as legal protector of believers at Cenchrea; they support a more generic sense. Furthermore, to fully spell out the duties of a patron here would distort the focus. However, the use of this term probably does point to Phoebe as being a woman of considerable wealth and influence. It is not certain what type of help she gave believers, but it was very likely financial. Likewise, it is not certain whether she helped only those who were believers. That is quite likely, but knowing that is not essential to the readers. Therefore in the display only 'people' is supplied as the object of the verb.

BOUNDARIES AND COHERENCE

The 16:1-2 unit is considered a separate paragraph from what follows. Semantically, it contains two APPEALS, even though the main verb συνίστημι 'I commend' is indicative and there are no imperatives. The nature of the APPEALS in these two verses is very different from the APPEALS in vv. 3-16. Here there is a request for action on the part of the believers, whereas in vv. 3-16 Paul is using imperatives for no reason other than to ask them to be his agents in giving the greetings that he would give personally if he were there.

PROMINENCE AND THEME

Most of the 16:1-2 theme is taken from the 2a and 2c EXHORTATION propositions of the two APPEALS. Since the 1a *basis* is crucial to the APPEALS and is represented by the only nonsubordinate finite verb in the paragraph, it also is included.

PART CONSTITUENT 16:3–16
(Hortatory Paragraph: Greetings of 16:1–27)

THEME: Greet many individuals among the believers there. All the congregations in this area greet you.

¶ PTRN	RELATIONAL STRUCTURE	CONTENTS
APPEAL$_1$	—'Priscilla, Aquila'	16:3a Greet Priscilla and *her husband* Aquila.
	└─description ─REASON─ NUCLEUS$_1$	16:3b They worked with me for Christ Jesus,
	NUCLEUS$_2$	16:4a and in order *to save* my life they exposed themselves [SYN] to great danger.
	RESULT NUCLEUS$_1$	16:4b It is not only I who thank them *for helping me*,
	NUCLEUS$_2$	16:4c but all [HYP] the non-Jewish congregations also *thank them for saving my life*.
APPEAL$_2$		16:5a *Greet* also the congregation *that meets* in their house.
APPEAL$_3$	—'Epaenetus'	16:5b Greet Epaenetus whom I love,
	└─description	16:5c who is the first man in *the province of* Asia who *believed* in Christ.
APPEAL$_4$	—'Mary'	16:6a Greet Mary,
	└─description	16:6b who has worked hard *for Christ* in order to *help you*.
APPEAL$_5$	—'Andronicus, Junia'	16:7a Greet Andronicus and Junia(f),
	├─description$_1$	16:7b who are my fellow Jews
	├─description$_2$	16:7c and who were also *previously* in prison with me.
	├─description$_3$	16:7d They are prominent/respected apostles,
	└─description$_4$	16:7e and they became Christians before I did.
APPEAL$_6$	—'Ampliatus'	16:8a Greet Ampliatus,
	└─description	16:8b whom I love *as one who belongs to* the Lord.
APPEAL$_7$	—'Urbanus'	16:9a Greet Urbanus,
	└─description	16:9b who works for Christ with us,
APPEAL$_8$		16:9c and *greet* Stachys whom I love.
APPEAL$_9$	—'Apelles'	16:10a Greet Apelles,
	└─description	16:10b whose *faith* in Christ *has continued after* it was tested.
APPEAL$_{10}$		16:10c Greet the *believers* who *live in the house* of Aristobulus.
APPEAL$_{11}$	—'Herodion'	16:11a Greet Herodion,
	└─description	16:11b who is my fellow Jew.
APPEAL$_{12}$	—'those'	16:11c Greet those who *live in the house* of Narcissus
	└─identification	16:11d who belong to the Lord.
APPEAL$_{13}$	—'Tryphaena, Tryphosa'	16:12a Greet Tryphaena and *her sister* Tryphosa,
	└─description	16:12b who work hard for the Lord.
APPEAL$_{14}$	—'Persis'	16:12c Greet Persis(f), whom *we* love,
	└─description	16:12d who has worked very hard for the Lord.

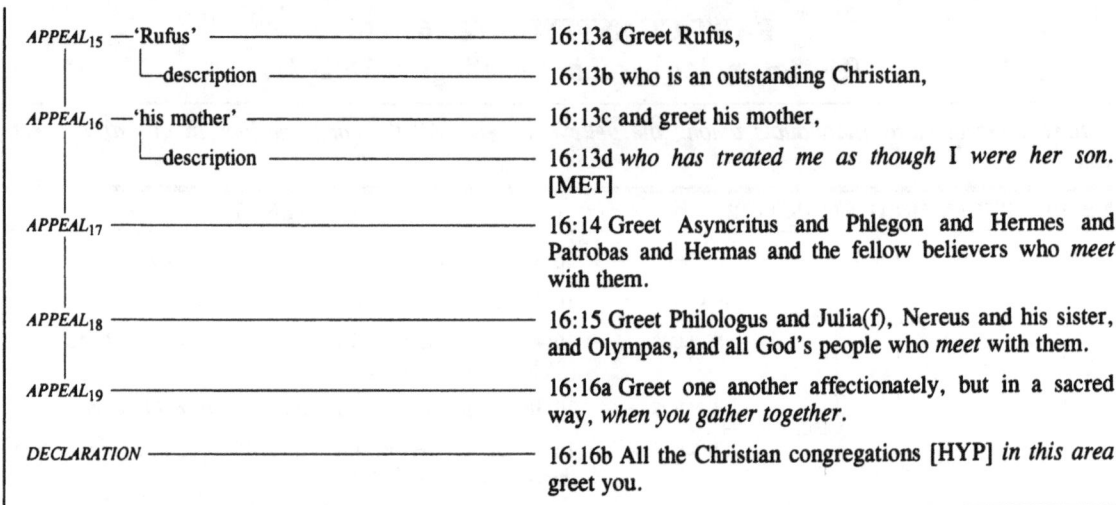

INTENT AND PARAGRAPH PATTERN

The 16:3-16 unit is hortatory as shown by the many occurrences of the imperative ἀσπάσασθε 'greet'. There are nineteen APPEALS, none of them supported by a *basis*. Proposition 16b represents a clause in which the verb is indicative; but since it is the same verb as the imperative 'greet' in the preceding APPEALS, it is included in this paragraph and called a DECLARATION.

The paragraph also is rapport-building. It is astounding that Paul can speak this knowledgeably of so many of the congregation at Rome where he had not yet visited. The unit could even be considered expressive in that it states Paul's feelings of oneness with, and interest in, these individuals. In fact, in some languages it may be unnatural to retain the imperatives. It is hortatory only because Paul cannot do personally what he asks them to do in his place.

NOTES

16:3-16 Greet The only difficulty with the verb ἀσπάζομαι 'greet' is how to translate it when it refers to greeting people in correspondence, not to greeting them in person. "Give my greetings to" (NCV, CEV, REB) may be better than "Greet." Inasmuch as Louw and Nida give the sense as "to employ certain set phrases as a part of the process of greeting," the appropriate greetings of the receptor culture may be used in translation. The following, for example, may capture the sense: 'tell them I am saying __ to them' or perhaps 'tell them I am thinking about them'.

16:3-4 It is very difficult to decide on the relational labels here. On the surface, it seems that 3b and 4a are descriptions and 4b and 4c are comments about them. Note, however, that there is a strong expressive component in v. 4 right along with the description, reason, and result ideas. The main focus here is not Paul's saying that they are the kind of people whom he and all the churches should give thanks for so much as actually taking this opportunity to thank them. It might be best to label 4b-c as EXPRESSIVE RESULT.

16:3a Priscilla The GNT has Πρίσκα here, the proper form of the name Priscilla, which is a diminutive. The Textus Receptus has 'Priscilla' here, as used by Luke in Acts, but it has very weak manuscript support. The translator would do well to use one form of the word in all references to this woman to avoid confusion or wrong meaning.

and *her husband* Aquila The display makes clear that Priscilla and Aquila were wife and husband, which obviously Paul would not have had to say. In four of the six times the two are mentioned in Scripture, her name occurs first, contrary to custom. Commentators speculate that either she was of a higher social status or that she was "more distinguished in Christian character and service" (Denney). Since such a connotation is uncertain, the translator is not at liberty to specify it. But the word order, which hints at it, should be retained if at all possible.

16:3b They worked with me for Christ Jesus The noun 'fellow workers' in the phrase τοὺς συνεργούς μου ἐν Χριστῷ Ἰησοῦ 'my fellow workers in Christ Jesus' could mean that they had the same occupation as Paul (see Acts 18:3), but the same word is used in vv. 9 and 21 in regard to others who did not have the same occupation, suggesting that Paul is referring here to his evangelistic ministry. The phrase 'in Christ Jesus' specifies the Christian nature of the work Paul is referring to. The display follows JBP in using the preposition 'for'.

16:4a *to save* **my life, they exposed themselves to great danger** The Greek is ὅιτινες ὑπὲρ τῆς ψυχῆς μου τὸν ἑαυτῶν τράχηλον ὑπέθηκαν 'who on behalf of my life risked their own necks'. This expression has been adopted into the English language. The display follows commentators such as Barnes, Hodge, and Lenski in avoiding the figure of speech and spelling out the meaning of 'risk'. Neck is considered a synecdoche, the part standing for the whole person (hence 'themselves' in the display), or the whole phrase could be considered a metaphor. In Greek 'for my life' occurs at the beginning of the clause and is thereby prominent. These words are similarly forefronted in the display.

16:4b **It is not only I who thank them** *for helping me* The words 'not I alone' occur before the verb and give emphasis by contrast. The emphasis is not so much on 'I' as on the phrase that follows, 'but they also'. The words 'for helping me' are supplied to specify what Paul was thanking them for. As Cranfield says, "it can scarcely be doubted that the gratitude spoken of in v. 4b is gratitude for the particular action to which v. 4a refers."

16:4c all the non-Jewish congregations also *thank them for saving my life* The Greek, καὶ πᾶσαι αἱ ἐκκλησίαι τῶν ἐθνῶν 'also all the churches of the Gentiles' is elliptical, not repeating the verb phrase 'give thanks to them'. What do these congregations thank them for? The answer, on which the commentators are in full agreement, is for saving Paul's life, as is made specific in the display. An alternative would be 'for what they did for me'.

The word 'all' is no doubt a hyperbole; if it is misleading to readers, it could be rendered as 'many'.

16:5a *Greet* **also the congregation** *that meets* **in their house** The Greek is καὶ τὴν κατ' οἶκον αὐτῶν ἐκκλησίαν 'and the church in their house', in which there is no verb. To indicate the implicit relation between 'congregation' and 'their house' most English versions supply 'meets'. LB is even clearer with "meets to worship."

16:5b whom I love The Greek is τὸν ἀγαπητόν μου 'my beloved'. A number of English versions use an adjectival form for 'beloved'. NIV has 'my dear friend'. In the display it is rendered as a relative clause. Dunn suggests that it is equivalent to ἀδελφός 'brother' (i.e., fellow believer), but the term seems to indicate a much deeper affection than 'brother' would.

16:5c who is the first man in *the province of* **Asia who** *believed* **in Christ** In the clause ὅς ἐστιν ἀπαρχὴ τῆς Ἀσίας εἰς Χριστόν 'who is the firstfruit of Asia in/for Christ', the word 'firstfruit' has a different sense than in 8:23. The meaning here is "the first convert in Asia" (BAGD, p. 81.1b), as REB and NRSV render it. Some translators may be able to shorten the phrase in the same way. The display follows NIV and TEV in specifying that Asia was a province; this may be necessary due to the fact that *Asia* has a different sense nowadays.

16:6b who has worked hard *for Christ* In the display it is made clear that the phrase ἥτις πολλὰ ἐκοπίασεν 'who labored many things' refers to Christian work.

in order to *help* **you** The preposition εἰς could mean 'among' (so RSV), but if that were Paul's meaning he would have used the preposition ἐν. It is better to take the preposition in its purposive sense, which then requires some verb (e.g., 'help') to be supplied, as in LB.

16:7a Junia(f) There is disagreement among commentators as to whether this name is masculine or feminine. The majority of versions and several commentators say it is masculine, a diminutive form of Junianus. However, Dunn points out that "the masculine form has been found nowhere else," which is conclusive evidence against that view. Moreover, there are over 250 instances of the occurrence of the feminine name Junia in extant Greek literature (and none of the masculine name Junias), and the Church Fathers all considered the name feminine (so Morris), hence the abbreviation *f* in the display (provided for translations in which such information is necessary). A number of commentators say that Junia was probably the wife of Andronicus.

16:7b my fellow Jews The phrase τοὺς συγγενεῖς μου 'my kinsmen' could mean either that they were relatives of Paul or that they were his fellow Jews. In 9:3 the term clearly has the latter sense, and also in v. 21, referring to four other individuals. Louw and Nida (11.57) give the sense here as 'fellow countrymen'. Morris notes, "it seems unlikely that there were so many members of Paul's family in Rome" and even more unlikely that there were so many of them who had been in prison with him. Therefore 'fellow countrymen' is the sense chosen for the display.

16:7c who were also *previously* in prison with me The words συναιχμαλώτους μου 'fellow captives of mine' could be taken in a metaphorical sense as referring to their being fellow slaves of Christ; but, as commentators note, there is nothing in the context which would lead us to take the word in any but a literal sense. Since they were not presently in prison with Paul, the reference must be to some previous imprisonment.

16:7d They are prominent/respected apostles The relative clause οἵτινές εἰσιν ἐπίσημοι ἐν τοῖς ἀποστόλοις 'who are notable among the apostles' can mean either 'respected by the apostles' or 'respected apostles', but Paul could have indicated the former much more clearly if he had used the preposition ὑπό. Harrison says that "['respected by the apostles'] scarcely does justice to the construction in the Greek."

16:7e became Christians before I did In the relative clause οἳ καὶ πρὸ ἐμοῦ γέγοναν ἐν Χριστῷ 'who also before me have been in Christ' the verb 'believe' could be considered implicit; but since the primary sense of the verb γίνομαι is 'become', it is better to assume the intended meaning as 'became Christians'. A few Western manuscripts have τοῖς πρὸ ἐμοῦ 'who were before me'. Arguments as to why the shorter reading might have been augmented or the longer reading shortened are inconclusive. The decision in favor of the GNT rests on the fact that manuscript support for the longer text is far stronger.

16:8b whom I love *as one who belongs to* the Lord An alternative rendering is 'whom I love because of his relationship with the Lord'. For the first part of this phrase (also in 9c) see the note on 5b; for the second part of the phrase see the note on 2a.

16:9b who works for Christ with us Since Paul uses the plural pronoun 'our' here, its referents must include both Paul and others. The others could be all Christian workers in general, in which case 'our' would be exclusive. But the others are probably all the believers in Rome. Therefore it is assumed that here the phrase τὸν συνεργὸν ἡμῶν ἐν Χριστῷ 'our fellow worker in Christ' must mean that at some time Urbanus did Christian work with Paul and has done or is still doing Christian work in Rome. Thus the pronoun 'us' is taken as inclusive.

16:10b whose *faith* in Christ *has continued after it was tested* The word δόκιμος means "approved (by test)" (BAGD, p. 203.1). It entails three separate events: (1) being tested by trials of some kind, (2) successfully enduring those trials, and (3) being approved by God as a result. For the display it is assumed that it was Apelles's faith that was tested. JBP has "who has proved his faith"; TEV, "whose loyalty to Christ has been proved." NCV's rendering, "He was tested and proved that he truly loves Christ," is slightly different. It is very difficult to indicate all three events succinctly and without use of a verbal noun such as 'faith'. An alternative might be 'who has been approved by Christ after successfully enduring trials'.

16:10c the *believers* who *live in the house* of Aristobulus The Greek is τοὺς ἐκ τῶν Ἀριστοβούλου, literally 'those from those of Aristobulus'. As Dunn notes, those who lived in Aristobulus's house, including his slaves, would be known as οἱ Ἀριστοβούλου 'those of Aristobulus', "and the Christians among them therefore as οἱ ἐκ τῶν Ἀριστοβούλου." It would include more than his family; REB's "the household of" is correct, though it doesn't specify them as Christians.

16:11b my fellow Jew See the note on 7b.

16:11c who *live in the house* of Narcissus See the note on 10c.

16:11d who *belong* to the Lord The phrase τοὺς ὄντας ἐν κυρίῳ 'those being in the Lord' is rendered here as in NJB. An alternative is 'who have a relationship with the Lord'. Relationally this proposition is considered an identification, though it could be argued that the label description would be better. However, the meaning is that not all those who lived in the house were necessarily believers.

16:12a Tryphaena and *her sister* Tryphosa Both names are feminine. Many commentators suggest they were probably sisters because of the similarity of their names. (Both come from the same root.) It would probably be well for a translator to indicate that they were women, as, for example, NIV's "those women who."

16:12b who work hard for the Lord The Greek is τὰς κοπιώσας ἐν κυρίῳ 'the ones working hard in the Lord'. A rendering based on semantic theory is about the same as the literal rendering. TEV, JB, CEV, NCV, and JBP also have "for the Lord."

16:12c Persis(f), whom *we* love Persis is a feminine name. The phrase τὴν ἀγαπητήν 'the beloved' has no indicator of agent; but since Paul does not say 'my beloved' as in 5b and 8b, it is assumed that she was loved not only by Paul but by the Romans. Thus 'we' is inclusive.

16:12d who has worked very hard for the Lord See the note on 6b. Note that the verb form here in 12d is a finite verb with the object πολλά 'many things, much', whereas the verb form in 12b is a participle with no qualifier. Most English versions translate ἐν κυρίῳ 'in the Lord' as 'for the Lord' here.

16:13b an outstanding Christian The Greek is τὸν ἐκλεκτὸν ἐν κυρίῳ 'the chosen in the Lord'. Commentators point out that since every believer is 'chosen in the Lord', Paul's use of the phrase here must have a special meaning. BAGD (p. 242.2) say, "Since the best is usually chosen," the meaning of the phrase in this verse is "the outstanding Christian." Barrett, Hodge, and Sanday and Headlam, as well as JBP, agree. If a more literal translation retaining the word 'Lord' is preferred, NEB's "an outstanding follower of the Lord" is good.

16:13c-d greet his mother, *who has treated me as though* I *were her son* Rufus's mother was not Paul's natural mother; thus the words καὶ ἐμοῦ 'and mine' are intended metaphorically. The point of similarity is the way she acted towards him. Many English versions retain the metaphor by rendering it as "who has been a mother to me." Others use a simile: TEV has "who has always treated me like a son"; CEV has "who has been like a mother to me."

16:14 and the fellow believers who *meet* with them The phrase τοὺς σὺν αὐτοῖς 'those with them' has no verb. Most English versions supply the verb 'to be', but this is ambiguous. Dunn says the phrase "is best understood as a reference to a house church." Goodspeed has "all God's people who meet with them." The word 'meet' implies meeting for worship.

16:15 Philologus and Julia(f) Nearly all commentators suggest that these two are husband and wife or possibly brother and sister. But rather than make this specific, the display only shows that Julia is a feminine name.

In the Greek construction the names are paired together, as are the next two names. In translating they should also be paired to indicate that there was some special relationship between the two in each pair.

all God's people who *meet* with them The word ἁγίων 'saints' could be rendered as previously: 'those who belong to God' (see the note on 8:27b) or 'God's people' (15:25). For 'meet' see the note on v. 14.

16:16a Greet one another affectionately The words ἀσπάσασθε ἀλλήλους ἐν φιλήματι ἁγίῳ 'greet each other with a holy kiss' are found either in this form or with slight variants four other places in the NT. According to ISBE (vol. 3, p. 1813D), "The kiss is common in eastern lands in salutation, etc, on the cheek, the forehead, the beard, the hands, the feet, but not (in Pal) the lips." Dunn suggests that "it is quite likely that Paul intended this counsel to be enacted at the conclusion of the reading of his letter." This is hardly likely! Others suggest that it was to take place during the worship service, "especially before the celebration of the Lord's Supper (Hodge; see also Lenski). Morris objects and says this liturgical function was not introduced until the second century. However, in the context of 'greeting', it could still refer to a worship service, and perhaps the words 'when you gather together for worship' should be supplied at the end. Some suggest the intention was that men kiss men and women kiss women, but there is evidence from the Church Fathers that it was not so understood. Lowery (p. 548) says, "The suggestion to separate the sexes for the exchange of the kiss arose in the late second century." However, since Paul clearly intended the function to be understood and carried out more than the form, the generic term 'affectionately' is used in the display without specifying the form of the action. CEV accomplishes this with "give each other a warm greeting." This seems better than trying to spell out the form or suggesting a substitute such as JBP's "a hearty handshake all around." An alternative for 'affectionately' is 'in a way that shows you love each other'.

but in a sacred way These words are intended to convey more clearly the sense of 'holy' but still collocate well with 'kiss'. It is not clear whether the word 'holy' "distinguishes it from all that is erotic and sensual" (Murray) or that it "distinguishes from an ordinary greeting of natural affection . . . [what is] specifically Christian" (Denney). But if kissing was a part of contemporary culture in biblical times, it is hard to see how a Christian type of kiss would differ from any other ordinary greeting. Therefore the sense proposed by Murray is chosen for the display.

when you gather together Since this chapter refers to individuals in various congregations, a clause is supplied to make specific what situations Paul almost certainly had in mind.

16:16b All the Christian congregations *in this area* The Greek is αἱ ἐκκλησίαι πᾶσαι τοῦ Χριστοῦ 'all the churches of Christ', which is an overstatement. Paul probably did not even know of the existence of *all* the churches, and he could hardly be the channel for their greetings. Thus the words 'in this area' are implied. LB has "All the churches here."

The phrase 'of Christ' is rendered 'Christian' because it is taken as a specification of their being Christians more than their belonging to Christ. Paul usually expresses the latter by the phrase 'in Christ'.

BOUNDARIES AND COHERENCE

The 16:3–16 paragraph consists mostly of requests to greet certain individuals. The last of these, in v. 16, concerns the manner of greeting one another plus a statement that the congregations in Paul's area also send their greetings, but v. 16 is considered part of the paragraph because the same verb ἀσπάζομαι 'greet' that occurs fifteen other times earlier in the paragraph occurs here twice.

The beginning of the next paragraph is marked by an *APPEAL* of an entirely different nature, introduced with παρακαλῶ ὑμᾶς 'I beseech you'.

PROMINENCE AND THEME

Though there is a long succession of *APPEALS* in this paragraph, they are all requests that individuals be greeted. None of them is particularly more thematic than another, so the list of individuals is summarized in the theme as "many individuals," and the many references to their being Christians is also summarized: "among the believers there." The final *DECLARATION* is thematic enough and different enough to be included in the theme as well.

PART CONSTITUENT 16:17-20
(Hortatory Paragraph: Generic appeal of 16:1-27)

THEME: *Note those who are causing quarrels among you and those who cause people to turn away from God. Avoid them, since they only want to satisfy their own desires and deceive those who do not suspect their motives. If you avoid such people, God will soon crush Satan under your feet.*

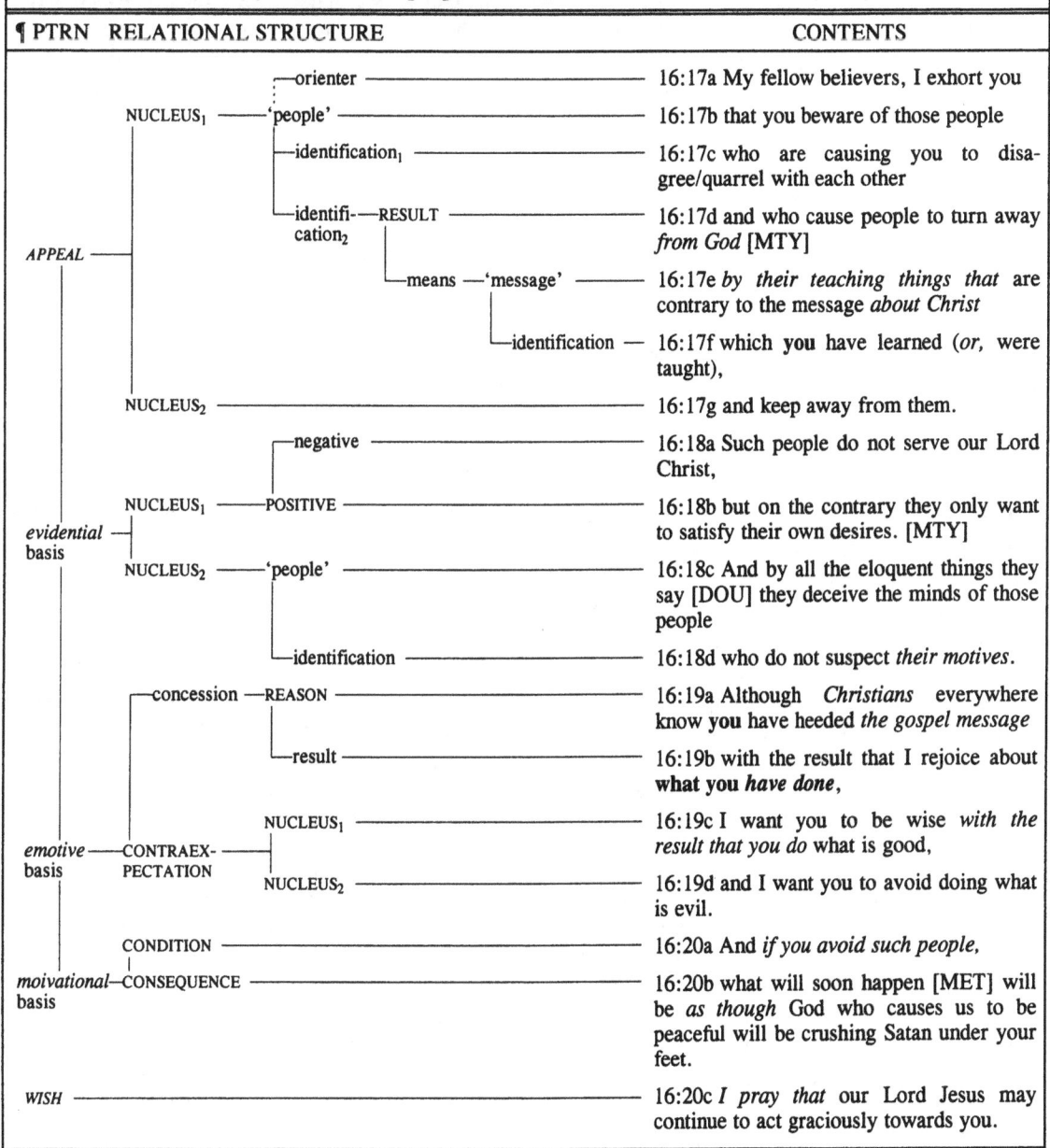

INTENT AND PARAGRAPH PATTERN

The 16:17-20 paragraph, like the preceding one, is hortatory. It opens with the performative παρακαλῶ ὑμᾶς 'I beseech you', followed by the infinitive σκοπεῖν 'beware' in 17b expressing the first part of the APPEAL. Then the imperative ἐκκλίνετε 'keep away from' in 17g expresses the second part of the APPEAL. These are clear signals that this is a hortatory paragraph. In 18a γάρ introduces the main statements in 18b ('they only want to satisfy their own desires') and 18c ('they deceive the people'), forming the *evidential basis* for the APPEAL. The verb θέλω 'I want' in 19c introduces the main proposition of the *emotive basis*, and the future tense of the verb συντρίβω 'crush' in 20b signals that this proposition provides the *motivational basis* for the APPEAL. The WISH in 20c for God's blessing on the readers is not substantially related to the rest of the argument in the paragraph.

NOTES

16:17b beware of The verb σκοπεῖν means 'take note of' in the sense of 'keep a wary eye on, beware of'. An alternative is 'watch out for'.

16:17c who are causing you to disagree/quarrel with each other The first object of the verb here is the phrase τοὺς τὰς διχοστασίας . . . ποιοῦντας 'those the dissensions . . . making'. A number of commentators and versions translate this as 'cause divisions'. This is no doubt correct because Paul is talking not just about differences of opinion, but the resulting separation into opposing camps. The article before the noun points to actual dissensions among the Romans, not just hypothetical ones, hence the present progressive tense in the display.

16:17d and who cause people to turn away from God The Greek noun here is the plural of σκάνδαλον. For this verse BAGD (p. 753.2) give its meanings as "temptation to sin, enticement to apostasy." These are quite different, even though related by cause and effect. In this context the latter seems more likely. Sanday and Headlam say that what is referred to are "the hindrances to Christian progress caused by these embittered relations." TEV, NCV, and LB have "upset people's faith." Another alternative is 'be hindered from following God'.

16:17e *by their teaching things that* are contrary to the message *about Christ* The phrase παρὰ τὴν διδαχὴν ἣν ὑμεῖς ἐμάθετε 'contrary to the teaching which you learned' could be taken as modifying the words 'dissensions and hindrances', but then one would expect the neuter article to precede the phrase. Many of the versions, however, show that they consider the phrase to modify the participle ποιοῦντας 'making'. For example, NRSV has "cause dissensions and offenses, in opposition to the teaching that you have learned" (see also NIV, LB). In the display a similar sense is conveyed. It is not the dissensions and hindrances to faith that were against the truth; Paul would hardly need to say that. It is what they were *doing* that was against the truth: "teaching things about Christ that are contrary to what you have been taught" (LB). The word διδαχή 'teaching' is rendered as 'message' here to avoid redundancy with the phrase that follows ('which you have learned'). The word 'doctrine' is a good alternative. With either one the phrase 'about Christ' should be understood.

16:17f which you have learned The subject in this clause is emphatic, as indicated by bold type in the display. The reciprocal of 'have learned', namely 'were taught', is equally acceptable. CEV has "by refusing to do what all of you were taught."

16:18b want to satisfy their own desires The phrase τῇ ἑαυτῶν κοιλίᾳ 'their bellies', rendered here as 'their desires', is the object of the verb 'serve' understood to be carried over from 18a. This is considered a metonymy, the body part standing for the event associated with it, namely desiring. Since in English the verb *serve* does not normally collocate with the noun *desires*, the display uses 'want to satisfy'. It may be that 'obey' could be used instead of 'serve' in 18a and instead of 'satisfy' in 18b.

16:18c by all the eloquent things they say The phrase διὰ τῆς χρηστολογίας καὶ εὐλογίας 'through smooth speech and fine speaking' is considered to be made up of a doublet. Moore (p. 42) classifies this as a borderline case of a near-synonymous doublet. Dunn also mentions this likelihood. Both terms mean eloquent speech.

deceive the minds The Greek is ἐξαπατῶσιν τὰς καρδίας 'they deceive the hearts', but what is deceived is people's minds, not their physical hearts. It is rendered 'minds' in TEV, NIV, NEB, and NCV.

16:18d who do not suspect *their motives* About τῶν ἀκάκων 'of the guileless', BAGD (p. 29) say that it refers to "the unsuspecting." If it is rendered with the verb 'suspect' that would require an object, hence 'their motives'. In many cases there will be some idiomatic expression such as the English *simpleminded* that would convey this sense.

16:19a Although *Christians* everywhere know The function of γάρ at the beginning of this verse is to indicate a shift of some kind. Here it introduces a new and different type of *basis* for Paul's APPEAL.

The verb ἀφίκετο 'has reached' is used in the extended sense of 'become known to', hence 'know' in the display. It is rendered in the present tense, but could be equally well rendered by 'has come to know'. NIV "has heard about." Note that πάντας 'all' (in εἰς πάντας ἀφίκετο 'to all has reached') is hyperbolic. It is rendered here as 'Christians everywhere'. The word 'Christians' is supplied since it is Christians, not people in general, who have heard this. NCV has "all the believers."

you have heeded *the gospel message* The subject of the verb 'reached' is ἡ ὑμῶν ὑπακοή 'your obedience', an abstract noun phrase expressing an event, hence 'you have heeded/ obeyed'. Semantically, it is the content of what the 'Christians everywhere' know. The verb 'heeded' requires some object such as 'the gospel message' to satisfy the case frame. TEV and JBP similarly supply "the gospel." The word ὑμῶν 'of you' is prominent by virtue of its position, and this is shown here by bolding.

16:19b I rejoice about what you *have done* In the Greek the positional prominence of 'over you' in ἐφ' ὑμῖν χαίρω 'over you I rejoice' is indicated by bolding. A full clause is used to render 'over you' to make it clear that Paul's happiness is over their actions.

16:19c-d I want you to be wise Paul's stating of his desire that they be wise is a rhetorical form by which he appeals positively to the emotions in order to influence behavior, hence the label *emotive basis* in the display.

***with the result that you do* what is good** The preposition εἰς in θέλω ὑμᾶς σοφοὺς εἶναι εἰς τὸ ἀγαθόν 'I want you to be wise unto the good' is taken as expressing result because if Paul had meant 'about', he would have used περί. The result relationship requires that some verb be supplied, hence 'do', following suggestions by Hodge and Barrett.

16:19d I want you to avoid doing what is evil The Greek is ἀκεραίους εἰς τὸ κακόν 'guileless unto the evil', exactly the same type of construction as in 19c; semantically, however, the two are not the same. Here ἀκέραιος, which is usually translated 'innocent', does not mean 'acquitted after a trial' but "not disposed to do wrong" (Barnes). A good alternative is CEV's "not have anything to do with evil."

16:20a And *if you avoid such people* Verse 20 provides a motivational basis for the v. 17 exhortation to shun those who cause divisions. The first part of v. 20 would not be relationally coherent with anything that precedes it if it were not taken in this way. Whedon's suggestion is "Assuming that you thus do," which is essentially the sense supplied in the display. Haldane more specifically ties v. 20 to v. 17:

> After the exhortation which the Apostle had just given to the saints at Rome to maintain peace among themselves, he here designates their heavenly Father, as in the conclusion of the preceding chapter, the God of peace.

16:20b what will soon happen will be *as though* God who causes us to be peaceful will be crushing Satan under your feet Concerning συντρίψει τὸν σατανᾶν ὑπὸ τοὺς πόδας ὑμῶν ἐν τάχει 'will crush Satan under your feet soon', some commentators think the reference is to Christ's eschatological defeat of Satan; they therefore presume that 'soon' intimates that Paul expected this to happen momentarily. But since the context says nothing regarding Christ's return, it is better to follow Sanday and Headlam, Morris, and Denney, who say that the reference is to overcoming false teachers who promote division. Haldane states the sense well:

> All the churches of Christ are to be hurt by factious people rising up among them, emissaries of Satan, under the cover of religion; and if the Church is not led away by the error of Satan, God, as the God of peace, will shortly deliver them from the malignant influence of this apostate spirit.

Erdman also takes the reference to be to false teachers: "False teachers, whom as the agents of evil Paul identifies with Satan, may come and cause dissensions." By defeating *them*, Paul says, true believers are defeating Satan. NCV's rendering, "defeat Satan and give you power over him," is well worth considering. In the display this metaphor is rendered as a simile; the words 'will be as though' are supplied to introduce the comparison with the generic expression 'what will soon happen'.

An alternative to 'God who causes us to be peaceful' would be 'God who causes us to live peacefully with one another'. (See the note on the identical phrase in 15:33.) The word 'God' here occurs with a definite article in Greek, but this is omitted in the display to avoid the wrong meaning in English that there is more than one God.

16:20c *I pray that* our Lord Jesus may continue to act graciously Theoretically a WISH does not belong in a hortatory paragraph, but it is included here because this is a brief blessing that closes off the preceding hortatory paragraph before Paul starts some more personal notes (see the notes on

15:33 and 1:7; see also CEV). The Textus Receptus follows manuscripts that add the word 'Christ' to 'our Lord Jesus'. There would be no reason to omit it if it had been in the original text, whereas it is known that there was a tendency to expand liturgical formulas such as this. A few other manuscripts place this clause at the end of the epistle. However, while one can see why it might have been moved to the end of the epistle, there is no reason it would have been moved here if originally it had been at the very end. The text followed in the display is given an A rating ("certain") in the fourth edition GNT.

BOUNDARIES AND COHERENCE

The 16:17-20 paragraph is relationally coherent in that it consists of an APPEAL (v. 17) followed by bases for the APPEAL. There are three bases: an *evidential basis* (v. 18), an *emotive basis* (v. 19) expressing Paul's desire, and a *motivational basis* (v. 20a-b) telling what will happen if the Roman believers heed his exhortation. The concluding WISH in 20c is a verbless clause expressing Paul's wish for a blessing on his readers (see note on 20c).

The boundary with the next paragraph is marked by the indicative verb ἀσπάζεται 'greets' in v. 21, indicating a change from the hortatory mode to the expressive mode.

PROMINENCE AND THEME

The theme of 16:17-20 is taken from the two NUCLEI (17b-d and 17g) of the APPEAL, the two NUCLEI (18b and 18c-d) of the *evidential basis*, and the *motivational basis* (20a-b).

PART CONSTITUENT 16:21-23
(Expressive Paragraph: Declaration of greetings)

THEME: *Several of those who are with me send their greetings.*	
RELATIONAL STRUCTURE	CONTENTS
NUCLEUS₁	16:21a Timothy, who works with me, greets you,
NUCLEUS₂	16:21b and Lucius and Jason and Sosipater, who are my fellow Jews, also greet you.
NUCLEUS₃ —'Tertius'	16:22a I, Tertius, *also* greet you as *one who belongs to* the Lord.
└─description	16:22b *I am writing this letter as Paul dictates it.*
NUCLEUS₄ —'Gaius'	16:23a Gaius greets you
└─description	16:23b in whose house I *Paul* am staying and in whose house the whole congregation *here meets.*
NUCLEUS₅ —'Erastus'	16:23c Erastus greets you—
└─description	16:23d he is the treasurer of *this* city—
NUCLEUS₆	16:23e and our fellow believer Quartus *greets you.*

INTENT AND PARAGRAPH PATTERN

It is very difficult to assign to the 16:21-23 unit one of the categories from the chart of paragraph patterns on page 10, and for that reason no paragraph pattern labels appear in the display: 16:21-23 consists simply of a series of greetings from Paul's companions to his readers. Conveyed with present tense verbs, these greetings are motivated by the respective individuals' love and concern for those at Rome. Hence this paragraph is considered to be expressive. In essence, Paul is putting into words what they themselves would express by words or actions if they were present in Rome.

NOTES

16:21a who works with me See the notes on 16:3b and 9b.

greets Here the greeting is a mirror image of the one in 16:3. Since it is not a face-to-face event but a greeting conveyed by correspondence, it may be necessary to say something like 'says he is thinking of you' or something similar.

16:21b fellow Jews See the note on 16:7.

16:22a as *one who belongs to* the Lord The phrase ἐν κυρίῳ 'in the Lord' follows the phrase 'the one writing this letter'. This would seem to suggest that the two go together, but 'write this letter in the Lord' makes no sense. It seems best, therefore, to connect 'in the Lord' with the main verb, 'greet', as all the versions and commentators do. The sense is very close to "send Christian greetings" (TEV, JBP). LB has "send my greetings as a Christian brother." Actually, having the words 'in the Lord' at the end follows the normal unmarked Greek clause order. An alternative is 'as one who has a relationship with the Lord'.

16:22b *I* am writing this letter *as Paul dictates it* By the words ὁ γράψας τὴν ἐπιστολήν 'the one who has written the letter' Tertius alludes to the fact that he has been Paul's amanuensis. This is made specific to avoid wrong meaning. JBP has "who have been taking down this epistle from Paul's dictation."

16:23b in whose house I *Paul* am staying The expression ὁ ξένος μου 'my host' means that Paul is a guest in the home of this man. Note that Paul resumes dictating here. This is made clear by 'I Paul'.

in whose house the whole congregation *here* meets The Greek is καὶ ὅλης τῆς ἐκκλησίας 'and of all the church'. This phrase is the second modifier of 'host'. The meaning here is not, of course, that the congregation were overnight guests, as Paul was. Thus, following TEV, JB, and LB, the word 'meets' is supplied in the display. Also 'here' is supplied to specify that the congregation Paul is referring to is the one in the place from which he is writing. JBP, LB, NCV, and NIV also supply 'here'.

16:23d treasurer of *this* city The word 'this' is implied (see NEB, NCV). If absolutely necessary, the translator may specify that the city was Corinth.

BOUNDARIES AND COHERENCE

The coherence of the 16:21-23 paragraph consists of its being a set of greetings in which the verb phrase ἀσπάζεται ὑμᾶς 'he greets you' is repeatedly used. It occurs explicitly four times and is implied twice.

The boundary with the next paragraph, which is a final expression of praise to God, is marked by τῷ δέ 'to the one who' in v. 25. (For the omission of v. 24, see the notes on 16:24.)

PROMINENCE AND THEME

Since the 16:21-23 paragraph consists of a set of greetings, the theme statement is simply a very brief condensation of them.

PART CONSTITUENT 16:25-27
(Expressive Paragraph: Doxology of 16:1-27)

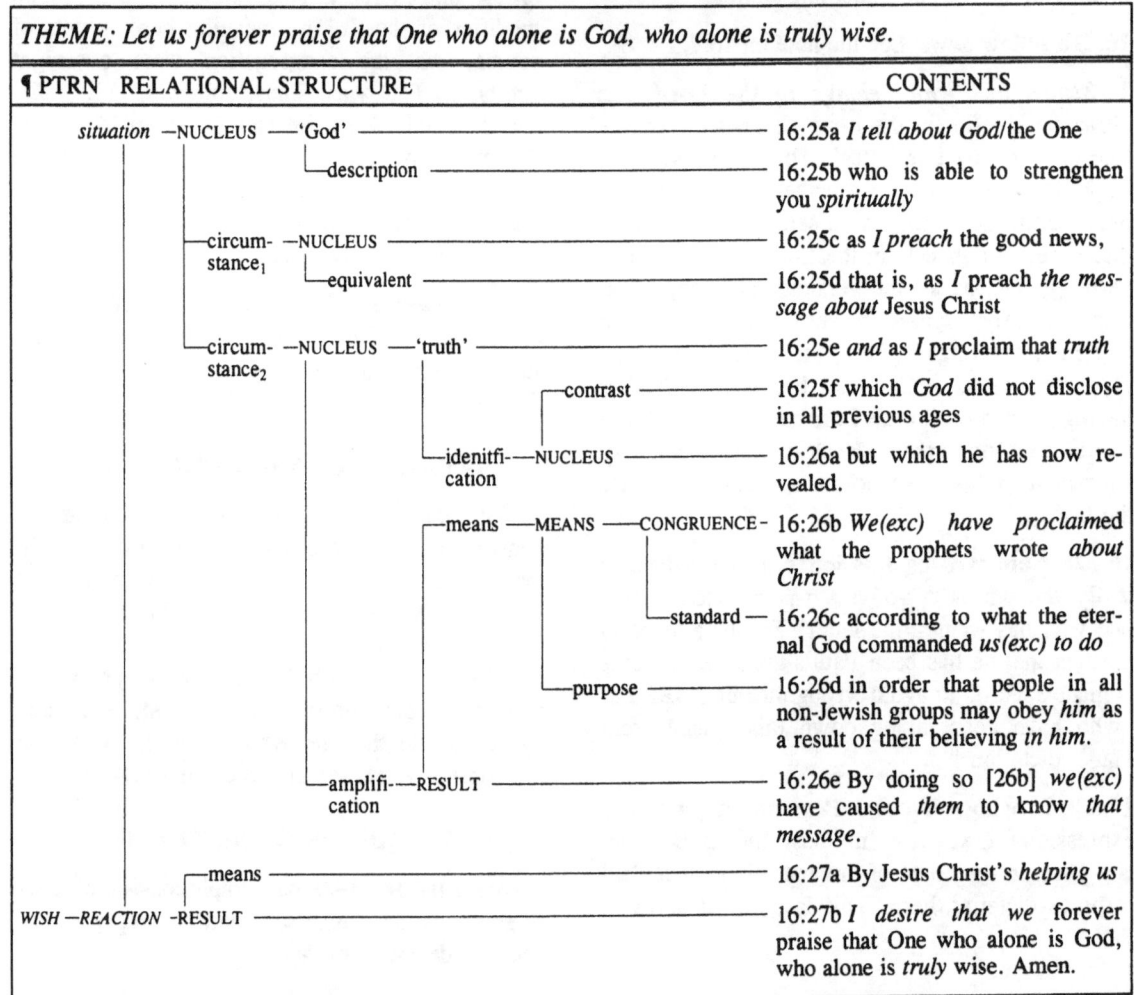

INTENT AND PARAGRAPH PATTERN

In spite of the grammatical problem in 16:25-27 (discussed in the notes), these verses clearly express a WISH that God be praised and this paragraph is thus considered expressive, with the WISH in v. 27 expressing the writer's REACTION to contemplating what God has enabled him to do. It is a doxology, and it follows the syntactical structure of other doxologies in the NT, with the beginning dative form τῷ introducing the one who is to receive the praise, the absence of a copulative verb, the abstract nouns encoding the events of praise, and the final εἰς τοὺς αἰῶνας 'unto the ages'. (Other examples of this structure are in Jude 24-25, Rev. 5:1, and Phil. 4:20.) Within the doxology Paul embeds what seems to be a validation of his message (25c-26e).

NOTES

16:24 A small number of manuscripts include v. 24, which eventually found its way into the KJV. It is rejected by all modern scholars. The fourth edition GNT omits mention of it entirely, and it is omitted in the display. For its contents, see the notes on 20c, which it substantially repeats.

16:25-27 There are difficult problems regarding this doxology. Metzger summarizes them (pp. 470-72):

> A full discussion of the problems of the termination of the Epistle to the Romans involves questions concerning the authenticity and integrity of the last chapter (or of the last two chapters), including the possibility that Paul may have made two copies of the Epistle, one with and one without chap. 16 (chaps. 1-15 being sent to

Rome and chaps. 1-16 to Ephesus). The doxology . . . varies in location; traditionally it has been printed at the close of chap. 16 . . . , but in some witnesses it occurs at the close of chap. 14, and in another witness (p⁴⁶) at the close of chap. 15. Moreover, several witnesses have it at the close of both chap. 14 and chap. 16, and in others it does not occur at all. . . . In evaluating the complicated evidence, the Committee was prepared to allow (1) for the probability that Marcion [whose edition of Romans apparently lacked the last two chapters], or his followers, circulated a shortened form of the epistle, lacking chapters 15 and 16, and (2) for the possibility that Paul himself had dispatched a longer and a shorter form of the epistle (one form with, and one without, chapter 16). Furthermore, it was acknowledged that, to some extent, the multiplicity of locations at which the doxology appears in the several witnesses, as well as the occurrence in it of several expressions that have been regarded as non-Pauline, raise suspicions that the doxology may be non-Pauline. At the same time, however, on the basis of good and diversified evidence . . . , it was decided to include the doxology at its traditional place at the close of the epistle. . . ."

Donfried (p. 50) has some good suggestions to offer:

The further suggestion made by some scholars that it is perhaps Marcionite in origin goes a long way in solving the textual difficulties of Romans. We know from Origen that Marcion cut off chapters 15 and 16, and thus Marcion's edition of Romans ended with 14:23. Since that is a rather abrupt note to end on, Marcion perhaps composed this closing doxology. Kümmel and Lietzmann are probably correct in suggesting that Paul's original Romans ended with 16:23 (without the doxology); Marcion then shortened this, so that his edition ended with 14:23, and expanded it with his doxology.

The question is far from settled, but it is probably correct to say there is a fair consensus that vv. 25-27 were added to an early version that ended at 14:23, and later moved to close the longer version that ended at 16:24. Dunn notes, "Paul nowhere else formulates such a long doxology, and its use to conclude a letter would be a departure from his usual style." But since it clearly contains Pauline ideas and language, "it is better to take it as simply the close of Romans as we know it and see what we can learn from that" (Morris).

Although Dunn may be right in saying about this doxology that it "is clearly liturgical in character" with its lines "structured for easy liturgical repetition," its semantic structure is extremely difficult to work out. No doubt the attempt here in the display has serious flaws, but it is an attempt with translators in mind.

Part of the difficulty in these verses is that grammatically they do not form a complete sentence. Verse 25 starts with τῷ δὲ δυναμένῳ 'Now to the one being able', and the rest of vv. 25-26 consists of a complex description of 'the one'. Then the first part of v. 27 is a little more definite in identifying the one who is able: μόνῳ σοφῷ θεῷ 'the only wise God. But nowhere is there a main clause; the antecedent that the three modifying phrases or clauses refers back to is not in an independent clause. The end of v. 27 has ᾧ ἡ δόξα 'to whom (be) the glory', but it is not a complete sentence, either. In order for it to be so, ᾧ 'to whom' would have to be absent—or else the third person singular present subjunctive form ᾖ of the verb 'to be' would have to occur instead of ᾧ. The Codex Vaticanus does, in fact, omit ᾧ. Some scribe must have recognized the problem. Other manuscripts have other readings apparently contrived to solve the problem. In all the versions this clause is rendered as though the text had omitted ᾧ or had ᾖ.

But even if the final relative clause is rendered as the independent clause in this three-verse passage, it is extremely awkward to show the relationships of 25-26 to 27 without violating the rule that requires a modifying clause to be preceded by the clause containing the antecedent to which the modifying clause refers. TEV solves the problem by beginning v. 25 with "Let us give glory to God," borrowing that semantic content from 27b. (Thus it occurs twice, in 25 and in 27.) JB handles it similarly, starting 25 with "Glory to him who." LB uses a slightly different approach, starting v. 25 with "I commit you to God, who." These are possible solutions, but they do violence to the form of the verses, which build up to a climax. The approach followed in the display reserves 'may we praise that one' until 27b, ignoring 'to the one being able' that introduces v. 25. An attempt is made to show the relationships and at the same time provide a more translatable form than the original Greek form.

There are a number of similarities between the 16:25-27 and 1:1-7 paragraphs. Both mention the gospel; both have the phrases 'all the Gentiles' and 'obedience of faith', and both mention the prophets. These similarities give support to the view that the epistle's overall pattern is a chiastic structure (see p. 35).

16:25a *I tell about* Here an independent verb is supplied in the display where the Greek has none. This verb encompasses all the nouns and verbs in vv. 25-26 that deal with making God's truth known: κήρυγμα 'preaching', ἀποκάλυψιν 'revelation', φανερωθέντος 'manifested', and γνωρισθέντος 'made known'. An alternative is "Praise God! He . . ." (CEV; cf. also NCV, TEV). The agent of the supplied verb is given as 'I' because of the words 'my gospel' in 25c, and this in turn calls for 'I' as the agent of the verbs in 25d-e as well.

***God*/the One** The Greek is τῷ 'to the one', leaving the identification of this 'one' to v. 27. The display supplies two alternatives, the first following TEV and LB and the other literal.

16:25b who is able to strengthen you *spiritually* The infinitive στηρίξαι follows δυναμένῳ 'being able'. It means "establish, strengthen" (BAGD, p. 768.2), but here its use is figurative; hence 'spiritually' is supplied to make the meaning clear.

16:25c as I *preach* the good news The Greek is κατὰ τὸ εὐαγγέλιόν μου 'according to the gospel of me'. The verb 'preach' is supplied to spell out the action implicit in the genitive 'of me, my'. As to the relationship indicated by κατά 'according to' (in the phrase 'the one who is able to strengthen you according to my gospel'), the sense is that when Paul preaches he tells people that God is able to strengthen spiritually. NCV makes it clear with "The Good News that I tell people."

16:25d that is, as *I preach the message about* Jesus Christ The Greek is καὶ τὸ κήρυγμα Ἰησοῦ Χριστοῦ 'and the preaching of Jesus Christ', which is considered to be either an equivalent of the preceding phrase or an amplification of it. Morris says that it "stands for much the same thing but from a different point of view." The preaching of Jesus Christ *is* the gospel, not something different. The supplied words 'the message about' express the relationship between the event of preaching and 'Jesus Christ'; a simpler alternative would be 'about'.

16:25e *and as I proclaim that truth* The phrase κατὰ ἀποκάλυψιν 'according to the revelation' is not preceded by a conjunction; but since it seems to parallel the κατά phrase of 25c, it is taken to be coordinate with it. Hence 'and' is supplied.

The noun ἀποκάλυψις 'revelation' expresses an event and is therefore represented by a verb. Although God is the revealer (Hodge, Morris), "the unveiling of [God's salvation purpose is] through Paul's preaching" (Dunn). Thus Paul is here considered to be the agent of this event in keeping with 25c, where 'my' occurs with 'gospel'. The word μυστήριον 'mystery' is rendered 'truth', since 'truth' is a meaning component of μυστήριον.

16:25f which *God* did not disclose in all previous ages Here there is a further explanation of 'mystery' parallel to 11:25. Since 'God' is supplied as the agent of the verb in the modifying phrase χρόνοις αἰωνίοις σεσιγημένου 'in eternal ages having concealed', a term less forthright than 'conceal' is used (an antonym with the negative).

The expression 'eternal times' sounds somewhat hyperbolic in English. Several English versions translate it as 'for long ages', but the sense is more specifically "in all past times" (Barnes). LB's "from the beginning of time" is idiomatic but expresses the meaning well.

16:26a but which he has now revealed The participle φανερωθέντος 'having been manifested' is passive. In the display it is represented as active, with 'he' (i.e., 'God') supplied as the agent to correspond with 25f.

16:26b The conjunction τέ here is seen as a weak connective introducing the 26b-e cluster. This cluster is postulated to be an amplification of 25e in view of the synonymy of the participle γνωρισθέντος 'made known' in 26e and the abstract noun κήρυγμα 'proclamation' in 25e.

***We(exc) have proclaimed* what the prophets wrote *about* Christ** The phrase διά τε γραφῶν προφητικῶν 'through the prophetic writings' expresses a means proposition. This requires some verb to be supplied. CEV has "God commanded his prophets to write." As Denney says, this is a reference to "the O.T. Scriptures of which Paul made constant use in preaching his gospel." The prophets wrote about many things, but what is in focus here is the Scriptures that foretold the coming of Messiah; thus 'about Christ' is implicit. 'We(exc)' is supplied as the agent of the verb 'proclaimed' and of 'caused them to know' in 26e because Paul was not the only one proclaiming the gospel as God had commanded (26c).

16:26c according to what the eternal God commanded *us(exc)* **to do** Since there is no καί 'and' here, the phrase κατ' ἐπιταγὴν τοῦ αἰωνίου θεοῦ 'according to the command of the eternal God' is considered to relate to the immediately preceding phrase: Paul and others have proclaimed Christ in accordance to what God commanded. The words 'the eternal' are descriptive, not identificational; in some languages this may have to be expressed by a nonrestrictive relative clause, 'who is eternal', or some other construction to avoid the wrong idea that there are other true gods who are not eternal.

16:26d in order that people in all non-Jewish groups may obey *him* **as a result of their believing** *in him* The phrase εἰς ὑπακοὴν πίστεως 'unto obedience of faith' is taken in all versions and commentaries to express purpose. It could go with either 26b or 26c, but it coheres better if taken as stating the purpose of 26b. The genitive 'of faith' is rendered here as it was in 1:5. Case roles require that objects of 'obey' and 'believe' be supplied, but they are not particularly in focus here.

Cranfield states that the phrase εἰς πάντα τὰ ἔθνη 'unto all the nations' must be taken with 'for obedience of faith', not with the participle that follows in 26e; otherwise it would be in a dative construction. This may be true, but there is little difference in sense either way.

16:26e we(exc) have caused *them* **to know** *that message* The passive participle γνωρισθέντος 'having been made known' is expressed as an active verb in the display, and Paul and others (e.g., other apostles) are considered the agents. Case frames require an object. The one supplied in the display is generic.

16:27a By Jesus Christ's *helping us* The phrase διὰ Ἰησοῦ Χριστοῦ 'through Jesus Christ' is taken as expressing a means proposition. This requires a verb, so the generic 'helping' is supplied in the display following Barnes: "through him now as mediator and intercessor in the heavens" (also Lenski). The pronoun 'us' is also supplied, although in the Greek there is no pronoun here or in 27b. In translating, whatever generic form is appropriate should be supplied (e.g., 'them', 'people', 'everyone').

16:27b *I* **desire that** *we* **forever praise** The Greek is ᾧ ἡ δόξα 'to whom (is) the glory' (see the 16:25–27 note on ᾧ). Since some languages do not have an optative 'may', and since this does express Paul's wish but is not a prayer, the sense is conveyed with 'I desire that' (see the 1:7 and 11:36 notes for this construction and the translation of δόξα).

that One who alone is God, who alone is *truly* **wise** The Greek is μόνῳ σοφῷ θεῷ 'to the only wise God'. In most translations this is rendered literally, but TEV has "To the only God, who alone is all-wise." Technically, if the first word had an adverbial sense (i.e., 'who is exclusively wise') it would be μόνον, but since it is adjectival here, both it and the word 'wise' must modify 'God' (cf. John 17:3: τὸν μόνον ἀληθινὸν θεόν 'the only true God'). The rendering in the display follows TEV, based on the assumption that the grammar is correct. Since there are wise people in the world, 'truly' is supplied in the display as a modifier of 'wise'.

At the epistle's close, several variations exist among the manuscripts. Short (a few long) identifications of the recipients, the writer, the place of writing, and the bearers of the letter are appended. The additions of the Textus Receptus all have poor manuscript evidence. The fourth edition GNT omits all references to such subscriptions.

BOUNDARIES AND COHERENCE

The 16:25–27 paragraph concludes the epistle. It consists of only one sentence in several English versions (e.g., JBP, RSV, NIV, NEB). In Greek it has no main verb and thus cannot grammatically be called a sentence. There is little in the way of lexical cohesion. However, it is important to note that this doxology contains many of the same elements mentioned in the first paragraph of the epistle: 'gospel', 'obedience of faith', 'writings' (of Scripture), 'Jesus Christ', and 'all the nations'. The best proof of its coherence is its formulaic doxology construction. The end of the unit is marked by the word ἀμήν 'amen'.

PROMINENCE AND THEME

The theme of 16:25–27 is drawn from the 27b RESULT proposition of the WISH.

BIBLIOGRAPHY

Reference Works, Commentaries, and Articles Relating to Romans

Alford, Henry. 1852. The Epistle to the Romans. In *The Greek Testament*, vol. 2, pp. 289–445. London: Rivington, Deighton.

Aune, David E. 1991. Romans as a *logos protreptikos*. In Donfried 1991, pp. 278–96.

Barnes, Albert. 1861. *Romans*. Notes on the New Testament. 1949 reprint. Grand Rapids: Baker.

Barr, James. 1988. 'ABBĀ isn't Daddy. *Journal of Theological Studies* 39 (April): 28–47.

Barrett, C. K. 1957. *A commentary on the Epistle to the Romans*. Harper's New Testament Commentaries. New York: Harper & Row.

Bauer, W.; W. F. Arndt; and F. W. Gingrich. 1979. *A Greek-English lexicon of the New Testament and other early Christian literature*. 2d ed. Transl., rev., and augmented by F. W. Gingrich and F. W. Danker from W. Bauer's 5th German ed. of 1958. Chicago: Univ. of Chicago Press.

Baur, Ferdinand C. 1836. Über Zweck und Veranlassung des Römerbrief und der damit zusammenhängenden Verhältnisse der römischen Gemeinde. In *Tübinger Zeitschrift für Theologie*, pp. 59–178.

Beekman, John, and John Callow. 1974. *Translating the Word of God*. Grand Rapids: Zondervan.

Beekman, John; John Callow; and Michael F. Kopesec. 1981. The semantic structure of written communication. Prepublication draft, 5th ed. Dallas: SIL.

Best, Ernest. 1967. *The letter of Paul to the Romans*. Cambridge Bible Commentary. Cambridge: University Press.

Blass, R., and A. Debrunner. 1961. *A Greek grammar of the New Testament and other early Christian literature*. A translation and revision of the 9th–10th German edition by Robert W. Funk. Chicago: University of Chicago Press.

Bornkamm, Gunther. 1991. The letter to the Romans as Paul's last will and testament. In Donfried 1991, pp. 16–28.

Bruce, F. F. 1963. *The epistle of Paul to the Romans*. Tyndale New Testament Commentaries. Grand Rapids: Eerdmans.

———. 1965. *The letters of Paul*. Grand Rapids: Eerdmans.

———. 1985. *The letter of Paul to the Romans: An introduction and commentary*. 2d ed. Tyndale New Testament Commentaries. Grand Rapids: Eerdmans; Leicester, England: Inter-Varsity.

———. 1991. The Romans debate—continued. In Donfried 1991, pp. 175–94.

Bullinger, E. W. 1898. *Figures of speech used in the Bible*. London: Eyre and Spottiswoods.

Bultmann, R. 1951, 1955. *Theology of the New Testament*. 2 vols. Tr. K. Grobel. New York: Scribner's.

Burton, E. D. 1900. *Syntax of the moods and tenses in New Testament Greek*. Chicago: University of Chicago Press.

Callow, John. 1983. *A semantic structure analysis of Colossians*. Dallas: SIL.

Callow, Kathleen. Forthcoming. *Man and message*. Lanham, Md.: University Press of America.

Campbell, William S. 1973–74. Why did Paul write Romans? *Expository Times* 85.

Conybeare, W. J., and J. S. Howson. 1950. *The life and epistles of St. Paul*. Grand Rapids: Eerdmans.

Conzelmann, Hans. 1975. *1 Corinthians: A commentary on the First Epistle to the Corinthians*. Translated from the German by James W. Leitch. Philadelphia: Fortress.

Cranfield, C. E. B. 1975–79. *A critical and exegetical commentary on the Epistle to the Romans*. 2 vols. New ICC. Edinburgh: T. & T. Clark.

Dana, H. E., and Julius R. Mantey. 1957. *A manual grammar of the Greek New Testament*. New York: Macmillan.

Dayton, Wilbur T. 1965. *The Epistle of Paul to the Romans*. Wesleyan Bible Commentary, vol. 5. Grand Rapids: Eerdmans.

Denney, James. 1967. St. Paul's Epistle to the Romans. In *The expositor's Greek Testament*, vol. 2, pp. 555–725. Reprint. Grand Rapids: Eerdmans.

Dodd, C. H. 1932. *The Epistle of Paul to the Romans*. The Moffatt New Testament Commentary. New York: Harper.
Donfried, Karl P., ed. 1991. *The Romans debate*. Revised and expanded edition. Peabody, Mass.: Hendrickson.
Dunn, James D. G. 1988. *Romans*. 2 vols. Word Biblical Commentary, 38A and 38B. Dallas: Word.
Erdman, Charles R. 1925. *The Epistle of Paul to the Romans*. Philadelphia: Westminster.
Friberg, Barbara, and Timothy Friberg. 1981. *Analytical Greek New Testament*. Grand Rapids: Baker.
Gamble, Harry. 1977. *The textual history of the letter to the Romans*. Grand Rapids: Eerdmans.
Gaston, Lloyd. 1991. Israel's misstep in the eyes of Paul. In Donfried 1991, pp. 309-26.
Gifford, E. H. 1886. *The Epistle of St. Paul to the Romans*. London: John Murray.
Greenlee, J. Harold. 1986. *A concise exegetical grammar of New Testament Greek*. 5th ed., revised. Grand Rapids: Eerdmans.
Haldane, Robert. [1874] 1970. *Exposition of the Epistle to the Romans*. Reprint. Marshallton, Dela.: Natl. Foundation for Christian Truth.
Harrison, Everett F. 1976. Romans. In *The expositor's Bible commentary*, vol. 10, ed. F. E. Gaebelein, pp. 1-171. Grand Rapids: Zondervan.
Hendriksen, William. 1980-81. *New Testament commentary: Exposition of Paul's Epistle to the Romans*. Grand Rapids: Baker.
Hodge, Charles. 1886. *Commentary on the Epistle to the Romans*. Grand Rapids: Eerdmans.
Hunter, A. M. 1955. *The Epistle to the Romans*. Torch Bible Commentaries. London: SCM.
International standard Bible encyclopedia. 1960. James Orr, ed. 5 vols. Grand Rapids: Eerdmans.
Jervell, Jacob. 1991. The letter to Jerusalem. In Donfried 1991, pp. 53-64.
Jewett, Robert. 1991. Following the argument of Romans. In Donfried 1991, pp. 265-77.
Karris, Robert J. 1991. The occasion of Romans: A response to Professor Donfried. In Donfried 1991, pp. 125-27.
Käsemann, Ernst. 1980. *Commentary on Romans*. Translated from the German by Geoffrey W. Bromiley. Grand Rapids: Eerdmans.
Klein, Günter. 1991. Paul's purpose in writing the Epistle to the Romans. In Donfried 1991, pp. 29-43.
Knox, John. 1978. The Epistle to the Romans. In *The interpreter's Bible*, vol. 9. Nashville: Abingdon.
Kümmel, W. G. 1975. *Introduction to the New Testament*. 17th ed. Nashville: Abingdon.
Lampe, Peter. 1991. The Roman Christians of Romans 16. In Donfried 1991, pp. 216-30.
Lenski, R. C. H. 1936. *The interpretation of St. Paul's Epistle to the Romans*. Minneapolis: Augsburg.
Levinsohn, Stephen H. 1992. *Discourse features of New Testament Greek*. Dallas: SIL.
Lightfoot, J. B. 1957. *Notes on the Epistle of St. Paul: Romans 1-7*. Grand Rapids: Zondervan.
Longacre, Robert E. 1983. *The grammar of discourse*. New York: Plenum.
Louw, J. P., and E. A. Nida, eds. 1988. *Greek-English lexicon of the New Testament based on semantic domains*. 2 vols. New York: UBS.
Lowery, David K. 1983. 1 Corinthians. In *The Bible knowledge commentary: New Testament*, pp. 505-49. Ed. John F. Walvoord and Roy B. Zuck. Wheaton, Ill.: Victor.
Manson, T. W. 1991. St. Paul's letter to the Romans—and others. In Donfried 1991, pp. 3-15.
Marxsen, Willi. 1968. *Introduction to the New Testament*. Philadelphia: Fortress.
Metzger, Bruce M. 1994. *A textual commentary on the Greek New Testament*. 2d ed. New York: American Bible Society.
Meyer, Heinrich A. W. 1881. *Critical and exegetical handbook to the Epistle to the Romans*. Translated from the German. Edinburgh: T. & T. Clark.
Michel, Otto. 1957. *Der Brief an die Römer*. Göttingen: Vandenhoeck & Ruprecht.
Minear, P. S. 1971. *The obedience of faith: The purposes of Paul in the Epistle to the Romans*. Studies in Biblical Theology 2/19. London: SCM.
Moore, Bruce R. 1993. *Doublets in the New Testament*. Dallas: SIL.
Morris, Leon. 1988. *The Epistle to the Romans*. Grand Rapids: Eerdmans; Leicester, England: InterVarsity.
Moule, C. F. D. 1959. *An idiom book of New Testament Greek*. 2d ed. Cambridge: Cambridge University Press.
Moulton, James Hope. 1963. *A grammar of New Testament Greek*. Edinburgh: T. & T. Clark.

Moulton, W. F., and A. S. Geden. 1926. *A concordance to the Greek Testament*. Edinburgh: T. & T. Clark.
Murray, John. 1968. *The Epistle to the Romans*. Grand Rapids: Eerdmans.
Newman, B. M., and E. A. Nida. 1973. *A translator's handbook on Paul's Letter to the Romans*. New York: UBS.
Nygren, A. [1944] 1952. *A commentary on Romans*. Philadelphia: Fortress.
Philippi, F. A. 1878. *Commentary on St. Paul's Epistle to the Romans*. Translated from the German. Edinburgh.
Robertson, A. T. 1925. *An introduction to the textual criticism of the New Testament*. Nashville: Broadman.
Sanday, W., and A. C Headlam. 1902. *A critical and exegetical commentary on the Epistle to the Romans*. 5th ed. ICC. Edinburgh: T. & T. Clark.
Shedd, William G. T. 1879. *A critical and doctrinal commentary on the Epistle of St. Paul to the Romans*. Reprint. Grand Rapids: Zondervan.
Stuart, Moses. 1836. *A commentary on the Epistle to the Romans*. London: Thomas Tegg and Son.
Stuhlmacher, Peter. 1991a. The purpose of Romans. In Donfried 1991, pp. 231-42.
———. 1991b. The theme of Romans. In Donfried 1991, pp. 333-45.
Taylor, Vincent. 1939. Greek texts reconsidered: Romans iii.25f. *Expository Times* 50:7:295ff.
Thomson, G. T., and F. Davidson. 1953. *The Epistle to the Romans*. The New Bible Commentary. Grand Rapids: Eerdmans.
Tuggy, John C. 1992. Semantic paragraph patterns: A foundational communication concept and interpretive tool. In *Linguistics and New Testament interpretation: Essays on discourse analysis*, ed. D. A. Black, pp. 45-67. Nashville: Broadman.
Vine, W. E. 1948. *The Epistle to the Romans*. London: Oliphants.
Watson, Francis. 1991. The two Roman congregations: Romans 14:1-15:13. In Donfried 1991, pp. 203-15.
Webster's new twentieth century dictionary, unabridged, 2d ed. 1978. N.p.: William Collins and World.
Wedderburn, A. J. M. 1991. Purpose and occasion of Romans again. In Donfried 1991, pp. 195-202.
Whedon, D. D. 1871. *Acts-Romans*. Commentary on the New Testament. New York: Phillips & Hunt.
Wiefel, Wolfgang. 1991. The Jewish community in ancient Rome and the origins of Roman Christianity. In Donfried 1991, pp. 85-101.

Texts and Versions

Aland, Barbara; Kurt Aland; Johannes Karavidopoulos; Carlo M. Martini; and Bruce M. Metzger, eds. 1993. *The Greek New Testament*. 4th rev. ed. Stuttgart: United Bible Societies.
Aland, Kurt; Matthew Black; Carlo M. Martini; Bruce M. Metzger; and Allen Wikgren, eds. 1975. *The Greek New Testament*. 3d ed. Stuttgart: United Bible Societies.
Beck, William F. 1964. *The New Testament in the language of today*. St. Louis: Concordia.
Bruce, F. F. 1965. *The letters of Paul*. Grand Rapids: Eerdmans.
Good news for modern man: The New Testament in today's English version. 1971. 3d ed. New York: ABS.
Goodspeed, Edgar J. 1923. *The New Testament: An American translation*. Chicago: University of Chicago Press.
The Holy Bible: Authorized (or King James) version. 1611.
The Holy Bible: Contemporary English version. 1995. New York: ABS.
The Holy Bible: New century version. 1991. Dallas: Word.
The Holy Bible: New Jerusalem Bible. 1985. New York: ABS.
The Holy Bible: New revised standard version. 1989. New York: ABS.
The Jerusalem Bible. 1968. Garden City: Doubleday.
Knox, Ronald A. 1944. *The New Testament*. New York: Sheed & Ward.
The living Bible, paraphrased. 1971. Taylor, Kenneth N., trans. Wheaton, Ill.: Tyndale.
The new American standard Bible. 1963. La Habra, Cal.: Foundation Press.

New English Bible, New Testament. 1961. Oxford: Oxford University Press; Cambridge: Cambridge University Press.
New international version of the New Testament. 1973. New York: Zondervan.
The NIV study Bible. 1985. Grand Rapids: Zondervan.
New living translation. 1996. Wheaton, Ill.: Tyndale.
Norlie, Olaf M., tr. 1961. *The New Testament: A new translation in modern English for today's reader.* Grand Rapids: Zondervan.
Phillips, J. B. 1972. *The New Testament in modern English.* New York: Macmillan.
The revised English Bible. 1989. Oxford Univ. Press and Cambridge Univ. Press.
Revised standard version. 1971. 2d ed. New York: National Council of Churches.
Septuagint. 1935. Alfred Rahlfs, ed. Stuttgart: Wurttembergische Bibelanstalt.
The twentieth century New Testament. 1904. Rev. ed. New York: Revell.
Weymouth, Richard Francis. 1930. *The New Testament in modern speech.* 5th ed., revised by J. A. Robertson. London: James Clark.
Williams, Charles B. 1963. *The New Testament in the language of the people.* Chicago: Moody Press.

www.ingramcontent.com/pod-product-compliance
Lightning Source LLC
Chambersburg PA
CBHW081756300426
44116CB00014B/2143